Medical Practice Management Handbook

Complete Guide to Accounting, Tax Issues, Managed Care, and Daily Operations

Eighth Edition

Reed Tinsley, CPA

ASPEN LAW & BUSINESS
A Division of Aspen Publishers, Inc.
New York   Gaithersburg

This publication is designed to provide accurate and authoritative information in regard to the subject matter covered. It is sold with the understanding that the publisher is not engaged in rendering legal, accounting, or other professional services. If legal advice or other professional assistance is required, the services of a competent professional person should be sought.

—From a *Declaration of Principles* jointly adopted by
a Committee of the American Bar Association and a
Committee of Publishers and Associations

Copyright © 2002 by Aspen Law & Business
A Division of Aspen Publishers, Inc.
A Wolters Kluwer Company
www.aspenpublishers.com

Portions of this work were published in previous editions.

Printed in the United States of America
1 2 3 4 5 6 7 8 9 0

Library of Congress Cataloging-in-Publication Data

Tinsley, Reed.
    Medical practice management handbook : complete guide to accounting, tax issues, managed care, and daily operations / Reed Tinsley.—8th ed.
        p. cm.
    Includes index.
    ISBN: 0-7355-3296-6
    1. Medicine—Practice—Accounting—Handbooks, manuals, etc. 2. Medicine—Practice—Finance—Handbooks, manuals, etc. 3. Physicians—Taxation—Handbooks, manuals, etc. I. Title.

R728.T548 2002
610'.68'1—dc21   2002016325

About Aspen Law & Business

Aspen Law & Business is a leading publisher of authoritative treatises, practice manuals, services, and journals for attorneys, corporate and bank directors, accountants, auditors, environmental compliance professionals, financial and tax advisors, and other business professionals. Our mission is to provide practical solution-based how-to information keyed to the latest original pronouncements, as well as the latest legislative, judicial, and regulatory developments.

We offer print and online products in the areas of accounting and auditing; antitrust; banking and finance; bankruptcy; business and commercial law; construction law; corporate law; criminal law; environmental compliance; government and administrative law; health law; insurance law; intellectual property; international law; legal practice and litigation; matrimonial and family law; pensions, benefits, and labor; real estate law; securities; and taxation.

Aspen Law and Business products treating accounting and auditing issues include:

Accounting Irregularities and Financial Fraud
Audit Committees: A Guide for Directors, Management, and Consultants
Construction Accounting Deskbook
CPA's Guide to Developing Effective Business Plans
CPA's Guide to Effective Engagement Letters
CPA's Guide to e-Business
Federal Government Contractor's Manual
How to Manage Your Accounting Practice
Miller Audit Procedures
Miller Compilations and Reviews
Miller European Accounting Guide
Miller GAAP Financial Statement Disclosures Manual
Miller GAAP Guide
Miller GAAP Practice Manual
Miller GAAS Guide
Miller GAAS Practice Manual
Miller Governmental GAAP Guide
Miller Governmental GAAP Practice Manual: A Guide to GASB 34
Miller International Accounting Standards Guide
Miller Local Government Audits
Miller Not-for-Profit Organization Audits
Miller Not-for-Profit Reporting
Miller Single Audits
Professional's Guide to Value Pricing

Aspen's Miller Comprehensive Online Libraries, available at www.millerseries.com or www.tax.cchgroup.com, include:

Miller GAAP Library—Miller GAAP Guide; Miller GAAP Practice Manual; Miller GAAP Financial Statement Disclosures Manual; and Miller GAAP Update Service

Miller GAAS Library—Miller GAAS Guide; Miller GAAS Practice Manual; and Miller GAAS Update Service

Miller Engagement Library—Miller Audit Procedures; Miller Compilations & Reviews; and CPA's Guide to Effective Engagement Letters

Miller Governmental GAAP Library—Miller Governmental GAAP Guide; Miller Governmental GAAP Practice Manual: A Guide to GASB 34; Miller Not-for-Profit Reporting; and Miller Governmental GAAP Update Service

Miller Governmental and Not-for-Profit Audit Library— Miller Single Audits; Miller Not-for-Profit Organization Audits; and Miller Local Government Audits

Miller International Accounting Library—Miller European Accounting Guide and Miller International Accounting Standards Guide

Original standards and pronouncements from **FASB** and **GASB** are also available with any Miller Online Library.

ASPEN LAW & BUSINESS
A Division of Aspen Publishers, Inc.
A Wolters Kluwer Company
www.aspenpublishers.com

SUBSCRIPTION NOTICE

This Aspen Law & Business product is updated on a periodic basis with supplements to reflect important changes in the subject matter. If you purchased this product directly from Aspen Law & Business, we have already recorded your subscription for the update service.

If, however, you purchased this product from a bookstore and wish to receive future updates and revised or related volumes billed separately with a 30-day examination review, please contact our Customer Service Department at 1-800-234-1660, or send your name, company name (if applicable), address, and the title of the product to:

ASPEN LAW & BUSINESS
A Division of Aspen Publishers, Inc.
7201 McKinney Circle
Frederick, MD 21704

▼ Contents

Part I: Medical Practice Financial Management

Part II: Medical Office Operations, Policies, and Procedures

Chapter 10. Basic CPT and Diagnosis-Coding Rules

Chapter 11. Filing Insurance Claims

Chapter 12. Accounts Receivable Management

Chapter 13. Keeping the Books

Chapter 14. Inventory and Purchasing

Chapter 15. Marketing the Medical Practice

Chapter 16. Personnel Management

Part III: Physicians' Contracts, Relationships, and Related Issues

Chapter 17. Buy/Sell Agreements for Medical Practices

Chapter 18. Physicians' Employment Agreements

▼ Preface

Another year has passed and the health care industry remains in a constant state of change. Reimbursement continues to change, governments continue to intervene and publish new regulations, competition is increasing, etc. In addition, there is pressure on medical practices not only to maintain their current profitability, but also to try to improve it as well. As such, medical practices continue to need expert guidance and management for both their internal management staff and their independent counselors. I hope this book helps you in this and other similar endeavors.

This book is written from my experiences working exclusively with health care clients for the past 16 years. Intended to be a field guide that can be used by any CPA, consultant, or health care employee, this book should be in the hands of any person working closely with physician medical practices. *Medical Practice Management Handbook* contains the tools necessary to give any medical practice up-to-date financial advice and counsel. Forms, checklists, letters, spreadsheets, and other documents on the disk enclosed with this book will enable you to put into practice what you are reading. By doing so, you will avoid spending hours of trying to reinvent the wheel.

Here are the major highlights of what is new in this edition; there are many others, including many new items on the CD-ROM.

- How to develop a formal marketing plan to build a health care client base.
- Creating a monitoring program to detect practice financial problems.
- New tips on cost containment.
- Expanded discussion on the importance of strategic planning.
- New information on CPT modifiers.
- An analysis of a recent U.S. Tax Court case involving physician bonuses reclassified as nondeductible corporate dividends.
- A review of the Office of the Inspector General's OIG Advisory Opinion No. 01-4, dealing with physician recruitment arrangements outside a safe harbor.
- Tips on estimating office start-up costs.

If you have any comments or questions, or if you need consulting advice, I hope you will not hesitate to call on me for assistance. Feel free to contact me at 281-379-5988 or by e-mail at reedt@rtcpa.com. Remember—the only foolish question is the one that never gets asked. I hope you enjoy the book.

Acknowledgments

I want to thank my wife Suan again for allowing me to indulge in my passion for writing. Year after year, she has steadfastly encouraged me during the time it takes to revise this book. Without her support, it would not be possible. This book is dedicated to her.

Reed Tinsley, CPA

Houston, Texas

▼ About the Author

Reed Tinsley, CPA, is the owner of Reed Tinsley & Associates, a Houston, Texas-based CPA and health care consulting practice. He works closely with physicians, medical groups, and other delivery systems on managed-care contracting issues, operational matters, strategic planning, and growth strategies. His entire practice is concentrated in the health care industry.

Mr. Tinsley has published books and numerous articles in national and regional publications, and has spoken frequently on a variety of health care topics including capitation, revenue enhancement, and integration services. His articles have been published in the *Journal of Medical Practice Management, MGMA Journal, Hospital Physician, Texas Medicine Family Practice Journal,* and *Group Practice Journal.* In addition to *Medical Practice Management Handbook,* he has written several other books, two of which have been published by the American Medical Association. Mr. Tinsley also serves on the Editorial Panel of Consultants for several publications.

Both the American Medical Association and the Southern Medical Association have sponsored Mr. Tinsley's seminars.

▼ PART I
Medical Practice Financial Management

Part I of this handbook details and discusses the financial management issues of a medical practice that practice administrators, physician leaders, and their advisors must know about. With the number of changes occurring within the health care industry, a careful eye must be kept on day-to-day operating issues. It all starts with finances.

Successful medical practices should surround themselves with a first-rate advisory team. This includes lawyers, accountants, financial planners, and practice management consultants. This team advises practice leadership on a myriad of issues, both internal and external. Practice leadership commits to meet with these advisors on a continuous basis. With the aid and counsel of the team advisors, the practice should be able to perform better, both operationally and financially. This is a real key to practice success.

Part I also includes a discussion of how to start specializing in the health care industry for those readers who consult with, or want to consult with, medical practices. The change from being a generalist to providing specialized consultative services to physicians and health care entities is not easy. Although every practice's situation differs, the guidelines given on how to develop a health care niche will be helpful for anyone preparing to enter this lucrative field.

▼ CHAPTER 1
Developing a Health Care Niche for the CPA or Consultant Reader

This chapter is dedicated to the reader who is a CPA or health care consultant. If you are not a CPA or health care consultant, proceed to Chapter 2.

Medical practices have a growing need for specialized services. The health care industry in most parts of the country is volatile and changing rapidly. This presents acute business problems for all medical practices. For example, as more and more health maintenance organizations (HMOs) are introduced and adopted into a physician's neighborhood, the physician will need to learn new insurance filing processes and all the administrative requirements of the plans.

Physicians need help increasing revenue and containing costs. They also need help adapting to a changing marketplace, because the changes will impact revenues and costs. This is why medical practices need more input and expertise from their advisors, especially their professional consultant. The consultant could be a certified public accountant, a full-time or part-time health care consultant, or any other related type of individual. The consultant's general "services" no longer meet the specific needs of many medical practices throughout the United States. Although services such as preparing basic financial statements and tax returns are necessary, they are no longer vital to the ongoing management of a medical practice. Medical offices are not presently demanding traditional accounting services to guide them through industry changes such as the continuous revisions to the Medicare payment program and the continued growth of managed care. To help their medical clients, professional consultants must develop and provide the knowledge, expertise, and services that their medical clients need.

Specialized Needs of a Medical Practice

The following is a partial list of the specialized services medical practices may need at some point. A good practice administrator should be able to perform many of these duties, but there will be times when independent expertise must be outsourced or engaged. One person cannot know everything, which is why it is so important to surround the practice with a first-rate team of advisors. All of these services and their related issues will be discussed in the chapters that follow.

Complete practice assessments/reviews   Periodically, a medical practice needs a complete review and assessment. The goal of this service is to evaluate the overall efficiency of the practice and to determine if it is losing revenue. A review attempts to improve the bottom line. For example, if cash flow decreases, the practice may want to hire a professional or health care consultant to conduct an independent assessment of its practice operations to determine the cause of the decrease. Think of a practice assessment in terms of a yearly tune-up of the physician's car. The objectives are to make sure that everything is running and operating as efficiently as possible, day in and day out.

Coding analysis   A coding analysis determines if the practice is coding all of its services correctly. If the office members do not code the services correctly, the practice may lose revenue. The analysis covers both procedural coding and diagnosis coding. A practice should be constantly reviewing the coding practices of its physicians. (See Chapter 10.)

Office policy and procedures manuals   A medical practice's efficiency can be traced directly to its internal operational systems. A lack of systems will often result in lost revenue. Thus, every medical practice should have a policy and procedures manual detailing how, when, and by whom certain office functions are to be performed. (See Chapter 16.)

Practice valuation   A practice valuation determines the value of a physician's ownership interest in a medical practice. Physicians, hospitals, insurance companies, and other entities or individuals who want to acquire medical practices can request such an engagement. A practice valuation could also be conducted for buy/sell situations. In that case, the practice will want to engage a qualified, experienced valuator of medical practices. (See Chapter 23.)

Mergers of medical practices Physicians who are contemplating merging their practices should seek someone to guide them through the process. (See Chapter 21.)

Physicians' contracts Medical practices need assistance with contracts such as those related to physicians' employment, buy/sell agreements, and managed care. Most of the provisions contained in physicians' contracts are financial in nature, such as tax considerations. Physicians need someone to review, and even help develop, such contracts. Some medical practices also may need assistance with contract negotiations with a potential employer, hospital, or managed-care plan. Again, this is where the practice's advisory team can be of assistance. (See Chapter 18.)

Development of individual practice associations (IPAs), management service organizations (MSOs), and other integrated delivery systems The health care industry is moving toward an integrated system of delivering health care. Physicians need to affiliate in order to compete. Physicians need assistance with all issues related to managed-care contracts. (See Chapter 22.)

Negotiation with managed-care plans Medical practices need to increase their own reimbursement from managed-care plans. This need is accomplished by negotiating an increase in price from these plans. This process includes the development of a managed-care strategy for the practice. New delivery systems require help with the initial facilitation of reimbursement rates. (See Chapter 19.)

Review of Medicare/Medicaid billing practices Many medical specialties are provided for a large number of Medicare and even Medicaid patients. Specific rules apply to Medicare/Medicaid billing. An office that is not aware of certain billing rules will lose revenue. Not only will revenue be lost, but this lack of knowledge could result in compliance problems for the practice. In other words, it might result in a reimbursement audit by the government. Therefore, Medicare/Medicaid billing must be reviewed periodically. (See Chapter 11.)

Review of the practice's receivables To optimize cash flow, a medical practice must manage its accounts receivable. All systems and procedures related to accounts receivable management must be monitored and reviewed, either continually or periodically. The aging of receivables also must be monitored. (See Chapter 12.)

Purchase and implementation of a computer system Practices are now realizing that proper management mandates a good computer system. Great care must be taken when purchasing and implementing a computer system or upgrading an old system. (See Chapter 7.)

Assistance with Occupational Safety and Health Administration (OSHA) and Clinical Laboratory Improvement Amendment (CLIA) compliance Myriad state and federal regulations relate to the daily operation of a medical practice. Examples are regulations associated with blood-borne pathogens and clinical laboratories. Medical practices must implement and maintain knowledge of these and other current and new governing regulations. (See Chapter 6.)

Interviewing and hiring personnel The success of most medical practices depends on their personnel. Many physicians do not have experience with hiring and neither do their office managers. Poor hiring decisions can hurt any office. (See Chapter 16.)

Implementation of internal controls Most medical practices are vulnerable to embezzlement. All medical practices must implement and monitor a basic system of internal controls. (See Chapter 4.)

Embezzlement review Fear of employee theft warrants an embezzlement review for some medical practices. This should be performed by an independent third party, such as the practice's CPA. (See Chapter 4.)

Purchase or sale of a medical practice Issues such as valuation, negotiation, taxes, contract development, and practice transition demand careful attention. (See Chapter 17.)

Design of physicians' compensation arrangements Because the medical industry is changing, old compensation systems may no longer be viable. An example would be the service area and the growth of capitation. Practices may need help revising their current compensation systems or developing new systems. Also, governmental regulations, such as the Stark laws, often require changes to current physician compensation systems. (See Chapter 18.)

Practice setup   New physicians need support in establishing and setting up their offices. (See Chapter 7.)

Education   To operate a successful medical practice, a physician and his or her office staff must be kept up-to-date on all the changes that occur annually in the health care industry, such as changes in Medicare billing policies and procedures. Internal education programs should be created and implemented by the practice.

Billing service review   Many physicians use outside billing agencies to bill and collect their services. These agencies are often left unaccountable. The physician's agency should be reviewed periodically to make sure that services are billed out correctly and that the agency puts in the time and effort required to collect these services.

Strategic planning   A medical practice needs help in order to strategically place itself in a position to take advantage of a changing health care marketplace. Today's successful practices are using strategic planning initiatives to their advantage.

Cost accounting   Every medical practice needs to know what it costs to perform a particular service, especially in areas where managed care dominates the marketplace.

Assembly of clinical data   To compete in a managed-care environment, practices must be able to demonstrate that they deliver cost-effective health care services. This allows practices to compete for managed-care contracts and to negotiate reimbursement rates successfully. (See Chapter 19.)

Capitation rate analysis   Capitation is a common way doctors are paid by HMOs and other delivery systems. When presented with a capitation rate, most doctors are unaware whether or not such a rate should be accepted and even more important, whether or not such a rate will be profitable.

Implementation of QA/UM programs As managed care grows, doctors and their practices must become "cost effective." This also applies to integrated delivery systems. Doctors who deliver cost-effective care will be the ones who will have the ability to negotiate managed-care rates and be in a position to compete for exclusive contracting arrangements. To become and remain cost effective, practices must implement quality assurance and utilization management (QA/UM) programs.

Managed-care marketing To compete for managed-care contracts, practices and other health care providers must market themselves to these payors. Development of a marketing document and a marketing program is essential.

Developing a Health Care Niche in a Small Professional or Consulting Firm

Health care is one of the fastest growing specialty areas for professional and consulting firms. The transition from generalist to specialist, however, presents a number of obstacles and demands a great deal of time and money. The most common obstacles are a lack of knowledge about the health care industry and the issues that are important to physician clients, and a lack of time to develop the expertise.

Limiting Factors

Because of the nature of a generalized practice, most CPAs and other consultants operating as sole practitioners or practicing in small professional or consulting firms are prevented from becoming more familiar with their clients and their clients' respective industries. Most consultants are forced to know a "little bit about a whole lot." In other words, consultants such as CPAs and generalist professionals service many different clients in a variety of industries. For example, a particular consultant may spend his or her day doing work for clients in medicine, retail, real estate, or law.

Because consultants must spend time with different types of clients (unless time is spent specializing in one industry), most cannot offer the time necessary to get to know any one client and the client's industry in depth, unless a consultant has a number of clients in a specific industry. Even then it is difficult to become familiar with an industry because of ongoing client obligations and responsibilities. A consultant must make the commitment to specialize in a particular client industry.

To determine how much or how little you know a particular client, try to answer the following three questions:

1. How does the client earn its revenue?
2. How does the client's business operate on a day-to-day basis?
3. Do I know everything about the client's industry? For example, do I know when a change within the industry will affect my client's revenue stream?

If you cannot answer these questions, you really do not know your client. And, if you do not know your client, you cannot advise that client. The definition of an *expert* is one who can walk into a client's office and run that office or business. An expert can perform the job of any of his client's employees. You, as the professional advisor and consultant, should strive to be an expert.

With limited staff and limited time, most small firms cannot take the nonchargeable time necessary to expand their specific knowledge of clients. This is one of the major dilemmas of a consultant who tries to become an expert in one field. It is a classic Catch-22. If the consultant spends nonchargeable time getting to know a medical client, he or she is not earning revenue for the practice. It is difficult for most consultants to reconcile the short-term impact with long-term benefits.

Personal Considerations

To develop a health care niche, a consultant must look first at the personal considerations and then at the business strategies it takes to create the niche. On a personal level, the consultant must decide if he or she wants to devote all or part of his or her time to health care. The consultant does not have to become an expert to enhance services to medical clients. The consultant has the flexibility to pick and choose the services he or she wants to render. However, each direction requires a certain amount of personal commitment. Unfortunately, most consultants do not have the luxury of dropping everything to concentrate on health care consulting. Therefore, the consultant will have to continue devoting time to tax and accounting issues while gaining knowledge about such areas as insurance reimbursement, Medicare, service coding, and the many government regulations that affect medical practices.

From a practical point of view, it is difficult to do both. Commitment requires a great deal of personal sacrifice, mainly in the form of time. You must therefore make the difficult decision of how much commitment you are willing to make. You will have to answer the following questions:

- Do I take time away from the practice?
- Do I take time away from family?
- Do I take time away from myself?

Even though a high degree of commitment may sound intimidating at first, the long-term benefits will far outweigh the short-term sacrifices. You will end up providing services no one else is capable of delivering to health care clients.

Educating Yourself

After facing the personal considerations necessary to develop a health care niche, your next step is to develop specific knowledge about medical practices and the health care industry. The two basic ways to do this are as follows:

1. Increase your overall knowledge.
2. Acquire hands-on experience by spending time in a medical practice.

To become aware of the specialized issues that affect the health care industry and medical practices, make a commitment to attend industry seminars and read industry publications. Call the state's medical association and the county's medical society to request a list of all upcoming practice management seminars. The state's Medicare and Medicaid insurance carriers also offer information on all upcoming seminars. Ask medical clients for seminar information they have received through the mail and attend as many seminars as time and money will allow.

Develop a health care library by subscribing to relevant publications. The list at the end of this chapter is a good place to begin. The consultant also should consider joining some of the listed organizations. These publications and association memberships will provide a foundation of knowledge of the health care industry and medical practices. Hard work and commitment are required in order to develop a knowledge of the industry.

Hands-on Experience

The next step in the learning process is to find out how a medical office operates daily. This will help you discover which services the medical client really needs, other than compilation and tax work. Learn how a medical practice bills and collects for its services. Then you will be able to tailor specific services your firm can offer to a physician's office. The best way to garner this knowledge is by spending time in the client's office observing and asking questions. Tell one of your clients that you want to become involved in the client's business and industry and ask if you could spend some nonchargeable time in the client's office. The client should appreciate the fact that you are willing to take an expanded interest in the practice. The office manager/administrator will be the best source of information.

These are the first steps in building a health care niche within a consultant firm. It is not an easy task, but eventually it is quite rewarding, both in terms of increased billings and personal and professional satisfaction.

Developing a Health Care Niche in a Large Firm

Securing Support

The first step in developing a health care niche in a large professional firm is to get a commitment from all of the firm's partners or shareholders to stand firmly behind its development. If they do not, the firm ultimately will not provide the resources, personnel, and energy it takes to develop a successful medical niche, and the results will be far less than spectacular. Securing the partners' complete commitment is arguably the most important issue related to developing a health care niche.

Getting all of the partners' commitment is difficult for many reasons. For example, partners who are nearing retirement seldom want to commit the working capital that is necessary to develop a new niche. This money will come out of their pockets, as reduced compensation, reduced equity interest, or possibly a reduced buy-out amount. Older partners may retain their own traditional views of public accounting, which often center on the conventional services of accounting, auditing, and providing tax advice. The development of specialized consulting services contradicts this traditional viewpoint. The firm's economics also will play a part in the partners' commitment. If a firm's net income has been stagnating or decreasing for several years, partners will not want to spend additional monies on the development of new services and capabilities. Owners in these situations often look at costs first and benefits later. Because most partners are unfamiliar with the various types of specialized health care consulting services, they may not see the long-term benefits of increased firm revenues, enhanced service to clients, and heightened consumer perception of the firm. Unfortunately, most discussions centered on the creation of a new niche never progress because everyone concentrates on the costs and how they will influence the bottom line. Although such an attitude is prudent, it is also shortsighted.

Catering to Clients

Owners of professional firms must realize that health care clients want more than just the typical accounting and tax services. In fact, many of these clients are beginning to question the true value of traditional accounting services. Health care clients need professional advisors who know something about their industry. This trend can be seen in other service industries as well. Large law firms, for example, are beginning to segment along industry product lines rather than by service lines. Instead of a lawyer being placed in the litigation, tax, or corporate department, he or she is now a part of the health care industry group, real estate industry group, and so on. This trend is the result of clients demanding such specialization. Physicians are practicing in turbulent times. Their revenues and costs are affected by many different factors. Even the way that medicine is practiced is changing. Medical clients need specialized help from their accounting and consulting firms. Consultants must risk expanding their firm's revenue base and service capabilities to clients. If firm owners are not willing to make the necessary commitments to develop a health care niche, their client base will begin to erode as other firms develop or expand their health care niche.

Assembling the Team

Assuming a firm can obtain the partners' commitment to develop a niche, the next step is to decide who in the firm will be groomed to provide the specialized services. This person or persons could be a partner, a manager, a senior accountant, or even a staff member. Make sure that the person who will be trained remains employed by the firm for a long time. It is not wise to invest resources in a person who is likely to leave the firm after a short while. If the firm will be spending money to send this person to specialized health care seminars, investing in nonchargeable time to build and expand its health care knowledge, or spending money to market its new service capabilities, the firm should make sure that the person is a safe and secure investment. The repercussions if the person left the firm could be disastrous. The partners may withdraw their commitment or the firm's reputation may be tarnished. The firm might even end up training someone who then leaves and competes against the firm.

Because of this risk, most firms first choose a person among the partner or manager group to head the health care department or industry group. The industry group will then pick its own personnel to train. The manager will need to decide if he or she wants to expand certain services already being provided to health care clients or develop entirely new, specialized consulting services. When selecting people to specialize in a particular industry, especially health care, the manager should gauge a person's interest in the industry. If a person is asked to specialize in health care but does not especially like the industry, he or she will not put forth the effort it takes to develop the expertise. In this situation, the niche will never be as successful as it could be, simply because of a lack of effort. In addition, the firm may face a heightened risk of personnel turnover because the individual does not especially like what he or she is doing.

One personnel option is to hire someone already experienced in health care. Firms have successfully hired health care consultants, practice administrators, office managers, and hospital practice management personnel to provide specialized services to their health care clients. If the firm decides to go this route, some issues need to be clarified. Most of these individuals are unaware of billable time and realization rate, so expect a learning curve in these areas and accept the fact there may be large write-downs of time in the beginning (assuming your firm bills projects by the hour). In addition, many individuals do not have a strong financial background. If the firm's reports and services are numbers-driven, there may be a learning curve here also.

Servicing All Health Care Clients

Finally, assuming the firm can garner the commitment of its owners and successfully set up a health care department or industry group, the firm must allow this group to service all of its health care clients. A problem can result in a large firm if compensation is somehow tied to billings or work-in-process runs. This is especially the case in accounting firms. If the health care group works with a particular client of another partner, that partner may want to get credit for the associated billings. When the industry group is penalized because it did the work but did not receive credit for it in the firm's compensation formula, this can, and often does, lead to frustration among the firm's personnel.

In addition, the industry group must establish uniform service protocols before beginning to service health care clients. Every person in the group must be taught to perform certain engagements, such as practice assessments, accounts receivable, management reviews, and coding analysis. If uniform protocols are not developed, the industry group and the firm will put at risk the quality of their work product. This could eventually tarnish the reputation of the firm within the health care industry.

A Common Obstacle—Making Time

Arguably, the biggest obstacle to the transition of becoming a specialist is time. Individuals want to make the commitment but just have not been able to find the time to do it.

The issue of time, however, may become a crutch for many individuals. Time is like the weather—it is something you will always have to deal with. Do not use time as an excuse for your failure or your firm's failure to commit to change.

To overcome the time problem, first look at the service list mentioned earlier in this chapter. Decide on the services you feel would be of most interest to your medical clients. For example, revenue enhancement engagements, such as fee schedule and accounts receivable reviews, can be performed for most medical offices. In areas where managed care dominates, physicians will need help with contracting issues. If you don't know what services to select, meet with a few clients and ask them directly. They will appreciate that you are taking a more detailed interest in their practice beyond typical tax and accounting.

Once you know which services you want to offer, make time to learn about those services and medical practices. Scheduling time to learn may be the best way to acquire knowledge about the services. For example, if you know that you have three hours every morning or evening to learn about medical practices, you will devote that time appropriately and you will be able to delegate other projects or schedule them at other times.

Finally, if you do not take the time and make the commitment to develop a health care niche, your competitors might. If local firms cannot provide these services, medical practices may hire a health care consultant or an out-of-town firm to provide the services. If you do not specialize, you may lose chargeable time and revenue.

Marketing Strategies

What are the best marketing strategies to get new business from physicians? The key to marketing success is first to determine what physician practices need right now. Then determine which of these services you can and want to deliver.

Once you have taken care of these two important issues, the next step is to create a marketing plan that will attract additional business and additional revenues. The marketing plan should target new business—not only from new physicians, but from existing physician clients as well. (For more information on marketing, see Chapter 15.)

The following are common marketing strategies you should consider; because service areas differ, some might work better for you than for others. However, the constant among all marketing strategies is this: success depends on proper implementation. Proper implementation includes not only the execution of the strategy but, more importantly, the commitment to continue with it even though it seems it is not working initially. One of the critical mistakes professional and consulting firms make with marketing is that they abandon a strategy too quickly when things don't seem to be going quite like they envisioned. Marketing is a long-term investment. Make sure that there is full commitment among the partner group to stick with some or all of the following marketing strategies before they are ever attempted.

Speeches   Be willing to speak anywhere, anytime. No marketing strategy is more effective than getting up in front of a group of people and being able to demonstrate your expertise by what you say and how you say it. Polish up your résumé. Then make a list of all local physician organizations (such as the County Medical Society) and meet with each. Let them know you are available to speak on a variety of physician practice management subjects, emphasizing the subjects that are presently hot buttons within the physician community.

Setting up your own speeches is usually difficult. You must find a good time for physicians to attend and it is costly. It is preferable to find a sponsor for your seminar who will send out the seminar announcement and take care of the speech location. It is always easier for you if you can just show up and talk.

Whenever you do speak, create a professional set of handouts for the attendees; you want them to take something back to their office with them. These handouts should include information on your firm and its service capabilities.

One final comment about giving speeches: Never, ever "sell" at these functions. The quickest way to lose credibility with your audience, and especially with your seminar sponsor, is to sell yourself openly to the participants. The seminar should demonstrate your expertise in the seminar topic, so selling is not necessary.

Publications　This is the number two marketing strategy (following speaking in public) to get new physician clients or even new business from existing clients. There is nothing that will give you greater credibility with a client or a potential client than authorship. Following are the keys to getting an article published:

1. Make a list of targeted publications. These are the publications in which you want to try to get your article published. These are the publications your physician clients and potential clients receive and read most often. Make a list of local publications first, statewide publications second, and national publications third. Find these by paying attention to what publications are in the physician's waiting area when you are there or simply ask the physician or the practice administrator. At a minimum, target the publications produced by the state medical association, county medical association, and the national academy of the physician's medical specialty.

2. Write about one of the current hot topics of the day. Health care is a rapidly changing industry; the important issues of the day seem to change quite often. For this reason, it is important that you know what is going on in the industry and what is currently impacting physician practices. Editors obviously want to publish articles that their readership will be interested in reading. If you meet with your physician clients regularly and if you keep up on your health care professional reading, you should have no problem knowing what the hot topics are within the industry.

3. Don't be afraid to submit an article to a publication's editor. Publications are always looking for articles or article ideas. Send either the complete article or a letter outlining your idea and asking if the editor would be interested in seeing the article.

One final note about publishing: If possible, never give up the copyright. Publications will usually try to get you to sign an agreement turning the copyright over to them. Try to avoid this because you will want to try to get your article published later in other health care magazines and publications.

Newsletters Newsletters are a good way to inform existing and potential clients about specific health care issues and to let them know a firm's service capabilities. A newsletter to a physician should concentrate on practice management issues (i.e., current needs) and not be diluted by tax, accounting, or personal financial planning issues. Another objective of the newsletter is to separate you from your competition. Focus the newsletter on what a medical practice needs. For example, it is doubtful that a discussion of compliance and planning issues will do this effectively, so you would probably avoid such a topic.

The following are the do's and don'ts of a successful newsletter:

1. Produce your own newsletter, even if it is a little more expensive. "Canned" newsletters look and read like "canned" newsletters and often cannot and do not talk about the issues of interest to your clients or potential clients. If you produce your own newsletter, make sure it is professional in appearance and content. People reading your newsletter are intelligent and will be able to spot a lack of professionalism. Strive for your product to measure up to or surpass your competitor's.

2. Produce and mail the newsletter at least quarterly; initially mail monthly if the intent is to go after new physician clients. The objective is to create an awareness within the physician community that you are an expert in medical practice issues. The more information you can get before them, the faster this may happen.

3. Mail the newsletter not only to existing physician clients, but to their administrators as well. Practice administrators are likely to read your newsletter sooner than the physicians will. (As a consultant, can you get to all of your professional reading?) If there is ever a practice management need within the practice, the administrator may influence the physician to give you a call. Also, for the same reason, send the newsletter to the physician's home address. Remember, the objective is to get the physician's attention.

4. Keep a good mailing list. First, make sure the mailing list includes all physicians you might want as clients. For example, target all the orthopedic surgeons in the city as potential clients; target all the office managers who are members of the local chapter of a medical organization. Make sure that the mailing list includes everyone who might be able to refer business to you. These are the people who deal with physicians on a regular basis, such as hospital administrators.

5. Send the newsletter to the editors at medical publications. You may receive offers to write an article for publication based on what an editor reads in a health care newsletter.

6. Tout your accomplishments. Let people know in the newsletter about articles you have published and speeches you have made. This will build up your credibility with the reader.

Client meetings   This is another excellent marketing strategy but one that many consultants fail to use. For marketing purposes, hold *ongoing* meetings with current physician or health care clients. The objective of any meeting is twofold: (a) to discuss an issue or solve a need and (b) to find out what other services the client may need from his or her consultant. One of the best marketing strategies is to get a client talking about what is going on with his or her medical practice. You will find that physicians will readily talk about their practice problems and issues when you show genuine interest. These discussions should provide a road map leading you to additional service opportunities and increased revenues.

Try to set up a meeting with each of your physician clients. No matter what the size of the practice is, conduct formal business meetings throughout the year, preferably once a month, though quarterly meetings may be enough. These meetings should have an agenda and a purpose—to let the practice know where it stands financially and to address the current issues affecting and impacting the practice.

Here is a simple practice agenda:

• Review of financial statements
• Review of practice management reports
• Review of accounts receivable

- Review of practice marketing efforts and physician referrals
- Employee issues
- Physician issues
- Revenue enhancement opportunities
- Managed-care contracting
- Other issues

Electronic communications As you probably know, newsletters and other related forms of print media can be an expensive form of marketing. However, a cheaper and arguably more cost-effective communication method is sending information to clients and prospects by e-mail through the Internet. For example, you can send out an electronic newsletter instead of sending one in a printed format. Many law firms do this now. Often, people will read an electronic newsletter (i.e., their e-mail), whereas a printed newsletter may get stuck on someone else's desk or under a stack of papers on the desk of the intended recipient.

Also, you can send other electronic forms of communication to your clients and prospects. For example, you can send a specific message that does not necessarily have to be in a "newsletter" format. This could be a specific message about billing and collection issues, a new regulatory announcement, etc. This is why it is so important that you collect and assemble as many e-mail addresses as you can from your clients and prospects. To facilitate your electronic communications with your prospects and clients, consider using a contact management software program such as ACT or Goldmine. If you are a larger organization, there are other very good contact management programs tailored for the size of your organization. These are usually called "CRMs"—customer relationship management programs.

Advertising The main objective of advertising is to create an awareness of your firm's service capabilities. You want to let your target clients know exactly what you can do for them. Then, when target (or even current) clients have a need, they will call on you to solve it because they know (through advertising) you can help. Advertising should target prospects instead of current clients because ongoing communications and meetings should serve to let current physician clients know what you can do for them. Most consultants do not get out of their offices and meet with their clients. Experienced rainmakers know that to get new business, all you have to do is get the client talking about his or her practice concerns; but first you have to be willing to meet with the prospective client and show interest.

Advertise in magazines and publications that your clients and prospects read most often. This could be the state medical association magazine or the county medical society's publication. Deciding where to advertise should be a part of your firm's marketing plan. The biggest mistake firms make is failing to see advertising (and other marketing strategies) as a long-term commitment and investment. Advertising less than six straight months in a particular publication is a waste of effort and money. Remember, the objective is to drill into the readers' collective minds that you can help them with their practices. Advertising only two straight months will not get this point across.

What should you advertise? If you can render the service, it is best to gear your advertising to one of the current hot buttons of the day. For example, this could be managed-care contracting, government regulation, compliance issues, or coding. At a minimum, your advertising should express your expertise in general practice management issues.

Here is a great saying about the objective of marketing strategies: *"When a client has an itch, they know who to call to scratch it."*

A follow-up program   Leads could come from a seminar at which you spoke, from an article you published, from your advertising, or from the Internet. Do you have a formal and accountable lead follow-up program? Every firm should develop a lead follow-up program, but, amazingly, most firms do not have one in place. Follow-up is sporadic, leading to many lost engagement opportunities.

Plan for follow-up. When you give a speech, always get a listing of the attendees, their addresses, and their phone numbers; always request this as a condition of your speaking engagement. With this list, you can send a follow-up letter or even add the people to your mailing list.

If someone in the firm obtains a lead on a potential client engagement, the firm should use an accountable follow-up process. This means that the lead (i.e., prospect) is contacted and placed into the firm's sales process. If your firm does not have a sales process, make sure the people responsible for selling are responsible for their efforts. This can be documented using a simple spreadsheet program, such as the following example:

PROSPECT	CONTACT PERSON	SERVICE/ PROPOSAL	POTENTIAL FEE	LAST CONTACT

This prospect tracking sheet is included on the CD-ROM.

In-house seminars This is in contrast to participating in a full-blown seminar, in which you rent space at a local hotel, have the event catered, print and mail fancy invitations, and hope somebody shows up. Instead, conduct seminars in your own office. Invite a small group of current clients and/or targeted potential clients. You could even invite referral sources. The seminar should last no longer than one hour. A good time to have this seminar is around 3:00 p.m. or 4:00 p.m.; the participants won't be rushed to get back to the office. Provide handouts. Consider holding a reception after the presentation.

A great marketing idea is to target your seminar efforts to practice office managers. Subject areas should be whatever are the hot topics of the day. A practice operations topic or a managed-care contracting topic are two examples. The invitee list should include current "A" or "B" clients and prospects. The session should last one hour and should be scheduled at a time that is convenient for the office managers. A good time is typically from 4:00 p.m. to 5:00 p.m. or from noon to 2:30 p.m.

Direct mail This is not always an effective way to garner new medical clients, but some consultants have done well with it. Each market is different and you will have to assess how receptive the physicians in your service area are to direct mail. If you do send a direct mail piece, the subject should be one that is foremost on physicians' minds at that time. If you don't know what these subject areas are, you have not kept up with what is going on with your medical client and what is going on within the health care industry. This is why it is so important to keep up with your professional reading and to meet with your health care clients on a regular basis. Sample "hot" subject areas are coding, revenue enhancement, practice growth strategies, and compliance. The direct mail piece should offer a service that can help the physician's practice.

When sending direct mail, it is also very important to include a postage-paid reply card. Make it easy for the reader to respond to your direct mail piece. Include on the card, for example, a list of services the reader could check if he or she might be interested in one or more of them. The card should include a request to be added to your firm's mailing list, as well as a request to be sent information about your firm.

Seminar/meeting attendance   As previously stated, the key to marketing success is your ability to forge relationships with your clients and referral sources. One of the best ways to do this is by attending health care seminars that these same individuals attend. For example, you could attend a health law course so you can develop relationships with health care lawyers who might be able to refer business to you. There is not a more powerful marketing tool than putting yourself in front of these individuals on a consistent basis. Just starting a conversation can lead to new business.

Build a web site   All professional practices should have their own web site. More and more people are going on the Internet to seek information and to seek assistance for a variety of problems and issues. However, do not expect to garner many clients with a web site that discusses the firm and lists its services. Most consumers do not select their professional advisor this way. However, if a firm understands how the Internet is being used for research, the opportunities do exist to attract potential new clients.

The more successful professional firms put on their web sites health care information that individuals (i.e., potential clients) can access simply by downloading or saving the information. For example, a web site should contain all health care articles written by firm personnel. One firm obtained a large practice merger engagement because a physician found and downloaded one of his medical practice merger articles from the firm's web site. Place anything on your web site that people can use, such as forms or checklists—things that will help the person. You don't want to give away the store, but on the other hand, one of the quickest ways to a sale is to help people get what they want. This is an age-old marketing technique that works quite well.

The Internet   Go out into the vast Internet to find potential clients. There are many listservs (such as Part B News) and discussion groups (such as MGMA) in which you can join and participate in. You can respond to questions (and sometimes proposal requests) and have your own questions answered. At other health care web sites, physicians or other individuals ask questions and you can respond to these specific questions. This interaction sometimes leads to new client opportunities.

Involvement in medical organizations   Get involved in medical organizations. Find out if there are local chapters of the Healthcare Financial Management Association, Professional Association of Healthcare Office Managers, and the Medical Group Management Association. Try to become an officer in one of these organizations or at least participate on a committee.

Scholarships   Create a scholarship fund for local medical residents or fellows or any other type of related scholarship. This type of marketing activity often results in great press and media exposure.

Client invoicing   Client invoicing is a way to market to existing health care clients. When sending out an invoice to a client regarding a health care matter, be as descriptive as you can about the services that you rendered and, more importantly, about the benefits achieved by the client. The client will find it hard to dispute your invoice when it states directly on it how the client benefited from your service. The objective is to demonstrate that the client did get a return on its investment. This is another way you let the client know the continuing benefits of his or her relationship with your CPA practice.

Results of your work product   The marketing strategy is similar to that of client invoicing. You want to communicate to your health care client, when possible, the tangible results of your work product. An excellent marketing idea is to quantify how you helped the client. How did you enable the client to make (or keep) more money? There is no better way to strengthen a client relationship than by showing the client exactly how you benefited them with your service or services.

For example, when you perform a coding review of a practice's evaluation and management services, you find that most physicians in the practice are not billing correctly for consultative visits. You meet with the office manager and billing personnel to discuss the situation, and then you meet with a few of the physicians. Everyone agrees that consultations are not being coded correctly. The next step should be to quantify lost revenues as a result of the practice's coding errors. You would calculate an average reimbursement difference between the correct coding method and how the services were actually billed, and multiply that figure by an estimated (or actual, if known) number of incorrectly coded visits. The resulting number is how much estimated revenue you found for the practice. You can imagine the client's perception of you and your service when this is communicated to the client.

CPA joint ventures   If your objective is to provide the highest level of service possible to medical clients, look for opportunities for joint ventures with other firms to provide the specialized services discussed previously in this chapter. Make this type of relationship a win-win situation. You will be able to serve your clients more effectively and most likely you will generate extra billable time as a result of the joint venture engagement.

Fax cover letters   Use your fax cover letter to assist you in making your services known. Consider how to place a list of your services on your fax cover letter as a reminder of your firm's capabilities.

The following is an example of how one firm listed these services at the bottom of its fax cover letters:

Consultants and Advisors in the following specialized areas:

- *Practice Administration*
- *Medical Billing*
- *Practice Valuation*
- *Practice Assessment*
- *Mergers and Acquisitions*
- *Managed-Care Negotiation*

- *Capitation Analysis*
- *Health Care Tax Matters*
- *MSO Development*
- *Medicare/Medicaid Issues*
- *Antitrust Issues*
- *Group Practice Creation*

- *IPA Development*
- *Physician Compensation*
- *Contract Review*
- *Physician Transition*
- *Systems Review*

- *Physician Recruitment*
- *Fraud and Abuse*
- *Strategic Planning*
- *Integrated Delivery Issues*
- *CPT and Diagnosis Coding*

Brochures   Use a health care services capabilities brochure in addition to your regular firm brochure. This is a brochure that is tailored to medical clients. It will be sent only to these clients, potential clients, and referral sources. The brochure should mention all of the specialized consulting services you offer. Designing and implementing this type of brochure is an excellent way to set you apart from your competition.

Nontraditional clientele   Physicians are the most obvious targets as new clients. In reality, many other health care providers need the same services. Dentists, D.O.s, chiropractors, and alternative health care providers all have some of the same needs as physicians. Your services can also be marketed to any entity or person that owns physician practices, such as hospitals and physician practice management companies.

The Best Marketing Strategy

The best marketing strategy is simple: *Be active*. This is true whether you are a multi-partner firm or a single individual. Do the following activities as often as possible:

- Meet with your clients
- Give speeches
- Write articles
- Attend local health care meetings
- Meet with prospects
- Implement new marketing strategies

The Plan Is Key

Whether you are an individual or have a firm, it's important to have some kind of a formal marketing plan to guide you through your marketing efforts. Marketing should be structured and accountable in order to be successful. You just can't try "this or that" and hope it works. You must have a plan! This applies to both individuals and the firm itself. Without a *formal* marketing plan, you could end up "winging" your marketing efforts, thus setting the stage for failure instead of success.

All marketing plans should be reduced to writing. Once done, these plans should be reviewed on a monthly basis and updated. In other words, the plan must be accountable. If you are a solo practitioner, you should still reduce your marketing plan to writing and review it each and every month. As the plan is reviewed, it should be refined as the months go by. Decide what is working and what is not working; add marketing ideas and delete others. A marketing plan should not become a stagnant document.

A Personal Marketing Plan

The following is an example of a personal marketing plan that can be used by professionals in larger organizations or even by solo practitioners. It is included on the CD-ROM that accompanies this book. Reminder: Make the person accountable for whatever is written down.

Individual Health Care Marketing Plan

_____, 2____

*Team Member:*_____

I.   *External Activities*

   Indicate activities that you will personally undertake to accomplish in the year ____ in the following categories:

A. Memberships

I will become an active member in:

1. Health Care Industry Associations

a. _____

b. _____

c. _____

2. Civic or Professional Organizations of Targeted Health Care Clients

a. _____

b. _____

c. _____

B. Leadership

I will work towards serving in a leadership position in the following:

Association/Organization	Position Desired Attained	Target Date

C. Seminars and Presentations

I will participate in the planning of the following FIRM or outside sponsored health care seminar, as a primary or panel speaker:

Seminar Topic	Target Audience	Target Date

D. Articles

I will prepare the following articles as a primary or co-author for publication in targeted health care publications:

Topic	Target Audience	Target Date

E. Personal Development

I will undertake the following activities to help me develop my personal skills and level of professionalism within the health care industry:

Health care CPE, courses, films or tapes:

_____

_____

_____

Health care teaching or lecturing opportunities:

_____

_____

_____

Other:

_____

_____

_____

II. Business Development Activities

A. Client Development and Retention

Identify existing health care clients who you will regularly entertain by way of lunches, dinners, etc.:

	Client Name	Contact
1.		
2.		
3.		
4.		
5.		
6.		

B. Client Visits

1. *Identify health care clients who would be appropriate targets for inviting to visit one, or more, of our offices and make a presentation about their businesses to our firm members; if convenient, we can visit their office:*

_____

_____

_____

_____

_____

2. *Identify health care clients who would be appropriate targets for a group of FIRM members to visit the offices of, and make a presentation to, on a timely issue of interest or concern; if convenient, we can visit their office:*

_____

_____

_____

_____

_____

B. Cross-selling

Identify existing health care clients that you will introduce to another FIRM members for cross-selling purposes:

	Client	Firm Member	Description of Action and Outcome Goal
1.			
2.			
3.			
4.			
5.			
6.			

C. Prospects and Referrals

Identify health care prospects or referral sources who you will regularly entertain by way of lunches, dinners, etc.:

Prospect or Referral Source	_Activity_
1.	
2.	
3.	
4.	
5.	
6.	

D. New Business Development

_Identify target health care prospects you will seek to develop new business from during the year _____:_

Target Prospect	_Type of Work_	_Activity_
1.		
2.		
3.		
4.		
5.		
6.		

A Firm Marketing Plan

The following is an example of an actual firm health care marketing plan. You will see the marketing ideas and how the plan slowly "evolved."

Horne CPA Group
Mason, TX Office—Marketing Action Plan
Strategy: In-House Seminars

Mission: _Public awareness of Horne CPA Group and to promote in a small setting our Firm's consulting services. To provide continuing business education to our clients and to become well known for providing such a service._

Action: _Committee members have agreed that every third Wednesday of each month, Horne CPA Group will present an in-house seminar, beginning in February 1999._

We have currently scheduled our first seminar for Wednesday, February 17, 1999 in the office's conference room entitled:

Evaluation and Negotiation of Managed Care Contracts Presented by Reed Tinsley, CPA

Future Seminars, Topics & Dates:

Compliance Programs: How to Evaluate Your Practice March 17, 1999

How to Assess the Health of Your Practice April 21, 1999

Other Topics: Practice Assessment & Y2K

Targeted Audience & Process: *Each member has provided Mr. Sanchez with a list of 15 names of persons within the Health Care Industry to invite (all ranks). The objective is to get 7 to 10 attendees at every presentation. The invitation list will be expanded throughout the year.*

Costs Incurred: $

Action	Delegated To	Date To Be Completed	Date Completed

Developing Relationships—The Key to Success

Once your marketing strategies are working well, success in developing a health care niche depends on one critical element: the ability to develop relationships with current clients, potential clients, referral sources, and other contacts. You may believe that you already have relationships with your clients, but do you have relationships that extend beyond the typical client/accountant relationship to the desired client/advisor/consultant relationship? In other words, do your clients know you are more than an accountant? You will know this is true when a client calls you for advice on the engagement subject areas mentioned earlier in this chapter. When you have this kind of a relationship with a medical client, you have created a bond in which the client feels he or she can call you about any matter concerning the medical practice. This is what creates the high-dollar service engagements and increases referrals from the medical client.

Clients who have a relationship with an accountant or consultant will almost always give new business to that person. One example of a relationship concerns a Southwest professional firm. A partner of the firm attended the annual conference of the Medical Group Management Association. At this meeting, he met the chief operating officer (COO) of a large ENT group practice. During this meeting, the partner discussed with the COO a very specialized service the professional could provide to the medical practice. The COO said he might be interested and asked the partner to send him some information. After getting back to the office, the partner mailed the requested information. He did not follow up with a phone call or set a meeting.

Another partner in the same firm happened to be working with one of his clients in the negotiation of a network provider contract with the same ENT group. The ENT group was developing a city-wide network of ENT physicians to compete for managed-care contracts. This negotiation brought the partner in contact with the chief executive officer (CEO), and the partner had three related meetings with the CEO. After the negotiation was completed, the partner asked the CEO to lunch for a general discussion on managed-care issues within the city and to discuss the specialized project. He asked the CEO if the firm could make a formal presentation to the practice on the project. The CEO agreed and the firm subsequently landed the lucrative project.

In this example, the second partner developed a relationship and the first partner failed to do so. A relationship is not created by sending out newsletters, direct mail, or any other external marketing effort. Although mailings are important, this is only the first step to creating the relationship. A relationship is developed through constant face-to-face contact. This contact allows the consultant to demonstrate his expertise in a way that external marketing efforts, such as advertising, cannot. It also allows the consultant to separate his or her firm from all other competitors.

The key to success in building your firm's health care niche is to create relationships with all the people who can either engage your services or refer clients to you. This is something you should never lose sight of. Nothing will dictate your success like developing relationships. Marketing strategies, attending seminars, and reading publications are ways to expand your health care knowledge, but developing client relationships is your path to closing the sale.

Tremendous opportunities exist for individuals and practices wanting to expand their practices into the health care industry. Many professional firms have not only doubled or tripled billings to existing medical clients, but have doubled or tripled their overall practice. A properly developed and motivated firm can experience these successes.

See the CD-ROM that comes with this book for samples of medical practice engagement letters to get you started in this lucrative field.

Health Care Organizations and Publications

Organizations

American Health Lawyers Association
>1025 Connecticut Ave., NW, Suite 600, Washington, DC 20036
>(202) 833-1100, www.healthlawyers.org

American Institute of Certified Public Accountants (AICPA)
>1211 Avenue of the Americas, New York, NY 10036-8775
>(212) 596-6200, www.aicpa.org

>Harborside Financial Center, 201 Plaza Three, Jersey City, NJ
>07311-3881
>(201) 938-3000

American Medical Association (AMA)
>515 North State Street, Chicago, IL 60610
>(312) 464-5000, www.ama-assn.org

American Medical Group Association
>1422 Duke St., Alexandria, VA 22314-3420
>(703) 838-0033, www.amga.org

American Society of Anesthesiologists
>520 N. Northwest Hwy., Park Ridge, IL 60068-2573
>(847) 825-5586, www.asaha.org/homepageie.html

Centers for Medicare & Medicaid Services
>7500 Security Blvd., Baltimore, MD 21244-1850
>(410) 786-3000, www.cms.gov

Healthcare Financial Management Association (HFMA)
>2 Westbrook Corporate Center, Suite 700
>Westchester, IL 60154-5700
>(800) 252-4362, www.hfma.org

Medical Group Management Association (MGMA)
>104 Inverness Terrace East, Englewood, CO 80112-5306
>(303) 799-1111, www.mgma.com

National CPA Health Care Advisors Association
>111 East Wacker Drive, Suite 990, Chicago, IL 60601
>(800) 869-0491, www.hcaa.org

Professional Association of Health Care Office
Management (PAHCOM)
461 East Ten Mile Road, Pensacola, FL 32534-9714
(800) 451-9311, www.pahcom.com

Society of Medical-Dental Management Consultants
3646 East Ray Road, #B-16-45, Phoenix, AZ 85044
(800) 826-2264, www.smdmc.org

Publications

Coding and Reimbursement for Physicians (for individual specialties)
(800) 765-6588, www.medicode.com

*Cost Accounting for Health Care Organizations: Concepts and
Applications*
(800) 638-8437, www.aspenpublishers.com

CPT and Diagnosis Coding Books
www.ama-assn.org, www.medicode.com

Group Practice Journal
(703) 838-0033, www.amga.org

Health Care Fraud & Abuse Newsletter
(800) 888-8300

Health Niche Advisor
(800) 638-8437, www.aspenpublishers.com

Health Law Alert
(410) 685-1120, www.ober.com

Managed Care Contracting & Reimbursement Newsletter
(800) 643-8095, www.brownstone.com

Medicaid Newsletters & Manual
(Contact your state's Medicaid carrier)

Medical Economics
Medical Economics Publishing
(201) 358-7200, www.medec.com

Medicare Newsletters & Manual
(Contact your state's Medicare carrier)

Medicare Compliance Alert
(301) 287-2700, www.compliancealert.com

Medicare RBRVS 2002: The Physician's Guide
(312) 464-5000, www.ama-assn.org

Modern Healthcare Magazine
(888) 446-1422, www.modernhealthcare.com

Part B News and *Part B Answer Book*
(301) 287-2700, www.partbnews.com

▼ CHAPTER 2
Financial Accounting and Management Reports

To manage a medical practice effectively, whether it be a solo or a group practice, the practitioner and his managers and advisors must have continual access to important financial information. The practice's finances generally can be summarized by preparing a practice statistical report, a balance sheet, and an income statement on a periodic basis (usually monthly). By using these reports, an accountant, consultant, practice administrator, or physician can evaluate the current financial health of the medical practice.

Medical practice performance can be tied directly to the numbers it produces. Poor statistics usually indicate poor performance somewhere in the practice. This is how you know that there is or could be a problem in the medical practice. Good statistics indicate good performance; it is that simple.

This chapter provides an overview of and discusses specific important statistics, statistical performance, what these mean, and how to improve them.

■ **Practice Point:** Remember this one axiom: NUMBERS DON'T LIE. If a medical practice (or any other health care provider) is not able to meet or achieve certain statistical benchmarks, you can rest assured there is some problem that warrants your investigation. This is why it is so important to monitor financial statistics on an ongoing basis.

Numbers and Benchmarking

As you read this chapter, keep the concept of benchmarking in mind. *Benchmarking* is basically goal-setting, and all medical practices and other health care providers need it. For the medical practice, determine where the practice should be in terms of financial statistics and numbers and where it should stand financially day to day, at the end of the month, and at the end of the year. For example, should the practice's overhead be 50 percent of collections?

Should only 15 percent of practice receivables be over 90 days old? Should the net collection percentage always exceed 90 percent? By constantly monitoring performance against these benchmarks, you can ensure the ongoing financial success of the medical practice.

■ **Practice Point:** It is preferable to monitor financial statistics and benchmarks on a monthly basis because, if a problem is detected, you will want to address it immediately.

	Charges	Collections	Coll %	Cont. Adj.	Adj. %	Net Coll.	% Bad Debts	A/R Ratio
Jan.								
Feb.								
Mar.								
Apr.								
May								
Jun.								
July								
Aug.								
Sept.								
Oct.								
Nov.								
Dec.								
Total								
Mo. Avg.								

Medical Practice Statistical Report

The medical practice statistical report summarizes a practice's clinical activities, production, collections, contractual adjustments, and accounts receivable data. Related financial percentages and ratios are then prepared from these data. The purpose of the statistical report is to provide you with a financial snapshot of the practice. By analyzing the information in the report, you should be able to detect potential financial problem areas and correct them. You should also be able to monitor the benchmarks established for the practice. A template for this report is found in Appendix A and on the CD-ROM.

You can use the statistical report as a stand-alone report or as a supplemental report to a compiled balance sheet and income statement (i.e., the one prepared internally or the one prepared by the practice's outside accountant). Following is a discussion of the financial figures in the report.

Production

The first step in the analysis and monitoring process is taking a look at production. An important consideration is overall consistency. For most established medical practices, production should be consistent from month to month unless the physician was out of the office for an extended period of vacation or illness. Production should not fluctuate much for most mature medical practices, especially those that have a consistent volume of clinical services monthly or yearly. For new medical practices, the report should indicate that production is growing each month. If not, investigate immediately.

If production is *not* consistent from month to month, look for the following possible causes.

The practice fails to bill patients on a timely basis   Work performed in one month should be posted and billed that same month. Inconsistencies may originate with hospital services. Many offices have difficulty billing hospital visits or surgical procedures on a timely basis. For example, a surgeon performs six surgeries during the third week of the month. He or she does not dictate the operative note that the office relies on to bill the surgery until the end of the last week of the month. As a result, these surgeries do not get posted and filed until the following month, and cash flow is delayed. In these situations, you may want to consider developing charge tickets so that the doctor or physicians can communicate exactly what they are doing to billing personnel.

The billing personnel lack expertise   Because of their experience and ability, some employees can prepare insurance claim forms more quickly than others. Look at the number of insurance claim forms prepared each day and determine if the number is adequate based on the office's production patterns. If it is not, determine if it is a people problem or an internal systems problem. Because medical practices are unique, you will have difficulty determining an adequate daily figure for claims preparation. You will need to use subjective judgment to determine if the volume of insurance claim forms prepared daily is adequate or not. For example, if two employees are performing a medical practice's insurance billing, and one is able to prepare twice as many insurance claim forms per month as the other, the office has a claims filing problem that needs investigation.

Be alert to situations in which the volume of claims prepared is impaired by something the physician does to hinder the billing process. For example, the physician may not communicate to the staff exactly which procedures he or she performed at the hospital. Also be aware of situations in which an employee may have more administrative duties than billing. For example, one reason an employee does not prepare as many claims as another employee may be that he or she is also responsible for answering the telephones.

As previously mentioned, for new medical practices, production should increase every month. This indicates growth. Production should definitely increase for a new medical practice that receives a financial subsidy from a hospital as part of a new physician recruitment agreement. Many new physicians do not feel the need to produce immediately because their income, at least in the first year, is subsidized in some way by the hospital. This often lulls physicians into a false sense of security. Many fail to realize they are going to be on their own within a relatively short period of time. This is why you, as the consultant or the practice manager, need to help the new physician build production as fast as possible in the first year. If the physician's production isn't increased, his or her salary will decrease.

It is important to prepare a budget for any new medical practice. The budget or cash flow forecast will set the production and revenue goals for the practice's first 12 months. If a new practice's production is stagnating or is not increasing at the desired rate, investigate immediately. If revenue is lagging, the practice may need to develop a strategic marketing plan to increase its revenue. (For a detailed discussion of marketing strategies, see Chapter 15.)

There is a decline in service volume Managed care encourages the management of clinical care. When managed care begins to penetrate a particular service market, many physicians see their volumes decrease. This is because either the managed-care plan can, and often does, decline a service when it must be precertified, or the primary care gatekeeper physician does a more effective job of managing the patient's condition before the patient is referred to a specialist. Also, competition can reduce production, especially in those situations in which a particular group obtained an exclusive managed-care contracting relationship and the related patients of the practice were transferred to this group.

> ■ **Practice Point:** One simple reason for a decline in service volume is that a physician has not signed up with managed-care plans. If managed care begins to penetrate a service area and the area's employers begin to contract with these plans for their health insurance needs, physicians will begin to lose patients if they are not credentialed providers on the plans.

Collections

The statistical report also lists collections and the gross collection percentage. Calculate the gross collection percentage (which must not be confused with the net collection percentage) by dividing the practice's collections by its production.

$$\text{Gross collection percentage} = \frac{\text{Collections}}{\text{Production}}$$

Monitor and analyze the gross collection percentage on a monthly and year-to-date basis. The gross collection percentage is one of the most important statistics of the practice because it indicates how much of the office's production is actually going into its bank account. Keep in mind that if the practice can increase its gross collection percentage, its cash flow will increase accordingly. Thus, each month, you should determine if the percentage is reasonable, after taking into account the practice's special characteristics.

The following are sample gross collection percentage benchmarks:

	Primary Care	*Specialty*
Concentrated fixed-fee environment	60–80%	45–60%
Moderate fixed-fee environment	65–80%	55–70%
Indemnity insurance dominates	75–90%	70–85%

Each medical practice has characteristics that affect the gross collection percentage. Some characteristics directly impact the practice's ability to meet the benchmark ranges, such as a concentrated fixed-fee environment. Also, the practice's fee schedule directly impacts collection percentages. These percentages assume a fee schedule that is at or near what is usual, customary, and reasonable for a particular service area. If the fee schedule is significantly below, the practice's actual collection percentage may be artificially high when compared to the benchmarks. For example, if a practice has a high gross collection percentage, and the practice's revenues mainly come from managed-care patients, the practice fee schedule probably is too low.

Another important characteristic is the practice's medical specialty. For example, a cardiology practice in which most of its revenue comes from treating Medicare patients cannot be expected to have a gross collection percentage greater than 80 percent. A practice that has a large number of patients with indemnity coverage, however, could and should expect to have a higher gross collection rate. Primary care practices often have higher gross collection percentages than do specialty-type practices, such as pulmonology.

If the practice's gross collection percentage does not meet expectations or expected benchmarks, look for the following possible causes.

A shift in the practice's payor mix   In some areas, patient demographics can suddenly switch from commercial insurance to managed care. Some geographic areas have been known to go from 20 percent managed-care penetration to 70 percent within a 12-month period. Because managed-care plans pay less (the contracted fee is less than the office's normal indemnity fee schedule), the practice's gross collection percentage should decline accordingly. Many offices fail to identify when their payor mix is shifting until it is too late to do anything about it. Remember that people move in and out of health plans throughout the year and that this could directly impact the medical practice. In the following example, a shift in the payor mix has occurred, and the medical office now has more patients with insurance policies that reimburse less than what the practice was getting paid the prior year. This will result in declining revenues for the medical practice.

Example of Shift in Payor Mix

Payor	Last Yr.	This Yr.
Medicare	11%	18%
Medicaid	5%	6%
Commercial Plans	68%	52%
PPO Plans	10%	15%
HMO Plans	1%	5%
Workers' Compensation	0%	0%
Self-pay	5%	4%
Other	0%	0%
Total	100%	100%

If a shift occurs, first try to pinpoint a breakdown of the practice's current payor mix, as in the example above. Determine what percentage of the revenue is derived from managed care, commercial insurance, self-paying patients, Medicare, Medicaid, and other insurance programs. Depending on the internal systems of the practice, obtaining this type of information can be an easy task or next to impossible. It may be difficult if the practice still uses a pegboard (i.e., manual) type of system. If a practice has a good computer system, you should be able to use it to conduct a payor mix analysis. If the practice does not have a computer, ask the physician or the billing staff for best estimates of the payor mix.

Next, determine how the practice can shift its payor mix to the type of patients for whom reimbursement is the highest. You can accomplish this by designing marketing strategies that target a specific payor class. The project's success will depend largely on the demographics of the practice's area and the willingness of the physician or physicians to participate in marketing activities. For example, if the practice is in an area that has moved toward managed care, there may not be much of an opportunity to change the practice's payor mix. The physician is stuck with managed-care reimbursement simply because no other alternatives are available. (For a more detailed discussion of demographic studies and marketing techniques, see Chapter 15.)

Failure to follow up on unpaid insurance claim forms   If insurance claim forms are filed and not followed up on a timely basis, insurance companies may delay payment. In turn, the office will not get reimbursed quickly. This is a common systems breakdown in many medical offices and it affects cash flow. The average time it takes a practice to prepare and file insurance claims for hospital services is 17 days from the last date of service. The benchmark, as will be discussed in Chapter 11, is five to seven days. (For more information on unpaid insurance claim forms, see the sections titled "Time Limit for Filing Claims" in Chapter 11 and "Unpaid Insurance Claims" in Chapter 12.)

Failure to collect monies from patients at the time of their office visit   For certain medical practices, such as family practice and pediatrics, office collection should be a mandatory policy. If patients do not make payments at the time of their office visit, insurance has to be filed for these services and, consequently, the office must wait for its payment. As a result, the gross collection rate will not be as good as it could have been if these payments were secured at the time of the visit. Thus, if the collection rate declines, the problem could be at the front desk. (See the section on front-desk collection analysis under "Collection Policies" in Chapter 12.)

Failure to send out patients' statements on a timely basis   Patients who do not receive statements every month cannot pay their accounts. If the statements are not mailed at the same time each month, cash flow could become erratic. (See the section titled "Patients' Account Statements" in Chapter 12 for more information.)

Change in insurance company reimbursement rates   Many insurance plans are changing the way they pay physicians. For example, many commercial insurance carriers and managed-care plans are adopting a resource-based relative value scale (RBRVS) system similar to the current Medicare payment system. There will be continuing pressure to reform the Medicare payment system and this could impact physician reimbursement. Other insurance plans annually decrease reimbursement rates, often without notifying physicians. (For more information on the RBRVS, see the section titled "Insurance Plans" in Chapter 11.)

■ **Practice Point:** If collections decline as a result of declining managed care reimbursement, decide whether or not the practice has the ability to renegotiate these rates. If not, develop a managed care strategy that will position the practice to accomplish this objective.

Failure to manage non-insurance receivables Many medical practices concentrate on collecting insurance receivables but do not make the same effort to collect patient-pay receivables. This, too, could result in a below-average collection percentage. These are receivables from treating self-pay patients (i.e., those with no insurance) or it could be monies due the practice by patients after their insurance has paid. It also includes annual deductibles and service co-payments. This could be a significant issue for larger medical practices, such as those with 10 or more physicians in it.

■ **Practice Point:** How well is the medical practice collecting co-pays and deductibles at the front desk? You might want to check it out.

Inexperienced billing and collection personnel Some employees of a medical practice are not skilled at medical billing and collection. This also could be said of front-desk personnel, many of whom are inexperienced in front-desk collections, scheduling, and so on. Always remember that if the office has implemented the proper business systems to ensure a successful and efficient operation, then collection problems could be directly tied to the people who are employed to carry out the business systems. (See Chapter 16 for more information on evaluating employee performance and for sample job descriptions.)

Possible embezzlement If the practice has a good payor mix, all the right business systems are in place, and the practice's personnel adhere to those systems, a declining rate could be the result of employee embezzlement. Instead of collected revenue ending up in the practice's bank account, it is diverted to an employee's personal account. (For a detailed discussion of avoiding embezzlement, see Chapter 4.)

■ **Practice Point:** Keep in mind that the gross collection percentage is affected by the practice's fee schedule. A fee schedule that is too high may result in what appears to be a low gross collection percentage. In other words, it may look like the practice has a poor collection performance when in reality it does not. If the fee schedule is too low, the result may be a gross collection percentage that appears to be too high. The point here is that when you analyze the gross collection percentage, not only must you take into account the practice's payor mix, but its fee schedule as well.

Contractual Adjustments

The next section of the medical practice statistical report summarizes the office's contractual adjustments. It also quantifies the related contractual percentage. A contractual adjustment is the difference between what a physician charges and what he or she is legally entitled to receive from the insurance plan. For example, if a surgeon's normal fee for a procedure is $1,000 and he or she signs a managed care contract agreeing to be reimbursed a fee of $800, the contractual adjustment is $200. The contractual percentage is calculated by dividing contractual adjustments by gross production:

$$\text{Contractual percentage} = \frac{\text{Contractual adjustments}}{\text{Gross production}}$$

As with the gross collection rate, evaluate the reasonableness of the contractual percentage. When conducting this evaluation, always keep in mind the practice's current payor mix. This will have a direct impact on the evaluation of this rate. A practice with a high volume of Medicare patients will have a higher contractual percentage than a practice with a high volume of patients who

have commercial insurance. For some general and cardiac surgical practices, the contractual rate could be as high as 50 percent.
This is simply because the contracted Medicare rates are less—
sometimes substantially less. The following are possible causes of
an unreasonable contractual percentage.

Using wrong figures You need to know what the contractual
adjustments include. If wrong figures are included, the contractual adjustment percentage could be artificially inflated. Contractual adjustments include the difference between what a physician
billed and what was approved for payment. The most common
category included in contractual adjustments is bad debts. For most
medical practices, however, bad debts should not be included because most practices have decided to write off a particular balance
as uncollectible. There are two exceptions to this: academic medical centers and nonprofit community health centers. Both of these
entities are committed to treating indigent patients. Generally, they
represent a significant portion of the entities' patient base. Therefore, their bad-debt write-offs will be recurring on a daily and
monthly basis. In this type of situation, bad debts might be included in the contractual adjustment category. Professional courtesy is another example of an adjustment that is not considered to
be a "contractual adjustment."

The practice's current payor mix If the practice has a high
volume of patients whose current insurance coverage pays less
than the practice's regular fee schedule (e.g., Medicare, Medicaid,
and managed-care plans), the contractual percentage may be lower
than anticipated. Also keep in mind that a high practice fee schedule will also contribute to a high contractual percentage.

A shift in the practice's payor mix To minimize the cost of health
care premiums, the employers in the practice area may be purchasing new types of insurance. Normally the switch is to some type of
managed-care plan. The shift to such coverage will result in an increase in contractual adjustments. In addition, the patients in the
practice's area may be getting older. Many may be on Medicare,
which will also result in contractual adjustments to the practice.

Incorrect posting of payments   The office staff may be writing off amounts as contractual adjustments when they should not be doing so. For example, a service is billed to the insurance company, which subsequently denies the charge. Instead of appealing the denial, the staff writes off the service as a contractual adjustment. Amounts due from patients also may accidentally get written off as contractual adjustments. This kind of incorrect posting results from a lack of knowledge of managed-care billing and collection. Sometimes employees believe that if a person has managed care insurance, he or she does not have to pay anything. (Refer to Chapter 13 for correct posting procedures.)

Possible embezzlement   To disguise embezzlement, an office employee may write off the full amount of a posted charge as a contractual adjustment while he or she embezzles the full amount. This is easily done in practices that have a high number of contractual adjustments. If a practice is writing off more than half a million dollars in contractuals, most people would not notice an additional $60,000. (Tactics for avoiding embezzlement situations are discussed in Chapter 4.)

Net Collection Percentage

To calculate the net collection percentage, divide the practice's collections by gross production (production less contractual adjustments):

$$\text{Net collection percentage} = \frac{\text{Collections}}{\text{Production, less contractual adjustments}}$$

The net collection percentage indicates how much of the practice's collectible production is actually being deposited in the bank. As previously mentioned, bad-debt expense is generally not included in this calculation. The net collection percentage should always be more than 90 percent for established medical practices. This is the benchmark. If the practice's net collection percentage is less than 90 percent, it could be experiencing a rise in its accounts receivable (i.e., the practice is not receiving payment), or the practice may not be writing off contractual adjustments. A net collection percentage of less than 90 percent indicates a problem within the billing and collection process.

For new medical practices, it will take a while to achieve the 90 percent benchmark. Each month, however, the net collection percentage should be rising toward 90 percent on a year-to-date basis. If it is not, investigate immediately.

	Total	Current	30	60	90+
January					
February					
March					
April					
May					
June					
July					
August					
September					
October					
November					
December					
Medicare					
Medicaid					
Commercial Plans					
Self-pay					
PPO Plans					
HMO Plans					
Workers' Comp					

Accounts Receivable

At the end of the medical practice statistical report is an analysis of the practice's accounts receivable. It is important to age and review the accounts receivable each month. With a manual peg-board system, the process is time consuming; someone in the practice must go through each patient's ledger card and determine the age of the account. A computer system automatically ages the accounts and an operator can easily print a report.

> ■ **Practice Point:** If a practice is not computerized, see that it gets a computer. Computerized systems and related medical billing software systems are very affordable. Manual systems are dinosaurs.

From the statistical report, you should look to see if the accounts receivable are getting older. This is called *bracket creep*. If the accounts are getting older, the office may have a collection problem. The practice may not have a procedure for receivables collection or, if it does, the office staff may not be following it. It could also mean that the office is understaffed and may need to hire someone to help with the billing and collection.

Also review the aging of the accounts receivable by insurance class. The receivables can be aged by such classifications as Medicare, Medicaid, commercial insurance, and managed care. Most good medical billing software systems should be able to produce such a report.

The purpose of this review is to determine if the practice is having trouble collecting from a certain payor. This process allows the office to identify a specific collection problem with a specific payor and to take immediate corrective action. For example, a practice electronically bills all of its Medicare-related charges. Typically, payment turnaround on an electronically filed insurance claim in the practice's state is 22 days. The aging worksheet shows $162,000 of Medicare-related receivables that are more than 90 days old. This obviously should not be happening if the claims were filed correctly and if Medicare patients were paying their co-payments on a timely basis. You will need to investigate the reason for this problem.

Besides printing an aging-by-payor class, see if the computer can produce a similar report by specific payor. Such a report will show you an aging for specific insurance companies, such as Prudential, Blue Cross/Blue Shield, Aetna, or PacifiCare. Again, this report allows the office to address a collection problem with a particular insurance company. The following is an example of such a report:

	Total	*Current*	*30*	*60*	*90+*
Aetna					
MetraHealth					
Blue Cross					
Prudential					
United					
Anthem					

A good indicator of how well the office is collecting its accounts is the percentage of receivables that is more than 90 days old. If the percentage is unusually high, something is wrong in the office. Again, a high percentage could be traced to a systems problem, a people problem, or a combination. A good benchmark for most medical practices is to keep receivables more than 90 days old at less than 15 to 20 percent of the total amount of accounts receivable. A good specific benchmark would be that no more than 18 percent of the accounts receivable should ever be 90 days or older. Medical practice statistical surveys, such as the one produced by the Medical Group Management Association, could be used for comparison.

One way to manage accounts receivable is to calculate the accounts receivable ratio. Divide accounts receivable by average monthly gross production over the past 12-month period:

$$\text{Accounts receivable ratio} = \frac{\text{Current accounts receivable balance}}{\text{Average monthly gross production}}$$

The accounts receivable ratio is mainly used as a tool to assess the reasonableness of the current accounts receivable balance. For primary-care medical practices in which revenue is mainly derived from office work, the ratio should be between 1.0 and 2.0. For surgical practices or others with a heavy concentration of hospital services, the ratio should be between 2.0 and 3.0. Under no circumstances should the accounts receivable ratio exceed three times the average monthly gross production. A ratio that exceeds this benchmark indicates a severe collection problem.

In addition to the accounts receivable ratio statistic, there are several other excellent A/R ratios you can and should be using to analyze not only your receivable balance, but the practice's collection efforts as well:

1. Average Days Receivable. This statistic is calculated by dividing the A/R balance by daily average charges [YTD Charges/ 365 days]. You can use 30.41 (365/12 months) in place of 365 days when calculating monthly ratios. You want to keep this figure under 90 days.

2. Accounts Receivable Turnover Rate. This is calculated by dividing the A/R balance by average monthly receipts. This statistic indicates the number of months of work that have not been collected as yet.

3. Accounts Receivable Ratio. Calculate this by dividing total accounts receivable by average monthly charges [either for the YTD or a rolling 12-month average]. For primary care and other office-based practices, this figure should be between 1.0 and 2.0 of average monthly charges. All other practices (e.g., specialty practices) should have between 2.0 and 3.0 of average monthly charges in their accounts receivable balance. Any practice that has over four times of average monthly charges in its accounts receivable balance has a collection problem!

Reviewing and analyzing practice receivables on an ongoing basis should be a commonplace occurrence and exercise for ALL medical practices. Unfortunately, quite often that is not the case. Size of practice does not discriminate here—larger practices can be just as guilty of this offense as smaller ones. If you are a CPA or consultant, make sure you and your clients are performing this task on a monthly basis. If you work in, or deal with, the management of a medical practice, you too must ensure that proper review and analytical procedures of the accounts receivable are in place and implemented each and every month. In today's health care operating environment, with all of its associated management pressures, you must pay strict and close attention to the practice's accounts receivables.

Clinical Activities

The statistical report should also summarize the practice's clinical activities. This includes encounters for office visits, hospital services, procedures, laboratory tests, and X-rays.

You can use the information from this report to determine where the practice's revenue is coming from and if there has been a reduction in clinical activities. For example, if the report shows a steady decline in office visits, especially new-patient office visits, investigate immediately. A decline in office visits could indicate an increase in managed care. If the practice is not attracting new patients, you will need to find out why. If the physician who experiences declines in consultations is a specialist, you would need to find out why referring physicians are not sending patients to the specialist. It may be a temporary situation, or the specialist could have done something to cause the other physicians to reduce their consultative requests. Because any decline in clinical activity results in a related reduction in the practice's revenue, reviewing this type of financial information is vital.

Here is a sample of a statistical report.

Month	NP Visits	EP Visits	Consults	Hosp. Visits	Procedures	Radiology	Lab	Other
Jan.								
Feb.								
Mar.								
Apr.								
May								

Month	NP Visits	EP Visits	Consults	Hosp. Visits	Procedures	Radiology	Lab	Other
Jun.								
July								
Aug.								
Sept.								
Oct.								
Nov.								
Dec.								
Total								
Mo. Avg.								

Summary of Financial Benchmarks

Based on the earlier discussions in this chapter, the following is a summary of financial benchmarking for a medical practice.

Gross Collection Percentage:

	Primary Care	Specialty
Concentrated fixed-fee environment	60–80%	45–60%
Moderate fixed-fee environment	65–80%	55–70%
Indemnity insurance dominates	75–90%	70–85%

Net Collection Percentage: Always greater than 90%

Accounts Receivable 90+ days: No more than 18% of total receivables balance

Accounts Receivable Ratio:

Primary care — Between 1.0 and 2.0

Specialists — Between 2.0 and 3.0

Any medical practice — Never above 3.0

Comparative Practice Management Report

As this chapter emphasizes, information is king. Information makes it possible to manage a medical practice, to identify problems within a practice, and to provide solutions to practice problems. To improve your ability to analyze the practice, create a Practice Management Report. This is basically a one-year snapshot of the practice's financial activity, and is an excellent way to monitor financial trends and to increase your ability to detect problem areas.

The following is an abbreviated version of such a report:

Month	Production— Current Year	Production— Prior Year	Variance	Collections— Current Year	Collections— Prior Year	Variance	Coll %— Current Year	Coll %— Prior Year	Variance
Jan.									
Feb.									
Mar.									
April									
May									
June									
July									
Aug.									
Sept.									
Oct.									
Nov.									
Dec.									

■ **Practice Point:** Make sure to include clinical activities in the comparative report. You will want to identify immediately any reduction in clinical volumes. For example, if surgical volumes decline, there may have been a drop in physician referrals that you will need to investigate. Any decline in new patient visits should also be investigated immediately.

Balance Sheet and Income Statement Preparation

The preparation of a balance sheet and income statement is vital to the financial management of any medical practice. The balance sheet is an indicator of a practice's assets, liabilities, and equity. The income statement summarizes the practice's income and expenses, resulting in a bottom-line net income figure.

Cash vs. Accrual Basis Financial Statements

Often a medical practice wants to know whether or not it should keep its books on the accrual basis of accounting, the cash basis of accounting, or the income tax basis of accounting. The answer often depends on the intended use of the financial statements. If required by a third party, such as a banking institution, the financial statements could be prepared on the accrual basis of accounting. However, cash basis statements or tax basis statements should be used for internal management purposes.

The accrual basis of accounting records revenues when they are earned and expenses when they have been incurred. In other words, revenues are recorded on the books when billed to patients, insurance companies, and other third-party payors, and expenses are recorded when incurred and there is an obligation to pay. Banking institutions or other lending institutions usually require accrual basis statements in order for a health care entity to receive and maintain a loan. The cash basis of accounting records revenues when the cash is received and other transactions, such as expenses, when they are actually paid.

The industry standard is to use the cash basis of accounting. This is because practices use their financial statements to manage and track their operations. For example, revenues and expenses are often compared to annual and monthly budgeted amounts. Even more important, published practice statistics are expressed on the cash basis of accounting. Reputable sources such as the Medical Group Management Association and the American Medical Association publish their statistical figures on the cash basis of accounting. Practices compare their own operational statistics to these surveys as a management tool. Practices need to know whether their collections are in line and whether or not their overhead is within reasonable limits.

Another reason medical practices use the cash basis of accounting is that it is difficult to account properly for a realizable accounts receivable figure. Accounts receivable are shown at their gross amounts; therefore you must record an "Allowance for Contractual Adjustments" to reflect the fact that the practice is not going to get paid by the insurance companies the same amount it billed them. (Refer to the discussion on contractual adjustments earlier in this chapter.) For some practices, this allowance can be significant. Any error in its calculation could result in a deep variance in the practice's accrual basis net income figure.

Financial statements for medical offices often are prepared on the income tax basis of accounting, because most industry statistics report income and expense on the same basis. This should not be confused with the cash basis of accounting, which requires adherence to all accounting principles except for the recognition of income and expense. The income tax basis of accounting deviates from the cash basis of accounting in many respects. The biggest differences concern the methodology for calculating depreciation expense and the amortization of intangibles. The manner in which certain prepaid expenses are recognized will also differ (e.g., in the case of the annual payment of a malpractice premium).

■ **Practice Point:** For CPAs to comply fully with generally accepted accounting principles, a compilation must include the statements of retained earnings and cash flow. These statements are rarely included in the compilation of financial statements for a medical practice. Therefore, the accountant's compilation report is modified to reflect such omissions. (See Appendix A for sample financial statements.)

The Purposes of Financial Statements

Medical practice financial statements generally are used for three purposes: (1) tax planning, (2) overhead control, and (3) internal control. Financial statements are prepared either monthly or quarterly, the frequency often depending on the practice's size and management needs.

Tax Planning

By tracking income and expenses on an ongoing basis via financial statements, the practice can implement tax strategies before year's end to minimize its tax burden. A formal tax planning review should be conducted for all medical practices. This usually occurs in October and November for practices that follow the calendar year.

Overhead Control

The income statement is primarily used for overhead control for most medical practices. Industry statistics for almost every medical specialty are available to show what is a reasonable overhead figure for a practice. This usually is expressed as a percentage of practice collections before physician's compensation. Therefore, you or the practice's accountant should format the income statement into the following categories:

Practice revenue (collections)
- Operating overhead

= Net income before physician compensation
- Physician compensation

= Practice net income

When the financial statements are prepared, the net income before physician's compensation can be compared to industry statistical surveys, such as those produced by the American Medical Association, the Medical Group Management Association, and the Medical Group Practice Association. (See Chapter 1 for phone numbers and addresses.) If the overhead percentage is in line with a statistical survey, there should be no cause for immediate concern. Substantial increases in specific expense categories, however, should be investigated immediately. (Refer to Chapter 3 for a more detailed explanation of cost containment.)

Physician's compensation generally is defined as actual payments to the physician as compensation plus related fringe benefits. This figure usually includes the physician's malpractice premium. Before comparing the practice's overhead to an industry survey, you will need to determine how the survey defines *physician's compensation* so the numbers you are analyzing will be comparable. (See Chapter 18 for more information on physician's compensation.)

If office overhead appears to be out of line after it is compared to an industry survey, investigate immediately. Before beginning the investigation, however, make sure that the collections per the survey are somewhat close to the practice's own collections. If a practice's collections are growing or are lagging, the related overhead percentage will be high. In this situation, the problem may not be overhead but rather a collections problem. The reverse is also true; if collections for a particular practice exceed the norm, the overhead percentage will be low, which could mask any overhead problems.

Assuming collections are not the problem, investigate specific overhead categories for reasonableness. Compare each category to the survey. At the same time, prepare a comparison of the practice's current-year expenses with the prior year's overhead expenses. Are there any substantial increases over the prior year? If so, can they be explained (e.g., pay raises to employees)? When preparing regular financial statements (or having them prepared) for a medical practice, make sure that a prior-year comparative report is prepared at the same time. This report compares revenue and expenses of the prior year with those of the current year, indicating variances in each category. Most general ledger software packages should be able to create this report.

■ **Practice Point:** Emphasis should be placed on the preparation of comparative financial statements, regardless of whether the practice is new or established. Comparative financials allow you to see practice trends and to detect overhead and revenue items that appear out of line. Comparative financials allow for immediate investigation.

Internal Control

When financial statements are prepared on the cash basis of accounting, internally documented collections for the financial statement period should be compared with what is shown as revenue on the practice's income statement. The practice's internal documentation of its collections should always agree with what actually was deposited into the bank account for the period. The deposit amount should agree with the collected revenue number shown on the practice's income statement. If the practice is computerized, collections shown on the practice's internal month-end management reports should agree with the collected revenue appearing on the income statement. If the practice is not computerized, total collections per the day sheets should agree with the revenue figure displayed on the income statement. This is a basic internal control for all medical practices. If the collections per the income statement do not agree with the practice's internal documentation, investigate the difference immediately. Generally, the reason can be traced to how the practice closes out its day and reconciles to the bank deposit. Many practices do not deposit daily or reconcile the bank deposit to internal documentation. Every medical practice must adhere to strict reconciliation standards, as discussed in Chapter 13.

A Proactive Stance

Balance sheets and income statements are important to large medical practices, but they may not be as useful to small practices as a practice management report. Balance sheets and income statements are compilations of history. How these historical numbers were created is what is important to most medical practices. Behind the income statements lies an office's production, collections, adjustments, accounts receivable, and internal office systems and efficiencies. By concentrating on and constantly analyzing these figures, you are taking a proactive service position with respect to the practice and not a reactive one. Reactive medical practices lose revenue; reactive consultants and CPAs lose medical clients. Therefore, many practice managers, consultants, and CPAs believe that the practice management report serves most medical practices much better from a financial and management standpoint. By using all three financial reports, however, you should be able to provide medical practices with top-notch accounting and consulting help.

Incurred But Not Reported (IBNR) Claims

One of the most confusing acronyms in the accounting profession today is IBNR. *Incurred but not reported* claims are found in situations in which a physician provider or an integrated delivery system is capitated by an HMO, and the provider has an obligation to pay for other health care services. For example, an orthopedic surgical practice receives capitated payments from an HMO, but out of this capitated money, the surgeon has to pay for all therapy services it refers out to physical therapists. There can, at times, be a significant lag between incurring an obligation to pay a service and actually receiving the insurance claim form from the provider. Using the above example, the orthopedic surgeon sends patients to physical therapy in March but does not receive the corresponding insurance claim forms from the physical therapist until April. This time lag is what creates IBNR.

IBNR is important because if a physician or integrated delivery system receives capitated revenues and turns around and spends all of the money, how are services going to get paid when claim forms for past services actually are received for payment? Unless monies are set aside in some sort of IBNR reserve, there may not be enough money to pay for these services and others that have been previously incurred by other providers. This is how providers and integrated delivery systems in a capitated environment can easily go bankrupt.

To protect the provider, an IBNR reserve must be set up, calculated, and funded each month, even though the entity might be on the cash or tax basis of accounting. Otherwise, the practice runs the risk of not being able to pay out claims when they are submitted by other providers. Generally these monies are put into an interest-bearing account. From an accounting standpoint, IBNR is accrued as an expense and is related as a short-term liability each month.

Calculating IBNR

Although calculating IBNR is not an exact science, IBNR can be estimated with reasonable accuracy. The estimation of IBNR becomes more accurate as time passes. This is because the calculation is usually based on historical data and the data accumulates as services are rendered over time to patients.

Following are the three basic methods are used for estimating IBNR.

Open-referral method   In most managed-care environments, a patient cannot be treated by a physician other than a primary-care physician (i.e., the gatekeeper) without an authorization. Under the open-referral method, IBNR is estimated as the cost of all open authorizations on file. Open authorizations are those services that have been approved but for which the provider or integrated delivery system has not received an insurance claim form. Once the number of open authorizations has been determined, it is then multiplied by the average cost per specialty to arrive at an approximate IBNR liability. To estimate IBNR most accurately, segregate open authorizations by medical specialty. This way, average costs per service can be matched with each related specialty and ancillary service (e.g., diagnostic technical component and facility charge for a CAT scan or MRI). Average costs per specialty are usually developed over time as actual claim history is accumulated. In the early stages of a capitated contract, however, you may have to engage an actuary to provide this cost data.

Projected historical cost method   This is probably the most common method used to estimate IBNR. It is based on the actual claims history on a member-month basis. *Member month* is defined as the total number of members who were covered within a specific time frame. For example, if an HMO had 10,000 members in January and 12,000 members in February, the total member months for the year-to-date as of March 1 would be 22,000.

To calculate IBNR using this method, you need to know the actual submitted costs for specialty services per member month. If the submitted costs were $2 and there were 10,000 member months during that period, IBNR would be estimated at $20,000. If the information is not available, IBNR can be estimated using actual-claims data. Any competent computer system can produce a report of actual-claims history. To be conservative, accrue at least twice as many average historical claims history as IBNR. This would allow sufficient cash reserves for future claims.

Actuarial data analysis   For this method, an actuary is engaged to estimate the IBNR. The actuary will use his or the insurance plan's demographic data, utilization history, and actual payment history to calculate IBNR. The problem with this method is the expense involved in hiring an actuary. Therefore, you should use this method only if capitated membership is large. If the group practice or an integrated delivery system is contracting directly with an HMO, the HMO may be able to provide you with actuarial data or an estimate of actual-claims history on a member-month basis in order to calculate IBNR.

Capitation Debits and Credits

At some point, you may be called on to account (from an accounting standpoint) for capitated revenue and all related transactions. For example, this may occur in a group practice that executes a full-risk capitation contract. If you are a CPA or consultant, you may be engaged to perform accounting services for either an independent practice association (IPA) or a physician/hospital organization that has secured a full-risk capitated contract. Generally, the purpose of this engagement is to prepare or to review compiled financial statements. In any event, the practice manager or the CPA must know the basic debits and credits involved when accounting for full-risk capitation.

Following are the basic accounting entries, which you must be aware of, and a corresponding explanation of each transaction. The transactions assume the accrual basis of accounting. For more information on this subject, refer to Statement of Position (SOP) 89-5, "Financial Accounting and Reporting by Providers of Prepaid Health Care Services," issued by the Association of Independent Certified Public Accountants (AICPA).

Debit: Cash

Credit: Capitation Revenue

This entry records capitation revenue in the month that it is received. Each month a check will be sent to the entity by the HMO per the terms of the HMO contract. If the HMO is late with its payment (e.g., a July capitation payment paid in August), the entry would be:

Debit: Accounts Receivable—HMO

Credit: Capitation Revenue

When the late payment is received, the entity would debit the cash account and credit the HMO receivable. If the HMO sends the payment early, the entry would be:

Debit: Cash

Credit: Deferred Revenue—Capitation

The entity would then record the capitation revenue in the month it is earned by debiting the deferred revenue account and crediting capitation revenue.

Debit: Payment to Other Capitated Providers

Credit: Cash

This entry is made when the capitated payments are made to other providers that are *subcapitated,* and these payments are the responsibility of the entity. For example, an IPA may receive capitation revenue and out of this revenue must pay capitated providers such as family practitioners, pediatricians, internists, and other medical specialists.

Debit: Reinsurance Recoveries

Credit: Reinsurance Revenue

Any entity with capitation revenue will purchase an insurance policy called *stoploss coverage.* This type of insurance protects the entity and its capitated providers from catastrophic illnesses. For example, if a physician is receiving $5,000 per month in capitated payments to treat approximately 250 enrollees and ends up incurring $40,000 of charges on one single patient, the stoploss coverage will reimburse the physician for those single patient charges that exceeded the reinsurance limit.

Some expenses will be incurred outside of the capitated payment, such as the fee-for-service (FFS) component for the delivery of patient care. When an entity receives a capitated payment under a full-risk arrangement, it will generally pay for the following:

- Payments to other capitated providers
- Payments to other providers that must be paid FFS (e.g., emergency care)
- Share of any hospitalization claims (e.g., the entity contracts for hospital risk-sharing)
- Administration expenses

Any leftover amounts are profit to the entity. Therefore, the entity must account for those FFS charges that have been incurred but have yet to be submitted to the entity by the providers (IBNR). For example, a surgeon gets to bill the entity for FFS. A capitated primary-care physician refers the patient to the surgeon, who in turn performs a procedure. The surgeon will submit his or her services for payment to the entity. Therefore, the entity must have set aside sufficient cash reserves to cover this and other services that have been rendered but not yet submitted to the entity for payment. Each HMO contract will spell out which services fall under capitated payments and which ones will not. The services that will not must be accounted for under the following IBNR entry:

Debit: Accrued Payments to FFS Providers

Credit: IBNR Accrual

When the checks are actually written to these providers, the IBNR liability account can be debited. Another way to account for this transaction is to debit the specific provider expense accounts when the payments are made, reverse the previous month's IBNR accrual, and accrue a new amount in the current month. Many entities prefer this method because they can see exactly how much has been paid to FFS providers during the year. An entity can increase its profit if it can control the amount of FFS expenditures through utilization management or some other manner.

Debit: Cash

Credit: Provider Withhold Payable

Some entities may withhold a percentage of a physician's capitated payment throughout the year as a way to control that physician's utilization. These amounts withheld are a liability until they are resolved at some point, generally at year's end. The payable will be debited if the physician is due a repayment of the withhold. Read the provider contract to find out how this can occur.

Special Group Practice Accounting

Generally, when physicians merge and create a clinic without walls, each physician maintains his or her own office and administration is centralized, including billing and collection activities. One bank account is opened to deposit practice revenues and pay the bills. The revenues of all of the physicians are commingled. For compensation, each office is considered a profit center. The physicians are therefore customarily paid on a straight productivity basis using the following formula:

Collections on physician's own production
- Direct office overhead
- Shared overhead
- Working capital retention
= Physicians' compensation

Of course, revisions may have to be made for governmental regulations, such as the division of ancillary revenue per the Stark II rules that became effective January 1, 1996. (The final Stark II regulations were released in 2001.)

Obviously, this type of physician compensation formula requires a very strict accounting of each physician's collections and the allocations of overhead to each profit center. The practice manager, consultant, and CPA for a new clinic without walls must ensure attention to detail, especially to the accounting for each of the physician's collections. This is important because payments received at each office location and the payments received through the mail at the centralized business office are deposited into one bank account. All of these payments are then posted to the respective patient accounts under each respective physician's name in the computer. It is this part of the process that commands such strict accounting by both internal practice personnel and the group's outside accountant.

To compensate the physicians properly, the deposits in the bank account must agree with the amount of collections indicated in the computer. Remember that the computer is used to show how much each physician collected. If collections are not properly accounted for, the compensation formula will not work. In addition, all transactions, including the payment of physician compensation, must be tied to the bank balance at any point in time. Otherwise, the practice may accidentally write and issue checks that could create a bank overdraft. To maintain the integrity of the physician compensation system in a clinic that is being shared by physicians, the accounts payable system must be set up correctly. When checks are written, the related expenses and costs must be allocated to the correct physician (i.e., profit center).

When collections are not reconciled properly and accounts payable are not allocated correctly, the physicians may lose confidence in the centralized business office, which could cause some physicians to leave the practice. Also, some physicians may micromanage the billing and collection activities because they no longer have faith in their employees.

To account for billing and collection activities, create a physician-reconciliation worksheet. To complete this worksheet, you will need to use the practice's daily computer report of collections by physician and the related bank deposit slips. These two documents must agree or must be reconciled. The worksheet allows you to break down payables and payments by physician. Direct costs are those expenses that can be tied directly to one office. The shared expenses are those split among the physicians, such as the costs of the centralized business office. The net amount is the amount of cash available to pay compensation to each physician.

Prior-Year Comparison

Whenever physicians merge their offices, they are naturally nervous about their collections. This is especially the case if compensation is based upon some type of productivity. Usually, the group as a whole, will be concerned about collections. Keeping this in mind, you should prepare a prior-year comparison report each month. Set up the report using the following headings:

Dr. Name   Prior Yr.   Current Yr.   Mo. 1   Mo. 2   Total

To prepare this report, obtain each physician's prior-year collection figures. Using this, calculate average collections per month for the prior year and insert that figure into the prior-year column for each physician. As the new group completes each month, each physician's current collections are inserted into each respective month. Then average monthly collections for the current year are calculated and inserted into the current-year column for each physician.

This report is used for two purposes. The first is to gauge how well the central billing office is collecting the physician's charges. If average monthly collections are lagging behind as compared to last year, investigate immediately. Unless production has fallen off, a substantial decrease should not occur. Second, use the report to give each physician some comfort level about how well the merger is working. Physicians need to see how their collections are doing with the merger as compared to when they were on their own. The group as a whole needs to know this information. If collections should drop, some physicians may become disgruntled and attempt to micromanage the business operations of the group. This will almost always cause friction within the group, so it should be avoided. On the other hand, the one major goal of any newly merged group practice is to make sure that each physician's current average monthly collections exceed last year's figures at the end of the group's first year of operations. If this report is prepared each month, you will be able to determine if the new group will meet or beat this important objective.

Special Tax Accounting Issue—Inventory

A common accounting issue in medical practices is when items must be "inventoried" and, as a result, the practice should use the accrual basis of accounting. In two court cases, the U.S. Tax Court ruled that cancer drugs administered to its patients were not "merchandise" under Regulatory Section 1.471-1, finding that the drugs were "inseparable from and subordinate to" the corporations' medical services.

The first case was *Osteopathic Medical Oncology and Hematology P.C. v. Commissioner,* 113 T.C. No. 26; No. 11551-98 (November 22, 1999). The most recent case was *Mid-Del Therapeutic Center, Inc. v. Commissioner of Internal Revenue,* and *D. Richard Ishmael, M.D., P.C. v. Commissioner of Internal Revenue,* where tax deficiencies resulted from the IRS' determination, pursuant to Section 446(b), that the taxpayers should have used the accrual method of accounting to report their taxable income. The ultimate issue, according to the Court, was to decide whether the IRS abused its authority under Section 446(b) by requiring the taxpayers to change from the cash receipts and the disbursements method of accounting (the cash method) to the accrual method. In order to decide this issue, the Court examined the question of whether chemotherapy drugs and related medications (the drugs), administered by the taxpayers to its patients during the course of medical treatments, were merchandise which must be inventoried.

Facts of the Mid-Del *Case*

The taxpayers in this case were Oklahoma corporations that operated a chemotherapy clinic. The clinic provided outpatient chemotherapy treatments to its patients. Dr. Ishmael employed a staff consisting of nurses, nursing assistants, laboratory technicians, physician assistants, administrative clerks, pharmacists, pharmacy technicians, and office maintenance workers. Mid-Del had no employees, but used contract nursing services leased through the Cancer Care Network and paid a common paymaster for doctors' services and other labor costs. Dr. Ishmael provided administrative services, including bookkeeping and billing, for both clinics. Mid-Del paid the doctor an annual fee for these administrative services.

Dr. Ishmael would examine the patient during the first visit to determine the proper chemotherapy treatment (if any) for that patient. When Dr. Ishmael prescribed a chemotherapy treatment, his order for the patient's individualized chemotherapy treatment was recorded in the patient's file, which was maintained at the clinic where that patient received treatment. Once a patient was evaluated and a chemotherapy regimen had been prescribed, the patient began regular, periodic treatments, which could continue for several months or years. Dr. Ishmael wrote prescriptions for any drugs a patient needed that were not administered by the clinic.

Accounting Issues According to the Court

As the Court stated, it is a customary and accepted practice in the health care industry for health care practitioners to use the cash method of accounting. Dr. Ishmael used the cash method of accounting for both income tax purposes and for bookkeeping purposes, and consistently reported the drugs used in patient treatments as supplies, not as inventory. Mid-Del also used the cash method of accounting for income tax purposes and consistently reported the drugs used in patient treatments as supplies, not as inventory. Mid-Del used the accrual method of accounting for bookkeeping purposes.

Following an audit, the IRS issued notices of deficiency to each of the taxpayers in which the IRS determined that they must use the accrual method. The notices of deficiency described the IRS' determination that the accrual method of accounting more clearly reflected the income than the taxpayers' current cash basis method of accounting.

The Court's Opinion

Section 446(b) vests the IRS with broad discretion in determining whether a particular method of accounting clearly reflects income.

The IRS' determination that a taxpayer's method of accounting does not clearly reflect its income was given great deference by the Tax Court in this case; however, the IRS, according to the Court, should not require a taxpayer to change from an accounting method which clearly reflects income to an alternate method of accounting merely because the IRS considers the alternate method to more clearly reflect the taxpayer's income. The issue of whether the taxpayer's method of accounting clearly reflects income is a question of fact to be determined on a case-by-case basis.

Under Section 471, the general rule is that whenever, in the opinion of the IRS, the use of inventories is necessary in order to clearly determine the income of any taxpayer, the inventories should be taken in such a way that clearly reflects its income. By regulation, the IRS has determined that inventories are necessary in every case in which the production, purchase, or sale of merchandise is an income-producing factor in the taxpayer's business. A taxpayer who is required to maintain inventories must use an accrual method of accounting with regard to purchases and sales of inventory according to Section 1.446-1(c)(2)(i) of the income tax regulations.

In this case, the IRS argued that the drugs were in fact "merchandise," the purchase and sale of which were income-producing factors in the taxpayers' businesses, and, therefore, the taxpayers were required to use the accrual method of accounting to report their taxable income. The term "merchandise" as used in Section 1.471-1 of the tax regulations encompasses goods purchased in condition for sale, goods awaiting sale, articles of commerce held for sale, and all classes of commodities held for sale.

Mentioning the *Osteopathic Medical* case, the Court stated that it held in a court-reviewed opinion that chemotherapy and other drugs, when used in the course of treating patients, are not held for sale and, therefore, are not merchandise. In that case, the holding was premised on the conclusion that the chemotherapy drugs and ancillary medications were both inseparable from the medical services provided to patients by the taxpayer and subordinate to the medical services provided.

According to the Court in this case, as in *Osteopathic Medical,* the furnishing of drugs and other medical supplies were inseparable from and subordinate to the medical services provided by taxpayers to their patients. Patients came to the clinic to receive medical treatment from Dr. Ishmael and not to purchase drugs per se, according to the Court. The drugs were administered to patients during the course of their treatment. At no point during the treatment process did a patient acquire title to the drugs or exercise control over them. A patient did not direct how or when the drugs were administered, nor could a patient simply purchase the drugs for self-treatment. Upon completion of each treatment, there was nothing left for a patient to acquire, sell, or otherwise exert ownership rights over. Although according to the Court there were some factual differences between this case and *Osteopathic Medical,* the key operational facts were virtually identical. Therefore, the Court held that this case was controlled by *Osteopathic Medical* and that, for purposes of Section 1.471-1 of the tax regulations, the taxpayers' chemotherapy drugs were not merchandise and the taxpayers did not have to use the accrual basis of accounting.

Possible Early Warning Signs of Practice Financial Problems

It is important for any physician medical practice to implement an ongoing monitoring program. Practice administration, physician management, or independent advisors can conduct this monitoring. The best approach is one that combines a team approach to management.

A good monitoring program should detect financial "problems" early so that they can be corrected "now instead of later." The following is a list of warning signs that should be part of any monitoring program.

Sudden change in accounts receivable tendencies Watch accounts receivable very closely. Benchmark what is "normal" for the practice to better recognize any irregularities. Each month, prepare or print summary accounts receivable reports showing comparisons over several months. In particular, look for either a significant drop in receivables (signaling a possible drop in production) or a steady increase in receivables over 90 days old. Also remember that comparing today's figures with last year's shows in which direction the practice is heading.

Abrupt changes in charges, adjustments, and receipts for an individual provider   If you notice a big jump or drop in these monthly totals, especially for two months in a row, investigate and find out why. It might just be a simple "bump in the road" (i.e., physician time off) or it could indicate serious underlying problems.

Late charges or other penalties   If the practice is getting assessed late charges or penalties, it could signal a cash flow problem. Is the practice paying bills on time? What does an aging of the accounts payable look like? Look at bank statements, too. Overdrafts or returned checks indicate critical problems.

Sharply rising overhead costs   Despite a practice's best cost-cutting efforts, overhead should continue to rise as the consumer price index slowly rises. Therefore, it's important to monitor practice expenses closely by categories like personnel, facility, office supplies, and medical supplies. Compare costs from month to month and from year to year. Overhead will be discussed in greater detail in a later chapter.

Inconsistent reporting   Finally, make sure information needed to run the practice is being made available on a timely basis each and every month. This includes all the financial information discussed in this chapter. If financial information is late or withheld, this could be an early warning sign of trouble.

▼ CHAPTER 3
Cost Containment in a Medical Practice

Any physician will tell you that overhead is, and always will be, a major concern. The overhead necessary to operate a practice must be contained or reduced in order to optimize a medical practice's net profit. Left unchecked, operating overhead can consume the gross revenue of any medical practice. It is thus important for office management and a medical practice's consultant to review overhead whenever a practice's financial statements are prepared.

As stated in Chapter 2, the operating overhead of a practice should be compared with overhead statistics of similar practices. Overhead statistics are summarized in survey form by medical practices around the country. If overhead, expressed as a percentage of the practice's collections or the total amount of overhead itself, appears to be out of line, conduct an investigation immediately. Probe specific overhead categories to identify significant or unexplained variances. Also review the transactional detail for each expense category to see where the practice is spending its money. This can normally be accomplished by reviewing the practice's general accounting ledgers.

■ **Practice Point:** Financial statements should be prepared on a comparative basis. This allows you to spot overhead items that appear to be out of line.

■ **Practice Point:** If you review practice overhead, be sure to have access to a year-to-date, detailed general ledger. This type of general ledger lists all financial activity, including journal entries, for each general ledger account for each month of the year-to-date. This is an excellent tool to use when analyzing the appropriateness of specific overhead categories. This type of report allows you to see if, in fact, entries to the account are realistic, necessary, or even misposted.

This chapter presents a review of the most common overhead categories of a medical practice and a related discussion of ways to reduce or contain overhead costs. When examining a practice's financial statements, especially the income statement, you will need to pay strict attention to overhead categories.

Payroll and Related Benefits

Arguably, one of the largest operating overhead figures is payroll. Salaries and related employee fringe benefits are two of the largest overhead expense items on the income statement. Thus, each should be monitored closely. If payroll and benefits appear to be higher than the norm, prepare an organizational chart that includes all employees, their job duties, and their related salaries and benefits. Next, based on the practice's specific needs, determine if all the employees are needed at the current time. Some practice managers, consultants, and CPAs first compare the number of the practice's employees to related personnel surveys, such as the one compiled by the Medical Group Management Association. Although this is a good start in the analytical process, keep in mind that what is good for one practice may not be good for another. For example, one physician's office may be a high producer, and another may be an average producer. The high producer will need more people in his office than would the average producer. Therefore, use surveys only as a starting point for evaluating personnel needs.

> ■ **Practice Point:** Surveys can be obtained from groups such as the Medical Group Management Association and the American Medical Group Association.

Determining Personnel Needs

An in-depth analysis of the practice's overall needs will indicate how many employees are actually needed to make the practice as efficient as possible. To conduct this analysis, you must have an intimate knowledge of how the office operates daily.

One area that should be reviewed is collections. Many times an office is understaffed and, therefore, personnel cannot devote enough time to collections. Even though adding collection personnel might look like an expensive maneuver, in the long run these individuals will more than pay for themselves. Analyze the office's billing and collection personnel needs by answering the following questions:

- Are insurance claim forms getting prepared and mailed (or electronically filed) on a timely basis (i.e., within two to three days for office visits and five to seven days from last date of service for all other charges)?
- Do current employees have the time to follow up on unpaid insurance claim forms each week? If so, how much time is being devoted?
- Do current employees have enough time to follow up on patients' unpaid balances?
- Are insurance appeals handled in a timely manner?
- Are patient-account statements mailed monthly in a timely manner?

Negative answers to any of these questions may indicate that the office is understaffed. Keep in mind, however, that negative responses to the questions could be attributed to the inexperience and incompetence of some of the individuals performing billing and collection duties. In such cases, suggest or consider personnel changes before recommending that the office hires new employees.

Another area to watch is the front desk. This is one of the most understaffed areas in many medical practices, especially those that operate in a heavy managed-care environment. Analyze personnel needs in the front-desk area by answering the following questions:

- Are there any problems with the patient check-in and check-out process?
- Are office charges and payments posted on a daily basis?
- Are the telephones answered in a timely manner?
- Are front-desk employees overwhelmed with managed-care related paperwork?
- Are front-desk employees overwhelmed by any other tasks?

Again, negative answers to these questions could be attributed to a lack of personnel in this area or to inexperienced or incompetent personnel.

■ **Practice Point:** One way to reduce overtime is to stagger the start times for practice employees. For instance, the practice might want nurses and other clinical staff to report at 8:30 a.m. with other employees. However, if clinic hours don't start until 9:00 or 9:30 and run until 6:00 p.m. or later, a practice is practically guaranteeing overtime pay. One way to avoid this problem is by staggering the nurses' arrival to different times so that everyone works just an eight-hour day. The same principle works with front office staff, too. Instead of looking at the 8-to-5 block, look at when employees are really needed. Chances are the practice doesn't need three front office people if the phone comes on at 8 a.m. and if patients don't start arriving until 8:30 a.m. or 8:45 a.m.

■ **Practice Point:** Tracking overtime by position and department is a way to identify and review individual productivity and related efficiency for each position and department.

Also keep in mind that the manner in which a physician practices medicine may result in higher employee needs than normal. Some physicians need personal secretaries or special assistants. Others might need additional nurses. For example, in some physician practices each physician has his or her own nurse, while in others the physicians share nursing staff. Some physicians even hire scribes to follow them around the hospital and record every chargeable procedure the physician performs. Your ultimate goal is to determine the practice's true needs and whether specific employees are an integral part of it. If they are not, they should be dismissed.

■ **Practice Point:** Many practices hire physician extenders to help in the practice. These individuals are either physician assistants or nurse practitioners. The first question to ask is whether this person is really needed to make the practice efficient or to add to its revenue stream. Some practices hire physician extenders thinking these individuals can become profit centers on their own. If this is the case, compare what this person has collected to the total costs to date of their compensation package (salary, benefits, malpractice insurance, etc.). Many times you will find that revenues do not cover costs. Discuss this with the physician(s) immediately.

Appropriate Compensation Levels

Next analyze what each employee is paid relative to his or her specific job duties in the practice. You may want to conduct a compensation survey at this point. A good place to start is by finding out what other physicians in the area are paying their staffs. This information will be available from personnel recruiters, hospital physicians relations personnel, hospital recruitment personnel, and the county medical society. Also use information from practices, especially ones in the same medical specialty. Many different types of compensation surveys exist. Compare the practice's compensation to surveys conducted by the Medical Group Management Association, the Health Care Group, and the Professional Association of Health Care Office Managers. (Refer to Chapter 1 for addresses and phone numbers.) If an employee is paid excessively more than employees with similar job duties in similar practices, the next step is to identify the reasons.

One reason the practice's overall payroll may seem excessive can be traced to employees' length of service. Long-term employees frequently earn higher salaries than employees with similar job descriptions in other practices. This is because long-term employees have received and continue to receive raises in their base pay each year. When reimbursement is at its peak, physicians have a tendency to give good raises. For example, an office manager who started out at $24,000 annually 10 to 15 years ago could now be making upwards of $40,000 per year in a one-physician practice. To prevent escalating salaries, annual raises should not be given haphazardly. Rather, an employee's total compensation package should be compared to what other people in similar positions make. As an employee approaches the salary ceiling, he or she must be informed that the rate of growth in salary will slow down. The percentage increase for the annual raise, however, cannot be eliminated entirely. Morale would almost surely decline in an employee who does not receive any compensatory increase each year, unless such lack of an increase is because of poor job performance. In place of a 6 percent raise, the employee may be limited to a 3 percent increase for the given year. A popular alternative used in many medical offices for highly compensated employees is replacing annual raises with a merit bonus. An office that uses merit bonuses can set performance standards; if they are met, the practice will benefit accordingly, and the employee is rewarded with bonus compensation.

Although raises and merit bonuses depend on a number of variables, such as employee performance, length of service, performance standards, and inflation, the bottom-line determinant is the generosity of the physician-owner. The physician must understand, however, that generosity has a price; he or she cannot complain about the practice's high payroll costs if salaries are set too high to begin with, and if annual raises are given each year without any thought to the practice's future.

Health Insurance

Group health insurance premiums can rise dramatically from one year to the next. In some small medical practices, the annual increase in premium rates can reach 50 percent. To lower the cost of insurance, review the practice's current insurance coverage. Coverage affects the premium dollar because rates increase when greater coverage is provided to employees. A policy with a $250 deductible generally costs more than one with a $500 deductible. A policy that includes dental coverage will cost more than one that does not. Again, the extent of coverage generally depends on the generosity of the physician-owner. In an era of skyrocketing premium rates, however, it may not make economic sense to provide expansive health insurance coverage to employees.

The next step after reviewing the practice's current insurance coverage is to solicit bids from different health insurance companies for comparable coverage. This is an especially good idea if the practice has had its insurance plan with the same company for a number of years. Consider using an independent agent to obtain bids. If the practice decides to switch insurance plans, lock in the premium rate for as long as possible. Generally, this can be done for at least one year after the new policy is purchased. Each year, however, monitor health insurance premium costs and any increase proposed by the insurance company. When such increases occur, evaluate the issues of coverage and the possibility of switching to a new plan.

Finally, a practice does not necessarily have to accept rate increases on its insurance premiums. Some insurance agents can remove proposed rate increases. This usually is done by showing that the employees did not use health care providers very often during the year.

As rates increase over a period of time, the practice may be faced with some difficult decisions in order to contain costs. It may decide to switch health insurance companies, even though it is perfectly happy with the one it has. The practice also may have to ask the employees to subsidize a part of the health insurance premium. In many practices, employees pay as much as 50 percent of the premium. However, you will want to check the employment laws of the state in which the practice is located to ensure that there are no limitations on how much of the premium employees can subsidize. The most difficult decision, however, is the one that limits coverage or eliminates the benefit altogether. Make sure that all possible alternatives have been explored completely before resorting to outright cancellation of health insurance as an employee benefit. Also consider current and pending legal requirements regarding health insurance.

Sick Leave Policy

Another employee fringe benefit that can increase costs is the practice's policy on sick leave. Many practices pay employees at the end of the year, or upon termination, for unused sick leave. As with employee compensation and the extent of health insurance coverage, the specifics of the sick leave policy depend on the physician-owner's generosity. The physician should keep in mind, however, that sick leave really should not be a compensated fringe benefit if the employees do not use it. Sick leave is a contingency for the benefit of the employee in the event of an illness. This is what a fringe benefit is all about. Some employees may object that not paying for unused sick leave penalizes healthy employees. The physician should remember that employees are initially paid for a full year's work. However, as an incentive to healthy employees, many practices have adopted the policy of carrying over unused sick leave to future years. This allows the employee to bank the unused sick leave and to use it in the case of an illness, especially a serious one.

Overtime Policy

A practice's overtime policy also can increase payroll costs. You will need to review its criteria for authorizing and paying for overtime by finding out the following information:

- Are employees made accountable for their overtime hours?
- How is overtime documented?
- Is overtime approved beforehand?
- Are exempt employees getting paid for overtime even though they are not entitled to it?

Retirement Plan

If the medical practice has a retirement plan, it must be analyzed for cost efficiency. A retirement plan is one of the most expensive fringe benefits offered to employees. Make sure that the type of plan currently in place is the right one for the practice. Also, make sure that the length of the plan's vesting schedule is to the physician's benefit. If a practice has a high turnover, the plan should be structured so that any unvested accounts are reallocated to the remaining participants based on the ratio of their own account balances. This would benefit the physician, because he or she will have the highest account balance. In addition, analyze the fees that the plan's administrator charges within the plan. If left unchecked, these costs can get quite high.

■ **Practice Point:** If retirement plan costs get too high, consider non-qualified, non-deductible retirement plan options.

Medical and Office Supplies

Another major operating expense for the practice is medical and office supplies. One of the first places to look for excess costs is vendor pricing, especially for medical supplies. Sometimes medical practices lock themselves in with one medical supply representative for a particular supply. Smaller practices may have a relationship with a supply representative to provide all of their medical supplies. The problem with exclusive relationships is that the practice may not be getting the best price available. Therefore, the practice should develop a list of its medical supply costs and bid out the supplies to various vendors.

Another option the practice has to reduce prices is group purchasing. For example, a group of independent physicians could get together to purchase selected items collectively and to take advantage of lower prices for larger orders. Members of individual practice associations (IPAs) or similar organizations often purchase, as a group, certain overhead items.

■ **Practice Point:** Many physicians are members of integrated delivery systems, such as IPAs. These so-called "groups" do in fact have group purchasing power and should use this kind of leverage to help reduce the overhead of their physician members. If the practice is involved in an integrated delivery system, find out whether or not such delivery system bids out costs for its members. If not, somehow get the physician to encourage this process with the delivery system itself.

■ **Practice Point:** The following are the most common overhead items bid out by delivery systems, such as IPAs: malpractice insurance, medical supplies, laboratory costs, radiology costs, and any other insurance.

Also, if the practice's computer system has the capability to generate its Superbills or patient charge tickets in-house instead of purchasing them from an outside vendor, the practice can save money. This is only recommended if the computer-generated Superbill can capture the same services as the purchased form. Do not recommend this option if it impairs the process of how physicians' services are captured. (See the section titled "The Superbill" in Chapter 9 for a detailed discussion of services to include on the Superbill.)

Besides the price of supplies, the quantities of supplies purchased should be reviewed. A medical office cannot afford to overpurchase and waste supplies.

Analyze the amount of supplies purchased each month and the method by which they are purchased. Begin by reviewing inventory on hand at the end of each month. If the inventory is and remains high, it may be necessary to limit the amount of supplies purchased each month. In addition, find out how the need for monthly supplies is determined and if purchasing is centralized with one or more persons in the office. If it is, assess the accountability of that person. The person who orders supplies should collect and assemble requests for supply purchases, place the orders, make sure the correct order has been received, and be responsible for checking all related vendor invoices. Also make sure the office has a clear purchasing policy. If it does not, suggest that the office develop and implement one.

For group practices with multiple offices, recommend that they centralize the purchasing of medical supplies and distribute the supplies to each office when they are delivered. If one office runs out of supplies, a designated employee should first call the other offices to secure additional supplies. Under no circumstances should an office be allowed to order more supplies. In effect, this arrangement forces each office to share and trade supplies. This is one way group practices can hold down medical supply costs. Also, make sure that an individual office does not have the ability to order its own supplies. This authority should always be centralized.

A clear purchasing policy should minimize duplication of ordering, avoid overstocking supplies, encourage price shopping with vendors, take advantage of purchase order discounts, and ensure that all invoices are properly prepared and ready for payment. This policy should apply to all supply purchases and should be monitored continually.

■ **Practice Point:** Don't forget to search the Internet for office and medical supplies. This is also a good way to compare pricing. The following are just a few examples of online suppliers: www.medicalartspress.com, www.esurg. com, and www.pssd.com.

Lease Agreements

Rental costs often are among the largest overhead items recorded on a medical practice's income statement. Incidental costs related to the practice's office lease often are overlooked overhead items. First review the operating stop provisions and insurance requirements in the practice's office lease document.

Under the typical operating stop provision, the landlord allocates to all of the tenants any excess costs needed to operate the medical office building in a particular year. Excess costs are those that exceed the base operating stop amount the landlord provided the practice when the lease was initially signed. So even though a practice agrees to a specific rental rate per square foot of space, the actual amount paid to the landlord may increase each year because of the operating stop provision. Therefore, review exactly what specific costs the landlord includes in the operating stop calculation. These usually are stated specifically in the lease. Look for costs that have nothing to do with operating the building. For example, unrelated payroll costs and management fees sometimes are included in the allocation. Also audit the landlord's operating stop calculation each year.

Besides the operating stop, check the lease for insurance the landlord may require the practice to purchase. Find out if the insurance is necessary and if there are alternatives. Although it is difficult to renegotiate both of these issues once a lease has been signed, they can and must be addressed before a medical practice signs a new lease or renews an old lease for office space.

Also assess whether the office space is designed as efficiently as possible. Often, physicians waste money on office space rental; the space they actually use is less than the amount of space they rent. Also, remember that rental expense can be expanded simply because of the building the physician is in. There is a difference between net rentable space and net usable space in each office lease agreement. The net rentable space includes the physician's share of common area space in the building, such as elevator space or unused atrium space. So, if a physician is in a building that has a beautiful atrium, he or she is paying for a part of this unusable space.

Review all other lease agreements in addition to the office lease document, especially equipment leases. Calculate the internal interest rate embedded in each lease. Do not forget to take into account any end-of-lease purchase requirements. Often, it is cheaper to purchase a specific item outright than to lease it over a period of time. Examine all related maintenance contracts on office equipment.

Determine if the same maintenance contract can be acquired more cheaply elsewhere or if the contract is necessary. Many practices pay for maintenance contracts long after the related equipment has lost its value or on equipment that is seldom used. Finally, analyze related repair costs on the practice's equipment, furniture, fixtures, and leasehold. Determine if these expenses were necessary and their likelihood of occurring again on the same asset. Also determine if it would be a better allocation of resources to purchase new assets rather than continuing to repair them.

Refunds to Patients

Since refunds to patients usually are listed in the collected revenue portion of the income statement and are thus netted against the practice's actual collections, they often are overlooked as overhead expenses. Nevertheless, if refunds to patients can be reduced, the practice's net income will rise. Together with the business office personnel, examine why the refunds were given and assess how such refunds can be eliminated in the future. They could have resulted from posting errors or from prepayments by patients before services were rendered. For example, some surgical practices require patients to pay a deposit before surgery is performed. You may want to select a few patient accounts and trace the related billing and collection transactions through the system to see how the refunds occurred and to make sure they are correct. By doing this, you will see if the refunds resulted from human error (such as incorrect posting of accounts) or internal systems error (such as guessing patients' co-payment amounts).

Other Costs

Many other costs of a medical practice should be reviewed for possible reduction or containment. Following is a listing of some of those costs:

- **Small overhead items** Pay special attention to any small overhead items, such as bank charges and penalties. These charges can and should be eliminated. Review the reasons for the charges and implement whatever steps are necessary to make sure that they do not happen again. A penalty may have been incurred because a payroll tax deposit was made late or a tax form was mailed late. Also, a bank charge may be assessed because the account does not maintain a minimum balance each month.

- **Advertising** Critique the cost and related benefits of advertising. Many offices spend money on advertising and similar marketing ventures but receive little benefit from them in the form of additional revenue. Look first at any costs related to display advertising, especially those in a telephone directory. Many offices pay for full-page or half-page advertising in several telephone directories. This can cost thousands of dollars per year. If the practice is not generating adequate revenue as a direct result of this form of advertising, the practice should either reduce the size of the advertisement or eliminate it altogether. Inspect other advertising costs and determine if they are necessary. For example, a firm could be incurring costs associated with specialty advertising, such as calendars or pens. (For a more detailed discussion of tracking and evaluating advertising expenses, see Chapter 15.)

- **Outside billing agency** If the practice contracts with an outside billing agency, determine whether the cost of paying an agency is worth the amount of recovered revenue. Compare the total amount collected by the billing agency less the agency's fee to the estimated internal billing and collection less the cost of personnel, equipment, paper, postage, and office efficiency.

- **Postage costs** Postage and telephone costs in the office rarely are controlled. Determine if employees are using office postage for personal correspondence. Also make sure that unnecessary correspondence is not being mailed out of the office, such as redundant communications to patients. Determine if the practice would benefit from some type of metered system.

- **Telephone costs** Telephone costs can be reduced with minimal investigation. The practice should have a system in place to detect whether employees are making personal long-distance telephone calls. If it does not, recommend one. Also, find out if the office is paying for telephone lines or other options it does not use. Finally, if it has not been done recently, have vendors submit bids for the answering and paging services to determine if a lower cost at the same quality service is available.

- **Petty cash** Assess how petty cash disbursements are controlled and if they are really necessary. Determine if an effective system is in place to govern petty cash disbursements.

- **Professional fees** Expenses related to professional fees must be inspected periodically. The necessity of these costs should be investigated. Determine which expenses are onetime costs and which ones are ongoing. For ongoing professional fees, search for less expensive alternatives. For example, a practice may be using an outside firm for retirement plan administration, whereas the practice's outside accountant may be able to provide the same service for a lower fee. The same can be said for costs related to ancillary services such as laboratory and radiology services. If the practice pays an outside company for these types of services, weigh the possibility of other similar companies providing the same service at lower cost. For example, have another laboratory bid for the practice's lab work.

Merging Practices to Reduce Costs

All practices have a duplication of overhead. Each has an office manager, each has similar staff, each has office space, supply needs, and so on. One way to reduce costs is for practices to merge and to integrate as much as possible. The following are a few obvious examples of cost reductions when practices merge:

1. Each office usually has its own office manager/administrator. A combined group practice only needs one.

2. Each office has billing and collection personnel. All of these individuals will usually not be needed after the offices merge.

3. Each practice has its own office space. Rental costs will be saved if practices can be combined into one location. In addition, if practices are combined into one location, all of the receptionists will probably not be needed at the new location.

These are just a few of the savings that can be achieved when practices merge. Regardless of format, when practices merge, the bigger group has greater group purchasing power. This should lead to a reduction of additional costs. (For more on this topic, see Chapters 21 and 22.)

Recruiting a New Physician to Reduce Costs

Another way to reduce practice costs is by recruiting a new physician to the practice and at the same time seeking financial assistance from the hospital where the practice sends its patients. As discussed in Chapter 20, it is legal for hospitals to provide this kind of financial assistance on either a gross income guarantee basis or a net income guarantee basis. Either way, it is possible to get a portion of the practice's overhead subsidized for a period of time under these arrangements. (See Chapter 20 for more information.)

Office Sharing with Another Physician to Reduce Costs

Many practicing physicians, solo to small practices, are looking to reduce their overhead. One way to do that is to share overhead costs by some type of office sharing arrangement. For example, physicians could share rent, personnel, supplies, etc., by practicing in the same office location. Solo practitioners or small practices should consider looking for physicians who may want to relocate their practice and share space. This could be on a full- or part-time basis. There are many sharing arrangements whereby a physician will see patients one or two days at the office of another practice. (See Chapter 21 for a detailed discussion of office-sharing arrangements.)

▼ CHAPTER 4
Internal Controls in a Medical Practice

Every medical practice must implement specific internal controls to protect it from revenue loss and potential employee embezzlement. Although there will never be a guarantee that employee embezzlement, fraud, or similar defalcations will be caught, a practice can still minimize these activities by implementing and monitoring sound internal controls. One of your duties is to make sure these controls are in place. This chapter discusses the basic internal controls that should be found in most medical practices. (See Appendix A for a sample internal control checklist for a medical practice.)

Computerized Practice

Controls detect and prevent embezzlements, such as an employee at the front desk who pockets the money from a patient's office visit and then manipulates source documents so that the charge fails to get entered in the computer. Someone should review the computer-generated daily report to ensure that charges related to patients' visits are actually recorded. Following are some controls that should be implemented to help detect and prevent embezzlement.

Prenumber all patients' encounter forms, or Superbills, and make sure they are accounted for on a daily basis   Accounting for the Superbills (i.e., charge tickets) used daily generally is done by checking the numerical sequence of the control numbers on each Superbill, then tracing them back to the patient sign-in sheet or the daily appointment record. Generally, a copy of each Superbill is kept in a separate file in numerical order. Then, when the Superbills are reviewed, it is relatively easy to pick out potential embezzlement situations by searching for a gap in the Superbill's numerical sequence. A gap may indicate that a Superbill was used for an embezzlement scheme. If the patient made a payment in the office but the visit charge was not entered in the computer, the patient's account would reflect no charge and no payment. In this case, the payment may have gone into an employee's pocket. If the charge had at least been entered, the billing employee would assume no payment was made at the time of the visit and would have sent a statement to the patient at the end of the month. When the patient then received the statement, presumably he or she would call the office and explain that the payment was in fact made at the time of the visit.

Divide job duties   One individual should not be allowed to both open the mail (i.e., initially handle the money) and enter payments in the computer. Dividing the two duties prevents an employee from stealing money from the practice and then manipulating patients' accounts in the computer, usually by writing off balances as contractual adjustments or bad debts. For example, an employee who is responsible for opening the mail and entering payments writes off an account as a bad debt after a patient's account statement has been mailed. The employee knows this patient will pay within 30 days, so the employee waits for the check to come in the mail so she can intercept it and cash it.

In an ideal situation, one person opens the mail, another person prepares the deposit slips, and a third person enters the payments to the patients' individual accounts in the computer. However, most small medical practices do not have adequate personnel to carry this out. What usually happens is that the person who opens the mail also enters payments into the computer or onto the ledger cards. Every medical practice should bond all personnel who will or may come into contact with money. *Bonding* is a type of insurance that will reimburse the practice for embezzlement by office personnel. It is typically referred to as *fidelity bond insurance*. This type of insurance can also reimburse the practice if money is ever stolen by someone other than a practice employee. For example, a receptionist takes the daily deposit to the bank. On her way to make the deposit, she stops to run an errand. While she is away from the car, her car is broken into and the deposit money is stolen.

■ **Practice Point:** Consider using a lockbox arrangement with your banking institution if you feel that duties cannot be properly segregated to ensure control measures. Under a lockbox arrangement, all mail receipts go to a "lockbox" at the practice's bank. They do not go directly to the medical office. The bank then makes copies of the checks and any EOBs (explanation of benefits) and sends them to the practice for posting. Some banks will even place these documents on CD-ROM for a practice. This is an excellent internal control methodology for any medical practice, especially larger ones.

Reconcile office visit payments, received during the day from patients, to source documents   Both the sign-in sheet and the appointment schedule should be reconciled to the computer-generated report of daily charges. In turn, the money from patients who paid for their office visits should be reconciled to the computer-generated report of daily payments. This may be a cumbersome daily task. Make sure it is done at least two to three times a month. Also, practices with multiple offices may not make deposits daily, resulting in the inability to reconcile the bank deposit slip to the daily computer reports. Branch banking by each office and corresponding cash transfers to a central operating account may solve this problem.

From an internal control standpoint, the practice needs to make daily deposits, if it can, so that the related reconciliation can be performed and situations, such as the following, can be avoided. An office manager reviews daily reports of charges and compares them to the appointment book. The manager finds a visit without a corresponding charge and subsequently locates the related office charge ticket. The ticket indicates that payment was made, so the manager assumes an employee embezzled money. As soon as the manager discovers this, internal controls are put in place. However, if the charge ticket did not indicate payment, the office manager could either post the charge and send the patient a bill or contact the patient directly. In either case, lost money is found.

Monitor contractual adjustments for reasonableness   Depending on the practice's payor mix, a high volume of contractual adjustments could indicate possible embezzlement. For example, an insurance claim for $1,000 is prepared and mailed to an insurance plan for services rendered by the practice. The plan approves 80 percent of the charge and subsequently sends a check in the amount of $800 to the practice. An employee in the practice takes the $800 check, deposits it into his or her own personal bank account, and then accesses the practice's computer to write off the $1,000 patient account balance as a contractual adjustment.

The best way to prevent embezzlement from occurring in this situation is to make sure the person who handles money is not responsible for entering it into the computer.

Also make sure that contractual categories are specifically identified. A medical office should not have one catch-all category called credit adjustment or contractual adjustment. Establish a credit adjustment category for each of the practice's major payors, for example, the categories could be credit adjustment—Medicare, credit adjustment—Medicaid, credit adjustment—Worker's Compensation, credit adjustment—Aetna, credit adjustment, and so on.

By specifically categorizing contractual write-offs, the CPA, consultant, or the practice manager can compare these adjustments to the practice's actual payor mix to look for inconsistencies. For example, 75 percent of the practice's revenues come from commercial insurance carriers. The computer records indicate that the practice is writing off 35 percent of its charges as contractual adjustments. This could indicate an embezzlement situation.

A final internal control measurement you can take is to print out and review patients' account ledgers periodically. Look for and investigate any balance that has been written off in its entirety without approval. If possible, use the practice's computer to scan for files that have been written off. If the office's computer does not have this capability, someone will have to go through each ledger to identify such charges.

Compare total monthly bank deposits to computerized report of monthly payments   Receipts posted to the medical billing software should agree with receipts actually deposited into the bank account. In other words, when the month is closed, the amount of receipts indicated on the management reports (e.g., Report of Monthly Charges, Receipts and Adjustments) should agree with what was actually deposited in the bank for that same month. If the numbers do not agree, investigate immediately and set up procedures to make sure they do. If receipts per the management reports are less than the bank deposits, it could indicate embezzlement (i.e., receipts were posted to the patients' accounts but never made it to the bank).

Necessitate mandatory consent of the physician for write-offs A patient's account balance should never be written off as a bad debt without the written consent of a physician. This avoids the situation in which monies can be diverted away from the practice without any kind of a trail. Write-offs are usually documented by printing out the patient's detailed account ledger and having the physician review and initial each ledger page as a way of approving the write-off. If this method is impractical, have the approval documented in the computer. The down side of this activity is that the physician has to become very active and hands-on in the receivable management process. Not all physicians have the inclination nor the time to become this involved.

Implement a password into the computer system Establish passwords in the computer system and allow access only to authorized personnel.

Encourage employees to take their vacation time in multiple days Having employees take extensive vacation leave may help uncover embezzlement tracks. When an employee is away from the office for an extended period, such as a week, the person who takes over the vacationing employee's tasks could stumble across errors and embezzlement caused by the vacationing employee. For example, an employee who is responsible for billing and collection takes a one-week vacation. While the employee is away, a patient calls about his account statement. The statement shows a deductible balance due, although the patient says he already paid. Because the vacationing employee was not able to intercept this type of call, the embezzlement was exposed.

Make sure the bank account is reconciled each month There are many medical practices today that do not reconcile their bank account or accounts each and every month. Failure to do so could indicate an embezzlement situation. Also with respect to the bank reconciliation, the best internal control would be to have the bank mail the monthly bank statement to someone who is not a check signer and have this person obtain the checkbook and reconcile the account "independently" of the practice administrator, practice controller, or a similar person. This may not be practical, in which case the practice should have its independent CPA review the bank reconciliation on a periodic basis.

Manual Practice

The same internal controls used for a computerized medical practice should be applied to a practice using a manual pegboard system. A pegboard system uses daysheets and patient ledger cards to post charges, payments, and adjustments. Thus, the daysheet activity should be reconciled to the sign-in sheet and to the appointment book. Review the patient ledger cards for write-offs of entire account balances.

Reconciling the accounts receivable balance to the daysheet and the total amounts due to the individual patient's ledger cards is the one major internal control that is specific to manual pegboard systems. When each daysheet is tallied, it maintains a running accounts receivable balance. Because the individual ledger cards are posted at the same time as the daysheet, the accounts receivable balance per the daysheet should agree with the total amounts due per the individual patients' ledger cards. Many times these two amounts do not agree. A charge or payment may be posted to the daysheet but not to the ledger card, and vice versa. The difference could result from innocent posting errors. History has shown, however, that much too often embezzlement occurs as a result of bad recordkeeping. In other words, the records are in such shambles that there is no way embezzlement could be detected. Thus, every month, have the practice add up all the balances due per the individual patient ledger cards and reconcile this balance to the daysheet.

Accounts Payable

Accounts receivable is not the only area in which embezzlement occurs; controls for accounts payable should also exist in every medical practice. Accounts payable controls prevent a practice's employee from preparing checks to an unauthorized vendor, which may in fact be in the employee's control. For example, a check could be made out to a fake office supply company and mailed to a post office box controlled by the employee.

The best internal controls for accounts payable are (a) to limit check-signing authority to the physician and (b) to attach a vendor invoice to each check when it is signed. In situations in which a physician refuses to take the responsibility for signing checks, make sure the endorsements on the back of the canceled checks are reviewed. Look specifically for third-party endorsements or endorsements that do not appear to match the payee on the check. Many times it is obvious when a business check is endorsed personally by someone other than the vendor. Have the bank statement and canceled checks mailed directly to his office for reconciliation.

As added protection, the physician may want to receive the bank statement and review it first, in which case the bank could send the statements directly to the physician's home. Just by scanning the transactions, a physician can sometimes detect that something is wrong.

> ■ **Practice Point:** Never, ever let practice personnel have access to a doctor's signature stamp. This is especially true for the person responsible for writing checks on the practice's bank account. This type of access just invites the temptation for theft.

Responsibility for Fraud and Embezzlement

The need to monitor internal controls often leads to a misunderstanding between the consultant and his or her physician-client. Once embezzlement is discovered, the physician usually blames the consultant for not catching the embezzlement. The misunderstanding occurs because physicians assume that establishing and monitoring internal controls is one of the accountant's normal duties. However, consultants do not normally include these services in general compilation and tax engagements, unless the physician expressly asks for and arranges to pay for them. For example, accountants may not make it a general practice to turn over the canceled checks to review the endorsements on the back when they reconcile the bank statement. Thus, the consultant should make sure that the medical client understands precisely the duties that will and will not be performed for the practice. The duties should always be spelled out in a detailed engagement letter. The following is sample wording to include in an engagement letter for medical clients; if you are a practice manager or physician, make sure that you understand what you are agreeing to if this clause is included in the proposal or engagement letter:

Clause for Responsibility of Fraud and Embezzlement

Our engagement cannot be relied upon to detect and disclose any errors, irregularities, or illegal acts, including but not limited to fraud, embezzlement, and defalcations. Therefore, we cannot be held liable for any direct, indirect, or consequential damages, losses, or penalties arising from the discovery or lack of discovery of any errors, irregularities, or illegal acts. It is your responsibility to apply and implement appropriately any recommendations we may give you concerning any area of practice management and accounting.

Real-Life Examples

The following are actual examples of fraud and embezzlement because of poor internal controls:

- An employee embezzled $800,000 from a management company in a three-month period, using the following:
  —A fake vendor scheme.
  —A sweep account with faulty transfer setup to create confusion over cash balances and interest income earned.
  —An investment account that only the employee had signature authority over.
- A pharmacy director at a hospital stole over $200,000 in prescription drugs and $500,000 in surplus equipment by:
  —Noting drugs as expired, then selling them to the local market.

—Cancelling the security contract for a closed hospital that served as storage site for the majority of the hospital system's surplus equipment inventory; inventory was then diverted.

- An office manager stole an undetermined sum from a medical practice by:

    —Using reconciling items to cover up theft.

    —Hiding unpaid payables for which a physician had signed checks.

- An office manager, on parole for prior embezzlement during her employment period at the practice, stole approximately $200,000 from a two-physician practice by:

    —Stealing outright cash received at the checkout window.

    —Overadjusting contractual adjustments and pocketing the excess adjustment amount.

    —Not recording patient visits into the system and pocketing the payments.

    —Not depositing daily, thus generating more cash.

Dealing With Employee Theft

While most employees are honest and trustworthy, occasionally a dishonest one gets through the hiring process and the situation of employee theft may arise. It is a good idea to have a plan in place to deal with employee theft, particularly because of the high stakes involved. On the one hand, not acting quickly enough might exacerbate theft losses and enable the thief to get away. On the other, acting too quickly might jeopardize a prosecution or even lead to legal liability if it turns out that the suspicions were unfounded.

Employee theft is any taking of employer property, including supplies, equipment, proprietary information, or funds. It can range from a one-time theft of petty cash to forging of signatures on checks to an ongoing complex embezzlement scheme.

The effect on the practice can be relatively minor in the case of an isolated low-level theft, or endanger the very well-being of the practice in extreme cases. No matter where in the spectrum a situation falls, there are three aspects to dealing successfully with any employee theft:

- Investigation
- Discipline
- Loss Recovery

The Investigation

An investigation must be initiated promptly if a theft is detected. The reasons for this include the following:

1. To minimize potential additional theft losses
2. To obtain evidence while it is still fresh
3. To avoid possible escape by those responsible for the theft
4. To avoid the running out of civil and criminal statutes of limitation

Scope of investigation   How extensive an investigation is required will depend on factors such as the nature of the theft (an incident of petty cash skimming will require a less extensive investigation than an incident in which theft is suspected because of circumstantial evidence), whether there are witnesses, and the elaborateness of any scheme. More extensive investigations may require a team of investigators, perhaps including management and third parties such as CPAs, investigators, and attorneys.

> ■ **Practice Tip:** Consider bringing in experts early on in serious situations. Legal advice may be necessary to preserve claims under any insurance policies and to avoid opening the practice to liability for missteps in the investigation. Accusations of theft are a serious matter, and can expose the practice to defamation claims if they turn out not to be true.

If an employee is caught in the act of theft, the investigation may be fairly simple and short. Unfortunately, most cases of suspected theft are based on indirect or circumstantial evidence and require larger-scale and more in-depth investigations.

Regardless of the extent of the investigation, certain guidelines should be observed:

- The investigation should be handled by a management employee other than the manager who first noticed the theft. If the nature of the loss justifies the use of outside experts, such as a CPA, attorney, or investigator, include them early in the process.

- Keep the investigation quiet. A breach of confidentiality can lead to defamation claims and may inadvertently alert accomplices.

- When conducting the investigation, interview any witnesses individually. Memorialize all interviews in writing and get the person interviewed to sign the memo. Warn employees to maintain confidentiality.

The employee suspected of the theft should be interviewed only during the final stage of the investigation. This will likely be the most difficult interview. Be sure to have a witness present. The purpose of the interview is to get the suspect's statement, not to obtain a confession. Avoid making any promises, even if the employee offers to make restitution for the loss. If the employee offers to return the property without strings attached, accept it without promises as to further action. Don't let the possibility of restitution detract from the need of a deliberative determination as to the proper resolution of the matter.

Discipline

Once the investigation is concluded, there are a number of questions to be answered, including the following:

1. Is there sufficient evidence that the theft occurred?

2. If so, is there sufficient evidence that the theft is attributable to the employee?

3. If so, what is the appropriate level of discipline? While in a minor incident a warning might be sufficient, often termination is the only alternative.

No matter how clear the evidence, avoid self-help remedies. Even if you are absolutely sure your suspicions of theft are justified, do not take the employee's property without written consent by the employee.

Finally, although it is not a form of employee discipline, you need to consider bringing in the law enforcement authorities.

Loss Recovery

Once it's determined that an employee theft has occurred, promptly contact the practice's insurer to determine the practice's rights under any fiduciary bond or employee dishonesty policy it has. It may be useful to have an attorney assist in reviewing the employer's rights under the policy in the case of a large or complicated loss.

What you need to determine with respect to coverage is whether the theft is a covered loss and what the policy's exclusions and deductibles are. You will also need to know the policy procedures and deadlines for filing a claim.

When there is no insurance or coverage is insufficient, it may be possible to recover the loss by civil lawsuit against the employee for theft or misappropriation. There may also be other parties with some liability for the loss. This should be discussed with legal counsel. Often, the easiest way to obtain restitution is through the criminal justice system. If the prosecutor files charges, restitution is often part of any plea bargain discussion.

▼ CHAPTER 5
Projecting the Practice's Cash Flow

A medical practice might want or need to prepare a cash flow projection for many reasons: (1) to budget income and expenses for the upcoming year, (2) for general business planning purposes, (3) to aid in the valuation of a medical practice, or (4) to fulfill a lender's requirement for granting a loan. Also, when a hospital recruits a new physician, the projection is used to structure an income guarantee that may be a part of any hospital recruitment agreement. For example, a hospital is going to offer a new physician $20,000 per month gross collections income guarantee. Before the hospital can make that offer, it will need to make sure that the amount is adequate to pay the physician's overhead, debt service, and personal compensation. To do this, the hospital will need a cash flow projection.

A cash flow projection can be prepared either manually or by using a computerized spreadsheet, such as Lotus or Excel. To create the spreadsheet or cash flow model, you must know what data to include and how to interpret the data.

To use correct accounting definitions, the preparation of a cash flow projection for medical practices is really a forecast of anticipated future results based on assumptions developed by either the accountant or the client, or by both. Refer to the AICPA's *Statement on Financial Forecasts and Projections* for further guidance on the proper reporting format. Because the forecast of future revenue and expenses is limited, it generally does not meet the strict definitions of a projected or forecasted financial statement per the AICPA guide. When a CPA is preparing a cash flow projection for a medical practice, such services should be treated as a compilation engagement. The CPA should always include the following compilation report:

Sample Compilation Report

[Date]

Personal & Confidential

[Physician's Name and Address]

We have compiled the accompanying projected first-year cash revenue and expense and related statement of assumptions for the new medical practice of Dr._____, in accordance with standards established by the American Institute of Certified Public Accountants.

The accompanying forecast and this report were prepared for Dr._____ for the sole purpose of obtaining a bank loan to start [his or her] new medical practice.

This forecast is limited to information that is the representation of Dr. _____ and does not include an evaluation of the support for the assumptions underlying the forecast. We have not examined the forecast and, accordingly, do not express an opinion or any other form of assurance on the accompanying forecast or assumptions. It is important to understand that there are differences between the projected and actual results, because events and circumstances frequently do not occur as expected, and those differences may be material. We have no responsibility to update this report for events and circumstances occurring after the date of this report.

Firm Name

Some issues affect only a medical office's cash flow. You must address the specific issues that follow when preparing a cash flow forecast for a medical practice. If they are not addressed, the cash flow forecast for the practice will not be accurate. In fact, a forecast of this type will only be your best estimate. (See Appendix A for a sample cash flow forecast.)

Gross Revenue (Charges)

Two components make up a medical practice's gross revenue: (1) office visits from patients and (2) the practice's fee schedule.

Office Visits

The number of office visits a practice has will depend on whether the physician is a primary-care physician, a specialist, or a combination of both (i.e., a multispecialty medical practice). Visits should be broken down into the specific services the practice expects to render during the year and should be segmented into office visits, inpatient visits, consultations, emergency room visits, procedures, radiology, laboratory, other ancillary services, and so on (similar to the layout of the CPT book). Office visits should be forecasted over each 12-month period, resulting in a total for the year. For example, the forecast should predict how many office visits the practice will have each month, broken down between new and established patients. For surgical practices, the forecast should approximate the number of surgeries each month, divided into specific surgical procedures.

Sample Office Visits for Orthopedic Practice

Service	Mo. 1	Mo. 2	Mo. 3
Consultations	8	14	21
New patient visits	2	6	11
Emergency services	14	21	28
Fracture care	4	9	15
Knee surgeries	1	3	6

Forecasting specific office visits for each 12-month period is arguably the most difficult part of preparing the cash flow forecast for a medical practice. The following are potential sources for forecasting information:

Physician   Estimate with the physician the services that will be rendered during the 12-month period. Have the physician be as specific as possible. Physicians just starting their own practice may have difficulty providing this information.

Office manager or billing clerk   Repeat the estimation discussion with the office manager or billing clerk. This person should also be able to estimate the number of office visits the physician will have over a particular period. The office manager or billing clerk can also be an excellent source for physicians who are setting up a new practice if the individual has previous experience in a medical practice.

Computer-generated service frequency report   This report lists, generally by current procedural technology (CPT) code and related description, the number of services that were rendered by month or year to date. The report is most useful when forecasts are prepared for established practices.

> ■ **Practice Point:** Maintain these reports for various medical clients. This way, if you need to prepare a cash flow forecast for another practice with similar characteristics, you can refer back to the frequency report for information on encounters with patients. Many CPAs and consultants maintain these reports in notebooks by medical specialty.

Hospital personnel   A hospital's recruitment director or physician relations director may be able to provide information or insight to service frequencies. He or she might be able to obtain this information from other physicians who are on the hospital's medical staff.

Other physicians' offices   Attempt to obtain the service frequency report from a similar practice or to speak with another practice's office manager or billing clerk. Again, establish some sort of database of these reports, if possible.

When forecasting office visits, your estimates should be conservative when dealing with new medical practices. Make the forecast as accurate as possible. Otherwise, it will not be useful for budgeting and monitoring income and expense goals. For example, when estimating the number of office visits for new patients for a family practice, it is common to place into the forecast one patient per day for the first month, two patients per day for the second month, and three patients per day for the third month. It is also important for new medical practices to analyze exactly where their revenue will come from. Primary-care practices generally get their new patients off the street. In other words, patients call the office for an appointment when they get sick. Specialists generally get their patients from referrals from other physicians. If a new family practitioner sets up a practice in the community, it will take a while for people in the community to (a) discover that the physician has set up the practice and (b) choose to see the physician for treatment. If a surgeon sets up a new practice, the established primary-care physicians will not start referring patients to the new physician automatically. It takes time to build up the trust of the referring physicians. By identifying where patients come from, it is easier for you to forecast prospective patients.

Fee Schedule

After establishing service encounters for each 12-month period, the next step is to quantify the total amount of gross revenue for each period. You can do this by multiplying the number of encounters by the fee the physician will charge for each particular service. Therefore, a practice's fee schedule will have to be designed before the cash flow forecast can be prepared.

Sample Fee Schedule

A cash flow forecast predicts that a new practice will have 90 office visits from new patients in one particular month. Of these visits, 40 will be allocated to CPT code 99212 and 50 to CPT code 99213. The practice will charge $60 for code 99212 and $75 for code 99213. Therefore, gross revenue will be $2,400 for code 99212 and $3,750 for code 99213.

Collected Revenue

The next step when preparing a cash flow forecast for a medical practice is to break down gross charges into collected revenue. The categories of collected revenue will depend on a variety of factors: payor mix, cash at the time of service, collections from billed services, and related estimated adjustments to billed charges.

Payor Mix

After you calculate gross charges, break down the charges into specific payor categories. The forecast should define how much gross revenue will be derived from patients with Medicare, Medicaid, workers' compensation, preferred provider organizations (PPOs), health maintenance organizations (HMOs), commercial insurance, no insurance (self-pay), and other insurance payors. This is accomplished by estimating the percentage of revenue in each category, which should result in a total of 100 percent.

Sample Payor Mix

A particular internal medicine practice has the following payor mix:

Medicare	60%
Medicaid	2
Commercial	20
PPO	15
Other	3
Total	100%

A practice's payor mix will be directly dependent on the practice's medical specialty. Ophthalmologists and cardiologists will see more Medicare patients than some other specialties. Pediatricians would not treat Medicare patients. They would, however, treat Medicaid patients. The practice's payor mix will also depend on the area in which the office is located. Some areas are heavily weighted toward managed care, and other areas may be dominated by people who have commercial insurance. An area with a population of low-income demographics may have a high percentage of people without insurance.

Collections from Cash at the Time of Service

Next, you will need to estimate, by payor category, the percentage of patients who will pay for all or a part of their visits while in the office (i.e., they will pay cash at the time of service). If patients pay for visits while in the office, these services will not need to be billed to an insurance company or directly to the patient. Estimating this percentage will depend on the medical specialty and area in which the office is located. Medicare patients owe a deductible each year, so a small percentage should be allocated to payment at the time of service for these patients. A pediatrician in an area dominated by commercial insurance most likely will require most parents to pay for children's visits before leaving the office. In this scenario, perhaps 80 percent would be allocated to payment at the time of service for commercial patients. A small percentage should be allocated to managed-care patients, because most will be required to pay small co-payments at the time of the office visits.

Collections from Billed Services

Two very important factors must be taken into account when calculating collections from billed charges: (1) the timing of payments by each specific payor category and (2) the actual and potential write-offs for each payor category. First, the forecast must define, for example, how quickly Medicare will pay the billed insurance claim, how quickly a PPO will pay, and so forth. Rarely will an insurance company pay in the first 30 days, and not every charge will be paid within 60 days. Thus, the forecast may estimate that Medicare will pay 80 percent of the overall billed charges in the first 30 days (especially if the practice bills these services electronically), and 20 percent in the next 30 days. Patients who do not have insurance may pay only 10 percent in the first 30 days after billing, 20 percent in the next 30 days, and so on.

Second, actual and potential write-offs must be considered for each payor category, mainly contractual adjustments and bad debts. For most payor classes, only a portion of the billed charges will be collected. The legally defined approved and contracted amounts often are less than what is billed to the insurance companies. In these cases, the remaining amounts are written off as contractual adjustments. In addition, not all patients pay their co-payments and deductibles, often resulting in bad debts. Every medical practice will have a certain percentage of write-offs as a result of professional courtesies. The following are common write-off percentages by payor class, each ultimately dependent on the office's medical specialty and locale:

Medicare	30%
Medicaid	50%
PPO	25%
Commercial	10%
Self-pay	40%
Other	20%

The forecast should separate charges and collections related to HMO patients. These charges are paid at a flat rate per month on a capitated basis and, thus, can be shown as a separate line item under the category of collections in the forecast.

After total collections have been calculated for a 12-month period, test the validity of this portion of the forecast by calculating the gross collection percentage as follows:

$$\text{Gross collection percentage} = \frac{\text{Collections}}{\text{Production}}$$

Make sure that the calculated gross collection percentage appears reasonable for the medical practice. If the percentage is too high or too low, recalculate estimated collections for the 12-month period.

Overhead and Other Cash Requirements

After gross charges and related collections have been calculated, the next step in preparing the forecast is to map out what the practice will pay out for overhead and other cash requirements each month. To prepare an accurate forecast, make sure that the office properly times all cash disbursements. For example, if the malpractice premium will be paid out in quarterly installments, do not take the total premium and spread it out equally over a 12-month period. Likewise, if a physician is going to take time off for continuing medical education (CME), place the related disbursements in the month in which they might be incurred. In addition to normal operating overhead, the forecast must include disbursements for items such as debt service and the purchase of assets. The forecast should also include all cash receipts other than those from patients, such as monies received from loans, expert testimony, and other outside income sources.

For new medical practices, the forecast should include purchases of fixed assets, such as medical equipment, office equipment, and furniture; start-up expenses that must be paid out before the office actually opens, such as for the purchase of medical supplies, payment of professional fees for start-up assistance, and the payment of rent and other deposits; and, if applicable, disbursements related to the payment of any debt service.

See Appendix A for a sample collection reconciliation letter, accounts receivable reconciliation letter, and actual-to-budget comparison worksheet.

The CD-ROM accompanying this book includes medical practice cash flow projection examples.

▼ CHAPTER 6
Business and Strategic Planning for Medical Practices

The demand of the marketplace is causing ongoing changes in the medical industry. These changes may cause old beliefs about how medicine should be practiced to become obsolete. Physicians must therefore pay attention to the business aspects of a medical practice. One way to accomplish this is through business and strategic planning. Although business planning should occur continuously throughout the year, it must occur at least once a year in the form of a formal business planning session. The purpose of this session is to review the internal operations of the past year and prepare for the upcoming year. The session should be attended by the physician-owner, the practice's office manager or administrator, legal counsel, and the practice's outside accountant. Other advisors can be included in the meeting, if need be. Business planning allows the practice to maximize revenues, minimize costs, and expand net income as much as possible. Without sound business planning, the future holds no guarantees.

In addition to ongoing business planning, at some point a medical practice should conduct a strategic planning session. This is particularly true for large medical groups. This session basically creates a blueprint of where the practice wants to go and how it is going to get there. As we all know, health care is a constantly changing industry; therefore it's important to keep an eye not only on the present, but on the future as well.

First, this chapter discusses the basics of diagnostic business planning for any medical practice. You can use this information to both diagnose and solve current problem areas and to prepare for the future. Without sound business planning, the continued success of a medical practice cannot be assured, nor can its success be predicted.

The last part of this chapter discusses the strategic planning process—from start to finish—as it applies to a medical practice.

Business Planning

Each of the following issues should be monitored on an ongoing basis. Successful practices discuss them at a monthly management-type meeting.

Finances

Diagnostic business planning begins with the evaluation of the overall finances of the medical practice. Particular emphasis should be placed on the following areas.

Charges, Collections, Adjustments, and Write-offs

Compare the practice's charges, collections, contractual adjustments, and bad debt write-offs to the same figures from the previous year and analyze significant changes. Pay strict attention to any increase in contractual allowances, because this could signal a change in the practice's payor mix. If a shift in payor mix is occurring, the practice may want to design strategies to shift the mix back to a more financially profitable type of patient. Whenever the practice's collections drop from one year to the next, warn the physician that it could signal a change in reimbursement patterns, a decrease in the number of office visits, or an internal problem with billing and collections.

Also conduct an analysis of production, collections, and adjustments by physician for a group medical practice. There is a tendency to analyze total group practice figures and not individual physician ones. Changes in each physician's productivity and collection statistics must be identified and addressed. A simple worksheet, like the following one, can be used.

	Prod.	*Prod. Variance*	*Coll.*	*Coll. Variance*	*Adj.*	*Adj. Variance*
Dr. A						
Dr. B						
Dr. C						

Only contractual adjustments should be included in the column labeled "Adj." Another column for bad debt write-offs could be added to the worksheet.

Financial Percentages and Ratios

Next, review the practice's gross collection percentage, net collection percentage, and accounts receivable ratio. (These statistics are explained in Chapter 2.)

$$\text{Gross collection percentage} = \frac{\text{Collections}}{\text{Production}}$$

$$\text{Net collection percentage} = \frac{\text{Collections}}{\text{Production, less contractual adjustments}}$$

$$\text{Accounts receivable ratio} = \frac{\text{Current accounts receivable balance}}{\text{Average monthly gross production}}$$

Assess whether all these statistics are reasonable for the practice's particular medical specialty, depending on the practice's payor mix. For example, a practice in which most of its revenue comes from treating Medicare patients cannot, in most instances, be expected to have a gross collection percentage greater than 80 percent, and the net collection rate should always exceed 90 percent; primary-care practices should have an accounts receivable ratio of 1.0 to 2.0; and surgical and other practices with large amounts of inpatient revenue should have a ratio between 2.0 and 3.0. Compare the practice's current statistics to the previous year's statistics and attempt to explain any significant shifts. Keep in mind that any improvement in the practice's statistics will result directly in an increase in revenue and related cash flow.

Contractual Adjustments

Review the distribution of contractual adjustments by the insurance company. Discuss and determine the practice's ability, if any, to lower its contractual allowances. Because contractual adjustments are actually a cash equivalent, any reduction will result directly in increased cash flow. Generally, a decrease in contractuals is accomplished either by shifting the practice payor mix or by renegotiating certain managed-care rates. Before deciding how to carry out the strategies agreed upon for reduction, develop a system to monitor the activities.

Monitoring these adjustments may alert you as to when specific insurance payors are beginning to dominate the revenues of the practice. Reliance on the revenues from a few insurance plans could put the medical practice at unintended financial risk.

Fee Schedule

Review the practice's fee schedule. For each current procedural terminology (CPT) code, decide fee increases for the upcoming year. Bear in mind that overhead will more than likely increase during the upcoming year, so a fee increase may be necessary to compensate for it. If the fee schedule has not been adjusted in a while, it may be a good idea to evaluate it completely. Chapter 8 discusses how to analyze a medical practice's fee schedule.

Evaluation and Management Coding Practices

Analyze the coding of evaluation and management services if it is not analyzed by someone in the office on a regular basis. An analysis worksheet is included in Chapter 10. As managed care continues to grow and as practices move more to a fixed-fee type of environment, proper coding becomes paramount. This is particularly true of patient-visit coding. Practices can lose significant amounts of revenue if services are not coded correctly.

Payor Mix

Reexamine the office's payor mix. Compare its current distribution to the previous year's distribution and identify shifts in specific payor classes. Any reallocation to payors that have fixed fees (e.g., Medicare and managed-care plans) will have a direct impact on the collected revenue of the practice. Thus, attempt to identify specific methods the practice can implement to shift its payor class away from insurance plans that could result in significant contractual adjustments. (Refer to Chapter 1 and Chapter 5 for additional discussions about payor mix.)

Revenue from Managed-Care Plans

Determine the percentage of revenue received from each managed-care plan. If the practice cannot readily obtain this information, reevaluate the office's current information system. Find out if most of the managed-care revenue is concentrated in a few plans. If a majority does exist, assess the financial risk to the practice should the plan drop the physician and, therefore, cause the practice to lose that managed-care revenue. For example, a practice collects $1,000,000 during the year, of which managed care makes up 50 percent. Forty percent of the $500,000 was collected from one managed-care plan. In this situation, the practice must assess whether or not it can afford to lose $200,000 of revenue all at once should it be deselected from the plan. At the same time, a majority in one plan may also indicate that the practice has leverage over the managed-care plan. If leverage does in fact exist, the plan may be willing to renegotiate payment rates and contract terms.

Managed-care renegotiation   Review all managed-care plans to assess their reimbursement rates and profitability. If the plan's rates or profitability are not acceptable, assess the potential for renegotiation. Remember, the fact that a practice treating a large block of enrollees from a particular managed-care plan could indicate that the physician may be able to renegotiate payment rates and contract terms. If cost and outcome data have been accumulated, as discussed later, assess the potential of using the data to renegotiate.

Quality assurance and utilization management activities   All medical practices must demonstrate cost effectiveness sometime in the future should a managed-care plan gain significant market share in their service areas. Therefore, practices must begin developing and implementing quality-assurance and utilization-management activities, which include the assembly of clinical outcomes. If the practice does have such a program, conduct a general overview of its success. This should not be too difficult to accomplish, as the office manager should have been assessing compliance and analyzing the success of the program on an ongoing basis. Plan quality-assurance and utilization-management activities for the next year and decide whether or not such data can be used to renegotiate any managed-care contracts.

If the practice does not have a quality-assurance and a management-utilization program, assess whether or not one should be implemented. This again will depend on the managed-care mix in the service area. For any practice, assess the benefit of having a utilization-management review conducted by a particular managed-care plan. The plan's utilization department should be able to provide this assessment. The department's assessment will be useful for any medical practice. (See Chapter 19 for more information about managed-care plans.)

Overhead

Compare each overhead category to the same overhead category from the prior year. Identify and question significant changes. In addition, decide how the practice's overall overhead can be reduced in the upcoming year. It is a good idea to review vendor pricing for all purchased supplies and services. Make sure that the practice is getting the best price or fee possible for all items. If necessary, obtain bids from current and prospective vendors. Finally, prepare a budget for the upcoming year that will serve as a management tool to control costs. Whenever the practice's financial statements are prepared throughout the year, make sure that the report that compares current overhead figures to the budget is prepared at the same time. Investigate significant variances. (See Chapter 3 and Chapter 5 for additional information on overhead control and budgeting.)

Cost Accounting

Every practice needs to know what it costs to render a particular service. These calculations should be prepared at least annually. (See Chapter 8 for additional information on how to calculate costs by service type.) Once calculated, analyze these figures and conduct a profitability analysis. This information also could be used to assess capitation rates, as discussed in Chapter 19, and to analyze a proposed capitation rate, should such a contract ever be proposed to the practice.

Accounts Receivable

An in-depth analysis of a current aging of the accounts receivable must be performed. Prepare and review a comparative report of monthly agings for the past 12-month period. Compare the receivables that are more than 90 days old to the same aging for the prior year. Discuss with the office manager significant shifts in the age of the receivables throughout the year. If receivables gradually aged, question the validity of the practice's collection policies. Also, identify any accounts more than 90 days old that are uncollectible and thus should be written off as bad debts. Make sure that the office is not wasting time on accounts it cannot collect.

Another diagnostic check related to the accounts receivable analysis is a critique of the front-desk collections. Calculate the percentage of patients who actually made some form of payment at the time of service. Then assess if this percentage is acceptable. (Refer to Chapter 2 for more information on accounts receivable statistical analysis.)

Banking

A final consideration is to determine how satisfied the office is with its current banking relationship. If all of the practice's banking needs are not being met, decide if a change to another banking institution is in order. If applicable, review all current outstanding notes payable. To reduce interest costs, assess whether or not any notes can be refinanced at a lower interest rate or paid off during the upcoming year.

Operations

Because physician-owners are busy practicing medicine, periodic breakdowns sometimes occur in the internal operations of the office. The following areas should be examined carefully.

Billing and Collection

Review all billing and collection policies to assess whether or not they have been successfully implemented throughout the year. If necessary, verify how well related office employees have complied with these policies. In other words, determine if the employees are doing the job they were hired to do. If it is the receptionist's duty to collect money from patients, find out if an acceptable percentage of money is collected. If it is the collection clerk's duty to follow up on unpaid insurance claims when they become 25 days old, find out if this is happening. Update and revise billing and collection policies, if necessary. If the practice does not use computers, assess the possibility of computerization for the upcoming year and identify whether the practice's efficiency could improve if a computer were purchased. Also assess whether the financial management of the office would improve if the practice had access to the kind of information a computer could readily provide.

Embezzlement Review

Determine the advisability of an embezzlement review. If the physician has never had this type of review done before, advise the physician to have it done. Also, a physician cannot be certain that his or her employees are not embezzling unless an embezzlement review is performed.

■ **Practice Point:** If the practice rejects such a review, the CPA or consultant should make sure that this rejection is documented in the client's file. A good way of documenting the client's rejection is by stating it in a letter and having the practice owner initial the letter.

Inventory

Prepare an inventory of all medical supplies in the office. Review the list and decide whether or not the practice is enforcing proper inventory control procedures. Make sure that medical supplies are not being wasted and that excess supplies are not being purchased and maintained in the supply inventory.

Compliance Regulations

Never assume that the office is in compliance with all Occupational Safety and Health Administration (OSHA), blood-borne pathogen, and worker safety regulations. If these rules are applicable to the office, conduct an internal OSHA audit. Make sure that the office is also in compliance with all other federal and state regulations, such as the federal Clinical Laboratory Improvement Amendment (CLIA) law for in-house laboratories.

Also analyze the records retention policies within the office. Identify records that can be disposed of, such as old tax records and clinical records. Likewise, identify records currently being disposed of that should be maintained by the practice. Keep in mind that records must be maintained to defend the practice in the event of an audit by an insurance plan, especially Medicare. Many practices maintain these records for 10 to 15 years at a minimum. Some consultants suggest that these records never be discarded.

Time Management

One major cause of inefficiency in many practices is excessive telephone calls from patients each day. Therefore, it is a good idea to review the internal management of these calls. The best way to do this is by interviewing the office staff. Staff members will be able to tell you specific problems they deal with in the office as a result of excessive calls. Identify problem areas and correct them immediately. If employees spend an inordinate amount of time on the telephone, they are less likely to perform their other assigned duties in a timely manner, if at all. In addition, review the internal management of telephone calls to and from insurance plans, especially managed-care plans. Are any office inefficiencies created by an excessive number of daily telephone calls related to insurance authorization, service precertification, and so on? Is the physician wasting time on the telephone?

At the same time, review the average time patients wait in the reception area before they are escorted to exam rooms and how long they wait in the exam room before the physician enters. Use the sign-in sheet as an opportunity for the patient to list his or her time of arrival. Then, have the nurse or technician who escorts the patient to the exam room jot down the time somewhere in the file, and have the physician do the same. Review these times and assess if the wait time is reasonable. If not, patients' satisfaction with the office may be affected, so immediately discuss how this time can be reduced. If patients are dissatisfied, they probably will not refer other patients to the practice. The problem can likely be traced to poor scheduling, bad time management on the part of the physician, or the physician's clinical style.

Human Resources

Business planning for a medical practice should include a look at a variety of human resources issues. A few important areas are discussed in this section.

Employee Evaluations

The preparation and review of employee performance evaluations is an often forgotten area of medical practice management. Most employees want feedback concerning their job performance. Without this feedback, they have no idea what impression the management has about how well they are doing their jobs. Assess and document the performance of each employee based on how well he or she performed all job duties during the past year and how well he or she complied with the office's operational policies and procedures. (See Appendix B for a sample employee annual performance review.)

Payroll

Review the employees' payroll and allot pay increases for the upcoming year. Compare employees' salaries to the current market rate for employees in similar positions within the medical community. This is especially important for long-term employees, who frequently are compensated at excessively high levels. Both performance and market rate should influence the percentage raise given to specific employees. In addition, the payroll records of the practice should be scanned each year to make sure that they are maintained properly and to make sure that such items as vacation time, sick leave, and overtime are being documented properly.

The following additional items require special attention.

Compliance with all OSHA-related documentation requirements OSHA requires quite specific recordkeeping for medical practice employees.

Compliance with federal and state labor laws Pay strict attention to the rules related to employee overtime, especially to employees who are entitled to overtime and those who are not.

Employee job descriptions Revise job descriptions if necessary. (See Chapter 16 for sample descriptions.)

Personnel manual Revise the manual if necessary. Ensure that it complies with all federal and state labor laws. (See Chapter 16 for more information.)

Contracts

First review the physicians' employment agreement and determine any need for revision. Pay strict attention to the physicians' compensation formula. It is important to discuss with the physicians on a yearly basis how satisfied they are with the distribution of net income. Dissatisfactions and disagreements over compensation are one of the main reasons groups break up.

Next, review the buy/sell agreement and decide if it needs to be revised. If the group does not have an agreement, one should be prepared immediately. Pay heed to the owner buy-out formula. It is critical to determine if the current formula makes sense in today's changing economic environment. In addition, quantify the buy-out amount for each physician as of the practice's year-end. Ask each physician-owner if he or she would be satisfied with being bought out at this price and in turn ask if each would be willing to pay out this amount. If not, the formula may have to be amended.

Also review and discuss other contracts the practice holds, especially managed-care contracts. Decide if any of these need to be revised. Assess whether the practice has leverage to renegotiate any of the managed-care contracts. If so, renegotiate both the terms of the contract and fee reimbursements.

Marketing

One significant result of the changes occurring to the landscape of medical practice is that offices must now pay more attention to marketing. As reimbursements are attacked and as pressures mount to control the growth of health care costs, physicians must look for ways to maintain and increase their revenue base. This often is accomplished by marketing. First, analyze patient satisfaction with the practice. If no current information is available to gauge satisfaction levels, have the practice survey its patients. Also identify the satisfaction level of other physicians who refer patients to the practice, which should be directly linked to referral patterns. If referrals have dropped from the prior year, investigate the reasons immediately.

Review current marketing activities and their successes or failures. Quantify all new revenue derived from each marketing activity. If this cannot be done, implement an information system that will document and compile data regarding where new patients first heard of the practice. Find out if the costs associated with the marketing activities have been less than the benefits received. At the same time, the physicians and their advisors should discuss specific marketing strategies for the upcoming year that might increase the revenue base. The need for new strategies will usually be tied to revenue projections for the upcoming year and may also be determined by any current or expected shifts in the practice's payor mix. Once marketing strategies are designed and implemented, be sure to monitor their success. Do not let a practice keep spending money on an activity that is not working. For more ideas on marketing, see Chapter 15.

Strategic Planning

Today, many physicians and their practices face new and complex challenges they did not have to deal with before. The emphasis on reducing the cost of health care, increasing access to care, the downward pressure on fees by third-party payors, increased competition among physicians and other alternative providers, and the movement toward strategic alliances are but a few of the factors which have changed the environment in which a doctor practices. Practicing quality medicine no longer assures a practice's success. Medical practices are becoming more of a business and that trend will continue if a practice is to survive. This means a practice must adopt techniques, processes, and systems that have been used in the business community for some time. This is why the first part of this chapter emphasized the need for business planning.

Strategic planning has become an ever-increasing critical process to assist medical practices. It is a proactive process whereby a medical practice actually takes control of shaping its future. It is the orderly, systematic review of the organization and the environment in which it exists. It is developing its best projections of how that environment will change, how external factors affect its environment, and an analysis of internal facts that impact its ability to adapt to change. In the end, it is identifying goals and objectives for the practice and the physicians, working out a "game plan" to accomplish those goals and objectives, and insuring that mechanisms are in place for measure progress.

In summary, the Strategic Planning Process is:

- An integrated set of activities or actions aimed at developing sustainable, competitive advantages for the medical practice.

- The orderly review of the organization in the environment in which it exists, developing its best projections of how that environment will change, and working out a game plan for how to accomplish those goals and objectives as defined by the organization.

- When achievements are the result of carefully developed plans.

- A commitment of financial and human resources.

Why Strategic Planning Does Not Occur Enough

There are many medical groups that have never conducted a strategic planning session or even thought about having one, even though the planning's overall importance and value to a medical practice can be quite extraordinary. There are several reasons.

First, physicians and managers have other numerous pressing issues to attend to in today's operating environment. This is why things like strategic planning do not gain attention until a crisis or problem occurs. Second, many physicians and their managers are reactive instead of proactive. One major responsibility of management today is to keep the practice "moving forward." Also, the strategic planning process requires a lot of honesty and objectivity to make it work right and this takes physicians out of their comfort zone. There is still a prevalent attitude out there that thinks strategic planning is a total waste of time, but a CPA or advisor can help change that attitude.

Hiring an Outside Facilitator

Once management has decided that it is in its best interest to conduct a formal strategic planning session, the first step should be to hire an outside facilitator. A qualified facilitator will bring independent information and perspectives to the planning process and related discussions. Since no consultant can form a strategy for the medical practice and expect it to be successful, it is important to select a facilitator that will concentrate on asking the right questions, focus the process, draw everyone's best ideas to the forefront, and articulate these ideas in ways that can make a difference for the practice. A facilitator can help overcome all of the reasons mentioned above on why strategic planning does not occur often enough.

The Strategic Planning Process

There are basically five steps to the strategic planning process:

1. Physician and staff interviews
2. Internal environmental analysis
3. External environmental analysis
4. The strategic planning retreat
5. Creation of the Action Plan

The first step is to conduct individual and group interviews with both the physicians and selected practice management, such as the practice administrator, billing manager, human resources manager, etc. These interviews can last anywhere from a half-hour to a full hour each. This is extremely critical in order to understand everyone's perceptions, to identify important issues, and to anticipate the best method to have everyone focused in the same direction. These interviews also help articulate who the practice is as an organization—its unifying purposes, ambitions and values.

An internal environmental analysis utilizes practice operational data, legal documents, and other information needed to review the medical practice internally. You will basically be seeking the same information as that discussion in the business planning section of this chapter. This information is then analyzed to identify specific issues that must be addressed during the planning process.

The external environmental analysis requires a detailed look at forces in the marketplace that will challenge the practice's viability, including other competing groups, additional physician partners, possible formation of multispecialty groups, changing physician/insurer relationships, changing demographics and physician/managed-care network relationships. You must determine exactly what is going on in the practice's service area from an external point of analysis. For example, are groups merging? Is insurer consolidation taking place? Are certain insurers beginning to dominate the service area and what effect might this have in the future?

The Retreat

Once all the information is gathered and has been analyzed, it is important to gather everyone together on a retreat. These retreats take from one to three days, depending on the size of the practice and what needs to be accomplished and decided upon to make the strategic planning process successful. The retreat should take place at a location away from the office. Solo practitioners need to get away and intake fresh ideas or dialogue regarding the future of their practice. Multiphysician groups benefit from tapping the collective knowledge and combined wisdom of group members as well as lessening the likelihood that vital matters are neglected because everyone thought someone else was attending to them.

Retreats will help get everyone focused at once, on the same page, and pulling in the same direction.

There is no "cookbook" agenda for a strategic planning retreat. The agenda is specifically designed by the facilitator and is based upon the interviews, internal analysis, and external analysis. However, the following are some issues that might get included on a planning agenda:

- How to preserve existing patient referral patterns.
- How to address specific competitive threats.
- How to improve billing and collections.
- How to improve employee morale.
- How to improve internal communications.
- Recruitment of new physicians or mid-level providers.
- Development of new services and ancillary services.
- Changes to the physician compensation plan.
- How to address declining managed-care reimbursement.
- How to improve patient relationships.
- Geographic expansion and new practice sites.
- Possible merger with other practices.
- Physician slowdown or retirement from practice.

This list is certainly not all-inclusive and as such, you need to keep one important thing in mind: A critical aspect of a successful retreat is determining and addressing all of the areas of concern for each participating physician.

The Action Plan

The most important step in the strategic planning process is the creation of an Action Plan. Whether it is in checklist or report format, the Action Plan makes the planning process accountable. It is a document that is used to make sure all of the issues and related decisions that were made at the planning retreat get implemented. Why go through this process and not implement? Believe it or not, it does happen. What happens is that after the retreat, everyone is excited and ready to get things rolling. However, as time passes by, this enthusiasm can wane and the decisions that need to get implemented are either put off or not made a priority. The Action Plan is something that can and must be reviewed each and every month by management until all decisions have been fully implemented.

The following is an example of an abbreviated report format that ends with sample Action Plan checklist.

Practice Observations

As part of the strategic planning process, the owners of the practice were asked about the positive points and negative points of the practice as it stands now. These observations were used as a catalyst for further discussions and the development of the overall strategic plan.

Positive Points

- *The practice is a "unified" group practice.*
- *The practice has a wide coverage area as a result of its multiple office locations and multiple hospital relationships.*
- *The practice has name recognition within the community.*
- *The practice has a well-known reputation for quality. The medical community as well as the public community knows this reputation.*
- *The practice has taken great strides in the development of personal relationships with physicians and the cementing of referral patterns.*
- *The practice has strong administration and owner hands-on involvement in the affairs of the practice.*
- *The practice has a history of adapting to a changing health care marketplace.*
- *The owners of the practice have trained many of the other podiatrists practicing in the Mason service area today.*
- *The practice is "managed-care friendly," and as such offers the following to the managed-care community: (a) easy access to appointments, (b) multiple locations, and (c) quality of care (i.e., cost-effective care).*
- *The practice will provide a service to any patient, regardless of his or her ability to pay.*

- *The practice is perceived as a major competitor in the market-place.*

Negative Points

- *The practice is perceived as a major competitor in the market-place. While this is a positive, it is also the target of other competi-tors and is not asked to participate in podiatry affiliations (e.g., IPA development).*
- *While the practice has much to offer in managed care, it is not adequately preparing itself for further market penetration. The practice does not know what it costs to render its services nor has it begun the process of accumulating clinical utilization and out-comes data. It has also not started the process of developing clini-cal pathways for selected podiatry surgical procedures.*
- *The practice has not developed community-based wellness pro-grams related to podiatry.*
- *The practice is slow in implementing ideas and suggestions, often as a result of the time it takes to obtain a collective agreement between the practice owners.*
- *For a managed-care payor, there are holes in the countywide pa-tient coverage area. This could impact the ability to obtain exclu-sive managed-care relationships.*

Top Issues Now Facing the Practice

Using information obtained from the overview of the practice, the owners' perception of the positives and negatives of the practice, and the current Mason health care marketplace, the practice must now identify the top issues it now faces. Once identified, the next section of this planning document will outline a strategy of how to address each. This is the overall objective of the strategic planning process.

During the strategic planning conference, the owners of the prac-tice identified these issues now facing the practice that demand im-mediate attention:

1. *Stagnant growth in practice revenue.*
2. *Changes in payor reimbursement patterns.*
3. *Development of other revenue/services.*
4. *Decision on whether or not to sell the practice to a third party.*

5. Competition for managed care contracts.

6. Reduction of practice overhead.

7. Improvement of internal operations.

The following report addresses each of these issues individually. Specifically, each discussion will include strategies the practice will execute to deal with each issue and highlight obstacles the practice must overcome to successfully implement these strategies.

Stagnant Growth in Practice Revenue

The owners of the practice are concerned about the growth in practice revenue. Much of this concern is based on the fact that the gross revenues of all of the practice locations, except for one, declined this year from that of the previous year. Competition from other providers and changes in reimbursement patterns will continue to impact the revenue stream of the practice. The reimbursement issue will be addressed separately on a different page. If left unchecked, the consensus among the owners is that practice revenues will either stagnate or even decline in future years unless this is dealt with immediately.

How the Practice Intends to Address this Issue

Add new patients by tracking current referral sources   The practice does not currently track referral patterns of existing doctors. As such, the practice is not able to identify and address situations where the referrals from a particular source have declined. This is critical in today's changing and competitive health care environment.

Action:

1. Make sure the practice strictly tracks who refers new patients to the practice and that such information is correctly entered into the computer system.

2. At the end of each month, print the referring doctor report and distribute to all providers for their review. This includes distribution to the associates.

3. Identify any changes in referral patterns.

4. Follow up with those doctors whose referrals show a decline; reward those doctors who have increased their referrals.

Add new patients by adding new referral sources *The practice is obviously not receiving new patient referral sources from every source. Therefore, the practice needs to target these individuals and sources in order to obtain new patient referrals. The following are potential sources of new referrals that were identified at the planning conference:*

—*Primary care and other doctors not currently referring to the practice.*

—*The Mason Methodist affiliation.*

—*Physical rehabilitation doctors.*

—*Diabetic support groups.*

Action:

1. *Develop an "accountability" program for the associates with a related contact marketing program.*

2. *Continue identifying new referral sources by the owner group and contacting these sources.*

The following is a brief description of the accountability program for the associates:

- *Identify current referral sources and sources that are not referring to each associate.*

- *Develop a plan on how each associate will contact the sources that are not currently referring to them in addition to those sources that are giving minimal referrals.*

- *Implement the contact program. Document results of each contact.*

- *Monitor the program by ongoing review of referring doctor reports, help the associates with their marketing activities, and make changes to the contact program as necessary.*

The owners will monitor their contact activities and related success by the ongoing review of the referring doctor reports on a monthly basis. This should take place at one of the monthly meetings.

Action:

In addition to the contract program developed for the associates, a similar contact program should be developed for the administrator.

One of the best ways to increase referrals is to have the practice's administrator contact her counterpart at other medical offices to find out why they are not referring and asking for new referrals. The information obtained can be valuable to the practice as it develops methods to increase referrals. Since the practice intends to hire an Assistant to the Administrator, this duty could be delegated to her or handled by the administrator directly. Like the associates, contacts must be documented and reviewed.

Increase revenues by adding additional doctors and additional locations *Revenues can increase if the practice adds additional providers with additional locations. This includes adding new associates and putting them in areas where the practice does not have offices. To do this however, the practice will have to invest a significant amount of capital. The best way to increase revenues is to add existing practices with their own established practice sites. This would add established practice revenues to the practice, provide for cost economies of scale, and may increase the practice's attractiveness to managed-care plans due to an increased coverage area.*

Action:

1. *Identify potential practices that may want to merge into the practice.*

2. *Contact these individuals to assess interest in such an affiliation.*

3. *If interested, implement merger process.*

Obstacles to Overcome to Ensure Success

1. *The willingness of the associates to market themselves to potential referral sources.*

2. *Making sure the associates are accountable for their contact activities.*

3. *Failure to monitor the program on an ongoing basis, with no exceptions.*

4. *Costs are too high to add new associates to the practice or opportunities do not exist for adding a new associate.*

5. *Unwillingness of established podiatrists to join the practice.*

6. *Unwillingness of current owners to allow other established podiatrists to have ownership in the practice.*

Changes in Payor Reimbursement Patterns

Practice revenues have been impacted by changes in payor reimbursement patterns. Many of the managed-care plans have begun the switch to paying doctors on the Medicare RBRVS system. Congress will continue its attempt to reform the Medicare system. Texas is beginning to implement its program to manage Medicaid. Physician reimbursement will continue to be attacked by all payors, both now and in the future. This will likely lead to a decline in practice revenues.

How Practice Intends to Address this Issue

Improve practice-coding patterns   *While insurance companies continue to change their reimbursement methodologies, it is imperative the practice does not lose revenues as a result of the improper coding of services.*

Action:

1. *Redesign the office charge ticket.*

2. *Centralize practice coding within the practice.*

3. *Provide a coding "in service" to all doctors and staff members.*

4. *Monitor payments in order to identify problems with service coding and develop a communication channel to inform doctors of coding problems.*

Assemble clinical outcomes and utilization cost data   *To gain advantage over declining reimbursement, the practice must begin the process of assembling clinical outcomes and utilization cost data. If the practice can demonstrate that it is more cost effective than the other podiatrists in the managed-care network, it may better its negotiation position. In other words, the practice may be able to parley a higher rate of payment. Outcomes and utilization data such as number of surgeries as a percentage of office visits, use of ancillary services, surgical complications, and the cost to treat certain conditions (i.e., podiatry-related diabetes problems) must be gathered.*

Action:

1. *Decide on what outcomes and utilization data information the practice will track and gather.*

2. *Determine if some of this information must be tracked manually. If so, create a manual tracking system.*

3. Obtain information from current practice billing system.

4. Obtain information from outpatient surgery centers.

5. Obtain information from hospitals.

6. Obtain information from managed-care plans.

7. Assemble data into a useable and presentable format.

8. Analyze data and make internal corrections to how services are rendered.

9. Present information to selected managed care payors to renegotiate payment rates.

Development of Other Revenues/Services

To increase revenues and net income, the practice must find other ways to increase its revenues and services. If the practice continues its same service pattern, revenues are expected to continue their decline mainly as a result of reduced reimbursement from insurance companies.

How Practice Intends to Address this Issue

Develop a Management Services Organization (MSO)   The development of a management services organization has many potential benefits. First, it can be used to recruit other doctors into an affiliation with the practice. Smaller podiatry practices may want to join the practice but may not want to give up independence and autonomy. In other words, they do not want to merge with the practice. Affiliation in an MSO relationship might solve this problem. The practice can increase revenues through the MSO fee it charges to these practices.

The MSO can also be used to manage other affiliate companies, such as a home foot care company. Finally, by moving all overhead and possibly assets to the MSO, another advantage to MSO formation is that it may become easier to offer practice ownership to the current associates.

Action:

1. Create legal entity and execute related legal documents.

2. Develop management service agreement.

3. Execute MSO agreement between practice and MSO entity.

4. Recruit doctors to the MSO.

Develop a home foot care company The practice has already identified this opportunity and is in the process of forming this company.

Action:

1. Create home foot care entity and execute related legal documents.

2. Finalize employment of the manager of the entity.

3. Execute MSO agreement between home foot care company and management services organization.

4. Begin company operations.

Continue affiliation with city health clinics As discussed at the planning conference, this affiliation is worth continuing. However, the practice must determine a way to increase its referrals from these clinics.

Action:

1. Determine potential referral sources.

2. Integrate into associate referral contact program discussed previously in this document.

3. Continue to monitor if doctor is best served elsewhere rather than at the clinics.

Obstacles to Overcome to Ensure Success

1. Practice is slow to implement these projects, thus missing opportunities.

2. Other doctors will not want to affiliate with the practice through an MSO arrangement.

3. The threat of potential competitors to the home foot care company.

Decision on Whether or Not to Sell Practice to a Third Party

One major issue facing the owners is practice transition. Either a program needs to be developed whereby the practice is transitioned to younger owners as the current owners leave the practice, or the practice must sell out to a third party in order for the current owners to receive some sort of payment for the value of their equity interest. Transition will someday become a major issue since the current owners could transition out of the practice within short time periods of one another. As such, the practice needs to at least begin looking at transition issues.

If the practice intends to sell to a third party, the issue then becomes one of timing. There has never been a ready number of buyers wanting to buy podiatric practices.

How Practice Intends to Address this Issue

Determine if and when the associates will be able to buy into the practice   If the associates will be allowed to buy into the practice, a buy-in price and related payments terms will have to be determined. The practice also needs to determine the qualifications to become a partner (e.g., Collections equal to $_____).

The development of a management services organization may make it easier for the practice to admit the associates (and other associates) as partners. The current owners of the practice will be the sole owners of the MSO. All assets of the practice will be owned by the practice; the practice only holds medical records and accounts receivable as its only real assets. As a result, the associates could buy into the practice at a lower price and make the transition to partner simpler and easier.

Action:

1. Determine whether or not the associates will be allowed to buy into the equity of the practice.

2. If so, determine when.

3. Determine buy-in price and related payment terms.

4. When appropriate, make buy-in offer to the associate(s).

Obstacles to Overcome to Ensure Success

1. Current owners cannot relinquish any part of their equity in the practice to the associates.

2. Associates do not want to buy into the practice.

3. Unrealistic buy-in terms are created for the associates (including future associates).

4. *Deciding how the associates will be compensated once they become an owner.*

Reduction of Practice Overhead

In light of the fact that practice revenues have stagnated and that reimbursements will most likely decline as more payors change how they reimburse providers, practice overhead must be minimized and contained. If not, practice net income will continue to get squeezed.

How Practice Intends to Address this Issue

Create Management Services Organization   *If the practice can recruit other podiatrists to its MSO, practice overhead should be reduced since more doctors will share billing and collection overhead.*

Review all cost categories and assess possibility for cost reduction   *The practice administrator should review **all** cost categories, using the bookkeeping general ledger as a guide. Go down each overhead category and determine if such category should be reviewed in either detail or the account bid out to assist in the determination of the lowest possible cost. Lowest cost may not necessarily take precedence; service and quality are major contributing factors in the selection of a particular vendor.*

Obstacles to Overcome to Ensure Success

1. *Failure to recruit of other podiatrists to the MSO.*
2. *Reluctance to leave a current vendor to someone whose costs is lower.*

Improvement of Internal Operations

The major concerns about internal operations revolve around personnel issues. At the planning retreat, the consensus was that improvements could be made in this area. Two immediate issues that require immediate attention are: (1) Improve the lines of authority, and (2) Improve employee training.

How Practice Intends to Address this Issue

Improve lines of authority *One problem that seems to occur are situations where a doctor attempts to handle certain employee is-*

sues. *For example, if the doctor is approached by an employee personally, the doctor should always refer the employee to the administrator for handling and disposition of the matter. If the administrator cannot adequately handle the situation, she will then ask for input from the practice owners.*

In addition, all doctors must understand that as owners, each has the responsibility to handle employee matters in the most effective manner possible. Each has a personal stake in the success of the employee group. While certain doctors may be "responsible" for a particular employee within the practice, a doctor should not get upset when that employee either approaches or is approached by another doctor. This is okay as long as what transpires is for the good of the group practice as a whole.

Implement new employee training program *The practice had problems internally when new employees were hired and were slow to grasp their job duties. To reduce errors and wasted time, the practice should design and implement a new employee-training program.*

Action:

1. *Create one- to three- page orientation sheet for new employees by job duty. This sheet will summarize the main duties of the employee and how certain duties are to be performed.*

2. *Administrator Assistant will conduct the orientation.*

3. *Administrator Assistant will monitor the performance of all new employees and will provide help to them when necessary.*

Practice Action Plan

Action	Delegated To	Date To Be Completed	Date Completed
Designate person in charge of practice coding			
Revise charge ticket			
Detailed review of practice payor patterns mix to assess revenue vulnerability to competition			
Print report detailing practice referral patterns			
Review referral report and determine changes in referral patterns from that of prior year			

Action	*Delegated To*	*Date To Be Completed*	*Date Completed*
Contact doctors whose referrals declined			
Implement program to increase these referrals			
Create contact program for the associates			
Conduct first meeting with associates to begin accountability program			
Monitor associate contact program on an ongoing basis			Ongoing
Create referral contact program for administrative staff			
Conduct first meeting with administrator to review results of initial contacts			
Make a list of podiatrists who may want to merge into the practice			
Contact targeted merger candidates			
Decide on what outcomes and utilization data information the practice will track and gather.			
Determine if utilization/outcomes data must be tracked manually. If so, create a manual tracking system			
Obtain utilization/outcomes data from current practice billing system			
Obtain utilization/outcomes data from outpatient surgery centers			
Obtain utilization/outcomes data from hospitals.			
Obtain utilization/outcomes from managed-care plans			
Assemble utilization/outcomes data into a useable and presentable format			
Analyze utilization/outcomes data and make internal corrections to how services are rendered			
Present information to selected managed care payors to renegotiate payment rates			
Perform cost accounting analysis for all practice services			
Determine feasibility of forming podiatric IPA			

Action	Delegated To	Date To Be Completed	Date Completed
Preparation of legal documents to create MSO			
Identify podiatrists to contract with MSO			
Recruit podiatrists to the MSO			
Preparation of Home Foot Care legal documents			
Implement home foot care operations			
Determine date for associate practice buy-in			

▼ CHAPTER 7
Setting Up a New Medical Practice

This chapter provides an overview of all of the tasks necessary to set up a new medical practice from start to finish. Doctors are setting up new practices all the time. Based on personal experience, I've found that how quickly the practice succeeds will depend on the attention given to all of the details in the setup. Establishing a new medical practice results from a variety of situations: a resident or fellow finishes his or her training and wants to enter into solo practice rather than join a group practice environment; doctors leave group practices to go off on their own; doctors are employed by hospitals that decide to divest themselves of their physician-owned practices; and doctors leaving a physician practice management arrangement.

When starting up a new practice, it is a good idea for the doctor to hire a qualified attorney, qualified CPA, and/or a qualified health care consultant to help set up the practice. "Qualified" means being able to demonstrate prior experience with assisting in the start-up processes of a new practice. Once the CPA or consultant is hired, the first step is to divide the duties between the physician and the advisor. However, there may be some situations where the physician will want to take on all of the responsibilities of setting up the new practice (e.g., the physician does not want to pay professional fees), even though this is not advisable.

Tasks Involved in Setting Up the Practice

Assign Responsibilities

If the new physician hires a CPA or consultant, the first task is to divide duties between the CPA (or consultant) and the physician. Generally, the CPA or consultant will be responsible for approximately 90 percent of the tasks it takes to open a practice. The physician and the new staff will probably purchase the majority of the hard and soft assets, such as furniture, medical equipment, and supplies.

After duties and responsibilities are divided, the CPA or consultant will begin the actual process of setting up the new practice. It generally takes two to three months to complete the necessary tasks. Enough time should be allowed so that the office can open on schedule.

■ **Practice Point:** Sometimes physicians will be cost-sensitive and will want to do as much of the setup as they can, which means paying out of their own pocket. If this is ever the case, the CPA or consultant should make sure that the physician performs his or her duties correctly and in a timely manner. In other words, review on an ongoing basis what the physician does.

Attend to Financial and Legal Matters

First, and if applicable, review the hospital recruitment agreement and assess potential tax consequences. This information will help you decide whether or not the practice should incorporate. Consider incorporating new practices. While there may not be many tax advantages, there are other advantages. Most important, the corporate format allows a legal shield between the practice and the physician individually. Here is a case in point based on an actual event. An employee went to the office supply store to run an errand and was in a car wreck. The person in the other car is killed. In this situation, the estate would have a claim only against the practice in most circumstances; however, if the practice is unincorporated, the estate would have a claim against the physician-owner, individually, since the employee was in effect an agent of the practice.

Besides providing a legal liability shield, a corporation gives a new physician financial discipline. This is particularly important when the new physician is getting paid extra by a hospital under a legal hospital recruitment contract. This is discussed in more detail in Chapter 20.

After selecting the practice's legal entity, obtain all employer identification numbers and prepare all applications for provider numbers. To apply for a Medicare provider number, obtain and complete Form 855. If ownership of a practice changes, a new 855 application must be submitted. For a practice name change, address changes, new Tax Identification number, etc., you only have to fill out an 855C (change) form. If a new physician is added to a practice and already has a Medicare number, Form 855R (reassignment) must be completed. The physician retains his individual Medicare number.

Applications for Medicare and Medicaid can be acquired from the related insurance intermediary in the physician's state. Allow about six weeks to obtain a Medicare provider number. The Medicaid number, which usually takes about two weeks to secure, cannot be obtained until after the Medicare number is obtained.

Next, prepare a schedule of asset needs and cash flow for the practice. List all hard and soft assets that the practice will need to acquire. The best way to do this is to obtain a copy of the architectural plan and list asset needs room by room. Use the cash flow forecast as a budgeting tool and as a way to determine the physician's estimated compensation if the hospital is providing a gross income guarantee. The forecast also will make the physician aware of any debt service responsibilities and the potential impact on compensation.

> ■ **Practice Point:** Try to have a list of qualified vendors ready to work with. This not only will cut down the time needed to set up the practice, it should also help ensure that the job is done right in the first place. You will need vendors to acquire hard assets, medical supplies, insurance, etc. These lists can be obtained from the local county medical society, from the hospital, or from the state medical association.

Hire Office Personnel

The next step is to hire office personnel, which is a difficult task. This part of the setup process can either make or break a new office. Hiring the wrong people, especially in the billing and collection areas, can virtually destroy a practice. Be careful during the interview process and allow enough time to recruit good people. The CPA or consultant should assist with interviewing each candidate and providing the physician with the top two or three candidates for each position. If necessary, prepare an organizational chart before recruiting prospective employees.

At the same time, prepare a detailed policies and procedures manual for the office. The manual should outline how the office will be operated, explain the office's personnel policies, and provide specific job duties for each employee. The goal is to create a document that will guide all practice employees in their day-to-day activities. The importance of this manual cannot be overemphasized.

Prepare Managed-Care Applications

If necessary, begin preparing managed-care applications. Find out which applications to prepare by calling the hospital's business office for the names of the top 10 to 15 plans for which the hospital is currently a participating provider. If the provider is an established physician, then these will be the plans for which the physician is already credentialled. Begin this process early, as it usually takes a while to receive credentials from the plans. However, if the service area demands it, the practice may have to sign up with all managed-care plans. Remember, the goal of any new practice is to obtain patients. Sometimes this can be accelerated simply by signing up with as many managed-care plans as possible. If a practice merger is involved, make a list of the managed-care plans for which each physician is currently a provider. Then determine the plans for which each physician is not a provider and try to obtain credentialling for all physicians in the same managed-care plan.

> ■ **Practice Point:** If the service area is dominated by managed care, the application process should start as soon as possible. Most new physicians do not get credentialled for at least five to six weeks after the application is submitted.

Keep in mind that an application is not complete until the new physician obtains hospital privileges (which takes time) and obtains a state medical license. These are usually the last things a new physician gets. To expedite the process, however, try to complete as much of the application as you can and mail it to the managed-care company. Attach a cover letter stating that the additional information will be sent as soon as it is received.

Choose a Computer System

Another important duty is to research and buy the practice's computer system. The system's quality will depend on how much the physician wants to spend. If the physician wants to be involved in the search, set up computer demonstrations and be prepared to advise the physician of each system's advantages and disadvantages. These demonstrations can take place in the office of the physician, the CPA, or the consultant. Make sure that everyone who will be using the new system is involved in the selection process. This includes both the receptionist and the billing personnel. This may or may not be feasible, depending on when these people are hired and if they are available to assist in this process.

The following are important issues when selecting a new system.

Batch entry   It is faster to post transactions in batches than one at a time. It is also important to be able to post charges, payments, and adjustments without having to move around to several different screens.

Moving through the system   Pay attention to how many menus and screens you have to go through to get where you want to go.

Commands   Determine if the commands are too complex throughout the system.

Setup time   Find out how long it takes to set up a new patient's file or account. The process should not waste the office personnel's time.

Patient look-up   Determine how easy it is to look up a patient, especially his or her detailed account balance.

Training   Determine the level of training the vendor offers.

Reporting   Find out what kind of day-end and month-end reports the system is capable of producing. These reports are critical to the management of a medical practice.

Back up   The system should be easy to back up.

- ■ **Practice Point:** Try not to let the physician be cheap when buying a new computer system. While it is tempting to go with a lower-end software package, investing in a good computer system will more than pay for itself in the long run.

- ■ **Practice Point:** People often ask for the names of a few good software packages. Here are a few, based on cost:
    - High end: Medic, IDX, and Medical Manager
    - Low end: Medisoft and Lytec

Other Tasks

Besides these duties, make sure the following is taken care of before the office opens:

- Develop a fee schedule.
- Purchase assets.
- Open a bank account.
- Establish an accounts payable system within the office.

One of the more important duties in setting up a new practice as a result of a practice merger is to notify all insurance companies that the physicians in question have merged and to inform them of the new group's identification number. All insurance companies should be telephoned at least one month before merged operations begin. To protect the billing and collection process, all initial paper claims should include a cover letter stating this same information.

- ■ **Practice Point:** If you are involved in a practice merger, the failure to notify insurance companies of the new entity's name, its federal identification number, and the physicians (along with their former federal identification numbers) who are now members of the new group practice, is usually the most critical error made during the implementation phase (i.e., merged entity setup). If done late or poorly, expect the new practice's cash flow to slow considerably.

The most overlooked facet of setting up a medical practice is marketing. Hospitals put a positive spin on how much they need the physician's services when they recruit, but this does not guarantee that the demand exists in the marketplace. Most hospitals recruit a physician, help set up the physician's practice, put announcements in the newspapers, and host an open house. After that, it is up to the physician to generate a patient base. Because many physicians are not experienced in acquiring new patients, some struggle financially during the first year of practice, unless the hospital has provided economic incentives. In such situations, the struggle occurs when the incentives run out. Therefore, the new physician needs to decide how he or she intends to attract new patients to the practice. In other words, help the physician develop a marketing plan. This plan can be developed in conjunction with the creation of the cash flow forecast, since the forecast will set the practice's initial monthly production goals. Marketing methods vary depending on whether the practice is primary-care or referral-based. (For more on marketing techniques, see Chapter 15.)

Timetable of Events

The following is a timetable for setting up a new practice. Remember that it will take at least three months to implement all setup activities and to prepare the practice for its opening day.

One Year Before Starting a Practice

If the new physician is just beginning to explore the possibility of starting his or her own practice, he or she should address the following issues at least one year before planing to open the new practice:

- Where does the physician want to live and where does he want to open a practice? Spouse and family desires should be considered. Practice considerations include managed-care penetration and community need for the physician's specialty.

- Does the physician want to purchase an existing practice? If so, begin a search with the local county and state medical societies, local residency programs, and brokers in the targeted practice locality.

Once a decision has been made, do the following:

- Gather demographic information about the community from local hospitals, local newspapers, and the Chamber of Commerce.
- If applicable, investigate the sellers' motivations. Talk with each seller if necessary.
- If applicable, determine the value of the targeted practice to purchase.
- Talk with physicians established in the community, especially new physicians. Assess the need for each physician's specialty and assess the potential for practice success.
- Explore interest in becoming employed by an established local medical practice, HMO, or other health care delivery system.
- Select legal counsel to represent the physician.
- Select a practice management consultant and/or an accountant to assist in the representation.
- If necessary, determine which banks are most likely to lend to physicians.
- If the physician is not recruited by a hospital, inquire with local hospitals in the targeted practice area about possible financial assistance.
- Determine the printing date for phone books and the length of time needed to reserve phone numbers.
- Execute the hospital recruitment agreement, if applicable.

Six to Nine Months Before Opening a Practice

- Prepare the practice's cash flow projections and expense/operating cost projections.

- If necessary, obtain a bank loan.
- If new office space is obtained or if existing rental space needs to be redesigned, meet with the architects and designer.
- If leasehold improvements are to be made, determine what they are, related costs, and time frame of construction.
- Purchase medical office and computer equipment. If applicable, check with state health agencies for X-ray regulations.
- Begin the process for obtaining a narcotic license, a state medical license, and a city business license, if applicable.
- Obtain a federal tax identification number.
- Request in writing an application for Medicare and Medicaid provider numbers.
- Obtain a listing of all managed-care plans in the practice area. Obtain provider applications and begin filling out the applications.
- If applicable, contact the state compensation insurance commission for information and forms for treating workers' compensation patients.
- See that the physician joins state and local county medical societies.
- Contact the state employment commission or the Department of Labor for wage and hour regulations.
- See that the physician obtains hospital privileges.
- Order copies of CPT and ICD-9 books.
- Begin researching computer systems and obtain bids from vendors.
- If applicable, execute an employment agreement with the medical practice or other employer.

Three Months Before Opening a Practice

- Select the computer system. Obtain implementation and training timetable.
- Hire employees.
- Purchase a medical records system.

- Implement accounts payable, payroll, and bookkeeping systems.
- Order all office forms, including charge tickets.
- Retain an insurance agent and obtain all practice-related business insurance.
- Obtain professional malpractice insurance.
- Obtain a phone number and install a phone system.
- Arrange with the bank to accept credit cards.
- Order office stationery, including announcements.
- Create the policies and procedures manual.
- Decide on the appointment scheduling system.
- Determine the practice fee schedule.
- Order patient information brochures.
- Open up the bank account.
- Have all office supplies and medical equipment delivered to the new office.
- Apply for a state unemployment tax number.
- Incorporate the practice, if the physician wishes to do so.

One Month Before Opening a Practice

- Begin marketing to the community or to physician referral sources.
- Train employees on office policies and procedures, especially billing and collection activities.
- Make sure all employees are adequately trained on the computer system.
- Test electronic billing.
- Provide CPT and diagnosis coding training.
- Publish an announcement in the local newspaper and in other local periodicals.
- Have office personnel begin answering telephones and making appointments.
- Send out announcements to other physicians and hospitals.

One Month After Opening a Practice

- Have an open house.
- Monitor all billing and collection activities on an ongoing basis.

Appendix A contains a comprehensive checklist for a new medical practice. Use this checklist for any setup engagement.

▼ CHAPTER 8
How to Set Physicians' Fees

Before a patient calls for an appointment or before the practice sends out an insurance claim form, the practice must have already established a fee schedule for its services. Unfortunately, if a physician is not using an appropriate fee schedule, his practice will lose revenue. The physician could be using a fee schedule from another practice. He could have purchased one of the many fee-schedule guides currently on the market. Or, an office member could have called around to various other offices on the pretense of being a potential patient and inquired about what the physicians charged for specific services. No matter how a fee schedule is developed, the goal of every medical practice is to set a fee for each of its services that is (a) fair and reasonable for its medical specialty, (b) fair and reasonable according to community standards, and (c) as close as possible to what insurance companies deem reasonable and customary. It is the fee schedule that drives the finances of a medical practice.

Any person with a working knowledge of the health care industry knows the tremendous pressures on physician reimbursement. You know how the health care market is continually reforming itself. Most physicians are seeing the growth in managed care and the proliferation of integrated delivery systems. Governmental intervention is becoming more prevalent, on the state level as well as on the federal level. The effect of these changes is that physicians are becoming more concerned about their futures and are paying less attention to the daily operations of their practices.

The advisor or manager of a medical practice must make sure the practice is not losing revenue. One area of constant neglect is the practice's fee schedule. You need to assess whether or not the physician's fee schedule is in line with the usual, customary, and reasonable standards in his or her market area. One way that you can determine this is by conducting a fee schedule analysis.

There are two easy ways to determine if the physician's fees are low. The easiest of the two is to find out when the fee schedule was last revised. The practice should revise its schedule annually. The second way is to review a sample of insurance EOBs. An EOB is the document that accompanies each insurance check. The document basically shows how much the physician billed, how much the insurance company approved for payment, and how much went to co-pay and to deductible. Following is a typical example:

Sample EOB

ABC Insurance Company
Address
Patient Name:
Account Number:

Date of Service	CPT Code	Service	Amount Billed	Amount Approved	To Patient Deductible	Patient Copayment	Amount Due Provider
8-31-0_	99214	Visit	100	100	0	10	90

Analyze commercial EOBs because commercial (or "indemnity," as they are commonly called) carriers do not pay physicians on a contracted fee basis. They pay a fee they consider to be usual, customary, and reasonable. Each insurance company has its own way of establishing usual, customary, and reasonable fee profiles. Some insurance companies use Medicare's RBRVS payment system, others use the Ingenix Relative Values for Physicians (formerly called the McGraw-Hill Relative Value System), still others use the payment profiles accumulated by the Health Insurance Association of America (HIAA), and some insurance companies employ their own internal methodologies. Whatever resource is used, make sure that the fees are considered usual, customary, and reasonable for the physician's service areas.

■ **Practice Point:** You might also want to review a sample of managed-care EOBs in addition to those from commercial-type carriers. If you ever see a situation in which the managed-care plan approved the billed fee 100 percent for full payment, you will know for a fact the physician's fee schedule is too low. Why? Because managed-care plans pay on a **discounted** fee basis. If a physician's normal fee is near a **discounted** fee, then most likely the fee schedule will need some type of adjustment. Remember, a managed-care plan will pay the lesser of what a physician bills and what the discounted rate is. Most physicians will bill their normal fee, knowing it will get discounted by the managed-care plan.

To assess whether or not the practice's fees are low, look at whether the commercial insurance companies are approving the physician's entire billed charges for payment. If the company is approving the whole fee, that means for that current procedural terminology (CPT) code, the physician has not yet reached the usual, customary, and reasonable threshold for the practice service area. Review EOBs located at the office or if you are a CPA or consultant, ask that 50 commercial EOBs be sent to the office. Use these EOBs to check if entire billed charges were approved for payment. If they were, some of the practice's fees might need to be adjusted upward.

The most important consideration should be what insurance companies will pay for the services rendered; not necessarily what patients will pay. If an insurance company says a fee is reasonable, it should then be considered reasonable within the physician's community and the practice's medical specialty. There are exceptions, and you should consider them when setting fees for the practice's area.

■ **Practice Point:** A resistance to increase fees generally occurs in small towns and communities. If the physician is balking at raising his or her rates, try to get a few changes made and not necessarily revise the entire fee schedule. For example, some physicians have changed a few of the office visit fees while leaving surgical charges alone.

It is also important to communicate to the physician that in most circumstances, the patient's portion of a fee increase is relatively small. For example, a physician raises an office visit charge from $40 to $60. If the patient is responsible for 20 percent, his or her out-of-pocket cost rises by $4 ($20 times 20 percent). This is not much of a difference. However, this could cause a problem for those practices that do a very good job of collecting monies at the time of a patient's visit. This is because patients in this circumstance will see and balk at the $20 increase. In this situation, it is important to communicate to the patient what the real out-of-pocket cost is after payment from the insurance company. Of course, this is a moot point if the practice is in the habit of billing the patient's insurance for all services rendered.

Medical and Laboratory Fees

Medical fees are charged for office visits, consultations, hospital admissions, hospital visits, and hospital charges. Laboratory fees are charged for tests such as a complete blood count, urinalysis, and cholesterol screening. When developing the fees for these services, complete the Medicine and Lab Fee Worksheet, which is included on the CD-ROM. This can be used to set a fee based on what insurance plans reimburse for the same services.

How to Use the Worksheet

1. On separate worksheets, list the most commonly used CPT codes for visits and laboratory services.

2. List the current fee for each service or leave the space blank if the practice is new and has not yet developed a fee schedule.

3. For each related CPT code, list the Medicare participating fee schedule amount taken from the practice's Medicare Disclosure Report (available from a Medicare carrier). Alternatively, if you are a CPA or health care consultant, you could use the report of another physician's practice in the same medical specialty and in the same practice area.

4. Next to Medicare's reimbursement, list the amount workers' compensation will pay for the same codes. The workers' compensation fee profile can be obtained from the state's workers' compensation commission.

5. From a selected number of managed-care plans, list the fees each plan will pay for each related CPT code. Obtain this information directly from the plans or from the EOBs from prior reimbursements. If EOBs are used, pay attention to whether a plan ever approved the full amount of the billed fee. If the full

Medicine and Lab Fee Worksheet

CPT	Service Description	Practice Fee	Medicare Par Fee	Workers' Comp.	Managed Care Payor #1	Managed Care Payor #2	Survey Fee

amount was approved, this indicates that the fee is too low because managed-care plans (preferred provider organizations) are supposed to pay a discounted fee to the medical office. The exception to this is when the office bills the actual contracted managed-care fee to the insurance company.

6. List fees from a fee survey or from another credible source.

After completing the worksheet, compare the fees in each column to the practice's current fees. The Medicare fee allowable generally is about 25 percent to 30 percent less than what a practice would normally charge its private patients. Most managed-care plans discount fees 20 percent to 30 percent. Workers' compensation fees are approximately 10 percent to 20 percent less than the practice's normal fee schedule. If a national fee schedule is used, remember that the fees shown are an average for the nation as a whole, unless the survey breaks out fees by region. Therefore, what might be reasonable in one part of the country may not be appropriate in another.

After comparing the fees in each category, determine what the fee should be for each CPT code based on the guidelines provided earlier. Then have the physician review and approve the new or revised fees. The physician must be comfortable with the fees he or she charges. Another way to set medical fees is by relative-value analysis, the method used to set procedure and radiology fees. These are discussed in the following section.

> ■ **Practice Point:** You can also use relative-value analysis, as described in the section below on evaluating surgical fees, to review and set laboratory fees. The easiest way to come up with a conversion factor is to use urinalysis code 81000. A typical fee for this service is $18. Using the Ingenix Relative Values for Physicians, divide the $18 by the number of assigned units and you will arrive at a conversion factor. Use this conversion to conduct your analysis for all lab charges.

You can do the same with medicine charges by selecting a medicine CPT code with a fee you know is near usual, customary, and reasonable. If you do not know, conduct a research of EOBs for medicine service reimbursements.

Procedure and Radiology Fees

Because insurance companies pay the majority of procedure and radiology fees, with the patient responsible for the deductible and co-payment, these fees are set differently from other fees. Therefore, an office should not experience the price sensitivity it would from office visit fees. In some cases, however, a patient will shop around for the best price (e.g., if the patient does not have insurance, has an extremely high deductible, or the medical specialty of the practice is obstetrics). If an insurance company will pay the majority of the fee, the office should set its procedure and radiology fees based on what insurance companies will pay. The maximum amount the insurance company will pay for a particular service is called the *fee profile* or the *usual, customary, and reasonable fee*. The main problem medical practices encounter when setting procedure and radiology fees is that some insurance companies will not disclose their fee profiles, forcing the office to look to other sources to set its fee limits.

One of the favored methods to set or to review procedure and radiology fees is to conduct a relative-value analysis. Many insurance companies now use relative-value guidelines to set their own fee profiles. Under any type of relative-value system, a fee is determined by multiplying relative-value units by a constant conversion factor:

$$\text{Fee} = \text{Relative-value unit} \times \text{Conversion factor}$$

Relative-value units can be obtained from a variety of studies already in the industry. The most common studies are the California Relative Value Study, Florida Relative Value Study, Ingenix Relative Values for Physicians, Medicare Resource-Based Relative Value Scale, and the relative value study produced by the American Society of Anesthesiologists (800-825-5586). The McGraw-Hill Relative Value Study is one of the most commonly used studies throughout the insurance industry, even though more insurance companies are adopting the Medicare scale.

In these studies, a relative-value unit is assigned to each medical service (CPT code). The unit can be based on a history of charges, how long it takes to render the service, how complicated the service is, the risks involved to both the patient and the physician, and the cost to render the service. The conversion factor is a dollar figure that is consistent for each type of medical service. In other words, the conversion factor should remain the same for each CPT code; it is the relative-value unit that will change. There generally will be separate conversion factors for medicine, surgery, laboratory fees, radiology, and anesthesiology.

To set or analyze existing procedure and radiology fees, use the procedure and radiology fee analysis worksheet, which is included on the CD-ROM.

How to Use the Worksheet

1. Use a separate worksheet for each procedure and radiology fee analysis.
2. For each worksheet, use the CPT codes most commonly used by the medical practice and list the related fee for each. Using the practice's year-to-date CPT frequency report, which can be printed from the office computer, select 30 of the most utilized codes in each category.
3. Using a relative-value study, list the relative-value units for each related CPT code. Calculate each service's current conversion factor by dividing the fee by the relative-value unit.
4. Total the fee and relative-value unit columns and calculate an average for each.
5. Calculate the average conversion factor for the fees selected.

Then determine if the practice's average conversion factor is reasonable for the office's medical specialty and service location. This often is the most difficult part of the analysis because no study has been conducted for conversion factors in this specific industry and especially for specific regions. One method for determining if the conversion factor is reasonable is to pull a sample explanation of benefits on which the insurance company or another company has specifically reduced a fee because it exceeded the usual, customary, and reasonable fee profile amount. Divide the approved fee amount by the related relative-value unit to calculate a geographic conversion factor.

Procedure and Radiology Fee Analysis Worksheet

CPT Code	Service Description	Practice Fee	Relative Value Unit	Conversion Factor
	Totals			
	# of Services			
	Average			

Compute average conversion factor for services analyzed using the following formula:

$$\frac{\text{Average fee amounts}}{\text{Average relative value units}}$$

As a starting point, the following are possible ranges of conversion factors, depending on a particular medical specialty, if the Ingenix Relative Values for Physicians are used:

Procedures $110–$155

Radiology $22–$24

If the calculated average conversion factor for the sample falls within an acceptable range, you will need to adjust the physician's fees that are below this range. These underpriced fees must be adjusted.

The conversion factor will depend on the physician's medical specialty and what he or she feels comfortable charging. For example, there should be a different conversion factor for a cardiovascular surgeon and a gastroenterologist. Why? Generally, because the services of some medical specialties are considered more difficult than others. Discourage the physician from bringing too much emotion into the decision to set procedure and radiology fees because the insurance companies will pay the majority of the billed amounts. For example, if a general surgery practice bills $1,000 for a particular procedure, and through relative-value analysis you determine that the fee should be $1,400, the increase in the fee will be $400. The physician may feel that some of his or her patients could not afford the increased fee and may want to leave the fee at $1,000. Explain that for commercial insurance plans, the insurance company would pay an additional $320 (80 percent) and the patient would pay an additional $80 (20 percent). As a rule, a patient needing surgery is probably not going to challenge the fee.

Once the fee schedule is analyzed, choose a conversion factor for the practice and revise the fees. The physician should be given a range of conversion factors to review before the fees are changed. For a surgical practice, for example, create a schedule with the following headings:

CPT Code Our Fee $110 $120 $125 $130 $135

Calculate the revised fees by using the conversion factor in each column. Then have the physician review the schedule and pick a conversion factor the practice would be comfortable charging. Getting the physician involved in the process and having him or her make the final decision is very important. Some physicians are uncomfortable raising fees, especially if such an increase is dramatic. They may prefer to start with a small increase and raise the fees again at a later date if further analysis warrants. However, some physicians want to revise their fees all at once. In each case, after a conversion factor is selected, revise the related procedure fees and the entire fee schedule if necessary.

Remember to keep the conversion factor for a particular line of service, such as surgery fees, constant throughout the fee schedule. However, the relative-value units will change for each service.

As previously mentioned, relative-value guidelines can be used to calculate medical and laboratory fees. Use the method already described, but be sure to select an appropriate conversion factor. The conversion factor usually ranges from $3 to $8, depending on the location of the practice, the medical specialty, and what the physician feels comfortable charging.

■ **Practice Point:** Once fees are set, they should be monitored on a constant basis. Do this by reviewing EOBs at least on a semi-annual basis, especially managed-care EOBs. Look for those services in which the payer paid the entire billed charge. When this occurs, the fee for the particular service or services needs to be adjusted.

■ **Practice Point:** Most physicians operate in a fixed-fee environment. In other words, their patients are insured by Medicare, Medicaid, or some type of managed-care plan. In these situations, there probably will not be that many opportunities to raise fees to increase practice collections, so CPT coding becomes extremely important. In other words, make sure that the practice is not losing revenue as a result of incorrect coding practices.

Physician Fee Analyzers

In addition to a relative analysis approach to analyzing, reviewing, and setting physicians' fees, there are commercial products that are also helpful. For example, one of the most popular products is Medicode's National Fee Analyzer (www.feeanalyzer.com and www.medicode.com). Available in both hard copy and Internet subscription basis, this book benchmarks current physician fee schedules against actual charge data for a practice's geographic area and specialty. It also references the 50th, 75th, and 95th percentiles of charge data to see where a practice's fees fall relative to those of its peers.

Pricing Charges When the -22 Modifier Is Used

The fee or payment allowable generally is increased by at least 25 percent when the -22 modifier is used along with the procedure code. Some practices even add on 50 percent. When the -22 modifier is used, the charge will probably end up in "Medical Review" and you will have to submit the appropriate documentation supporting the use of the modifier.

Closely monitor reimbursement on these charges. Some payors refuse any additional reimbursement. Their rationale is that lesser reimbursement does not occur for the "bunnies," so why should a physician demand more for the tough cases? Some payors will give an extra allowance but often an appeal is necessary to receive appropriate reimbursement.

▼ PART II
Medical Office Operations, Policies, and Procedures

This section of the book provides a basic framework for how a medical practice should be managed and the specific policies and procedures that can and should be implemented. It also outlines the basic day-to-day operations of a medical practice. The manner in which the policies and procedures are implemented will depend on the size of the practice and the physicians' medical specialty. What may work for a large practice may not work in a small practice, and vice versa. However, no matter what the medical specialty or the size of the practice, basic policies and procedures are common to every medical practice. For example, every medical practice should have a policy on the follow-up of unpaid insurance claim forms. At a minimum, use this section of the book to make sure that the basic systems are in place. You may need to adapt these systems to the practice's specific needs.

The success of any medical office, no matter what the physician's medical specialty, depends on a system of policies and procedures. Equally important is the continuous administration and management of the medical practice. A medical practice without policies, procedures, and management almost always experiences the following: (1) lost revenue, (2) constant internal inefficiencies, and (3) poor employee morale. If proper systems are put into place and followed by the office staff, a medical practice has no reason not to be successful. If the right policies and procedures are in place, and the practice still has problems, this is often the result of a personnel problem and not the fault of the internal systems. Also, if the particular policies and procedures that are implemented are not managed on an ongoing basis by someone in the office, the intended efficiencies will never be achieved. Most physicians prefer to delegate policy design and related management to an office manager or administrator. True practice success, however, mandates the physician's involvement in the office's administration and management.

▼ CHAPTER 9
Basic Medical Office Procedures

Each medical practice, no matter what size, has certain basic office procedures that every practice manager or advisor must understand. Knowing how a medical practice works and operates on a day-to-day basis is the beginning point for any person wanting to assist a medical practice with its management. A paramount goal for any practice manager or advisor is to make sure that the office is operating as efficiently as possible. Whenever a medical office is inefficient, no matter how minute the inefficiency may seem, the operating net income of the practice may feel the impact. By understanding these basic medical office procedures, you can be in an advisory position to help the physician eliminate inefficiencies and optimize the bottom line.

Office Hours

Designated office hours should be established for every medical practice. Generally, normal office hours for medical practice employees are 8:00 a.m. to 5:00 p.m., or 8:30 a.m. to 5:30 p.m., Monday through Friday. Of course, hours may vary from one medical practice to another. For example, some practices allow their employees a half-day off each week, especially if patient hours regularly run past office hours. This is one way to reward employees for staying late. Some practices are open on Saturdays for the convenience of patients who prefer weekend appointments. Likewise, other practices extend their office hours into the evening.

> ■ **Practice Point:** Many, many patients prefer after-hours availability. To add volume, consider adding after-hour appointment slots. This can be either on a Saturday, as mentioned above, or one night a week.

Medical offices pay their employees for a 40-hour week, and office hours should reflect this fact. If a practice closes Friday afternoons, it may be paying its employees as if they were working 40 hours when, in fact, they are not. If this occurs, you must make sure the employees are being paid only for the hours they work. Also, if the office is not open 40 hours a week, make sure employees have enough time to perform all their job duties. If not, this will directly impact the operating efficiency of any medical practice.

■ **Practice Point:** If employees do not have enough time to perform their duties, first make sure that the office has the right operational systems in place. If the right operational systems are in place and the office is still having a problem getting tasks accomplished, it is a personnel problem and not a systems problem. In this case, either the office is understaffed or the employees are unskilled. Explore both possibilities.

Management must make sure that all employees arrive at the office on time and that they do not leave the office before their shifts are complete. Because the practice pays employees for a 40-hour week, the office manager must make sure employees are working 40 hours. Inefficiencies can and do occur because employees are not spending sufficient time on their designated job duties. One way to solve this problem is to speak to those employees who habitually arrive late for work.

■ **Practice Point:** If excessive overtime is a problem, and the problem cannot be traced to an operational issue, try using a time clock. It works to cut down wasted overtime dollars.

Other problems include excessive lunch hours and physician time off. Many practices give their employees more than one hour for lunch because the physicians often use this time to get caught up and make hospital rounds. If this occurs, and the employees cannot finish their duties, suggest to the office manager that the lunch hour be shortened to an hour. You must make sure all employees are maximizing their time during the day on their own job duties.

Physician time off can also be an issue. Some physicians, for example, take a day off or an afternoon off each week. Make sure that the employees are working as efficiently as they can when the physician is not in the office. Unfortunately, some employees do not work as hard when the physician is out of the office. This is a simple fact of life. If employees complain that they do not have enough time to perform their job duties, never take this at face value. Solutions always require some investigation.

■ **Practice Point:** Do not let whining employees cloud your judgment. Find out if the culprit is an operational problem or employees just slacking off when the physician is not around.

■ **Practice Point:** Some offices are in fact understaffed. This could be your problem to identify and to solve.

Preparing for the Office Day

The telephone should be taken off the answering service when the office is opened. Generally, this is the receptionist's responsibility, but the first person to arrive in the office should make sure the phone is taken off the service. Patients and potential patients may get upset when they call the office during designated office hours and they get the answering service. The telephone should always be answered by the office staff during office hours and placed on the answering service after hours.

Assigned employees should carry out the following functions first thing in the morning:

- Unlock the front door to the office.
- Bring the computers on line.
- Check the cash drawer. This includes reconciliation of the cash drawer from the previous day.
- Begin filling in open appointment slots with walk-in appointments or phone call appointments.
- Pull the medical charts for the day's appointments if they were not gathered the night before.
- Prepare charge slips for the day's patients.

■ **Practice Point:** These may seem like trivial duties, but they are critical to the overall daily efficiency of any medical practice. For example, if the receptionist does not pull medical charts until the patient arrives for his appointment, the office will start to run behind schedule. Usually, this means that the patient will have to wait longer, because the physician will need some time to review the medical chart. The receptionist will also be affected, because this additional duty takes time away from normal duties. If the receptionist gathers the charts the night before or first thing in the morning, the office's processes will run more smoothly. The patients will not have to wait longer, the physician will be able to review the charts in a timely manner, and the receptionist can perform duties without being interrupted.

■ **Practice Point:** Many medical offices forget about customer service. Patients are their customers and should be treated as such. A lackadaisical attitude toward these duties impacts service.

Shutting Down the Office

The office door should remain open until the last patient has left the office. Once the office is closed, the telephone should be put on the answering service and the cash drawer and front door should be locked. Office keys should be issued only to office staff members and must never be loaned out to others, unless specifically authorized by the owner of the practice. These duties are just some of the many internal controls for a medical practice.

■ **Practice Point:** Make sure no cash or checks are left unattended in someone's desk drawer. This happens often in busy practices. The person who posts checks that come in the mail or cash that has been received from patients after their visits just cannot get to all of the postings in one day. Unposted checks remain in the office and are not deposited. Make sure this does not happen. All cash and checks should be deposited each day.

Telephone Management

For busy medical practices, the telephone can become a hindrance to the efficiency of daily office operations. One of the biggest problems encountered by a medical practice, especially an office with many physicians, is managing the volume of phone calls from its patients. If employees must spend a majority of their time fielding telephone calls, they will not be able to devote enough time to their normal job duties, and compliance with the offices' internal operating systems might be impaired. For example, a receptionist is having difficulty answering telephone calls and checking out patients at the same time. In this situation, the receptionist's ability to record office visit charges and collect payments can be and usually is hindered.

> ■ **Practice Point:** If the office is having problems checking patients in and checking patients out, determine if telephone calls are the problem. Telephone calls could also contribute to nurses not having enough time for patient care and other office duties.

Minimizing Redundant Telephone Calls

Excessive telephone calls to a medical practice come from many sources. The most obvious source is from patients who call to make appointments. However, do not attempt to reduce these calls, as the income they generate is important. Other types of phone calls, however, can and should be cut short or bunched together. For example, to minimize the distraction that results from patients calling for lab test results and to improve efficiency, designate a time during the day or week when patients can call specifically for this purpose. The office manager should then assign one person to answer phone calls about test results. This policy would allow other employees to perform their office duties with minimal interruptions. An alternative solution is for the office to adopt the policy of informing patients of their lab test results in writing only.

Calls from patients who want to discuss their medical problems over the phone, without making an appointment, can also waste office time. If patients call the office seeking free advice regarding their medical problems, insist that they make an appointment. An office visit allows the physician an opportunity (a) to diagnose and treat the problem properly, (b) to avoid losing revenue by giving free advice over the telephone, and (c) to avoid malpractice claims if advice that has negative consequences is given over the telephone. If a practice's physician is giving out advice over the telephone, suggest that he or she discontinue doing so. A physician cannot make a proper assessment of the patient's condition over the phone, and the physician could be held accountable if his or her advice is incorrect. If the physician continues to give advice over the phone, make sure that the physician documents the call in the patient's medical chart.

Another way to cut down on unnecessary telephone calls is to begin charging for them. Although a practice cannot charge for this service under certain insurance plans (such as Medicare and Medicaid), it may for others. Even if an insurance plan does not pay for the call, the patient could be responsible for payment because the telephone charge is a noncovered benefit. When patients have to pay for these services out of their own pockets, they usually quit making unnecessary calls, or at least reduce the number of calls to the office.

> ■ **Practice Point:** If you implement a telephone policy, make sure the practice informs its patients before implementation. If the practice does not inform its patients, it may be inundated with calls from angry patients when they are billed for services not previously explained. This is especially true if the practice begins to charge for telephone calls.

Sample Telephone Call Policy

When a physician orders tests for a patient, the patient is asked to return to the office for the test results and for possible treatment orders. Only under special circumstances will a physician discuss test results over the telephone. If you insist that the physician discuss the results with you by telephone before your office appointment, and the physician has not asked for the information to be handled by phone, you will be charged for the telephone conference. If you would like to discuss your lab tests with other office clinical personnel, call the office between the hours of ____ and ____.

It is the policy of this office for the physician to communicate with the patient directly regarding the patient's medical status. If you have a clinical problem requiring a physician's attention, call the office to make an appointment. Please refrain from calling the office strictly for advice except in cases of medical emergency. If the patient is not capable of discussing his or her medical course of treatment with the physician, the family will need to designate one person to act on the patient's behalf.

Unless otherwise designated, the following policies will apply:

- *If the patient is married, the physician will communicate with the spouse, and the spouse will then be responsible for relaying the information to other family members.*

- *If the patient is not married, but has adult children, the physician will discuss the patient's condition with one designated child.*

- *If the patient is not married and has no children, the physician will discuss the patient's status with his or her parents.*

- *If the patient is a minor, the physician will communicate with the parents or court-appointed guardian. Any other person will need to contact the parents or guardian for an update.*

- *If you are a personal injury patient and have an attorney, the physician will not discuss your case with the attorney by telephone or by office conference. Any communication with your attorney will need to be in writing, and you will be charged for the time.*

[Insert here the office's policy on charging for telephone calls.]

■ **Practice Point:** A question that is often asked is whether or not the practice should invest in an automated telephone attendant to eliminate excessive phone calls. Some practices have had success with this type of system while many others have not. Success can be achieved if (a) the prompts are kept to a bare minimum and (b) a receptionist is readily available when the prompt asks the patient to press a button to access this person.

One further word about automated telephone systems. No matter how much you might dislike such a system, there may come a time when a practice must implement one. For example, there are instances when the phones are literally overwhelming the practice and other tasks are not getting done. Here is an actual example of one medical practice.

The practice has 10 lines (six open lines, two private, one hospital, and one billing line) and it is always putting patients on hold because it is working on the calls that came in prior (such as scheduling appointments, patient referrals, taking messages, as well as checking in and out patients at the same time). Like many practices, the physicians prefer a live person answering the phone. This practice has four front-desk employees.

This is an example where a practice might want to look at implementing an automated attendant and call routing system. This assumes all other ideas on how to manage the telephone have been looked at. Whenever such a system is implemented, there will be some complaints from patients and even the practice's own doctors. However, there was one instance after a year, where the practice sent out a patient satisfaction survey about its automated system and received a 94 percent favorable response. Although a consultant may not be a fan of such systems, they can help an overburdened medical office.

Confidential Information

Any medical practice must be aware at all times of its duty to keep patients' medical information confidential. This is a basic ethical and legal requirement for all medical practices. Nonetheless, some offices are careless with confidential information. One control feature of a medical office is to protect the medical status of its patients. In addition, there are office matters that should also remain confidential, such as the practice's finances and payroll.

Confidentiality of Patient Information

Any and all information about patients' illnesses or personal lives must be kept completely confidential. Following are guidelines for a medical practice:

1. A conversation with a patient about his or her medical condition should not be overheard by other patients in the office. This is a problem in offices in which front-desk conversations can be overheard by people sitting in the waiting room. Make sure the front-desk staff and other personnel do not discuss patients' information in this area and that they keep their voices down.

■ **Practice Point:** To test whether this is a problem, sit in the practice's waiting room and listen. If you can overhear the patients' conversations, the practice has a confidentiality problem. Suggest that the office either ask its patients questions in the exam room or create a form on which the patients can write their ailments. If employees of the practice overhear conversations, make sure the employees understand that this information is completely confidential and should not be told to anyone inside or outside the office.

2. Loose paper should never be allowed to remain in a patient's medical records. Such papers could fall out and be seen by unauthorized personnel. Make sure the office anchors all papers into the medical record.

3. Medical records should be kept in a place where passing patients will not see them during office visits. Allowing medical charts to be left lying around the office could result in a breach of patient confidentiality.

4. Patients' files should be maintained in the business office or near the front desk and should be accessible only to the physician; designated staff, such as the nurses and referral physicians; or patients, upon request. Any other request for a patient's information (such as requests coming from news media, a patient's relatives, or insurance companies) should be honored only after the practice has obtained appropriate permission, including, if necessary, a written release by the patient.

5. The office should have a policy for assessing a charge for copying a file for, or on behalf of, a patient. The request could be made by a patient, an insurance company, an attorney's office, or another third party. The charge could be by the page or a set fee. For example, some offices charge 10 cents a page, while others charge a flat fee of around $35 to $50. The fee should be paid before the file is released. The charge for a workers' compensation matter will, in most instances, be dictated by each state's related rules and regulations governing workers' compensation reimbursement.

■ **Practice Point:** Some medical specialties should not have a sign-in sheet, in order to protect patient confidentiality. Oncology and psychiatric practices are two of the most common.

Intraoffice Confidentiality

All matters pertaining to the inner workings of the office must also be treated as confidential information. The following types of confidentiality issues should be adhered to by all medical practices:

1. Business records should be kept in the business office and must not be discussed with, or made available to, outsiders unless authorized by the physician or his or her designate.

2. Personnel matters are always especially sensitive. Payroll information is confidential and should be available only to the physician or his or her designate. The office manager should inform the practice's employees that they are not to solicit information concerning other employees' wages or terms of employment. When one employee finds out that another employee is making more money, internal chaos can erupt.

3. Discussions among the office staff or between employees and outsiders regarding the skills or performance of other employees in the practice should be prohibited. This will help to prevent employees from gossiping, which wastes time and negatively impacts productivity.

4. Office personnel must be told and made to understand that any information received through the mail from the practice's accountant or other designated sources should be opened only by the office manager or by the physician. Information on practice finances should remain confidential. This policy will prevent the following situation: The accountant mails year-end W-2 forms to the office. The receptionist opens the package and sees the compensation levels of all employees for the year. Unless the receptionist is a uniquely honest person, there will be ensuing discussions among the employees and internal consequences will follow.

■ **Practice Point:** Review these confidentiality issues with the physician or physicians annually and determine if the employees are adhering to the practice's confidentiality policies. If they are not, help the practice develop solutions.

Violating any of the confidences listed earlier can, and often should, result in the termination of the violator's employment. There should be no exceptions. As previously mentioned, the main reason for the strict policy is the demoralizing effect on the employees of the medical office, which inevitably results in turmoil within the office, consequently reducing employee productivity and morale. Therefore, the office manager should stress to each employee that all compensation matters are confidential and any violation of this policy will result in job termination. Make sure this is mentioned in the office's personnel policy manual.

Scheduling Office Appointments

If one commonality exists among medical offices, it is scheduling appointments. Physicians do not generate income unless they see patients. Unless the practice is an urgent care center (e.g., minor emergency clinic) in which patients walk in off the street to see a physician, you will need to help the office develop a policy for scheduling appointments. There is a right way to schedule appointments and also many wrong ways. Problems in the scheduling process will always disrupt a medical office and could ultimately impact its bottom line.

■ **Practice Point:** If a practice's daily operations appear chaotic, first observe how appointments are scheduled. Improper scheduling can cause practices to fall behind. For example, if too many patients are scheduled in the same time slot, patients will complain about their wait time and may not see the physician again. They will also tell friends about the long wait. This bad reference may affect the physician's business.

How to Decide Between Accepting a Patient and Issuing a Referral

The front-desk employees will need guidelines to help them decide between scheduling an appointment for a patient or referring the patient to another physician. For new patients, the front-desk employee needs to determine whether or not the physician can fulfill the patient's needs. For example, if the physician's field of expertise is cardiology and the patient needs an annual exam, the employee would refer the patient to a general practitioner. The employee can determine the patient's problems by listening to the patient. Instruct the employee that, when in doubt, the employee should refer the patient to a physician or nurse in the office. The front-desk employee should use the following guidelines:

1. If the case clearly falls within the physician's field of expertise, schedule an appointment.

2. If a specialty outside of the physician's field is clearly indicated, communicate the situation to the patient. Offer to have the physician discuss the matter with the patient.

If a referral is necessary, the front-desk employee should refer the patient to a physician who has been preapproved by the practice. The practice should maintain a list of these physicians by medical specialty. If the patient belongs to a health maintenance organization (HMO), a preferred provider organization (PPO), or some other managed-care plan, make sure the front-desk employee knows to refer the patient to a contracted physician within the same managed-care program. Otherwise, the physician will not get paid if he or she treats the patient as an out-of-network provider.

The front-desk employees should never refer established patients to another physician unless the physician expressly directs them to do so. In these situations, the physician must determine whether or not the patient needs to be seen by another physician.

■ **Practice Point:** Make sure that all employees responsible for making appointments know the duration of the practice's most common clinical office visits. This is important because if an employee schedules too many lengthy appointments in one day, the patients will have to wait a long time or the office may be forced to cancel some appointments that same day. Neither of these options would promote good public relations with the physician's patients. If necessary, set a meeting with the practice's staff members and the physician to review the most common visits and their duration. This will help the employees to schedule all appointments appropriately. The appointment guidelines in the following section will help you develop guidelines for the medical practice.

Appointment Length

The estimated length of an appointment could end up being the single most important issue in many medical practices, especially those that treat a large number of patients in the office (e.g., pediatrics, family medicine, internal medicine). When a patient calls the office for an appointment, it is the duty of the front-desk employee to determine the nature of the patient's problem and to schedule a related appointment time. Errors in the scheduling process can wreak havoc on a medical practice. As previously mentioned, problems in scheduling can cause the office to run behind on its appointments, resulting in a crowded waiting room and angry patients. Scheduling problems can also result in the uneven distribution of patients during the day, often leaving office personnel standing around with nothing to do for hours at a time. For busy offices, scheduling problems increase the stress level of both the physician and the office staff.

Determining the nature of the patient's clinical complaint can be one of the most difficult aspects of running a medical practice. If a simple clinical problem is scheduled for a lengthy time slot, or if a complicated clinical problem is scheduled for too short a treatment time, this could result in underbookings, overbookings, office delays, and frustrated patients. Front-desk employees should use the following guidelines to determine the length of time needed for an appointment:

New patients with complicated problems needing extensive evaluation	60 minutes
All other new patients	45 minutes
Established patients with no complications or routine hospital follow-up	15 minutes
Established patients with complications or needing extensive evaluation	30 minutes
Surgical postoperative visit	15 minutes
Complete physicals	60 minutes
Samples for lab tests	10 minutes
In-office procedures	45 minutes
Medication check	15 minutes

Since every practice operates differently, these guidelines will differ for each individual medical specialty, and the time schedule should be adjusted accordingly. If the office staff is unsure of the time schedule for specific clinical situations, the physician should give appropriate guidance and instruction.

> ■ **Practice Point:** If a particular physician does not see many patients in the office, go first to the appointment book to see how his or her patients are scheduled. Many offices block out the same time for all appointments, no matter why the patient came to the office. For example, one practice blocked 20 minutes for every patient—for routine follow-up, simple problems, and other conditions. Scheduling time according to a specific schedule, as mentioned above, should alleviate this problem.

Office Appointment Policy

Another aspect of an appointment policy is determining when to schedule appointments. Appointment days will depend partially on (a) the physician's personal preferences (e.g., working around days off, hospital rounds, and surgery days) and (b) the practice's medical specialty. Some specialties, such as pediatrics, have many walk-in appointments or appointments that are made the same day. In these cases, the scheduling staff must leave a certain number of appointment slots open each day to take care of walk-in and same-day appointments. Also, you should know that rarely do medical specialists have office visit hours on the weekends or on every day of the work week. Many primary care practices, however, have office visit hours six or seven days a week.

The appointment policy will also need to address the issue of what times of the day the office will see patients. One basic element of scheduling patients is that appointments should not be made past a designated time. For example, if the office is open until 5:00 p.m., appointments generally should not be scheduled after 4:00 p.m. This allows the office staff to finish up its clinical work and to close out the business aspects of the practice's day. If the practice accepts appointments until the office closes, the physician runs late and the office remains open late, resulting in unnecessary employee overtime. Employee morale is also impacted when employees cannot leave work at a reasonable hour. Exceptions to this scheduling rule should be permitted only if all other slots are filled, if the patient is unable to come in earlier or at a later date, or upon approval by the physician for other reasons.

■ **Practice Point:** If the office is paying too much overtime, determine if the appointment schedule is the cause.

Once the front-desk employee has scheduled an appointment for a patient, the employee should repeat this information to the patient to avoid misunderstandings. If the patient is in the office when he or she schedules an appointment, the front-desk employee should give the patient an office card with the appointment date and time written on it. The front-desk employee should instruct new patients to arrive for their appointments at least 15 minutes early to complete necessary paperwork. The employee should write in the appointment information (i.e., date and time) either on a manual appointment book or in the computerized appointment scheduler. Besides the date and time, the receptionist should include each patient's telephone number so the office can call to remind patients of their appointments. The phone numbers also allow the office employees to follow up on patients who do not show up for their appointments. Finally, when a patient calls the office for an appointment, he or she should be given the appropriate financial instructions (i.e., office visit payment policy).

■ **Practice Point:** Find out if the office has a problem with no-show appointments by periodically reviewing a sample of daily appointments. Make sure one of the staff members calls patients the day before their appointments to confirm the appointments. Also, if a patient cancels an appointment or does not show up, an employee needs to follow up with the patient to reschedule the appointment.

■ **IRS Note:** The medical practice should keep appointment books for at least three to seven years. This period mirrors the various IRS statutes of limitation. Appointment logs may be necessary in the event of an IRS examination.

Financial Instruction

When a patient calls for an appointment, the receptionist should inform or remind the patient of the practice's collection policy regarding office visits. This is especially important for new patients. The practice manager or advisor should make sure that the receptionist knows the practice's collection policy and that he or she relays that information to each patient when an appointment is scheduled. The receptionist could use the following phrasing: "I just want to mention that it is our office policy to collect full payment, or the co-payment, at the time service is rendered. Is that a problem?"

By having the receptionist state the office policy each time a patient schedules an appointment, it reminds the patient that he or she will be expected to make some kind of payment at the time of the visit. This procedure should cut down on the common problem of patients not paying the office-visit cost when they come in.

■ **Practice Point:** The success of front-desk collections should always be tested from time to time. Is the office **really** doing a good job collecting monies and co-payments from patients at the time of their visits? If not, you can be sure accounts receivable are suffering. Not instructing the patients about the practice's payment policy could be one of the culprits.

If the receptionist mentions the practice's policy each time an appointment is scheduled, it will be difficult for patients to claim that they forgot their checkbooks or that they were under the impression that no payment was expected. Asking each patient if the practice's payment policy is a problem is a friendly way of allowing the patient to object or to say that he or she cannot pay for the visit because of a specific reason. If the patient cannot pay for the office visit, depending on the practice's policy, the receptionist could either schedule the patient and bill him or her personally or bill the patient's insurance plan for the visit.

With the exception of the hospital-based specialties, every medical practice should have a definitive collection policy for office visits. The receptionist should be trained to communicate the policy to patients who call to make an appointment and should then be monitored to determine how well the front-desk staff is actually enforcing the policy. (See the section titled "Office Visits" in Chapter 12 for more information.)

The front-desk personnel should be trained and prepared to give the approximate fee for the office visit, should a patient request it.

However, the receptionist should always provide an appropriate caveat about potential charges for laboratory tests, X-rays, medication, or other services that the physician may deem necessary upon examining the patient.

■ **Practice Point:** You should remember that many employees are uncomfortable talking about financial matters to people needing a clinical appointment. Ask the receptionist if he or she is comfortable with such duties and then monitor the receptionist's work.

Delays Caused by Physicians

If the front-desk staff has been given the proper instruction and training on how to schedule appointments, but problems persist in the office, the physician could be the source of the problem. Some physicians chronically run late. In such cases, you will need to show the physician the specifics regarding how this behavior affects the practice and the patients' perception of it.

■ **Practice Point:** To document time delays in the reception area because of the physician's or office staff's behavior, use the worksheet in Appendix B, Worksheet for Analysis of Patients' Waiting Time in Reception Area. Have the receptionist use this worksheet to log in when the patient arrives in the office and when the patient is escorted to the exam room for the appointment. You will then need to quantify the average waiting-room time and determine if the time is reasonable. Ask the following question: "Would I be upset if I had to wait this long for my appointment?" If the waiting-room time appears unreasonable, investigate immediately.

Make the Office Visit a Pleasant One for Patients

Every medical office should do what it can to make a patient's appointment wait time as pleasant as it can be. For example, let the patients know that the physician is running late. Provide reading/viewing materials for patients to occupy their time. Offer coffee, tea, water, cookies to all patients in the waiting room. If applicable try to utilize an area of the waiting room for children, toys, etc. Medical practice is a business, patients are customers, and everyone likes and appreciates excellent customer service.

The Patient's Office Visit

Understanding the flow of patients in a medical office is mandatory for anyone who manages a medical practice or provides consultative services to physicians. This knowledge provides insights necessary to detect problems in the office. The challenge of effective daily medical practice management is to identify and remedy situations that create inefficiencies in the office and contribute to lost revenue and cash flow.

Before the Appointment

The general flow of the office day can be greatly upset by patients who do not show up for their designated time slots. Therefore, someone from the office should call all patients the day before their appointments to confirm the dates and times. The phone calls also provide a good opportunity to remind new patients that they should arrive at least 15 minutes early so they can fill out the necessary paperwork. If a patient does not show up for his or her appointment, the receptionist should call the patient as soon as possible to reschedule or at least to find out why the visit was missed. This could help the office prevent scheduling unnecessary visits in the future.

■ **Practice Point:** Some practices utilize the Internet to allow patients to complete their paperwork. For example, a practice may allow a patient to complete a new patient information form on its web site. This enables the practice to have this information several days before the appointment, thus saving a lot of time when the patient finally arrives at the office.

■ **Practice Point:** Some offices charge a fee if a patient does not show up for his or her appointment. The norm is usually $5 to $10. Keep in mind that if this is occurring, the practice may be violating not only its managed-care contracts, but Medicare law as well. Read a sample of managed-care contracts to see if this amount can in fact be collected from the patient. Know that a practice may get in trouble if it collects more than what is allowable from a Medicare patient.

One helpful time-saver is to pull the patients' charts for the current day's scheduled visits either at the beginning of the day or the night before. In addition, the Superbill, office charge ticket, or patient encounter form should be placed on top of each medical chart to avoid potential delays. If the practice is computerized and uses a computer-generated Superbill, another option is to print the Superbill when the patient arrives in the office. This avoids wasting a Superbill if a patient does not show up for the appointment. The Superbill and patient chart should be together when the physician sees the patient.

The Superbill

The *Superbill* (also referred to as the *patient encounter form* or the *charge ticket*) is a form used in the office to indicate which services are rendered, mainly pertaining to those services rendered in the office. (See Appendix B for a sample Superbill.) Some offices also use the Superbill to record hospital, surgery, laboratory, and radiology charges. When a physician examines a patient, the physician records the services and the related diagnoses on the Superbill. The front-desk employee uses the Superbill to check out the patient, extracting the necessary information from the Superbill to determine the appropriate charges for the visit before obtaining the payment from the patient or before billing the patient's insurance plan.

If the Superbill is not completed correctly, the front-desk employee cannot check out the patient, determine the accurate fee, or collect the correct payment. This creates unnecessary accounts receivable in the practice. Even missing diagnosis codes create inefficiencies in the office. If the front-desk employee cannot input all the information into the computer while the patient is checking out, another employee will need to do it later in the day or even the next day. This wastes valuable office time.

Recording services To optimize revenue in the medical practice, the physician must record accurately and completely all of the services rendered to the patient. If any services are not recorded on the Superbill, revenue will be lost. This is because if the services are not documented on the Superbill, the receptionist cannot bill the services either to the patient or to the patient's insurance plan. Because the easiest and most efficient way to record services is by using a checklist, make sure that the Superbill includes all of the services that can be rendered in the office. An 8½ × 11-inch form usually is the most appropriate size to use, because it is small enough to be manageable yet large enough to list all the services the practice offers (and corresponding CPT codes). A complete list of services may be more difficult to come by if the practice uses a computer-generated Superbill as the charge ticket because these Superbills have limited space on which to print the codes.

> ■ **Practice Point:** Have a physician review the CPT book and checkmark each and every service he or she can render in the office. Make sure these codes are included on the Superbill.

Diagnosis codes In the interest of saving time, a comprehensive list of the diagnosis codes should also be printed on the Superbill. If the diagnosis codes are not listed on the Superbill, the physician will have to write in the diagnosis or diagnoses manually for each encounter with a patient. This will entail someone in the office taking the time to look up the related diagnosis codes in the *International Classification of Diseases and Related Health Problems,* 10th Revision (ICD-10), before the charge can be input into the computer and, if required, billed to the insurance company. Besides the regular Superbill, many surgical practices also use a surgical Superbill, or surgery charge card. (An example of a surgery charge card can be found in Appendix B.)

Template completeness One of the best ways to ensure that all services are being captured on the Superbill is to have the physician review the CPT book and indicate all the services that he or she could render in the office. (This is also an excellent exercise for the physician because many physicians are not schooled in CPT coding.) Because the CPT book is revised each year, the office manager must compare the codes on the Superbill to the codes in the revised CPT book to make sure there have not been any changes to the codes the office uses. This includes any changes in the word descriptions to the codes. If codes have been changed, the Superbill template must be revised immediately. The same goes for the diagnosis codes; if an office bills a code that has been changed or deleted, the insurance company could deny or delay payment.

Prenumbering   Every Superbill in the office should be prenumbered. This is one of the most basic internal controls for a medical practice. Each day, the office manager should account for the Superbills used that day. Generally, this is done by accounting for the numerical sequence of the control numbers on each Superbill and tracing them back to the patient sign-in sheet or the daily appointment record. (See the sample daily control sheet in Appendix B for an example of one way to account for these numbers.) If an office does not account for the Superbills used each day, it could be susceptible to embezzlement. (For more information on employee embezzlement, refer to Chapter 4.)

■ **Practice Point:** The CPT codes change every year. The Superbill may have to be revised to take into account any changes to related codes or the possible addition of new codes. Make sure that the medical office reviews the new ICD book each year.

The Flow of Patients in the Office

One of the most important aspects of keeping the flow of patients smooth throughout the office day is keeping to the appointment schedule. Patients become upset when they must wait a long time in the reception area for their appointments. As a general rule, patients should be escorted to examination rooms within 10 minutes of the appointed times and should wait in the examination rooms no more than another 10 minutes before examinations begin. Patients should be given the common courtesy of an explanation if the wait is longer than 10 minutes. If an office is having difficulty following this guideline, investigate the reasons for the delayed waiting period. Some reasons for this problem could be that the physician is working inefficiently or the scheduling process is too tight at certain times. (See the Worksheet for Analysis of Patients' Waiting Time in Reception Area in Appendix B.)

Does the Medical Office Design Accommodate Fluid Patient Flow?

There are many medical practices where the layout of the office is not conducive to fluid and efficient patient flow. For example, architects inexperienced in designing medical offices begin drawing the layout with little understanding of how doctors and their support staffers actually work. There may be instances when the physician spends too much time educating the designer, or ends up working in an office that is so inefficient that he or she is deterred from assisting the medical practice in reaching its potential.

Managing patient flow lies at the heart of good medical office design. When the physician begins to look at patient flow, he or she should see if the physical layout of the office is somehow causing any of these type of inefficiencies. This is especially true when and if a practice can design its own office space, since a poorly designed office cannot be changed "after the fact" without great expense.

Sign-in

Patients should sign in at the receptionist's desk when they first arrive. Exceptions generally are made for psychiatry and oncology practices in order to maintain patient confidentiality. A sign-in sheet can be a prepared form, a small spiral notebook, or even a blank piece of paper.

The following chart is an example of a sign-in sheet.

Practice Name: _____

Date: _____

Please Sign In

Patient's Name	Address Changed?	Appointment Time	Arrival Time	Doctor today?	New Insurance?
	Yes or No				Yes or No
	Yes or No				Yes or No
	Yes or No				Yes or No
	Yes or No				Yes or No
	Yes or No				Yes or No
	Yes or No				Yes or No
	Yes or No				Yes or No
	Yes or No				Yes or No
	Yes or No				Yes or No
	Yes or No				Yes or No
	Yes or No				Yes or No
	Yes or No				Yes or No
	Yes or No				Yes or No
	Yes or No				Yes or No
	Yes or No				Yes or No
	Yes or No				Yes or No
	Yes or No				Yes or No
	Yes or No				Yes or No
	Yes or No				Yes or No
	Yes or No				Yes or No
	Yes or No				Yes or No

■ **Practice Point:** At the end of each office day, the sign-in sheet should be placed in a folder and kept as a permanent record. The sheet will serve as a paper trail for the office and also as a method for internal control. (For a detailed discussion of how the sign-in sheet is used for internal control purposes, read the section titled "Closing the Books" in Chapter 13.)

It is also a good idea, for internal-control purposes, for the office manager to match each patient's visit to the control number that is preprinted on the Superbill. The receptionist can write the Superbill number beside each patient's name on the sign-in sheet or, if the practice is on a manual system, the receptionist should write the number on the daysheet beside each patient's name.

New Patient Information Sheet

Each new patient who arrives for an appointment must complete an information sheet. (See the sample new patient's information sheet in Appendix B.) For management purposes, the most important part of the information sheet is the patient's specific insurance information, including the name of the insurance company and the patient's insurance policy number. If the patient has any type of secondary insurance coverage (such as Medicare), it too should be included on the sheet. The front-desk employee must make sure the patient completes the sheet correctly and signs the authorization statement to pay benefits to the practice. The authorization statement section of the sheet is critical because unless the patient authorizes the insurance company to pay the benefits directly to the physician's office, the insurance company will pay the benefits to the patient. If this occurs, the office must go through the added trouble of obtaining payment from the patient, instead of collecting only the patient's co-payment amount.

> ■ **Practice Point:** If the practice has a problem getting insurance claim forms prepared and mailed on a timely basis, you should determine if the problem is because the office is having problems collecting initial information from the patient. If the patient information form is not filled in correctly and completely, the billing staff will have to take more time to retrieve this information.

Consolidate the new patient information sheets at the end of each month and summarize them to track from where new patients are being referred. (See Appendix B for a sample new patient tracking form.)

Accurate Insurance Information

The front-desk employee should always ask established patients whether they still have the same insurance coverage or if they have switched to a different health insurance policy. If practices make the mistake of assuming that patients still have the same insurance coverage when in fact they do not, the initial insurance claim will be denied and staff members will need to obtain the new insurance information and refile the claim. To circumvent this problem, the office's sign-in sheet should have a statement written at the top that asks the patients to inform the receptionist if their insurance coverage has changed since the last office visit. In some offices, the receptionist is responsible for obtaining this information from the patients. Another idea is to have patients who have not been in the office within the last year complete new patient information sheets. This ensures that the insurance information is correct in patients' files.

> ■ **Practice Point:** Another idea is to make sure the waiting area has a sign, visible to all patients, that reads: "Please let the receptionist know if your insurance has changed since your last visit."

When a new patient arrives in the office, the receptionist should make a copy of the patient's insurance card for the practice's records. Not only does this card contain the patient's relevant insurance policy information, but it also designates the patient's co-payment amount, if any. If the receptionist has this information, he or she can more easily collect the co-payment while the patient is in the office. The receptionist should try to collect the co-payment because if it is not collected, it must be billed and collected from the patient. Not only is billing more costly than simply collecting the payment when the patient is in the office, but some practices have a tendency toward inefficiency when they bill for a number of $10 to $15 co-payments. The receptionist also should make copies of established patients' insurance cards. The office manager should consider adopting the policy of making a copy of each patient's drivers license to keep in the patient's file. The information on the license can be used in case the patient cannot be located (such as if the patient has skipped on the receivable).

> ■ **Practice Point:** If charges are denied due to incomplete or different insurance coverage, first determine if the receptionist is having difficulty collecting this information from patients.

> ■ **Practice Point:** To identify problems with incorrect insurance information or problems recording patient information by the front desk, constantly review EOBs. You will be able to spot the denials resulting from these problems and correct them immediately.

Checkout

When the patient's examination is complete, the patient should be escorted to the reception counter for checkout. When a patient checks out, the receptionist should complete the following procedures:

- Schedule hospital admission or future appointments.
- Verify the status of current insurance (unless verified beforehand).
- Collect office visit fees or co-payments.
- Complete any further instructions as directed by the physician or by clinical staff.

To create the most efficient office possible, the receptionist should input charges and payments related to a patient's visit into the computer or record them on the manual daysheet. If an office is doing a poor job of collecting payment at the front desk, assess whether or not the problem lies with the physician. Sometimes a physician will give checkout instructions to the patient while he or she is in the examining room. For example, a physician might say, "Don't worry, we will bill your insurance for you." Often, a physician will circumvent office policy. In addition, make sure the physician or a nurse is making the effort to escort patients to the front desk. If the patient does not go through the front desk, the necessary checkout procedures cannot be performed.

■ **Practice Point:** Many practices will say they have trouble collecting co-payments because the receptionist does not know what the amount really is. In these situations, adopt the policy of asking for at least $10. If the practice has to issue a refund, so be it; at least it has its money.

The Importance of a Recall System for Medical Practices

An effective recall system is critical to avoid potential liability, provide better service, and provide additional revenue. Medical practices run a serious malpractice risk if patients are not recalled for follow-up as required by medical protocol. For example, a gastro-enterologist has seen a patient with early indications of potentially cancerous polyps. Professional protocols call for regular re-examination. If the patient dies of colon cancer, an effective malpractice attorney will ask if the gastroenterologist recalled the patient.

Recall systems can be manual or computerized. Many practices have a simple manual system in which the receptionist pulled the charts of patients listed for recall when they checked out from their first visits. Major problems with this kind of system are that the receptionist in a busy front office may miss some names or may not check to see if the patients made and kept their recall appointments. Worst of all, the system might fail if the receptionist quits.

The best recall systems are computerized. Practices can develop a recall system using their own computer system. A computerized system should ensure that patients will not "fall through the cracks." The practice's computer billing system is one type of application to use for effective patient recall. A physician could mark the recall time (e.g., "3 months," or "one year") on the patient's fee slip, and the instruction could be entered into the system along with the fee for the current visit.

Ideally, a computerized recall system should also allow for the following:

- Storing the reasons for recall, using a set of codes, until the patient is actually re-contacted.
- Printing out recall letters a set time before the visits are due. These form letters should include pre-drafted sentences or paragraphs keyed to the reason for recall and telling the patient why the visit is necessary.
- Printing out a checklist of patients to be recalled so that staff can check them off as they are scheduled and seen.

Some systems can even automatically check off recall patients as they are later billed for their visits and generate a list of patients who have not responded to the recall and who should thus be followed up further.

If appropriate, the practice should send a final warning letter to each patient who fails or refuses to honor the recall effort. The computerized system should be able to generate this letter as well. A copy should be retained in the patient's chart.

An effective recall system can be handled by most medical software systems. If a practice's system cannot handle this, consider upgrading or at least make sure that an effective manual recall system is in place.

Referrals from Other Physicians and Patients

When a new patient schedules an office visit, the receptionist needs to find out exactly how the patient was referred to the office. This is one of those basic Marketing 101 principles. You should track the office's patient referrals on a continual basis. By doing so, you can evaluate the practice's marketing efforts and analyze its referral patterns at any point in time. (See Chapter 15 for more information about marketing techniques.)

Flagging Referrals

The medical practice should have some type of file-flagging system so it can track new patients who are referred by another physician. This system will allow the practice to send a letter to the referring physician immediately after the office visit, thanking the physician for the referral and briefly describing the patient's condition and prescribed treatment plan. If the referral comes from a patient, it is also good policy to send a thank-you note to the patient and encourage additional referrals. Remember that the benefits that come from thank-you letters—namely, more referrals—are greatest if the letters are sent in a timely manner by the office. To make sure the office is sending thank-you notes promptly, obtain copies of some referral thank-you letters and compare the dates on the letters to the dates the physician treated the patients.

Tracking Referral Patterns

The practice must also have a system in place that captures and summarizes patient and physician referral patterns. The information usually is best summarized either in the computer or by hand in a log book. The source for documenting referral patterns is the new patient information sheet. The sheet should include a line item that asks the patient how he or she heard of the practice. This allows the practice to keep track of which physicians are good referral sources and to determine if the telephone directories or other types of marketing efforts are worth the advertising costs. Then, a special effort can be made to stress to the top referring physicians that the practice appreciates their business. This could be conveyed with a simple thank-you note or in the form of a gift. Keeping track of referral patterns also allows a practice to address any decline in referrals from specific physicians. Only then can corrective measures be implemented. Some offices, however, get careless when documenting this information. You must stress to the receptionist the importance of collecting this information.

■ **Practice Point:** Make sure that whenever a new patient fills out the new patient information sheet, the section on where he or she came from (i.e., a physician referral) is complete. Review a sample of the most recently completed forms to verify that the new patient information sheets are complete. (See Appendix B for a sample new patients' information sheet and a sample physician referral tracking form.)

■ **Practice Point:** Print out the patient referral listing or the physician referral listing. If it does not look complete, talk to the receptionist and make sure he or she collects this information. Also use this report to identify a decline in referrals from a specific physician or group of physicians. This is extremely important for any office that relies on physician referrals for patient encounters. If a decline is identified, it should be dealt with immediately. Either the practice's physician can speak to the referring physician and find out why referrals have declined or the practice's administrator can talk with the referring physician's own administrator.

Referral Tracking Worksheet

While most medical software billing systems can print a Referring Doctor Report, most cannot show a decline or increase in referrals. The following is a sample worksheet that can be used to analyze a decline in referrals. Also use this format to create a worksheet to analyze an increase in patient referrals; the practice will want to make sure these doctors are thanked and rewarded in some way.

Referring Doctor/Source	Referrals Current Year	Referrals Last Year	Referrals for Year	Reason for Decline in Referrals

Terminating a Patient Relationship

There may come a time when a practice must terminate a patient relationship. In these cases, the practice should be aware of relevant state laws and anything contained in a contract related to patient abandonment (to be sure it is not violating these provisions). When in doubt on how to do this, the practice should contact the state's medical association.

If a patient relationship has to be terminated, obviously this must be communicated to the patient. This is usually done in form of a letter. The following is a sample letter the medical practice can use (however, be sure any written correspondence meets state law guidelines).

Dear _____:

I regret to inform you that I must withdraw as your _____ [e.g., Cardiologist].

Since your condition requires medical attention, I suggest that you place yourself under the care of another cardiologist without delay. In the event of an emergency, I shall be available to attend you until _____ [date]. After _____ [date], I can no longer be responsible for your medical care.

This period of time should give you ample opportunity to select a physician of your choice from the many competent practitioners available. If you will sign an authorization, I will make available to this physician your case history and information regarding the diagnosis and treatment which you have received from me.

I request that you or the physician of your choice inform me immediately in writing upon your transferal to his services.

Very truly yours,

Physician's Name, M.D.

▼ CHAPTER 10
Basic CPT and Diagnosis-Coding Rules

Whether a physician treats a patient in the physician's office, in the hospital, or at some other location, the physician must communicate to the patient or to the patient's insurance company exactly which services were rendered and why. The physician communicates this by using current procedural terminology (CPT) codes and explains the reasons behind the various services by using diagnosis codes or *International Classification of Diseases and Related Health Problems,* 10th Revision, Clinical Modification (ICD-10) codes. This chapter provides a brief review of these coding systems, along with a discussion of the most common coding errors. To supplement this overview, you should obtain publications that provide detailed explanations of CPT and ICD-10 coding.

Medical Terminology

Billing a physician's services requires a general working knowledge of medical terminology. For example, if a surgeon performs a cholecystectomy, the person billing the procedure at the physician's office must have an idea of what the procedure entails to know which CPT code to choose and whether or not any additional services might have been performed during the operative session. Knowledge of medical terminology is especially important when billing employees must read an operative report or a physician's inpatient communication of other hospital charges to find out exactly what services the physician performed.

Knowledge of medical terminology is also important for anyone responsible for reviewing a practice's billing activities. To make sure that charges are being billed correctly, someone needs to review the work of the practice's billing employees periodically. The reviewer could be someone in the practice, the practice's outside accountant, or the practice's health care consultant.

■ **Practice Point:** To get a firsthand view of how difficult and important it is to bill procedures, obtain an operative re-

> port, read it, and try to determine which codes to use. This is a good way to see the integration of medical terminology, CPT coding, diagnosis code, and charge billing. If you attempt this task, you will understand how easy it is to make mistakes when billing physician services.

In medical terminology, the root element is the main subject of the medical term and often is related to a body part. The prefix of an element is used to change the meaning of the medical term or to make it more specific (e.g., *hemi* means half). The suffix of an element frequently describes a condition of the body part or an action to a body part.

The following is a list of some of the most common elements found in medical terminology:

aden-	gland
angi-	blood vessels
arthr-	joint
cardi-	heart
cerebr-	brain
cholecyst-	gallbladder
dermat-	skin
enter-	intestines
gastr-	stomach
hepat-	liver
megal-	enlarged
nephr-	kidney
path-	disease
plast-	plastic repair
rhin-	nose
-ectomy	surgical removal of all or part of
-itis	inflammation
-oma	tumor
-osis	condition
-otomy	cut into, incision into

Many excellent books are available on the subject of medical terminology. If you want to become even more familiar with the terminology, consider attending a class on the subject.

CPT Codes

CPT was introduced and published by the American Medical Association in 1966. It assigns numeric digits to descriptions of specific medical services. As CPT gained acceptance within the insurance industry, physicians began using these codes to identify the services and procedures they performed. Almost every insurance company now requires physicians' offices to use CPT codes to describe and bill their services. In 1993, the insurance claim form was revised to eliminate word descriptions; only the CPT code is used to describe the service rendered to a patient.

The CPT Book

Each year the American Medical Association updates its list of CPT codes. Generally, 400 to 700 revisions are made to the coding system annually, including the addition of new codes, the deletion of existing codes, and the revision of the word descriptions of other codes. The CPT book indicates which codes are new by placing black dots beside them. Revised codes are indicated with a black triangle.

The CPT book is divided into the following six sections:

1. Evaluation and management services
2. Anesthesia
3. Surgery
4. Radiology
5. Laboratory
6. Medicine services

CPT books can be acquired from the American Medical Association or from the Practice Management Information Corporation. (See Chapter 1 for addresses and phone numbers.)

The Most Common CPT Coding Errors

The most common CPT coding errors found in medical practices and a related discussion of CPT coding basics are as follows.

Error: Coding at the wrong level of service for office visits

A physician must choose among a number of CPT codes to represent the services rendered to each patient during an office visit. The most common visit codes physicians use are as follows:

Office or Other Outpatient Services	
New patient	99201–99205
Established patient	99211–99215
Hospital Inpatient Services	
Initial hospital care	99221–99223
Subsequent daily hospital visits	99231–99233
Hospital discharge management	99238
Consultations	
Office consultations	99241–99245
Initial inpatient consultations	99251–99255
Follow-up inpatient consultations	99261–99263
Confirmatory consultations	99271–99275

When a physician treats a patient, the practice's billing employee must choose one of the CPT codes to bill the patient or the patient's insurance company. The most frequent problem in medical practices is that the wrong codes are chosen. For example, if a new patient is treated in the office and the staff member selects code 99202 when he should have chosen 99203, the practice loses revenue. In the reverse situation, if the staff member chooses code 99203 when he should have chosen 99202, and the employee consistently overcodes these services, the practice could be risking an audit by an insurance carrier, especially if this occurs in Medicare and Medicaid billing.

Each CPT code has its own definition. Acquire a CPT book, familiarize yourself with it, and attend courses on basic CPT coding.

One of the best ways to avoid coding errors is to conduct a meeting with the physician or physicians and the billing employees to discuss specific CPT coding for visits. At this meeting, take the 10 to 20 most common clinical situations that occur in the office and the hospital and match them with the CPT definitions for the related evaluation and management service. For example, a new Medicare patient has diabetes. Using this clinical case, discuss the treatment protocols at the meeting and arrive at an appropriate CPT code. This meeting will alert the physician and employees about what specific codes to use for specific clinical situations.

Another good idea is to review the month-end service frequency report that most computerized medical software packages can produce. This report lists the CPT codes that were used for the particular month and year-to-date, along with a count of how many times the codes were used. By scanning this report, even a person with limited knowledge of CPT coding should be able to see if a practice is undercoding or overcoding its visit services. In most cases, the coding practices of an office should be distributed among the various CPT levels, because different people are treated with different problems and symptoms throughout the month and year. Not everyone is treated for the same problems; thus, one code should not be used all the time. If it looks as if the codes are unevenly distributed, investigate the situation along with the billing personnel.

You can analyze undercoding or overcoding of office visits by creating a worksheet similar to the following one. List the related CPT codes under each category. For example, list all the new patient CPT codes under the heading "New Visits."

CPT Code	Description Utilization Percentage
New Visits	
Established Visits	
Consultations	
Hospital Admits	
Hospital Visits	

A practice that treats sick patients often or treats patients with difficult clinical problems should have a code distribution weighted more heavily toward the higher-level evaluation and management-visit codes. A physician specialist should use consultative codes more often than new or established patient visit codes, in most circumstances. Try to find out the type of clinical situations the office treats most often, review the practice's current coding distribution for related services, and determine if it makes sense. For example, a cardiologist has a very busy inpatient practice. While reviewing the CPT frequency report, you notice that 98 percent of all hospital visits are coded at the highest level of service (99233). This leads you to suspect that overcoding may be occurring and you investigate immediately.

If the medical practice uses a manual system, and a frequency report is not available, review CPT coding practices by scanning insurance claim forms related to evaluation and management services. By scanning these forms, you should be able to tell whether the practice is coding at only one level of service or at various levels of service.

Error: Incorrectly coding a consultation as an office visit

Consultations have a higher standard fee than regular office visits or hospital visits. One way medical specialists lose revenue is by billing a consultation as an office visit. This error is usually caused by the physician or the billing employee not fully understanding the difference between the two services. Coding consultations properly is critical for anyone who treats patients with insurance coverage involving contracted fees, such as Medicare, Medicaid, and managed care. In these situations, physicians cannot increase revenue by increasing their fees; however, they can increase revenue by coding their services properly.

A consultation generally occurs when a physician provides advice or an opinion on a case in response to another physician's request. The request must be documented in the patient's medical record and a written report must be sent to the requesting physician. For example, a person is out jogging and twists his knee. He goes to his family physician, who decides the problem might be a severe sprain or a cartilage tear. The family physician sends the patient to the orthopedist for an opinion of what the problem really is (i.e., the family physician is asking for an opinion of a suspected problem). The orthopedist should code the service as a consultation.

> ■ **Practice Point:** Most consultations are requested of medical specialists, such as cardiologists, pulmonologists, neurologists, and surgeons.

Following are Medicare's guidelines for billing CPT codes for consultations (99241 through 99275). Many other payors adopt these same guidelines for billing consultative encounters.

Medicare will pay for a consultation when all of the criteria for the use of a consultation code are met. First, the consultation must be provided by a physician whose opinion or advice regarding evaluation and/or management of a specific problem is requested by another physician or other appropriate source (unless it is a patient-generated confirmatory consultation).

Second, the request for a consultation from an appropriate source and the need for consultation must be documented in the patient's medical record.

And third, after the consultation is provided, the consultant prepares a written report of his or her findings which is provided to the referring physician.

Consultation followed by treatment   Medicare will pay for an initial consultation if all the criteria for a consultation are satisfied. Payment may be made regardless of treatment initiation unless a transfer of care occurs.

A transfer of care occurs when the referring physician transfers the responsibility for the patient's complete care to the receiving physician at the time of referral, and the receiving physician documents approval of care in advance.

The receiving physician would report either a new or established patient visit depending on the situation (a new patient is one who has not received any professional services from the physician or another physician of the same specialty who belongs to the same group practice, within the past three years) and setting (e.g., office or inpatient).

A physician consultant may initiate diagnostic and/or therapeutic services at an initial or subsequent visit. Subsequent visits (not performed to complete the initial consultation) to manage a portion or all of the patient's condition should be reported as established patient office visit or subsequent hospital care, depending on the setting.

Consultations requested by members of the same group Provided all of the requirements for use of the CPT consultation codes are met, Medicare will pay for a consultation if one physician in a group practice requests a consultation from another physician in the same group practice.

Documentation for consultations As noted, consultations must be properly documented. This includes a request for the consultation from an appropriate source, documentation of the need for consultation in the patient's medical record, and a written report furnished to the requesting physician.

In an emergency department or an inpatient or outpatient setting in which the medical record is shared between the referring physician and the consultant, the request may be documented as the following:

- Part of a plan written in the requesting physician's progress note
- An order in the medical record
- A specific written request for the consultation

In these settings, the report may consist of an appropriate entry in the common medical record.

In an office setting, the documentation requirement may be met in the following ways:

- By a specific written request for the consultation from the requesting physician
- By a specific reference to the request in the consultation record

In this setting, the consultation report is a separate document communicated to the requesting physician.

Consultation for preoperative clearance   Provided all of the requirements for billing consultation codes are met, Medicare will pay for the appropriate consultation code for a preoperative consultation for a new or established patient performed by any physician at the request of a surgeon.

Postoperative care by physician who did preoperative clearance consultation   After a preoperative consultation in the office or hospital, if the consultant assumes responsibility for the management of a portion or all of the patient's condition(s) during the postoperative period, then the consultation codes should not be used. For example, in the hospital setting, the physician who has performed a preoperative consultation and assumes responsibility for the management of some or all of the patient's condition(s) during the postoperative period should use the appropriate subsequent hospital care codes and not the follow-up consultation codes to bill for the concurrent care being provided. In the office setting, the appropriate established patient visit codes should be used during the postoperative period.

Provided all of the criteria for the use of the consultation codes are met and a primary care physician or specialist has not already performed a preoperative consultation, the primary care physician or specialist who performs a postoperative evaluation of a new or established patient at the request of the surgeon may bill the appropriate consultation code for evaluation and management services furnished during the postoperative period following surgery.

Surgeon's request that another physician participate in postoperative care   If a physician who has not seen the patient for a preoperative consultation is asked by the surgeon to take responsibility for the management of an aspect of the patient's condition during the postoperative period, the physician may not bill a consultation. The surgeon is not asking the physician's opinion or advice for the surgeon's use in treating the patient. The physician's services constitute concurrent care and should be billed using the appropriate level visit codes.

The following examples should clarify the rules as to the billing of consultation codes.

Examples of consultations

1. An internist finds a new skin lesion on a patient he has been following for 20 years for mild hypertension and diabetes mellitus. The internist sends the patient to a dermatologist for further evaluation. The dermatologist examines the patient and removes the lesion, which is determined to be an early melanoma. The dermatologist sends a report to the internist regarding his evaluation and treatment of the patient.

2. A general ophthalmologist diagnosed retinal detachment. Because he does not treat this specific problem, he sends the patient to a retinal subspecialist for evaluation. The retinal subspecialist evaluates the patient and schedules surgery. He sends a report to the referring physician explaining his findings and the treatment option selected.

3. A family physician diagnoses a patient with diabetes mellitus. In response to a request from the physician, an ophthalmologist conducts a baseline evaluation to rule out diabetic retinopathy. The ophthalmologist examines the patient and sends a report to the family physician on his findings. If the ophthalmologist tells the patient at the time of service to return in one year for a follow-up visit, this subsequent follow-up visit should be billed as an established patient visit in the office or other outpatient setting, as appropriate.

4. A rural family practice physician diagnoses a new onset of atrial fibrillation in a long-term patient and sends the patient to a cardiologist at an urban cardiology center for advice on his care and management. The cardiologist examines the patient and suggests a cardiac catheterization and other diagnostic tests, which he schedules. He then sends a written report to the requesting physician.

   Subsequent annual follow-up visits provided by the cardiologist should be billed as an established patient visit in the office or other outpatient setting, as appropriate.

5. A family practice physician diagnoses a breast mass in a female patient who has been under his care for some time. The family practitioner sends the patient to a general surgeon for advice, management of the mass, and related patient care. The general surgeon examines the patient and recommends a breast

biopsy. Then he sends a written report to the requesting physician. The general surgeon subsequently performs a biopsy.

The surgeon routinely sees the patient once a year as follow-up, which should be billed as an established patient visit in the office or other outpatient setting, as appropriate.

6. An internist diagnoses a thyroid mass in a patient who has been under her care for some time. She refers the patient to a general surgeon for advice on management of the mass and related patient care. The general surgeon examines the patient, orders diagnostic tests, suggests a needle biopsy of the mass, schedules the procedure, and sends a written report to the requesting physician. The general surgeon subsequently performs a thin-needle biopsy and then routinely sees the patient twice as follow-up for the mass. Subsequent visits provided by the surgeon should be billed as an established patient visit in the office or other outpatient setting, as appropriate.

7. A patient with underlying diabetes mellitus and renal insufficiency is seen in the emergency room with fever, cough, and purulent sputum. Since it is not clear to the emergency room physician whether the patient needs to be admitted, he requests an opinion by the on-call internist. The internist may bill a consultation. This occurs regardless of whether the patient is discharged from the emergency room or admitted to the hospital provided the criteria for consultation have been met. If the internist admits the patient to the hospital, he may bill either an initial inpatient consultation or initial hospital care code, but not both for the same date of service.

The criteria for consultations will not be satisfied if there are standing orders in the medical record for consultations, if there is no order for a consultation, or if there is no written report of a consultation. For example, an internist receives a call from her patient with a complaint of abdominal pain. Although it is after hours, the internist believes this requires immediate evaluation and advises the patient to meet her in the emergency room, where she evaluates him. The emergency room physician does not see the patient. The internist should bill for the appropriate level of emergency care.

To make sure that consultations are billed correctly, first determine whether the practice sees patients referred by other physicians. The service frequency report produced by the computer should be helpful in this regard.

If the medical practice is having trouble identifying consultative visits, train the front-desk employee to identify these situations. The intake process should reveal why the patients are in the office and whether they were referred to the office by other physicians. If the front-desk employee determines that the patient is in for a consultation, the employee could make a note on the Superbill to alert the physician to the possible consultation. The physician then makes the final decision on whether the visit is a consultation.

> ■ **Practice Point:** If a practice uses the consultation codes often, make sure that the office's Superbill lists these CPT codes first. This will immediately bring such codes to the physician's attention. If the consultation codes are buried in the middle of the charge ticket, a consultation often is miscoded as a regular office visit, and the physician loses revenue.

One of the most common billing errors and misinterpretations involves the billing of critical care services. It is important to keep up on these issues in order to prevent a compliance problem resulting from the improper coding of these services or, more importantly, prevent missed revenue due to billing the wrong CPT code when it should have been the higher paying critical care code.

The following highlights important points on critical care CPT codes from the Program Memorandum (Transmittal Number B-99-43), issued by the U.S. Department of Health and Human Services in December 1999.

Use of the Critical Care CPT Codes 99291 and 99292

(A) Definition of Critical Illness or Injury

The AMA's CPT defines a critical illness or injury as follows:

A critical illness or injury acutely impairs one or more vital organ systems such that the patient's survival is jeopardized. Please note that the term "unstable" is no longer used in the CPT definition to describe critically ill or injured patients.

(B) Definition of Critical Care Services

CPT 2000 has redefined critical care services as follows:

> *Critical care is the direct delivery by a physician(s) of medical care for a critically ill or injured patient. . . . The care of such patients involves decision making of high complexity to assess, manipulate, and support central nervous system failure, circulatory failure, shock-like conditions, renal, hepatic, metabolic, or respiratory failure, postoperative complications, overwhelming infection, or other vital system functions to treat single or multiple vital organ system failure or to prevent further deterioration. It may require extensive interpretation of multiple databases and the application of advanced technology to manage the patient. Critical care may be provided on multiple days, even if no changes are made in the treatment rendered to the patient, provided that the patient's condition continues to require the level of physician attention described above.*

> *Critical care services include but are not limited to, the treatment or prevention or further deterioration of central nervous system failure, circulatory failure, shock-like conditions, renal, hepatic, metabolic or respiratory failure, postoperative complications, or overwhelming infection. Critical care is usually, but not always, given in a critical care area, such as the coronary care unit, intensive care unit, pediatric intensive care unit, respiratory care unit, or the emergency care facility.*

(C) Guidelines for Use Whenever Medical Review Is Performed in Relation to Critical Illness and Critical Care Service

There must be a high probability of sudden, clinically significant, or life-threatening deterioration in the patient's condition which requires the highest level of physician preparedness to intervene urgently.

> *Critical care services require direct personal management by the physician. They are life and organ supporting interventions that require frequent, personal assessment and manipulation by the physician. Withdrawal of, or failure to initiate these interventions on an urgent basis would likely result in sudden, clinically significant or life-threatening deterioration in the patient's condition.*

> *Claims for critical care services will therefore be denied if the services are not reasonable and medically necessary. If the services are reasonable and medically necessary but they do not meet the*

criteria for critical care services, then the services should be re-coded as another appropriate E/M service (e.g., hospital visit).

Providing medical care to a critically ill patient should not be au-tomatically determined to be a critical care service for the sole reason that the patient is critically ill. This is a common billing mis-take made by many medical offices. The physician service must be medically necessary and meet the definition of critical care ser-vices as described previously in order to be considered covered.

EXAMPLE: A dermatologist treating a rash on an ICU patient who is maintained on a ventilator and nitroglycerine drip which are being managed by an intensivist should not bill for critical care.

(D) "Full Attention" Requirement for Critical Care Service

The CPT critical care codes 99291 and 99292 are used to report the total duration of time spent by a physician providing critical care ser-vices to a critically ill or critically injured patient, even if the time spent by the physician on that date is not continuous. For any given period of time spent providing critical care services, the physician must de-vote his or her full attention to the patient and, therefore, cannot pro-vide services to any other patient during the same period of time.

(E) Reporting of Physician Time Toward Critical Care Time

Time spent with the individual patient should be recorded in the patient's record. The time that can be reported as critical care is the time spent engaged in work directly related to the individual patient's care whether that time was spent at the immediate bedside or else-where on the floor or unit.

Time spent in activities that occur outside of the unit or off the floor (e.g., telephone calls, whether taken at home, in the office, or elsewhere in the hospital) may not be reported as critical care since the physician is not immediately available to the patient. Time spent in activities that do not directly contribute to the treatment of the patient may not be reported as critical care, even if they are performed in the critical care unit (e.g., participation in adminis-trative meetings or telephone calls to discuss other patients).

(F) Non-Critically Ill or Injured Patients in a Critical Care Unit

Services for a patient who is not critically ill but happens to be in a critical care unit are reported using other appropriate E/M codes. This too is another common billing error made by medical offices. Many doctors and their billers assume that just because they see a patient in ICU they can bill critical care codes.

More Coding Errors

Error: Failure to use CPT modifiers

Modifiers are numerical descriptors that are added to CPT codes to provide further detail about a patient's visit. These modifiers help to explain further the services rendered.

Here are two common modifiers:

-24   Unrelated evaluation and management service by the same physician during a postoperative period

-25   Separately identifiable evaluation and management service by the same physician on the same day as a procedure

Example

Proper Use of the -25 and -76 Modifiers

The following modifier is used to report an Evaluation and Management (E&M) service that resulted in a decision to perform a minor surgical procedure or to indicate the patient's condition required a significant, separately identifiable E&M service.

-25 Modifier—Significant, separately identifiable evaluation and management service by the same physician on the same day of the procedure or other service   The physician may need to indicate that on the day a procedure or service, identified by a CPT code, was performed the patient's condition required a significant, separately identifiable E&M service above and beyond the other service provided or beyond the usual preoperative and postoperative care associated with the procedure that was performed. When these conditions exist and the procedure is a minor procedure (has a one-day or 10-day global period), use the -25 modifier. Primary considerations for using the -25 modifier are:

- Why the physician is seeing the patient.

- If the patient exhibits symptoms from which the physician diagnoses the condition and begins treatment by performing a minor procedure or an endoscopy on that same day, the -25 modifier should be added to the correct level of the E&M service.

- If the patient is present for the minor procedure or endoscopy only, the -25 modifier does not apply.

- If the E&M service was to familiarize the patient with the minor procedure or endoscopy immediately before the procedure, the -25 modifier does not apply.

- If the E&M service is related to the decision to perform a major procedure, the -25 modifier is not appropriate. The correct modifier for decision for surgery is -57.

Finally, note the -25 modifier is meant to be used with E&M services associated with procedures.

-76 Modifier—Repeat procedure by the same physician   The physician may need to indicate the procedure or service was repeated subsequent to the original procedure or service on the same date. This circumstance may be reported by adding the -76 modifier to the repeated procedure or service. For Medicare purposes, this modifier is an informational modifier used for a procedure/service other than surgical. The following are a few examples of how this modifier is used in practice:

Example

A patient comes into the emergency room with complaints of chest pains. At 9:00 a.m. the physician orders a chest X-ray. Later that afternoon, the physician sees the patient again and orders the second chest X-ray. This would be coded to Medicare as:

71010 Single view chest X-ray

71010-76 Second single view chest X-ray

Example

A patient visits the physician on Wednesday morning for a bladder infection. She is treated and sent home. That same afternoon, the patient returns to the physician's office with a twisted ankle. Proper coding would be:

99213 Bladder irrigation

99213-76 Established patient office visit

In certain cases, if modifiers are not attached to the related CPT codes, the physician's billed charges might be denied. Billing personnel and even the practice's accountant should be knowledgeable in modifier billing. To determine whether or not a practice is using modifiers properly, review a sample of the explanation of benefits (EOBs). Look for denials of billed charges. If specific charges have been denied because modifiers were not attached to the CPT codes, inform the practice and investigate the situation further.

> ■ **Practice Point:** One area of lost revenue for surgeons is the failure to bill for postoperative visits resulting from a complication of the surgery. One example is a return visit due to an abscess of the suture area. While carrier policy varies, most times this visit can be billed as long as the appropriate modifier and diagnosis code are used. Refer to Medicare regulations for instructions related to Medicare patients.

Error: Incorrectly billing multiple surgical procedures

A surgeon may perform more than one procedure during an operative session. Most insurance companies believe that it is less expensive to perform multiple surgical procedures during one operative session than it is to perform the procedures at different times. Therefore, the companies will not pay the physician's full fee for all the procedures performed. Most insurance companies will pay the complete fee for one procedure, 50 percent of the fee for another procedure, and 25 percent of all other procedures. Some billing employees fail to fill out the insurance claim form properly to maximize charge reimbursement.

Example

A patient has surgery in which the physician performs two procedures. The normal physician's fees are $2,500 for procedure C and

$1,000 for procedure D. The billing employee prepares the insurance claim form by listing procedure D first and procedure C second. The insurance company pays the entire $1,000 and only 50 percent of the $2,500 charge, for a total payment of $2,250. However, if the employee had listed procedure C first and procedure D second, the physician would have received $3,000 in payment, an additional $750.

To maximize reimbursement, the billing employee should always list on the insurance claim form procedures with the highest fee first. The physician's full standard fee should always be listed on the form. If the second procedure is reduced by 50 percent by the billing employee, he or she should inform the insurance company about this. Otherwise, the insurance company will only reimburse 50 percent of the already reduced fee. Many practices inform the insurance company by writing directly on the claim form that they have already reduced the fee. The billing employee should also use the appropriate CPT modifier for multiple surgical procedures (modifier -51).

To make sure that the practice is properly billing multiple surgical procedures, scan a sample of insurance claim forms to see whether the procedures are properly ranked from highest surgical fee to lowest surgical fee. This exercise assumes that the practice's surgical fee schedule has been properly developed. Also make sure that the physician's fees are appropriate. Sometimes a low surgical fee will be attached to a procedure that deserves a higher fee. When scanning the claim forms, make sure that the multiple procedure modifier is used.

Error: Incorrectly billing incidental surgical procedures

Incidental surgical procedures are services insurance companies feel are secondary in importance to the other surgical procedures that the physician performed, and thus are not considered medically necessary. The best example is an appendectomy. Frequently, when surgery is performed in the abdomen, the surgeon will remove the appendix to ensure that the patient will never have appendicitis. Because insurance companies say that the procedure is not medically necessary, they will not pay for it. The practice must then decide to bill the patient or write it off. Most practices write it off, because patients balk at paying for anything their insurance companies have not deemed to be medically necessary.

A problem that occurs in most surgical practices is that the billing person reviews the operative note before preparing the insurance claim form. He or she then bills for every procedure listed on the note. If an incidental surgical procedure is listed on the claim form, the insurance company will deny payment and the charge will remain in the practice's accounts receivable balance until the physician or the office manager decides to bill the patient or write it off. If the practice does not write it off, accounts receivable will have a tendency to inflate. Therefore, advise the practice not to bill incidental surgical procedures unless the billing employee knows that the insurance company will pay for such procedures. To determine if the company will pay for incidental procedures, have the billing employee call the insurance company before an incidental procedure is billed and find out if the service is going to be paid. (The billing person should compile a list of the specific circumstances under which various insurance companies pay for incidental procedures.) The practice can also bill incidental procedures if the patient has been informed of the insurance company's denial to pay, and the patient agrees beforehand to pay for the service.

Error: Incorrectly billing outpatient observation services

Observation services are those services furnished on the premises of the medical office, including use of a bed and periodic monitoring by nursing or other staff, which are reasonable and necessary to evaluate an outpatient's condition or determine the need for a possible admission as an inpatient. Such services are covered only when provided by the order of a physician or another individual authorized by state licensure law and hospital bylaws to admit patients to the hospital or to order outpatient tests. Observation services include acute care services.

One day or less of outpatient observation services Generally a person is considered a hospital inpatient if formally admitted as an inpatient with the expectation that he or she will remain at least overnight. When a patient is placed under observation but not formally admitted as an inpatient, the person is initially regarded as an outpatient. Many observation patients recover sufficiently to be discharged on the same day that observation services began. Clearly, they are classified as outpatients. Others worsen or are found, on evaluation, to require inpatient care and are formally admitted as inpatients on the same day. The day of admittance is counted as the first inpatient day.

Second day of outpatient observation services   Some observation patients continue to require observation overnight. They may be discharged, or formally admitted, on the following day. If patients are not admitted but are released on that day, they are classified as outpatients. If a patient is formally admitted on that day, this is counted as the first inpatient day.

Services denied on third day of outpatient observation services   If a patient is retained in observation status for a second night without a formal inpatient admission having occurred, further observation services are denied. If a medical practice bills for observation room services that span more than two days, the bill will be rejected. A physician may request an exception to the denial of services from the intermediary.

The following services are not considered observation services and, therefore, are not covered:

- Services that are not reasonable or necessary for the diagnosis or treatment of the patient but are provided for the convenience of the patient or a physician

- Services which are covered under Part A or as part of another Part B benefit, such as services that are defined as facility services and subject to the ambulatory surgical center (ASC) payment rate or, in the case of patients who undergo diagnostic testing in a hospital outpatient department, routine recovery procedures/services furnished prior to the testing

- Services for routine postoperative monitoring during a normal recovery period (four to six hours)

- Any substitution of an outpatient observation service for a medically appropriate inpatient admission

Examples

1. A patient comes to the emergency room complaining of difficulty breathing. The patient is seen by the physician on duty, who orders laboratory tests, including a blood gas analysis, and an injection to help the patient breathe more easily. The physician then has the patient placed in an outpatient observation unit to determine whether this intervention produces normal breathing. Six hours later the patient is again seen by the physician, who determines from the patient's chart and his own observation that the patient's vital signs are normal and the patient has resumed normal breathing. The patient is released. Under these circumstances, the outpatient observation services are covered, and the bill submitted by the hospital may include charges for those services.

2. A patient comes to a hospital's outpatient department to undergo a scheduled surgical procedure which is not a covered ASC surgical procedure. After surgery, the patient is taken to the recovery room, where he exhibits difficulty in awakening from anesthesia and an elevated blood pressure. These conditions persist, and the patient is seen by a physician, who has him placed on observation. The physician leaves orders for the nursing staff to monitor the patient's condition and note any continued abnormalities that could indicate a drug reaction or other post-surgical complications. After a few hours, the patient no longer is lethargic, has a normal blood pressure and shows no other signs of post-surgical complications. The physician, upon being advised of these conditions, orders the patient released from the hospital. Under these circumstances, coverage of outpatient observation services begins when the patient was placed in the observation bed. Services received in the hospital's outpatient surgical suite and recovery room cannot be covered as observation services, because they are otherwise covered under Part B.

3. A patient is scheduled to have an uncomplicated cataract extraction on an outpatient basis. The patient expresses a preference for spending the night following the procedure at the hospital despite the fact that the procedure does not require an

overnight stay. The hospital may register and treat the patient on an outpatient basis and permit the patient to remain at the hospital overnight. The overnight stay cannot be covered as observation services because it is not medically necessary. When this is the case, the patient must be notified that the overnight stay is not medically necessary and may be charged for the additional services. If unforeseen complications necessitate inpatient admission, the patient is admitted and a Part A claim is submitted.

4. A patient comes to the emergency room in the evening with a complaint of sudden severe flank pain which radiates to the inner thigh, nausea, vomiting, and urinary frequency and urgency. Examination reveals soreness over the kidney area, spasm of the abdominal muscles, and microscopic hematuria. Additionally, an X-ray reveals the presence of a stone in the ureter. The patient is admitted to the hospital as an inpatient at 11:00 p.m. He is treated with I.V. fluids, IM Morphine, and an antispasmodic every four hours. Further diagnostic studies are scheduled for the following morning. During the night, the patient passes a stone through the urethra without complications. The patient is then comfortable without nausea or urinary symptoms. Therefore, the patient is discharged at 9:00 a.m. and scheduled for follow-up in the physician's office. Although the patient was able to be discharged in less than 24 hours, the admission was appropriate, because it was reasonable to expect at the time of admission that the presenting problem would require more than 24 hours to resolve.

CPT Modifiers

As previously mentioned, problems can occur with CPT modifiers. A modifier provides a means by which a physician or other practitioner can indicate that a service or procedure was altered by specific circumstances. Modifiers can be reported in two ways:

1. Appended to the procedure number usually reported. If the practice's computer system allows the practice to use eight or more digits to report a service on one line, it may choose to append the two-digit modifier; or

2. Reported by using a separate five-digit code along with the procedure code. If the computer does not allow the practice to report more than five digits on one line, then it should list the procedure on the first line and the five-digit modifier on the next.

The following is a summary of the most common modifiers used by practicing physicians:

-21 Prolonged Evaluation and Management Services: Use this modifier when a face-to-face service provided is prolonged or otherwise greater than that usually required for the highest level of E/M (evaluation and management) service.

-24 Unrelated Evaluation and Management Service by the Same Physician During a Post-Operative Period: Use this modifier if a patient is seen during the global surgery period for a condition that is unrelated to the original surgery.

-25 Significant, Separately Identifiable Evaluation and Management Service by the Same Physician on the Same Day of the Procedure or Other Service: The physician may need to indicate that on the day a procedure or service identified by a CPT code was performed, the patient's condition required a significant, separately identifiable E/M (evaluation and management) service above and beyond the other service provided or beyond the usual preoperative and postoperative care associated with the procedure that was performed. The E/M service may be prompted by the symptom or condition for which the procedure and/or service was provided. As such, different diagnoses are not required for reporting of the E/M services on the same date. This circumstance may be reported by adding the modifier "-25" to the appropriate level of E/M service, or the separate five-digit modifier 09925 may be used.

-26 Professional Component: Certain procedures are a combination of a physician component and a technical component. Used when the physician component is reported separately, the service may be identified by adding the modifier "-26" to the usual procedure number.

-50 **Bilateral Procedure:** Unless otherwise identified in the listings, bilateral procedures that are performed at the same operative session should be identified by adding the modifier "-50" to the appropriate five-digit CPT code.

-51 **Multiple Procedures:** When multiple procedures are performed at the same surgical session by the same provider, the primary procedure or service may be reported as listed. The additional procedure(s) or service(s) may be identified by appending the modifier "-51" to the additional procedure codes.

-54 **Surgical Care Only:** Used when one physician performs a surgical procedure and another physician provides preoperative and/or postoperative management services.

-55 **Postoperative Management Only:** Used when one physician performs the postoperative management and another physician has performed the surgical procedure.

-56 **Preoperative Management Only:** Used when one physician performs the preoperative care for a patient and another physician performs the surgical procedure.

-57 **Decision for Surgery:** Used when an E/M service resulted in the initial decision to perform a surgery. The modifier is attached to the E/M CPT code.

-76 **Repeat Procedure by the Same Physician:** Used when a physician may need to indicate that a surgical procedure was repeated subsequent to the original procedure.

-77 **Repeat Procedure by Another Physician:** Used when a physician has to repeat a procedure performed by another physician.

-78 **Return to the Operating Room for a Related Procedure during the Postoperative Period:** Used when a physician may need to indicate that another procedure was performed during the postoperative period of an initial surgical procedure.

-79 **Unrelated Procedure or Service by the Same Physician during the Postoperative Period:** Used when a physician has to perform a surgical procedure during the postoperative period that is unrelated to the initial procedure.

Carriers' CPT Coding Policies

Many medical practices try to guess which CPT codes insurance companies will pay for and, accordingly, which CPT codes should be billed. To assist a medical practice in optimizing revenue from proper CPT coding, list the practice's most commonly billed insurance plans and determine their CPT coding preferences. One of the best ways to do this is to call or write to each carrier and ask for its specific policies about CPT coding rules. Most medical practices should know the answers to the following questions:

1. **Does the insurance company use the current version of the CPT book?**   This alerts the practice to what codes it can and cannot use. If the practice bills codes that are not in the insurance company's computer, payment will be denied simply because the code is not recognized.

2. **Does the insurance company currently allow providers to bill the new CPT codes and modifiers added per the last revision to the CPT book?**   If needed, the practice should inquire about specific codes and modifiers that apply to the practice. If the billing employee does not know this information, he or she should have the physician review the CPT book and indicate specific new codes and modifiers that can be used in the practice. Again, the practice should use the insurance company's answer to determine the correct codes and modifiers to bill.

3. **How does the insurance company define the global surgical package?**   The insurance company's answer tells the practice when it can bill certain services (e.g., hospital admission and postoperative complications) and when it cannot (e.g., hospital discharge and visits in the postoperative period).

4. **Does the insurance company allow the billing of follow-up visits in the postoperative period if they are the result of complications of the original surgery?**   The answer alerts the practice to bill a charge any time a patient is treated in the office because of complications. For example, some insurance companies pay for treating an infection in the suture area, and some include the service as part of the global surgical package.

5. **What, if any, is the insurance company's standard postoperative period for most surgical procedures?** The practice may want to ask about specific surgical CPT codes the practice bills most often. This tells the billing employee when the practice can bill a postoperative visit and when it cannot.

6. **Does the insurance company allow the billing of Medicare Health Care Financing Administration Common Procedure Coding system (HCPCS) codes for specific services? If so, which ones?** Because HCPCS codes are quite specific in their descriptions, especially for medical supplies, they can be more informative than CPT codes.

7. **What is the insurance company's policy on the billing of medical supplies? Are there any specific limitations for this medical specialty?** Find out if the insurance company will pay for any and all supplies used in a specified patient visit (e.g., the removal of a foreign body from the eye). Will the insurance company pay the ophthalmologist for the surgical tray and eye patch separately? Also, find out if the insurance company wants the physician to bill supplies using CPT code 99070 or HCPCS code A4550.

8. **How are multiple surgical procedures reimbursed?** The practice needs to make sure it ranks the surgeries correctly on the insurance claim form (with the most expensive service first).

9. **Does the insurance company allow a visit on the same day as a surgical procedure?** For example, if a cardiologist sees a patient in the emergency room and performs a heart catheterization on the same day, the practice will need to make sure that it bills for the visit or finds out under what circumstances the insurance company will pay for the visit. Also, find out if the insurance company wants the practice to bill supplies using CPT code 99070 or HCPCS code A4550.

10. **Does the insurance company use a relative-value system to determine fee profiles? If so, which one?** The answer to this question will help the practice set its own fee schedule. For example, the practice should revise its fee schedule using the Ingenix Relative Values for Physicians study if most of the insurance

plans the practice works with are using the study to set their reimbursement profiles.

11. **Does the insurance company plan to adopt the Medicare RBRVS payment methodology any time soon?** If a carrier plans to adopt this system, you will want to calculate the practice's internal current conversion factor. When the change is made, compare the practice's conversion factor to the carrier's conversion factor and analyze the payment discount.

12. **Are there any cases in which the insurance company will not pay for an assistant at surgery?** Again, the practice needs to make sure it bills only for those services for which it will be reimbursed.

13. **Does the insurance company "bundle" any CPT codes?** If so, the practice should find out which ones so that billing mistakes will not occur in the future.

Once answers to these questions are obtained, summarize them on one sheet of paper for the billing staff. Finally, talk to the physician and other personnel to find out if there are any other important billing questions that need to be answered.

■ **Practice Point:** The information obtained from insurance companies and other information related to the practice's most commonly used insurance carriers can be kept in a notebook. The notebook should contain the answers to the 12 questions, reimbursement rates for the top 25 utilized CPT codes, and the provider contract, if one was executed (e.g., for managed-care plans).

Diagnosis Codes

A diagnosis code is used to explain the reasons behind the service being rendered. Every CPT code must have a related diagnosis code or codes. Diagnosis codes can be found in the *International Classification of Diseases and Related Health Problems,* 10th Revision, Clinical Modification (ICD-10), which is published by the World Health Organization and released by other commercial vendors such as the Practice Management Information Corporation.

Diagnosis codes are made up of three-digit categories and four- and five-digit subcategories.

An insurance claim form must always include a diagnosis code. The absence of diagnosis codes will result in payment denials and delays. Each time a service is billed, the employee must select the most specific diagnosis code possible and make sure that the code goes out to the fourth or fifth digit, if necessary. One of the best ways you can detect problems with diagnosis coding is to review the explanation of benefits (EOB) periodically. (For more information about EOBs, see Chapter 13.) For example, a practice bills an insurance company, and the charge is denied. The reason given on the EOB is "Diagnosis does not relate to the service billed." In this situation, the billing employee will have to change the diagnosis code and rebill the insurance company.

HCPCS Codes

The Health Care Financing Administration Common Procedure Coding System (HCPCS) is a coding system used by Medicare. The HCPCS coding system has three levels:

1. CPT codes
2. National codes
3. Local codes

CPT codes are the same codes developed and updated by the American Medical Association. National codes are designed and implemented by the Health Care Financing Administration. These codes are used to bill Medicare only. Other insurance companies rarely accept Medicare codes. Local codes are designed and implemented by each state's Medicare carrier. These codes are being phased out because of the national standardization of HCPCS coding. Review a book on HCPCS coding to become familiar with this coding system. Use this book to determine if the practice can bill specific services using HCPCS codes instead of using CPT codes. Because HCPCS codes are more detailed in many circumstances (e.g., supplies), an office treating Medicare patients may be able to increase its reimbursement levels. Many HCPCS books are released by commercial vendors such as the Practice Management Information Corporation. Also review the Medicare newsletters, past and present. They will give specific information on how and when to bill these codes. Finally, review the Medicare manual produced by the state's Medicare carrier. It should have specific information regarding the use of HCPCS codes.

Documenting Services Rendered

The services the physician performs must be documented in a patient's medical record. The documentation in the medical record must always support the CPT and diagnosis codes that were billed to the patient or his or her insurance company. For example, if a physician bills over two-thirds of her established patient office visits at the next-to-highest CPT code (99214), the documentation in the patient charts should support this level of service.

The policy of most insurance companies is that if the service is not documented, it did not happen. Medicare's policy on this issue is especially strict. A medical record could be the patient's office chart, the operative report, the hospital medical record, or any type of progress notes. If the practice is audited by an insurance carrier, insufficient documentation may result in the practice having to reimburse the insurance company for what it may consider overpayments. If the practice is using an inordinate percentage of the higher levels of visit services, make sure that the documentation in the medical records supports the use of these higher codes.

For evaluation and management services, medical records must include documentation of the following:

- The patient's chief complaint
- The patient's history
- The physical examination and review of systems
- Medical decision-making
- The treatment or management plan
- The consultation/coordination of care

The principles of proper medical record documentation can be found in *Principles of Medical Record Documentation*, which was coproduced by the American Medical Association, Health Insurance Association of America, and other related entities. Contact the American Medical Association for more information.

The following list summarizes the medical record documentation principles:

- The medical record should be complete and legible.
- The documentation of each encounter with a patient should include the following:
  —Date
  —Reason for the encounter
  —Appropriate history and physical examination
  —Review of laboratory, X-ray, and other ancillary services
  —Assessment
  —Plan for care, including discharge plan if appropriate
- Past and present diagnoses should be accessible to the treating and consulting physician.
- The reason for and the results of laboratory tests, X-rays, and other ancillary services should be documented.
- Relevant health risks should be identified.
- The patient's progress should be documented.
- The written plan of care should include, when appropriate, treatments, medications, any referrals and consultations, patient/family education, and specific instructions for following up.
- Documentation should support the intensity of the patient's evaluation and treatment, including thought processes and the complexity of medical decision-making.
- All entries to the medical record should be dated and authenticated.

The medical office should have its medical records reviewed periodically. The practice should either engage a consultant or have an employee familiar with coding guidelines and chart documentation review a sample of the office's medical records, both inpatient and outpatient. The reviewer should compare what was billed with the related documentation in the medical record. If the documentation does not support the billing, the reviewer should investigate immediately and institute corrective action. The reviewer should also determine if the problem lies with the physician, the billing personnel, or both.

Every year, numerous changes are made to CPT codes, diagnosis codes, and HCPCS codes. These changes affect many areas of a medical practice. Therefore, each year, a practice must review code changes and assess which internal documents must be revised. Almost every year the practice's chargemaster, Superbill, hospital or surgery encounter forms, and ancillary service forms (such as laboratory and X-ray forms) must be revised. If these forms are not revised to take into account annual code changes, the practice could experience denials of its billings or, at a minimum, delays in payment. Remind the practice that most insurance plans do not implement these annual changes until at least March 31 of each year.

Finally, every medical practice must purchase a new CPT, ICD-10, and HCPCS book every year. These publications are absolutely essential for a practice to implement coding changes. One easy way to determine if a medical office is up-to-date with its coding practices is to ask the office manager to show you a copy of the practice's CPT and diagnosis coding books. If the manager can produce only old copies, the practice is more than likely experiencing coding problems that you can help solve.

▼ CHAPTER 11
Filing Insurance Claims

A patient's insurance coverage generally falls into one of three groups of insurance carriers: commercial, managed care, or governmental (Medicare, Medicaid, or Workers' Compensation). Some patients might have a combination of insurance coverage, such as Medicare and commercial insurance, also referred to as *Medicare supplement, Medigap,* or *secondary insurance.* Before a medical office files an insurance claim for a patient, a staff member needs to find out which insurance is the patient's primary insurance and which is the patient's secondary insurance by verifying the patient's coverage with the insurance company.

Insurance Verification

A staff member should verify all insurance coverage with the carrier in each of the following situations:

1. If a patient is going to be admitted to a hospital
2. If a patient will have many visits to the office over an extended period
3. If the office believes the patient's insurance coverage might have terminated, might be limited, or might have changed in any way
4. If the physician will perform a procedure on the patient, even if it is performed in the office
5. If the office believes the patient may become personally responsible for payment of the service, such as in the case of a deductible or when coverage for the particular service has terminated

Insurance is usually verified before a patient arrives for an appointment. The patient's insurance information can be obtained over the telephone when he or she makes an appointment. However, the front-desk employee can verify insurance coverage for each patient while the patient waits in the reception area or is in the exam room. For example, a patient calls the obstetrician for an appointment. She has tested positive using a home pregnancy test and wants to verify her pregnancy. When the patient checks in, the employee asks for her insurance card and calls the insurance company to verify coverage. This can all be done before the patient leaves the office.

If a patient requires admission to a hospital, insurance coverage needs to be verified with the carrier before the patient is admitted. The best time to do this is before the patient's office appointment. If the office implements the policy to verify the coverage before a patient's appointment, the receptionist will need to obtain the insurance information from the patient when the appointment is scheduled. This way, if coverage for the service is limited, the office can determine how much of the fee the patient will ultimately have to pay, and the office can discuss a payment arrangement with the patient before the service is rendered. For example, a patient needs an appendectomy. Based on the insurance verification of coverage, the patient will be responsible for 20 percent of the physician's surgical charge. When the patient goes to the office for a pre-op visit, the receptionist informs the patient that he has to pay 20 percent of the surgical charge. The patient pays half of the amount owed as a surgical deposit.

■ **Practice Point:** You should encourage the practice to collect the entire amount paid. At a minimum, a surgical deposit should be obtained or a payment agreement reached.

Finally, an insurance verification form must be completed and filed as part of the patient's record every time insurance coverage is confirmed. (See Appendix B for a sample verification of insurance coverage form.)

■ **Practice Point:** One excellent way to detect verification problems is to review the explanation of benefits (EOBs) periodically. Look specifically for denied charges with the following or similar denial messages on the EOB: "Patient no longer covered under this insurance plan" or "This service is not covered."

To determine which system would be more efficient for a particular medical practice, speak with the receptionist or the individual responsible for verifying insurance coverage. Find out if the verification process causes the office to fall behind in other important responsibilities and discuss possible solutions. Often, verification can be eliminated for many new patients' office visits as long as the office obtains a copy of the insurance card. However, there will be exceptions in some offices. For example, an obstetrics/gynecology office must know the details of an expectant mother's insurance coverage so that the appropriate financial arrangements can be made for the co-payment amount related to the delivery.

Some insurance companies require precertification before a surgical procedure is performed or before a patient can be admitted to the hospital. Basically, managed-care plans require precertification; it is their way of clearing a physician to perform the surgery, admitting the patient into the hospital, or performing another type of service. In such cases, the patient should be precertified either before hospital admission or at the time of insurance verification, if possible.

■ **Practice Point:** If the practice is having trouble verifying insurance in a timely manner, first speak with the receptionist. The receptionist may be having difficulty obtaining all of the patient's insurance information or may not have the time to do so. If that is the case, you or the manager of the practice and the receptionist should try to solve this problem.

Preparing an Insurance Claim Form

If a patient does not pay for the visit at the time of service, the office will need to prepare and file an insurance claim form with the patient's insurance company to receive payment. (See Appendix B for a sample health insurance claim form.) The manner in which the insurance claim form is completed will depend on the type of insurance.

To receive payment from the insurance company, the office must prepare the insurance claim form correctly. This is what is known as filing a clean claim. Every relevant box on the form must be completed, with special emphasis on such items as the patient's insurance information, the patient's authorization to pay benefits, the name of the referring physician, the referring physician's identification number if the patient has Medicare coverage, the diagnosis code, the current procedural terminology (CPT) code, the dates of service, the place of service, and the type of service. Any error in these or other boxes will cause payment to be denied or delayed. For example, for a Medicare claim submission, the referring physician's name and related unique provider identification number (PIN) must be shown in line items 17 and 17a. If placed in another location on the claim form, the claim will be rejected. Also, the office should always prepare claims using a typewriter or a printer. Handwritten claims may delay payment of the claim because of illegibility.

To aid in prompt claims processing, the office should do the following:

- Change computer toner frequently to maintain dark print.

- Avoid dot matrix printers if possible, since the printing is light.

- When typing, make sure that data is in the appropriate box and that the typing does not cross the lines.

- Always maintain clear separation between letters and do not squeeze information between lines.

Following are some of the items that must be included on the related line items on the insurance claim form (officially called the "HCFA 1500 Insurance Claim Form"). If the practice is having difficulty receiving payment from insurance companies, first make sure it is filing clean claims.

Item 1 This item on the claim form indicates the patient's type of health insurance coverage. For example, if a Medicare claim is being submitted, the Medicare box should be checked or marked.

Item 1a This is either the patient's Social Security number or Medicare health insurance claim number. The patient's insurance card contains this information.

Items 4 and 6   Item 4 is the name of the person who is actually insured. Item 6 states the patient's relationship to the insured. For example, if a child who is covered as a dependent on the father's health insurance policy is taken to the pediatrician, the father's name would go on line item 4, and the child would be indicated on item 6.

Items 11 and 11c   These line items list the group and policy numbers and must always be completed if the patient has a primary insurance policy other than Medicare. If the patient is covered under Medicare, the word "none" should be entered if the patient does not have a primary insurance policy. Circumstances under which Medicare may be a secondary payor include: (a) if the patient is covered under a group health plan, (b) if the claim should be filed first with no-fault and/or other liability carrier, and (c) if the claim relates to a work-related injury.

Items 12 and 13   The patient or authorized representative must sign and date this line item unless his or her signature is already on file in the physician's office. Generally, this information is included and signed by the patient on the new patient form completed during the initial office appointment. The authorizations could be in the hospital's records, if applicable. If the signature is on file, the words "signature on file" should be entered on these line items.

Items 17 and 17a   These items, if applicable, list the referring or ordering physician's name and PIN. This applies only to Medicare patients. The PIN is issued by the Medicare carrier to all physicians who apply for a Medicare provider number. Most states have a book listing physicians' names and their PINs.

Item 21   This item designates the patient's diagnosis using the ICD-9 codes.

Item 23   If a service must be preauthorized by an insurance company, the related preauthorization number assigned by the carrier is included here. Preauthorizations are common with managed-care plans.

Items 24a and 24g Item 24a is the date or dates the service was rendered. When "from" and "to" dates are shown with a series of identical services, the number of days is entered on line 24g. These items are commonly used for hospital visits.

Item 24b This line contains the two-digit place-of-service code, which tells the insurance company where the service was performed.

Top Ten Billing Errors

Many of the errors found in Medicare Part B audits are attributed to billing errors. To eliminate these errors, Medicare published a list of the ten most common billing errors. Provide the following list to practice personnel, because even though it was produced for Medicare, any practice may find common errors that apply to other insurance companies.

1. **CPT modifiers are either incorrect or missing.** The billing employee must pay special attention to modifiers -24, -25, -57, -78, and -79. Modifiers go on line 24d of the HCFA claim form.

2. **Diagnosis codes are either incorrect or missing.** Diagnosis codes explain why the physician performed a particular service. The billing employee should always be as specific as possible and use a fifth digit when available. Use the "v" codes when necessary. Diagnosis codes go on line 21 of the claim form.

3. **Procedure codes are either incorrect or missing.** Sometimes an office actually forgets to include the CPT code on the claim form or uses incorrect codes, such as deleted or revised CPT codes. The billing employee should make sure the practice's chargemaster agrees with both the codes and related descriptions contained in the CPT book. CPT codes go on line 24d of the claim form.

4. **Referring/ordering physician's name and PIN are missing.** If an office gets referrals from other physicians, most of its Medicare claim forms should include the referring physician's name and PIN. The billing employee must include

the physician's name and PIN if services are ordered, such as lab tests. If the office does not have a PIN, the manager will need to order a book from the Medicare carrier. This information goes on lines 17a and 17b of the claim form.

5. **The place of service code is either incorrect or missing.** This code tells the carrier where treatment was performed. If the place of service was the office, the billing employee should not use the hospital visit code. These codes go on line 24b of the claim form.

6. **Provider's name and Medicare number are missing.** Group practices billing under one provider number should pay attention to this. Besides this number, the name of the physician rendering the service usually must be included on the claim form.

7. **Quantity billed amounts are either incorrect or missing.** If multiple services are rendered for a single CPT code, the billing employee must either itemize each service on a separate line or place the total number on line 24g of the claim form. Line 24g is the indicator for total days or units related to the service. For example, if a physician sees a patient for five straight days in the hospital, and CPT code 99231 should be billed, the billing employee could either put each day on a separate line or put the number "5" on line 24g. If the practice decides to use the total number, it will need to make sure the correct date range is included on line 24a.

8. **Extra information is missing.** The billing employee should make sure all of the necessary information is supplied. For example, if a surgeon bills the -22 modifier, he or she must attach the operative note to the claim form.

9. **The date of service is either incorrect or missing.** This is line 24a of the claim form.

10. **The practice does not provide timely answers to development letters.** If Medicare sends the practice a letter, the office should respond to it immediately.

To ensure payment from Medicare or any other insurance carrier, the billing employee should make sure every insurance claim form is prepared perfectly before it is mailed or transmitted electronically. One of the advantages of electronic billing is that most times a claim cannot be transmitted unless it is filled out correctly. To give reimbursement a chance and to improve practice cash flow, make sure the practice files clean insurance claim forms each and every time.

■ **Practice Point:** Make sure that the practice electronically bills as many of its insurance claim forms as possible, especially if a practice treats many Medicare and Medicaid patients. Filing claims electronically will speed up the process and usually will improve a practice's cash flow.

Billing Medicare Correctly

In 1997, the Health Care Financing Administration, through its Medicare carriers, implemented what is known as the "National Correct Coding Initiative." The goal of the initiative was to identify and eliminate the incorrect coding of medical services. This initiative was implemented via the installation of a set of new edits into each of the Medicare carriers' automated claims processing systems.

The new package of claims processing edits focuses primarily on comparing the CPT codes for those situations where two or more services are provided to one beneficiary on the same day. These edits identify situations in which outdated codes are being used, the CPT definitions for some services may have been misunderstood or misinterpreted, or mutually exclusive procedures have been coded together, or a simple coding mistake has been made.

Physicians and others who have been correctly coding for their services and who routinely keep abreast of changes in the CPT coding system should experience little or no disruption in the processing of their Medicare claims, save for an occasional mistake.

The CMS has already developed the new package of edits under a contract with a Medicare contractor. The contractor has reviewed the code definitions for all CPT codes. In addition, the CMS sought the advice of a broad range of physicians and specialists concerning current standard medical and surgical practices. The CMS intends to make periodic revisions and updates to the coding package. The CMS suggests that physicians work through their local medical society to make suggestions concerning corrections and/or improvements to this initiative.

Coding edits can be put in the following general categories:

1. Coding based on standards of medical/surgical practice
2. Coding included in medical/surgical packages
3. Coding within CPT definitions, such as separate procedures, families of codes, most extensive procedures, and sequential procedures
4. Coding with designation of sex
5. Coding of mutually exclusive procedures

According to the HCFA, the following are reasons some claims may be affected:

- Unclear understanding or misinterpretation of some CPT coding definitions of services
- Use of outdated versions of CPT to code services
- Mistakes in coding

The table on the next page is an example of the coding edits.

The Initiative

Obviously, some practices will have trouble working with the coding edits. The first step is to identify these coding problems, if they exist, as soon as possible. Review a sample of the Medicare Explanation of Medical Benefits and look for charge denials. A lack of knowledge of the new coding edits could be the problem. Solving this type of coding error requires that you become familiar with the coding edits. Forassistance, acquire the *National Correct Code Policy Manual for Part B Medicare Carriers*. The manual consists of two volumes. These volumes include a table of contents, 12 chapters, an index, and two attachments. The chapters are organized by CPT coding for medical procedures and services—except for Chapter I, which contains general correct coding policies, and Chapter XII, which addresses HCPCS Level II codes under the Part B carrier's jurisdiction. To order the manual, call the National Technical Information Service sales desk at 703-605-6000 or (800)363-2068; or visit the web site at www.ntis.gov. For a paper copy of the manual, ask for item number SUB9576INQ. For a diskette, ask for item number SUB5408.

Sample of Coding Edits

CPT Code for Comprehensive Service	CPT Code for Component Service Billed on the Same Day as the Comprehensive Service	Explanation
90780—IV Infusion	36000—Introduction of needle or intracatheter	The comprehensive code describes services involving infusion. Because the placement is of peripheral vascular access devices integral to vascular infusions, the CPT code or placement of needle or intracatheter is not to be billed separately.
93731–93736—Pacemaker Analysis	93041—EKGs; 93042—EKGs; 93012—EKGs; 93014—EKGs	The codes for pacemaker evaluation and analysis include in their definition the electrocardiographic recording and interpretation of recordings.
71020—Radiologic Examination, Chest, Two Views	71010—Radiologic Examination, Chest, Single View	The frontal view is included in the two-view chest X-ray.

Insurance Plans

The process of filing insurance claim forms is complicated by the multitude of insurance plans available. The patient could have insurance through Medicare, Medicaid, a managed-care plan, or a commercial insurance plan, or the claim could be associated with a workers' compensation case. There are a number of other plans besides these. This multitude of plan types is one important reason every office needs to verify a patient's coverage before filing the insurance claim.

■ **Practice Point:** To help a practice quickly identify the patient's type of insurance, make sure the insurance categories are listed on the practice's Superbill. The categories can be marked for each patient visit. This will help the office identify not only the type of patient, but also the related billing rules for the particular insurance carrier, which will aid the entire office in billing and collecting for a service.

Commercial Plans

Under a commercial plan, the insurance company pays for the services rendered on a regular fee-for-service basis. This type of insurance plan generally is called an *indemnity plan*. The insurance company will usually pay 80 percent of the billed charge, and the patient usually pays the remaining 20 percent. The commercial insurance plan, however, will pay only fees that it considers to be usual, customary, and reasonable (UCR). If a physician's fee does not meet the company's criteria, the patient is responsible for the remaining payment.

■ **Practice Point:** Find out how the office handles charges that are above the UCR limit. The charges are either billed to the patient or they are written off. Make sure the office attempts to collect the fee from the insurance company if the office believes its fee is UCR. If UCR reductions occur frequently, the practice's fee schedule could be too high.

Managed-Care Plans

There generally are two types of managed-care plans: preferred provider organizations (PPOs) and health maintenance organizations

(HMOs). PPOs pay physicians on a discounted fee-for-service basis. HMOs pay physicians on a capitated basis, which generally is a fixed dollar amount each month based on an actuarially calculated per-member, per-month amount.

Government Plans

Medicaid and Medicare are government programs that provide insurance coverage for individuals whose incomes fall below a certain level (Medicaid) or for individuals who are 65 years old or older or who become disabled (Medicare). Workers' compensation insurance applies to those who are injured on the job. When the physician treats a patient who was injured on the job, the practice should file the employer's workers' compensation insurance claim if one is in force.

Medicare

Medicare consists of two separate types of insurance: hospital insurance (Medicare Part A) and medical insurance (Medicare Part B). Medicare Part B governs the payment of physician services, regardless of whether the patient receives the service at home, in the physician's office, in a clinic, or in a hospital. When a Medicare patient sees a physician, the patient is required to pay the first $100 (the annual deductible) of charges each calendar year. The deductible must represent charges for services and supplies covered by Medicare. It also must be based on the Medicare-approved amounts, not the actual charges billed by the physician or medical supplier.

Medicare-Approved Amount

After the patient pays the Medicare deductible, Medicare generally pays 80 percent of the Medicare-approved amount for covered services the patient receives the rest of the year. The Medicare-approved amount is based on a national fee schedule, called the "resource-based relative value scale" (RBRVS). The schedule, which went into effect January 1, 1992, assigns a dollar amount to each physician service based on work, practice costs, and malpractice insurance costs. It was developed by the Health Care Financing Administration pursuant to the Physician Payment Reform Program legislated by Congress in the Omnibus Budget Reconciliation Act (OBRA) of 1989. Under this payment system, physicians are reimbursed for their services according to a national fee schedule. Medicare will then generally pay 80 percent of that amount.

Participating Physicians

Physicians who agree to accept assignment on a Medicare claim agree to accept the Medicare-approved amount as payment in full. The Medicare carrier pays 80 percent of the Medicare-approved participating amount, and the Medicare patient must pay the remaining 20 percent, the co-payment, and the deductible (if applicable). Also, physicians who sign Medicare participation agreements, and become "participating physicians," must accept assignment on all Medicare claims.

> ■ **Practice Point:** When a practice files an insurance claim form for a Medicare carrier, the billing employee can use the physician's normal fee. Medicare still will pay only 80 percent of the participating approved amount, but this will allow the practice to minimize the number of fee schedules it has to keep up with. This is the suggestion you can offer to practices that want to simplify their billing process.

Nonparticipating Physicians

If a physician does not sign as a Medicare participant, the physician is known as a "nonparticipating physician." A nonparticipating physician can accept assignments (i.e., accept the nonparticipating Medicare-approved amount as payment) on a case-by-case basis, except in certain situations. For example, all physicians must accept assignments for Medicare-covered clinical diagnostic laboratory tests. If a physician does not accept such an assignment, however, the benefits will be paid directly to the Medicare patient, and the office must collect full payment from the patient.

■ **Practice Point:** If a nonparticipating physician decides to accept a Medicare assignment and wants to be paid directly by Medicare, the physician should mark the "accept assignment" box on the insurance claim form. The physician will be paid 80 percent of the nonparticipating Medicare-approved amount and the check will be sent directly to his or her office.

A physician who does not accept assignment of a Medicare claim is limited as to the amount he or she can charge a Medicare patient for covered services. This is called the "limiting charge" and is calculated as a percentage above the national fee schedule amount for nonparticipating physicians. There is a specific column on the Medicare payment report showing the limiting charge for each CPT code. Nonparticipating physicians who do not accept assignment and knowingly, willfully, and repeatedly charge Medicare patients more than the limiting charge are subject to severe sanctions by Medicare. In other words, nonparticipating physicians cannot bill Medicare patients more than the limiting charge. In addition, federal law requires nonparticipating physicians who do not accept assignment to provide Medicare patients with written estimates of charges before performing any type of elective surgery.

■ **Practice Point:** If a nonparticipating physician accepts a Medicare patient, the practice can only bill the limiting charge on the insurance claim form. Make sure that the practice has the Medicare payment report and that the billing employee knows when he or she must use it instead of billing the physician's normal fees.

■ **Practice Point:** If the provider is a nonparticipating physician, review a sample of Medicare insurance claim forms to see how often the physician is accepting assignments. Many nonparticipating physicians accept numerous assignments, especially if hospital charges are involved, because by accepting assignment, physicians ensure that the Medicare checks will be sent to their offices instead of to the patients' homes. If you notice that the physician accepts a lot of assignments, you should ask the physician to consider becoming a participating member, because participating physicians are reimbursed more than nonparticipating physicians for assigned claims.

■ **Practice Point:** If a nonparticipating physician does not accept assignment for a service but treats the patient,

Medicare will send the payment check to the patient. The patient is thus responsible for paying the physician for her services. In this situation, find out how often the practice receives full payment for such services. If possible, determine the collection percentage for this group of patients. If collections are poor, discuss the possibility of the physician becoming a participating provider in the next year so that the practice can receive direct payment from Medicare, and its collections can improve.

The national fee schedule, called the "Medicare Combined Disclosure Report," summarizes what a physician can bill and collect for services rendered to a Medicare patient. All medical practices receive this report at the beginning of each year. (See Appendix B for an example of a Medicare Disclosure Report.)

Waiver of Liability

When a service is furnished to a Medicare patient, and the provider (usually the physician) of service knows that the patient's condition does not meet the necessary medical requirements for the service, the provider must notify the patient that Medicare will not provide coverage and give the reason why coverage will not be provided. A sample format (waiver of liability statement) can usually be found in the *Medicare Provider Manual*, which should be in every physician's office.

In such cases, the patient must agree to accept liability for the service and sign a waiver of liability statement, which the practice must keep in the patient's file. If there is no indication on the claim that the patient has been notified of the noncoverage, the physician cannot bill the patient for the service. Medicare will send the Medicare patient an Explanation of Medical Benefit form (EOMB), which will explain to the patient that he or she does not have to pay for the service. If the patient has been notified, the EOMB will indicate to the Medicare patient that he or she is liable for the charges.

In the past, the -ZU modifier was used to advise Medicare that the patient had been notified of Medicare services and supplies that are not considered medically reasonable and necessary. A new national modifier has been established to indicate to Medicare that the patient has been notified. If the modifier is not used, Medicare will assume that the patient was not notified and a message will be sent to the patient indicating he or she does not have to pay for the service. The national modifier is -GA.

Medicare Appeals Process

Any Medicare beneficiary or his or her representative has the right to appeal action taken on claims if (1) he or she is dissatisfied with the amount of payment, (2) if payment was denied, or (3) if the original request for payment was not acted upon promptly. A physician who has accepted assignment on a claim may also appeal the amount of the Medicare payment.

To take proper advantage of Medicare appeal rights, make sure every physician's office does the following:

- Reviews all Medicare explanations of benefits (EOBs) for reduced reimbursement and payment denials.

- Communicates any discrepancies to the carrier, preferably by telephone.

- Researches and gathers all pertinent information regarding claims in question and thoroughly reviews all information in charts, medical records, and operative reports.

- Prepares the appeal request, if necessary.

Nonparticipating physicians are required to attain patients' authorization to submit requests for reviews for all unassigned claims. Several types of Medicare appeals are available.

Review

Because Medicare procedures vary from state to state, refer to the Medicare manual for the state in which the practice operates for specifics on requesting a review. Although there is no dollar limit to request a review, the appeal must be filed within six months of the date of the processing notice (EOB or similar remittance advice). Reviews generally occur whenever Medicare initially denies a claim. If the request for a review fails to meet the six-month requirement, good cause must be shown to grant a review. Good cause consists of the following situations:

- Circumstances beyond the individual's control, including mental or physical impairment, advanced age, or death
- Incorrect or incomplete information about the subject claim furnished by official sources (such as the Health Care Financing Administration)
- Delay that results when an individual tries to secure supporting evidence and does not realize that such evidence could be submitted after filing a request
- Unusual or unavoidable circumstances
- Destruction or other damage to records

Hearing

A request for a hearing with Medicare must be made within six months of the final review determination. A hearing is limited to a dollar amount of $100 or more on an aggregate claim basis for one or more patients, and the carrier must respond to such a request within 10 days of receipt. The three types of hearings include: (1) on the record, (2) by telephone, and (3) in person. All hearings are presided over and conducted by a hearing officer who must abide by the Health Care Financing Administration policy. Since this is a national policy, the conduct of the hearing should be the same in all states.

Administrative Law Judge Review

Petition for an administrative law judge review must be made within 60 days of the final hearing decision. Claims in question must be at least $500.

Fraud and Abuse

Any medical office treating Medicare patients must be aware of the strict fraud and abuse rules governing Medicare billing. Congress established the Office of Inspector General (OIG) under the Department of Health and Human Resources in 1976 for the purpose of identifying and eliminating fraud, abuse, and waste in Health and Human Services programs and to promote the efficiency and economy in departmental operations. The OIG carries out this mission through a nationwide network of audits, investigations, and inspections of physicians' offices.

The most common inspection is the Medicare audit. It is used to detect inconsistencies in billing, coverage, and payment of bills for particular services. It is also used to evaluate the propriety of certain Medicare payments and to determine that actual services billed were appropriately rendered to a Medicare patient.

For example, an office bills every new patient visit at the highest level of service. Medicare flags the office's bills and audits a sample of related patient charts to see if the office is using the correct CPT code.

Medicare fraud is defined by the HCFA as "knowingly and willfully making or causing a false statement or representation of a material fact made in application for a Medicare benefit or payment." Fraud often occurs when a physician knowingly or willfully makes or causes to be made a false statement or representation of a material fact for determining rights to a Medicare reimbursement. For example, a practice bills Medicare for a service that was not rendered. The practice wrote off the patient's 20 percent co-payment, so the patient never got a statement. It also occurs when a physician or another individual pays any other person directly or indirectly for referrals or solicitations of Medicare patients. The following list contains some common examples of Medicare fraud:

- A deliberate application of duplicate reimbursement
- Any false representation with respect to the nature of charges for services rendered
- A claim for uncovered services billed as services that are covered
- A claim involving collusion between the physician and recipient resulting in higher costs or charges

Medicare abuse refers to activities that, while not considered fraudulent, may directly or indirectly cause financial losses to the

Medicare program or to the beneficiary. Abuse generally occurs when the physician operates in a manner inconsistent with accepted business and medical practices and in such a manner that these practices result in an unnecessary financial loss to the Medicare program. The most common types of abuse are the overuse of medical services (e.g., repeated lab testing when results are normal or not used, or the unintentional upcoding and overuse of office visits) and a breach of the Part B (medical insurance) assignment.

To avoid a Medicare audit, look for the following red flags:

- *Waived co-payments*—Physicians are required to collect the 20 percent Medicare co-payment from the Medicare patient. Barring exceptional cases, such as extreme financial hardship, routinely waiving the co-payment is considered a fraudulent activity.

- *Discriminatory billing practices*—Medicare patients cannot be billed a greater charge for similar services than patients who have commercial insurance or no insurance.

- *Additional necessary medical services*—Look for an abnormally high number of occurrences of the same service and the same diagnosis.

Developing a Compliance Program

Physicians, billing clerks, and health care consultants all should understand the importance of complying with Medicare regulations. The federal government is actively pursuing incidents of fraud and abuse within the Medicare system. In the past, physicians were generally unaffected by Medicare compliance issues because investigations were few and far between. Today, physicians are increasingly being investigated by the Office of Inspector General, the Federal Bureau of Investigation (FBI), and state and local law enforcement agencies in relation to Medicare fraud and abuse issues. In addition, Qui Tam laws have been implemented. These laws offer significant financial incentives to individuals who report physicians who are subsequently found guilty of violating Medicare regulations. Additionally, federal laws have increased fines for Medicare fraud and abuse from $10,000 per incident to

$25,000 per incident and imposed jail time as a possible punishment for such violations. As a result of these developments, obtaining an understanding of Medicare fraud and abuse issues is now essential for most health care practitioners.

The excuse that the billing department incorrectly billed Medicare does not absolve the physician of his or her responsibility. Medicare holds the physician ultimately responsible if he or she could have or should have known of billing violations. For corporate health care entities, responsibility for billing errors rests not only with physicians, but also with billing clerks, upper management, corporate officers, and others within the organization.

Besides Medicare billing issues, managed-care organizations are generally required to comply with National Commission on Quality Assurance (NCQA) guidelines which require, among other things, that physician practices meet certain minimum chart documentation standards.

Compliance programs not only help to identify and prevent billing errors, but also show the physician is making a good faith effort to submit claims appropriately. While no federal mandate requires that a practice have a compliance program in place, it is unquestionably to the practice's benefit to have one. Because a compliance program requires close monitoring of the billing and payment process, it can also serve as an important management tool that gives the physician a better grasp of the business side of the practice.

First, a compliance program will facilitate a better cash flow by ensuring that claims are filed correctly the first time, making them less likely to be returned unpaid. Second, even the well-intentioned physician who tries to follow Medicare guidelines religiously will occasionally make mistakes. If such mistakes follow a pattern, they may attract the attention of fraud investigators. But to convict a physician of billing fraud, there must be a finding of intent to commit an illegal act. The physician's participation in an effective compliance plan will stand as solid evidence that any mistakes were unintentional, and the investigating agency will consider this evidence in determining what action to take.

By the same token, an ineffective or inactive compliance program would be worse than no program at all. Such a program would be more likely to generate errors than to correct them. Not only that, but fraud investigators might well consider the program to be a bad-faith effort to circumvent, rather then enforce, compliance.

Elements of a Basic Compliance Plan

An effective compliance plan should include the following elements:

- A general statement of conduct that promotes a clear commitment to compliance.
- Appointment of a trustworthy compliance officer with the authority to enforce standards.
- Effective training and education programs for all professional and support personnel.
- An auditing and monitoring process.
- Internal investigation and enforcement through publicized disciplinary guidelines and actions.
- A process to respond to identified offenses and apply corrective action initiatives.
- Specific and effective lines of communication between the compliance officer and professional and support personnel.

While these requirements may seem daunting, they are relatively simple to implement. For example, the physician or office manager can serve as the compliance officer so a full-time employee need not be dedicated to that. Similarly, discussion of compliance-related issues can occur as a segment of regular staff meetings.

Here are basic steps for setting up educational objectives:

- Determine who needs training in billing and coding, and what kind of training is needed.
- Budget the money to pay for such education.
- Determine the type of education service that best suits your needs, whether it is seminars, in-service training, self-study, or other programs.
- Determine when the education is needed and how much each person should receive.

- Reward the staff members for achieving their goals.

Participants in billing and coding educational programs should be held accountable for demonstrating tangible results. Billing staff should learn how to avoid errors in filing claims, which will result in a low rate of claim denials. Physicians should learn and understand Medicare guidelines for demonstrating medical necessity, which will lead to fewer claims being denied as medically unnecessary.

A Step-by-Step Billing Compliance Program

1. Each quarter the compliance officer should review a random sample of 25 to 35 charts per physician, along with all associated encounter documents, claim forms, and their respective explanations of benefits and payment stubs.

   - Are necessary elements documented to support the level of care billed?
     —If a test has been ordered, is the reason for the test evident through the chart note? If not, can the reason be clearly inferred?
     —Does the chart contain documentation to support ordered ancillary services, such as physical therapy?

2. Review the associated claim forms or transmittal documents (computerized claims my have to be printed on paper for review). Did unbundling occur? To determine if a code has been unbundled, refer to the Correct Coding Initiative, which lists the codes and codes pairs that are mutually exclusive and cannot be unbundled. This document can be ordered from the National Technical Information Services by calling (703) 605-6585 or on the web site www.ntis.gov.

3. Review the internal procedures for billing for consultation. Are these requirements met? The request and need for the consultation must be documented.

   —The consulting physician's findings must be documented in the medical record and communicated to the referring physician.

—Once the consulting physician assumes management of one or all of the patient's conditions, the billing codes for consultations should not be used. Instead, use the standard evaluation and management codes.

4. Check that each encounter has a clear, written diagnosis. Physicians should include all diagnoses on the internal encounter form. Do not simply use a diagnosis from a previous encounter, because this may have nothing to do with the present encounter. Check the medical record and ask the physician to submit complete information on the internal encounter form.

5. Make sure the chart has a clinical and clerical audit trail. This means that every billed charge should be evident from the clinical record, and each clerical transaction should have all the necessary support documentation.

6. Ensure that an educational and training program is in place for all staff responsible for posting charges and payments. Personnel should have a solid coding background and need to be aware of the code pairings and listings mentioned in Item 2.

7. Neatness and organization weigh heavily in your favor. Consider the review officer who has to read an illegible, disorganized, and sloppy record versus one that is neat, well-organized, and legible. If the officer can't read the chart, the likely conclusion is that the service was never performed.

8. Examine the number of claims your billing personnel resubmit to the carrier each month for review or appeal. A high number of these could indicate an unacceptably high level of internal billing errors.

9. Periodically review the practice's daily and weekly charges. Determine whether all of the services claimed to have been rendered by your practice in one day were actually completed within the given time frame. Conduct a similar review on your hospital charges, especially with time sensitive services such as critical care services.

10. Keep necessary reference manuals in the office for clarification about how to bill for the services you perform. In particular, keep the Medicare Part B Manual and newsletters handy. These newsletters should be routed to, and initialed by, all billing and

coding personnel as well as physicians. For the sake of efficiency, the compliance officer can flag important items that are relevant to your specialty.

11. Make certain all necessary waivers are in place and on file in the patient's chart if you are providing services that are not considered medically necessary by the carrier or not covered. Waivers are also necessary if the practice provides screening lab tests.

12. Check your use of modifiers. Modifiers are two-character digits that are added to procedure codes to modify the scope, definition, circumstances, or charges associated with services provided. Properly used, modifiers allow physicians to communicate with automatic processing systems and can increase or decrease payment for a specific service. Improper use of modifiers can lead to claim denials, payment reductions, and time-consuming claim appeals. So make sure you and your staff are up-to-date on the rules for usage of modifiers.

13. Check credit balances and refunds. If the practice owes money to Medicare or to a Medicare patient, refund it promptly. Don't use credit balances in lieu of refunds, as this can lead to problems.

14. Ensure that all requirements are met for nurse practitioners, physician assistants, and clinical nurse specialists who bill for services incident to those provided by a physician. Some of these services should be reported using the "YR" modifier to indicate that services were ordered by the physician but performed by auxiliary personnel under the physician's immediate supervision. In these cases, the physician does not have to be physically present with the patient at the time of service but must be within the confines of the office.

15. Review the internal charge documents such as encounter forms or Superbills. Are the codes current? Do you have all coding levels available for use or just the higher reimbursing codes? If the lower levels are not included, providers are forced to use only the higher paying codes. Incorrect internal documents can be another source of billing and coding errors.

Documenting Compliance Measures

The compliance officer should keep an ongoing log of compliance activities. This log should, at a minimum, entail compliance meetings, educational activities, and internal audit results. Particular attention should be paid to documenting violations uncovered by the compliance program and the resulting remedial action. Should outside investigators later uncover these violations independently, a clear record that the practice discovered and corrected the problems on its own may well dissuade the investigators from taking further action.

The following steps are necessary to perform a chart review:

1. Randomly select 10 to 20 patient charts for review. In most cases, only Medicare charts are selected.

2. Determine that a "Signature on File Lifetime Authorization for Medicare and Medicaid" form is on file. This must be signed by the patient giving the physician permission to bill the Medicare program on the patient's behalf. Generally this can be found on either the new patient information form or the office charge ticket itself. Also, determine whether Medigap insurance exists. If so, determine that a Medigap Benefits Authorization form has been completed. This authorization allows the physician to submit claims to the patient's primary payor with crossover to Medicare. In reality, nine out of ten charts will not have either of these forms, yet both are required by the HCFA.

3. Request billing data from the practice. Select one Date of Service (DOS) from each chart and request all records related to that DOS. The charts should include billing information, claim forms (HCFA 1500), Explanation of Medicare Benefits (EOMB), Superbills (or charge slips), physician medical notes and any other relevant information related to the DOS selected.

4. A reviewer who is experienced in medical billing and coding and has extensive knowledge of federal and state regulations should review the documentation prepared for the DOS selected and determine that charges per HCFA Form 1500 are consistent with the documentation maintained in the medical

file. Compare the HCFA Form 1500 to the Superbill to determine that all procedures per the 1500 are documented on the Superbill. Review the medical documentation to determine that all procedures billed can be substantiated. The reviewer must determine the following:

a. That the level of care billed is appropriate (i.e., the accuracy of the evaluation and management code (E&M code)). The E&M code is based on HCFA requirements for Medicare, Medicaid, Champus, and other federally funded programs. Currently, most of the practice's billing risk relates to federally funded programs, especially Medicare, rather than commercial and managed-care plans. HCFA guidelines might possibly include all payors (commercial, managed care and federally funded programs) in the future. In addition, many managed-care contracts currently contain performance and audit guidelines that must be adhered to.

b. That procedures performed were medically necessary. Certain procedures are diagnosis specific, accordingly diagnosis codes must be consistent with procedure codes (i.e., ICD-10 code must be consistent with CPT code).

c. That appropriate payment was received from Medicare. The reviewer should examine the EOMB to determine this. Denials should also be examined to determine if resubmission is necessary. This is the revenue enhancement aspect of the chart review. If denials are identified, the reviewer might suggest the following:

1. Correcting the billing problem identified and rebilling the procedure.

2. Requesting that Medicare review the denial.

5. When the chart review is completed, a findings and recommendations report should be prepared. This report should always be reviewed by physicians and appropriate management level personnel. The medical practice has no obligation to share this findings report with others, as it is an internal audit. The consultant has an obligation to keep his audit findings confidential.

Because the internal chart review is the only way of identifying potential problems before Medicare does, *every practice* should conduct such audits. Common problems identified in chart reviews include the following:

- Truncated Diagnosis Codes—Claims are not coded to the highest specificity. For example, a claim for reimbursement is made for hypertension rather than benign or malignant hypertension. Or a claim is submitted for diabetes rather than for adult onset, insulin dependent diabetes.

- Unbundling of CPT codes—Many CPT codes encompass various procedures performed. In such cases, if the various procedures are unbundled (broken out and billed separately), increased charges might result. The Correct Coding Initiative, a Medicare Regulation under HCFA, prohibits the unbundling of charges.

- Lack of documentation to substantiate procedures billed or level of care provided.

- Lab work performed—Medical necessity and diagnosis must be consistent with the lab work performed.

The Main Objective of a Compliance Plan

Remember these three, simple words:

PREVENT—DETECT—CORRECT

These three words are the foundation of any compliance plan a medical practice implements. The plan, on an ongoing basis, must prevent fraud and errors, detect fraud and errors, and correct fraud and errors.

■ **Practice Point:** Many practices are adding to their physician employment agreements language stating that a contract may be terminated if the physician does not comply with the practice's compliance plan and related initiatives.

■ **Practice Point:** The Office of Inspector General (OIG) for the Department of Health and Human Services has officially released its latest model compliance plan. The document is entitled "Office of Inspector General's Compliance Program Guidance for the Durable Medical Equipment,

Prosthetics, Orthotics, and Supply Industry." The document is available at the OIG's web site at the following web address: http://www.dhhs.gov/progorg/oig/modcomp/index.htm

This Compliance Program Guidance is the fifth such model compliance plan to be officially released by the OIG. The OIG has previously released Compliance Program Guidance documents for the following health care providers:

Clinical Laboratories

Hospitals

Home Health Agencies

Third-Party Medical Billing Companies

Additionally, the OIG has released a voluntary Provider Self Disclosure Protocol.

Inspector General Issues Voluntary Compliance Program Guidance for Physician Practices

The Department of Health and Human Services' Office of Inspector General (OIG) has issued final guidance to help physicians in individual and small group practices design voluntary compliance programs. The intent of the guidance is to provide a road map to develop a voluntary compliance program that best fits the needs of an individual practice. The guidance itself provides great flexibility as to how a physician practice could implement compliance efforts in a manner that fits with the practice's existing operations and resources.

The final guidance—*Compliance Program Guidance for Individual and Small Group Physician Practices*—can be found on the Internet at http://oig.hhs.gov/oigreg/physician.pdf.

The government is encouraging physician practices to adopt the active application of compliance principles in their practice, rather than implement rigid, costly, formal procedures. The government's goal in issuing this final guidance was to show physician practices that compliance can become a part of the practice culture without the practice having to expend substantial monetary or time resources.

Under the law, physicians are not subject to civil, administrative, or criminal penalties for innocent errors or even negligence. The Government's primary enforcement tool, the civil False Claims Act, covers only offenses that are committed with *actual knowledge* of the falsity of the claim, *reckless disregard* or *deliberate ignorance* of the truth or falsity of a claim. The False Claims Act does not cover mistakes, errors, or negligence. The OIG is very mindful of the difference between innocent errors ("erroneous claims") and reckless or intentional conduct ("fraudulent claims").

A voluntary compliance program can help physicians identify both erroneous and fraudulent claims and help ensure that submitted claims are true and accurate. It can also help the practice by speeding up and optimizing proper payment of claims, minimizing billing mistakes, and avoiding conflicts with the self-referral and anti-kickback statutes.

Unlike other guidance previously issued by the OIG, the final physician guidance does not suggest that physician practices implement all seven standard components of a full-scale compliance program. While the seven components provide a solid basis upon which a physician practice can create a compliance program, the OIG acknowledges that full implementation of all components may not be feasible for smaller physician practices. Instead, the guidance emphasizes a step-by-step approach for those practices to follow in developing and implementing a voluntary compliance program. As a first step, physician practices can begin by identifying risk areas which, based on a practice's specific history with billing problems and other compliance issues, might benefit from closer scrutiny and corrective/educational measures.

The step-by-step approach is as follows: (1) conduct internal monitoring and auditing through the performance of periodic audits; (2) implement compliance and practice standards through the development of written standards and procedures; (3) designate a compliance officer or contact(s) to monitor compliance efforts and enforce practice standards; (4) conduct appropriate training and education on practice standards and procedures; (5) respond appropriately to detected violations through the investigation of allegations and the disclosure of incidents to appropriate Government entities;

(6) develop open lines of communication, such as discussions at staff meetings regarding erroneous or fraudulent conduct issues and community bulletin boards, to keep practice employees updated regarding compliance activities; and (7) enforce disciplinary standards through well-publicized guidelines.

The final guidance identifies four specific compliance risk areas for physicians: (1) proper coding and billing; (2) ensuring that services are reasonable and necessary; (3) proper documentation; and (4) avoiding improper inducements, kickbacks, and self-referrals. These risk areas reflect areas in which the OIG has focused its investigations and audits related to physician practices.

Recognizing the financial and staffing resource constraints faced by physician practices, the final guidance stresses flexibility in the manner a practice implements voluntary compliance measures. The OIG encourages physician practices to participate in the compliance programs of other providers, such as hospitals or other settings in which the physicians practice. A physician practice's participation in such compliance programs could be a way, at least partly, to augment the practice's own compliance efforts.

The final guidance also provides direction to larger practices in developing compliance programs by recommending that they use both the physician guidance and previously issued guidance, such as the *Third-Party Medical Billing Company Compliance Program Guidance* or the *Clinical Laboratory Compliance Program Guidance,* to create a compliance program that meets the needs of the larger practice.

The final guidance includes several appendices outlining additional risk areas about which various physicians expressed interest, as well as information about criminal, civil, and administrative statutes related to federal health care programs. There is also information about the OIG's provider self-disclosure protocol and Internet resources that may be useful to physician practices.

■ **Practice Point:** The model compliance plan is included on the disk that accompanies this book.

Preparing for Government Investigations

Recent developments in regulatory enforcement have made it painfully obvious that any person who is involved in providing health care services or advising health care providers regarding regulatory issues is exposed to potential involvement in civil or criminal proceedings. This involvement can be either as a witness, a subject, or as a target of an investigation. Every entity that participates in the health industry, therefore, should develop policies and procedures that prepare the entity for regulatory intrusion.

Development of policies and procedures for response to government audits and investigations is a complex matter, and one system may not suffice for all entities. The following describes some general policies and procedures that could help an entity respond to regulatory activities and service of legal process.

Subpoenas

Subpoenas can come from several sources: the Department of Health and Human Services, the Office of the Inspector General; a federal grand jury; or private litigants. Regardless of the source, subpoenas are merely documents that request the production of documents or the presence of a person at a deposition and do not require an immediate response. If served with a subpoena, do not turn over documents called for, do not discuss the case with the individual who served you with the subpoena, and do not discuss the subpoena with anyone other than the entity's Corporate Compliance Officer and legal counsel.

Search Warrants

Unlike subpoenas, search warrants can be executed immediately by the agents who present the warrant to the entity. It is likely that several agents will descend on the entity at the same time and actually carry away files, records, and sometimes even computer systems without advance warning.

If someone representing a government agency attempts to execute a search warrant, the following steps should be taken:

- Do nothing to interfere with the agents.
- Demand a copy of the search warrant and the business card (or name) of the agent in charge.

- Be sure the office manager or highest ranking employee on the premises is informed of the situation.
- Call an attorney approved by the entity, and follow the attorney's instructions carefully. If the entity has a Corporate Compliance Plan, a report should also be made to the Corporate Compliance Officer.

The employees need to be present while the search is conducted. Employees should take steps to assure the following:

- Only those items referred to in the search warrant are taken.
- Company documents are not photocopied on the premises.
- A correct and complete inventory of all items taken is given to an employee before the agents leave the premises.

Although the agents have the right to be on the premises to execute a warrant, this does not mean that employees must submit to interviews. Employees are not required to explain entity operations, bookkeeping, records, or the meaning of any document. Employees should cooperate in locating those items called for in the search warrant, but no more. If an agent makes requests or demands something inconsistent with these instructions, employees should seek the advice of legal counsel.

Contact with Government Agents and Investigators

You and your employees should be prepared for the possibility of being approached away from the work place. It is quite common for investigators to arrive unannounced at someone's home and then try to make the person feel guilty unless the person consents to an interview. Occasionally, investigators will try to suggest that someone must speak with them "or else." No one is required to submit to questioning by government investigators or employees. Beware of any investigators who say you have nothing to worry about or suggest that by talking to them things will go easier for you. Investigators do not have any authority to promise anything to a witness. Only a government attorney working with your attorney can make promises binding on the government.

If someone claiming to represent the government contacts you at work or at home, follow these simple steps:

- First, ask for identification and a business card.
- Second, determine precisely why this person wishes to speak with you.
- Third, tell the person you wish to make an appointment for a date and time in the future. The investigator will probably attempt to talk you out of delaying the interview, but you have the right to schedule a future time. The common ploy is to suggest that honest people have nothing to hide and there is no reason for innocent people to consult an attorney. The simple response to such a claim is that honorable government investigators have nothing to fear from a simple delay of an interview.

After the investigator leaves, promptly contact the Corporate Compliance Officer or one of your attorneys.

Remember, investigations by the government are commonplace and seldom result in criminal prosecutions. The mere fact that an inquiry is made does not in any way suggest that any entity has acted negligently or improperly. The government has a right and obligation to conduct inquiries, just as you have the right to demand that it be done in an orderly and proper fashion. Each provider or consultant to the health industry is well advised to assess its regulatory risk and develop a Corporate Compliance Plan that includes procedures for responding to government audits and investigations.

Billing Hospital Services

A record of services rendered to hospital patients is normally compiled by the hospital when a patient is discharged and by the physician on an ongoing basis. To compile and bill a physician's hospital charges accurately, the practice needs to develop an effective form of communication. Otherwise, the physician's office may lose revenue. The billing employee can determine the charges and related fees for the hospital services by reviewing the physician's communicative record. If this record is easy to read and clear, the patient or his or her insurance carrier can be billed in a timely manner.

■ **Practice Point:** Find out how a physician communicates hospital and surgical charges to the billing employee. This is the first step in determining if there is a problem in the billing process.

The manner in which the physician communicates his or her hospital charges to the billing employee can take many forms. For example, if a surgery is performed, the employee must wait for the operative note to know exactly which services the surgeon rendered. For hospital visits, the billing employee does not know what the physician is actually doing in the hospital unless the physician informs the office. The physician can relay this information by calling the practice, by recording the information in a hand-held tape recorder, or by providing the office with a written communication. Unless the physician communicates the information accurately, charges will be lost. For example, the billing employee could bill the wrong level of service or not bill a charge because the physician did not notify him about the charge.

Medicare Billing for Physician Assistants, Nurse Practitioners, and Clinical Nurse Specialists

As a way to improve practice and clinical efficiencies, many medical practices around the country are employing physician assistants (PAs), nurse practitioners (NPs), and clinical nurse specialists (CNSs). As such, it is important to know how to bill these services and how they will be paid.

Payment for Services

The payment for PAs, NPs, and CNSs is up to 80 percent of the lesser of either the actual charge or 85 percent of the physician fee amount. For assistance at surgical services, payment equals 80 percent of the lesser of either the actual charge or 85 percent of the physician fee schedule amount paid to a physician serving as an assistant at surgery.

Billing Requirements for PA Services

Medicare payment for PA services is made only to the PA's employer, regardless of whether the PA is employed as a W-2 employee or whether the PA is a 1099 employee who is acting as an independent contractor. Accordingly, while a PA has an option in terms of selecting employment arrangements, only the "employer" (W-2 or 1099 as the case may be) can bill a carrier or intermediary for the PA's services.

When PAs are rendering service(s), Form HCFA-1500 must contain the provider identification number (PIN) of the PA as well as the employer's name, address, where payment is to be directed, etc. If the employer is a group practice, the employer must include its group PIN, including the name, address, where payment is to be directed, and list the individual PA's PIN on the form.

Billing Requirements for NP and CNS Services

Medicare requires that NPs and CNSs submit claims to the Part B carrier in their state under their own respective billing number for professional services furnished in a facility or other provider settings, except when the services of these non-physician practitioners are clearly facility services and are specifically included in the costs that are covered by the intermediary payment to the facility. Only the facility may bill and be paid for non-physician practitioner services when the services are billable as facility services and are bundled or included in the facility payment.

"Incident to" Services Not Affected by These Provisions

Services provided "incident to" physicians' services are not affected. "Incident to" services must still be provided by employees of the physician under the physician's direct supervision. Also, those services should continue to be paid for under the physician fee schedule as though physicians personally performed them. This means that payment for those services is based on 100 percent of the physician fee schedule amount. Such "incident to" services may be provided by PAs, NPs, CNSs, nurses, medical assistants, technicians, etc., who are employed by physicians.

Time Limit for Filing Claims

In order to collect payment from patients promptly, the practice needs to file and receive payment from the insurance plan as quickly as possible. Therefore, all insurance claims should be prepared and mailed to the insurance carrier within five to seven working days from the last date of service or hospital discharge.

Tracking Insurance Claim Forms

To test how rapidly a medical office prepares and mails its insurance claim forms, pull a sample of at least 25 claim forms from the unpaid insurance file. After obtaining the sample, prepare and complete a worksheet that tracks the claim form. The worksheet should contain, at minimum, the following headings:

Patient's name

Preparation date

Last date of service

Time difference

You can obtain the preparation date from box 31 and the last date of service from box 24a located on the insurance claim form. On the worksheet, count and document the difference in days and calculate an average for the overall sample of claim forms. If the average is more than seven days, the practice is most likely having a problem getting its claims out, resulting in impaired cash flow and accounts receivable.

Check for any wide variations in the filing of claims for certain services. For example, using a sample that includes both office and hospital charges, a CPA found that a practice was preparing and mailing claims within the seven-day average. Upon a closer analysis of the sample, however, the CPA noticed that the practice was getting its office charges out quickly but was having a problem with the timely filing of hospital charges. The CPA began investigating why hospital charges were not being filed on a timely basis.

■ **Practice Point:** The following are benchmarks for filing insurance claim forms:

Office visits: 2–3 days from date of service

All other services: 5–7 days

Example

Susan Henry needs reconstructive surgery on her nose; the procedure has been deemed to be medically necessary. She has surgery on June 25 and is discharged June 27. The plastic surgeon's office bills the claim 10 days after Susan is discharged and does not follow up with the insurance company. Sixty days pass before the practice calls the insurance company, which states that it has no record of receiving the original claim. Even though the practice immediately faxes a copy to the carrier, the practice does not receive payment until 10 days later—80 days after Susan is discharged. Because Susan's account receivable with the practice is 80 days old before the insurance payment arrives in the office, the co-payment amount is more than 90 days old when she is finally billed. Research shows that a practice is lucky to collect 50 cents on the dollar whenever an account reaches 90 days old.

To improve both the practice's collections and its accounts receivable, the medical office needs to tighten up the billing process. The goal is to prepare and mail insurance claims quickly and then work to receive payment quickly from the insurance company.

Common Causes of Delay and Possible Solutions

Insurance claims are not prepared and mailed on time for a variety of reasons. The following list presents the most common causes with corresponding solutions:

Problem The person responsible for billing in the office is not experienced in filing insurance claim forms for a medical office. For example, an orthopedic practice hires Suann as its billing employee. The office manager assumes Suann has the appropriate billing experience because she was responsible for billing for Dr.

Havens, a proctologist. However, Suann has never billed orthopedic services and she needs some training.

Solution Most people do not realize that the position of billing clerk is quite specialized. The billing clerk must know CPT and ICD-10 coding, along with myriad rules pertaining to managed care, Medicare, Medicaid, and other insurance programs. A person who is inexperienced in these areas of billing generally takes a longer time to prepare insurance claim forms. The most obvious solution is to hire someone with appropriate experience. (See the section titled "The Hiring Process" in Chapter 16.) The office's current billing staff member must be made accountable for his or her job duties, one of which is the timely filing of insurance claim forms. Therefore, make the person aware that the office's policy is to prepare and mail all claims within the required time limit of five to seven days. Then monitor the employee's success at meeting this time requirement by completing the insurance claims forms tracking worksheet on a periodic basis. If a problem still exists, and the employee is filing the forms in a timely manner, search for some other possible cause, such as the proper billing systems not being in place, as discussed throughout this section.

If the problem is due to the employee's lack of knowledge of the billing rules for specific managed-care plans, have the employee complete the summary of managed-care plan requirements form for each plan. (See Appendix B for a sample form.) Then, the billing personnel can refer to the form in the future when billing managed-care plans and thus prevent claims filing delays.

Problem The physician is not completing all services rendered on the Superbill in a timely manner. Perhaps the physician does not record office charges while the patient is in the office or does not complete the Superbill in its entirety. Sometimes the physician completes the CPT code but does not complete the diagnosis code requirement. When this occurs, the billing employee must look in the patient's medical record to determine exactly what the physician did in the exam room. Only then can the physician's services be coded.

Solution You will need to solicit the physician's cooperation. Explain to the physician the consequences of failure to complete the encounter form while the patient is in the office. If you can show how cash flow and receivables are being impacted, the physician may be more cooperative.

Problem   There is a lack of communication between the physician and the billing staff regarding what the physician did when visiting a patient in the hospital. For example, Dr. Gorman, a critical care pulmonogist, has a very busy inpatient practice. She sees approximately 10 patients per day in the hospital. Her billing staff has no idea what she does at the hospital and cannot bill for services until Dr. Gorman informs the staff of such activities. The staff usually waits three to four days to bill Dr. Gorman's services.

Solution   The billing employee needs to capture the physician's hospital charges in a timely manner. The physician should relay her services the same day she performs them. Whenever possible, the physician should document the charges on paper. The physician may want to try using hospital charge cards or surgical charge sheets. (See Appendix B for sample hospital and surgery charge cards.) If the physician cannot or is unwilling to write down the charges, the next best solution is to set aside some time (preferably the first thing after the physician arrives in the office) for the physician and a billing employee to discuss and document the physician's most recent hospital charges.

Problem   The billing staff waits for the operative report before preparing an insurance claim form. For example, Dr. Murphy performs a hysterectomy. Dr. Murphy relies on her billing staff to do its own follow-up in order to bill the procedure, because she is so busy.

Solution   One reason the operative note is needed is because the staff does not know what the physician actually did in the operating room. Using the office's surgery schedule that lists the preliminary procedure, the billing staff should meet with the physician and ask her the following questions:

• Was the listed procedure performed?
• Were any additional procedures performed?

- Were there any complications?
- What is the diagnosis?

The billing staff can complete an insurance claim form by using this information. This solution also eliminates the need to wait for the operative report. For checks and balances, review a selected number of claim forms to be sure that what the physician communicates to the billing staff is actually contained in the operative report.

Another reason a billing employee may wait for operative reports is the misconception that he or she must attach the report to the claim form in order to be paid by the insurance company. However, according to most insurance company representatives, attaching an operative report to an insurance claim form will only delay payment. For example, the Medicare manual states specifically that if an operative report is attached, payment will be delayed. However, an operative report should be attached to the insurance claim form in the following situations:

- When CPT modifier -22 is used
- When an unlisted procedure CPT code is used
- When an insurance company routinely requests the operative report for a specific procedure

If the insurance company routinely requests the operative report, make sure the company is not requesting the report because there was a problem with the insurance claim form. Unbundling charges is a good example of when this might routinely occur. Also, just because one insurance company routinely requests the operative report does not mean all other insurance companies will do the same. Therefore, unless there is a specific reason for doing so, the billing employee should not attach the operative report to an insurance claim form.

Problem The office waits for the hospital or other facility to file its insurance claim first to avoid having the patient's deductible apply to the physician's services. For example, at the start of a new year, all patients have their deductibles in force. A physical medicine physician, whose practice is mainly inpatient at the rehab hospital, holds claims for the first three months of the year so the rehab hospital will be assessed the patient's deductibles.

Solution This policy will always delay claim filing and impair cash flow. Help the practice implement and monitor a filing policy that allows the office staff to collect the deductible as soon as possible after the service is rendered or before the service is rendered. For hospital-based physicians, work with the hospital's business office to have it try to collect these payments for the practice.

Problem The physician wants to review all insurance claim forms before they are mailed, and he does not review them in a timely manner. For example, Dr. Camp has informed his staff that he wants to review all insurance claim forms before they are mailed, because the office has had some problems with incorrectly filed forms. However, Dr. Camp is busy and cannot review the files immediately; he usually returns the forms in a week.

Solution If a physician is confident that the billing employees are correctly preparing claim forms and are not missing any charges, then a final review by the physician should not be necessary. However, if the forms are filed incorrectly, either review the forms or encourage the physician to speed up the review process by showing how the delay is impacting the practice and its cash flow. The best solution is to hire competent and experienced billing employees.

Another sure way to speed up the claims filing and payment process is to have the practice file the forms electronically. Medicare, Medicaid, and a variety of other insurance carriers have electronic capabilities. Electronic filing can be useful for practices with multiple physicians filing numerous insurance claim forms or any practice that sees a large number of Medicare or Medicaid patients, regardless of the office's size. For more information on electronic billing, contact the practice's computer vendor or the state's Medicare or Medicaid office. The practice's computer vendor should also be able to provide a list of commercially available insurance claim clearinghouses that can bill claims electronically, directly to other insurance carriers. If you need more information, then contact the state's medical association.

Filing Primary Insurance Claims

In the interest of keeping accounts receivable low, it is generally best to avoid filing an insurance claim for office visits if a patient has commercial insurance, unless special circumstances require that certain arrangements be made with the patient. Remind the office manager or the physician that billed services become accounts receivable and that it is always preferable to receive payment immediately. Special circumstances include situations in which patients are clearly incapable of filing claims, when the law requires the office to file the claim, or when patients forget to bring their checkbooks or credit cards, or have no other way of making a payment. Other reasons to bill services are if charges are too high to collect at the time of service (e.g., surgical charges, in which case the receptionist should at least collect the deductible and/or co-payment) or if other physicians in the area bill the insurance company instead of collecting monies at the time of service.

> ■ **Practice Point:** Some physicians play follow the leader. For example, physicians in a particular service area bill the patient's insurance before collecting any monies from the patient. Physicians do this because it is a community standard. However, assess the current practice and determine if following such standards is the best office policy for the practice.

If necessary, reemphasize the point: The reason to avoid filing commercial insurance claims is to maximize cash flow. If an insurance claim is filed for commercial insurance, it becomes an accounts receivable to the practice and thus is subject to all the office policies and procedures necessary to obtain payment from the insurance company. If the office collects payment for the visit, there is no accounts receivable for that transaction. The more money the office can collect at the front desk, the better the practice's cash flow will be. A detailed discussion of how to use the front-desk collections monitoring form is found in Chapter 12 under the section titled "Front-Desk Collection Analysis." (See Appendix B for a sample front-desk collection analysis worksheet.) The front-desk employee should be able to collect some payment for at least 90 percent of its visits, even if a patient only pays $5. If the percentage of collections at the front desk is lower than 90 percent, investigate immediately.

The practice must file insurance claims for patients covered by Medicare, Medicaid, workers' compensation, and almost all managed-care plans, as required by law or by the plan's contract with the physician. A practice generally files primary insurance claims for hospital charges. The billing employee should take special care to make sure that billings for hospital services are compatible with the hospital's own records. This protects the office in the event of an audit by an insurance company.

Before mailing insurance claims, the billing employee should make sure all of the patient's forms that are required by insurance companies have been completed and mailed. For example, some insurance plans have their own authorization statements that must be signed by the patients and submitted to the insurance companies before the physicians can be paid. If the patients were referred by other physicians within HMOs or PPOs, the billing employee should make sure the appropriate referral forms have been completed and mailed, if applicable. Many managed-care plans require primary-care physicians to complete physician referral forms when patients are referred to specialists. In order to be paid, the specialists' offices must attach these forms to their own insurance claims.

■ **Practice Point:** Make sure that insurance filing information is collected in a notebook. The notebook should contain the specific billing requirements and guidelines for each of the practice's major insurance carriers it bills. All staff members should be aware of this information and where they can find it.

Filing Secondary Insurance Claims

Most medical practices file secondary insurance claims for their patients. Secondary insurance policies generally cover the services not covered by primary insurance plans. In almost all cases, these types of policies act as a supplement to Medicare coverage. Medicare supplemental insurance, or a *Medigap policy*, is a health insurance plan designed specifically to supplement Medicare's benefits by filling in some of the gaps in Medicare coverage. All supplemental policies do not provide the same benefits. Some pay for the Medicare deductible, while most pay the coinsurance amount. Some policies even cover a limited number of services not covered under the Medicare program.

The practice needs to have a process for detecting when a patient has a supplemental insurance policy. If it does not, the practice will mistakenly bill the patient for the remaining amount that Medicare did not cover. After waiting a period of time, the practice will find out that the patient has not paid because he or she thought the office was filing the secondary insurance claim. This activity drags out a practice's cash flow and creates older accounts receivable. The new patient information form must include a section that indicates if a secondary insurance policy is in force. In addition, front-desk personnel should be trained to ask the patient if he or she has a supplemental policy, whether the patient is new or established.

■ **Practice Point:** On a periodic basis, review an aging of the practice's Medicare accounts receivable. Review small account balances in excess of 90 days. The problem may be that the practice is having difficulty identifying secondary insurance claims.

The most important aspect of filing a patient's secondary insurance is timeliness. Because secondary insurance claims are for relatively small amounts of money, many practices do not pay strict attention to such filings. All this does is delay the office's reimbursement and impede its cash flow. Delayed filings could also create inefficiencies because the billing employee will have to spend time collecting a large number of small-balance accounts. One of the best ways you can find out if the office is not filing secondary claims in a timely manner is to review an aging of accounts receivable. Look for small balances in the over-90-days column. If these are secondary insurance filings, the practice most likely is not filing these claims on a timely basis. If the practice has this problem, suggest that it implement the policy of having the Medicare patient pay the office for his or her deductible and co-payment while the office extends the service of preparing and mailing the secondary claim for the patient. Attempting to collect the co-payment also helps physicians' offices document these attempts, which is required by Medicare. Another solution is to make the billing personnel accountable for the timely filing of the claims, if the practice decides not to collect the money directly from the patient. Monitor the timing of Medicare reimbursements and make sure the office files the secondary claims within two days after receiving payment from Medicare.

Organizing Office Copies of Insurance Claim Forms

Often, copies of filed but unpaid insurance claim forms are scattered throughout the office. In some offices the copy is kept in the patient's chart. This activity creates internal inefficiencies and is a prime indication that the office is most likely not doing its follow-up work on a timely basis. The practice's copies of all filed but unpaid insurance claim forms should be kept in a centralized location in the office so that anyone can access the unpaid insurance claims. Centralizing the insurance claim forms allows for (a) easy access when performing insurance follow-up procedures, (b) a quick review of the claim forms if such a review is required, and (c) the easy tracing of the unpaid claims to other source documents in the office. For example, the hard copies of the insurance claims should be traced to the computer-generated unpaid insurance report to ensure the report's accuracy. The hard copy of the insurance claims can be used to trace to the patient's ledger accounts for internal control purposes. In this situation, insurance claim amounts must always agree with the patient's accounts receivable on the account ledger.

One easy way to centralize the unpaid forms is to keep the office copies in an alphabetized or numerical expandable folder until payment is received. For insurance claims that are filed electronically, the electronic claim submission edit report or a printout of the actual insurance claim forms should be maintained in the centralized file. As practical as this all sounds, it may prove impractical for some medical offices. This is especially true for those practices that file a large number of claim forms and for those offices that file most of their claims electronically. No matter how an office files its claims, an important practice management goal is to make sure all unpaid insurance claim forms are somehow centrally maintained.

> ■ **Practice Point:** Centralization of insurance claim forms is often impractical for larger medical practices or for those that file numerous claims. In this situation, make sure that copies of claims can be printed on demand (without interfering with the reporting) and the practice can at any time print an aging of unpaid insurance accounts receivable from its computer.

Billing Process Questionnaire

The following is a list of questions about the billing process that should help you improve the efficiency of billing third-party payors, while at the same time improve or maintain cash flow. Each question must have an answer since each is vital to the billing process. If you are a new medical practice, sit down with the billing staff and go over these questions. If you are an existing practice, do the same. Again, the objective is to streamline the billing process and make it as effective and efficient as it can be.

- When should a patient's insurance information first be obtained?
- When should a patient's insurance be verified?
- How should an office determine if a patient's insurance coverage has changed since the last visit?
- Should an office make a copy of the patient's insurance card?
- Should new patient demographic information be input into the computer before a patient is escorted to the exam room?
- Must each doctor be required to complete all information on the charge ticket after he or she treats a patient?
- When the patient checks out, is all the charge and payment information entered into the computer before the patient leaves the office?
- How should surgical or procedural charges be captured so that they may be billed properly and timely?

- How often should insurance claim forms be filed each week?
- Will each doctor be required to dictate notes on a timely basis?
- If yes and the physician is in non-compliance, what will be the penalty?
- Does the practice utilize electronic billing?

▼ CHAPTER 12
Accounts Receivable Management

If a practice has a good collection system within the office, and employees follow the system, theoretically, the practice should not have a problem with cash flow and receivables. This is not the case, however, for many medical practices. Some offices do not have a defined collection system or their collection duties are delegated among employees. In some practices, collection activities take a back seat to other office activities. In larger practices, the sheer volume of revenue tends to mask certain collection inefficiencies within the billing and collection department. In other words, when cash flow is good, most offices do not pay much attention to potential problems that might be occurring within the collection department. This chapter provides an overview of accounts receivable management and related collection policies.

Information First

It is important to remember that accounts receivable management *starts* with information. In other words, a practice must adopt the policy of printing and reviewing accounts receivable aging reports in detail each month. This is the only real way to assess how well the office's collection efforts are doing. However, many offices, even large practices, have a lax attitude toward this simple issue. Besides the simple aging report, a practice should also print and review an aging by insurance company and separate agings for patient receivables and insurance receivables. Unfortunately, most practices' computer systems cannot print these specialized reports which are so important to good receivables management. Without good information about a practice's receivables, it is almost impossible to manage its overdue accounts adequately.

■ **Practice Point:** Make sure that these reports are printed and reviewed on a regular basis. Many practice managers, CPAs, etc., are so consumed with other duties that they sometimes forget about a few basics, such as making sure accounts receivable are not getting out of hand.

Handling Billing Inquiries by Phone

At various times during the day or week, patients will call the medical office regarding their accounts. The last thing an office wants to do is upset patients, especially those who are voluntarily calling about their account balances. Multiple account balance requests, however, could hinder the collection process. The protocol for handling account inquiries by telephone is an important, and often overlooked, element in the collection process. Make sure that the practice's employees use the following simple guidelines when answering the patient's telephone calls:

1. Always respond in a courteous manner and express willingness to help. One reason patients either leave a practice or delay making payments on their accounts is because a staff member was rude or unhelpful.

2. Use the patient's information in the computer or on the patient ledger cards to help answer questions. This is where the billing detail is located.

3. If it is necessary to call back a patient, specify a time convenient for the patient.

4. Never tell patients that the office cannot locate their accounts or other relevant information. Such a response sounds like the office is either putting patients off or is unorganized.

5. The staff members should never ask patients to call back later. Instead, staff members should express a willingness to return patients' calls. Patients will either accept or offer to call back.

Patients' Account Statements

The employee responsible for billing should send account statements each month to all patients who have balances due. There should not be any exceptions to this rule.

■ **Practice Point:** Do not assume that the office is actually sending the statements. A number of offices do not send out patient statements consistently each month.

Many practices like to prepare and mail the statements no later than the 25th of every month so that the statements will arrive before the first of the next month, when most patients typically pay their bills. Under no circumstances, however, should the billing employee send the patients' statements later than the 10th day of the following month. Some surgical practices like to mail patient's account statements as soon as the patients' insurance companies have reimbursed the practice. The practices' collections will improve if the billing employee can send the patients' account balances as early as possible. In larger practices, statements usually are sent out weekly in batched cycles. This is done either by the age of the accounts or in cycles using the patients' last names. For example, balances of patients whose last names end in A through K are mailed out during the first week of the month.

A practice may want to continue to send account statements if a balance is due and even if the patient's insurance company will pay for the services. Account statements should state clearly that insurance reimbursement is pending. This alerts patients about the billing and what their ultimate liability might be. If there is no mention of the insurance pending, patients may pay the balance and create a problem with multiple credit balances in accounts receivable.

■ **Practice Point:** Watch for practices that collect reimbursement from a patient's insurance and write off the remainder of the balance without sending the patient an account statement. The routine writing off of co-payments and deductibles is usually considered an illegal practice, especially according to Medicare. The practice should always make an effort to collect these balances, unless the practice can demonstrate a patient's particular financial hardship.

■ **Practice Point:** A question that often gets raised is whether or not a practice should use some type of finance charge for overdue accounts. The answer generally is "no." One reason is that according to most state laws, a person must legally contract (i.e., agree) to pay a finance charge. The main reason is that finance charges violate most provider agreements with insurance carriers. For example, finance charges violate Medicare law because a physician would collect more than the allowable from the Medicare patient. This applies to both participating and nonparticipating physicians. Also, finance charges likely violate managed-care arrangements because most provider contracts state the physician cannot collect more than the co-payment and/or deductible from the patient.

The practice can use its computer to print out patients' statements. If the practice does not have a computer system, an employee should make copies of the patient ledger cards and mail them to the appropriate patients. All patients' statements should include some type of dunning message on them. A *dunning message* is a short message on the statement, usually at the bottom. "Your insurance is still pending" and "Your account is overdue" are examples of dunning messages. Like collection letters, each message should be tailored to the age of the account. This provides basic communication with patients and it may improve the practice's collection activity.

■ **Practice Point:** Make sure that the practice's employees know the difference between a dunning message and a collection letter. Collection letters are considered a much stronger form of account collection; dunning messages are friendly reminder messages.

Collection Policies

The following is an overview of the most common forms of collection systems and policies for medical offices.

Office Visits

A major collection policy goal for a practice should be to collect something from every patient who comes to the office for an appointment, unless payment is not allowed by law. This was briefly discussed in the section on patient appointment scheduling in Chapter 9. Conduct a periodic check of the front-desk collection activity to determine if the front-desk employee is collecting the necessary monies.

Front-Desk Collection Analysis

One way you can check the effectiveness of the front-desk collection policy is to analyze the percentage of potential office visit payments that are actually paid (at least partially) while patients are in the office. You can do this by using the following process:

1. Select a sample of patients' office visits, generally covering 20 to 25 separate days.
2. Count all the visits in which patients could have made payments, no matter how small. This includes patients who could have paid in full, made a partial payment, paid their co-payment, or paid their deductible. Exclude visits in which the office cannot legally accept payment from the patient (e.g., Medicaid and workers' compensation). If you are unsure whether or not a particular patient could pay at the time of service, ask the billing or front-desk employee.
3. Count the number of visits in which patients actually made payments, regardless of the amount.
4. Divide the number of payments by the number of potential payment situations to compute the percentage of patients who made a payment at the time of their visits. (See Appendix B for a sample front-desk collection analysis worksheet.)

A practice should be able to collect some form of payment for at least 90 percent of the visits for which a payment can legally be accepted. If your analysis indicates a lower percentage, investigate immediately. Find out if the front-desk employee has been properly trained on collections and whether the employee is complying with the office's collection policy. Keep in mind that some people feel uncomfortable asking patients for payment. Such personnel should not be at the practice's front desk.

■ **Practice Point:** Remember that service-area politics often dictate the practice's collection policy. In some communities, especially smaller ones, the standard is to bill a patient's insurance first before attempting to collect directly from the patient.

Delinquent Accounts

If a patient who is making an appointment has a balance due on his or her account, the receptionist should note this fact and try to collect the receivable at the time of the visit. If the balance is a large amount, the office manager should discuss the delinquent account with the patient. Staff members should never embarrass a patient by talking to him or her about an overdue account in front of other patients. The front-desk staff should be as discreet as possible. The patient's promise to pay should be documented, preferably by having the patient sign some type of installment agreement.

■ **Practice Point:** Suggest usage of the following sample office policy regarding delinquent accounts: If the overdue balance is less than $250, the front-desk employee is responsible for collecting the balance or partial payment. If the balance is $250 or more, the patient should be directed automatically to the office manager for financial counseling.

■ **Practice Point:** For noncovered services or denied services, make sure that the patient is liable for the balance that is due. Most managed-care contracts state a patient is liable for noncovered services, but sometimes they are not liable for denied services.

Bad Debt Control

With the financial pressures inherent in modern medicine, it is imperative that a practice collect every dollar it is entitled to. Mechanisms and systems need to be in place to avoid bad debt situations to the greatest extent possible. The following checklist will help determine whether or not a medical practice is at undue risk for bad debts. Any "no" answers should be investigated immediately and solutions should be recommended.

Do written guidelines exist on the collection of self-pay accounts? Every practice should have written guidelines on how to handle self-pay and patient-pay accounts. These are accounts in which the patient has no insurance or the patient owes a balance after his or her insurance has paid.

Are collection guidelines periodically reviewed and revised? The modern medical practice environment is in a state of flux, and internal policies of a practice, especially collection policies, need to keep pace if the practice is to thrive. Policies should be reviewed and revised at selected times.

Are collection guidelines clear, concise, and sufficiently detailed to serve as a working reference to personnel? Medical practices should have clear documentation of guidelines that employees can read and understand easily. This reduces training time and provides employees with a useful ongoing reference guide.

Does business office personnel receive adequate initial training on collection guidelines and procedures? Up-front training can help avoid and eliminate many day-to-day problems within the practice. Good practices take the time to train new employees.

Do employees receive periodic supplemental training on collection guidelines and procedures? After initial training, periodic supplemental training is recommended. This training is appropriate after revisions to the guidelines or procedures. It should also occur at regular intervals, say annually, even if there is no revision. To determine whether supplemental training is necessary, consider whether the guidelines are being followed. Are the guidelines working? Monitor the collection results as part of an ongoing assessment to ensure that the guidelines and procedures are effective.

Are employee suggestions for changes in policies and procedures encouraged? Good practices encourage and recognize employee feedback.

Do exceptions to guidelines require the case-by-case approval of management? Guidelines should be followed "to the letter," although, there could be situations in which an exception to the policy may be called for. However, the decision to deviate from the guidelines should not be made by the employee. Exceptions should be reviewed, approved by management, and properly documented.

Do self-pay guidelines allow payments over time on certain accounts? A sound collection policy will allow for installment payments. A review mechanism should be in place to make sure that installment payments are actually being made as scheduled.

Do self-pay guidelines cover minimum payment amounts and the maximum number of payments that will be accepted? The installment payment policy should be fair to both the patient and the practice. Set a reasonable length of time for patients to pay off their accounts.

Do collection guidelines specify what action should be taken if a patient misses a payment? The policy should specify at what stage additional collection actions are taken. And it should be followed diligently. For example, if the policy is to turn the patient over to collection if two consecutive payments are missed, then this should be followed in each case. If exceptions are made, then they should be made only with management's approval.

Does management support the collection guidelines, even when a patient complains? All the doctors within the practice must support the guidelines. It is self-defeating to implement a policy that doctors will not follow. Policies and guidelines become ineffectual if employees receive disparate instructions from different doctors and administrators.

Hardship Cases

In hardship cases, the practice can make special arrangements with patients on a case-by-case basis. However, the office manager should do this only if it is in accordance with the practice's established guidelines. The front-desk employee should know the practice's collection guidelines and how to implement them. The patient's promises to pay should be documented in his or her account whenever practical. If necessary, the patient could sign some form of an installment agreement. The billing employee will need to follow up on these promises to make sure that the patient continues to make installment payments.

Professional Courtesy

Various legal issues are raised by the practice of professional courtesy—taking care of the families of other physicians without charge—and providing discounts for medical care. While professional courtesy is good for the medical profession in that it builds bonds between physicians and reduces the incentive for physicians to treat their own families, the U.S. Congress and private insurance companies have greatly reduced the permissible scope for discounting charges for medical care. Practices must review their policies to assure that they are in compliance with the appropriate requirements. Violating restrictions on reduced charges can subject violators to steep penalties, including the following:

- Denial of the claim
- Deselection from the plan
- Fines
- Imprisonment

Private insurers and the federal rules both impose basic restrictions on how patients are charged for medical care. There is no exception to these restrictions for professional courtesy. So, in general, if you cannot reduce the cost of care for anyone else in your practice, you cannot reduce it for physicians. On the other hand, there are situations in which it is allowable to reduce the cost of care for everyone except physicians.

Waiving Co-pays

The most common way physicians reduce the cost of care for patients is waiving the co-pay ("insurance only") and giving the patient a discount on the care. Private insurers and the federal government generally ban waiving the co-pay. The reason is that the co-pay is meant to discourage casual trips to the physician. The theory is that patients will be more sophisticated health care consumers if they share the cost of treatment. The reality is otherwise. The co-pay limits access to care for many people. Note that Medicare has some provisions allowing the co-pay to be waived for documented indigency. Insurers and Medicare both require reasonable efforts to collect co-pays.

Discounts

Giving a discount—that is, taking a set amount or a percentage off the bill—raises certain risks. The practice must be aware that the discount must apply to the total bill, and not just to the patient's portion. For example, if the patient owes a 20 percent co-pay on a $50.00 charge ($10.00) and the practice gives a $10.00 discount, the patient pays $8.00 and the insurance company pays $32.00. If the patient owes a $10.00 co-pay regardless of the amount of the charge, the patient must pay $10.00 and the insurance company pays $30.00. So, in this situation, the discount would only benefit the insurance company.

Discounts raise issues as to the practice's customary charges for a procedure. Many private insurers and some federal programs have a so-called most favored nation clause in their contract which entitles the plan to pay the lowest charge the practice bills to anyone. The practice runs the risk that a pattern of discounts could reduce the allowable reimbursement schedule to the discounted price.

No Charge

There is no private-insurer ban on waiving the entire charge for the care. Practices are free to charge for some visits and not for others. For example, many pediatricians do not charge for the first follow-up visit for otitis media (inflamation of the middle ear). This increases the likelihood that the child will be brought back for the recheck. The insurance company is also getting a free ride, but at least the patient is getting the care.

No-charge visits that are part of a fraudulent scheme are prohibited. Also, a no-charge visit is still a patient-care encounter that must be fully documented. For example, a patient has severe asthma and is subject to a one-year preexisting illness exclusion in his health insurance policy. If the practice provides necessary treatment a month before the end of the year-long waiting period, it must document the treatment fully, even if it does not charge the insurance company for the treatment.

Practices can also deliver non-reimbursable care as part of an otherwise justified office visit and bill the company for the authorized part of the visit. For example, if the insurance doesn't cover immunizations, a practice could do the immunizations at the time it does an authorized well-child check-up or when the child is in for some other medical condition. It cannot, however, bill for an office visit when the only reason the patient is being seen is to deliver care that is not authorized under the policy.

Kickbacks and Inducements to Refer Patients

Federal law and the laws of some states govern financial transactions between health care providers. These laws, which include the Medicare Fraud and Abuse laws and Stark I and Stark II (applying to care paid for in whole or in part by the federal government), prohibit any inducements or kickbacks that could influence the decision of a physician (or others) to refer patients or affect a patient's decision to seek care. Violations are punishable with fines and imprisonment. Further, any claims submitted for the care of the patients gotten through the scheme are deemed false claims.

Courts construe these laws broadly. Even if it has other valid purposes, any payment or inducement that might have a tendency to affect referral decisions is prohibited. The following example is based on one of the leading cases in this area: A lab providing Holter monitor services charged a fee for providing the monitor and hired outside cardiologists to read the record. This was perfectly proper. However, the lab also allowed the ordering cardiologist to be the reading cardiologist. There was no allegation that the service cost more or was not properly done. The arrangement was ruled illegal solely because paying the ordering physician could induce the physician to order the test. According to the court, an otherwise proper payment is illegal if it can also have the purpose of affecting referrals.

Otherwise permissible discounts or no-charge visits can also run afoul of these laws. Here are some examples:

- A surgeon gives professional courtesy only to physicians who referred business. This constitutes a clear violation of the law.
- A physician gives professional courtesy only to physicians on the same hospital staff. This raises the same issues, although the link to referrals is more tenuous.
- A physician gives professional courtesy to all physicians without conditions. This approach is more defensible, but there's still a risk if the government can show that a disproportionate number of physicians receiving the courtesy were also referring physicians. A court might well rule that this was a prohibited inducement.

Penalties

The penalties for running afoul of the kickback and inducement rules can be steep. They include the following:

- Private insurers can refuse to pay the claim based on violation of the contract.
- Private insurers can deselect the physician from the plan.
- The insurer could sue the physician for fraud.
- In extreme cases, the government could prosecute the physician for mail and wire fraud for using the mail and electronic communications to file the fraudulent claims.
- The Health Insurance Portability and Accountability Act of 1996 (HIPAA), better known as the Kennedy-Kassebaum bill, makes it a federal crime to defraud private insurance companies. Violations of the contracts with a private insurer are criminal fraud under HIPAA and could result in fines and criminal prosecution.
- The federal government can refuse to pay a claim and can ban the physician from participation in Medicare and Medicaid.

- Filing a claim for services that were provided in ways that did not follow the federal regulations violates the False Claims Act (FCA). Violations of the FCA are punishable by a $5,000 fine per claim and imprisonment. The large financial settlements that have been paid recently to the federal government, such as the $17.5 million paid by Baptist Medical Center in Kansas City, are based on false claims allegations.

How great is the risk? While so far there have been no reported cases, prosecutions, or settlements based solely on professional courtesy to health care providers, in the general patient care arena, private insurance fraud cases have been based on waiving co-pays and/or providing discounts that were not passed on to the insurer. There have been federal actions for the same violations, as well as for using waivers and discounts to induce Medicare patients to use other health care services.

Recommendation

Practices must examine their professional courtesy policies to assure that these do not violate either the contractual terms in private insurance policies or the Medicare/Medicaid laws and regulations. Practices should make sure that professional courtesy is not linked to referrals, either in reality or in appearance.

Collection Procedures

The following is a basic, general procedure used to collect payment from overdue accounts in a medical practice if the patients do not present themselves for office visits.

Accounts Receivable

Each month, the billing employee should age the accounts receivable to determine the priority for collection. The employee's ability to age the accounts receivable easily into the categories of current, 30 days old, 60 days old, and 90 days old will depend on whether the practice is computerized. If it is computerized, the aging should not be difficult, because the computer has the capability to calculate accounts' ages automatically. If the practice uses a pegboard system, the employee will have to age the accounts manually using the individual patient ledger cards. This will take an enormous amount of time (which illustrates one distinct advantage of purchasing and using a computer system). One way to age accounts manually is to segregate the patient ledger cards physically by their respective ages.

> ■ **Practice Point:** If the practice is still using a pegboard system for billing and collection, suggest that it buy a computer. Using the cheapest medical software system is still better than a manual system. Computerized practices are more efficient, more accountable, and can be better managed.

Telephone Calls and Past-Due Notices

After using accounts receivable aging to determine past-due payments, the person in the office responsible for collections should make an initial friendly phone call to the patient. Because of personnel shortage, busy schedules, or other reasons, calling all patients sometimes is impractical. If this is the case, try setting a limit on the telephone calls. For example, the office policy may be that the collection employee will call patients whose account balances exceed a particular dollar amount. For most practices, the balance is between $200 and $500. However, if the practice is large, you may have to raise the balance limit to make the number of phone calls manageable.

> ■ **Practice Point:** Stress the importance of having the front-desk employee collect overdue receivables at the time of a patient's visit. Because of the time required to collect individual patient accounts (not insurance accounts), the office could increase productivity and cash flow if the front-desk employee collected money on overdue accounts.

If a practice is too busy to make telephone calls, the office should send friendly past-due notices to patients whose accounts are 30 days delinquent. (See Appendix B for sample collection letters.)

The collection employee should send past-due notices to patients whose insurance has not yet paid, assuming the employee has filed insurance claim forms. The employee responsible for the practice's collections needs to document his or her follow-up conversations with the patients. He or she can do this on the computer, or on the ledger cards if the practice uses a pegboard system. This not only documents any patient promises, but also is a way to make the collection person accountable for follow-up duties. If this documentation does not exist or is sporadic, it could be because the collection employee is not following up with collection calls.

> ■ **Practice Point:** Make sure that the practice makes its collection employees accountable for their collection efforts. This is one of the best ways to maximize collection activities.

If patients do not respond to the friendly 30-day approach, and if their accounts become 60 days old, the billing employee should send stronger collection letters. The employee should continue to place collection calls to the patients and to document all conversations. Review this documentation periodically to assess what patients are saying about not paying their accounts. This way, the practice's collection policies can be fine-tuned to improve collection efforts.

After accounts are 90 days old, the practice's billing employee should begin to work the accounts rigorously. The 90-day and final collection letters should be sent to all patients who have not yet contacted the office about their delinquent accounts. (See Appendix B for sample collection letters.) Many practices utilize what is normally called a "10-day letter." This letter is automatically sent to all patients who have received three statements. The letter basically tells the patient the following information:

1. The account is seriously overdue.

2. The practice is understanding and thus is willing to work with the patient to come up with a mutually favorable payment plan.

3. The patient should call the office within 10 days to discuss the account; otherwise the office will have to pursue a more serious form of collection effort.

If a patient does not call within the 10-day period, he or she probably is not going to pay the account. In other words, it is a bad debt. The practice may opt to write off bad debts (but only with a physician's approval) or, if appropriate, the practice may turn over the accounts to a collection agency.

Collection Agencies

Many practices are reluctant to turn accounts over to a collection agency, perhaps because they fear that the patient may threaten a lawsuit or because the physician is simply uncomfortable about taking this step. Remind the practice that as long as it is doing its job trying to collect overdue accounts in both an efficient and timely manner, patients who do not pay are probably trying to skip out on their bills. Essentially, these people have stolen the office's services, and the office should not feel guilty about resorting to a collection agency.

Many medical offices express a lack of confidence in the agency or agencies they use or have used in the past. The most common cause of such poor results is that accounts are turned over too late to be collected. To obtain the best performance out of a collection agency, the office manager should turn over accounts to the agency when they are 90 days old (or after the 10-day letter has been sent out, as discussed earlier). By handing the accounts over in a timely manner, the agency can work on delinquent accounts and the office staff can work on more current accounts. It does not make good collection sense for employees to spend a majority of their time trying to collect accounts that are 90 days old or older. The practice should let someone else do it. Medical practice collections will improve if the majority of time and effort is spent on collecting accounts less than 90 days old.

The following is a worksheet to see how well the practice's collection agency has been performing; if the numbers are not up to your expectations, it may be time to change agencies.

Total balances turned over to collection: _____

Total amount collected by the agency: _____

Percent collected: _____%

Total individual accounts turned over to collection: _____

Total individual accounts where collection occurred: _____

Percent collected: _____%

Other Collection Options

Some offices utilize two other collection methodologies: small claims court and a collection bureau. The first option, small claims court, is used when the practice files a lawsuit against the patient for the amount owed. Many physicians do not like to use this approach because they fear this may cause patients to consider some type of malpractice claims against them.

The next collection method is to turn the bad-debt information over to a collection bureau. When this is done, the bad debt goes on the patient's own credit record. A patient faced with bad credit will often attempt at some point in the future to contact the office regarding settling his or her delinquent account.

Potential Problems with Hospital Consults

One area of problem collections is hospital consultations. In a typical scenario, one physician asks another physician (usually a specialist, such as a neurologist) to step in and see his or her patient who is already in the hospital. The specialist will usually then bill the patient or patient's insurance for a hospital consultation. Many times the patient is totally unaware that the physician is going to bill them. This leads to a collection problem. Patients usually do not want to pay for a service for which they did not ask or pay a physician with whom they are not acquainted.

If the physician is a referral-based physician, the following letter could be sent to a patient's home address as soon as possible after the consultation occurs. This should improve collections related to hospital consultations.

Sample Hospital Consult Letter

Dear Patient:

Your attending physician, Dr._____, asked that I see you in consultation regarding _____(state condition). I have reviewed your medical chart and have examined you at the hospital. I have submitted a report of my findings to Dr._____.

As a physician practicing independently of Dr._____, I will be paid for my services separately. Your insurance will reimburse me its amount, and I will bill you for any additional co-payment and/or deductible. If you should have any questions, please do not hesitate to contact my office at your convenience.

Unpaid Insurance Claims

The following general system can be used to collect on unpaid insurance claims.

Identifying Unpaid Claims

Every week the collection employee should identify unpaid insurance claims that are at least 25 days old. If the practice is computerized, the employee can print a report that lists these claims; other offices should have a centralized location, usually an alphabetized expandable file, for unpaid claims. Some offices may keep the office copies in patient's charts. Unless the office has access to a list of the unpaid claims, however, keeping the forms in the charts will often create inefficiencies. This is because the collection personnel will have to pull charts in order to follow up on accounts and will not know at any one time which claims are 25 days old.

Telephone Calls

For each claim that is at least 25 days old, the collection employee should place a call to each insurance company. This conversation must always be documented in the computer or in some other location. The employee should include the name of the contact at the insurance company, why the claim has not been paid, and when payment can be expected. (See Appendix B for a sample insurance follow-up form.) If the documentation is made on paper, the employee should attach it to each office copy of the unpaid claim until payment is received. If the office files a large number of claims electronically, the forms can be attached to the computer edit report that lists the electronically filed claims. The reason for starting with claims that are 25 days old is that the office must find out as soon as possible whether claim forms even got to the insurance companies and were entered into their computers. A chronic problem for many practices is that insurance companies will say they have no record of receiving claims. By starting with claims that are 25 days old, the collection employee can refile claims early. In addition, the earlier the employee starts the follow-up process, the quicker the claims will be paid on balance. A major goal of every medical practice is to obtain payment within 30 to 45 days for all insurance claim forms filed.

■ **Practice Point:** Accountability for follow-up calls is important for collection success. Monitor how many follow-up calls the collection employee makes during the week. If left unaccountable, many employees will not make such calls. Instruct the office to print its related notes from the computer for review.

Whether the employee responsible for collections should make telephone calls to every insurance company that has accounts that are 25 days old depends on how many claims are filed each week, how large the balances are, and the capabilities of the office's collection personnel. The goal of any office should be to try to make all the phone calls. If all of the calls cannot be made, the employee should first call those insurance companies with balances greater than a specified dollar amount. Otherwise, the *tracer method* can be adopted. In this case, the collection employee makes a copy of the insurance claim form and the word *tracer* is stamped in red on it. The date of the tracer should also be written on the claim. These claims are then refiled with the respective insurance companies. A tracer designation indicates to most insurance companies that the office is inquiring about the status of an unpaid claim.

Follow Up Using the Fax Machine

Besides phone calls, a practice could also follow up on unpaid insurance claims by using what is normally called a "Claim Inquiry Fax Form." This form is normally used for large unpaid balances, usually those exceeding $2,500. The form is reproduced in Appendix B and included in the enclosed diskette.

Refiling Claims

Depending on the follow-up call, the collection employee should refile claims (via facsimile, if possible) or do whatever is necessary to get claims paid as quickly as possible. The employee who makes the calls must document who he or she talked to at the insurance companies. That way, the employee will have names of people to call if the claims continue to be delinquent.

> ■ **Practice Point:** Periodically review claim refilings and appeals. Make sure that they are done correctly and in a timely manner.

Appealing Claims

In the accounts receivable you will find certain accounts for which the insurance company denied the charge and the practice is attempting to get the balance from the patient. It would be prudent not to assume a medical practice consistently appeals denied charges. This point is highlighted by detailed review of unpaid insurance balances. If the balance is due to a denied charge, make sure that the practice has first properly appealed the denial before attempting collection from the patient.

There is a right way to appeal a denial and a wrong way. The wrong way is to resubmit the claim without explaining why the claim should be reconsidered for payment.

You may want to attach the original claim form and the related Explanation of Benefit (EOB) to the appeal letter. It is always a good idea to ask for a sample of their appeal letters just to make sure that the format and content are correct. This is one way you can help a practice prevent wasting time on receivables collection that was meant instead for insurance appeals.

> ■ **Practice Point:** Make sure that a practice learns from the appeal process. It makes no sense to appeal a claim if the same thing is going to happen again and again. The easiest form of receivables management is to make sure that the service is billed correctly the first time.

Collection Process Questionnaire

Like the billing process, the following is a list of questions about the collection process to help you improve the ability to collect monies from third-party payors and patients. Remember, any improvement you can make to the collection process should increase practice cash flow. If you are a new medical practice, sit down with the billing and collection staff and go over these questions. If you are an existing practice, do the same. Again, the objective is to streamline the collection process and make it as effective and efficient as it can be.

- What should be the standard office visit payment policy?
- If the patient is on a managed-care plan, how should the front desk determine the co-payment amount to collect from each patient?
- If the patient has an overdue balance, should there be an attempt to collect this amount from the patient while the patient is in the office?
- If a patient is scheduled for surgery, should the office attempt to collect a surgical deposit?
- Should patients receive any type of financial counseling before a procedure is performed?
- When a patient checks out after the office visit is complete, should the front desk (or check-out desk) attempt to collect full payment, deductibles, and/or co-payments?

- How will claim denials be handled?
- When will the practice begin following up on unpaid insurance claim forms?
- What will be the practice's follow-up procedure for unpaid insurance accounts?
- How will the practice follow up on unpaid patient receivables and how often?
- When will patient account statements be mailed out?
- Will collection letters be used by the practice?
- If yes, how often should the collection letters be sent out and what types of collection letters should be sent out?
- Does the practice use a collection agency?
- If yes, how often will accounts be sent to the collection agency?

▼ CHAPTER 13
Keeping the Books

Chapters in Part II of this book discussed the basics of appointment scheduling, the day-to-day activities in a medical office, the procedures for filing insurance claim forms, and suggestions for collecting payment from patients and insurance companies. Equally important are such items as posting payments, handling denied charges, and closing out the books—all of which are discussed in this chapter.

Posting Payments

When payments are received in the medical practice, either from insurance plans or from patients themselves, a billing employee must post them to the respective patient account ledgers. Payments are received through the mail or from patients at the time of their office visits. Payments will be posted either on the computer or on the individual patient ledger cards, if the practice still uses a pegboard system.

Insurance Payments

An insurance carrier normally sends an explanation of benefits (EOB) along with its payment. The EOB indicates how much of the charged fee was approved for payment, how much was applied to a deductible, how much was applied to a co-payment, and how much was applied to other sources, such as a withhold in managed-care plans. Most EOBs will indicate how much of the charged fee the patient is ultimately responsible for paying. EOBs also provide data essential to the collection process in the office.

Preposting Operations

Before posting any insurance payment to the patient's account, the billing employee should be sure to perform and document the following:

1. Compare the EOB with the original insurance claim and review each carefully. All charges on the claim form must be included on the EOB. Look for changes in current procedural terminology (CPT) coding by the insurance company (e.g., determine if a service was downcoded). The goal is to identify charges that can be appealed.

2. Investigate all denied charges and appeal them, if necessary (these will appear as zeros on the EOBs).

3. Appeal all usual, customary, and reasonable (UCR) reductions, if necessary. UCRs are filed when the insurance company reduces the physician's fee because the company feels it is too high for the practice area.

4. Any carrier request for additional information that appears on the EOB must be taken care of quickly. The goal is to get paid as quickly as possible by the insurance company.

5. The information contained on the EOB should be posted on the computer or manual patient ledger card promptly and carefully upon receipt. An error in the posting process may cause the patient's account balance to be incorrect.

Is the Practice Getting Paid Properly?

How does a practice know it is receiving the correct reimbursement from its managed-care payors? According to an informal polling of practitioners at a health care conference, more than 50 percent of the participants indicated they found errors regarding what the medical practice was contracted to receive as payment and what the managed-care company actually paid for the service. For example, a practice was contracted to receive $44 for visit code 99213 from ABC Managed Care Company, but the EOB indicated only $38 was paid. This type of situation seems to be occurring more and more often.

Managed-care companies make mistakes and it is up to the practice to catch these mistakes and file an appeal for the additional reimbursement. Catching reimbursement errors can be extremely difficult for many practices, however, especially for smaller ones. Small practices often do not have the time or the personnel to pay attention to this type of activity, as important as it is. A software system can help.

At a minimum, a practice should have a system in place to spot-check managed-care reimbursements. The easiest is a manual system whereby each week a sample of managed-care reimbursements is reviewed. Here is the process for a manual system:

1. Obtain reimbursement rates for the practice's top 25 revenue-producing CPT codes. Place them in a spreadsheet for easy access. These should be obtained from the top 10 to 15 managed-care plans from which the practice generates revenues.
2. Each week, take a sample of reimbursements from these plans (the practice can decide which ones) and compare the reimbursement per the EOB to the spreadsheet.
3. If an error is found, file an appeal immediately.
4. If errors continue consistently for a particular payor, meet with payor representatives, if possible, to discuss why such mistakes are occurring and how they can be corrected.

A manual system of this type can be cumbersome, so each practice will need to decide how to implement such a system. The point is that managed-care payors are making mistakes, and practices must have a way to detect the errors in order to get paid correctly. It would be most desirable if the practice's computer system, rather than a manual system, could detect the errors.

Unfortunately, most software systems cannot compare managed-care reimbursements and detect payment errors. Most cannot even tell you what a particular payor pays for a particular service. This is because most software systems used by practices today were built for a fee-for-service environment. As managed care grows, however, the level of sophistication needed increases, and these systems cannot provide the minimal critical information needed to succeed in this type of environment. So far, for most practices, a manual system will not be sufficient over the long haul. The burdens are often too great. Therefore, practices everywhere should begin evaluating their current system and defining what the practice needs both now and in the future as managed care continues to penetrate the marketplace. Physicians must realize this process is an investment in the practice and not just another piece of overhead. To be successful, you will need to convince the physician or physicians of the long-term benefits of investing in new computer software.

> ■ **Practice Point:** If a practice has a number of managed-care payors who reimburse providers using the Medicare RBRVS payment system, consider changing the practice's customary fee schedule to the same type of system. For example, many practices set their commercial fee schedule at 200 percent of current practice Medicare rates. This is the fee that is charged all payors. This way, a person who posts can visually compare managed-care reimbursement to the fee billed. Here is an example: Let's say a managed-care payor reimburses the practice at 120 percent of current Medicare rates. When the payment arrives, the person who is posting the payment can visually divide the billed charge "by 2" and know this number equals 100 percent of the current Medicare rate. If the payment is at, near, or below this 100 percent amount, the posting person will know the practice may not have been reimbursed correctly. This is one way to "flag" the EOB for further investigation.

Contractual Adjustments

After the EOB has been carefully reviewed, the billing employee should post the insurance payment to the patient's account. On the patient's account balance record, the employee must account for the difference between the charge submitted on the claim and the amount allowed contractually. Each time this is done, the employee should indicate in the patient record what type of adjustment was made (e.g., Medicare, HMO, PPO, professional courtesy, or a UCR). These types of adjustments generally are called *contractual adjustments*. A contractual adjustment is the difference between what a practice bills and what it is legally entitled to collect. For example, if a physician's normal fee is $1,200, and she signs with a PPO that has a contractual reimbursement of only $1,000 for the same service, the contractual adjustment would be $200.

Make sure that the practice does not lump all of its adjustments into an account called *credit adjustments*. The practice needs to make sure that it can identify each contractual adjustment and other write-offs because this ability is critical to the management of a medical practice. Instead, suggest that the practice use the following individual credit adjustment categories: *Cr. Adj.—Medicare, Cr. Adj.—Medicaid, Cr. Adj.—Blue Cross, Cr. Adj.—Prudential.*

By having separate adjustment categories, you can determine which insurance programs are reducing charges the most. If the practice is writing off a large number of adjustments for a specific plan, investigate and assess whether or not it makes sense to continue with the specific insurance plan. At the same time, determine if such write-offs are reasonable and, if so, whether or not they can be reduced. Identifying write-offs is also a smart way to account for withhold adjustments made by managed-care plans.

> ■ **Practice Point:** Remember that some practices accidentally write off denied charges as contractual adjustments. This could explain why a particular contractual adjustment amount appears unreasonable. In some cases, the practice would have been paid if it had appealed the denial. Review a periodic sample of denied claims to make sure that the billings were corrected and the respective claims refiled.

Withhold Adjustments

A *withhold* is an amount withheld from a physician's reimbursement that may or may not be reimbursed depending on the managed-care plan's criteria for reimbursement. For example, if a physician's normal charge for a procedure is $1,000, and he signs a managed-care contract that will reimburse only $800 for the same procedure, the managed-care plan will approve $800 for payment and may subtract another 10 percent as a withhold adjustment. Therefore, the practice receives a check for $720 instead for $800. The $80 that was withheld should be accounted for separately in the office's computer or by way of other documentation if the practice is on a manual system.

At the end of the year, review how much was withheld by each managed-care plan and then have the billing employee appeal for reimbursement of the withhold. If a plan will not reimburse a withhold, the billing employee should have a plan representative explain the plan's withhold policy. The practice also must know if the true discounted fee not only is the approved amount, but also is reduced by the plan withhold. A billing employee should never write off a charge that has been denied by an insurance company until the employee has fully investigated such denial.

Fractional Payment of the Allowed Charge

After the insurance provider considers contractual adjustments and other reductions, an insurance plan usually pays only a fraction of the allowed charge. Medicare, for example, pays 80 percent of the allowed amount. Some indemnity plans pay 90 percent. An office employee should post the amount paid by the insurance plan to the patient's account in the computer or on its manual ledger account card. The balance of the account is the patient's responsibility. If the balance is not paid, it should be billed in the next round of monthly statements. Therefore, the employee needs to pay strict attention to the amount the patient is responsible for when posting insurance payments. This amount should be identified clearly when posting payment and contractual adjustments to the computer or on the patient's manual ledger account card. If errors are made during the posting process, the aging of accounts will be unreliable. Thus, when patient's statements are mailed, they may contain incorrect balances due. This is guaranteed to upset patients. In most cases, the patients' insurance plans will also send them their own copies of the EOBs for the patients' records.

Filing the Explanation of Benefits

After the EOBs are posted, the office employee should file them with the respective copies of the insurance claim forms either in the patient's clinical file or in a separate business file set up for each patient. Some practices may find it more efficient to maintain the EOBs in notebooks referenced by the insurance company. The practice will need to keep the insurance claim forms and related EOBs together so that it can easily audit a patient's account history when such a need arises. In addition, a copy of the EOBs should be kept in a manner that will allow someone to review them on a periodic basis. (For a detailed discussion of the EOB periodic reviews, see the section titled "Reviewing the Explanation of Benefits" in this chapter.)

■ **Practice Point:** Keep the practice from filing the EOBs in the patient charts. The EOBs are not easily accessible in such files, which makes reviewing them difficult.

■ **Practice Point:** Charge tickets, Superbills, and EOBs should be kept for a minimum of six years, since the False Claim Act has a statute of six years.

Patients' Payments

Payments received from patients should be posted to the patients' accounts in the computer or on their manual ledger cards on the same day they are received. This policy includes payments received through the mail and payments received from patients at the time of their office visits. In other words, all payments, including those received from insurance companies, should be posted on a daily basis. This strict policy is necessary because one of the best internal controls in a medical practice is to have the daily bank deposit agree with total collections posted for that particular day. Otherwise, you may have a difficult time reconciling posted payments in the patients' records to the practice's deposits. One easy way you can check the timing of payment postings is to compare total posted collections for a month against total deposits per the bank account reconciliation. If payments are posted timely, the two numbers should agree.

■ **Practice Point:** Periodically look through the desk drawers of the business personnel. The objective of this review is to make sure that checks are not in desk drawers or files, sitting and waiting to be posted. Believe it or not, this occurs quite often, especially in busy medical practices that are understaffed.

Postdated and Returned Checks

The practice should not accept postdated checks. Not only does postdating prevent timely posting to the patient's account, but most times the check bounces anyway, thereby exasperating the collection efforts in the office. Returned checks should also be posted to the computer or to the patient's ledger card. Before doing so, the billing employee should be instructed to run the check through the bank one more time. If it bounces a second time, the employee should remove the corresponding payment posting from the patient's account. This usually is done by posting it through a credit adjustment called *returned check.*

Collection Agencies' Checks

Payments from collection agencies must be posted correctly. Most agencies will send a lump-sum check to the practice identifying which patients paid on their accounts. When an account is sent to a collection agency, a medical practice generally writes off the account as a bad debt so that a realistic receivables balance is maintained. If the account is not written off, the portion of the agency's lump-sum check applicable to each patient can be posted to the respective account. If the balance is written off, the office employee must first restore the balance to the patient's account; otherwise, if the payment is posted, it will create a credit balance in the patient's account. Generally, the balance is added back by posting it to a debit adjustment account called *bad debt recovery.* After this is done, the payment can be posted and the balance zeroed out.

For example, a practice engages a collection agency to collect its overdue accounts. In one particular month, the agency sends a check for $671 to the practice for prior collection efforts. Because the practice did not write off the accounts, the billing employee can simply credit each of the accounts listed on the agency's check.

Auditing Payment Postings

A goal of every medical practice is to secure the correctness of its patients' accounts, and thus its accounts receivable. As previously mentioned, if payments are posted carelessly, the practice risks sending out patient account statements with incorrect balances. This will do nothing but upset the patients and may cause them not to return or not to refer other patients. If the practice's referring physicians find out that the practice sent out wrong bills, the referring practices may stop referring patients, especially if the physicians believe their patients will not being taken care of properly.

To ensure the correctness of the amounts due on the patients' account ledgers, each month or on some periodic basis, someone (the CPA or an office employee) needs to audit the payments to patients' accounts. Any posting error can wreak havoc on the accounts receivable balance. A designated employee, the practice's office manager, or the outside accountant should take a sample of at least 20 to 25 EOBs and trace each item to each respective patient's account. Trace the payment and the contractual write-off from the EOBs to the patient ledger account and determine if the amounts were posted correctly. The reviewer should make sure that the balance on the patient's detailed account ledger is correct.

For example, the CPA audits the payment postings and finds that contractual write-offs are not being correctly adjusted off the patients' accounts. Because of this, patients are accidentally (and illegally) being billed for these amounts. The CPA's audit catches the error and corrects it.

Reviewing the Explanation of Benefits

On a periodic basis, preferably monthly, the practice's administrator, billing clerk, outside accountant, or consultant should review EOBs. Reviewing EOBs is one of the most important, yet most often overlooked, duties in a medical practice. EOBs provide the practice with a wealth of information, such as how quickly insurance companies are paying claims, how they approve practice charges, whether or not charges were denied, and any discounts taken off billed charges.

Reimbursements from Insurance Companies

To review EOBs to determine how insurance companies are actually reimbursing the practice, look for situations in which the insurance company, especially managed-care companies, approved all of a billed charge for payment. This generally indicates that the practice's fees are too low. Remember, when a practice signs with a PPO, the practice agrees to accept a discounted fee that ranges from 20 percent to 30 percent off the practice's regular fee schedule. Managed-care plans, however, will pay the lesser of the amount billed or the contracted fee. Therefore, when a managed-care plan approves the full amount of the billed charge for payment, this indicates that the practice's fees are too low. The same could be said for other insurance plans that approve all of the billed charges for payment, including commercial insurance plans.

> ■ **Practice Point:** Make sure that the EOBs are easily accessible to review and that they are not filed in the patient's file. It is very difficult and time-consuming to go through patient charts each month to retrieve EOBs.

Analyze EOBs to determine how quickly insurance plans are reimbursing the practice. Find out (a) if there is a problem with specific insurance companies (e.g., companies that routinely deny a particular service for a particular reason, such as not attaching an operative note to the insurance claim form), (b) if there is a problem receiving payment for specific services, and (c) whether the practice's collection employee is following up on unpaid insurance claims. (See Appendix B for a sample insurance claims filing analysis worksheet.) Take a sample of EOBs and compare the EOB control dates with the last dates of service. The control dates can usually be found in the upper right or left corner of the EOBs. The average turnaround should be no more than 30 to 45 days. If it is more, investigate the reasons behind the delay.

> ■ **Practice Point:** If the practice is not receiving payment within 45 days, first determine if the billing employee is following up on unpaid insurance claim forms in a timely manner. Remember, the practice should be following up on unpaid insurance bills 25 days from the date of service. Also make sure that insurance claim forms are being prepared and mailed within five to seven days from the last dates of service.

Payment Denials

One of the most important tasks involved in reviewing EOBs is to look for payment denials, no matter what the reason. Page through a sample of EOBs and look for zeros as the approved charges. After finding them, investigate why the insurance companies denied payment. One reason could be errors by the practice's billing personnel or errors by an insurance company. If payment was denied because of errors made by the practice, find out where the errors originated and make sure that they do not happen again.

For example, the billing employee files a service as a preventative medicine visit. The insurance company denies this charge because it does not cover such services. In such cases, find out if errors can be corrected and the claims refiled. If they are refiled, make sure that the appeal letters are properly drafted (see "Appealing Claims" in Chapter 12). Many times, the billing employee will refile claims without supporting the case for having the insurance companies pay the billed amounts. Without additional information, the insurance companies will probably deny the claims again.

Finally, make sure that any denied claims were not automatically written off as contractual adjustments to the patients' accounts. The practice's billing employee sometimes will assume that the insurance companies must have been right in their denial of charges. If denials show up on EOBs and they look like they could be appealed, trace them to the patients' detailed accounts to make sure that they were not written off without appeals or explanations. If errors were made by the insurance companies, have the billing employee refile or appeal the claims, if possible.

■ **Practice Point:** As stated in the last chapter, on a periodic basis, obtain a sample of the practice's appeal letters. Review them for format and content. Make sure that the appeal letters state why the original claims should be paid.

Practice Fee Schedule

Also analyze EOBs to make sure that the practice's billed charges are not too low. (For a detailed discussion of fee schedule development, see Chapter 8.)

■ **Practice Point:** If the physician's full fee is approved for payment by an insurance company, the physician's fees are probably too low because the insurance company usually reimburses on a discounted-fee basis. If a managed-care plan reimburses a physician's full fee, then the fees are too low and they should be changed.

Recommend that the physician revise fees for a select number of CPT codes or possibly for the entire fee schedule. Never let the practice lose money simply because its fee schedule is too low.

Billing and Collection Personnel

An EOB review can also be used to evaluate the billing and collection personnel in the office. If the EOBs reveal numerous denials and long payment turnaround, it could be the fault of the billing and collection personnel. Make sure that the staff members know how to prepare insurance claim forms and that they are experienced in CPT and diagnosis coding. Also find out if they know how to read operative notes and if they know Medicare billing rules. The staff members should also know how to follow up on unpaid insurance claims, if that is the policy in the practice. If the staff members do not know how to do these things, the practice could be losing both revenue and cash flow.

Banking

Because the medical practice will need to deposit its payments daily, no matter how small the deposit, it should establish a banking relationship as close to the office as possible. The office manager should use standard bank deposit slips when making deposits and endorse each payment with an approved stamp, usually a rubber stamp that can be acquired from the practice's bank.

If the practice collects a large amount of money during the year, suggest to the physician that he or she consider having both a checking account and a money market account to maximize the practice's earnings potential on unused funds. In this situation, all monies are deposited into a money market account until they are needed.

To maximize interest income, the practice should make payments at specific intervals, twice a month if possible. When it comes time to disburse funds, the total amount required to pay the bills is transferred from the money market account into the checking account. In other words, the checking account becomes an *imprest fund*. When exploring this opportunity, be sure to find out how many account-to-account transfers the bank will allow before it begins charging a service fee. In some cases, this fee may be higher than the amount of interest that can be earned.

Closing the Books

After all the transactions have been posted, the office manager or another employee needs to make sure that the practice's books and records are closed out. This is done both daily and at the end of the month, whether the office is computerized or is still using a pegboard system.

Daily Closeout

Failure to close out the day could create problems if the system were to go down (or if information were to be otherwise lost) and would make it more difficult to balance the books at the end of the month.

Before closing out the day, the manager or employee should post all of the day's charges, payments, and adjustments to the computer. Many offices like to post the next day or at another more convenient time. Discourage this because the practice needs to balance to the bank deposit slip every day. After the day's activity is posted by the employee, the next step will depend on whether the practice is on a manual or computerized system. If it is on a manual system, the employee should total and summarize all columns on the daysheet, making sure all balances are properly carried forward. If the practice uses a computer, the employee should print all of the daily reports. These reports usually consist of the following:

- Daily report of charges
- Daily report of payments

- Daily report of adjustments
- Deposit slip

These reports, or the daysheets, should be maintained in a centralized location in the office on permanent record. They must never be discarded.

For some practices, it may be beneficial to summarize cash postings on a single sheet of paper such as the following:

Sample Daily Cash Posting

ABC Medical Practice
Daily Cash Posting
Date: _____

	Patient Name	Insurance Company	Office Receipt	Mail Receipt
Totals				

Using this schedule, the employee can balance/reconcile the practice's daily report of payments and its appointment book.

The following is another example of a closeout form:

Business Date: _____

Morning Time of Service	Batch #_____		
Total Charges	$ _____	**Batch Report Total**	$ _____
Cash	$ _____		
Checks	$ _____		
Credit Cards	$ _____		
Total Deposit	$ _____	**Batch Report Total**	$ _____
Afternoon Time of Service	Batch #_____		
Total Charges	$ _____	**Batch Report Total**	$ _____
Cash	$ _____		
Checks	$ _____		
Credit Cards	$ _____		
Total Deposit	$ _____	**Batch Report Total**	$ _____

Mail Payments

Batch #_____

Total Deposit	$ _____	**Batch Report Total**	$ _____

Batch #_____

Total Deposit	$ _____	**Batch Report Total**	$ _____

Batch #_____

Total Deposit	$ _____	**Batch Report Total**	$ _____

As indicated above, charges for all services and all payments received are in agreement with their respective postings on the computer system as evidenced by the Batch Report Totals.

Signed:_____ Date:_____

Once the records have been reconciled, the manager or employee should deposit the money received in the office during the day. These payments might have arrived through the mail or made by patients who paid for their visits. Even practices with multiple offices should attempt to deposit daily. Deposits must be made daily, whether the deposit amount is $10 or $10,000, because daily deposits ensure that the practice has proper internal controls in place. One of the best internal control measures is to make sure that all source documents relate to one another (see worksheet above). What was deposited into the bank account must always agree with the daily reports. The deposit data must balance with the daily computer report of payments or the total amount of receipts as shown on the manual daysheet. In addition, the daily report of charges and any related payments should agree with the patient listings on the appointment book and the sign-in sheet. This is why the practice should never throw away the sign-in sheet. The practice's outside accountant or the office administrator should cross-check these source documents periodically and investigate any discrepancies. (See Chapter 4 for a more detailed discussion of internal controls.)

Finally, the computer files must be backed up. Many computerized practices do not back up their files on a consistent basis. Such practices run the risk of their computers crashing and subsequently losing a large amount of financial and practice data. To protect the practice in the case of fire or vandalism, the office should store the backup files off-site. Many offices use a tape backup system to copy computer files. The office manager should check the tape backup periodically to make sure that the system is properly backing up onto it.

Monthly Closeout

Similar to the daily closeout, the month-end closeout should also be performed by the practice. After the last day's activity has been posted, and the day closed out, a computerized practice should perform its closeout function as directed by its software operating instructions. For manual systems, the office manager or designated employee should total and summarize the last day of the month's daysheet (where the month-to-date information is located). In addition, a practice on a manual system must reconcile the end-of-the-month accounts receivable balance listed on the daysheet to the total balances per the individual patient's ledger cards. In other words, the practice should be able to total up all of the balances due per the individual ledger cards. This number should agree with the accounts receivable balance on the daysheet. If the numbers do not agree, staff members or the practice's outside accountant needs to investigate.

For computerized practices, print the following reports (or print reports in a similar format):

- Aged accounts receivable
- Listing of unpaid insurance claims
- Procedure productivity report
- Listing of charges, collections, and adjustments
- Insurance payment analysis report
- Referring physician report

At the end of each month, the practice statistics should be summarized and analyzed by the office manager or the CPA. (For a more detailed discussion of the analysis of these reports, see Chapter 2.)

■ **Practice Point:** The collections per the monthly cash basis income statement should agree with the month-end total of payments posted. If they do not, determine whether they can be reconciled. If they cannot, you will need to investigate.

▼ CHAPTER 14
Inventory and Purchasing

A system for purchasing and maintaining the medical practice's inventory needs to be carefully planned and monitored. A lack of such a system or a breakdown in the current system could result in a waste of both money and physical inventory. The ultimate impact will be on the practice's bottom line.

Inventory

To ensure proper control, medical supplies should always be kept in a central medical supply stockroom. Business supplies generally are kept in a centralized supply closet. This type of centralization will provide some control over the inventory process. If inventory is spread around the office, some waste will result. If an office maintains large quantities of supplies, it should keep a formalized inventory record. This record might be maintained on index cards, in a notebook, or in a computer file. Review the written record periodically to determine usage, pricing, and so forth. This review is one basic control over inventory management.

Most medical practices, especially large ones, should have a set, specific minimum quantity of each inventory item so that staff members know when to reorder supplies. As a general rule, the office manager or designated employee should reorder when inventory is down to a two-week supply. Always get a physician's (or his or her designate's) approval before ordering supplies. Generally, a nurse or the practice administrator is placed in charge of inventory management, including the ordering process.

All rooms requiring medical supplies, such as examining rooms and the laboratory, are stocked with the necessary items from the central stockroom, usually once a week.

■ **Practice Point:** If it ever appears that the office is ordering the same medical or office supply over and over again, determine if inventory waste is occurring. It could be that certain inventories are not being properly handled or used in the office.

Controlling Inventory for Multiple Site Offices

One of the biggest areas of waste in a medical practice is medical supply inventory. Often, individual offices in a group practice have control over their own acquisition of medical supplies. Unfortunately, this system is not very cost effective. The problem lies in the fact that when one office site purchases a medical supply, another office may have an oversupply of the same item. Instead of having one office repurchase a supply item when it needs it, the office should first find out if another office has a surplus of the supply and get it from the other office. Therefore to contain medical supply costs, a group practice with multiple sites should consolidate its medical supply inventory. This is done very easily using the following methodology:

1. Establish one office as the supply purchaser. At a designated time, each office is asked exactly what supplies it needs for the upcoming period.

2. Each office is instructed to call another office *first* to see if that supply is available, possibly in exchange for another supply.

3. If the supply cannot be found at another office, the office manager and administrator purchase the supply in bulk. The supplies ordered by each office are then delivered to each respective site.

Having the offices trade or transfer supplies helps to keep supply costs down. If another office cannot provide a supply because of its own inventory needs, the practice sites should have the ability to reorder the supply.

Purchasing

The office should have a system in place to pay and account for vendor invoices. The practice should create and maintain an approved list of vendors. This prevents employees from making unauthorized purchases of supplies from vendors that might not give the practice the best quality or price. In smaller medical practices, supplies should not be procured without a physician's approval. In larger offices, this approval can be delegated to the office manager; however, there should always be a physician who both approves the purchase of any item over a certain dollar amount and reviews disbursements at periodic intervals.

> ■ **Practice Point:** Large medical practices, especially those with numerous departments, should consider implementing a purchase order system to procedure supplies, inventory, etc. This is even true for small practices that need to make a number of large purchases.

Immediately after supplies are delivered to the office, the shipment should be inspected by the office manager. He or she should compare the delivery ticket with the purchase order that accompanies the delivery. All items that are listed on the delivery ticket should be enclosed in the package.

Another purchasing policy the medical practice should have is a bidding policy. On a periodic basis, the office manager should solicit bids for office, medical, and any other supplies used in the practice. One of the problems that often occurs in a medical practice is that the office consistently purchases a particular supply from a single vendor. As time passes, the vendor may not provide the practice with the price discounts that another vendor might. On the other hand, the practice should not sacrifice quality and service for a lower price.

> ■ **Practice Point:** If the practice has been ordering supplies from the same medical supply vendor for a long time, make sure to compare the vendor's prices to those of other vendors.

Expenditures

Invoices should be maintained in a central location until they are paid. Many smaller offices use an alphabetized expandable folder to keep unpaid vendor invoices together. Larger practices should use a computerized accounts payable software program. When it is time to pay invoices, all expenditures should be paid by check, unless this is clearly impractical. Once an invoice is paid, the billing employee should attach it to the check and send it to be signed.

Recommend that the person signing checks be a physician-owner and not another individual in the office delegated to perform the task. A physician-owner's involvement is critical to the internal control function of accounts payable.

Once an invoice is paid, it should be marked "paid" and placed in a related vendor-paid file. The check number should also be indicated on the vendor invoice. Smaller offices usually set up alphabetized vendor files. Larger offices usually set up individual vendor files. At the end of the year, all paid invoices are boxed up by the billing employee and kept as part of the practice's permanent records.

To simplify the practice's accounting, disbursements should be posted on the related check stubs and maintained for reconciliation with the monthly bank statements. The billing employee should make sure that a complete description is included on the check stub. For example, if payment is made to the practice's outside accountant, "accounting fee" should be written in the description column. If a practice uses a computer to pay its vendors' invoices, each check should be assigned an accounting code as required by most computerized accounts payable systems. If the payables are computerized, make sure that the practice prints and maintains a month-end report of payables and a list of the computerized check disbursements as a part of its permanent record. These reports are used for internal accounting and cash reconciliation.

■ **Practice Point:** Carefully review the endorsements on the backs of canceled checks. This is an excellent way to detect embezzlement by an employee who writes a check to a vendor that doesn't exist and then endorses and cashes the check.

▼ CHAPTER 15
Marketing the Medical Practice

As the health care industry changes and new payment patterns evolve, the revenue streams of many medical practices may stagnate or decline. Therefore, maintaining the revenue base should be a priority, and increasing revenue takes on even more critical importance. How a practice markets itself will depend on whether it is a primary-care practice or a referral-based practice. Primary-care practices, such as family practices and pediatrics, get their patients directly from the area. In other words, revenue comes directly from patients who are ill and call the practice for an appointment. Referral-based practices, such as general surgery, get their patients from other physicians who have referred the patients to the practice. In many service areas, patients rarely go directly to a specialist, especially in service areas that are dominated by managed-care plans. Regardless of the specific type of practice, some marketing efforts are common to all medical practices. Even though you may not have a degree or experience in marketing, you can still assist a medical practice with its marketing efforts.

Premarketing Considerations

Before a practice begins designing a marketing plan, it needs to know something about its target market. This can be achieved by conducting a demographic study of the practice's geographic area. As a first step, contact the neighborhood hospital's marketing department to see if it has conducted its own demographic study of the practice area. If it has, determine if the hospital's study contains enough information for the practice to formulate its own marketing plan. If not, recommend that the practice hire a qualified professional to perform the study (even if the practice's staff feels it can conduct the demographic study itself).

A demographic study should answer the following questions:

1. Who are the practice's main competitors, and how many physicians in the same medical specialty are in the practice area?

2. What is the population's general age, sex, household size, and household income in the practice area?

3. What changes have occurred in the last five years to the area's demographics?

4. Which insurance companies have the largest market share in the area?

5. What has the employment trend been in the area over the last five years?

6. What has the managed-care trend been in the last five years?

The information gathered from the demographic study, although most valuable to primary-care practices, is also useful for referral-based practices. A referral-based practice will need to know how its referring physicians may be affected in the future and it will also want to know something about the patient population. The practice can use this information to forecast any future impacts on its revenue. For example, suppose a medical specialty currently treats a significant amount of patients who have commercial insurance. The demographic study indicates a rapid growth in managed care or an increase in the overall ages of the patient population. Because the practice's base of patients is shifting to managed care or Medicare, both of which reimburse less than commercial insurance plans, the medical practice's future revenue could be affected.

Internal Marketing Strategies

Most of the internal marketing strategies a medical practice can adopt are basic, but sometimes their importance is understated. For example, the internal decor, the behavior of the staff members, and the policies of the practice must create a friendly and professional impression in the minds of its patients and referring physicians. As you conduct an analysis of the internal office environment, answer the following questions:

1. Is the reception area comfortable for the patients? (Ask yourself: If I was a patient, would I feel comfortable?)

2. Are patients provided with activities, such as a television or magazines, while they wait for their appointments? Are the

magazines in the waiting room current and do they cover a variety of interests that are appropriate for anyone? Are refreshments, such as coffee or water, provided?

3. Do the patients have to wait a long time in the reception area for their appointments? Long waiting periods upset patients and create the impression that the practice is inefficient and inattentive to its patients' needs.

4. Is the front-desk staff courteous and willing to help the patients and the offices of the referring physicians? Poorly trained, discourteous front-desk personnel can quickly give patients a negative impression of the practice.

5. How do the nurses and other clinical staff treat and interact with patients? Do they go out of their way to help patients? Are they friendly and composed? How helpful are they over the telephone?

6. Are the office's policies and procedures creating bad impressions? For example, an office in a small community adheres to a strict policy to collect payments from patients at the time of their office visits. It is a standard practice in the community to bill the patients' insurance plans first. Patients and referring physicians may avoid the medical practice simply because of its collection policy.

7. Are thank-you cards for new patient referrals—both to physicians and patients—routinely and consistently mailed out? Physicians and patients want to be recognized for their referral efforts.

8. Does the physician spend adequate time with the patients in the exam rooms? In some practices, physicians are in and out of the exam room so quickly that the patients are left unclear as to whether the examinations are complete.

9. Does the office have a recall system? Many primary-care practices lose revenue simply because they do not have a system in place that will prompt patients to come back to the office for visits. For example, a dentist's office or gynecology practice should have a recall system informing patients that it is time for their annual checkups or examinations.

External Marketing Strategies

Following are some external marketing strategies that you could recommend or consider.

Brochures

Every practice should have a professional brochure it can give to patients, mail out, or give to referring physicians. The brochure should provide general information about the physician, the practice, its services, and its policies. It can also convey an image about the practice. A primary-care practice could mail its brochure to a targeted list of people in the local area. A referral-based practice can distribute the brochure to its current and potential referring physicians. Again, the goal is to create positive visibility for the practice.

Unfortunately, the number of poorly produced practice brochures outnumber the good. One reason is because many practices try to design their own brochures without seeking professional guidance. This is no time to be stingy when addressing such an important project. Practices with a brochure often fail to keep it up to date or even list new services the practice provides. The following are a few tips garnered from successful brochures:

- The cover design is extremely important. Most readers won't look past a poorly designed, unattractive cover.
- Use photographs and illustrations when possible, especially photographs of the physicians.
- Emphasize the benefits a patient will receive if he or she visits the practice.
- Use color whenever possible.
- Include a small map to the office location(s), if possible.
- Emphasize the practice's web site, especially any and all the clinical information a patient might be looking for.

Direct Mail

A primary-care office, in particular, needs to create visibility and name recognition in its community. To create instant and ongoing visibility with direct mail, the practice could mail its brochure, or a similar marketing tool, to targeted patients in the area. You need to inform the practice that one mailing will not create visibility. Any direct-mail campaign must be consistent and long term. Otherwise, potential patients will not remember the practice. Marketing takes time. Cost limitations will usually dictate how many times a practice can send direct-mail pieces. Make sure that the practice budgets adequately for these expenditures.

For example, a family practice wants to increase its visibility. With the help of its consultant or practice manager, the practice creates a brochure and implements a direct-mail strategy to households with two working spouses. One major goal of the practice is to promote the availability of its office visits after 5:00 p.m. on certain days. The practice does one mailing and stops the direct mailings when the after-hours appointments don't increase immediately. The practice's failure to commit to a long-term strategy prevented it from reaching its targeted audience.

Newsletters

Both primary-care practices and referral-based practices could create newsletters to mail to patients and referring physicians. Newsletters are usually created and mailed on a quarterly basis. They serve to inform patients and referring physicians about clinical issues and the office. The newsletter does not have to be fancy or long. Many are just one page and are printed on the practice's letterhead. You could recommend a number of inexpensive graphics software packages or word processing software packages that contain graphics capabilities for the practice to use to create its newsletter.

■ **Practice Point:** Determine if the physician's medical academy has a newsletter the practice can purchase and distribute to patients and/or referral sources.

Season's Greetings

The practice should send year-end thank-you letters to all patients and referring physicians. The letters are notes of appreciation to patients for their patronage and to both patients and physicians for their referrals. The thank-you letters also serve as reminders that the practice is growing and would like to receive additional referrals. The office needs to make sure that patients and other physicians do not have the impression that the practice is so busy it does not need new patient referrals. Gifts are appropriate for referring physicians.

For example, a general surgery office sends out three sets of gifts at Christmas time to its referring physicians. It breaks its referring physicians into three groups: The A list, B list, and C list. The A-list physicians refer the most patients to the practice, the B-list physicians refer the next highest amount, and the C list refers the least amount of patients. The A-list physicians receive the most expensive thank-you gifts and the physicians in the other lists receive other designated gifts.

Advertising

The success of an advertising campaign will usually depend on a lot of different criteria. If an office is receiving almost all of its new patient referrals from other physicians, it may not make sense to spend money on advertising. For example, some physicians may spend a huge amount of money on full-page ads in telephone directories when almost all of their referrals are coming from other physicians. However, if a practice does not receive much new revenue from referrals, investigate developing an advertising program in telephone directories, a local newspaper, or a periodical. Another option, especially for practices located near a busy intersection, is advertising on bus stop benches or using other signs to increase the visibility of the practice.

Remind the practice that the success of any advertising campaign is a direct result of its consistency. If an advertisement is run once or twice and then stopped, the practice will not maximize its visibility and the results of the advertisement will be poor. Like direct mail, advertising is a long-term marketing strategy.

■ **Practice Point:** Before the practice begins a marketing program, it should have a system for tracking new patients and where they come from. If it does not have such a system, help the practice develop one. The tracking system will help you compare the new patients received versus the advertising costs expended, which will let the practice know if its marketing program is successful.

A Word About Yellow Pages Advertising

Many medical practices spend hundreds and thousands of dollars on Yellow Pages advertisements. In large urban areas, a practice may advertise in two, three, or four different Yellow Pages directories. Yellow Pages advertising is, or can be, a large overhead expense. As such, it makes business sense to know if the expense is worthwhile or not. How can a medical practice determine the return on investment (ROI) for its advertising and decide whether or not its advertising investment is paying off?

As we all know, Yellow Pages advertising has become extremely expensive for many medical practices around the country. Yellow Pages advertising is considered an easy way to make the public aware of a medical practice and to give a prospective patient practice information if he or she wants to find a doctor. Although simple in nature, practices are often pressured to buy increasingly larger displays. Either the Yellow Pages account executive is applying pressure or the practice is applying its own pressure simply because it believes it is not receiving enough new patients from the Yellow Pages. In this situation, the practice probably thinks the reason is that the original ad is too small and by increasing its size, more patients might notice the practice. As mentioned above, Yellow Pages costs are increasing as the number of phone books needed to reach the practice's patients and potential patients in its service area keeps growing.

Where's the Cost-Benefit?

Spending a large amount of practice overhead on Yellow Pages ads is fine if it actually brings new patients to the practice and the related work is gainful. In my experience, many physicians and practice managers often take it for granted that these ad dollars are a good investment. Believe it or not, many others do not even know how much money they are spending on Yellow Pages ads each year and some don't even know how many patients, if any, were obtained from the advertising. Unfortunately, many practices continue or expand their listings each year out of the misconception that they must do something in order to remain competitive or that they won't get any new patients if they do eliminate their Yellow Pages advertising.

Yellow Pages advertising is worth its cost if, at the very minimum, it brings in enough business to pay for itself. Still better, if a medical practice can determine which size ads and which local or regional directories are productive, it might be able to make even more effective advertising decisions. For example, a practice can drop or reduce ads in some directories, increase ads in others, and perhaps hire an advertising or marketing professional to help improve the displays.

Good marketers attempt to gauge each marketing strategy based on its ROI. For example, a marketing strategy with a three-to-one ROI produces $3 of revenue for each dollar spent. This clearly justifies continuing or expanding the effort. An ROI of only $.40 for each dollar spent probably isn't worth the cost, and, as such, these dollars should be committed elsewhere.

Get the Data

Like any marketing strategy, Yellow Pages advertising should be based on this sort of cost/benefit analysis. Unfortunately many practices cannot use this analysis because the practice cannot identify what really is bringing in their new patients.

The first step is to look at the practice's new patient registration form. This is key in obtaining this kind of information. You must make sure that the form asks very specific questions so you can make the ROI calculations. The form must prompt the new patient to write down how he or she found out or was referred to the practice. For example, the form could ask "Why did you choose our practice?" and then list a number of possible choices to check off. One of the choices should be "From the practice's Yellow Pages listing." After that, ask the new patient to identify the local book from among a list of those in which you advertise.

Front-desk personnel must be instructed that this section of the patient registration form must be completed in all instances—there are no exceptions! A lack of attention here will result in the practice not obtaining all of the data it needs to calculate its ROI for any and all of its marketing activities, not only just Yellow Pages advertising. Periodically, someone in practice management should review these completed forms to make sure this section of the registration form is getting filled out each and every time.

Calculate ROI

Now it is time to calculate the return on investment on your Yellow Pages advertising costs. The first step is to identify each patient that has come to the practice because of the Yellow Pages advertising. The practice's computer system, if this information is being tracked properly as discussed above, should be able to provide this listing. If applicable, be sure to segregate out these patients by each separate Yellow Pages book. Next, add up the fees collected related to these individual patients. The collection could come from third-party payers and/or the patients themselves. Now calculate the return on investment by dividing these collections by the related costs to advertise in the Yellow Pages. Analyze this figure. Was the investment worth it? Could the dollars have been better spent elsewhere?

As with any advertising, keep in mind that it may take months, or even a year or two, for revenue to be generated from any form of advertising. This is why marketing professionals vigorously stress that only a full and complete commitment should be made to advertising. This is because many practices advertise for a little while and then pull the ads when they don't see the results they think they should be seeing. This is a big mistake. If you are going to do it, just remember that advertising is a long-term commitment.

Relationships with Other Physicians or Physicians' Offices

For a practice that is based on referrals, the best marketing strategy is for the practice's physician to go out of his or her way to meet potential referring physicians. Developing relationships is the key to generating patient referrals. The physician should eat in the physician lounge or nearby hangouts where the other physicians regularly eat. The practice's physician should take referring physicians to dinner at regular intervals or go to the offices of potential referring physicians to discuss the possibility of developing cross-referral relationships. Make sure that the practice's brochure is mailed to all potential referring physicians.

■ **Practice Point:** Determine if the practice has a marketing plan for acquiring referral physicians. The plan's budget should include money for reimbursing physicians for their marketing costs.

■ **Practice Point:** Sometimes a practice's physician compensation system actually discourages physicians from marketing for the practice. A productivity-based formula encourages a "me" mentality and not a group mentality. This causes each physician to look out for himself or herself because of the internal competition for patients. In this type of situation, it is difficult to get physicians to commit to a group marketing plan.

The practice's office manager should develop business relationships with the office managers of the referring physicians' practices. Specialty physicians sometimes forget that staff members of primary physicians' offices frequently are the ones who choose where to send patients. For example, a primary-care physician examines a patient whose EKG reading indicates that she could have a problem with her heart. After the exam is complete, the physician instructs a front-desk employee to refer the patient to a cardiologist. The physician usually does not state the specific name of a cardiologist, simply because the employee knows who the physician has previously selected as the referring physician. If more than one cardiologist is on that list, the front-desk employee often is the one who makes the selection.

■ **Practice Point:** Marketing is useless if you don't track doctor referrals. The practice should make a list of all doctors who can refer patients, then monitor referrals from these individuals. You can also use this as your "contact list" for marketing purposes. The following is a sample referral tracking worksheet:

Referring Doctor/Source	Referrals Current Year	Referrals Last Year	Referrals for Year ____	Reason for Decline in Referrals

Managed-Care Plans

When physicians sign with managed-care plans, they often feel that no further marketing efforts directed toward managed-care enrollees are necessary. Usually, when a person with managed-care insurance gets ill, he or she chooses a physician by looking in the physician roster book or asking a fellow employee to give a referral.

The goal of marketing in a managed-care atmosphere is to eliminate both of these customs. In other words, the goal is for a managed-care enrollee to choose a practice before a medical need arises, so that the enrollee can call it directly when he or she needs medical attention. To achieve this, the practice must concentrate on marketing efforts that increase its visibility. The physicians, the practice manager, or the practice's advisor should call the human resources directors at the companies that pay premiums to the managed-care plan and inquire about presenting a seminar to the employees. If the employer or managed-care plan has a newsletter, the physicians may be able to submit articles. Finally, the practice can offer free or reduced-rate services to the employees of the companies. Examples include cholesterol testing and blood pressure screening. These kinds of activities will bring much needed visibility to the practice and generate patient visits to the office.

If the practice is a referral-based practice in a managed-care setting, review the providers on the plan. If no referral relationship with the providers is in place, the practice should attempt to establish a relationship so it can expand its list of potential referring physicians.

■ **Practice Point:** If managed-care plans become predominant in a physician's community, the physician should consider signing up with one of them to maintain and increase revenues.

As managed care continues to increase in many service areas, physicians and their advisors should keep a simple fact in mind: Integrated delivery systems are developing and competing for managed-care contracts. In some areas, marketing involves joining a local PHO or IPA. Some practices are even developing their own IPAs or group practices. Once these entities are established, you and the physicians can develop a marketing plan for contracting with managed-care plans.

For example, a group of physicians form a new IPA and recruit more physicians. After developing its provider panel, the group obtains a contract with the largest HMO in the area. An OB/GYN who decided not to participate in the IPA loses 30 percent of his practice; the OB/GYN physicians who did sign up gain this 30 percent. This is a good example of how *patient shifting* occurs as managed care grows in a particular service area and how a practice can add revenues simply by participating in integrated delivery systems.

Managed Care and Marketing to Employers

You may think there's nothing medical practices can do if a desirable employer group in its area is considering joining a plan and the practice is having trouble contracting with that plan. But a strategy is available to the practice so that it doesn't have to just sit by and wait to see what happens—and possibly lose any chance of treating the employer group's employees and their families. It may pay for it to contact the employer directly about the practice's difficulty in hammering out an agreement with the plan and to tell the employer about other, more responsive plans that the medical practice already belongs to. The employer may decide it would be better off joining one of those other plans instead.

When employers switch their health insurance coverage to a different or new managed-care plan, the practice must decide to become or remain a provider with this plan to keep treating its patients. However, there may be times when it is difficult negotiating with the managed-care plan, times when the plan refuses to compromise on several substantial issues, times when agreed-upon changes are not included in the revised draft of the contract, or times when the managed-care plan will flat out refuse to negotiate. In other words, the practice may determine that getting a reasonable contract won't happen.

Here is a marketing idea: Consider talking with the employer about how much trouble the practice is having contracting with the managed-care plan. Employers are open to hearing about this type of information. For example, you might disclose that the managed-care plan had taken a very hard line on certain provisions, failed to incorporate previously agreed-to changes, and unilaterally changed contract language from draft to draft without notifying the practice. In other words, you are pointing out that the managed-care plan might be as tough to work with for its members as for providers. At the end of the discussion, suggest that the employer group compare the managed-care plan with several other plans in the area that the practice already has contracts with and could vouch for as better contract partners.

How to Contact Employers

If a medical practice thinks that an existing or new employer group in its service area is switching insurance coverage or is otherwise shopping for a new plan, the practice can and should use its contracting experiences to help it persuade the employer group to join a plan it already belongs to. If a plan has a good relationship with its providers, it's also more likely to treat its members fairly. Set up a face-to-face meeting with the employer. But keep in mind you can call or write instead. Contact the employer's employee benefits manager. And if the employer group is using an insurance broker to get health insurance coverage, also contact the broker.

Tell the manager why you've contracted with some plans and not others. If you're already treating some of the employer group's employees, either under a plan contract or not, point out that the employees would get to stay in network if the employer contracted with a plan the practice belonged to. Give the manager a list of the plans you recommend and the names and telephone numbers of plan representatives to contact. Then follow up with each plan on your list to let them know the employer may contact them. This also gives the plan the opportunity to contact the employer group directly. You should consider using this strategy, even if you think the chances are slim that the employer will listen to you. If the employer hears the same concerns from other providers, it may follow your advice.

Tracking the Effectiveness of Marketing Efforts

Keep track of how new patients heard of the practice. The easiest way to do this is by asking on the new patient information sheet how the patient first heard of the practice or who referred the patient to the practice. Keep track of every person who has referred a patient to the practice and record when marketing activities, such as telephone directories, direct mail, and advertising, worked to bring in a new patient. Never let a new patient leave without knowing how the patient was referred to the office.

■ **Practice Point:** Review the practice's information form for new patients. The form should contain a line item asking where the new patient heard about the practice or who referred the patient. If it does not, the practice is probably not tracking its marketing efforts. You can confirm this by printing the referral listing from the computer. If the list is not detailed and complete, the practice is not tracking its marketing efforts. Ask the physician if he or she is interested in finding out how the practice's marketing program is doing. If the physician is interested, have the office manager add to the new patient information form the question regarding where patients heard about the practice. Explain to the physician that this answer will help him or her determine which marketing programs are working best.

If a practice does not track its new patient patterns, it can neither evaluate its current marketing efforts effectively nor determine the best course for future marketing tactics. For example, many offices advertise in telephone directories. Depending on the size of the advertisement, the cost can be high. Before the practice continues to place an ad in the directory, it should know how many new patients it has received as a direct result of the advertisement. Conduct a cost/benefit ratio. A medical practice should know how many patients are a direct result of its marketing efforts. If the practice continues to spend money on marketing programs without determining how effective they are, the practice could be wasting money on activities that are not working and it should explore other marketing activities.

For example, a practice spends $80,000 per year on advertising. When someone asks the physician if the program is working, the physician does not know the related new revenues the practice has received as a result. With the physician's permission, you can conduct an analysis to determine if the practice is losing money or making money on this marketing activity.

If the practice's referrals are increasingly coming from one or more physicians, the practice needs to show its gratitude. Likewise, if it appears referrals have dropped from these physicians, the practice must find out the reasons behind the drop and take corrective action. Otherwise, future revenue will become impaired. The practice should never let a change in referral pattern go unattended. It must be addressed immediately.

■ **Practice Point:** One way you can determine if the practice's referral patterns have changed is to print the practice's referring physician list or report. If you notice an increase or decrease in referrals, you should investigate and, working with the physician, find a solution to the problem.

▼ CHAPTER 16
Personnel Management

Besides operational policies, every practice should have defined personnel policies in place. Employees must know what their employer's specific policies are in order to avoid unnecessary confusion and disagreement. In some states, it is important to have personnel policies, from a labor-law standpoint. Remind physician-owners that, in most cases, if a practice has documented its personnel policies in writing (for example, in the form of a personnel manual), and the employees rely on what is documented as policy, *then what is documented becomes the labor law for the practice.* For example, suppose a personnel manual states that an employee who is chronically late for work will first be given an oral warning, then a written warning, and then terminated. If the office immediately fires the employee without following these guidelines, the practice may risk a wrongful termination lawsuit. Unfortunately, many practices put together personnel manuals without giving thought to the consequences if management does not comply with the contents. At a minimum, a practice's written personnel policy manual should be reviewed once a year to make sure that it complies with both federal and state labor laws.

However, no matter how many office policies and procedures are put into place in a medical practice, they will not work unless the staff members are qualified and responsible enough to implement and follow them.

The Hiring Process

Many problems that occur in medical practices could have been avoided if the office had hired qualified people from the start. Unfortunately, often there is a lack of qualified personnel capable of performing such duties as front-desk operations, billing, collection, managing, and nursing. The importance of the hiring process should never be overlooked or underestimated. Helping medical practices hire the right people has been a service neglected by most practice advisors. The first step to aiding the practice is to understand the hiring process itself.

Americans with Disabilities Act

The Americans with Disabilities Act (ADA) was passed by the federal government in July 1992. Both federal and state laws now restrict employers with at least 15 employees from discriminating against applicants with disabilities (including pregnant women) that do not impair job performance.

The ADA defines *qualified individuals with disabilities* as those who meet the practice's skill, experience, and education requirements with or without reasonable accommodations, and those who can perform the essential functions of the position. Therefore, written job descriptions that accurately reflect the functions of each position in the firm help determine whether a candidate is qualified. (See the section addressing job descriptions later in this chapter.)

Addressing Other Legal Issues

Make sure that each phase of the hiring process is reviewed for compliance with the law. Here are some points to remember:

1. **Provide reasonable access to the office for all applicants being interviewed.**

2. **Revise job applications.** Make sure that all questions pertain to specific job functions applicants would be expected to perform. Eliminate questions regarding previous medical or mental health, because past injuries or conditions may not be indicative of the candidate's present abilities.

3. **Review interview scripts.** Discuss new policies with anyone in the practice who will participate in the interview process. The interviewer cannot inquire into an applicant's medical or workers' compensation history during the pre-offer stage, nor can the interviewer ask if the candidate will require time off

for treatment of a condition. However, the interviewer may state the practice's policy regarding time off and ask if the individual expects to comply.

4. **Test properly.** The practice needs to provide a detailed job description and review the required tasks. The applicant can be asked to demonstrate competence in each area of assigned responsibility with or without reasonable accommodation. Include a tour of the office and a visit to the workstation for all qualified prospects. If accommodation is needed, the degree of accommodation can be mutually decided at that time.

Job Applications and Interview Questions

Review the practice's job application form periodically to ensure that it is in compliance with current federal and state employment laws. To keep up with changes to current law, contact a local attorney or chamber of commerce. The categories listed below must be *omitted* from interviews and job application forms:

- Marital status
- Dependents/children (number and age)
- Childcare plans
- Parenthood plans
- Preferred means of address (Mr., Mrs., Miss, Ms.)
- Maiden name/former name—unless previously employed by the organization to which he or she is applying
- Names of spouse or parents
- Head of household/principal wage earner
- Living arrangements
- Request for recent photo with application
- National origin, birthplace, naturalization
- Native language
- Age or date of birth
- Height/weight
- Sex

- Religion
- Race
- Arrest record
- Non-job-related club/lodge memberships
- Home or car ownership
- Type of military discharge
- Handicaps that are not job-related
- Non-job-related education or experience requirements
- Credit check—the applicant must sign a release or be notified in writing and must be allowed to either see the credit information or be given the address of the information source

Hiring the Right People

The following tips are useful when hiring personnel for the practice:

1. **Place a complete ad.** When advertising for a new employee, make sure that the help-wanted ad communicates exactly what the practice is looking for. To weed out candidates in large cities the ad can indicate the part of the city in which the practice is located. If computer experience is needed, state it in the ad. Always state that prior experience in a medical practice is a must. Also, have the prospective employee submit a salary history. This will be important when establishing the appropriate level of compensation.

2. **Review résumés closely.** Has the prospective employee changed jobs often? Does the résumé communicate specific job experience? Are references included on the résumé? If the office uses a computer, make sure that computer experience is indicated.

3. **Call the prospective employee's references.** Generally, most people will include in the résumé only people who will give a good reference. Additionally, references are not required to disclose any information about the individual's performance. Many offices may have reference policies that disclose only the

individual's dates of employment and employment position and, because of legal reasons, the primary reference may be hesitant to say anything negative about the applicant. Therefore, it may be difficult to get a truly honest assessment of the prospective employee's performance. If the practice is not satisfied with the information given by the references the applicant supplied, it may try to find someone who is not on the prospective employee's reference list who can provide more input about the person's performance. Ask each reference if he or she knows the name of any other person with whom the prospective employee worked. These secondary resources may provide a more detailed, two-sided reference that can give the practice a better idea of the work performance of the applicant.

If the practice's efforts fail to generate enough information to make a hiring decision, consider retaining the services of a professional. Fees for professional reference checks begin at about $75 to scan the background of support- or staff-level personnel, and may extend to about $500 for management and partner-level candidates.

4. **Ask situational questions when interviewing prospects.** Situational questions present the prospect with circumstances that occur in the practice and ask how the individual would deal with the problem. This will distinguish applicants from one another. If the prospective employee is interviewing for a billing position, ask the applicant to explain the difference in the various levels of office evaluation and management CPT codes. Ask specific questions about Medicare billing and insurance verification and precertification. If the position is for collection clerk, ask the applicant how he or she would follow up on unpaid insurance or on patients' overdue accounts. Ask the applicant how he or she would manage a practice's accounts receivable on an ongoing basis.

5. **Offer competitive salaries.** Remember, a practice gets what it pays for; if a practice is unwilling to compensate an employee fairly, job performance might be impaired simply because the best person was not hired in the first place. Asking for a salary history in the employment advertisement helps to establish the going rate for the position for which the practice is hiring.

The practice's accountant should always be involved in the hiring process. This is just one of the extra services he or she can provide. Ideally, having both the accountant and physician interview prospective employees will reduce the number of errors that can occur in the hiring process.

Personnel records documenting position and pay history, performance review, persons to be notified in case of emergency, and other information essential to sound employment practice should be maintained for each employee. These records should be maintained in separate files, usually by the office administrator.

Personnel Manuals

If a practice decides to have a personnel manual, it should include, at a minimum, the following sections:

1. The firm's history, organizational chart, goals, equal employment clause, and overall philosophy
2. Roles of employees in operation of the practice, reporting responsibilities, and professional obligations
3. Rules, policies, and safety and emergency procedures
4. Office hours and compensation
5. Employee benefits and bonus programs
6. Performance standards and review procedures
7. Procedures for termination of employment
8. Work procedures, grievance procedures, and other fairness issues such as AIDS discrimination, harassment, disability discrimination, and smokers' and nonsmokers' rights
9. General job responsibilities and backup functions for each staff level

Hours and Compensation

Working hours and lunch breaks should vary with an employee's job responsibilities and patient load and require coordination among the staff so that the office is covered with adequate nursing and business personnel until all patients have been seen at the close of the day.

Employees should normally work 40 hours per week, but may work more or less if authorized by a physician in advance. For example, unauthorized overtime should not be allowed. Unless specifically exempted, employees who *do* work more than 40 hours in one single work week must receive overtime not less than time-and-one-half their regular rates of pay. As a general rule, administrative employees are exempted from overtime pay if they are paid at least a weekly salary and are responsible for work directly related to the management of the practice. The practice's office manager is almost always an exempted employee. Professional employees are exempted under the law if their job requires advanced knowledge in a field of science or learning customarily obtained by a prolonged course of specialized instruction. This includes nurses in most cases. Many practices use so-called flex time instead of monetary compensation for overtime. Because most states have laws governing this issue, you should contact the state's employment commission for clarification if the medical practice is using flex time.

Practices generally do not have to pay employees for being on call unless they are not free to use the on-call time for their own personal purposes. For example, if the office requires an employee to carry a beeper, but the employee enjoys complete control over the free use of his or her time, the practice is not required to pay overtime.

A practice must pay employees for attendance at meetings or training if (a) attendance is during regular work hours, (b) attendance is mandatory, (c) the meeting or training is directly related to the employee's job, or (d) the employee performs productive work during the meeting or training. A more difficult issue involves employees who are required to attend meetings and educational programs after work hours. In almost all cases, the practice must pay for the employee's work time. If the employee falls into the exempt category, however, overtime pay is not required. Again, because this is such a complicated area, contact the state employment commission for clarification.

Also, employees usually are compensated for business-related expenses, but only if the expense was authorized beforehand.

Employee-related expenses include seminars, office supplies, automobile expenses, and professional publications.

Benefits

Many benefits are available for medical-practice employees. What a practice offers its employees will depend on its financial circumstances and the generosity of the physician-owner. You and the physician should always keep in mind that the overhead necessary to operate a practice must be contained or reduced to optimize the net profit that could be available for distribution as physicians' compensation. Benefits are a major operating cost to the medical practice. (For more information about cutting costs through benefits, see the section titled "Payroll and Related Benefits" in Chapter 3.)

Vacation

In most medical practices, no vacation benefits are available in the first year. After the first year of continuous employment, full-time employees become eligible for one week of paid vacation, and they are eligible for two weeks of paid vacation after 24 months of continuous employment. For long-time employees, most practices limit vacation leave to three weeks. Any vacation time should be scheduled as far in advance as possible and finalized at least six weeks prior to the date it is scheduled to begin. (See the sample employees' time-off request form in Appendix B.)

For internal control purposes, each employee should be required to take his or her entire vacation leave each year. One reason for this policy is that an employee's absence is a good time to evaluate internally his or her job performance. In many cases, the people who fill in for the absent employee find mistakes and errors that would not normally have been found had the employee not taken a vacation. In these situations, the problems can be corrected once the employee returns.

To maximize office productivity, employees in small offices should be encouraged to schedule their vacations at the same time as the physician's vacation, CME study, jury duty, and the like.

This mainly applies to single-physician practices that are more inactive when the physician is out of the office for a prolonged period. However, vacation time should *not* be encouraged at these times if the office needs to catch up on filing or other procedures while the physician is away. Also, employee vacations should be taken before the end of the employee's anniversary year and should not carry over to the succeeding year. In other words, employees should "use it or lose it."

Holidays

A practice should have a set holiday schedule that allows employees to receive days off with pay. Most medical practices give full-time employees six paid holidays a year. Generally, these holidays are New Year's Day, Memorial Day, Independence Day, Labor Day, Thanksgiving Day, and Christmas Day. Holidays that fall on a weekend usually are observed either on the preceding Friday or the following Monday. The physician-owner(s) reserves the right to add paid holidays at his or her discretion.

Sick Leave

Regular, full-time practice employees generally are eligible for sick leave. Personnel should emphasize to the employees that this leave should only be taken when the employee or a family member is sick—not when the employee feels like taking the day off. Most medical practices provide a maximum of five days of paid sick leave per year only after the first three months of continuous employment; new hires are not eligible for paid sick leave. Usually, unused sick leave does not carry over to the next year nor do the employees receive compensation for unused sick leave. Some offices are more generous in their sick-leave policy. Another common policy is for the practice to provide five sick days per year and to allow employees to carry forward the unused leave to a maximum of 20 days. The purpose of this type of policy is to provide a cushion for normally healthy employees in the case of a catastrophic illness. As with the previous policy, employees are not compensated for unused sick leave.

Hardship Leave

Any office must be flexible enough in its personnel policies to grant additional leave for hardship or other reasons, provided that no additional staff is employed to carry on the work during such time. This, along with personal time off for death or serious illness in the employee's family or for other emergencies, should be evaluated for pay eligibility by the physician or management on a case-by-case basis. (See the section "Family Leave Policy" later in this chapter.)

Jury Duty

Employees must be encouraged to serve when called to jury duty. They should receive time off with pay. If an employee is selected for jury duty, his or her compensation should be adjusted for jury duty pay if the duty extends beyond one week. Service beyond three weeks may require an adjustment in compensation if additional staff is employed to carry on the work.

Paid Time Off (PTO)

Many practices combine all of the leaves and time-offs described above into one category called "paid time off." With PTO, an employee is allocated an amount of time to use as he or she wishes. There is no designated leave for vacations, sick time off, etc. The following are examples of actual PTO polices of various medical practices.

Example

For the first year of employment: 80 hours
2nd year thru the 5th year: 120 hours
5 years: 160 hours

Example

Employees can sell PTO time accrued in excess of 80 hours twice yearly. They do get paid for PTO accrual if they resign. Accrual begins at date of hire but is not available to employee until after they have been employed for 90 days.

Example

Hourly employees accumulate 4.615 PTO hours per pay period, but it does not include sick time. Employees accumulate one sick day per month.

Example

0–5 years	*3 weeks*
5–10 years	*4 weeks*
10+ years	*5 weeks*

Incentive Programs

Incentive programs, such as bonuses or profit sharing, may or may not be offered as an added compensatory benefit. However, the practice should not award bonuses unless employees earn them. A bonus can be used as a motivating device in the office. The practice can develop a set of goals that, if met, will entitle employees to receive bonuses. For example, some practices set a fixed-dollar collection goal for the billing and collection staff. Others award a bonus to the practice manager based on net income before physician compensation. In this case, the manager is motivated to increase collections and reduce overhead. In any event, the practice's bonus program should be achievable. Unreachable goals defeat the purpose of the bonus program, which is to motivate employees to do a better job.

Sample Administrator's Incentive Compensation Plan

Practice administrators are often frustrated because they feel they are not paid what they are worth. This usually occurs when the practice has done well but the physician or physicians have failed to recognize financially the efforts of the administrator. The following is a sample incentive bonus plan for a practice administrator. Compensation is not only a sensitive issue, but it can be a divisive one as well. The last thing a practice can afford is to lose a good administrator simply because he or she feels they were not adequately compensated for their continued efforts for the practice. Administrator compensation is one issue you (especially the physician, CPA, and consultant reader) need to always keep in mind. Remember that finding a new administrator is often an arduous task.

Sample Incentive Bonus Plan

5 percent of current base salary *Incentive bonus if operating expenses at the end of the year equal 52 percent to 58 percent of practice collections. Operating expenses do not include physician-related expenses and physician compensation.*

10 percent of current base salary *Additional incentive bonus if operating expenses at the end of the year are less than 52 percent of practice collections.*

5 percent of current base salary *Incentive bonus if practice's net collection ratio equals or exceeds 95 percent.*

5 percent of current base salary *Incentive bonus if accounts receivable ratio at the end of the year is equal to or less than 1.5 times average monthly production for the 12-month period immediately preceding.*

Collections Growth Incentive *This is 3 percent of all collections exceeding a designated collection target. In developing the target, you would start with practice collections for the prior year and add a targeted growth rate (for example, 10 to 25 percent). If the administrator can get collections over the targeted growth rate, he or she will receive 3 percent of the excess. For example, if practice collections for the prior 12-month period were $1,000,000 and you wanted to target a 10 percent increase in the next year, the administrator would get 3 percent of all collections that exceeded $1,100,000. The objective here is to motivate the administrator to build the gross revenues of the practice.*

Discretionary Bonus *The practice can allocate a $2,500 discretionary bonus. This bonus will be based upon a designed grade point system and each physician will complete the Administrator Satisfaction Grading Form. Based on how each physician grades the administrator, he or she will receive all or part of the $2,500 bonus. Each practice should individually tailor its grading form to those issues that are important to them. For example, a rating on how the administrator deals with staff and interacts with people could be included on the form.*

Health Insurance

Many medical practices offer group health insurance as an employee fringe benefit. While some practices will pay 100 percent of the premium for the employee only, some pay only 50 percent of the premium. This is because the cost of providing employees with health insurance coverage is becoming more and more expensive. Coverage for the employee's spouse and dependents is almost always at the employee's expense. (See the "Health Insurance" section in Chapter 3 for information on keeping costs down.)

Performance Reviews

All employees should be given performance reviews. New hires should receive one at the end of the first 90 days of employment and all employees should receive formal annual reviews at the time of their anniversary dates. A sample employees' annual performance review form is in Appendix B.

Generally, when new employees are hired, the initial 30- to 90-day employment period is probationary. Depending on state law, new employees are not eligible for benefits during the probationary period. This allows the practice to see first what kind of employees the individuals are going to be. The probationary period is an often-overlooked management tool.

It is important that the physician or office manager provide positive feedback as well as constructive criticism during employee reviews. Employees are part of the office team and should feel free to provide their comments and suggestions about the practice. Constructive employee suggestions should never be discouraged, because employees are the ones who see how the office runs and performs on a daily basis and can provide valuable insight into correcting problems and inefficiencies.

Daily Reviews

Related to 90-day and annual reviews are daily performance reviews. When an employee performs exceptionally well during the day or continues to excel and follow office policy, someone in the office should provide positive reinforcement. If morale is a problem in the medical practice, lack of encouragement could be one of the biggest reasons. Employees often feel unappreciated for the work that they do for the office. Consequently, many have the attitude that it is useless to put out so much energy for the practice if the physician does not appreciate the effort. The result is an unproductive, inefficient office. The office manager or the physician should periodically let employees know they have done a good job and that the office appreciates the hard work they are putting forth.

Raises and Promotions

Raises and promotions should be used to recognize individual performance. Before an employee's review, analyze what he or she is paid relevant to his or her specific job duty in the practice. (For more information about evaluating appropriate salary levels, see the section titled "Payroll and Related Benefits" in Chapter 3.) The appropriate monetary raise and job title change is based on these figures, the length of time the employee has been with the practice, and especially the employee's individual performance.

Termination of Employment

Employees should be expected to give at least two weeks' notice prior to voluntary resignations. To avoid wrongful discharge suits or other legal complications, every medical practice should familiarize itself with the labor laws in the state in which it operates. Most offices will reserve the right to terminate employment without notice, however, for causes such as, but not limited to, dishonesty, theft, violation of office policy, breach of confidentiality, and any action considered detrimental to the patients' care. In most normal situations, the practice has the right to terminate employees because of unsatisfactory job performance. Such termination should be preceded by counseling sessions and probationary periods, during which employees have the opportunity to show significant improvement. The office manager or the physician should make sure that the reasons for the probation are documented and signed by employees. If employees are eventually terminated for a recurring problem, the practice must be able to show the patterns of behavior and related disciplinary actions.

Family Leave Policy

Federal law prohibits employers from discriminating against employees based on pregnancy. Essentially, this means the following:

- Employers must treat disabling conditions related to pregnancy the same as other disabilities covered by benefit plans.
- Employers cannot require pregnant employees to take leave unless the employees are unable to perform their jobs. In such cases, employers should arrange for physical examinations before determining whether employees are unable to perform their jobs because of their pregnancies.
- Employers must fully reinstate employees returning from the firm's specified pregnancy leave. In other words, employees must be able to return to the same or comparable jobs and be credited with previous service for purposes of seniority, accrued vacation, retirement benefits, and so on.
- Before employment, employers cannot ask female applicants if they are pregnant or are planning to have children in the future.
- Employers cannot base hiring decisions on pregnancy alone, regardless of how close the birth is.
- Employers should let the length of temporary disability be determined by the pregnant employees and their physicians—or, in some cases, the companies' physicians.

Many states also have laws and regulations pertaining to family leave. Firms are advised to have their policies reviewed by labor attorneys to ensure compliance with state laws.

The Equal Employment Opportunity Commission (EEOC) has issued guidance to clarify the confusion surrounding the issue of family leave. The EEOC's statement concludes that leave policies that treat male and female employees differently with regard to time off violate Title VII. This means that if a practice grants paid or unpaid leave to employees, it must provide equal benefits to male and female employees.

As a result of the enactment of the 1993 Family and Medical Leave Act, many practices have had to revise their personnel policies. The Act entitles designated employees to take extended leaves of absence, without pay, to care for seriously ill family members. It also obligates the firm to restore such staff members to the same or equivalent positions, benefits, rates of pay, and status when they are able to return to work.

All firms with 50 or more employees must comply with the Act. This includes multi-office firms with branches within a 75-mile radius that total 50 or more staff members. Some states, however, have enacted legislation that requires companies with fewer total employees to comply. Contact the state's department of labor for details about the state's legislation before revising any practice's policy regarding leave.

In brief, the Act does the following:

- Provides up to 12 weeks of unpaid leave to employees who qualify. Check state law, however.

- Defines *qualifying employees* as individuals employed by a firm for a minimum of 1,250 hours within a 12-month period.

- Recognizes *covered family members* as sons or daughters (biological, adopted, stepchildren, or legal wards under the age of 18, or beyond 18 with mental or physical disabilities), parents, spouse, or self.

- Requests medical certification by employers and monthly updates on the status of the health conditions from employees during the leave period, if necessary.

Free copies of the Act are available from both the state and federal departments of labor. A sample policy should be available upon request from the state legislature where the practice is located.

Harassment Policy

Physician-owners must express an interest in the human dignity and protection of their employees. Many employers now are particularly concerned about the possibility of employee harassment, whether it be sexual, racial, ethnic, or some other type. The definition of *harassment* in any form—verbal, physical, or visual—should be stated and known by everyone who works in the practice. A harassment policy should be a part of every personnel policy manual. Violation of this policy should *always* result in disciplinary action. If an employee feels that he or she has been the victim of harassment or knows of another employee who has, the employee should be instructed to report it immediately to the office manager or a physician.

Employee Job Descriptions

The efficiency and success of a medical practice are directly dependent on the job performance of its employees. To ensure success and to eliminate miscommunication, all employees should be given written descriptions of their job duties. Job descriptions should explain what is expected of employees and can be used as a tool to evaluate the employees' job performance. Another essential function of job descriptions is that they can be used as evidence to show why employment decisions were made if discrimination charges are brought against the practice.

The following basic set of job descriptions outlines the duties for various personnel in a medical practice. Each practice, however, should tailor its job descriptions to meet the unique characteristics of its own office operations. Job descriptions can also be used to make sure that employees are properly cross-trained.

Office Manager—Small Practice

- Orient, train, and supervise all office personnel, in conjunction with physicians.
- Maintain employee records, including résumés, employment history, salary or wage history, sick leave, and vacation time.
- Handle the majority of calls from patients regarding billing, balance due, and secondary insurance.
- Assist with checking in and checking out patients.

- Prepare disbursement for the payment of accounts payable and give it to physicians for signatures.
- Prepare thank-you letters to referring physicians and patients.
- Close out the computer at the end of the day and print reports.
- Prepare the month-end computer closeout and print reports.
- Open mail and prepare deposit slips. Take deposits to the bank.
- Make sure that the computer's daily receipts agree with deposit slips and the appointment book.
- Code check stubs with the general ledger account numbers as requested by the practice's outside accountant. Mail copies of bank statements and checks to outside accountant each month.
- Make sure that all tax reports are prepared and filed on a timely basis.
- Handle physicians' correspondence unrelated to office billing and collection activities.
- Maintain and reconcile the petty cash fund monthly.
- If requested, reconcile the bank account or accounts each month.
- Manage the operation of all office and medical equipment.
- Maintain appropriate quantities of business supplies.
- Assist insurance/billing clerks, when necessary.
- Ensure that all employees are cross-trained.
- Provide financial counseling to patients requiring hospital admission or regarding delinquent account balances.
- Periodically review EOBs to detect potential problem areas.
- Make sure that insurance claims are filed on a timely basis.
- Make sure that billing and collection personnel are complying with related office policies.

Administrator—Large Practice

- Establish ongoing planning policies and procedures that expeditiously modify objectives to meet changed circumstances.

- Formulate a system for communication of adopted objectives to all personnel.

- Determine the means for implementing policies and procedures to accomplish the practice's objectives.

- Monitor and report the practice's progress in attaining its objectives.

- Develop and recommend base, bonus, and fringe compensation policies and procedures applicable to all employees.

- Develop and recommend policies dealing with recruitment of physicians, nurses, secretaries, and administrative personnel.

- Develop and recommend written job descriptions and personnel policies applicable to all employees.

- Administer periodic reviews and evaluations of all employees.

- Establish policies and procedures for employee relations (e.g., holiday luncheons, presents, staff meetings, etc.).

- Recommend the selection and employment of outside consultants.

- Prepare an organization chart.

- Directly supervise the administrative personnel employed by the practice.

- Develop and recommend business origination and group contracting goals for the practice.

- Pursue, analyze, and recommend managed-care contracting opportunities which support the goals of the practice.

- Develop a positive patient relation philosophy for all personnel employed by the practice.

- Define the practice's internal and external markets. Examine the packaging of the practice's services, physical plant, policies, and procedures from a marketing standpoint. Evaluate business promotion expenses and purposes.

- Publish a brochure for use in the practice's recruiting and marketing activities.

- Project and determine office space, equipment, and other physical requirements.

- Adopt maintenance policies and procedures.

- Establish budgets for office furnishings and policies and procedures applicable thereto.
- Establish purchasing policies and procedures.
- Establish internal housekeeping requirements, office appearance, and enforcement policies.
- Establish nonmedical training programs and maintain secretarial and other manuals.
- Establish new employee introduction programs for medical and nonmedical personnel.
- Systematize common forms.
- Handle internal and external complaints.
- Prepare an annual business plan and budget.
- Supervise the preparation of monthly and annual financial reports.
- Supervise the preparation of financial reports necessary to develop managed-care contracts and proposals.
- Recommend investment policies and procedures to the Executive Committee.
- Establish overtime control procedures.
- Establish policies and procedures to identify and collect delinquent accounts receivable.
- Prepare and file all tax returns and other governmental reports required in the conduct of the practice's business.
- Prepare and maintain all corporate minutes, records, and other data.
- Implement automated general ledger, accounts receivable, accounts payable, timekeeping, payroll, and other accounting systems.
- Establish and maintain filing and information retrieval systems appropriate for the practice's needs.
- Minimize the time demands on physicians for firm administration and facilitate the resolution of scheduling conflicts.
- Create a confidence level and attitude which encourage medical and nonmedical personnel to bring problems to the administrator for solution.

- Research issues and make recommendations to the Board of Directors with respect to the adoption of policies and procedures.

- Consider the interests of all of the employees of the practice in the administration responsibilities and deal fairly with each employee of the practice.

- Address problems on a timely basis and promptly institute approved solutions.

- Be a sounding board for all of the employees of the practice.

- Seek additional education and competency in medical group administration.

- Expeditiously implement decisions.

- Communicate problems to those in a position to solve them and solutions to those in a position to implement them.

- Support the practice's primary business of practicing medicine by producing an administrative staff which is a service organization within a service organization.

Nurse

- Inspect patients' files to ensure completeness of the clinical record before examination.

- Set up clinical files for new patients.

- Escort patients to exam rooms and prepare them for the physicians' examinations.

- Note the patient's complaints and take weight, height, other vital signs, and medication history.

- Prepare medications and give injections.

- Assist physicians with patients' examinations.

- Instruct patients regarding where to go for their tests if they are not performed in the office.

- Record and maintain laboratory, X-ray, and other test data in the patients' charts.

- Upon approval by physicians, communicate test results to patients. Document interaction on the patients' charts.

- Maintain adequate medical supplies. Initiate orders for replenishment as needed.

- Make sure that the office is in compliance with all federal and state clinical regulations, including Occupational Safety and Health Administration (OSHA) guidelines.

- Screen clinical calls for physicians and handle those that do not require their input. Advise the patients according to the office's clinical protocols.

- Meet with drug representatives and maintain sample inventory, especially tracking expiration dates.

- Maintain the neat appearance and cleanliness of exam rooms.

- Ensure that all necessary equipment, instruments, supplies, gowns, and linens are ready for use. Arrange for waste disposal and laundry services as needed.

- Help with telephone calls.

- Retrieve mail from the hospital.

- Fill in for or assist other staff members during absence or work overload.

Billing and Collection Personnel

- Keep abreast of Medicare rules and regulations, if applicable to the practice. Keep the office manager and physicians informed of significant changes.

- Send out all patients' statements and insurance claims on a timely basis in accordance with office policy.

- Prepare and mail secondary insurance claim forms as soon as payments are received from primary insurance carriers.

- Fulfill requests for medical records or any other information by insurance carriers.

- Handle business and insurance carrier correspondence. Reply promptly.

- Post and reconcile EOBs promptly upon receipt.

- File all EOBs in notebooks, patients' clinical charts, or patients' business files as set up in the office.

- Analyze accounts receivable and follow up with effective, timely phone calls and collection letters in accordance with office policy. Contact patients by telephone regarding their delinquent accounts if the balance exceeds a designated dollar amount.

- Prepare and mail collection letters to patients each month in accordance with office policy.

- Prepare a list of patients' accounts to send to the practice's outside collection agency for follow-up. Have physicians approve the list before the accounts are sent to the collection agency.

- Promptly prepare appeal letters to insurance carriers that deny patients' billings.

- Follow up weekly on all insurance claims not paid within 25 days.

- Maintain office business records, including insurance folders, billings, income, and accounts receivable. Furnish information to physicians and the outside accountant upon request.

- Post payments to patients' accounts on a timely basis.

- Verify patients' insurance coverage before hospital admission or in accordance with office policy.

- When applicable, obtain authorization numbers for insurance companies before hospital admission.

- Prepare hospital and other institutional inpatient cards for use by the physicians when making rounds.

- If applicable, schedule surgeries at the hospital.

Front-Desk Personnel

- Take phones off the answering service first thing in the morning and put them back on during the lunch hour and when the office closes at the end of the day.

- Answer all telephone calls.

- Schedule daily appointments and provide patients with appropriate instructions as required per office policy.

- Ensure that the reception room is organized, neat, and ready for patients. Greet patients and visitors, determine needs, and respond accordingly.

- Have first-time patients complete the new patient information sheet.

- Make a copy of the patients' insurance cards and drivers' licenses.

- Instruct new patients of the office collection policy when they make their appointments.

- Make sure that established patients who arrive for their appointments have not changed insurance coverage.

- Have established patients complete the new patient information sheet if they have not made appointments within the last 12 months.

- Maintain the appointment book and the daysheet.

- Call patients to remind them of their appointments.

- Prepare charge tickets and retrieve and file charts for each day's patients.

- Check out patients; post charges; collect payments, co-payments, or deductibles related to the visit; post receipts.

- Collect overdue accounts receivable from patients when checking them out or before their appointments. Refer patients with overdue balances exceeding a designated amount to the office manager for financial counseling.

- Follow up on no-shows with letters or phone calls as appropriate.

- Retrieve the office mail each day.

- Fulfill requests for medical records from patients. Obtain the patients' signatures on requests for records to be sent or to be obtained from other physicians.

- Assist in filing patients' charts.

- Make copies as requested by the physicians.

- Stamp and send outgoing mail.

- Substitute for other staff as needed.

Employee Retention

Many medical practices are looking for ways to stop the cycle of hiring one good employee only to have two others resign. As health care organizations strive to deliver quality health care, retaining key employees is an ongoing concern.

A study conducted by the Gallup Corporation received the following responses to the question of what employees are looking for:

- Having the opportunity to do what I do best
- Having the sense that someone cares about me
- Knowing what's expected of me
- Getting recognition for what I do
- Having opportunities to learn and grow
- Being productive

A common thread runs through these responses—effective performance management. Managers do not intentionally ignore employees' needs for recognition and professional development. Usually absent are both a system and accountability for ensuring that employees understand expectations, receive feedback about their performance, receive recognition for good performance, and have a plan for professional growth and development.

You can advise physicians and office administrators on ways to maintain quality employees. Following are some areas medical practices should give attention to in order to prevent high employee turnover.

Professional Growth and Development

Professional growth and development plans for the employee should be written and reviewed in formal and informal performance discussions. Today's employees understand that job security may be a thing of the past, so instead they want to be assured that their professional abilities will be marketable in the future. Retaining good employees today is often dependent upon an employer's ability to provide opportunities for an employee to grow and develop.

Business Goals and Plans

A performance management system should include time for the manager and employee to discuss the organization's business goals and planned organizational changes. Doing so enhances the employee's sense of ownership in the organization and helps the employee plan for changes that may impact his or her job. Having sound information about business plans also can counter the "rumor mill factor," which often focuses on negative information that can impact an employee's decision on whether to stay or leave the company.

Recognition

Employees who perform well or make progress in professional growth deserve to be recognized. Each individual will respond to different forms of recognition. A simple pat on the back may be fine for some, while others may appreciate some form of public recognition. An effective manager knows his or her employees and what will work best for them. It is also important for organizations to have specific recognition programs in place that regularly recognize individual or group achievements, contributions, or performance.

The focus of these recognition programs should be on achievements, contributions, or behaviors supporting the company goals and plans. Rewards and recognition will not replace competitive salaries, but they can help create a greater sense of loyalty and make employees feel that they are important members of the team.

The following is a simple example of a recognition program one medical practice has actually used. This and other programs are also intended to increase staff morale, which should never be overlooked.

Example

The medical practice will occasionally buy lunch for all staff members. It also lets them leave early occasionally if the practice is not seeing patients. This practice also takes a day off and goes to a local flea market together. The staff is paid for the day and the practice buys lunch for everyone. In addition, it has also given $10 video gift cards on a Friday.

The following are a few other recognition and morale boosters used by medical practices:

- *Donuts in the office on Fridays.*
- *Not only free coffee for employees, but tea and hot chocolate as well.*
- *Keep saltines and pretzels available in break room.*
- *Provide a summer picnic for staff and families with food catered in or cooked by doctors; include soda, drinks, and games with prizes.*
- *Christmas party for staff and spouse/guest at the country club.*
- *Provide tickets to the county fair for staff and family.*
- *Buy wreaths for employees at Christmas time.*
- *Provide gift certificates from a grocery store at Thanksgiving time.*
- *Have a monthly Positive Employee Recognition award (doctors and manager choose the employee to receive the award).*
- *Frequently buy bags of candy and put them next to the coffee pot.*
- *Provide memberships to Sam's Club or other wholesale outlet.*
- *Occasional "happy hour" parties for staff only.*
- *Recognize birthdays and anniversaries at staff meetings.*
- *Don't forget Birthdays, Secretaries Day, Nurses Week, etc.*
- *Participate in Bring Your Daughters (Children) to Work Day.*
- *Car wash gift certificates.*
- *Pot luck dinners for holidays.*

Employee Surveys

Conducting an employee survey can be an effective way to retain quality employees. By focusing on recognition needs, the effectiveness of supervisors, the work environment, work and family balance, or time-off benefits, the survey results can help a medical practice direct its retention efforts and at the same time create a better place to work. Administrators will find out what currently is working (and should be continued), as well as identify some opportunities to change some things.

Employee surveys can be a double-edged sword if not implemented properly. It is important to share the survey results with employees and address the top issues identified. If survey results are not communicated or used in a purposeful way, employees become cynical and will be less inclined to give an opinion the next time asked.

The following is a sample employee survey in its simplest form. It makes sure that the employee knows his or her duties and solicits feedback on what is good and bad about the practice:

Employee Survey

*Name*_____ *Title*_____

What are your responsibilities?

1. _____
2. _____
3. _____
4. _____
5. _____
6. _____
7. _____
8. _____
9. _____
10. _____

What do you think works well in the office?

_____
_____
_____
_____

What do you think needs improvement?

_____
_____
_____
_____

What are ways to improve?

_____

_____

_____

_____

Are there any specific coding issues that, in your opinion, are still unresolved? If yes, explain.

_____

_____

_____

_____

Are you aware of any compliance issues that need to be addressed in the office? If so, please explain.

_____

_____

_____

_____

Other ways for physicians to retain their best employees include the following:

- Competitive salaries
- Incentive (bonus) programs for all levels in the organization
- Improved benefits
- Alternative work arrangements such as flexible scheduling or compressed work weeks
- Improved personal time-off policies

Overtime Pay

One of the most pervasive yet least understood federal laws governing the workplace is the Fair Labor Standards Act of 1938 (FLSA). The main thrust of this law is to prescribe a minimum wage and an overtime wage to be paid on all hours worked in excess of 40 per week. Because the overtime wage of time-and-a-half is expensive for medical practices, what type of employee is and is not exempt from this overtime pay requirement continues to be a question for many employers. Unfortunately, many physician employers are either unaware of the basic overtime laws, do not understand them, or choose to ignore them. As such, many physician offices are not in compliance.

Salary alone does not determine overtime status. The most common, though not the only, exemptions from overtime pay are for executive, administrative, and professional employees, the so-called "white collar" exemptions. Employees in these categories are often paid a set monthly salary as opposed to an hourly wage, but many employers assume that because they have classified a worker as "salaried," the worker automatically qualifies for one of the white collar exemptions. This is not necessarily true.

The United States Department of Labor (DOL), enforcement agency for the FLSA, cautions against assuming that any particular job title or position will automatically be considered exempt. DOL regulations give examples of positions generally considered exempt: physicians, attorneys, artists, personnel directors, lease buyers, executive assistants, financial experts, and teachers. Examples of jobs considered non-exempt include clerks of various kinds, errand runners, bookkeepers, secretaries, inspectors, trainees, reporters, and lab and X-ray technicians. But how does an employer know how to classify a job that is not one of these examples? For starters, an employer should be familiar with the tests that the DOL itself uses in making these determinations.

General Requirements

Unless specifically exempted, employees covered by the Act must receive overtime pay for hours worked in excess of 40 in a workweek at a rate not less than time-and-one-half their regular rates of pay. The Act doesn't limit the number of hours employees aged 16 and older may work in any workweek. The Act does not require overtime pay for work on Saturdays, Sundays, holidays, or regular days of rest, as such.

The Act applies on a workweek basis. An employee's workweek is a fixed and regularly recurring period of 168 hours—seven consecutive 24-hour periods. It need not coincide with the calendar week, but may begin on any day and at any hour of the day. Different workweeks may be established for different employees or groups of employees. Averaging of hours over two or more weeks is not permitted. Normally, overtime pay earned in a particular workweek must be paid on the regular pay day for the pay period in which the wages were earned.

The regular rate of pay cannot be less than the minimum wage. The regular rate includes all remuneration for employment except certain payments excluded by the Act itself. Payments which are not part of the regular rate include pay for expenses incurred on the employer's behalf, premium payments for overtime work or the true premiums paid for work on Saturdays, Sundays, and holidays, discretionary bonuses, gifts and payments in the nature of gifts on special occasions, and payments for occasional periods when no work is performed due to vacation, holidays, or illness.

Earnings may be determined on a piece-rate, salary, commission, or some other basis, but in all such cases the overtime pay due must be computed on the basis of the average hourly rate derived from such earnings. This is calculated by dividing the total pay for employment (except for the noted statutory exclusions) in any workweek by the total number of hours actually worked.

Where an employee in a single workweek works at two or more different types of work for which different straight-time rates have been established, the regular rate for that week is the weighted average of such rates. That is, the earnings from all such rates are added together and this total is then divided by the total number of hours worked at all jobs.

Where non-cash payments are made to employees in the form of goods or facilities, the reasonable cost to the employer or fair value of such goods or facilities must be included in the regular rate.

Compensable Work Hours

A major issue related to overtime pay is the question of "hours worked." In other words, what goes into the total number of hours worked for a week? It is clear that an employer must pay for all the time an employee spends actually performing work for the employer. Questions arise because some employees think (and some employers worry) that they should be paid for travel to and from work, coffee and lunch breaks, preparatory and concluding activities, and time spent on calls, to give just a few examples. The DOL and the courts have made some specific rulings on these issues.

For example, travel time going to work and returning home is not compensable, but time spent getting from one worksite to another during the workday must be paid. Meal breaks are usually 30 minutes to an hour in length and are not counted as hours worked, but if morning and afternoon breaks are allowed, they count as work time if they last 20 minutes or less. A word of warning however: Not all meal breaks are created equal. If the employer expects the employee to perform work such as answering phones while sitting at his or her desk, the DOL may well consider that to be compensable work time. The test is whether the employee is completely relieved from duties while eating. Preparatory and concluding activities must be paid if they are an integral (i.e., indispensable) part of the employee's principal activities at work. Time spent "on call" must generally be paid if the employee must wait for assignments in such a way that he or she is unable to use that time effectively for his or her own purposes.

Types of Overtime Pay

The most common form of overtime pay is the one specified in the statute, i.e., time and a half for all hours worked in excess of 40 in a week. Overtime must be paid in cash unless the employer somehow qualifies to pay sometime in the future. DOL regulations permit other ways to figure overtime pay, but they involve complex technical requirements. If you would like details on these and other methods for calculating overtime pay, request a copy of Part 778 of the wage and hour regulations from your nearest DOL office.

Overtime Exemption Tests

The DOL has adopted both long and short tests for determining whether a given position qualifies for an administrative, executive, or professional exemption. Employees who meet the criteria for either of the tests are exempt from receiving overtime pay under the white collar exemptions.

Executive

Long Test

a. primarily manages an operation *or* subdivision
b. routinely supervises two or more employees
c. has hiring, firing, and promoting authority
d. routinely exercises discretion in the workplace
e. spends at least 80 percent of workday in above listed activities
f. earns at least $155 per week, not including board, lodging, or other facilities

Short Test

a. primarily manages an operation or subdivision
b. routinely supervises at least two other employees
c. earns at least $250 per week

Administrative

Long Test

a. routinely exercises discretion and independent judgment in performance of job duties
b. duties consist mainly of office or nonmanual work related to management policies or general business operations or duties involve administrative work in a school system or individual school which provides academic instruction
c. duties involve the direct and routine assistance of an executive or administrative employee in the performance of specialized

or technical work, requiring special training, experience, or knowledge

d. performs duties under general supervision only

e. spends 80 percent of workday in above listed activities

f. earns at least $155 per week

Short Test

a. duties are described in the long test

b. duties must include work requiring the exercise of discretion and independent judgment—a slightly lesser standard than the long test which requires "routine exercise of discretion and independent judgment"

c. earns at least $250 per week

Professional

Long Test

a. primary duties include: (1) work requiring advanced knowledge normally acquired through a prolonged course of specialized intellectual study; this criterion is not met by a general academic education, routine training, or apprenticeships; (2) original and creative work stemming primarily from invention, imagination, or talent; or (3) teaching, tutoring, lecturing, or instructing for an educational institution

b. work must require the consistent exercise of discretion and independent judgment

c. work must be intellectual and varied in character

d. work does not lend itself to standardization by time, i.e., how much time any part of the overall task should take cannot be determined

e. at least 80 percent of the employee's workday must be devoted to the type of work described above

f. employee must earn at least $170 per week

Short Test

a. duties are as described in the long test

b. duties need only include work that requires use of discretion and independent judgment

c. employee must earn at least $250 per week

DOL Wage and Hour Investigations

You should keep in mind that a medical practice can be investigated by the DOL because of complaints from current and former employees, reports from competitors, or the DOL's targeting of a specific industry. In addition to overtime pay complaints, the DOL handles complaints concerning basic minimum wage and child labor violations. A DOL investigator has the authority to view an employer's records and interview employees and managers. Although the employer must furnish all records requested, he can be assured that the investigator will not reveal information contained in employer records to employees or third parties.

Penalties or Noncompliance

An employer who has mistakenly or intentionally misclassified a non-exempt employee as exempt will be liable for the payment of back overtime wages. The same is true if an employer has failed to pay the minimum wage. If an employer refuses to pay, either the DOL or the individual employee may bring suit to enforce the determination. At this point, the employer may be liable for the employee's attorney fees and double the amount of wages owed.

Getting Help

The Fair Labor Standards Act is complex. When in doubt, you may contact the U.S. Department of Labor with specific questions about the law's requirements or to obtain a copy of the booklet, *Handy Reference Guide to the Fair Labor Standards Act.*

Overtime Pay Examples

Fixed sum for varying amounts of overtime   A lump sum paid for work performed during overtime hours without regard to the number of overtime hours worked does not qualify as an overtime premium even though the amount of money paid is equal to or greater than the sum owed on a per-hour basis. For example, no part of a flat sum of $90 to employees who work overtime on Sunday will qualify as an overtime premium, even though the employees' straight-time rate is $6.00 an hour and the employees always work less than 10 hours on Sunday. Similarly, where an agreement provides for six-hours' pay at $9.00 an hour regardless of the time actually spent for work on a job performed during over-time hours, the entire $54 must be included in determining the employees' regular rate.

Salary for workweek exceeding 40 hours   A fixed salary for a regular workweek longer than 40 hours does not discharge FLSA statutory obligations. For example, an employee may be hired to work a 45-hour workweek for a weekly salary of $300. In this instance the regular rate is obtained by dividing the $300 straight-time salary by 45 hours, resulting in a regular rate of $6.67. The employee is then due additional overtime computed by multiplying the five overtime hours by one-half the regular rate of pay ($3.335 × 5 = $16.68).

Overtime pay may not be waived   The overtime requirement may not be waived by agreement between the employer and em-ployees. An agreement that only eight hours a day or only 40 hours a week will be counted as working time also fails the test of FLSA compliance. An announcement by the employer that no overtime work will be permitted, or that overtime work will not be paid for unless authorized in advance, also will not impair the employee's right to compensation for compensable overtime hours that are worked.

▼ PART III

Physicians' Contracts, Relationships, and Related Issues

Contracts are part of physicians' everyday lives. One of the first actions that new physicians coming out of residencies or fellowships take is to sign some type of contract, such as employment agreements or hospital recruitment agreements. Physicians already in practice also must confront contractual issues. Such contracts might include managed-care contracts, hospital recruitment agreements, employment agreements, partnership agreements, or corporate buy/sell agreements.

Physicians should look for expert guidance on all issues related to the contracts they sign. Many people believe that most contracts contain vast amounts of legalese, and thus only attorneys should be involved in their review and development. A majority of the terms and clauses of most physicians' contracts, however, are financial in nature. In fact, about 80 percent of the content of physicians' contracts contain financial terms and issues. Therefore, individuals experienced with such financial issues should be involved in the development and review of such contracts. Legal counsel should still be consulted, however, about the terms of the contract that specifically relate to legal issues.

Besides contracts, physicians have many other kinds of relationships, such as those relating to the formation of group practices, the development of independent practice associations, and their involvement in physician/hospital organizations, medical foundations, and management service organizations. In today's health care environment, the number of these relationships is increasing rapidly. Physicians entering into these relationships need expert guidance on the specifics of the related financial issues that directly impact on them.

Part III of this book is a discussion of the primary contracts physicians encounter in private practice, including a brief discussion of the various relationships physicians may be considering. The focus is on the financial issues related to these contracts, along with any other specifics physicians must be aware of before signing contracts or entering into contractual relationships.

▼ CHAPTER 17
Buy/Sell Agreements for Medical Practices

Any medical practice with more than one physician-owner needs a buy/sell agreement. The agreement explains the manner in which an owner can buy into the practice and how the practice will buy out an owner. Corporations have buy/sell agreements, which sometimes are called "shareholder agreements." Partnerships generally have similar provisions incorporated into their partnership agreements. Buy/sell agreements must be reviewed and updated to take into account any changes that have occurred in the health care industry since their last revision. Physicians in group practices should review their agreements at least once a year, generally at the end of the practice's fiscal or calendar years. Health care reform, the continued attacks on service reimbursements, Medicare cuts, and the adoption of the resource-based relative value scale (RBRVS) payment system by other payors are just a few of the changes that affect the value of physicians' ownership interests. In addition, physicians forming group practices must understand the specific issues in buy/sell agreements so that they can be drafted properly. (See the buy/sell agreement checklist and sample contract in Appendix C.)

> ■ **Practice Point:** For a group practice, determine when the group's buy/sell provisions were last reviewed. This is often an overlooked task, especially for new group practices. Many individuals feel only an attorney should conduct this review. However, many of the provisions in the agreement are financial in nature and thus might require a CPA's review as well. Make the effort to review all of the buy/sell provisions (or at least discuss them) at least once a year. For newer practices, insist on reviewing the provisions as soon as possible.

The Practice's Buy-Out Amount

The most obvious issue the physicians will need to address in any type of buy/sell arrangement is what to pay a physician-owner should he or she leave the practice. Death, disability, retirement, voluntary termination, or the involuntary termination of an owner can all result in a buy-out. A buy-out agreement generally values a departing physician's interest based on either appraisals of the practice or some type of fixed-formula approach. A continuing problem with the appraisal approach is that the buy-out amount is not determined until a practice is actually faced with a buy-out. In other words, most physicians are not willing to have independent appraisals conducted each year just to see how much the physicians would be obligated to pay departing owners should buy-outs occur. Waiting until a buy-out materializes, however, may result in a physician's equity interest being appraised at a value that is too high in the minds of the remaining owners and their subsequent refusal to pay it. Such disagreements can and often do lead to litigation. Therefore, an accurate appraisal of the practice is needed if the agreement values ownership interest at an appraised value.

■ **Practice Point:** Most buy-out provisions were created when the health care industry was quite different from what it is today.

Changes in the industry demand that a practice's buy-out agreement also change. Physician-owners must understand that changes in the industry have had a direct impact on the present and future revenue streams of medical practices. Therefore, you need to determine if the practice's buy-out calculation should be revised.

■ **Practice Point:** Be aware that if you do not address the buy-out issue, you may face a substantial amount of litigation over the buy-out issue if major changes continue to occur in the health care industry. For example, a successful practice buys out a physician. Because the practice was successful, the physicians did not expect their revenue to change over the coming years. However, the practice began to experience financial difficulty because of changes in the industry, and its revenue began to decrease. The practice now has difficulty making payments to the departed physician, and the remaining physicians are frustrated because their compensation continues to decline while the departed physician continues to receive a substantial "salary" from the practice. In such cases, owners will probably balk at continuing to make buy-out payments when they see their own incomes declining, and they may take legal action to stop the payments.

Appraisals

If the buy-out of a physician will be based on an appraisal, the practice will need to hire a qualified appraiser in order to receive an accurate medical-practice valuation. For example, many agreements name the practice's accountants as appraisers. However, not all accountants who have health care clients have experience or expertise in medical-practice appraisals; they may not possess the necessary in-depth knowledge of the health care industry to arrive at accurate appraised values. Although valuation formulas generally are the same for all industries, the techniques of applying and interpreting them are radically different from industry to industry. These factors can and do affect the ultimate outcome of an appraisal. In addition, if appraisers are also personal accountants or advisors to one or more of the owners involved, conflicts of interest may arise. Chapter 23 discusses in detail how to value a medical practice.

> ■ **Practice Point:** As mentioned, be aware of potential conflicts of interest when the person or firm preparing a valuation also has as a client one of the physicians already in the group. In this situation, who is the "client" of the valuator? The same can be asked when designing a buy-out arrangement. Does the professional look after the best interests of the group entity or the individual physician-owner who is also a client? In these situations, it is often best to engage an independent professional.

Formula Approaches

If the practice uses the fixed-formula approach, the physicians will generally pay a departing owner his or her interest in the net book value of the practice, plus a value for goodwill if the physicians agree that such a value exists. Whether the buy-out is decided by appraisal or by fixed formula, the practice's accounts receivable and fixed assets need to be valued. (See "Valuing Fixed Assets and

Accounts Receivable" in Chapter 23.) Goodwill can be valued at a percentage of the physician's or the practice's collections for the prior 12-month period or for some other period. For example, the agreement may set a physician's goodwill value at 20 percent of that physician's prior 12-month collections. Another formula approach is to value the buy-out amount at a multiple or percentage of the departing physician's average annual compensation for an agreed-upon number of years.

The advantage of any type of fixed-formula approach is that the owners can quantify the buy-out amount at any time. Many owners calculate the amount at the end of the tax year so that each owner can determine whether the buy-out amount is fair. If any owner believes it is not fair, all of the owners should meet to discuss and resolve the matter. Thus, at the end of each year, the buy-out amount should be calculated and the following questions asked of each owner:

- If you were to be bought out today, do you believe that the calculated buy-out amount is reasonable?

- If you had to pay a departing physician the calculated buy-out amount, do you believe it is a reasonable amount to pay?

Examples of Formula Approaches

The following are real-life examples of medical practice buy-out formulas:

Example 1

The term "Option Price," unless otherwise defined by later agreement as indicated herein, shall mean the amount, per share, equal to the net book value per share of the Company computed on the accrual basis of accounting, excluding accounts receivable and goodwill as determined by the Company's accountant. Each party to this Agreement agrees that annually, Shareholders may negotiate and agree upon, by unanimous vote, a different value for the Option Price. Such agreement altering the value hereunder shall be attached to and become part of this Agreement.

Example 2

The Shareholders and the Association agree to determine the value of the Shares according to the following formula:

A. Fixed Assets (Book Value):

One (1) divided by number of Shareholders multiplied by Fixed Assets Valuation

PLUS

B. Goodwill:

Highest annual collections for the Shareholder in the previous three (3) calendar years of full-time employment by the Association multiplied by six percent (6%).

Example 3

Computation of Value

1. *The term "Value" as used herein will be an amount that bears the same proportion to the amount of the Net Worth of the Association (as defined below) as the number of Shares to be purchased bears to the total number of the Association's Shares outstanding on the Valuation Date.*

2. *The term "Net Worth" as used in Paragraph 1 of this Exhibit "A" will be an amount equal to the book value of the Association's assets as of the Valuation Date determined using the accrual method of accounting, less the amount of its liabilities on the Valuation Date as disclosed by the Association's books of account regularly maintained in accordance with generally accepted accounting principles consistently applied, but adjusted as follows:*

   a. *Insurance, if any, owned by the Association on the life of a deceased Shareholder whose Shares are the subject of purchase under Paragraph 5 ("Disposition Upon Death of a Shareholder") or Paragraph 8 ("Disposition Upon Death of Shareholder's Spouse") of this Agreement will be valued at its cash value on the Valuation Date and not its face value.*

   b. *No adjustment will be made on account of any event occurring subsequent to the Valuation Date, whether the event constitutes an adjustment to the state income tax liability of the Association or otherwise.*

   c. *Reserves for contingent liabilities will not be treated as liabilities.*

   d. *No amount will be included for goodwill.*

   e. *No amount will be included for accounts receivable.*

    f. The Association's fixed assets will be valued based on the fair market value (as determined by an independent appraiser), less any debt owed by the Association on those assets. The independent appraiser must be agreed upon by the Association and the selling Shareholder. If the parties are unable to agree upon an appraiser, then each will select an appraiser and the value determined by the two appraisers will be averaged.

Example 4

Value. The term "Value" means an amount that (i) bears the same proportion to the amount of the Net Worth of the Company (as defined below) as the number of Membership Units to be purchased bears to the total number of the Company's Membership Units outstanding on the Valuation Date.

Net Worth Computation. Subject to an agreed-upon determination in accordance with Paragraph 6, the term "Net Worth" as used in Paragraph 2 means an amount equal to the value of the assets of the Company, determined as follows:

    a. Real estate assets shall be appraised as of the Valuation Date by an independent appraisal agreed upon by the Company and the selling Member. If the parties are unable to agree upon an appraiser, then each shall select an appraiser and the values determined by the two appraisers shall be averaged.

    b. All other assets and liabilities will be valued at accrual basis book value as of the Valuation Date.

    c. Goodwill will be excluded from the calculation.

Example 5

Upon the occurrence of an Operative Event, the Affected Member will be entitled to receive the balance, if any, of such Member's capital account increased or decreased, as the case may be, by the Member's share of the amount of any profit or loss that has been incurred by the Company for the portion of the year for which the Member was a Member but has not yet been allocated to the Member's capital account, and any amounts accrued up to the date of the Operative Event under the Guaranteed Payment Plan. In the event that such overall balance is negative, the Member (or Tendering Person, if so obligated) shall pay the negative balance to the Company, unless this payment is waived or reduced at the sole discretion *of the Directors. The closing shall, thereafter, take place at a time designated by the Company, which shall not be more than one hundred twenty (120) days from the date of the qualification of an executor or administrator, if applicable; provided, however, that in any event the closing shall take place within six (6) months of the date of the occurrence of the Operative Event.*

Accounts Receivable

Practice advisors and physician-owners often wonder if accounts receivable should be included as part of the buy-out amount. The answer is "yes." How it is structured is an important issue. Your goal is to structure the accounts receivable as a form of deductible deferred compensation to the practice. This would allow the practice to deduct the payments on its business federal income tax return. Accounts receivable is, in reality, an income asset. It is not an equity asset. In other words, the practice reports income and pays out compensation to the physician as receivables are collected. Therefore, accounts receivable should be part of the physician's employment agreement and should be paid out over time as deferred compensation. (See Chapter 18 for further details on this issue.)

Whether to include accounts receivable when a physician buys into the practice, however, is a different issue. The inclusion of accounts receivable only inflates the value of the buy-in and, therefore, it should not be included as part of the new physician buy-in. Instead, existing accounts receivable should be declared a bonus to the owners of the practice and should be paid out to them over a period of time (generally, three to five years) as a regular overhead disbursement. A bonus is declared because the owners of the practice are the ones who really own the practice's accounts receivable. This way, all the new physician actually buys into is the practice's net fixed asset value and goodwill, reduced by any debt. When determining the buy-in for any new physician, the appraiser should realize that the new physician will be concerned mainly with the dollar amount of the buy-in. Rarely will the new physician concentrate on what makes up the buy-in value. (Buy-in arrangements are further discussed in Chapter 18.)

Payout Terms

Should a buy-out occur because of a shareholder's death, the buy-out amount usually is paid as soon as the practice receives the proceeds from a life insurance policy. Most medical practices obtain insurance on the lives of each physician-owner, with the practice named as beneficiary under the policy. If life insurance on each owner does not exist, the payout will have to be paid through installment payments. Depending on the amount of the buy-out, however, the practice may want to pay the buy-out immediately rather than in installments. Buy-outs also occur in the event of disability, retirement, and voluntary or involuntary withdrawal.

Payments related to these events are almost always paid through installment payments, generally over a five-year period at the prime rate of interest. The interest rate sometimes is capped at 12 percent to protect the cash flow of the remaining shareholders.

Examples of Payout Terms

The following are real-life examples of payout terms from actual medical practice buy/sell agreements:

Example 1

Payment of Option Price at Death and Disability. *All payments of all or some percentage of Option Price shall be paid, at the option of the Company or Other Shareholders, by one of the following methods:*

1. *To the extent that insurance proceeds are available, all such proceeds shall be payable immediately to the estate of Deceased Shareholder and his or her Spouse or to Disabled Shareholder and his or her spouse*

2. *In cash*

3. *By installment payments as set forth in Paragraph 5.3.B.2 below*

4. *By any method of payment agreeable to the Company and the selling Shareholder or his or her estate*

Payment of Option Price Under All Other Circumstances. *All payments of all or some percentage of Option Price shall be paid, at* the option of Shareholders or the Company, whichever party is the purchaser or redeemer, by one of the following methods:

1. All in cash

2. By installment payments. If the purchaser or redeemer elects to pay Option Price in installments, the payments shall be represented by a promissory note providing for the payment of the balance of the purchase price in equal monthly installments, over a period of five (5) years from the date of the note, together with interest thereon at one (1) point above the prime rate of interest charged from time to time by [Name of bank] of [City, State], as established by the President or any Vice President of the Bank ("Stated Rate") with a cap of ten percent (10%). Notwithstanding the foregoing, if during any period Stated Rate exceeds the nonusurious maximum rate of interest that could be charged ("Maximum Rate"), the rate of interest in effect on this note shall be limited to Maximum Rate during each such period, but at all times thereafter the rate of interest in effect on the note shall be Maximum Rate until the total amount of interest accrued on the note equals the total amount of interest which would have accrued thereon if Stated Rate had at all times been in effect, at which time Stated Rate shall then be applicable. Said promissory note shall be secured by either a pledge of Stock for which said note is given as consideration or by other assets having an unencumbered value at least equal to the amount of the promissory note given hereunder, as the parties shall mutually agree.

3. Any method of payment agreeable to the purchaser, Shareholders, Company, and the selling Shareholder.

Example 2

Terms of Payment.   The terms of payment by the Association for any Shares offered by the offering Shareholder pursuant to this Paragraph shall be, at the option of the Association or purchasing Shareholders, either on the terms set forth in the notice of proposed sale or as follows:

1. Terms of payment by the Association shall be payable at the price set forth herein on the following terms: 20 percent of the purchase price shall be payable in cash on delivery of the Shares certificates to the Association, and the balance shall be payable in sixty (60) equal monthly installments commencing one year from the date of delivery of the Share certificates to the Association.

2. *Should any Shareholder(s) exercise an option to purchase, the purchase price of the Shares shall be paid on the following terms: 20 percent of the purchase price shall be payable in cash on delivery of the Share certificates to the purchaser(s) and the balance shall be payable in sixty (60) equal monthly installments commencing one year from the date of delivery of the Share certificates to the purchaser(s).*

3. *The portion of any purchase price not paid in cash shall be evidenced by the promissory note(s) of the purchasing Association, or Shareholder(s), bearing interest at the rate determined pursuant to Paragraph 21 on the unpaid balance. Payment of the Association's promissory note shall be personally guaranteed by the Remaining Shareholder(s). The purchasing Association or Shareholder(s) shall have the right to prepay the note or notes, in whole or in part, at any time without penalty.*

Example 3

Payment of the Purchase Price. *The purchase price for the Membership Units purchased under Section 3.03 hereof must be paid in cash, except that, at the option of the purchasing party or parties, eighty percent (80%) of the purchase price may be deferred and paid in installments with twenty percent (20%) paid at closing. The number of installments may be up to twenty-four (24) equal monthly installments. The outstanding balance of the purchase price will bear interest at the General Interest Rate. If Code sections 483 and 1274A apply to this transaction, the interest rate on the outstanding balance of the purchase price will be fixed at the interest rate then required by law. The first installment of principal, with accrued interest, will be due on the first day of the month following closing. Subsequent monthly installments, with accrued interest, will be due on the first day of each month that follows until the entire amount of the obligation, principal and interest, is fully paid. The purchasing party may prepay any part of the remaining balance at any time without penalty.*

Life Insurance Proceeds. *If the purchasing party is the beneficiary of any life insurance on the life of a deceased Member from whose estate the purchasing party is purchasing Membership Units, then it shall pay in cash an amount equal to the death benefits payable to the beneficiary under the policy or policies. If the insurance proceeds of the purchasing party-beneficiary exceed the purchase price of the Membership Units, the excess is the property of such beneficiary. If* *the Company is prohibited by law from using all or any portion of the proceeds of the insurance policy or policies it owns on the deceased Member's life, this subsection shall apply only to insurance proceeds that the Company may, by law, use to apply on the purchase price of the Membership Units.*

Covenants Not to Compete

Related to payout, the buy-out agreement should specify the procedure to follow should a physician leave the group and practice medicine in competition with the practice. Generally, this is covered in the agreement by a covenant not to compete. For example, this provision may state that should a physician compete against the practice some time in the future, the installment payments cease immediately if the buy-out has not been paid in full. The inclusion of a covenant will depend mainly on the laws of the state in which the practice is located. Also, many physicians believe that the covenant is not worth the time and money necessary to enforce it.

Whether a covenant not to compete is in place or not in the buy-out agreement, if a physician leaves the practice and immediately competes against the practice, there should be limitations on the buy-out amount. Because the departing physician will probably take patients, and thus revenue, away from the practice, it is not fair to pay out his or her full share of the ownership. Many buy/sell agreements include a clause stating that if a physician leaves the practice and immediately competes against the practice, the physician will be entitled to receive only his or her share of the practice's fixed asset value. In other words, the physician's share of accounts receivable and any goodwill would be forfeited.

The following is an example of a restrictive covenant provision from an actual medical practice buy/sell agreement:

Each Shareholder agrees that upon any transfer of Shares pursuant to this Agreement, the selling Shareholder, for a period of five (5) years from the Purchase Date of the Shareholder's Shares, shall not, directly or indirectly, disclose to any person or entity any confidential information obtained or learned as a result of the Shareholder's affiliation with the Association. For purposes of his Agreement, confidential information shall include patient lists, technology, proprietary information, and trade secrets of Association or any information of any kind, nature or description concerning any matters affecting or relating to the Association's business, its manner of operations, its plans, processes or other data of any kind, nature or description. Confidential information shall not include information that is: (1) generally available to and otherwise known by the public other than as a result of Shareholder's unpermitted disclosure; (2) available to Shareholder on a nonconfidential basis from a source other than Association or the other Shareholders, provided that, Shareholder is not aware that such source was bound by a confidentiality agreement with Association; or (3) independently acquired or developed by Shareholder without violating any confidentiality obligations to Association.

Association and each Shareholder acknowledge and agree that the purchase by Association or any other Shareholder of a selling Shareholder's Shares will include valuable consideration in recognition of the goodwill of the Association and the Shareholder. Each Shareholder also acknowledges that Association will incur substantial costs in providing equipment, support services and personnel, management and other items and services required for Association to provide professional services and to recruit a physician to replace any selling Shareholder. Each Shareholder acknowledges that the purchase of Shares was a voluntary decision made by Shareholder in order to receive the benefits of ownership in the Association. Each Shareholder and Association acknowledges and agrees that Association provided valuable, special and unique assets to Shareholder, and that such assets greatly affect the effective and successful conduct of the business of the Association and its goodwill. In exchange for Shareholder's covenant not to compete, each Shareholder and Association acknowledges and agrees that, in addition to Shareholder's compensation, valuable consideration was furnished including:

   i. access to confidential and proprietary information and trade secrets of Association;

   ii. full access to an established medical practice and a large patient base;

   iii. availability of medical equipment, office equipment and a trained and adequate staff; and

   iv. specialized training to provide medical services according to Association's standards.

Shareholder and Association agree that if Shareholder should set up an office and practice medicine in competition with Association, it would cause economic harm and loss of goodwill to Association resulting in immediate and irreparable loss, injuries and damage to Association, and that neither the general public nor any patients will be adversely affected by the noncompetition covenant, in that other similar providers of professional medical services are readily available within the restricted area. Therefore, each Shareholder agrees that during the term of this Agreement and, in the event of a transfer of the Shareholder's Shares pursuant to this Agreement for the period of the purchase payout from the Purchase Date of Shareholder's Shares hereunder, except as allowed hereunder, the Shareholder will not, indirectly or directly, for the Shareholder, or for any other person, firm, corporation, association, or other entity, as owner, employer, employee, principal, agent, partner, consultant or substantial stockholder (as defined herein) start or engage in any business similar to or of the same nature as Association's business within one (1) mile of the Association's office, except for any employment on part-time or other basis with the Association. Each Shareholder stipulates that the scope, territory and time period specified in this covenant are reasonable. This covenant shall be construed as an agreement ancillary to the other provisions of the Agreement.

In the event that a Shareholder, except a retiring Shareholder, shall violate any of the provisions of (a) or (b) above and without limiting other possible remedies available to Association for breach of these covenants, the Shareholders specifically understand and agree that the Association shall be entitled to an injunction from any court having competent jurisdiction to legally enforce the covenants and agreements stated herein, without prejudice to any of the rights or remedies which the Shareholder may have and without the necessity of the Association having to allege or prove irreparable harm or injury or the absence of an adequate remedy at law. The existence of any claim or cause of action of a Shareholder against the Association, whether predicated on this Agreement or otherwise, shall not constitute a defense to the enforcement of these covenants by the Association.

Substantial stock ownership, as used herein, shall mean ownership, either legally or beneficially, by the Shareholders or by any person acting under a Shareholder's control, of more than one percent (1%) of the outstanding capital stock of a corporation.

The provisions above may be waived by the Association upon unanimous consent of all of the Remaining Shareholders of the Association.

Any such waiver shall be in writing signed by all of the Remaining Share-holders.

If a Shareholder, other than a retiring Shareholder, violates the terms of this agreement, the amount of damages will be difficult to determine and therefore the Shareholder agrees that appropriate liquidated damages, and not a penalty, to be paid by Shareholder to Association will be equal to the remaining amount to be paid by Association and/or the Remaining Shareholders to Shareholder under the purchase terms of this Agreement in addition to any other damages set forth herein. The amount payable to Shareholder under any promissory notes shall be credited against the amount of liquidated damages due from the Share-holder. If a retiring Shareholder violates (b) above, the sole penalty will be the reduction of the amount to be paid pursuant to purchase of Shares hereunder to an amount equal to the depreciated value of the fixed assets multiplied by the percentage interest of the retiring Share-holder. It shall not be a violation hereunder for a retiring Shareholder to work for the Association on a part-time basis or for a governmental agency on a part-time basis.

Notwithstanding (a) and (b) above, a selling Shareholder shall:

i. *have access to a list of the Shareholder's patients whom Shareholder had seen or treated within one (1) year of the Purchase Date;*

ii. *have access to medical records of the Shareholder's patients upon authorization of the patient and any copies of medical records for a reasonable fee as established by the Texas State Board of Medical Examiners;*

iii. *have access to the list of patients or to medical records in the format which such records are maintained by the Association; and*

iv. *be permitted to buy out of the covenant not to compete at a reasonable price or, at the option of either Shareholder or Association, as determined by a mutually agreed upon arbitrator, or, in the case of an inability to agree, an arbitrator of the court whose decision shall be binding; and not be prohibited from providing continuing care and treatment to a specific patient or patients during the course of an acute illness after the Purchase Date.*

Tax Deductibility of Buy-Out Payments

The remaining physician-owners will need to maintain the tax deductibility of the buy-out payments. Otherwise, the remaining owners not only must make cash payments to the departing owner but also face an additional economic burden if the payments are not deductible. The physicians should never assume that buy-out payments are deductible. Payments to repurchase a physician's ownership interest generally are not deductible by the practice. For example, payments to buy back a physician's stock in a professional corporation are not deductible. These payments are classified as treasury stock. This is why structuring the buy-out payments is such a critical issue. In fact, the Internal Revenue Service (IRS) has been cracking down on group practices that try to deduct nondeductible buy-out payments. Amendments to the tax code were enacted in 1990 to make it mandatory to report to the IRS the specific details of a buy-out transaction. Under Section 1060 of the Internal Revenue Code, if a departing physician owns 10 percent or more of the practice and, in connection with the buy-out, enters into an agreement with the practice, then the transaction must be reported to the IRS.

Examples

1. Dr. Brown owns 100 percent of X corporation. As a step toward semi-retirement, Dr. Brown sells 90 percent of her X corporation stock to Dr. Jones and enters into an employment agreement with X corporation. Although there has been a transfer by a 10-percent-or-greater owner, there is no reporting requirement because there is no transferee.

2. Dr. Kim owns 50 percent of Y corporation. He sells half of his shares to Dr. Tyler, and Dr. Tyler enters into an employment agreement with Y corporation. Although an owner of 10 percent or more of an entity has transferred an interest in the entity, there is no reporting requirement, because the owner (Dr. Kim) has not entered into the employment agreement with Dr. Tyler.

3. Dr. Miller is the sole shareholder of Z corporation. Z corporation issues new shares to Dr. Delgado and enters into an employment agreement with her. The reporting requirement applies. Under Section 318(a)(3)(c) of the Internal Revenue Code, if any person owns 50 percent or more of the stock of a corporation, the corporation is considered as owning such person's stock by attribution. Accordingly, Z corporation is deemed to

be a 100 percent shareholder in itself for purposes of Section 1060(e), and it has transferred an interest in itself and entered into an agreement with the transferee (Dr. Delgado).

Remember that if Section 1060(e) of the Internal Revenue Code applies to the buy-out or buy-in transaction, the corporation and the shareholder or buy-in partner will have to attach an IRS form to each of its tax returns.

Other Provisions in Buy/Sell Agreements

There are other provisions in buy/sell agreements, many of which require attorneys' services. Besides the obvious legal considerations, one goal of the person evaluating the agreements is to assess how these provisions will affect the daily and continuing operations of the practice. Another goal is to achieve fairness among the parties.

Involuntary Removal

The buy/sell agreement should address how an owner will be involuntarily removed from the practice. Termination of employment is different from termination of a physician's ownership interest in the practice. If a physician is dismissed from the practice, he or she will also need to be removed as an owner of the practice. Some agreements provide that an owner be removed if a certain percentage of the owners (e.g., two-thirds or three-fourths) vote to do so. Other agreements specify that the physician's ownership interest is terminated immediately when his or her employment or compensation agreement is terminated. If a vote to remove a shareholder is not an option, the agreement should state specific instances in which an owner can be involuntarily removed from the practice's ownership. For example, a physician-owner must automatically surrender his or her ownership interest in the practice if the physician loses hospital privileges, loses medical licensure, becomes uninsurable for malpractice coverage, or is convicted of a crime. Involuntary withdrawal also occurs when a physician becomes permanently disabled, often as defined in the physician's disability policy. Generally, the issue of permanent disability is addressed separately in the agreement.

Temporary Disability

The buy/sell agreement should discuss when an owner can be removed from ownership in cases of a temporary disability. Situations of temporary disability occur more often than situations of permanent disability. For example, a physician who contracts multiple sclerosis can be out of the office for long periods of time. During a period of temporary disability, the physician generally remains an owner but at some point his or her compensation is reduced.

Many agreements fail to address the issue of physician-owners who test positive for HIV, for example. This could lead to a potentially explosive situation if the other owners believe it is in the best interests of the practice for the physician to leave, but the infected physician refuses to do so. Before addressing a situation such as this in the buy/sell agreement, make sure that any provisions are not in violation of the Americans With Disabilities Act of 1990.

Adding a New Owner

The agreement must also include a provision about the process in which a new owner is added to a practice. Generally, admitting a new shareholder requires the unanimous vote of the existing owners of the practice. Internal disharmony might arise if a physician who other physicians do not want as a fellow owner is admitted. The agreement should not state specifics about how the buy-in amount would be calculated for the new owner. Generality gives the practice the flexibility to design a buy-in based on changing economic and market conditions in the health care industry. Thus, the agreement should state that the buy-in amount will be determined by the practice at the time a new physician-owner is admitted.

Sale of the Practice

While practice acquisitions are not as common today as they were a few years ago, the buy/sell agreement still needs to address this issue. First, the agreement should state the vote of the owners to affirm a sale of the practice. For small practices, the vote to sell is usually unanimous. For large practices, the vote is usually two-thirds or three-fourths of the current owners.

The buy/sell agreement may address how the sale proceeds will be distributed among the owners. The assumption usually is that sale proceeds will be split according to equity ownership. The problem is that disputes often arise because physicians are usually not equal in their production and their overall contributions to the practice. Internal strife can occur if a physician feels he or she is not receiving a fair share of the sale proceeds.

▼ CHAPTER 18
Physicians' Employment Agreements

With the implementation of the resource-based relative value scale (RBRVS) and in light of the continued attacks on physicians' reimbursements, many physicians are responding by forming or by joining group practices. Many physicians, especially new physicians, do not want the problems or the risks and uncertainty involved in solo practice.

Every group medical practice should have an employment agreement in place for each physician. Although this contract, like a buy/sell agreement, contains legal issues, the majority of the clauses concern financial matters. This chapter discusses the major financial arrangements in an employment agreement for a group practice. Although the emphasis here is on group practices, even an incorporated single physician should have an executed employment agreement as part of the corporate records. (See the sample new physician letter of intent, employment agreement outline, and employment agreement in Appendix C.)

Compensation

The employment contract should clearly define how all physicians, both new and established, are compensated. Whether payment is based on production or straight salary, the method of compensation should be documented in the employment agreement. For new physicians, many health care consultants promote the use of an incentive bonus besides regular salary. The typical incentive bonus pays a percentage of the collections on the new physician's production when the collections exceed a certain level. This level is typically two to two-and-a-half times the physician's total compensation package, which includes allotted fringe benefits such as payment of the physician's malpractice premium. This way, the physician pays for himself or herself, adds at least an equal amount to the overhead of the practice, and shares in the rest. The medical practice should encourage the new physician to develop a patient or referral base on his or her own.

■ **Practice Point:** If you review a physician contract that includes an incentive bonus, make sure that the bonus is attainable. It makes no sense to include a bonus provision that can never be met; this type of situation could end up discouraging the physician.

■ **Practice Point:** For new physicians (e.g., those hired out of residency), setting an attainable and reasonable incentive bonus that is based on collections is very important in managed-care settings. Keep in mind, it may take a while to get a new doctor credentialled on managed-care plans. Sometimes this takes up to four to six months for some managed-care plans. In this situation, it is unlikely a new doctor would be able to participate in his or her collection-based incentive bonus program if the collection target is set too high.

The following is an example of a physician incentive bonus provision taken from an actual employment contract:

Bonus. *During each year of employment hereunder, the Association will pay to the Doctor a bonus in an amount equal to forty percent (40%) of the Doctor's Excess Gross Collected Revenue (as defined below). Such bonus will be (i) paid to the Doctor on an annual basis, within thirty (30) days following each one-year anniversary of employment hereunder if any such Doctor's Excess Gross Collected Revenue exists, and (ii) net of appropriate employment and federal withholding taxes and retirement plan contributions. "Doctor's Excess Gross Collected Revenue" means that portion of Total Gross Revenue (as defined below) that is in excess of Four Hundred Thousand Dollars ($400,000). "Total Gross Revenue" means all fees for professional services rendered by the Doctor hereunder that are collected on behalf of the Association during such one-year period of employment.*

Death, Disability, or Termination of Employment

The employment contract must make clear the amount of compensation that is owed in the event of death, disability, or termination of employment. This is especially important if incentive or other bonus clauses are in place. The physician's failure to plan for and understand this contract provision could cause the physicians and their families severe financial hardship. Most contracts provide that if a physician leaves the practice, he or she is entitled to accrued compensation, earned but unpaid bonuses, and accrued vacation pay.

One of the most important issues in an employment agreement is the provision addressing how much and for how long a physician will be paid in the event of his or her disability, whether permanent or temporary. Generally, a disabled physician receives full compensation for one to three months after the disability occurs. After this period, compensatory payments cease. The physician or the practice should have a disability insurance policy that will pick up the payments to the disabled physician after this period elapses. To protect the practice and the physician, the employment agreement should include a clause stating that an employed physician must have disability insurance. The one- to three-month period could be extended if the physician is compensated on some sort of productivity formula in which overhead is shared. In such a case, the disabled physician is still responsible for his or her share of the practice's overhead. As long as the physician's collections can pay for this share of the overhead, there is no reason the term cannot be lengthened. The only issue that must be addressed in this situation is if the practice plans some type of capital expenditure, such as for equipment. The disabled physician's collections may not be enough to contribute his or her future share. In that case, the one- to three-month compensation period may remain intact.

Temporary disability is more common than permanent disability. When the physician is temporarily out of work, such as for a broken leg or a strained back, the other physician-owners expect that the disabled physician will be returning to the practice. Like a permanent disability, the employment contract generally provides that the physician will be paid full compensation for a limited period of time. Clauses in the employment agreement addressing temporary disability, however, often overlook an equally important issue, compensation for the able-bodied physician in small practices should another physician become disabled.

Example of the Effect of Temporary Disability on an Able-Bodied Physician

Dr. Bower and Dr. Havens own an obstetrics/gynecology practice. They each receive compensation of $10,000 per month, with year-end prof-its divided equally. Their employment agreement states that a physi-cian will be paid his full $10,000 per month in the event of a disability for three consecutive months. After three months, the payments will cease.

While on vacation, Dr. Bower breaks his leg in a skiing accident. He is expected to be out for two to three months. While he is at home recuperating, Dr. Bower receives his full $10,000 salary for the two- to three-month period. Dr. Havens, however, also receives his full salary but has to cover for Dr. Bower. Thus, Dr. Havens gets paid his regular salary but has a double workload. Dr. Havens may become disgruntled with this situation. One could argue that Dr. Bower would do the same for Dr. Havens should he ever become temporarily disabled, but dis-abilities to separate physicians in the same medical practice rarely occur.

To anticipate a contingency such as that in the example, the employment contract may state that the able-bodied physician or physicians be paid additional compensation at an agreed-upon compensatory rate. This arrangement is based on the idea that the practice would have to pay extra for a *locum tenens* (substitute) physician if it had to bring in one to cover for Dr. Bower's prac-tice. Issues such as these mainly apply to physician-owners of the practice. Rarely are provisions made if a nonowner has to provide the coverage. The owner or owners of the practice, however, may want to give a bonus to the nonowner physician to compensate for the additional coverage. Make sure that this contingency and re-lated cross-coverage issues are discussed among the physicians and, if necessary, a related provision is included in the employ-ment contracts.

To protect small medical practices in the event of the temporary or permanent disability of a physician-owner, the practice should acquire an overhead disability policy. This policy will pay the prac-tice a specific amount to subsidize ongoing overhead. If the prac-tice already has this type of policy, assess the length of time before the policy is required to pay monies to the practice. To help the practice in the case of a temporary disability, the policy should begin paying after at least 30 days. It does not make sense to set the policy at 90 days because if a physician is out for more than three consecutive months, it is likely that the disability is permanent rather than temporary. The purpose of an overhead disability policy is to assist the practice during the most crucial time of need, and that usually is during the first three months that the disabled physician is not working.

Deferred Compensation

An employed physician who is also an owner of the practice should have a provision dealing with deferred compensation included in his or her employment contract. This would apply only if the practice is going to pay the physician his or her share of the practice's accounts receivable when the physician leaves. This provision ensures the deductibility of payments to a departing owner. In most buy-out situations, part of the buy-out amount is tied to the physician's own accounts receivable or his or her share of the practice's accounts receivable. As discussed in Chapter 17, accounts receivable is considered an income asset, not an equity asset. This is because accounts receivable is ordinary income to the physician-owner as it is collected. Therefore, a physician-owner's employment contract should include a deferred compensation provision related to his or her share of the practice's accounts receivable and should be excluded from the physician's buy-out per the practice's buy/sell agreement.

The following is an example of a deferred compensation provision from an actual physician employment agreement:

11.05. *Compensation Payable.*

(a) *Upon Death.* Upon termination of this Agreement under Section 11.01(d) hereof, (due to the death of the Doctor), the Doctor's estate will be entitled to receive the compensation computed in accordance with Article III hereof for the Doctor's services provided during the term of this Agreement, but unpaid as of the effective date of termination. In addition, if the Doctor was a Shareholder of the Association as of the date of the Doctor's death, the Doctor's estate will be entitled to receive additional compensation in an amount equal to the Doctor's Accounts Receivable (as defined below). The Doctor's Accounts Receivable will be paid to the Doctor's estate within thirty (30) days after the date of collection by the Association. In no event will the Doctor, upon termination of this Agreement, be entitled to additional compensation or payment for vacation leave, sick leave, CME leave or other leave accrued but not taken.

(b) *Upon Disability.* Upon termination of this Agreement under Section 11.02(c) hereof, (due to the disability of the Doctor) the Doctor will be entitled to receive the compensation computed in accordance with Article III hereof for the Doctor's services provided during the term of this Agreement, but unpaid as of the date of termination. In addition, if the Doctor is a Shareholder of the Association and the ownership of the Doctor is terminated in accordance with the Association's Bylaws (as may be amended), then the Doctor will be entitled to receive additional compensation in an amount equal to the Doctor's Accounts Receivable (as defined below). The Doctor's Accounts Receivable will be paid to the Doctor within thirty (30) days after the date of collection by the Association. In no event will the Doctor, upon termination of this Agreement, be entitled to additional compensation or payment for vacation leave, sick leave, CME leave or other leave accrued but not taken.

(c) *Without Cause.* Upon termination of this Agreement by the Association or the Doctor pursuant to Section 11.04 (without cause at least sixty (60) days' advance written notice), the Doctor will be entitled to receive the compensation computed in accordance with Article III hereof for the Doctor's services provided during the term of this Agreement, but unpaid as of the date of termination. In addition, if the Association terminates this Agreement pursuant to Section 11.04 or if the Doctor gives at least twelve (12) months' advance written notice of such termination, the Doctor will be entitled to receive additional compensation in an amount equal to the Doctor's Accounts Receivable (as defined below). The Doctor's Accounts Receivable will be paid to the Doctor within thirty (30) days after the date of collection by the Association. In no event will the Doctor, upon termination of this Agreement, be entitled to additional compensation or payment for vacation leave, sick leave, CME leave or other leave accrued but not taken.

(d) *By the Doctor with Cause.* Upon termination of this Agreement by the Doctor pursuant to Section 11.03 ("Optional Termination for Cause by the Doctor"), the Doctor will be entitled to receive the compensation computed in accordance with Article III hereof for the Doctor's services provided during the term of this Agreement, but unpaid as of the date of termination. In addition, the Doctor will be entitled to receive additional compensation in an amount equal to the Doctor's Accounts Receivable (as defined below). The Doctor's Accounts Receivable will be paid to the Doctor within thirty (30) days after the date of collection by the Association. In no event will the Doctor, upon termination of this Agreement, be entitled to additional compensation or payment for vacation leave, sick leave, CME leave, or other leave accrued but not taken.

(e) *All Other Termination Events.* Upon termination of this Agreement pursuant to any provision other than as described in Section 11.05(a), (b), (c), and (d) above, then the Doctor will be entitled to receive the compensation computed in accordance with Article III hereof for the Doctor's services provided during the term of this Agreement, but unpaid as the effective date of termination and will not be entitled to additional compensation or payment for vacation leave, sick leave, CME leave or other leave accrued but not taken.

Compensation Formulas

The physician's employment agreement should specifically state how a physician is going to be compensated. A number of compensation formulas exist in the industry. Which formula the physicians decide to use will depend on the practice's medical specialty and the physician-owners' business philosophies. The following brief discussion examines the most popular forms of physicians' compensation formulas. These formulas are directed to the physician-owners of a medical practice, because generally, new physicians are paid a base salary and possibly a bonus. Keep in mind, however, that the formula used today may not fit into tomorrow's health care environment. Thus, you should strongly recommend that the physicians' compensation formula be reviewed each year. If the physicians are happy with the formula, there should be no reason to change it. Any disagreement over the formula, however, should be discussed and the formula revised, if necessary. Many group medical practices have dissolved over the practice's compensation formula. Although there is no such thing as a perfect compensation formula, you can develop one that is deemed fair and reasonable by all the physicians.

Whenever you address compensation plans or income distribution plans with a medical practice, it is imperative that you have an understanding of the physician's perception concerning that plan. Therefore, as part of the practice assessment, it may be beneficial to gather some information on the physician's current perception of the compensation plan.

An analysis of this information can aid a medical practice in addressing sensitive issues and sometimes provides a building block for addressing changes that need to be made within the compensation formula. Shown below is a questionnaire which can be used successfully during practice assessments, as well as in individual physician compensation analysis engagements. It may have to be modified for each separate practice assessment so as to address unique compensatory issues and situations of the practice being evaluated.

After compiling information on the compensation plan and performing some of the compensation analysis shown previously, you may uncover additional issues that need further investigation. Sometimes this leads to a review of the current physician employment agreements. If you elect to review the physician employment agreements, the review generally should be limited to standardization issues, benefit issues, and physician availability issues, which can be reviewed and noted in a short period of time. This review should in no way equate to a complete analysis of the physician employment agreements. Legal counsel should be retained to review all other aspects of the agreement.

Equal Compensation

Under an equal compensation formula, the physician-owners equally share the practice's net earnings. This method generally is used by medical practices in which all physicians contribute equally to the earnings of the practice or in practices that do not want to foster an aura of competition among the physicians. For example, a cardiovascular surgical practice may want to split income equally in order to eliminate the possibility of the physicians fighting over physician referral sources. In this situation, the physicians would try to share the workload equally. The equal compensation method typically is used more by smaller medical practices than by larger ones.

The main advantage of the equal compensation formula is its obvious simplicity. It also fosters an environment of teamwork. The main disadvantage of this formula is that it does not reward productivity and it rewards physicians who are not as productive as the other physicians. When one physician begins to feel he or she is working harder and thus producing more than the other physicians, problems may arise.

Example of Equal Compensation

Dr. New	$333,500
Dr. Slowdown	333,500
Dr. Steady	333,500
Dr. Needs Cash	333,500

Production with Fixed, Variable, and Direct Costing

Under a straight productivity method, each physician earns income from the collections on his or her production. Overhead is then allocated to each physician based on an agreed-upon formula. Generally, the straight productivity formula is as follows:

> Collections on physician's own production
> − Shared overhead
> − Share of variable overhead
> − Direct overhead
> − Retained earnings
> = Gross physician compensation

Shared overhead, otherwise known as *fixed costs,* is shared equally. These expenses, such as rent and personnel costs, continue whether the physician produces one dollar or hundreds of thousands of dollars. Variable overhead generally is split based on productivity. Expenses are categorized as variable when they cannot be costed directly to the physician (e.g., medical supplies). Direct overhead includes those expense items that can be costed to the physician directly, such as malpractice premiums, lab fees, and continuing medical education costs. Retained earnings generally are the amounts needed to pay for debt service and capital expenditures. This usually is split evenly among the physicians.

The advantage of this formula is that it rewards producers; it rewards a physician's direct financial contribution to the practice. In most medical practices, not everyone is equal. Some physicians contribute more than others, both in terms of revenue and the pace of their work. The disadvantage of this formula is that it does not foster teamwork in the practice; in fact, it could actually foster unhealthy competition among the physicians. Another danger is that physicians may overuse services to boost their own compensation. The success of this formula will depend on the physicians' maturity. As long as they believe that everyone is contributing differently to the practice, there probably will not be a problem using the formula.

■ **Practice Point:** Make sure that the productivity-based formula is Stark-compliant. Collections received from rendering designated health services cannot be distributed based upon the volume or value of the physician's referrals, even if the referral is within the practice entity.

PHYSICIAN QUESTIONNAIRE

Compensation Plan

Physician's Name: _____ Date _____

1. How would you rate your medical practice's distribution plan?
   ❏ Generous ❏ Reasonable ❏ Marginal ❏ Unfair ❏ Disastrous

2. How would you rate your level of compensation?

   ❏ Extremely overcompensated
   ❏ Overcompensated

❑ Basically fair
❑ Undercompensated
❑ Extremely undercompensated

3. Do you understand the present income distribution plan?
❑ Yes ❑ No

4. How would you rate the level of complexity of your existing income distribution plan?
❑ Extremely complex
❑ Complex
❑ Moderate
❑ Simple
❑ Very simple

5. Do you feel that your income distribution or compensation plan is adequately achieving its goals?

_____

6. What do you like most about your existing plan?

_____

7. What do you like least about your existing plan?

_____

8. What would you recommend as a change to the existing income distribution or compensation plan?

_____

Production with Equal Share

This is another productivity-based formula where a doctor is paid based on his or her collections less an allocated equal share of practice overhead. Again, make sure this type of formula is compliant with the Stark II law.

Production with Incentive Pools

This formula carves out a percent of the practice collections and places them in an incentive pool. The money in the incentive pool is then paid out based on agreed-upon criteria. The money that is not allocated to the incentive pool is then allocated to the doctors based on net production, their own collections, etc. The following is an example of this formula:

Sample Plan

Distributable Income from Productivity Plan	$ 1,000,000
Less: 20% for Incentive Pools	(200,000)
Distributable Income Per Production Basis	$ 800,000

Incentive Pools (20% of Available Income):

1. Cost Effectiveness	$ 80,000
2. Patient Satisfaction	$ 50,000
3. Seniority	$ 20,000
4. Group Meetings and Administration	$ 50,000

Equal Compensation Plus Productivity Bonuses

An equal compensation plus productivity bonus formula provides each physician with an equal monthly draw, or base compensation. Each quarter, agreed-upon profits or monies are divided among the physicians based on the ratio of the physician's own collected production to total practice collections for the period. The advantage of this method is that it fosters teamwork and equal commitment, while rewarding individual performances. Again, the disadvantage is that it does not solely reward total individual performance and thus will not work if material productivity differences exist among the physicians.

The following is an example of this formula:

Incentive Compensation Formula. Physician shall receive the following "Specified Percentages" of Physician's Net Professional Fee Collections within the following specified levels, respectively:

Level	Net Professional Fee Collections	Specified Percentages
Level 1	$325,000–$350,000	25%
Level 2	$350,000–$400,000	30%
Level 3	$400,000 and up	35%

Therefore, if a physician's net professional fee collections were $450,000, then the Physician's Incentive Compensation payment amount for Level 1 would be $6,250 (25% × $25,000); for Level 2 would be $15,000 (30% × $50,000), and for Level 3 would be $17,500 (35% × $50,000), for a total incentive compensation of $38,750 ($6,250 + $15,000 + $17,500), subject to any applicable incentive compensation limitations.

Net Production

The net production method is a straight productivity formula without any allocations of overhead. Under this method, the net earnings of the practice are split based on the ratio of each physician's own net gross production (after contractual allowances are subtracted) to the practice's total net gross production.

The advantage of this formula is that it is not based on collections but rather on the amount of production that will be collected. The physicians do not have to worry about the practice doing a good job of collecting their individual revenues. The main disadvantage of the formula is that the highest producer pays for more of the practice's overhead, even if he or she does not use the overhead as much as the other physicians.

The following is an example of the net production methodology used to compensate a physician:

Gross Charges	$3,000,000
Gross Collections	2,300,000
Overhead (42%)	966,000
Net Income	1,334,000

Production %

Dr. New	22%
Dr. Slowdown	17%
Dr. Steady	25%
Dr. Needs Cash	36%

In this example, Dr. New would get 22 percent of $1,334,000, Dr. Slowdown 17 percent of $1,334,000, etc.

Part Equal, Part Productivity

The part equal, part productivity method takes a part (generally 10 to 50 percent) of the practice's gross collections and splits it evenly among the physicians or a select group of physicians. The remainder is split based on the straight productivity formula discussed earlier. This formula is used often in small multispecialty group practices in which the physicians reward the primary-care physicians for referring patients to the surgical physicians. The formula attempts to create a culture in which the physicians operate as one unit and each works toward the success of the group in his or her own manner.

Relative Value Units

Practices could use relative value units (RVU) to measure productivity and incentivize employed physicians. Relative value scales are used by Medicare to determine the fee for a particular medical procedure by factoring together certain components of work, expense, and risk. You may want to include in the employment agreement an exhibit with the RVU values for the anticipated CPT codes utilized in the physician's practice. The contract language below may be used when a physician is to receive both a base salary based upon a standard amount for each RVU generated, plus incentive compensation based on a bonus rate for any RVUs generated over a stated, threshold amount.

1. *Base Salary. Employer shall pay Physician a base salary equal to $_____ (the "Normal Compensation Rate") times the number of professional RVUs generated by Physician; plus*

2. *Incentive Compensation. Physician shall be entitled to receive incentive compensation equal to $_____ (the "Bonus Rate") times the number of professional RVUs generated by Physician in excess of the RVU Incentive Threshold.*

3. *Definition: RVUs shall mean the Relative Value Units factors utilized by Medicare associated with professional medical services personally provided by Physician as defined in accordance with the Physician's Current Procedural Terminology Codes using solely*

> the "Work RVU" factors published by the Health Care Financing
> Administration.
>
> 4. The RVU Incentive Threshold amount shall be $_____.

Capitated Plans

A complex problem when designing compensation formulas for physician groups is how to divide the monies received from capitated plans. As discussed in Chapter 19, *capitation* means the practice is paid on a per-member, per-month basis, and will be paid the same amount no matter how many patients the physicians see in any particular month. The capitated amount is actuarially defined by the health maintenance organization (HMO). Primary-care physicians are capitated based on the number of patients in the HMO plan who sign specifically with the physician. Specialists are capitated based on the total number of patients in the HMO plan or are sometimes paid on a discounted fee-for-service basis.

As capitation grows, it will affect many current physician compensation formulas. This is particularly true if the practice's current formula is productivity based. The reason is that the incentives in both systems are at opposite ends of the spectrum. Incentives in productivity compensation formulas encourage high utilization, patient competition, individual goals, specialization, and a sell-sell attitude. In a capitated environment, the incentives are to optimize the use of the practice's resources, lower costs, control utilization, satisfy patients, practice quality medicine, reduce specialization, and emphasize preventive health care. The incentives in a system whereby the physicians are paid equally fall somewhere between these two extremes. Whenever a compensation formula has to be changed due to an increase in capitation revenues, the incentives necessary to reward the physicians who truly manage the delivery of health care need to be built into the formula.

As capitation grows, there are many different types of transitional models to choose from. One model is to allocate fee for service (FFS) and capitated revenues on a FFS equivalent. Another is to allocate FFS revenues based on physician production and divide capitated revenues equally. A third model is to allocate FFS revenues based on production and allocate capitated revenues based upon the number of patients assigned to each physician. This model is mainly applicable to primary-care groups, because these physicians are "panelized," whereas specialists are not. In other words, employees do not choose a specialist when they initially sign up with an HMO insurance product.

Some larger groups designate certain physicians as *capitated physicians*. The problem with this model is that it does not work well in smaller group practices and it can be very divisive. Also, it is hard to imagine true integration within a practice when this type of system is put into place. Another model is a combination of models utilizing two pools of income, FFS and capitation. The FFS pool is allocated on actual collections. Capitation is allocated on actual capitation. Revenues are totaled and direct and indirect costs are subtracted to equal total physician compensation. A bonus pool could be added to this type of formula system.

The goal of any group practice should be to design a capitation-based formula whereby all of the physicians are working together to control utilization, minimize costs, eliminate competition, and improve the bottom line. Arguably, the best way to do this is to pay the physicians a base salary and divide up any net income (i.e., *bonus pool*) based on a set number of capitation-based incentives. In many cases, practices in transition will use the physician's base salary from the previous year as the new base salary. However, this is only a starting point and the salary should be set based on a tightly prepared financial cash projection. If all physicians are receiving a base salary, this should minimize competition for patients. If the physicians know they will share in the practice's bottom line, it forces them to work together to do what is necessary to create a healthy bottom line to divide up amongst themselves.

The next step is for you to develop a set of criteria that will be used as a basis to split up and distribute the net income of the practice (or bonus pool if this methodology is selected). The following are the most common:

1. Contribution to profitability
2. Risk sharing
3. Cost per patient
4. Performance—leadership, effort, efficiency, administrative duties, workload

5. Contribution to the group

6. Patient satisfaction

7. Seniority

8. Referral patterns

9. Utilization—bed days, tests ordered, etc.

10. Quality/outcomes

These criteria can be used to begin the process. Ultimately, it will be the physicians themselves who decide what is important to them and their group.

The following is an example of a provision in a physician employment contract that incentivizes the physician based on quality indicators:

> **Additional incentive compensation.** *In addition, Physician shall be entitled to earn additional Incentive Compensation as follows: (i) up to $_____ per quarter for scoring ninety percent (90%) or above on patient satisfaction surveys as determined by the Employer; (ii) up to $_____ per quarter from the Employer's discretionary bonus fund based upon overall cost effectiveness, utilization review, peer interaction, office staff relations, Medicare/indigent patient care, compliance with medical records protocols, and other factors determined by Employer; and (iii) up to $_____ per quarter for participating in Employer management and/or medical staff committees.*

Unfortunately, there is no such thing as a perfect compensation plan. The group will need to experiment and try different plans, especially if it will start working with HMOs. Before developing a plan, the physicians should review the incentives discussed in this chapter, design a formula that is unique to the group, and remember the group is more important than the individual.

Factors Impacting Physician Compensation

Physician Employed by a Hospital

Hospitals that employ physicians must be concerned about the Anti-Kickback provisions and if the hospital is also tax exempt, it must take into account the IRS private inurement rules when setting physician compensation. To comply with these rules, the amount of base salary will need to be a fair market value amount and not take into consideration the value of any referrals by the physician. Overall compensation, including any bonuses, must also be commercially reasonable.

The risk increases for hospitals that employ physicians when compensation becomes partially tied to productivity or the achievement of other criteria. The terms of the bonus arrangements, or any salary that includes an incentive compensation amount, including both the base salary and the anticipated bonus amount, will require a review for inurement, private benefit, Stark and Anti-Kickback concerns. As such, a reasonable cap or ceiling should be included in the agreement's compensation provisions to prevent possible windfalls in incentive compensation. Agreements should specify that in no event will the employer be obligated to pay the physician incentive compensation that would cause the physician's total compensation amount to exceed the total compensation cap.

The following is an example of a cap provision in a physician employment agreement:

> *Base salary. Employer shall pay to Physician a base salary equal to $_____ dollars per year, or pro rata portion thereof plus:*
>
> *Incentive compensation. As a bonus, Physician shall receive an amount equal to $_____, or percent (_____%) of the physician's net professional fee collections in excess of the Incentive Threshold. The Incentive Threshold shall be an amount equal to _____ dollars.*
>
> *Cap. In no event shall the total compensation payable to Physician, including base salary and Incentive Compensation, be greater than $_____ per year.*

Partial Retirement of a Physician

It is not uncommon for physicians to want to slow down after a certain age. This reduction in their production can cause problems in the income distribution formula. How should this slowdown be accounted for? What overhead should be applied to the physician? How long should partial retirement be allowed to continue? Should ownership continue during this period of partial retirement? What if the group needs to add another full-time physician to take up the slack? Answers to these questions will, of course, vary from practice to practice since each practice situation is unique.

Generally, it is recommended by many consultants that when partial retirement exceeds a 35 percent reduction in production, the group practice should consider utilizing an annual salary for the physician. This salary should be reviewed each year and evaluated on the basis of production, referrals, seniority, and other contributions to the practice.

Special problems can also develop concerning expansion plans when a partially-retired physician retains his or her same ownership interest in the practice. A physician in this situation generally does not want to continue investing in the practice. Therefore, a group may want to consider purchasing this physician's interest after a period of time. You should make sure that the group's buy/sell agreement addresses this issue.

Physician Extenders

Physician extenders such as nurse practitioners and physician assistants are becoming more prevalent in medical groups. How should this piece of overhead, as well as what the person collects, be accounted for by the group and how does it integrate into the compensation formula? Many groups will credit the physicians who are actually using the physician extender. Other groups will departmentalize the physician extender. His or her collections are offset against his or her direct compensation and possibly some variable operating costs. This net amount, whether it be a profit or a loss, is allocated back to specific physicians in the group. This allocation can be based on any number of factors.

Seniority

Should a medical group recognize seniority and what value should be placed on it? If the compensation formula is productivity based, this usually applies when a physician decides to slow down. Some groups compensate for this but most do not. Overall contributions to the group must be reviewed and a decision made whether or not an extra payment based on seniority is justified.

Administration

There are many physicians today who are actively involved in the management of the medical practice at the expense of their own productivity. Should physicians be compensated for administration? Generally the answer is "yes," and the payment is usually in some form of a monthly stipend or extra salary.

Call Schedule

A normal physician compensation arrangement in a group practice assumes that all the doctors in the group are on the group's call schedule. But what happens if one doctor decides he or she cannot or does not want to take calls? The answer is that this doctor needs to take some kind of a reduction in his or her compensation. It is simply not fair from a compensatory standpoint to allow a physician to be "off duty" when the other doctors are not. How to address this issue is arguably one of the thorniest situations when it comes to physician compensation.

In many groups, the doctor who does not take calls receives a percentage reduction in his or her compensation. The norm seems to be anywhere from 10 percent to 30 percent. Some groups even go so far as to reduce a physician-owner to employee status if he or she does not take calls for a period of time, for example, two or three years.

What to Pay New Physicians

New physicians are generally paid at the current salary level for their particular medical specialty for the local area. Sources of this information locally are hospital administration personnel, the county Medical Society, and other physician practices. You might also check with the state Medical Association. A national source is the annual compensation survey conducted by the Medical Group Management Association.

Generally a new physician is paid a salary with a bonus incentive. The bonus is usually calculated as a percentage of that physician's own collections when such collections exceed a certain amount annually. This collection target is usually equal to two to two-and-a-half times the new physician's compensation package. In addition to the salary, it would include such items as malpractice insurance and health insurance, and all direct employee benefits such as dues and licenses. The following is an example of such a bonus formula.

> You will be entitled to an incentive bonus of 40 percent of each dollar collected on your production when collections exceed $380,000 annually. This amount will be paid on a monthly basis through the end of your twelve-month employment period.

Integrating the New Physician Employment Agreement with a Hospital Recruitment Agreement

When a new physician is recruited by a group practice, the group may have gone to its hospital and obtained a financial recruitment package in order to engage the new physician. This is common in the health care industry. However, because of fraud and abuse rules, the hospital contract has to be executed by the individual physician and the hospital, even though the group is the one employing the new doctor. In this case, the hospital will pay over any monies due under the contract to the new doctor, who will then endorse the same monies over to the group. The group then takes these monies and pays the new doctor's salary each month.

Therefore, it is important to address this issue in the new doctor's employment agreement, which, in fact, is rarely done. It must be addressed because of a well-known IRS rule called "assignment of income." If the new physician is not contractually obligated to turn any monies received under the hospital contract over to the employer group, he or she would most likely have to report these monies as income on his or her personal income tax return. As such, a clause needs to be added to the new physician's employment agreement in order to avoid this unexpected tax consequence. The following is an example of such a clause.

> **Physician Recruitment Agreement.** *For the initial twelve- (12) month term of this agreement, Physician and Company acknowledge that the Physician is a party to that certain Physician Recruitment Agreement by and between the Physician and _____ Healthcare System within an initial one- (1) year term. Pursuant to such Physician Recruitment Agreement,_____ Healthcare System will be paying the Physician certain sums on a monthly basis for one (1) year. The Parties understand that such agreement is a material basis for the Company and the Physician to enter into this Employment Agreement. The Physician's salary herein is based upon the Company receiving all funds paid by _____ Healthcare System pursuant to section ___ of the Physician Recruitment Agreement. The Physician, as a condition of employment, agrees to immediately turn over to the Company all sums received from the guaranteed minimum income payment as stated in section ____ of the Physician Recruitment Agreement. The Physician shall endorse over to the Company all such sums, which shall become the property of the Company.*

Components for Better Compensation Plans

Medical groups and entities integrating with physicians (physician practice management companies, hospital systems, health plans, etc.) are struggling with the challenges of implementing a physician compensation plan that promotes critical group success factors while operating in an environment of constantly changing reimbursement methodologies. Organizations have moved from productivity-based models to salary models to capitation pools and back again. Organizations are realizing that future physician compensation plans must incorporate something besides a complex set of incentives for various desired behaviors. Most are realizing that physicians can manipulate any plan within a short period of time once it is understood by the physicians. Any compensation plan that tries to reward all the critical success factors quickly becomes too complex. Most of the time, the incentives for desired behaviors are not adequately compensated to induce any significant behavior change.

Three components can provide any organization with a compensation plan that will meet the challenges of today's changing market and changing reimbursement methodologies. Every successful plan needs to have *accountability, empowerment,* and *market* components. This concept promotes a salary/bonus model that incorporates incentives for practice patterns that promote group success. This concept requires strong physician leadership, as does *any* successful compensation plan in this ever-changing environment.

Accountability

Base compensation (salary portion) must promote overall accountability to the group. Three benchmarks that should help establish base compensation for any group include: (1) hours worked in direct patient care, (2) relative value units produced or production defined by the group (i.e., gross charges, number of visits/surgeries/consults, etc.), and (3) actual cash collected for services rendered. These three benchmarks should be weighted depending on the group's perception of each component's value in establishing accountability in base compensation for the group. This base compensation should make up between 50 percent and 80 percent of an individual physician's total compensation. The base should never exceed 80 percent to allow for adequate reimbursement for other components of physician compensation. This base compensation is founded on the premise that a group or organization has to have highly productive physician members to be successful and yet each group can measure that accountability in different ways.

Empowerment

Physician groups are notoriously slow decision-makers due to the need to build consensus with all or a majority of the physicians in the practice before they can move forward on an issue. Even today, most compensation models still promote this concept, as productivity-based models result in establishing each physician or specialty as its own profit center. This does very little to promote the overall success of the medical practice itself.

Successful groups must empower their physician leaders and the best way to do that is to give them the ability to monitor and set compensation. In this model, the incentive bonus pool for physician compensation is completely *discretionary.* The key reason for this is to empower the physician leaders. This alone will move a practice toward proactive management and governance. Since this incentive pool should be at least 20 percent of total compensation, it will allow the physician leaders to promote and adequately reward the team players.

This discretionary model of incentive bonuses allows the practice to monitor and reward more areas of behavior without trying to place an insignificant amount of incentive on each one. It also requires the individual physicians to concentrate on the overall group success rather than on two or three areas of behavior in an attempt to game the plan.

Here are ideas for critical success factors:

- Peer coding analysis
- Peer patient satisfaction results
- Peer costing analysis
- Individual goal setting
- Group contribution (meetings, committees, etc.)
- Administrative duties
- Attitude
- Patient management
- Peer ancillary utilization

Whatever factors the group chooses, these should be closely tied to the capabilities of the management information system. The compensation committee should be at least 50 percent physician members with equal voting rights. This committee does not have to represent every specialty in the group. The whole purpose is to empower the real physician leaders. The peer data has to be provided to the physicians on a regular basis. Since this can be a tough concept to get all physicians to accept, consider first-year and/or second-year safeguards in which underperforming physicians are guaranteed at least 90 percent of prior year income if productivity is also comparable.

Medical practices must develop a common vision and start to focus on their control of medical management. This requires strong physician leadership and a commitment of financial and human resources. Empowerment of these leaders with a discretionary incentive bonus plan will make a difference.

Market

Physician compensation should approximate market value. This concept is particularly important for organizations that have acquired physician practices that regularly refer to their facilities. The concept of implementing a market-based compensation plan requires the utilization of external benchmarks. These benchmarks are becoming more sophisticated and relevant to compensation planning. Some of the more common benchmarks used today are the following:

- *Physician Compensation and Production Survey,* Medical Group Management Association

- *Group Practice Compensation Trends and Productivity Correlation Survey* and *Group Practice Survey of Key Medical Management Information,* The American Medical Group Association

- *Physician Marketplace Statistics* and *Socioeconomic Characteristics of Medical Practice,* American Medical Association

- *Statistical Report,* Society of Medical-Dental Consultants

- Individual Specialty Associations

In the future, these benchmarks will become even more sophisticated and will probably be available online.

The value of the market concept is to provide an external objective benchmark for the practice to consider when establishing an individual's overall compensation. It is impossible to please everyone and the group or organization cannot afford to compromise the success of everyone for the demands of an individual physician. External benchmarking allows the leadership to assess its establishment of overall compensation. In cases in which overall compensation is being questioned by a physician, external benchmarking helps add credibility to the compensation plan. It reduces the risk that a practice will lose key physicians to the market if compensation is maintained at a fair market rate. It is usually better to use at least two external benchmarks to be sure a reasonable target is established. Internal past performance should weigh significantly in establishing these targets and the external benchmarks should serve more in a check-and-balance role.

By implementing accountability, empowerment, and market components into physician compensation plans, you can assist physician organizations in meeting the challenges of today's health care market. This limits the ability of physicians to manipulate the plan. Credibility is established with external market benchmarks. The compensation plan considers the overall performance of the physician. This method is generally perceived as fair with a high degree of security for the physician and promotes group success. Not every group will have the leadership or trust level to implement a compensation model like this. It requires subjective decision-making and physician performance evaluations.

Physician Compensation and a New Tax Wrinkle

When a group of doctors practice in a corporation that is taxed for IRS purposes on its own (i.e., taxed as a C-Corporation), it is customary for these doctors to distribute as much of the corporation's profit as possible in order to avoid having to pay corporate-level federal income taxes. However, in a recent U.S. Tax Court case, the IRS reclassified physician bonuses as nondeductible corporate dividends. This is an extremely important tax development and all "C-Corporation" group practices need to be aware of it.

In Pediatric Surgical Associates P.C. v. Commissioner, T.C. Memo. 2001-81; No. 12743-98 (April 2, 2001), the U.S. Tax Court held that profits earned from nonshareholder physicians but that were allocated to shareholder physicians in the form of bonuses and classified as deductible officers compensation on the Clinic's corporate return were, in fact, a distribution of earnings and profits—or nondeductible dividends.

The pediatric surgical clinic ("the Clinic") included (1) shareholder surgeons who received monthly salaries and cash bonuses and (2) non-shareholder surgeons who received only monthly salaries. The Clinic deducted the amounts paid to the shareholder surgeons as officer compensation. The IRS disallowed a part of those deductions, finding they should have been characterized as dividends instead. The Tax Court agreed with the IRS's interpretation.

The years under review by the IRS were 1994 and 1995. In 1994, the Clinic reported gross receipts of $2,080,008 and taxable income of $29,255 on Form 1120. For 1995, on gross receipts of $2,405,718, the Clinic reported taxable income of $49,323. The Clinic computed taxable income under the cash receipts and disbursements method of accounting.

During the audit year 1994, the Clinic consisted of four shareholder surgeons and in 1995 the Clinic employed three shareholder surgeons for the entire year and one shareholder surgeon up until his retirement date of June 30, 1995. In addition, the Clinic employed a non-shareholder surgeon from January 1, 1994 through July 14, 1994. The Clinic also hired another non-shareholder surgeon on July 1, 1995 and this physician was employed throughout the remainder of 1995.

In the middle of each month, the Clinic would determine the amount remaining in its bank account and the amount of cash necessary to meet anticipated cash-flow needs for the immediate and near future. The balance in the account, if any, was paid out, in equal amounts, as bonuses to the shareholder surgeons, according to the shareholder employment agreements. During the audit years 1994 and 1995, the full-time shareholder surgeons were compensated on average $353,455 and $451,743, respectively. Additionally, the non-shareholder surgeons were compensated at $72,000 in 1994 and $76,061 in 1995. Total compensation of shareholder physicians, reported on the Clinic's tax returns as officer compensation for 1994 and 1995, was $1,300,231 and $1,528,125 respectively.

The original notice of deficiency received by the practice from the IRS on June 25, 1998 assessed additional taxes and penalties of $247,746 in 1994 and $345,127 in 1995. The principal adjustments giving rise to the deficiencies in each year were the IRS's disallowance of a portion of officers' compensation. The amounts disallowed were $598,710 and $805,469 for 1994 and 1995, respectively. The IRS auditor limited deductible officers' salaries based on the theory that the salary paid to the new non-shareholder physicians established reasonable shareholder physicians' salaries.

Ultimately, the IRS sharply reduced the proposed deficiencies to amounts determined to represent the Clinic's profits attributable to services rendered by the non-shareholder surgeons. The IRS conceded the deductibility of all but $140,776 and $19,450 of the disallowed amounts. The IRS's position was that a portion of what the Clinic had treated as compensation to the shareholder surgeons was profit attributable to services performed by the non-shareholder surgeons, which should have been treated as nondeductible dividends rather than as deductible compensation.

The Clinic's principal argument was that payments made to the shareholder surgeons were clearly compensation for services rendered and not dividends. This was because the payments to the shareholder surgeons were reasonable in amount since they did not exceed the corporation's profits, calculated by subtracting all corporate expenses except officers' compensation from corporation's gross receipts (which were exclusively from providing services). The practice also made the same argument in different terms: "Petitioner's shareholder surgeons were paid compensation in an amount less than their gross collections, which proves that they were reasonably compensated."

The Clinic's treatment of the reported amounts was consistent with the board's intending such amounts to constitute payments purely for services. The Clinic also argued that the shareholder employment agreements tied base compensation and bonuses to the number of months worked during the year, which, the Clinic argued, signified compensation for services.

The case revolved around Internal Revenue Code (I.R.C.) Section 162 concerning trade or business expenses. I.R.C. Section 162(a)(1) establishes a two-pronged test for the deductibility of payments purportedly paid as salaries or other compensation for personal services actually rendered. To be deductible as compensation for services, the payments must be (1) "reasonable" and (2) "in fact payments purely for services." The IRS indicated that according to the second prong test, the disallowed amounts were not, in fact, payments purely for services that concerned them. To prevail according to the court, the practice had to show that the remaining amounts were paid to the shareholder surgeons purely for their services. This was difficult because the shareholder surgeons were not the only service providers employed by the practice. There were also the non-shareholder surgeons, whose contribution to corporate profit could not be assumed to be zero, according to the court.

Section 1.162-7(b)(1), Income Tax Regulations, states: "Any amount paid in the form of compensation, but not in fact as the purchase price of services, is not deductible." The regulations further provide that an ostensible salary may, if paid by a corporation, be a distribution of a dividend on stock, or may be in part a payment for property. Therefore, the medical practice must prove its intent (i.e., the intent of the members of the board) to pay compensation. Whether such intent had been demonstrated was a factual question to be decided on the basis of the particular facts and circumstances of the case.

As previously mentioned, the practice argued that the shareholder employment agreements pegged base compensation and bonuses to the number of months worked during the year, which, the practice argued, signified compensation for services. According to the court, a payment pegged to time worked may be nothing more than a payment for services. It may, however, include a distribution of profits, if the only recipients of such payments are the owners of the enterprise. Here, all of the recipients of such payments were shareholders of the petitioner (shareholder surgeons). Three were full-time employees, who were entitled to equal payments, while the fourth was a part-time employee, entitled to a proportionate payment. That disparity did not eliminate the possibility of a disguised distribution of profit according to the court, but reflected only an implicit redistribution of ownership upon the decision of a shareholder surgeon partially to retire.

Ultimately, the court reallocated deductible shareholder compensation as nondeductible dividends equal to the "profit" generated by the non-shareholder physicians. The court took the collections generated by these physicians and deducted expenses, which consisted of the salary paid to the physicians plus one-tenth (one-fifth for the one-half of the audit year during which each physician was employed) of other expenses considered equally apportionable to the five surgeons employed during each year. The court ruled there should be a pro rata (one-tenth) allocation of rent, repair, and maintenance expense, depreciation of office equipment (other than shareholder automobiles), telephone expenses, and equipment lease expenses to the non-shareholder surgeons' collections.

The court found the net profit attributable to the non-shareholder surgeons was as follows:

	1994	1995
Collections	$171,918	$129,806
Expenses	(110,684)	(120,769)
Profit	$ 61,234	$ 9,037

As mentioned above, this case has the ability to impact any group medical practice that employs both shareholder physicians and non-shareholder physicians. Characterizing all payments to physician shareholders as compensation could not only result in additional corporate taxes, but in penalties as well. Keep in mind the court sustained the IRS's accuracy-related penalty against the practice. The court, finding a lack of good faith, held that the penalty was justified based on the shareholder surgeons "utter indifference" to the possibility that part of their bonuses were derived from the non-shareholder surgeons. Group practices are therefore cautioned and advised to seek tax counsel regarding this extremely important matter.

Physician Compensation and the Stark Laws

Generally, a physician in a group practice cannot be compensated based on the volume or value of her referrals if designated health services are involved. This is the essence of the Stark Laws, which are discussed in detail in Chapter 21. Therefore, any group practice that utilizes a productivity-based formula could be in violation of the Stark Laws. Generally, under Stark, physicians can only be compensated based on the work they actually perform, if the compensation is based on referrals (i.e., productivity based). There-fore, many group practices will have to revise their productivity-based formula to comply with the Stark Laws.

The Health Care Financing Administration has given little guid-ance on how this should be done, and Stark II regulations have just been issued. If physicians want to maintain their productivity for-mula, they could do this by putting net income from ancillary ser-vices into some type of a bonus or separate pool. Net income would be the actual collections less direct expenses related to the ancil-lary billings. This pool could then possibly be divided based on the following:

1. Production from non-designated health services
2. Number of visits
3. Patients seen
4. Percentage ownership
5. Equal shares
6. Seniority
7. Any other methodology that is not based on the value or vol-ume of referrals

Nothing in the Stark Laws requires groups to solve this com-pensation problem on the revenue side alone. Some groups may use their net ancillary profits to reduce other overhead expenses, depending on how the expenses are allocated in the production formula. In any event, productivity-based compensation formulas are currently a gray area. All of these types of formulas deserve close scrutiny.

Sample Stark Compensation Formula

The following is a sample productivity compensation system that takes into account the Stark regulations. The formula is for a multispecialty group practice with multiple locations.

An ancillary profit center will be established for each specialty and each physical location of the group practice. All ancillary pro-duction from services that the physician did not perform, that are not incident to his services, or that he did not supervise in his exam area will be pooled in his specialty/location ancillary pool profit center. All payors are included in this formula.

- The ancillary profit centers will pay all expenses using the following expense types: (1) direct and (2) pro rata.

- The physician will pay his share of production expenses that are allocated directly to him using the following expense types: (1) direct, (2) equal, and (3) pro rata.

- When there are fewer than four providers (physicians and physician extenders) in a pool, then that pool's net profits will be combined with a similar specialty or the location's net profits and the combined dollars will be the amount distributed to the two specialties or locations based on the formula prescribed. This formula will distribute net profit from each ancillary profit center pool based on the ratio of the physicians' non-ancillary production.

- Additional positive and negative incentives will be used. The following are incentives to contain costs and increase efficiency:

  —A monthly tax will be charged to the physician.

  —A tax on each patient visit will be charged to the physician.

  —A tax on each nonbillable visit per month in the ancillary department will be charged back to the physician, to the location, or to whomever requested the nonbillable service. The monies will be used to offset expenses in that location's specialty ancillary profit center pool.

  —Physicians who are boarded or double boarded will be given bonuses.

  —The ancillary directors will be paid a fee.

  —Physicians who serve on committees or who are officers will be given bonuses.

- All ancillary taxes will be added to the ancillary net profit pool of that specialty and kept separate by pool and will be redistributed using the non-ancillary production formula, after the additional bonuses are distributed.

- Any ancillary service specifically mentioned as a designated service in the Stark self-referral regulations will be placed into the ancillary pool for that specialty and location.

- Each ancillary pool will pay expenses at the location where the expenses are incurred, either directly or pro rata. Pro rata expenses will be calculated using a ratio of ancillary charges to the total ancillary charges at the location determined for each profit center pool. Direct expenses will include any expense incurred from production that is allocated directly to that specialty pool and location and is not considered part of the professional physician services. Expenses incurred from the services designated as the physician's professional services will be allocated on a direct basis whenever possible and pro rata if direct is not possible.

Two Stark-Related Bonus Pool Examples

EXAMPLE I: Established plan for physician compensation—Orthopedic Group

Identify and allocate all the designated health service revenues (Medicare and non-Medicare) to a separate cost center. Operating expenses, direct and indirect, will be charged to this cost center. The net profit or net revenue from this cost center will be distributed to the physicians based upon their equal stock ownership in the professional corporation.

Total group revenues from Evaluation & Management (E&M) and surgery services which are not designated health services will be allocated to a separate cost center. Operating expenses (direct and indirect) and physicians' base salaries will be charged to this cost center. The net profit or net revenue from this cost center will be the basis for a productivity bonus based on a formula that recognizes a percentage of each physician's revenues from E&M and surgery services to the total group revenues from E&M and surgery services. This is illustrated as follows:

Facts	E&M & Surgery Dr. A	E&M & Surgery Dr. B	Total E&M & Surgery	Designated Health Services (X-ray)	Total Group Practice Revenues & Expenses
Revenues	600,000	1,200,000	1,800,000	200,000	2,000,000
Overhead Expenses			(900,000)	(100,000)	(1,000,000)
Profit before distribution to physicians			900,000	100,000	1,000,000
Base salary paid monthly ($25,000 per month x 2 physicians)			(600,000)		
Net profit before bonus calculation			300,000		

Bonus calculation based upon established written plan:
Total E&M and Surgery revenues per physician divided by total E&M and Surgery revenues for the group. Designated health service revenues (X-ray) are not included in the total of E&M and surgery revenues.

Physicians Revenue from E&M & Surgery	+	Group Revenue from E&M & Surgery	=	Physician % of Revenue	x	Profit before Bonus Calculation	=	Bonus
Dr. A: 600,000	÷	1,800,000	=	33 1/3%	x	300,000	=	100,000
Dr. B: 1,200,000	÷	1,800,000	=	66 2/3%	x	300,000	=	200,000

Recap of compensation per physician:

	Dr. A	Dr. B	Total
Base salary (paid monthly)	300,000	300,000	600,000
Productivity bonus (calculated quarterly)	100,000	200,000	300,000
Total compensation before distribution of designated health services net profit	400,000	500,000	900,000
Designated health service net profit — Distribution based on equity ownership	50,000	50,000	100,000
Total compensation	450,000	550,000	1,000,000

Example I is permissible, in part, because the E&M and surgery revenues used in the calculation of the bonus due each physician as shown above are not designated health service revenues. The predetermined formula for distribution of the designated health services revenues is permissible because the distribution is based on the equity shares of the physicians, rather than on their designated health service referrals.

EXAMPLE II: Established plan for physician compensation—Orthopedic Group

In this example, we distribute the designated health services revenues (X-ray) as part of the distribution of the overall profits of the group practice.

Facts	E&M & Surgery Dr. A	E&M & Surgery Dr. B	E&M & Surgery	Designated Health Services (X-ray)	Total Group Practice Revenues & Expenses
Collections	600,000	1,200,00	1,800,000	200,000	2,000,000
Overhead Expenses	(1,000,000)				
Profit before Physician compensation distribution			1,000,000		
Base Salary- paid monthly					(600,000)
$25,000 per month x 2 physicians					
Net Overall Profit before Bonus Calculation			400,000		

Bonus calculation based upon previously determined established plan:

Total E&M and surgery revenues per physician divided by the total E&M and surgery revenues for the group. Revenues do not include any designated health service revenues (x-ray):

	Physician Revenues from E&M Surgery	÷	Group Revenues from E&M & Surgery	=	Provider % of Revenues	x	Profit before Bonus Calculation	=	Bonus
Dr. A:	600,000	÷	1,800,000	=	33 2/3%	x	400,000	=	133,000
Dr. B:	1,200,000	÷	1,800,000	=	66 2/3%	x	400,000	=	267,000

	Dr. A	Dr. B	Total
Base salary (paid monthly):	300,000	300,000	600,000
Bonus (calculated quarterly):	133,000	267,000	400,000
Total compensation	433,000	567,000	1,000,000

Example II is permissible because a physician can be paid a share of overall profits of the group under the Stark Law, even if the profits include designated health service revenue, as long as the share is not determined in a manner that is directly related to the volume or value *of that physician's designated health service referrals to Medicare and Medicaid patients. In this example, we have used only the revenues from E&M and surgery services personally performed by each physician to determine the division of the overall profits above the base monthly salary.*

Additional Examples of Physician Compensation Formulas

The following are examples of physician compensation formulas taken from actual physician employment contracts.

Example 1

Productivity Bonus. *In addition to base salary, the Doctor shall be entitled to a bonus based on his productivity according to the following formula:*

The Productivity Bonus shall be based on the total collections received by the Association attributable to each Doctor's efforts from seeing private patients, including monies received for work performed by the Doctor from individual private patients, all payments by insurance companies for patient care and services rendered by the Doctor and all payments from any Health Maintenance Organization or any PPO and revenues from shots and extracts. The Productivity Bonus shall be determined and paid quarterly based upon the percentage ratio of each Doctor's collections, according to the formula set forth below. The formula may be changed from time to time upon unanimous agreement of the parties.

Total Collections:

Less:	Operating Overhead
Less:	Primary Bonus Pool
Less:	Asset Acquisition and Debt Service Payments
Less:	Doctor Base Compensation
Less:	Working Capital Holdback
Equals:	Productivity Bonus Pool

Primary Bonus Pool: *The Primary Bonus Pool shall be equal to $75,000 and shall be allocated among the senior physicians of the Association as they may determine.*

Example 2

Base Salary. *The annual base salary will be One Hundred Eighty Thousand Dollars ($180,000), payable in equal monthly installments.*

Bonus. *During each year of employment hereunder, the Association will pay to the Doctor a bonus in an amount equal to forty percent (40%) of the Doctor's Excess Gross Collected Revenue. Such bonus will be (i) paid to the Doctor on an annual basis, within thirty (30) days following each one-year anniversary of employment hereunder if any such Doctor's Excess Gross Collected Revenue exists, and (ii) net of appropriate employment and federal withholding taxes and retirement plan contributions. "Doctor's Excess Gross Collected Revenue" means that portion of Total Gross Revenue (as defined below) that is in excess of Four Hundred Thousand Dollars ($400,000). "Total Gross Revenue" means all fees for professional services rendered by the Doctor hereunder that are collected on behalf of the Association during such one-year period of employment.*

Example 3

Physician's Base Compensation: *Physician shall be paid Base Compensation equal to the Physician's Professional Fee Income less Physician's Direct Practice Expenses, Physician's Portion of Association's Overhead Expenses and Physician's loans or other monies due Association. Such Base Compensation shall be payable on a monthly basis during the term of this Agreement, or at such more frequent intervals as the Association's Board of Directors may determine. Such salary may be adjusted from time to time if Physician and Association agree in writing by amendment to this Agreement.*

Incentive Compensation: *Physician shall be paid incentive compensation according to the following formula:*

Physician's Professional Fee Income

(plus) Physician's Portion of Ancillary Services

(less) Physician's Base Compensation

(less) Physician's Direct Practice Expenses

(less) Physician's Portion of Association's Overhead Expenses

(less) Physician Loans or Other Monies due to the Association (if any)

= Physician's Net Profits

"Ancillary Services" means the technical and professional component of laboratory services, diagnostic imaging services and other ancillary services (including infusion pumps and crutches, but excluding all other durable medical equipment and parenteral and enteral nutrients, equipment and supplies) that are furnished by a physician employed by Association in one of the Association's office locations.

"Association's Overhead Expenses" means all operating expenses and costs incurred by the Association in its operations and other items generally considered overhead, depreciation, interest, amortization and federal and state taxes, but excluding Physician's Direct Practice Expenses.

"Physician's Direct Practice Expenses" means payroll taxes, benefits, professional liability insurance premiums, professional dues and subscriptions, continuing medical education expenses and all other direct or indirect expenses attributable to Physician.

"Physician's Portion of Ancillary Services" means the total amount of annual payments collected and received by the Association from the performance of Ancillary Services multiplied by a fraction where the numerator is the total number of Professional Service Encounters by the Physician and the denominator is the total number of Professional Service Encounters by all of the physician employees of the Association.

"Physician's Portion of Association Overhead Expenses" means the overhead expenses of the Association for the Incentive Compensation period multiplied by a fraction (i) the numerator of which is Physician's Professional Fee Income (1) and (ii) the denominator of which is the Association's Professional Fee Income.

"Physician's Professional Fee Income" means the total amount of payments collected and received by the Association, attributable to any professional services personally provided or services incident to those personally provided by Physician to patients of the Association.

"Professional Service Encounters" means all actual individual patient appointments, visits and other encounters which are recorded and documented by the physicians employed by the Association.

Example 4

Compensation. *As compensation for services rendered to the Association during the term of this Agreement, the Doctor will receive* and the Association will pay the compensation recited in this Article. In general, the Doctor will be paid a pro rata share (based on the number of physicians employed by the Association) of ten percent (10%) of the Association's net profit (as determined by the Association) and will be paid a portion of the remaining ninety percent (90%) of the Association's net profit based on the Doctor's adjusted production, as described in greater detail below.

Pro Rata Payment. *Subject to Section 3.09 ("Compensation in the Event of Disability") hereof, once each quarter, on a date to be set by the Association and that will be as soon after the end of a Computation Period (as defined below) as is reasonably practicable, the Doctor will be paid a pro rata share of ten percent (10%) of the Association's net profit (as determined by the Association) for the Computation Period. The Doctor's pro rata share will equal a fraction, the numerator of which is equal to one (1) and the denominator of which is equal to the number of physicians then employed by the Association.*

Doctor's Adjusted Production Payment. *Subject to Section 3.09 ("Compensation in the Event of Disability") hereof, once each quarter, on a date to be set by the Association and that will be as soon after the end of a Computation Period (as defined below) as is reasonably practicable, the Doctor will be paid the Doctor's Adjusted Production Payment, which will be determined by multiplying ninety percent (90%) of the Association's net profit (as determined by the Association) by a fraction, the numerator of which is equal to the Doctor's Net Collected Revenues (as defined below) and the denominator of which is equal to Total Collected Revenue (as defined below) and then subtracting from that amount the following: (i) the Doctor's Pro Rata Share of Overhead Expenses (as defined below), (ii) the Doctor's Allocated Share of Business Overhead Expenses (as defined below), and (iii) the Doctor's Personal Business Expenses (as defined below).*

Salary/Draw. *The Doctor will receive a monthly Salary or Draw ("Salary/Draw") against the quarterly computation. The Salary/Draw will be deducted from the computation for the quarter and the balance due will be paid to the Doctor. If the computation results in a negative balance (the Doctor receiving more Salary/Draw than was due to the Doctor), the negative balance will be repaid immediately upon calculation. Any such negative balance that is not repaid immediately by the Doctor in accordance with this Agreement will be offset against future compensation due to the Doctor hereunder and the*

Doctor will be charged interest on such un-repaid amount at a rate equal to two percent (2%) per annum plus the New York prime rate in effect at that time. Any current overdraws attributable to the Doctor as of the effective date of this Agreement must be repaid to the Association by the Doctor upon the effective date of this Agreement. The amount of the Doctor's Salary/Draw will be determined by the Association based on the compensation paid to the Doctor for the previous quarter. The Association reserves the right to adjust the Doctor's monthly Salary/Draw as needed or as collection patterns deviate.

Definitions.

(a) "Computation Period" is a three-month period beginning and ending on calendar year quarters.

(b) "Doctor's Pro Rata Share of Business Overhead Expenses" means the Doctor's pro rata share (determined by dividing the number one (1) by the sum of the number of shareholders in the Association) of certain business overhead expenses of the Association incurred during the Computation Period including, but not necessarily limited to, property and liability insurance coverage; facility rent, utility services for the Association's facility (if any); maintenance and repairs for the Association's facility; security and janitorial for the Association's facility; equipment purchases; equipment leases; maintenance and repairs on the Association's equipment; fees for accounting costs for the Association's taxes, consulting and legal services; advertising and marketing; telephone expense for the Association's facility, answering service fees, storage rent expense; provided, however, that such term will not include Doctor's Allocated Share of Business Overhead Expenses (as defined below) or Doctor's Individual Expenses (as defined below).

(c) "Doctor's Allocated Share of Business Overhead Expenses" means the Doctor's allocated share (which equals a fraction, the numerator of which is the Doctor's Net Collected Revenue and the denominator of which is the Total Net Collected Revenue for the Association) of certain Business Overhead Expenses of the Association incurred during the Computation Period including, but not necessarily limited to, staff wages and salaries, payroll taxes, benefits and profit sharing contributions; workers' compensation premiums; advertising and fees related to employee recruitment; employee seminars, continuing education and licensing fees; patient billing and collection expenses, including mainte-

nance on billing system; office expenses and supplies; office forms and printing; medical supplies; photo lab supplies; postage and delivery expenses; transcription service; and medical waste removal; provided, however, that such term will not include Doctor's Individual Expenses (as defined below).

(d) *"Doctor's Individual Expenses" means all expenses directly attributable to the Doctor individually including, but not limited to, auto expense; cellular phone expense; meals and entertainment; dues for professional organizations and associations; individual subscriptions; individual professional liability insurance premiums; personal health, life, dental and disability insurance premium; individual 401(k) and profit-sharing contributions; individual expenses related to continuing education and seminars; individual donations and contributions; individual payroll taxes; and individual office expenses and delivery expenses.*

(e) *"Doctor's Net Collected Revenues" means all fees for professional services rendered by the Doctor that are collected on behalf of the Association during a Computation Period, less any cash adjustments and less any refunds to patients or third-party payors.*

(f) *"Total Net Collected Revenue" means all fees for all professional services that are collected on behalf of the Association during a Computation Period, less any cash adjustments and less any refunds to patients or third-party payors.*

Fringe Benefits

A physician's employment agreement should explain exactly which fringe benefits the practice will pay for on behalf of the physician-employee. The following benefits are most commonly offered to a physician:

- Retirement plan
- Health insurance
- Life insurance
- Disability insurance
- Annual medical licensure
- Reimbursement of board certification expenses

- Malpractice insurance premium
- Dues and publications
- Continuing medical education
- Vacation leave, generally three to four weeks
- Sick leave, generally 10 working days
- Time off to take board exams
- Auto reimbursement
- Car or cellular phone and/or pager purchase and allowance
- Entertainment allowance
- Reimbursement of relocation costs

Malpractice insurance policies come in two forms: occurrence policies and claims-made policies. Under an *occurrence policy,* the insurance carrier remains responsible for any allegations of malpractice that occur while the policy is in force. Under a *claims-made policy,* however, the insurance carrier is responsible only if a malpractice claim or notice of a claim is filed before the policy's termination date. To protect the physician when a claim is made after his or her coverage under the claims-made policy is terminated, the insurance carrier will offer a *tail policy.*

If the practice pays for the physician's malpractice insurance premium and if the policy is a claims-made policy, the employment agreement should state who will be responsible for the tail-end premium. If this issue is not addressed, the departing physician may assume the practice will pay for the premium when the practice will not. For some medical specialties, the premium can be high. The potential disagreement over who pays for the insurance can and often does lead to litigation. If the employed physician is a not an owner of the practice, the practice generally will pay for the tail-end premium. This is because the nonowner physician is expected to generate profits for the practice. In other words, the practice benefits from the physician's service. However, all physician-owners should be responsible for their own malpractice tail-end premiums. The owners' employment agreement and the group's buy/sell agreement may include a clause that states that the practice will pay the tail-end premium, but the departing physician's buy-out will be reduced by that amount.

■ **Practice Point:** If you review the contract of a new physician recently graduated from residency or fellowship, make sure that the contract clarifies whether or not the physician will be paid for the time off needed to take his or her board certification exams and any related board certification study courses. This time off should be in addition to any agreed-upon vacation leave.

Practice Buy-In

The physician-owners will have to decide whether to include in the employment agreement how a new physician will buy into the ownership of the practice. Many contracts do not include such a provision in order to allow the practice some flexibility should circumstances change. Whether the method of buy-in is included in the contract or not, all parties should at least understand how the amount of the buy-in will be calculated and how it will be paid. Clarifying this at the beginning of the employment relationship can head off potential problems when the matter is ultimately discussed and negotiated.

The group practice will have to make three basic decisions related to the admittance of a new owner:

- What percentage of the practice will be purchased by the new owner and when will it be effective?
- How will such interest be valued?
- How will the purchase price be paid?

Percentage of the Practice

How much of the practice a physician can acquire, and when he or she can do so, usually depends on the medical specialty. Generally, hospital-based practices and surgical practices allow a quicker buy-in than primary-care practices. Buy-in generally is allowed after one year of employment for hospital-based practices and up to two years of employment for primary-care practices.

The trend in the industry, however, is to defer the decision to buy-in until *after* the first two years of employment. This is because the practice usually cannot tell if the physician is a candidate for long-term ownership after only one year of employment. In some situations, however, a new physician clearly shows all the characteristics and the commitment necessary to be an owner after one year. Therefore, the employment contract should state that at the end of the first year of employment, the owner or owners will evaluate the situation and may or may not make a buy-in offer to the new physician. This clause gives the practice the flexibility to make a physician an owner after the first or second year of employment.

The ownership percentage that a new physician will be allowed to acquire will depend on the current owners of the practice and what the new physician can afford to buy. The trend in the industry is to allow the new physician to purchase an equal ownership share. Some practices, however, stagger the buy-in percentage over a number of years to make sure that the practice is making the right decision by offering ownership to the new physician. For example, a physician eventually will be allowed to acquire 33 percent of the practice but will acquire this total percentage evenly over a two- to three-year period.

Valuing Interest

The owners of the practice must decide how to value the interest the new physician is buying. First, however, the practice must specify which of its assets will be included in the buy-in. Generally, the buy-in includes all of the practice's assets and liabilities. The practice may want to eliminate accounts receivable from the buy-in amount, however, as was discussed in Chapter 17, primarily because including it will unnecessarily inflate the amount of the buy-in. As previously discussed, instead of including accounts receivable, a more efficient way to handle the practice's current accounts receivable at the time of the buy-in is to declare a bonus of the net realizable receivables to the current owner or owners. This amount can be paid for over time (generally five years) and becomes a regular overhead item. This strategy effectively reduces the cost of the buy-in. The manner in which a physician buys into the group should, at a minimum, mirror how a physician is bought out of the group.

Method of Payment

Finally, a decision must be made about how the new physician will pay for the buy-in. Payment of the buy-in amount generally takes two forms: before-tax funding and after-tax funding. The new physician's share of the practice's fixed assets, and possibly other balance sheet assets, should always be paid for on an after-tax basis. Because after-tax dollars will be used, these payments will create the physician's tax basis in his or her ownership. If accounts receivable is included in the buy-in formula, the buy-in that can be tied to the practice's goodwill usually is paid for on a before-tax basis. This is accomplished through income differentials between the new physician and the current owners of the practice. The theory behind the strategy is that the current owners are being compensated for their share of the practice's accounts receivable, which is an income asset of the practice. As discussed in Chapter 17, the buy-in transaction may have to be reported to the Internal Revenue Service. Therefore, appropriate tax research and documentation are needed to support the structure of the buy-in.

Another Approach to a Buy-In

Instead of designating when a physician is eligible to buy in, say in one, two, or three years, another approach is to tie when the physician can buy in and the amount of the buy-in to the physician's actual financial performance. The most common methodology here is to allow (or even sometimes guarantee) the buy-in to occur when the physician's own collections have paid for his or her compensation package and an equal amount of the practice's overhead from the first day of employment. On the accompanying CD-ROM is a sample worksheet showing how this is done.

Keep in mind that until the physician's collections build up, there will be numerous deficits in this monthly calculation. However, as the physician builds his or her production, the collections each month begin to exceed the physician's compensation and his or her equal share of the overhead. When this occurs, the physician begins to pay back the deficits incurred in prior months until the net collections have extinguished the cumulative deficit. At this moment, the new physician is eligible for buy-in.

Now that the timing of the buy-in has been settled, the next step is to determine the amount of the buy-in.

Keep in mind that when the physician pays back the cumulative deficit, it means that he or she has paid for himself or herself (i.e., covered the physician's compensation and benefits) and paid in an equal share of the practice's overhead *incurred from the first day of employment*. Depending on the physician's ability to produce, the existing practice owners benefit directly from this subsidy in that the excess funds usually will be added to their compensation. Therefore, it is the amount of this overall expense subsidy that should be analyzed to determine and assess the buy-in amount. Most practices have adopted the policy that when the physician pays back the cumulative deficit, the buy-in is at the practice's net book value calculated in the month the deficit is zeroed out. Others only charge the new physician his or her share of equipment value. Some have charged only the par value of the stock shares to be purchased.

> ■ **Practice Point:** Every practice buy-in situation will be unique to that particular practice. It is very difficult to establish a standard formula that can apply to any buy-in arrangement. The buy-in plan should be tailored for each separate practice.

Other Contract Provisions

Every physician's employment agreement must address other issues, such as covenants not to compete and nonsolicitation clauses. How they are addressed will most often depend on the laws of the state in which the physician practices. The physician-owners should retain an attorney experienced in physicians' employment agreements to draft the employment contract.

Covenants Not to Compete

Most employment contracts contain a noncompetition provision. The enforceability of a covenant not to compete will depend on state law and related litigated case law. If the contract contains a noncompetition clause, the owners of the practice should assess the potential effects of having to enforce the covenant. In other words, enforcement could backfire within the physician's own medical community. For example, suppose a relationship between a physician and the practice does not work out for a variety of reasons. The physician leaves and attempts to set up a practice. The original practice sues on the covenant and is able to obtain an injunction against the physician. However, other physicians in the medical community have strong ties to the departing physician, and the original practice loses referrals and respect simply because it bullied a physician that other medical professionals liked and respected. Also, the physician-owners should consider the legal costs involved in any enforcement action.

If you represent a new physician, obviously the new physician will not want to sign a covenant not to compete. This is because, if the employment relationship (as opposed to an ownership relationship) does not work out for any reason, the physician will most likely have to uproot his or her family and move out of the service area. However, most practice employers will demand that any new associate execute an agreement that includes the covenant. This just makes good business sense.

In this type of situation, your objective in representing the new physician will be to eliminate or water down the covenant as far as possible. You can usually eliminate a covenant when the employer or the new physician has executed a recruitment assistance agreement with the hospital. In this situation, the hospital will provide financial assistance to help the practice employer get the new physician started in practice. Therefore, hospitals do not like covenants because the hospital has made an investment in the new physician. The last thing a hospital wants is for this investment to have to move away because a covenant is being enforced.

The covenant can be watered down simply by reducing the radius in which the new physician cannot practice medicine. This radius is often dictated by state law or related court rulings. If a practice has multiple sites, make sure that the radius applies only to one site and not to all of them. You may be able to water down the covenant further using zip codes. Find out where most of the practice's patients come from by zip code and try to apply the covenant to other zip codes. In other words, have the covenant apply to zip code areas from which the practice does not get most of its patients.

Nonsolicitation Clauses

If the physician-owners decide not to include a covenant not to compete in the physician's employment agreement, they should at least include a nonsolicitation clause. This contract clause provides that when the physician leaves the practice, he or she can take his or her patients. The departing physician, however, agrees not to solicit the other physicians' patients in any manner and also agrees not to make an offer of employment to any current employee of the practice. Some agreements state that, should a physician depart, the practice and the physician will send out a joint announcement to the departing physicians' patients or referral sources. This action attempts to secure the cooperation of all parties and prevent solicitation.

Outside Income

The employment contract should also address outside income that could be earned by the physician. Generally, the contract allows the physician to keep whatever income he or she earns on his or her own time. However, any income earned during the practice's time remains within the ownership of the practice and is allocated based on the practice's compensation formula. Outside income could include earnings from honorariums, royalties, and expert testimony.

Termination of Employment

Finally, the contract should discuss how a physician's employment can be terminated by the group. This policy will depend on the labor laws of the state in which the practice is located. If the practice is in an employment-at-will state, the contract generally does not have to state specifically how a physician's employment can be terminated. If state law does not have employment-at-will statutes, however, the contract should give specific cases for which a physician can be terminated. Examples include the following:

- The physician loses his or her hospital privileges.
- The physician becomes uninsurable for medical malpractice coverage.
- The physician is convicted of a crime.
- The physician does not work for three consecutive months.
- The physician breaches any term of his or her employment agreement.

Each physician in a group practice should sign an employment agreement. Those without contracts expose themselves to litigation. The ultimate sign of a good contract is that it is fair to both the physician and the practice.

A Final Word About Physician Compensation

When designing a physician compensation plan for a group medical practice, keep in mind these important points:

There is not a perfect plan.   There will almost always be some bias and you will not be able to please everyone.

Each group is unique.   The compensation plan should be unique to each group. Rarely are two formulas ever the same.

Compensation plans are not governance tools.   A group practice needs leadership and it must have common goals to succeed in the future.

Compensation plans must address the group's goals and mission.   If it does not, you may be creating separate practice units (i.e., the physicians) masquerading as a group practice.

A "perfect plan" would encourage:

- maximum net income generation

- minimum overhead
- efficient practice
- quality medical care and services
- appropriate utilization
- fair distribution of income
- harmony

▼ CHAPTER 19
Managed-Care Contracts and Contracting

For many physicians, managed care now dominates their practices and their patients' lives. In some communities, managed care now represents up to 80 percent of the insurance market share. Managed care was proposed by insurance companies and employers to control the growth of health care expenditures. Employers want to keep their health-insurance premiums low, and insurance companies want to contain the costs associated with hospitals, physicians, and other health care providers. As managed care advances on the marketplace, physicians and physician groups will have to decide whether to participate in managed-care plans. Should they decide to participate, physicians will want to know how participation will affect their practices, they will need help with their contracts, and they may need help renegotiating the agreements. (See the sample managed-care contract in Appendix C.)

Managed-Care Definitions

Before assessing any managed-care contract or relationship, you must become familiar with the terminology that applies specifically to managed care:

Administrative costs   A managed-care plan's costs related to utilization review, insurance, marketing, medical underwriting, agents' commissions, premium collection, claims processing, quality assurance programs, and risk management.

Adverse selection   Among those applicants for a given group or individual program, the tendency for those with an impaired health status or who are prone to a higher than average utilization of benefits to be enrolled in disproportionate numbers and in lower deductible plans.

Age/sex rating   A method of structuring capitation payments based on the age and sex of the enrollee/member.

Alternative delivery system (ADS) A method of providing health care benefits that differs from traditional indemnity (commercial insurance) methods. A health maintenance organization (HMO), for example, is an alternative delivery system.

Anniversary The beginning of a subscriber group's benefit year. A subscriber group with a year coinciding with the calendar year would be said to have a January 1 anniversary.

Appeal Process available to a provider under a payor's utilization management program, which allows the provider to ask for reconsideration of the original precertification decision by a peer reviewer. In addition, appeals apply to decisions by the payor to not cover or not pay for services already provided.

Attrition rate Disenrollment expressed as a percentage of total membership. An HMO with 50,000 members experiencing a 2 percent monthly attrition rate would need to gain 1,000 members per month in order to maintain its 50,000-member level.

Basic health services Benefits that all federally qualified HMOs must offer.

Benefit package A collection of specific services or benefits that the HMO is obligated to provide under the terms of its contracts with subscriber groups.

Benefit year A 12-month period that a group uses to administer its employee fringe benefits program. A majority of subscribers use a January-through-December benefit year.

Board certified A physician who has passed an examination given by a medical specialty group and who has, as a result, been certified as a specialist in his or her clinical area of practice.

Break-even point The HMO membership level at which total revenues and total costs are equal and, therefore, produced neither a net gain nor a loss from operations.

Capitation The per capita cost of providing a specific menu of health services to a defined population over a set period of time.

The capitated payment generally is a fixed payment received each month by the physician-provider. This payment is the same regardless of the number of services rendered by the physician or physician group.

Cash indemnity benefits   Sums that are paid to insureds for covered services and that require submission of a filed claim.

Catchment area   The geographic area from which an HMO draws its patients.

Claims review   The method by which a provider's service claims are reviewed prior to reimbursement by the health plan. The purpose is to validate the medical necessity of the services that were provided.

Closed panel   A managed-care arena in which members are required to see only physicians who are contracted with the plan. Members cannot see physicians outside of this set of providers for routine care covered by the plan.

Coinsurance   The portion of the cost for care for which the insured is financially responsible. This usually is determined by a fixed percentage, as in major medical coverage. Often, coinsurance applies after a specified deductible has been met.

Community rating   A method for determining health insurance premiums based on actual or anticipated costs in a specific geographic location as opposed to an experience rating that looks at individual characteristics of the insured.

Composite rate   A uniform premium applicable to all eligible members by a subscriber group regardless of the number of claimed dependents. This rate is common among labor unions and large employer groups and usually does not require any contribution by the union member or employee.

Concurrent review   Monitoring of the medical treatment and progress toward recovery once a patient is admitted to a hospital.

Contract   An HMO agreement executed by a subscriber group. The term may be used in place of subscriber when referring to penetrations within a given subscriber group. The term also designates an enrollee's coverage.

Contract mix   The distribution of enrollees according to contracts classified by dependency categories (e.g., the percentage of singles, doubles, or families). It is used to determine average contract size.

Coordination of benefits   Establishes procedures to be followed in the event of duplicate coverage, thus assuring that no more than 100 percent of the costs of care are reimbursed to the patient.

Co-payment   A modest payment that an enrollee with an HMO or preferred provider organization (PPO) makes at the time selected services are rendered.

Credentialling   The process whereby a health plan reviews the provider's credentials before allowing the provider to become a member of the plan's provider panel. Credentials would include training, experience, malpractice history, etc.

Deductibles   A pre-defined flat-dollar amount paid by enrollees in a health plan toward the cost of covered services before the plan itself begins to pay for any of the benefits.

Direct contracting   The situation in which individual employers or business coalitions contract directly with providers for health-care services without the use of HMO or PPO intermediaries. This enables employers to include in their plans the specific services preferred by their employees.

Enrollment   The process of converting the eligible members of the subscriber groups into HMO members or the aggregate count of HMO enrollees as of a given time.

Experience rating   A method to determine an HMO premium structure based on the actual utilization of individual subscriber groups. Age, sex, and utilization experience are the principal determinants in setting rates when using this method.

Exclusivity clause A part of a provider's contract with the health plan prohibiting the provider from contracting with more than one managed-care organization (e.g., HMO, PPO, IPA, etc.)

Fee for service The amount that the patient is charged according to a fee schedule set for each service or procedure to be provided.

Fiscal intermediary The agent that has contracted with providers of service to process claims for reimbursement under health care coverage. In addition to handling financial matters, the fiscal intermediary may perform other functions, such as communicating with providers.

Gatekeeper A primary-care physician in an HMO who makes referrals to other physicians. His or her function is to reduce health care use and costs.

Group model HMO An HMO that contracts exclusively with a multispecialty medical group to provide care to the HMO members. The members are required to receive medical care only from these doctors unless a referral is made to another physician.

Health maintenance organization (HMO) An organization of health care personnel and facilities that provides a comprehensive range of health services to an enrolled population for a fixed sum of money paid in advance.

Indemnity carrier Usually an insurance company that offers selected coverage within a framework of fee schedules, limitations, and exclusions as negotiated with subscriber groups.

Managed care A planned and coordinated approach to providing quality health care at lower cost.

Market area The targeted geographic area or the area in which the principal market potential is located.

Market share The part of the market potential that an HMO or PPO has captured. Usually market share is expressed as a percentage of the market potential.

Open enrollment period   The period of time stipulated in a group contract in which eligible members can choose a health plan alternative for the coming benefit year.

Open panel   A managed-care arena in which private physicians contract with a plan to provide care in their own offices.

Outcomes management   A clinical outcome is the result of medical or surgical intervention or nonintervention. It is believed that through a database of outcomes experience, providers will be able to determine which treatment protocols result in consistently better outcomes for patients.

Outlier   One who does not fall within a pre-described norm. This term is used mainly in connection with utilization review. A provider who uses either too many (e.g., many surgical procedures) or too few services (e.g., few hospital admissions) may be described as an "outlier."

Out-of-area benefits   The scope of emergency benefits available to HMO and PPO members while temporarily outside their defined service areas.

Peer review   Evaluation of a physician's performance by other physicians, usually within the same geographic area and medical specialty.

Penetration   The percentage of business that an HMO captures in a particular subscriber group or in the market area as a whole.

Per member, per month (PMPM)   The cost or revenue from each plan's member for one month.

Point-of-service (POS) plans   A POS plan encourages, but does not require, members to choose a primary care physician. As in traditional HMOs, the primary-care physician acts as a "gatekeeper" when making referrals. However, in a POS plan, members can opt to visit non-network providers at their discretion. However, members in a POS plan must pay a higher deductible and a higher co-payment if non-network providers render medical care to them.

Practice patterns   A historical record of diagnoses and treatments provided by doctors to their patients. Managed-care plans monitor and analyze these records to determine which circumstances yield the most positive outcomes for patients.

Precertification   Process used by the managed-care plan or organization to review nonemergency provider services before such care is given by the provider.

Preferred provider organizations (PPOs)   Contractual arrangements between physicians and insurance companies, employers, or third parties in which physicians provide services to a designated area with set fee schedules.

Primary-care physician (PCP)   The family practice doctor who is the initial source for diagnosis, screening, testing, treatment, and referral for a patient. In certain managed-care plans, such as HMOs, the PCP must be chosen by a member to act as the coordinator of all health care services given by other providers in the network.

Utilization   The frequency with which a benefit is used (e.g., 3,200 physicians' office visits per 1,000 HMO members per year). Utilization experience multiplied by the average cost per unit of service is capitated costs.

Utilization management   A process that measures use of available resources to determine medical necessity, cost-effectiveness, and conformity to criteria for optimal use.

The Growth of Managed Care

Managed care is a part of almost every physician's life. To appreciate its significance, one must first understand why managed care is growing. Most employers provide health-insurance benefits to their employees as a fringe benefit. Thus, the employers pay health-insurance premiums to a selected insurance plan. These premiums often increase at an accelerated pace. In some parts of the country, employers are faced with 25 percent to 50 percent premium increases every six months. To combat the rising cost of health care, an employer can (a) eliminate fringe benefits, (b) make the employees subsidize part of the health insurance premium, or (c) look for cheaper insurance. The employer who opts to look for cheaper insurance generally will find it in a managed-care plan, such as a PPO or an HMO. In other words, the increase in managed care in a physician's practice area is employer-driven.

To gain a basic understanding of managed care, it is important to understand market evolution and the related provider/payor actions under each. Physicians, payors, hospitals, and other providers are faced with different challenges as markets continue to evolve throughout the country. This is particularly true for those markets that are moving toward managed care. Providers, especially physicians, make strategic decisions based on the particular stage of managed care in a particular service area.

Stage 1: Unstructured Market

- Indemnity insurance is most prevalent.
- There is little hospital integration.
- Most physicians in the service area are independent.
- There are mainly unsophisticated purchasers in the market.
- There is generally an overuse of inpatient care.
- HMO penetration is generally less than 10 percent.

Stage 2: Loose Framework Market

- Managed-care penetration increases.
- Hospital consolidation begins, generally as loose affiliations.
- Physicians begin to organize in groups, primarily single-specialty group practices.
- Excess inpatient capacity begins to develop.
- Payors begin to acquire or partner with providers.
- HMO penetration is generally 10 percent to 20 percent.

Stage 3: Consolidation

- Employers begin to reduce managed-care options.
- A few large, selective HMOs/PPOs emerge.

- There is an alignment/consolidation of payors and providers.
- Physician group practices become capitalized.
- Health systems link with physicians.
- Provider net income margins begin to erode.
- HMO penetration is generally 20 percent to 30 percent.

Stage 4: Managed Competition

- Employers form coalitions to purchase health services.
- There is continued consolidation of provider systems and health plans.
- Integrated network develops full continuum of care.
- Solo physician practices become isolated.
- There is a dramatic decline in specialty utilization.
- Providers begin to compete on value, quality, and outcomes.
- HMO penetration is generally 30 percent to 40 percent.

Stage 5: Population-Based Delivery Reform

- Networks with market share form true partnerships with payors.
- Providers focus on core competencies.
- Integrated systems manage patient populations.
- There is comprehensive care delivery.
- HMO penetration is greater than 40 percent.

As managed-care plans begin to increase in a particular market, physicians will need to sign up with managed-care plans for two basic reasons: (1) to get patients and (2) to keep patients. If a particular practice area is shifting toward managed care, a physician must become a managed-care provider to establish a revenue stream. To enroll with a managed-care plan, begin by calling the business offices at the hospitals in which the physician has admitting privileges and ask for a list of the managed-care plans with which the hospital has signed (usually 10 to 15). The physician should be a participating provider for all of these plans. Besides gaining new patients, an established physician may have to sign with managed-care plans to keep his or her returning patients. If the employers in the physician's practice area are switching to managed-care plans, the physician must become a provider on these plans to keep a segment of his or her patient base. If a physician does not become a participating managed-care provider, the patients who are enrolled in the plan will be forced to switch to physicians who are plan providers.

> ■ **Practice Point:** All medical practices must create a managed-care strategy. This strategy will outline how the practice intends to handle the increase of managed-care plans in its service area. Practices that are prepared and proactive are usually the ones that are successful in dealing with managed care.

Assessing a Managed-Care Plan

The physician or the physician's consultant should meet with the plan's provider representative and ask the following questions:

- What is the plan's current market share in the physician's practice area?
- What is the anticipated market share in each of the next five years?
- How does the plan attempt to secure this market share?
- Which employers are currently signed up with the plan?
- Which other managed-care plans does this plan compete against in the practice area?
- Which other physicians in the physician's medical specialty are also participating providers in the plan?
- Which hospitals participate in the plan?

The answers to these questions should give you some indication of whether it would be financially sound to sign up with the managed-care plan. The analysis of market share is critical because the physician needs to know something about the growth trend in managed care in his or her practice area before he or she can make a decision. If managed care's market share has grown and will continue to grow, the physician probably should sign with the plan.

Another factor the physician should consider before enrolling is the plan's reputation. Determine the quality and stability of the specific employers enrolled in the plan.

Look at the other physicians who participate in the plan. If participants are respected peers, this indicates that it is a high-quality plan.

■ **Practice Point:** The analysis above applies to existing plans in a particular service area. It does not apply to new managed-care plans that come in to a particular service area. However, every physician should analyze and attempt to negotiate terms and rates with new plan providers just as he or she would with any other contract.

■ **Practice Point:** Evaluating a managed-care payor sounds good in practice but is usually irrelevant in practical terms. As managed care grows in a particular area, or if it is anticipated to grow, physicians will **need** to sign up with these plans just to have access to a patient base. This is the reality of a changing health care marketplace.

The physician should strive for two specific goals when signing up with managed-care plans: (1) to obtain the most favorable terms possible and (2) to limit financial risk as much as possible.

Leverage

The physician's success in achieving these goals will be directly dependent on whether the physician or physician group has any type of leverage in the medical community. A physician who has leverage should be able to negotiate or renegotiate better contract terms. A physician who does *not* have leverage will not be able to obtain the most favorable terms possible when negotiating the managed-care contract. The plan's manager may adopt a "take it or leave it" attitude, and refuse to negotiate with the physician. This is particularly true when a new physician signs the initial contract.

Leverage in the medical practice area generally becomes a factor in the following situations: (a) when the physician is the only physician, or one of the few physicians, in his or her medical specialty; (b) when a definite difference in clinical capabilities exists among physicians (i.e., the physician can demonstrate with data that his or her practice is more cost-effective than other practices in the same specialty that are on the provider panel); (c) when the plan wants to concentrate physicians' services within a specific group practice or practices; or (d) when, after signing up with the plan, the physician ends up treating too many patients enrolled with the plan.

> ■ **Practice Point:** Before negotiating a managed-care contract, determine if the practice has leverage. If a physician knows he does not have leverage, then he must position himself so that he can negotiate. Positioning strategies include joining or forming an independent practice association (IPA) or accumulating practice clinical data to demonstrate how cost-effective the practice is.

Leverage can take many forms. Practice owners, their managers, and their advisors need to be on the look out for them or begin the process of positioning the practice for leverage. If no preparation is made for leverage, contract negotiations will most likely fail.

Leverage in Numbers

The first form of leverage is the so-called *numbers strategy*. Practices or delivery systems that have a significant amount of the managed-care plan's provider panel usually have some form of leverage. This is because the managed-care plan runs the risk of losing a portion of its panel if these physicians terminate the contract. If physicians leave a network, the patients they treat will have to seek other providers. This is generally undesirable. Parents often do not want to have to find a new pediatrician. Patients get to know their primary-care physician and do not want to change. Women do not want to be forced to change their OB/GYN physician. Primary-care physicians often do not want to be forced to change their referral patterns to other specialists.

If physicians leave the plan and patients have to switch physicians as a result, patients will complain to their employers. This often gives a negative impression about the managed health plan.

This may impact the health plan's ability to keep certain employers as customers in the future.

To gain this type of leverage, physicians have formed independent practice associations and group practices. They can also attempt to expand their existing practices or delivery systems by adding physicians. Hospitals have attempted to create PHOs (physician hospital organizations) with their medical staff. In doing so, practices and delivery systems must always be aware of the federal antitrust rules. The federal government basically does not look favorably on situations in which physicians come together simply to negotiate against a managed-care plan. A detailed discussion of antitrust rules is presented in the chapter on integrated delivery systems (Chapter 22).

When negotiating using the numbers strategy, keep in mind this important point: If the payor perceives that it has alternative provider choices should a particular physician or number of physicians leave the network, contract negotiations will be difficult. For example, an IPA of 20 ophthalmologists may decide to reject a particular contract by submitting their termination notices to a payor. The issue of a possible termination by the physicians probably came up during contract negotiations. If the payor feels it would have adequate ophthalmology coverage should these physicians leave the network, the payor is asking itself why it should concede anything during the negotiation. Success during this type of negotiation would depend on whether the IPA had possible geographic leverage or leverage through documented clinical quality.

Geographic Leverage

Managed-care plans generally do not want to run into a situation where the patients will not have easy access to the physicians within the health plan's provider network. When this occurs, the network has what is often called *geographic holes* in the provider service area. Payors want to avoid this predicament because in time patients will begin to get very upset if they have to drive a perceived long distance to see a physician; the result will be patient complaints to their employers. This could have a negative impact on the managed-care plan because employers want their employees to be happy with their health insurance benefits. If the problem is not cured, it could cause the employer to switch to another plan with a broader, more complete, provider panel. As a result, the health plan could lose some business.

No Competition

Not having competition is another form of negotiation leverage. If the practice is the only medical specialty in a particular service area, it usually has leverage against the managed-care plan because the managed-care plan has no or few contracting alternatives. For example, take the pediatric subspecialty practice that is the only subspecialty practice in the service area. In this situation, the managed health plans are usually agreeable to a negotiation because they know the practice has the ability to stay out of the network. This means the practice will be paid at higher reimbursement rates. The payor will have to concede something if it wants these physicians in its network at a negotiated discount off the practice's regular fee schedule. Becoming an *in-network* provider could be an advantage to a practice because it reduces the amount of red tape often associated with out-of-network providers (i.e., the difficulties associated with getting approval to treat a patient as an out-of-network provider).

Circumstances become somewhat clouded when there is more than one physician of a particular medical specialty in the service area. The first one willing to go in-network will reduce the leverage of the other practice(s) because the payor now may have a contracting choice. This choice could be limited if the practice going in-network does not provide adequate geographic coverage as described above. Also keep in mind that the recruitment of a new provider to the area might impact future contract negotiations. This is one reason a practice with real leverage may want to go in-network if favorable rates and terms can be negotiated. Any new physician to the area, assuming the physician will set up a competing practice, just might accept managed-care contracts freely. In this situation, the practice that decided to remain out-of-network could have difficulty with future contract negotiations.

■ **Practice Point:** If the physician or the practice is the only game in town for a particular medical specialty, negotiate to get the practice in-network by offering a 10 to 20 percent discount off the practice's current fee schedule.

Quality

The next form of leverage is utilization and outcomes data (i.e., quality). Practices and their owners who are progressive enough to obtain, assemble, and analyze outcomes data will have a significant amount of leverage against managed-care plans. Why? As stated above, managed-care plans usually pay all physicians at the same rate schedule. If a practice or delivery system can present data showing it is a lower cost provider than the other physicians of the same medical specialty on the panel, the managed-care plan will usually consider giving the physicians some kind of an increase in reimbursement. If the managed-care plan does not do this, it indicates to the community that is does not care about quality.

The following are a few samples of the most common quality indicators:

- Cost per patient for a particular series of diagnosis codes
- Surgeries performed as a percent of patient encounters
- Usage of ancillary services
- Lengths of stay in the hospital
- Specialist referrals as a percent of patient encounters or by diagnosis codes (for primary-care physicians)
- Number of repeat visits due to surgical complications

Keep in mind that quality can also be defined by clinical outcomes, as well as by hard figures. One example is asthma and allergy. How many work days are missed by those patients the practice is treating? For glaucoma specialists, an indication of quality care is how well eyesight is restored after glaucoma surgeries and how often complications arise. For psychiatrists, quality could be seen in how well addictions are cured and the incidence of relapse.

It is important to remember that managed-care plans do not initiate an increase in reimbursement rates. Physicians must ask for such an increase. Medicine needs to become more efficient, but this is a process that is not going to happen overnight. However, the practices that do become efficient and cost-effective will most likely end up the true winners in the managed-care reimbursement playing field.

■ **Practice Point:** Quality is a powerful tool when negotiating with a managed-care payor simply because if a provider can prove it is more cost efficient than its competitors (i.e., delivers better quality of care) and the payor still does not negotiate fairly with the provider, then it shows the employer community, the consumer community, and the provider community that the payor does not really care about "quality." This is one issue a payor does not want revealed.

Patient Volume

Treating many patients enrolled with the payor is another form of leverage. If a group of physicians is treating many of the plan's enrollees as patients, obviously the plan does not want to lose this group. If so, the patients will have to find other physicians, and most do not want to do this.

Conduct a study of the practice using the 20 percent rule to see if this form of leverage exists. Under this rule, no more than 20 percent of the practice's total managed-care revenue should come from one managed-care plan; otherwise, the practice may be at financial risk. This study should be performed yearly to keep a check on the practice.

Example of the 20 Percent Rule

At the end of a year, ABC group practice had collected $1,000,000 in patient revenue. Of this total, 50 percent ($500,000) of the revenue came from managed-care plans. Of the $500,000 in managed-care revenue, half came from one single plan (25 percent of the total revenue).

In the example, this group of physicians must assess whether its practice can afford to lose $250,000 of revenue (50 percent of the managed-care total) if one or more of its providers are removed from the plan. Many physicians may not realize that a substantial amount of their revenue is at risk if one particular managed-care contract is terminated or if the payor decides to change the terms of the arrangement. However, while this is a definite negative, it is also a positive because it means that the practice treats many patients of the plan and therefore may have some negotiation leverage. In this situation, attempt to negotiate or renegotiate contract rates and terms.

> ■ **Practice Point:** When using patient volume as a leverage tool in managed-care negotiations, it is also a good idea to bring cost accounting to the negotiation table with it. In other words, be sure to conduct a cost accounting study by CPT code and use this information when negotiating with the managed-care plan. It is very difficult to treat a large number of patients when reimbursement for these patients barely covers the cost to treat them.

Termination

Another form of leverage is contract termination by the physician or the practice. As obvious as it is, this is the most dangerous form of leverage. There will be situations in which a physician, practice, or delivery system will terminate a contract just to force the managed-care plan back to negotiating table. But what happens if the plan calls this bluff? Obviously the physicians will lose revenue in this instance since they will lose access to patients. Therefore, before considering such a move, a practice or its owner should analyze carefully whether or not this leverage will work and the ramifications if it does not.

Perils of Hospital (or Entity) Control

Attempts to gain leverage over managed-care health plans are often impacted by who owns the medical practice. If physicians own the practice, they usually will have the flexibility to do what they believe is best for the practice. In other words, a practice most likely will attempt to obtain some of the leverage strategies discussed in this section. But what if the practice is somehow controlled by a hospital, physician practice management company, delivery system, or some other third-party entity? Here the ability to gain leverage becomes somewhat cloudy. Situations such as these include direct ownership of the medical practice or participation by the practice in a delivery system controlled by the hospital or entity. The issue is whether the controlling party will look out for the economic interests of the physician practice or for the overall organization instead.

The best way to examine this is to look at a few examples using a hospital as the controlling party. Take the example of the hospital which has acquired medical practices. In this example, the acquired physicians are usually paid a base salary along with an annual incentive bonus equal to a percentage of collections when such collections exceed a particular collection threshold. Assume that the practice operates in a concentrated managed-care market. Question: What will be the reaction of the hospital owner if the managed-care payors decide to decrease what they are currently paying their in-network physician providers? Question: What will the hospital owner do when asked to sign up acquired physicians at a poor reimbursement rate schedule?

Each of the above examples has a direct impact on the compensation of the physicians. If the hospital does nothing, the physicians may have to take a pay cut because collections will go down unless somehow production can be increased. In the short term, the physicians might not receive a bonus because the collection threshold might not be achieved. This is a fact of life in most discounted fee-for-service reimbursement contracting environments.

The major issue in these examples, as well as in a PHO, is whether or not the hospital will allow itself to position its acquired medical practices for managed-care contracting success. Unfortunately, this is doubtful in most of these situations because the hospital may be fearful to negotiate with a payor on behalf of its acquired physicians when the hospital facility itself has a contract with the same payor. Once a hospital (or possibly other entity) owner attempts to negotiate or renegotiate contract rates and terms, a payor will probably not react favorably because the hospital facility does not want to run the risk of having its own reimbursement schedule attacked by the plan.

Utilization and Outcomes Data

The physicians who will eventually win in the managed-care arena are those who can demonstrate they practice in a higher quality, more cost-effective manner than their peers and competitors. Arguably the most powerful form of leverage a provider has in managed-care contracting is the ability to submit utilization and outcomes data. If a practice or delivery system can present data showing it is a lower cost provider than the other physicians of the same medical specialty on the panel, the managed-care plan will usually consider giving the practice some kind of an increase in reimbursement. If the managed-care plan does not do this, it indicates to the consumer and employer communities that it does not care about quality as defined by cost-driven issues. Obviously, health plans do not want such negative publicity and physicians can use this situation effectively during the negotiation process.

Unfortunately, most health plans today consider only what it costs to render care to patients; few seem to care about quality measures defined by clinical outcomes as well as by hard financial figures. Assuming that health plans consider only cost numbers, providers must assemble this information if they desire an increase in reimbursement rates (i.e., an increase in what they get paid to treat patients).

Evaluating Risk

Managed-care plans shift risk to the physician. This is one way in which the plan makes its profit and contains its health care expenditures. Risk will take many forms, usually depending on whether the plan is a PPO or an HMO.

If the plan is a PPO, evaluate the fee discount on the physician's most commonly used services. Discounting fees is one way a PPO shifts risk to a physician. Appendix C contains a managed-care plan fee request form that can be used to obtain fee information from the PPO. Request the PPO's fees for the current procedural terminology (CPT) codes the practice most commonly uses. Analyze the percentage discount of the practice's normal indemnity fee for each service. Assess whether the discounts are reasonable. If they are not, the physician may not want to sign with the plan.

■ **Practice Point**: Set up the following simple worksheet to analyze PPO fee rates. The worksheet will help you analyze the practice's top 25 utilized services:

CPT Code	Description	Practice Fee	PPO Fee	% Discount

■ **Practice Point:** If the discount is too steep, the physician can choose not to sign the agreement or she can attempt to negotiate better rates. If the physician does not have leverage, she probably will not be able to negotiate for better rates. However, she should consider joining or forming an IPA to facilitate the negotiation of managed-care contracts.

Determine whether the PPO (or even HMO) will deduct an additional withhold from the physician's reimbursement. A withhold is an amount that is deducted from the already discounted fee. For example, a physician's normal fee for a service is $1,000. The physician signs with a managed-care plan, for which the approved fee for the same service is $800 (a 20 percent discount). However, the plan also withholds an additional 10 percent from the physician's payment, in this case $80. Thus, the physician's reimbursement will not be the expected $800, but rather $720 ($800 – $80).

The withhold is usually intended to control a physician's behavior or to provide financial security to the payor. It generally goes into a pool, out of which the physician will receive reimbursement if predefined goals are met. These goals usually are tied to the physician's utilization of services or the profitability of the plan. Thus, if a withhold exists, determine under which circumstances the withhold will be returned to the practice at the end of the year.

The practice must account for all managed-care withholds properly during the year. A computerized practice can do this by having the office manager set up a credit adjustment for each plan that deducts a withhold. If the practice is on a manual system, the manager will have to tally the information on a paper ledger for each managed-care plan. At the end of the practice's year, meet with each of the plan's provider representatives and determine if the withhold will be returned to the practice. If it will not, more risk has been shifted to the physician because the fee discounts were steeper than originally planned.

Assess the potential financial risk to the practice if it will be reimbursed on a capitated basis. Under a capitated arrangement, a physician is paid a flat amount each month, regardless of the number of patients treated. Most HMOs use capitation contracts, and the contracts are based on an actuarially computed per-member, per-month basis. Assessing potential financial risk when evaluating an HMO capitated contract is probably one of the most difficult tasks you will perform. Unless an actuary assesses the risk, it is almost impossible to determine the reasonableness of the per-member, per-month payment.

A different approach you can take to assess the risk is to anticipate utilization, quantify it using the practice's indemnity fee schedule, and compare it to the capitated payment. An HMO's representative can provide information on anticipated use based on the HMO's past experience locally and possibly on a national level.

■ **Practice Point:** Make sure to account for any withholds on the practice's financial statements. These should be recorded as accounts receivable from the respective health plans that deduct them from the practice's reimbursements. This is an excellent way to keep track of what is owed the practice. The withhold can be expensed once the amount that will not be returned to the practice at the end of the year is determined. This determination is made through discussions between the practice and the respective health plans.

Evaluating the Contract Terms

You will need to analyze many issues before the physician signs the managed-care contract. Here are some items to look at carefully when evaluating a contract.

• The payor

Ensure that the term *payor* is adequately defined. Does the definition include the minimum requirement that the payor is bound by written agreement to the Physician Agreement, both financially and otherwise? Ensure that the health plan is obligated to provide the practice with a payor listing and with appropriate updates and that the practice has the ability to terminate nonpaying or late paying payors, as well as those who engage in unfair payment practices. The practice should also have the ability to monitor the financial solvency of payors.

- Contract term

  Run a contract term off the plan year cycle. If the contract is tied to the plan year, will patients be locked into their selected plan at the time that possible contract termination becomes effective? Health plan concerns over movement of enrollees to different plans based on physician participation may provide the practice with additional leverage.

  Complex risk agreements may merit longer contract terms, while "low" risk agreements (i.e., fee for service, or fee for service with a withhold) may merit a shorter contract term.

- Voluntary termination provisions

  Consider whether a voluntary termination clause is in the best interests of the practice. A voluntary termination provision effectively reduces the term of the agreement to the length of the notice period. For example, an agreement providing for termination at any time upon 90 days notice effectively is a 90-day contract. On the other hand, the clause also reduces risk and prevents unilateral termination by the health plan. But make sure that the plan cannot unilaterally terminate the physician by removal from the Provider Directory.

- Credentialling

  A big issue with medical practices is the time it takes to get a new doctor credentialled with their contracted managed-care payors. Sometimes it takes up to six months to get a new doctor on a managed-care provider panel. Therefore, the practice should seek to speed up the credentialling process by getting the plan to rely on outside credentialling. For example, the practice should attempt to insert into their managed-care contracts that instead of requiring the practice's physicians to submit to the plan's credentialling process, the plan instead will rely on a certification from a hospital attesting to the fact that the practice's physicians have been properly credentialled in accordance with the hospital's credentialling policies and procedures.

Voluntary termination clauses also have significant disadvantages, especially when they are included in a complex risk agreement. They reduce commitment and can result in loss of time and resource investment.

■ **Practice Point:** Also make sure the agreement addresses how a practice can close itself to accepting new patients from the health plan. In most cases, all the practice has to do is notify the payor that it is no longer accepting new patients from the health plan.

- Involuntary termination provisions

Make sure that termination is expedited in the event of nonpayment. The contract should also allow for termination for breach (other than for nonpayment) upon expiration of a notice and cure period. Consider a clause preventing a second instance of the same or a substantially similar breach within a specified period of time (e.g., six months) after the date that the earlier breach was cured. There should be selective termination as to particular payors.

- Continuation of care provisions

Determine under what circumstances the provider is obligated to continue providing care after the termination of the contract. Consider these options:

—To all members until the end of the applicable plan year

— Only to those members who are under treatment or are inpatients on the date of termination

Does the contract conform to state law requirements for continuation of care? List any times that the continuation of care provisions do not apply (e.g., a provider termination for health plan nonpayment or breach).

Determine what rates apply for continued care. Consider the effect of applicability of "contract rates" if the continuation provision applies only to certain members or if the rate was a capitated rate.

- Renewals

Review and decide advantages and disadvantages of the automatic renewal provisions. The big advantage of an automatic renewal clause is that it avoids the inadvertent lapse of the agreement. There should be some provision for rate adjustment (or expedited termination, if the parties cannot agree upon rates) upon the automatic renewal. Automatic renewal is potentially disadvantageous if the health plan goes into bankruptcy.

Evaluate the practice's ability to terminate the contract on 60 days' notice (even in a contract which otherwise does not contain a voluntary termination clause) if the parties are unable to agree upon renewal rates within a specified period of time.

- Noncovered and disallowed services

    How far-reaching is the hold-harmless clause? Does it prohibit the physician from seeking payment for noncovered services or services which are "non-reimbursable" due to technical default? Hold-harmless provisions typically prohibit the physician from billing the patient, or any other person acting on the patient's behalf, in the event of the health plan's nonpayment.

- The provider manual

    Check to ensure the agreement specifies that if there is any inconsistency between the provider manual and the contract, the contract supersedes and controls. Because many provisions typically contained in a "provider manual" (such as benefit plan descriptions and administrative requirements) can significantly affect the economic expectations of the physician, under both fee-for-service and risk agreements, attention should be paid to these provisions.

    The practice should not agree to adhere to provisions in a provider manual unless, at a minimum, it will be provided with prior written notice of any material changes and there is some ability to reject the modification through contract termination or other mechanisms.

- Emergency services

    Is the definition of "emergency services" tied to the patient's presenting symptoms, rather than to the ultimate diagnosis? Many states now mandate the "prudent lay person" standard.

- Gag clauses

    Gag clauses are those that restrict or appear to restrict, in any way, the physician's communications with his or her patients.

These might be contained in provisions dealing with non-solicitation or non-disparaging remarks. Physicians should at all times be free to advise patients regarding which plans they participate in and which plans may be the "best" for them, considering marketing guidelines for Medicare Risk Agreements, when appropriate. Physicians should also be free to conduct general "advertising," so long as no advertisement is directed toward a particular enrollee.

- Confidentiality clauses

  Confidentiality clauses can protect both physician and the plan so long as they are mutual and reasonable in scope. Consider limiting confidentiality clauses to proprietary information (such as customer lists and rate information) and make sure that public-domain information is not included. Ensure that disclosure is allowed in connection with lawsuits, and to comply with a court order, subpoena, or other compulsory process. It is not unreasonable for the provider to require prior notice of these disclosures.

  Consider whether a provision should be included in the contract that physician profiling data or other information regarding physician performance under the agreement should be considered confidential information. The contract should then state that such information should not be disclosed unless the physician has had an opportunity to review and comment or the information does not identify the specific physician.

- Rendering of care

  A physician should be free to provide care deemed appropriate in his or her medical judgment. The contract should not contain any language which limits, or *appears* to limit, that ability. The contract should preserve to the greatest extent possible the distinction between the clinical provision of care and the administration of benefits. Watch for clauses that indicate that the physician will "adhere to" the health plan's utilization management determinations.

- Liability issues

  Evaluate malpractice insurance coverage requirements. Will coverage need to increase? If so, calculate the cost involved.

Check to see whether there are any restrictions or liability involved with the release of patient medical information. Physicians can be liable for professional negligence if they deviate from the standard of care. And juries may be inclined to award punitive damages if a physician appears to have allowed economic interest to override medical judgment. Physicians open themselves up to breach of contract claims when contracts appear to make "promises" regarding quality.

- Indemnification clauses

  Look carefully at indemnification clauses that require the physicians to indemnify the health plan for the acts and omissions of the physicians and the physicians' agents, servants, and employees. Check with the physicians' insurance policy. Many policies specifically exclude coverage for "contractual indemnification."

- Plan administrative responsibility

  Note whether the contract clearly sets forth who is responsible for making medical management/coverage determinations, verifying eligibility and benefits, adjudicating claims, and making claims payment. Are the requirements of the medical management program fair and reasonable?

  Look at who is responsible for dispute resolution. Consider different dispute resolution processes for different types of disputes. Must the physician exhaust internal plan appeals first?

  Who is responsible for ensuring that the physician is not prohibited from seeking injunctive or other equitable relief?

  The contract should also clarify who will determine what time limits are applicable and what happens if one party delays or otherwise fails to cooperate; who will determine who pays the cost under what circumstances; and who will coordinate benefits and third-party liability.

  The contract should state who will try to recover the difference between what the primary payor pays and the practice's billed charges, not to exceed the secondary payor's contract amount.

- Arbitration

  Ensure that the contract contains a clear description of the process and a statement of who will determine where the arbitration is to be held? This is critical for out-of-state payors. The contract should also state who will determine whether arbitration applies if one party desires to seek injunctive relief.

Consider the following issues:

—Is it clear how arbitrator(s) or mediator(s) are selected?

—What rules apply?

—Is arbitration binding or nonbinding?

- The rate

  Does the contract refer to a specific rate or merely to the then current "allowable" under the plan? What notice will the practice receive of rate changes? Does the practice have the ability to terminate prior to the effective date of any rate change?

  Managed-care plans are paying many physicians as a percent of the current Medicare RBRVS rates. These rates are anywhere from 105 percent of Medicare rates upward to 150 percent for certain services. As these and other forms of reimbursement are adopted, physician reimbursement is being cut anywhere from 30 percent to 50 percent. As Medicare reduces its rates in the future, related managed-care rates will decline also.

  The managed-care contract should state which RBRVS rate year the schedule is based on and under what conditions the schedule can change from year to year. The problem is that the rate will change automatically each year as Congress changes Medicare payment rates. In this case, a practice could experience a decrease in pay simply because Congress decided to cut its Medicare budget. Therefore, the managed-care contract should tie reimbursement to a particular RBRVS year and at the same time state this rate cannot change for a period of time. The managed-care contract should state that the plan cannot change rates without first notifying the physician *in writing*. This way the practice will at least have advance notice of a rate change and will be in a position to negotiate a different rate.

- Case rate and risk agreement issues

  Rewrite or delete phrases with lack of specificity or broad references to the "Benefit Plan." Determine whether certain high-cost procedures or high-cost drugs are excluded and what happens in the event of a dual diagnosis. Determine whether the plan can down-code and what happens if new technologies are developed. What happens if there is a change in the standard of care?

- Member co-payments/co-insurance

  Determine what charges are the Member's responsibility. Can these go up or down? Determine how changes affect overall compensation.

- Benefit plan issues

  Determine whether the physician is obligated to participate in all health plan products. If so, how does that impact compensation?

- Capitation

  Determine which members are covered by the payment. Are credits given for the unassigned member? Determine whether there are limits on retroactive additions/deletions. Clarify which members are covered under each monthly payment (i.e., those enrolled as of the first of the month or fifteenth of the month).

- Physician audit rights

  Determine whether the agreement contains the audit rights necessary to assess the health plan's compliance with the agreement and to ensure the proper and accurate accounting of all financial matters. Consider the frequency of the audit rights and who bears expenses in connection with those audit rights. For instance, if an audit reveals a discrepancy in actual costs against debits in favor of the health plan, does the plan pay the cost of the audit?

- Department of Insurance grievance processes

  Review physician appeal rights and rights to contact the Department of Insurance should a dispute arise with the payor.

- Direct patient access

  Does the member have direct access to the physician? If not, make sure that the practice understands the payor's referral/authorization requirements.

- Co-payments

  Determine whether the co-payment, co-insurance, and deductible levels are acceptable.

- Network issues

  Determine whether the network is broad enough to include the providers to whom the practice generally refers patients.

- Solvency issues

  Determine whether the health plan insolvency insurance covers participating providers. Obtain and review the payor's annual and quarterly Department of Insurance filings and look for early indicators of insolvency (i.e., initial denials, claims payment lags, requests for additional information). Does the contract require the physician to hold harmless and indemnify any third party? If so, the physician may be subject to a contingent liability.

  ■ **Practice Point:** Practices must decide the importance of the issue of hold harmless. Many attorneys state that a physician should never sign a contract that includes a hold-harmless provision. While this makes good business sense, sometimes the practicalities of managed-care contracting cause a physician or practice to choose what is important. If a managed-care plan is adamant about not changing this provision, does it make sense to walk away from the contracting opportunity? Probably not. If you are able to negotiate a favorable reimbursement structure, will the practice want to execute the contract even though the managed-care plan will not change the hold-harmless clause? It is important to decide which contract terms are the most important and on which ones the practice will compromise.

  ■ **Practice Point:** A question that often arises is how to remove the hold-harmless clause. There are generally two ways. First, cross out the provision, initial it, execute the contract, and mail it to the managed-care plan. Some plans will accept this and some will not. Another way is to call the payor and state that you would like this provision eliminated. A practice's success either way will depend on how much leverage it has in the service area.

- Malpractice insurance

  Per the contract, how much malpractice insurance coverage must the physician have in place? To participate in the plan, the physician may have to increase his or her malpractice insurance coverage. Also remember that if a physician reduces malpractice insurance coverage limits, the physician may violate this provision in some or all of the practice's managed-care contracts.

- Contract termination

  How can the contract be terminated by either the physician or the managed-care plan? If the contract can be terminated simply by giving notice, a practice may be taking a risk by increasing its reliance on managed-care patient revenue. (See the related discussion on the 20 percent rule earlier in this chapter.)

- Disclosure of information

  Does the contract prohibit the managed-care plan from disclosing any information about the physician in connection with any credential-related or peer-review deliberations, unless such disclosure is required by law?

- Standard of medical practice

  Does the contract hold the physician to a standard of medical practice that is higher than that applied to a reasonable physician acting under the same or similar circumstances?

- Right to refuse to treat patients

  Does the contract protect the practice's right to refuse to accept a member of a health plan or to terminate the patient? For example, some contracts allow a practice to terminate a patient if the patient displays hostility or improper behavior toward a doctor, the doctor's staff, or the practice's other patients.

- Nonmedical requirements

  Does the contract require the physician to perform any other services besides medical services? For example, a physician may be required to participate in peer-review activities.

- Changes in the medical practice

  Does the contract contain any provisions that may require the physician to alter the practice significantly, such as increasing the physician's availability, altering physician referral practices, or increasing or decreasing office staff?

Other Managed-Care Issues

When deciding whether to participate in a managed-care plan, you must evaluate additional issues. Many involve billing the plan for the physician's services. These issues may or may not be contained in the written managed-care contract. Following are some issues that should be addressed:

- Which clinical services must the physician render?

- Which services are not covered by the plan?

- Is the plan required to notify the physician when a patient leaves the plan? For example, an employee leaves a job and her insurance coverage ends. If the patient goes to the physician the next day for an office visit, will the plan still pay the physician until the physician's office is notified of the disenrollment?

- Must the physician accept all patients from the plan or can the office limit the number? If the practice is overrun by patients from a specific managed-care plan, the practice may need the flexibility to limit the volume of visits with patients.

- Which services must be precertified with the plan before the physician can provide them?

- Are there any referral restrictions?

- What, if any, is the time limit for filing claims with the plan?

- Does the contract define what is considered to be a submitted "correct and clean" claim?

- How quickly does the plan usually pay claims?

- Is there a provision for late payments by the plan? Attempt to negotiate that if payments of clean and complete claims are made after 30 days of receipt they will be considered late and subject to an interest charge.

- What special forms must be submitted to the plan before it approves payment?
- Which services require a second opinion?
- How does the discounted fee schedule change each year?
- How are these changes communicated to the physician?
- What are the patients' co-payments and deductibles, if any?

> ■ **Practice Point:** Another important issue in managed-care contracting involves group practices that recruit new physicians. Never assume that a new physician to the practice will be able to get on a plan just because the physicians in the group practice are contracting with that managed-care plan. Many managed-care plans now are closing their provider panels to new physicians because they believe they already have enough physicians contracted in that particular medical specialty. Therefore, group practices should include in their managed-care contracts a provision that if the practice recruits a new physician, that physician will become a member of the plan as long as he or she passes the normal credentialling process.

Renegotiating Managed-Care Contracts

What if the medical practice does not like the financial and nonfinancial terms of the contract? Can the practice change them? What if the managed-care plan changes the terms of the contract after it is signed? Can the practice change them again?

Success in changing managed-care contracting terms usually varies from locale to locale. However, as previously mentioned in this chapter, success can be achieved if the practice has the *leverage* to negotiate or renegotiate favorable contract rates and terms. Otherwise, practices will have to accept what is offered to them by the managed-care plan. More often than not, this will have a major impact on the finances of the practice.

Capitation

Capitation is a payment system whereby a medical provider is paid for his or her services based on a fixed, flat rate, termed "per member, per month." This type of payment system can apply to both primary-care physicians as well as specialty providers, such as surgeons and cardiologists. For example, a managed-care payor might pay a family practitioner 53 cents each month for each enrollee who signed up with that family practitioner. A surgeon could get paid $1.00 per member, per month for all enrollees assigned to it by the payor. Capitation used to be a growing form of reimbursement in the managed-care markets. While capitation is still prevalent in areas such as California, Florida, and some east coast states, by and large capitation has not grown to represent a significant percentage of most medical practices' overall revenues.

The following is a sample capitation rate contract provision that highlights how a medical practice might be paid under a capitation arrangement.

> *Physician shall be paid Capitation Compensation for all Members in the ABC Care Commercial Health Plan assigned to Physician in the amount of One and 54/100 Dollars ($1.54) per Member per month in full consideration for all Medical Services performed by Physician for such Members. Such Capitation Compensation is for all services rendered by Physician, including drugs and supplies.*

It is important to understand and realize that numerous medical providers and integrated delivery systems throughout the United States have lost money working within the capitated reimbursement system. Why is this? For one, most medical providers do not "change" how they clinically treat "capitated" patients after taking on a capitation contract. In other words, utilization does not change after this type of payment system is introduced. When paid at a flat rate, physicians must become efficient in their clinical work, which most do not understand how to do. Keep in mind that when a payor wants to pay its providers on a capitated basis, it really wants to "shift the risk" of care away from the payor to the providers themselves. What usually happens is that after the initial twelve months of a capitated contract, a provider will compare its patient utilization (i.e., fee for service charges that would have been incurred) against what the practice received as capitation, only to find out that the practice earned "25 cents on the dollar."

Another reason for lost revenues is that the capitation payment that was offered and paid to the medical practice was not adequate to cover the utilization that was actually incurred. Also, maybe the actual utilization of the patient base exceeded the expected or budgeted utilization that the capitation rate was originally based upon.

This is why it is so important to analyze the contract terms and capitation rate before accepting the contract and why it is also important to analyze the capitation contract and rate, year in and year out. This section of the chapter reviews the important financial and nonfinancial issues that you should address before a medical practice accepts a capitation contract. This discussion focuses on a capitation arrangement between a medical practice and a payor that applies to the rendering of the clinical services by the medical practice itself; the discussion does not involve full risk contracting, IBNR, and integrated delivery system capitation.

Finally, remember that if a contract has already been accepted, the issues about to be discussed should be reviewed annually. If great care is not taken with respect to the financial and nonfinancial segments of the arrangment, rest assured that the practice will have set itself up for the potential to lose money under the capitation contract.

Capitation Nonfinancial Issues

The nonfinancial issues in any capitated contract are just as important as the capitation rate itself. As you will soon see, consider these issues "little land mines" that if stepped upon could cause the economics of the capitation arrangement to "blow up" at any point in time in the future. In other words, failure to address these issues adequately could result in significant financial losses in the future. The following are a few of the most significant nonfinancial issues that you should address, review, analyze and, if necessary, negotiate. As you will see, some of these issues appear to be financial in nature, but make sure they are adequately addressed in the capitation contract. The section on financial issues will deal mainly with how to evaluate a capitation rate and related subject areas.

Service Obligations

First, you must find out the total array of clinical services that are included as part of the capitation rate. In other words, the practice will receive a fixed payment each month and in exchange for this payment, it must render a defined set of clinical services to the patients. The contract should spell out exactly what these services are. If it does not or is vague, then simply ask the payor what clinical services are included in the capitation rate as it relates to the practice's medical specialty. The following is a sample contract provision.

> **Provision of Covered Services.** Group shall provide to Members, through Participating Group Providers, those Covered Services which are within the scope of the respective Participating Group Provider's license and certification to practice. A Services Schedule may be attached hereto and made a part hereof, when applicable. Company and Physician Group may mutually agree in writing at any time, and from time to time, either to increase or decrease the services described in the Services Schedule. A Group Provider may not provide any Covered Services to Members unless and until said Group Provider has been fully credentialled and approved by the applicable peer review committee. Participating Group Providers shall provide Emergency Services to Members, as necessary. It is understood and agreed that Company, or, when applicable, the Payor shall have final authority to determine whether any services provided by Participating Group Providers were Covered Services and to adjust or deny payment for services rendered by Participating Group Providers to Members in accordance with the results of such determinations.

Before accepting a capitation contract, find out exactly what of the following, by CPT code, are included in the capitation rate:

1. Which evaluation and management codes are included?
2. Which medicine codes?
3. Which surgical procedures, both in and out of the office setting?
4. Which radiological procedures?
5. Any in-office drugs included?
6. In-office supplies included?
7. Diagnostic and laboratory services?
8. Any other services included?

This issue is extremely important because:

1. you want to identify services you do not want to be responsible for under a fixed fee arrangement,

2. determine if the practice can perform all of the services, and

3. decide if there are any services that you want paid on a fee for service (FFS) basis.

For example, drugs are sometimes omitted because the actual cost of the drugs can change (i.e., rise) during the contract, but the capitation rate does not change accordingly. There may also be a time when a payor will try to get a medical practice to be responsible for a service it cannot deliver itself. The following are two examples:

Example 1: The Ob/Gyn practice that was responsible for gynecology services. It did not employ a gynecologist.

Example 2: The cardiology practice that was responsible for heart surgical procedures, such as heart bypass surgeries. It did not employ a heart surgeon.

If a practice accepts responsibility for services it cannot render itself, the practice must then go out and subcontract for these services. In other words, the cardiology group would have to go out and negotiate and enter into a contract with a heart surgery doctor or group. Can the practice negotiate a subcontract with another provider at favorable enough rates to allow it to profit under the capitation arrangement? Most times the answer is no, which is why it is very important to identify in the capitation contract those services that the medical practice cannot perform.

Finally, identify the services that can be "carved out" of the capitation rate and paid on a fee for service basis. Generally these are subspecialty services, tertiary care services, infrequently performed services, or high-cost services or products. The following are a few examples of services that have been carved out of a capitation rate and paid on an FFS basis:

Cardiology: Nuclear medicine services.

Urology: Cancer-related drugs.

Ear, Nose, and Throat: Total parotidectomy with facial nerve dissection and a radical maxillectomy with orbital exenteration.

Otology: Surgery for cerebellopontine angle abnormalities.

Ophthalmology: Ocular and orbital implants.

Service Area

It is important to define the relevant service area in the capitation contract. Service area is important because the medical practice will have to render services to patients within this defined area and also determine if it can cover the hospitals included in the service area and whether "out of area" services are included within the capitation rate. Generally, a service area is defined by zip code or by hospital coverage. The contract itself should list these zip codes or hospitals by name. If it does not, you must make sure that it does. The following is a sample contract provision.

> *SERVICE AREA—ABC HMO's Service Area for its Medicare line of business includes those counties or portions of counties in which ABC HMO is under contract with the Health Care Financing Administration, Department of Health and Human Services, to provide services as a health maintenance organization to Medicare beneficiaries. ABC HMO's Service Area for its Commercial line of business includes those counties or portions of counties in which ABC HMO is licensed to provide services as a health maintenance organization by the State of Texas that are described in Attachment B.*

The practice must make sure that it can cover (and service patients at) the hospitals that are included within the service area. If it cannot, the practice runs the risk of having to pay the physicians who actually treat a capitated patient at the non-covered hospital.

Here is a simple example: Suppose a two-doctor cardiology group accepts a capitated contract that covers a service area that includes two hospitals that are geographically close to one another. The group has an office on one hospital campus but does not at the other; however the group is on the active medical staff at the other hospital.

Suppose one doctor is treating patients in the office one day and the other is in surgery. During that day, an ambulance takes a heart attack patient (who is on the capitated health plan) to the emergency room at the other hospital. The two doctors are unable to get to the emergency room, so the ER physician contacts another cardiologist for treatment. This cardiologist is obviously not part of the capitated contract. Since the two-doctor group is responsible for its capitated patients within the service area, it is financially responsible to pay the cardiologist who actually treated the patient, usually at that doctor's full fee. That's why it's important to make sure a medical practice can cover all of the hospitals in the defined service area if the capitation contract makes it responsible for such coverage.

As mentioned above, a practice is only responsible for rendering service to patients within the defined service area. But what happens if one of its capitated patients is treated outside of this service area? Is the practice responsible for these services or is somebody else? The answer depends on what the capitated contract says about "out-of-area" services. This is usually mentioned in the Service Obligation portion of the contract that was discussed previously.

> ■ **Practice Point:** You should never ever accept financial responsibility for "out-of-area" services in a capitated contract.

If services are rendered out of area and the practice is responsible for these services, then it must pay the doctors of the same medical specialty who treated the patient. Here is another simple example: A cardiology group accepts responsibility for out-of-area services. Erin Granberry goes out-of-town to visit relatives and unfortunately has a heart attack. The cardiology group is financially responsible for paying for any out of town services rendered to Erin that are listed in the Service Obligation section of its own capitated contract with the payor. All of these services will usually have to be paid at the treating physician's full commercial fee schedule. This shows how the economics of a capitated arrangement can get destroyed by accepting as included in the capitation payment responsibility for services outside of the defined service area.

Minimum Enrollment

How many capitated patients does a practice need in order for it to be able to be profitable? One part of the answer obviously depends on the amount of the capitation rate that is negotiated and accepted by the medical practice. The smaller the cap payment, the more patients that are needed to be profitable and vice versa. However, in general, a primary-care practice needs to receive capitation for at least between 500 and 1,000 enrollees and a specialty practice needs at least 7,500 to 10,000 patients. Again, the actual number will be dependent on the capitation rate that is accepted by the medical practice.

As such, it is often a good idea to negotiate a minimum enrollment number that must be met before the capitation payment becomes effective. The following is an example.

> After eight hundred (800) Members have been assigned to provider under the ABC Care Commercial Health Plan, Physician shall be paid Capitation Compensation for all Members in the ABC Care Commercial Health Plan assigned to Physician in the amount of One and 54/100 Dollars ($1.54) per Member per month in full consideration for all Medical Services performed by Physician for such Members. Capitation Compensation will begin the month immediately succeeding the month in which eight hundred (800) Members are assigned to provider under the ABC Care Commercial Health Plan. Such Capitation Compensation is for all services rendered by Physician, including drugs and supplies.

This is especially true for surgical practices. In the beginning of a capitation contract, it does not take that many surgeries to occur early to severely impact the profitability of the capitation arrangement. If a minimum enrollment provision cannot be negotiated into the agreement, then you must attempt to negotiate internal stop-loss protection as will be discussed later on in this section on nonfinancial capitation issues.

Termination

The following is a typical termination provision in a capitated contract.

> This Agreement may be terminated by either party at any time without cause upon at least ninety (90) days' prior written notice to the other party.

Keep in mind to ask yourself when this time period should be lengthened. As a medical practice continues its relationship with a payor that pays it on a capitated basis, the percentage of revenues the practice derives from this payor should increase. For some practices, the capitated revenues received from a payor could become very significant and, as such, end up representing a large percentage of the practice's total overall revenues. This is the time to renegotiate the contract to increase the termination notice requirement.

If a payor's capitated revenues are significant, the practice will need time to address how to replace this revenue should the payor ever decide to terminate the arrangement. Otherwise, the physicians risk a loss of compensation if the practice cannot replace this revenue somehow. Keep in mind, however, increasing the termination notice is a two-edged sword—the practice is also bound by this notice period even though it may want out of the contract some time in the future.

Finally, make sure the contract allows a "cure" of a breach before it can be terminated (i.e., the reason for the termination can be fixed first). This protects the practice from what might appear to be an involuntary termination. The following is an example.

> *This Agreement may be terminated at any time by either party upon at least thirty (30) days' prior written notice of such termination to the other party upon default or breach by such party of one or more of its obligations hereunder, unless such default or breach is cured within thirty (30) days of the notice of termination.*

Payor's Ability to Change Capitation Rate

If left unaddressed, a payor could have the ability to change the capitation rate in the middle of the contract. We have seen payors do this many times, often to the detriment of the medical practice. For example, one payor was paying $1.10 PMPM (per member, per month) to a specialty practice and dropped the capitation rate to $.87 after eight months into the contract. After monitoring the situation, it turned out the payor was paying more in capitation payments than the related utilization warranted in their opinion. The medical practice was offered a "take it or leave it" proposition. In another situation, a payor eliminated the capitation payment arrangement altogether and started paying the medical practice on a fee for service basis in the middle of the third year of the capitation arrangement.

Using actual utilization, most payors will conduct an annual review of their capitated relationships and during this review process compare what they paid out in capitation in relation to "what they would have paid out" if the medical practice had been paid on a discounted fee for service basis (e.g., 130 percent of current Medicare rates). In the example previously mentioned, a payor found out it would have paid a lot less if the practice were paid on discounted FFS, so it changed how the practice was going to get paid in the future. Keep in mind one of the problems related to capitation from the payor side is that a payor could "give away profit" if utilization is less than expected, which is what happened in this example. By making the practice convert to an FFS payment system, the practice lost over $200,000 in actual cash flow.

Therefore, to protect the practice, consider adding a provision that states that the payor cannot change the rate before the end of the contract year or term without the written consent of the medical practice or adding a provision that states that the payor can only change the rate within 30 days before the end of the contract year or term. Like the termination provision previously mentioned, locking in a date is also a double-edged sword in that the ability or inability to change the capitation rate also applies to the medical practice itself. If the medical practice is losing money and wants to change the rate, it too must wait until the prescribed time period, unless of course it threatens or actually does terminate the contract arrangement as a way to force the payor to change the rate in the middle of the contract year or term.

Ability to Close the Practice to New Patients

This provision mainly applies to primary-care practices but can apply to other medical practices as well. There may come a time when a practice is "overrun" by patients of a particular plan in which it is capitated. In other words, the primary-care practice is seeing a significant number of the patients who have enrolled in the health plan. If the capitation rate is a good one, this is not necessarily a bad thing since the contract arrangement should be profitable as patients are added and the related utilization risk is spread out over a large patient base. However, this situation could be an economic disaster if the capitation rate is a bad one and/or utilization is much higher than expected. In a situation where the practice does not want to terminate the contract or cannot get the payor to change the capitation rate, the practice needs the ability to cut itself off from accepting any new patients. Therefore, be sure a clause is inserted into the agreement allowing the practice to do this with the appropriate written notice to the payor. The following is an example.

> **New Members.** *With good cause acceptable to Company, a Primary Care Physician may decline to accept new Members as patients (excluding persons already in his or her practice who become Members) by providing at least ninety (90) days prior written notice to Company, provided, however, that each office where a Primary Care Physician practices shall accept a minimum of two hundred fifty (250) Members to the extent that two hundred fifty (250) Members select or are assigned to said office. Nothing in this Agreement is intended to or shall be deemed to guarantee the selection or assignment of two hundred fifty (250) Members to such office. After a Primary Care Physician office has notified Company that said office will accept no additional Members, said office shall not accept as patients additional members from other managed care organizations. Any request for a re-opening of said office for the enrollment of additional Members must have the prior approval of the applicable peer review committee.*

Retroactive Adjustments or Disenrollments

When a medical practice is paid capitation, the capitation check is based upon the capitation rate times the number of eligible members, usually at the beginning of the month. However, there are times when an employee leaves a company and the actual recording of the termination by the payor (i.e., removal from the eligibility list) does not occur for months later. This can happen when a large employer delays getting this information to the payor and/or the payor itself delays deleting the terminated employee from the eligibility list.

When this delay occurs, the medical practice is receiving a capitation payment for the terminated employee for a number of subsequent months. When the employee is finally removed from the eligibility list, the payor will then conduct a review to determine if capitation was overpaid to the medical practice for this particular person. If so, it will then deduct the overpayment from the practice's next capitation check. This is typically called a "retroactive adjustment." Therefore, be sure the contract addresses the following issues:

1. Limit the time period a payor can go back and take away capitation from the medical practice. *A medical practice should not be penalized for the administrative inefficiencies and errors by a payor. Therefore, the contract should attempt to limit the time period a payor can go back and take away capitation, which is usually 90 to 120 days. This is the time period from when the employee left employment to the date he or she was removed from the eligibility list. Or, the contract can state the payor only has only 60 days from the date of termination to identify an employee as ineligible and make the appropriate capitation adjustment.*

   ■ **Practice Point:** Any medical practice receiving a capitation check must also receive an eligibility list with the check, either on paper or by electronic access. Without the list, how can the practice review and audit the retroactive adjustments? This is very important obviously for any practice that receives a significant capitation check each month from a single payor.

2. Ability for the practice to bill an ineligible patient on a fee for service basis. *If a patient is declared ineligible and related past capitation monies are taken away, you must make sure the practice has the legal right to bill the patient for these services. Some contracts actually fail to address this issue.*

The following is a sample contract provision regarding billing members.

Nothing in this section is intended to prohibit or restrict Group from billing individuals who were not Members at the time that services were rendered.

The previous section addressed the instance of a payor taking away capitation payment for a disenrolled employee. What happens in the case where a person becomes enrolled in the health plan but the practice does not receive its appropriate amount of capitation payment for a period of time?

You would think this should not be a problem for primary-care practices because a new employee must "designate" his or her primary-care physician at the time of enrollment. This is what the primary-care practice's capitation rate will be based on; however, there have been instances where a person designated a primary-care physician but the related capitation payment was not adjusted. Therefore, not only does this issue apply to specialty practices that are capitated, but it could apply to primary-care practices as well.

How does a medical practice know that it has received "all" of the capitated payment for a particular patient? In other words, how does a practice know that it has received all of the capitation payment it is entitled to after a new patient became enrolled? The answer to this question requires a medical practice to pay strict attention when a new "capitated" patient arrives at the office for his or her first appointment:

1. Can the medical practice immediately identify a capitated patient with a specific health plan? The answer must be "yes!"

2. Next, the practice must make a copy of the new patient's insurance card, which should state when the practice became eligible on the health plan.

3. Next, the practice needs to trace the eligibility date to the eligibility lists it has received or has access to from the health plan.

   ■ **Practice Point:** Do not throw away eligibility lists if received on paper.

Next, when a patient is first treated in the office, see if the patient is on the eligibility lists corresponding to the date shown on the insurance card; if not on the list(s), the practice did not receive the related capitation payments. The practice then should appeal to the payor for these additional payments.

Building Internal Stop-Loss Protection into the Contract

If you are offered a capitated rate, say $1.00 PMPM, how do you know this is a "good" rate? In other words, how do you know this is a rate the medical practice can expect a reasonable economic gain from? Is this a rate that is guaranteed to lose the practice money? Unfortunately many practices around the country accept a capitation rate blindly and eventually end up realizing it was not worth getting "twenty cents on the dollar." This is why any capitation proposal must be closely scrutinized and great care must be exercised before a medical practice accepts any such contract.

The reality is that most practices have absolutely no idea whether the capitation rate it is being offered is reasonable or not. Of course there are national statistics, but this has no relation to the utilization that is unique to each service area and medical specialty that capitation rates are built upon. Comparing a rate to statistical information is a good first step, but by no means is it the final step. This is why it is so important to analyze the capitation rate that is offered, as will be explained in the section on "Capitation Financial Issues," further on in this chapter.

If you are ever unsure whether or not the capitation rate is reasonable, then you must build into the contract economic protection for the medical practice. While this may appear to be a financial issue, it is discussed here because of its importance as a legal provision to the capitation contract. This type of protection is called "stop-loss" protection; consider it a form of insurance in case the economics of the arrangement do not turn out like you want it to (i.e., you lose money on the contract!). This is not like stop-loss or reinsurance protection, or an IPA or other entity accepting full risk capitation. Reinsurance is a form of insurance for medical practices or IPAs that accept risk for other medical services that it cannot render; in other words other providers will bill the IPA or medical group for their own services under the capitation arrangement.

To build internal stop-loss into the capitation contract, base it on either a fee for service equivalent or utilization targets. The first is a fee for service equivalent and this type of stop-loss provision compares what the practice receives in capitation to an FFS target. For example, say a practice wants to guarantee itself at least Medicare rates in each year of the capitation contract. To do this, the practice would negotiate a provision to the contract that says that at the end of the contract year, the payor will take all of the utilization by the practice rendered to the eligible patients and multiply it by current Medicare rates. This total figure would then be compared to the capitation payments it received. If the capitation payments are less than the Medicare FFS equivalent, then the payor would pay the difference to the practice.

The other form of stop-loss is based on utilization targets. Remember that all capitation rates are based on actual or expected utilization. As such, this is an excellent way to build internal stop-loss into the contract. If the payor has prior utilization history on its enrollment population, then try to obtain this information and conduct the rate analysis as will be discussed later on in this chapter. You can then create a "floor" whereby if the actual PMPM, based on actual utilization, ends up higher than the rate that is offered to the practice, then the offered rate will change into the actual PMPM or some percentage thereof. Or, you can negotiate a provision whereby the payor reverts to an FFS arrangement if certain utilization targets are hit; the following is an example.

> *ABC HMO agrees to pay provider $1,700 for each obstetrical delivery when such deliveries exceed 24/1,000 enrollees in any one year of the contract.*

If utilization statistics cannot be obtained, the practice will be "flying in the dark" as it relates to the economics of the arrangement. This should be obvious by the discussion above. In this situation, obviously try to negotiate the back-end FFS equivalent. If this is unsuccessful, try negotiating a "look back" arrangement, whereby the payor will sit down with the practice after six to eight months and compare actual utilization to the capitation rate. This forum may allow for a change in the rate.

Capitation Financial Issues

The obvious financial issue is that any capitation rate that is offered to a medical practice must be reviewed and evaluated before the contract is accepted. If the rate cannot be analyzed, then remember to build in internal stop-loss protection as discussed previously.

A capitation rate can easily be analyzed if actual prior utilization for the practice's specialty can be obtained from the payor. However, you must keep the following in mind:

If utilization data are not made available to the medical practice, it must build internal stop-loss protection into its contract!

■ **Practice Point:** If a payor is unwilling to provide the practice with any utilization data, whether actual or budgeted, then consider this a RED FLAG. My experience in this situation says that most payors are trying to make money by offering a "low ball" capitation rate to the medical provider. They know that the actual PMPM is based on prior utilization; as such, they try to reduce their own health care costs by offering a lower PMPM the next year.

Analyzing the Capitation Rate

Assume that utilization data are available to the medical practice. The following discusses how to use this information to analyze the rate that is offered or if need be, to submit a bid for a capitation arrangement. The first step is to create a worksheet like the partial one below:

CPT CODE	PROC. DESCRIPTION	PROC. COST OR PRICE	ACTUAL UTILIZATION	USAGE RATE PER 1,000	PRICE RATE PER 1,000	PMPM RATE
33207	INSRT HRT PCMKR, VENTRICU	602.88	2.57	0.15	90.13	0.0075109
33208	INSERT PACEMAKER-2 WIRE	616.12	2.57	0.15	92.11	0.0076759
33210	INSERT, HEART ELECTRODE	227.44	3.43	0.20	45.34	0.0037781
33213	INSERT PULSE GEN - 2 CHAM	418.14	0.86	0.05	20.84	0.0017365
33233	PM GENERATOR REMOVAL	197.98	0.86	0.05	9.87	0.0008222
33249	INSRT/RPL CD/DF LEADS/GNTR	1028.96	0.86	0.05	51.28	0.0042731

The following describes how to prepare this analysis worksheet:

Procedure Price (or Practice Costs)   In this column, you will enter either the "cost" it takes to render the service or the target or procedure price. A discussion of how to calculate service costs will be provided later. However, instead of cost, you can insert any type of target price you wish. For example, you can calculate a Medicare equivalent PMPM simply by inserting the practice's current Medicare rates into the worksheet. Some practices want to know for example that a PMPM equivalent is based on 130 percent of current Medicare rates. Keep in mind that "price" generally has nothing to do with how much it "costs" to render a service. This is why you will want to enter the cost for each CPT code in this column instead of a target price.

Utilization Rate per the Payor   This column is the utilization obtained from the payor for a designated period of time. In the worksheet above, this utilization is for a 12-month period, but it can be for a lesser time period. (*Important Point:* Always be on the lookout for "dirty data." Many payors do not track data very well, believe it or not.) When obtaining payor utilization, it is very important for the services to be scanned and to search for commonly utilized services that do not appear on the list. The capitation calculation will be flawed if certain services are not included. In this situation, you will need to include these additional services on the worksheet.

Usage Rate per 1,000   The utilization obtained from the payor in the worksheet represented 17,200 enrollees. The next step in the worksheet is to convert the utilization to a per 1,000-member basis. The figures in this column were derived by using the following formula: (utilization rate × 1,000) ÷ 17,200.

Price Rate per 1,000 Members   Multiplying the usage rate per 1,000 members times the cost or target price derived the figures in this column. To reemphasize, you should at a minimum use "costs" instead of target price when you can. If so, you might title this column as "Service Cost per 1,000 Members."

PMPM Rate Estimate   The final step is to convert the "Price Rate or cost per 1,000 members" to a per member, per month figure. Do this by dividing the price rate by 12,000 since the utilization shown on the worksheet was for a 12-month period (i.e., 1,000/12,000 = 1/12). Once you have made these calculations, then add up all of the figures in this column for all services to arrive at a PMPM rate estimate. If the utilization was for a six-month period, the denominator in the calculation would have been 6,000 instead of 12,000.

How to Calculate Service "Costs" Instead of Target Price

As mentioned above, it is best to insert the "actual cost" it takes to render a service since price generally has little relation to what it costs to render the service. However, it is recommended that you at least calculate the worksheet using regular Medicare rates to find out if the payor is offering a capitation rate that is actually below what Medicare pays.

There are many good books and articles on cost accounting by CPT code. The most common cost accounting analysis is based on relative value units. The following is how to calculate costs per CPT code:

Using the medical practice's CPT frequency report, calculate the total RBRVS units for all of the services that were rendered by the practice. For each CPT code, multiply the service frequency by each RBRVS unit. This includes work, malpractice insurance, and overhead relative value units (RVUs), adjusted by each related geographic practice cost index (GPCI).

The following table is an example showing three services and then a total for all the CPT codes:

CPT Code	Description	Frequency	RVUs	Total RVU
10060		159	1.56	248.04
10061		10	3.10	31.00
11750		208	3.84	798.72
Total for all services and all CPT codes				9,913

Next, divide the total RBRVS units into total practice overhead, including physician compensation. This calculates an overhead dollar figure (cost multiplier) per RVU. For example, total overhead is $350,722. It is divided by total units calculated (9,913), which equals 35.38 (cost multiplier).

Keep in mind that total overhead in this calculation must include "normal" physician-owner compensation. This is because if you include "total" physician-owner compensation, it includes the "profit" taken out of the practice. Therefore, add back physician-owner compensation and then deduct normal physician-owner compensation based on current medical practice surveys. These surveys can be purchased from the Medical Group Management Association or the American Medical Group Practice Association.

Next, multiply the overhead cost multiplier calculated by total RVUs for each CPT code. This calculates a unit overhead cost for single occurrence for each CPT code. The following is an example:

CPT Code	Description	RVUs	Cost Multiplier	Cost/ Occurrence
10060		1.56	35.38	55.19
10061		3.10	35.38	109.68
11750		3.84	35.38	135.86

Evaluating the Rate

On an ongoing basis, review and analyze the capitation arrangement. The last thing you want to have happen is to wait 12 months and find out that the practice received twenty cents on the dollar (i.e., enrollment practice utilization at the regular practice fee schedule compared to the capitation payments that were received). Therefore, the practice must compare the capitation payments it receives against an FFS comparison. This comparison could be again the practice's normal commercial fee schedule or a percentage of desired RBRVS reimbursement. If the percentage is low, either the rate is inadequate and/or utilization has been excessive. To avoid further losses, the practice must attempt to renegotiate the capitation rate and/or internal stop-loss provisions.

How to Develop a Capitation Term Sheet

The time will come when a practice or other similar delivery system will need to submit some form of capitation proposal to a managed-care plan. This usually will occur when a payor has begun discussions with a medical practice or other health care provider before issuing the Request for Proposal. One of the simplest and most useful ways to continue the dialogue is to prepare and submit a Capitation Term Sheet. This document basically lays out all of the financial and nonfinancial terms of a proposed capitation relationship.

The following example shows the term sheet prepared by an ENT practice that was asked to submit a proposal to an HMO. Pay strict attention to each contracting category; these categories are usually the same for almost all capitation agreements.

■ **Practice Point:** This document can also be used as an analysis tool for almost any capitation contract. Use each category to assess the contract. It would even be a good idea to create a checklist using these categories and refer to it when analyzing capitation agreements.

Capitation Contract Term Sheet Example

[Date]
Mr. Paul McBride
ABC Health Maintenance Organization
[Address]
[City, State, Zip]
Re: Ear, Nose & Throat Contract Proposal—ENT Affiliates

Dear Paul:

The following is ENT Affiliates' proposal to ABC Health Maintenance Organization for an exclusive ENT (otolaryngology) contracting relationship. I attempted to respond to the categories I feel will comprise most of the contract. These proposed terms are to be used to form the basis of a final contract between ABC Health Maintenance Organization and the practice. I am sure we will need to discuss them further in order to arrive at a final contract with which everyone is comfortable.

Contract Proposal

Global Exclusivity

Nothing contained in the agreement shall preclude the physicians from participating in or contracting with any other health care provider organization, managed care plan, health maintenance organization, insurer, employer, or any other third-party payor, or directly with any payor.

In-Area vs. Out-of-Area Coverage

The practice will be responsible for all in-area coverage but out-of-area coverage will be excluded from the practice's capitated rate.

Evaluation and Management Services

All evaluation and management services applicable to otolaryngology care will be included in the capitation rate we propose. This includes the following: Office Visits, Consults, Hospital Care, Nursing Facility Care, Phone Advice, and Emergency Care.

Drugs—In Office

The practice of ENT is dependent on the pharmacist for its prescribed pharmaceutical therapy. Any prescribed drugs would be excluded from our proposed capitation rate. For that reason, we need to agree on a pharmaceutical source to which we will refer the patient, or on a price for specific drugs or items dispensed in the office. The physicians in turn will bill ABC Health Maintenance Organization for specifically identified items on an agreed fee-for-service basis. If prescriptions requiring drugs must be referred to an independent pharmacy contracted with ABC Health Maintenance Organization, such providers will not bill ENT Affiliates and ENT Affiliates will not be responsible for the payment of these costs.

All in-office drugs incidental to the delivery of ENT services will be included in the capitation rate.

Supplies—In Office

Any disposable supplies used during the treatment in a participating practice site will be included in the capitation rate.

Diagnostics/Laboratory

Any diagnostic or laboratory service performed in the office shall be included in the capitation rate. However, if these tests must be referred to an independent laboratory contracted with Healthsource, such providers will not bill ENT Affiliates and ENT Affiliates will not be responsible for the payment of these costs.

Special Procedures & Diagnostics Related to ENT

Audiological studies and testing (professional component only) are integral to the practice of otolaryngology and will be considered to be part of the capitated contract. The practice would like to ensure that a proper protocol is followed before the patients' referral for such procedures. If a patient should need a hearing aid, the hearing aid evaluation and the cost of the hearing aids will be excluded from the capitation rate.

Neuro-otological vestibular studies (balance loss profiles), voice studies, specialized otology procedures (i.e., cochlear implants), speech/hearing therapy, allergy testing and immunotherapy, facial plastics, and head and neck surgeries for cancer are related to, but not integral to, the practice of otolaryngology and will be excluded from the capitated rate.

ENG and ABR studies will be excluded from the capitation rate.

Procedures—In-Office and In-Facility (Inpatient)

An agreed-upon list of in-office and inpatient procedures will be in-cluded in the capitation rate, and the list will be considered part of the capitation contract. However, tertiary-related services will be ex-cluded. A partial list of some of these exclusions is attached to this letter. ABC Health Maintenance Organization and practice members will work together to make a complete list of these specialized ser-vices the group will contract for outside of the capitation rate. ABC Health Maintenance Organization will be responsible for the costs that are excluded from the capitation rate. Likewise, artificial devices and prosthetics will be carved out until a good utilization history can be captured and priced.

Otolaryngology services related to cochlear implants shall also be excluded from the capitation rate.

Rates

Based upon the utilization data provided to the practice, we pro-pose a capitation rate of $1.02 per member, per month. Until we can gather specific utilization data on our group for one complete year, ABC Health Maintenance Organization will guarantee the prac-tice in the first year of the contract reimbursement equal to current Medicare rates. At the end of the initial 12-month period, the prac-tice will calculate its utilization at current Medicare rates. Healthsource will verify this calculation and agree to pay immedi-ately to the practice the difference between this fee-for-service (FFS) calculation and actual capitation payments made during the same time period.

The proposed capitation rate excludes an allowance for ABC Health Maintenance Organization's transference of certain of its administra-tion costs to the practice. If ABC Health Maintenance Organization intends to transfer claims adjudication and all other contract admin-istration functions to the practice, the proposed capitation rate will be $1.08 cents per member, per month.

After one year, the agreed-upon, first-year capitation rate will be re-viewed by all parties.

Bonus

The practice will be eligible for a bonus if certain utilization targets are met and maintained. This can be discussed in greater detail at a later time.

Reimbursement

As mentioned above, we propose to carve out specific services that will be reimbursed on a fee-for-service basis. In addition to the services listed above, ABC Health Maintenance Organization and practice can work together to create a specific list of carve-out services.

We propose the following FFS reimbursement:

130 percent Current Medicare Rates for E&M Services

150 percent Current Medicare Rates for all Other Services

These rate arrangements will be fixed and cannot change unless agreed upon by both parties.

Noncovered services will be the final responsibility of the patient and will be paid at the physicians' current practice rates.

Contract Term

The proposed contract term is for three years.

Quality Assurance/Utilization Management

The practice agrees to work with ABC Health Maintenance Organization on quality assurance and utilization programs related specifically to otolaryngology care. This includes the development of protocols for the primary-care physicians contracted with Healthsource.

Operations

The practice will be responsible for the following:

1. *Approval (authorization) of initial referral to one of the participating physicians*
2. *Authorization/precertification of additional service requests (e.g., surgeries and testing) by the participating physicians*
3. *Review of submitted charges before a claim is paid*
4. *Cash administration*
5. *ENT Affiliates' own provider fee schedules and contract*

Conclusion

As a reminder, contract terms that are tentatively agreed upon will have to be ratified by the practice before we can execute a final agreement.

The physicians are excited about this contracting opportunity and the development of a win-win relationship with ABC Health Mainte-

nance Organization and its patients. By working together, I am sure we can develop a contract that will be mutually beneficial to all parties.

I look forward to working with you on this project.

Very truly yours,

Specialist Capitation Schedule Exclusion List for HMO Plans for Otolaryngology

The Capitation amounts listed in the contract will exclude the following services and procedures that may be performed by some of the practices' contracted providers.

- Excision tumor of ear and mastoid, unless benign
- Partial temporal bone resection
- Radical temporal bone resection
- Excision pinna and neck dissection
- Total parotidectomy with facial nerve dissection
- Total parotidectomy without nerve graft
- Total parotidectomy with nerve graft
- Partial maxillectomy
- Total maxillectomy
- Radical maxillectomy with orbital exenteration
- Abbe-Estlander flap
- Partial glossectomy
- Partial mandibulectomy
- Composite resection—primary and tumor with RND
- Radical neck dissection
- Extended radical neck dissection (transsternal mediastinal dissection)
- Diverticulectomy (cervical)
- Subtotal laryngectomy
- Thyrotomy (laryngectomy)
- Supraglottic laryngectomy
- Hemilaryngectomy
- Wide field laryngectomy
- Total laryngectomy with neck dissection

- *Cervical esophagectomy with neck dissection*
- *Tracheal resection with repair*
- *Major vessel grafting*
- *Arterial infusion procedure*
- *Resection acoustic neuroma (translabyrinthine, middle cranial fossa, etc.)*
- *VII Nerve section via middle fossa*
- *Reconstruction external ear*
- *Otoplasty*
- *Rhinoplasty*
- *Laryngoplasty*
- *Tracheoplasty*
- *Mentoplasty*
- *Rhytidectomy*
- *Blepharoplasty*
- *Pedicle flap procedures*
- *Implants (including chest, neck, shoulder, forehead, scalp, cheek)*
- *Facial sling procedures*
- *Prognathism correction*
- *Retrognathism correction*
- *Cleft lip repair*
- *Cleft palate repair*
- *Mediastinoscopy*
- *Dacryocystorhinostomy*
- *Hypophysectomy*
- *Allergy testing and immuno-therapy*
- *Cochlear implants and* all related *pre/post testing procedures*
- *All neuro-otology services*
- *Hearing aid dispensing*

Keys to Success Under Capitation

Whether the physician is presently receiving revenue under a capitation arrangement or is evaluating a capitation contract, he or she must remember the real keys to profiting under this type of payment system:

- Rate evaluation
- Service carve-out
- Communication
- Practice efficiency

Use RBRVS and HMO utilization statistics to evaluate a capitated rate. The physician should make sure that he or she will be compensated adequately. If necessary, hire an actuary. The physician should profit financially by carving out as many services as possible from the capitated rate. These are services the physician could bill on a fee-for-service basis. For example, family practitioners have been successfully carving out well-woman exams from their capitated rate. Ophthalmologists carve out the cost of inocular lenses from their capitated rate. Oncologists carve out the cost of certain expensive drugs. Primary-care physicians carve out certain services related to the treatment of HIV patients. The physician should review his service list and negotiate a carve-out of his or her own. If the service is not on the responsibility grid, the physician should bill it as a fee-for-service charge.

Proper communication can also increase profitability under a capitation contract. The physician should communicate with his or her patients. A practice makes more profit under capitation when it renders fewer services to capitated patients. Many patients, however, especially Medicare patients, tend to use physicians more when they switch to an HMO plan. This is especially the case for patients whose plans do not require a patient co-payment or deductible. Therefore, patients must be educated about when to come to the physician. The office manager or front-desk person should explain which services are included, when to make a phone call instead of a visit, and so on. The physician wants to avoid the situation in which the patient comes into the office with a sore joint and says, "By the way, Doctor, while I'm here can you . . . ."

Good communication is also needed between specialist physicians and their primary-care counterparts. Specialists who receive capitated payments must make sure that the primary-care physicians are rendering the services they are getting paid to render within their own capitated rate. Profitability gets reduced when physicians cannot switch from a fee-for-service mentality to a capitation mentality. Primary-care physicians cannot, nor should they, send patients to specialists without proper consideration.

Finally, a medical office must be efficient to profit under capitation. Practices must begin looking at the feasibility of using physician extenders, such as physician assistants and nurse practitioners. The practice must become efficient in the process of health care delivery, with both capitated patients and other patients. Excess time could be spent on capitated patients at the expense of other fee-for-service patients. This situation ends up doubly impacting practice profitability.

Utilization

One definite way a practice can succeed under a capitated arrangement is to make sure that its utilization is controlled. The first step is to monitor clinical behavior. Primary physicians must control referrals to the specialists and must watch the use of ancillary services. The goal for primary-care physicians is to enhance overall profitability so that their own capitation rate will be increased, or so they will receive periodic bonuses as a direct result of good utilization management. Physician specialists must make sure that the primary-care physicians are not carelessly referring patients to them. Primary-care physicians are usually compensated very well to manage care. If they are not managing their practice well, the specialist should identify these patterns and communicate them back to the HMO. Failure to manage care by primary-care physicians is what causes specialists to lose significant revenues in a capitated environment.

One way specialists can enhance their own profitability is to develop clinical protocols for the primary-care physicians. By working with primary-care physicians, the specialists can show them how to manage certain clinical situations themselves before a referral has to be made to the specialist.

Gathering Data

It is a challenge for many medical practices to gather the information necessary to prove to a third-party payor that the practice is indeed cost effective. A practice may have to gather utilization and outcomes data, usually by clinical episode or diagnosis code. This type of information will be critical when competing for contracts and can also be extremely valuable in the negotiation and renegotiation of managed care rates.

For example, an OB/GYN group wanted to negotiate rates with a managed-care plan. The plan armed itself with the following limited practice data: (1) C-section rates, (2) VBAC rates, (3) average length of stay in a hospital, (4) rate of surgical complications, and (5) length of stay and complication rates for laparoscopic hysterectomies. At the same time, the OB/GYN group was able to obtain national utilization data for its specialty. The data proved that the group beat the national average in every category. Obviously, this is an enviable situation for a medical practice because it can demonstrate, with actual statistics, that it is a cost-effective provider. In this situation, the managed-care plan will probably listen to proposed changes to the group's reimbursement schedule. Also, it is doubtful that this group will ever be removed from the plan, because of its cost-effective patient care.

As managed care grows, the need for and analysis of utilization and outcomes data becomes more and more important. A practice may need to buy an expansive computer system. This need will obviously be dictated by a particular market. This is why the practice and its advisors must keep up-to-date about the managed-care movement in the physician's service area. One reason physicians are continuing their affiliation activities is so that they can have access to this type of data in the future. For example, one advantage of practice mergers is the fact that a group can acquire a more expansive management information system. This is a more cost-effective way of upgrading a system. Other practices are affiliating with management-service organizations in order to have access to utilization and cost information.

Managed-care rates can be negotiated or renegotiated with supportable utilization and outcomes information. If practices want to bid on and acquire managed-care contracts, they will have to provide this information. If physicians want to remain on managed-care panels, they must pay strict attention to utilization and outcomes data. The data cannot be ignored.

Sample Provider Utilization Reports

By CPT code

CPT Code	# of Patients	Total Charges	Avg. Chg. per Patient	# of Visits	Avg. Chg. per Visit
99212	5	280	56	11	25.45
99070	1	15	15	1	15.00
99214	6	330	55	4	82.50
Total	12	625	52.08	16	39.06

By diagnosis code

ICD-10 Code	# of Patients	Total Charges	Avg. Chg. per Patient	# of Visits	Avg. Chg. per Visit
386.02	30	2395.00	79.83	40	59.88
V76.1	11	1060.00	96.36	11	96.36
558.9	18	8019.84	445.55	19	422.10

For hospital services

DRG Number	Description	Total # of Cases	Avg. Length of Stay	Avg. Charge per Case (hospital)
083	Major Chest Trauma	1	8.0	25,070
148	Major Small/ Large Bowel	2	7.0	14,307

After the Contract Is Signed

After a physician becomes a plan provider, monitor the office's relationship with the plan, both financially and nonfinancially. This is especially necessary for those physicians who are forced to sign with managed-care plans because of the increase in managed-care participation by the employers in the physician's practice area.

Daily Operations

After a managed-care contract is signed, you will need to make sure that the office staff handles these payors and their patients correctly. You also will need to make sure that the office continues to operate efficiently. As managed care continues to grow, many medical offices may become inefficient, mainly because of all of the administrative burdens placed on them by managed care. Practices may lose revenues as a result of these inefficiencies. After signing managed-care agreements, you will need to monitor practice compliance. First, the office manager should place all of the managed-care information in notebooks for easy access so that he or she can effectively monitor these relationships. For each managed-care payor, the notebook should contain the following:

- A copy of the executed managed-care contract
- Reimbursement schedule for the practice's most commonly utilized services
- Any of the payor's specialized forms, such as provider referral forms and patient authorization forms

Once the office manager has gathered this information, the manager should create a managed-care reference chart. The chart summarizes the major requirements of the practice's managed-care plans. This chart can be used by the practice's personnel to keep up on all of the administrative requirements of the plans, which should help reduce mistakes within the office and maintain its revenues. The following is an example of a reference chart:

Plan Name	Effective Date	Co-Payment	In-Network Laboratory	In-Network Hospitals	In-Network Radiology	Referral Form Required?	Time Limit to File Claims

On an ongoing basis, also compare the practice's managed-care reimbursements to the agreed-upon reimbursement schedules included in the managed-care notebook. Payors make mistakes reimbursing providers, more often than physicians realize. What was approved for payment may be different from the reimbursement schedule. This is why the practice manager or its CPA should monitor managed-care reimbursements. Therefore, each week take a sample of managed-care EOBs and compare the reimbursement to the amount shown on the reimbursement sheet in the managed-care notebook. Differences should be appealed immediately by the office manager.

Continued Participation

Determine whether it makes sense for the practice to continue participating in the managed-care plan by answering the following questions. This assessment should be done annually.

- Is the volume of patients higher than expected? If yes, evaluate the potential effects on other aspects of the practice. Determine if the practice's payor mix is shifting dramatically to managed care.
- Is the volume of patients too small to warrant continued participation in the plan?
- Review the PPO reimbursements and assess the level of fee discounts. Are such discounts acceptable to the practice?
- If applicable, is the withhold reasonable? If not, and the practice has not received any reimbursement of the withhold, take this into account when evaluating the fee discounts.
- Assess any administrative burdens the plan places on the practice. Do these burdens interrupt the efficiency of the practice?
- Is the plan adding competing physicians in the practice's service area? If so, assess the potential impact on the practice's future revenue.
- Evaluate the profit or loss on capitated contracts.
- Evaluate how quickly the plan pays the claims submitted by the practice.

The 20 Percent Rule

Each year the practice must conduct a study of the so-called "20 percent rule." No more than 20 percent of the practice's total managed-care revenue should come from one managed-care plan; if it does, the practice may be at risk financially.

Example of a Violation of the 20 Percent Rule

At the end of a year, Dr. Gralitzer's practice collected $500,000 in patient revenue. Of this total, 40 percent ($200,000) of the revenue came from managed-care plans. Of the $200,000 in managed-care revenue, half came from one single plan (20 percent of the total revenue).

In the example, Dr. Gralitzer must assess whether his practice can afford to lose $100,000 of revenue (20 percent of the total) if he is removed as a provider from the plan. Many physicians may not realize that a substantial amount of their revenue is at risk if one managed-care contract is terminated. Remember that most managed-care contracts state that the physician's contract can be terminated with only 90 days' notice. Contracts can be terminated for a variety of reasons, the most common being a dispute over a utilization issue or the employers in an area switching between PPO and HMO plans.

If it appears that the practice may be at financial risk after performing the year-end analysis, consider taking the following actions:

1. Assess the possibility of the physician's contract being terminated. Meet with plan representatives to determine if the plan is satisfied with the physician. Also, monitor the growth of HMO market share in the practice area.

2. Attempt to reduce the percentage of revenue coming from one plan. You could do this by shifting the mix of patients away from the plan. This often requires the development of a marketing plan that specifically targets other types of payors and insurance plans.

3. Determine if the physician has any leverage with the managed-care plan. While the 20 percent rule has a definite down side, it also has a positive side: leverage. A practice that is at

financial risk because of the 20 percent rule is treating a good number of patients from one plan. If the plan is happy with the physician, the last thing it wants is for the physician to terminate the contract voluntarily. If the physician terminates, his or her patients will be forced to seek out other physicians. In many cases, these patients will complain to their employers. The employers, in turn, may complain to the plan on behalf of their disgruntled employees. Thus, a physician who treats many patients from one single plan may have the opportunity to renegotiate the terms of the managed-care contract. At a minimum, the physician may be able to renegotiate a higher reimbursement from the managed-care plan. The best way to begin the renegotiation process is to meet with the provider representative or the local plan administrator and ask for a specific increase in reimbursement or a specific change in contract terms.

■ **Practice Point:** When practices treat many patients from a particular managed-care plan, they often forget the potential impact of a termination of the contract. If a particular contract is terminated, a practice could lose a significant amount of revenue. This is why the 20 percent rule is so important. Therefore, if a particular managed-care plan represents a major portion of the practice's revenue stream, it is imperative for a practice to renegotiate the termination time period in the contract. For example, if a payor represents a major revenue source, it is always a good idea to try to extend this time period. For example, you may need to extend out the normal 90-day termination notice period to, say, 180 days or even one year. This is a negotiable issue. If for some reason the contract is ever terminated, this extended time period should allow the group time to replace the lost revenue stream.

Scoring the Health Plans

Once a managed-care plan is executed, it is a good idea to monitor the performance of the health plans the practice participates in. While much emphasis is placed on reimbursement for obvious reasons, there are numerous other issues that affect the daily operations of the practice. The following is a sample of a portion of a

Health Plan Scorecard that is included with this book. This information will be useful if the practice needs to (1) address specific issues with the health plan or (2) assess whether or not to continue its participation with the plan in the future.

Scoring

(PP) Promptness of Payments: Pays claims promptly, without unreasonable information requests or re-submissions.

(A) Accessibility: Able to reach a provider relations or customer service representative in a reasonable period of time.

(C) Competence: Provider relations is able to provide timely, definitive answers to questions.

(N) Network: Referral panel is not restrictive (selection of participating physicians and hospitals).

(MM) Medical Management: The plan has a user-friendly utilization management program (efficient system for obtaining referrals, authorizations, pre-certifications, etc.).

Plan Name	PP	A	C	N	MM
Accountable Health Plan PPO					
Aetna Managed Choice PPO, POS, and HMO					
Affordable Health Care (First Health)					
Affiliated Health Plan (Unicare PPO)					

What to Do If the Practice Is Deselected

In many areas of the country, managed-care health policy premiums sold to employers continue to remain competitive. However, health care costs continue to increase in many of these markets. In order to maintain profitability, these health plans have changed their philosophy toward provider reimbursement and network development.

Since the control of provider utilization has been difficult, payors are reducing their costs in these competitive areas by reducing their payments to health care providers. For example, many payors are beginning to use the Medicare RBRVS payment methodology to pay physicians, resulting in significant payment reductions for surgical care and other services. This has led to an explosion in physician affiliations, such as IPAs and practice mergers.

Traditionally, the focus of network development was to have as broad a provider network as possible without diluting the health plan's leverage to secure favorable rates from employers. Easy access to medical physicians at one time was the rule. Now, because of a competitive payor environment and because health consumers are beginning to get used to having fewer provider choices, health plans have begun to pare down their network in order to achieve greater cost savings. To reduce health care costs, payors therefore have begun the process of weeding out the physicians they feel overutilize medical services. These payors feel this will allow them to monitor and control a fewer number of providers, which in turn should help achieve long-term profitability. Also, accreditation services like the National Committee on Quality Assurance (NCQA) and the Joint Commission on Accreditation of Healthcare Organizations (JCAHO) have established guidelines requiring participating plans to evaluate and manage their provider networks more closely.

In order to bring about this change, health plans have become aggressive in canceling provider agreements. This process is known in the industry as "deselection." When a payor looks at its physicians' utilization history at a time when it wants to reduce its service costs, those physicians who are perceived to overutilize services are generally targeted for deselection. Generally, health plans look at provider utilization annually but many review utilization on an ongoing basis throughout the year. On page 19.68 is a sample report used by one payor to compare utilization among a group of otolaryngological physicians.

In this example the health plan, which was a payor with significant market share in the service area, targeted one of the physicians for deselection because the physician performed more surgeries per visit than the other ENT physicians on the panel. In other words, the physician was perceived as being "surgery happy."

As a result, the physician indeed received a letter from the health plan terminating his provider agreement. If deselected, this physician would lose a significant amount of practice revenues.

With shrinking reimbursements and growing overhead, it is natural for every physician to want to preserve his or her managed-care contracts in order to maintain a steady stream of revenues. Some practices are extremely vulnerable to deselection because they have allowed themselves to become too dependent on the revenue receipts from a small group of payors. Some practices actually receive more than 70 percent of their total revenues from only four to seven managed-care payors. Therefore, if a health plan or other third-party payor decides to terminate its contract with a physician, the physician can only hope he or she can appeal the deselection decision; otherwise, practice revenues will be lost.

Most managed-care contracts allow the payor to cancel a physician's contract simply by giving notice to the physician. A typical contract states that the contract can be cancelled by giving 90 days' written notice to the physician. Typically, the payor does not need a reason to terminate in these instances. However, many contracts state the agreement can only be terminated "for cause." In other words, the payor must establish and provide a reason to the physician for the contract being terminated. Therefore, a physician should attempt to negotiate a termination provision in future managed-care contracts that require the payor to demonstrate a specific cause for termination. If the contract can be cancelled by giving notice, there is usually nothing a physician can do about it, unless of course regulatory rules allow otherwise.

If a physician receives written notice of deselection, the first step is to seek professional help. This includes the hiring of legal counsel and a qualified health care consultant who has experience in these matters. The next step is to review the contract to verify that the plan has followed the contractual provisions for termination. Was the termination without cause? If so, appealing will probably not be successful for the reasons previously discussed. However, if the termination was with cause, the next step would be to investigate why in fact the physician was deselected and help build a case for appeal. The objective is to get back on the provider panel by getting the health plan to reconsider its decision. Each state has rules governing the appeal process. Contact your state's

Insurance Commissioner's office for this information. Usually the physician will ask for an appeal hearing; this is the usual forum to appeal the deselection.

If the termination was with cause, determine why the plan has decided to terminate this contract. One reason could be that the termination was a business decision to form an exclusive contract with the physician's competitor in exchange for a more favorable contract. It is also possible that the payor feels its network is not in line with the needs of its members. Most likely, however, the network has used some form of economic credentialling and decided that the physician's practice patterns are too costly. Immediately obtain information on the payor as to why the deselection occurred.

ABC Health Plan Inc.

ENT Comparison—Surgical Encounters per Members Seen

Date Range: 1/1/01 to 12/31/01

Provider Number	Mbrs Seen	Surg Enc	Surg Proc	Surg Proc per # of Enc	Surg Enc/ Mbrs seen	Surg Enc per 1000 Mbrs seen
111421	216	117	346	2.96	54%	541.61
100310	102	120	161	1.341	118%	1176.47
111934	328	168	319	1.90	51%	512.20
114233	217	126	215	1.71	58%	580.65
111347	102	22	28	1.27	22%	215.69

If the health plan has terminated the contract because the physician is deemed an overutilizer, review the grounds and information on which the deselection was based. For example, a surgical specialist's contract might be terminated because the health plan has determined that he or she performs too many surgeries as a percent of office visits. Request all reports used by the health plan in making its decision. In particular, focus on all internal utilization reports pertaining to the physician.

When reviewing these reports, do not automatically assume that they are accurate. First, compile practice statistics and compare them with those of the health plan. You may be able to demonstrate that the health plan's decision was based upon faulty information. For example, suppose an internist was deselected based on the overutilization of hospital services and the continued use of the high-level office visit CPT codes. After gathering relevant practice statistics and the payor's own utilization figures, you find this particular practice is different because it specializes in the treatment of HIV-positive patients. Therefore, the practice's coding patterns and utilization are justified. This was confirmed by analyzing the diagnostic codes the practice utilizes.

Another part of the appeal strategy is to compare the practice data with any available industry averages and with peers of the physician, if possible. One word of caution in this area: Be careful when selecting peers for comparison purposes. Within the same medical specialty the patient mix can vary significantly; this often makes it almost impossible to compare two physicians in the same specialty. This could be seen in the example above. It would not have made sense to compare an HIV-positive internal medicine practice with the statistics of a general internal medicine practice. Finally, if the data support the health plan's decision to terminate, be willing to admit it and see if the health plan would be willing to contract with the physician on a temporary basis and work together to correct the physician's utilization problems.

If the physician is a specialist, he or she may have strong referral relationships with the plan's primary-care physicians. Therefore, get these primary-care physicians to write letters on behalf of the physician asking for reinstatement. The physician might also want to have some of these physicians attend the appeal hearing to speak as to why they want the physician to remain on the provider panel. Another important part of the appeal is to find out the plan's own utilization review procedures and to see if they were followed. Most payors will notify a provider first if there are utilization problems before terminating the contract. For example, some plans will notify the physician in writing of the problem and ask that it be corrected. Others will have the physician meet with a person in the Utilization Review Department to discuss any problems. This is important because the physician can say he or she was unaware there was a problem and that he or she would surely have corrected the problem had it been known beforehand. This is why all practices should meet regularly with the utilization representatives from its top five health plans—those plans that provide the patients the practice sees most often. Have the health plan give the practice a utilization report card. This way, a practice can know beforehand if there is a potential problem and begin to correct it.

After gathering this information and developing the appeal strategy, the next step is usually attendance before a panel of individuals at the appeal hearing. This is the time to present the physician's case as to why the notice of deselection is incorrect and to ask for reinstatement to the provider panel. However, determine what the appropriate process is for appealing the health plan's decision. It could be a formal hearing or it could be a submitted written appeal. The physician and his or her representatives need to attend the appeal hearing fully armed and ready to present the physician's case for reinstatement. This includes presenting the information discussed previously. Finally, check state laws and regulatory agencies for special provisions or procedures that must be followed by the physician and the health plan itself. You might also want to find out what agencies have accredited the health plan and inquire about their requirements for provider grievances. If the appeal is unsuccessful, the physician may want to file a grievance.

Health plans everywhere are looking to reduce their costs. This means physician utilization patterns are going to be scrutinized much more closely now than in the past. Practices must begin the process of reviewing their own utilization patterns, developing internal cost-effective strategies, and working with payors to develop win-win relationships. If ignored, physicians may soon find themselves locked out of access to the patients of certain health plans in the service area. Rest assured, provider deselection is one method payors will use as a way to reduce their future health care costs.

▼ CHAPTER 20
Hospital Recruitment Agreements

Today's competitive health care environment demands that hospitals recruit physicians almost year-round. To remain competitive, hospitals must improve utilization, increase inpatient occupancy, and develop clinical services. An expanding medical staff is necessary to carry out these tasks. It has long been a standard in the industry for hospitals to provide an array of incentives to recruit physicians. Physicians often can use these incentives to ease their transition into private practice.

Each year hospitals determine their medical staff needs and recruit physicians, both new and established. A physician or his or her advisor can find information regarding hospital staffing goals in their written strategic plans. Hospitals offer recruitment incentives to physicians in the form of written contracts. When physicians receive contracts, they should have them reviewed by legal counsel. Attorneys often overlook the financial aspects of the contracts, however, and these incentives have the greatest impact on the recruited physicians. Remember that recruitment incentives vary among hospitals and geographic regions. The incentives also vary if the hospitals are for-profit entities or not-for-profit entities and on how the hospitals view the current regulatory environment. Tax status and the regulatory matters are discussed later in this chapter. (See the sample hospital recruitment agreement checklist and contract in Appendix C.)

General Recruitment Issues

When probing into the particulars of a hospital recruitment agreement, keep in mind that all hospital recruitment contracts are negotiable. Often, a recruited physician accepts and signs a contract without negotiating, even when the financial terms in the contract are not in the best interest of the physician. To obtain the best terms, a recruited physician will have to negotiate.

Even though a hospital specifies a need for the recruited physician, the physician should never assume the need is real. During the recruiting process, a hospital may emphasize the existing need for the recruited physician in its practice area when, in fact, such a need does not exist. A hospital may think there is a need or may believe that the need will occur some time in the near future. To make sure that such a need exists, ask to see the hospital's demographic study of the area and its related documentation for the necessity of the recruited physician's specialty. If the hospital cannot produce this information, it may have other information that shows the recruited physician is needed in the area. Be skeptical if the hospital's reasons for the recruitment are not concrete and realistic.

During the recruitment process, the physician should investigate and inspect the clinical capabilities of the hospital. Physicians sometimes are blinded by the financial incentives a hospital offers during the recruitment process. Many do not take into consideration what clinical life will be like once they are on the medical staff, and disillusionment often occurs. For example, many physicians become upset at the level of nursing care at the hospital. They may be troubled by substandard surgical care or the lack of updated technology and equipment. The quality and delivery of care at the hospital should always be investigated thoroughly by the recruited physician before signing the recruitment agreement.

The financial aspects of a hospital recruitment agreement must always be reviewed by a qualified professional before the agreement is executed. While the legal aspects are undeniably important, financial issues make up about 90 percent of the hospital recruitment agreement.

A recruited physician should never relocate without first executing an agreement. A verbal agreement to the terms of the contract is not sufficient to warrant a relocation. In such cases, the final written document may not coincide with what was agreed upon verbally, and negotiating a contract after the fact places the physician in a vulnerable position.

Financial Contract Issues

A hospital most commonly offers the following financial recruitment incentives to a physician:

- Income guarantees
- Overhead subsidies
- Reimbursement of relocation expenses
- Marketing allowances
- Practice start-up assistance
- Loan guarantees
- Interest-free and interest-bearing loans
- Recruitment bonuses
- Signing bonus
- New equipment loans
- Loan forgiveness for service
- Management services
- Repayment of student loans

Income Guarantees

The most common recruitment incentive is the income guarantee. This guarantee provides the practice with working capital to pay both general operating overhead and compensation to the physician. There are two types of income guarantees: a gross income guarantee and a net income guarantee.

A *gross income guarantee* provides the practice with a minimum level of collections each month. For example, assume the contract guarantees the practice a gross income of $15,000 per month. In one month, the practice collects revenue of $5,000. At the end of the month, the hospital will make up the income difference by paying the practice $10,000 ($15,000 – $5,000).

Out of the *minimum gross income guarantee*, the practice must pay overhead, the physicians' compensation, and any debt service. Therefore, when reviewing the contract, the recruited physician must make sure that the gross guarantee will be enough to pay himself or herself a desired level of compensation. For example, if Dr. Hopper anticipates making $100,000 in the first year of practice, she must determine whether the practice will be able to pay operating overhead, any debt service, and her $100,000 salary at the offered level of guarantee. If it cannot, the gross income guarantee is too low. You will need to prepare a cash flow forecast to evaluate the reasonableness of the offered guarantee. Also, the physician should remember that under a gross income guarantee, the physician bears all of the risk to pay overhead and debt service. It will be the physician's responsibility to control these payouts.

A *net income guarantee* provides a physician with a guaranteed level of compensation after the payment of overhead and, sometimes, debt service. This frequently is called a "turnkey contract" because the physician often does not bear the risk of the overhead.

In the illustration below, the hospital makes up the difference between actual net income for the month and guaranteed net income for the month. This example does not include the payment of any debt service, which is an issue often overlooked by physicians in the negotiations of the recruitment agreement. The physician should determine if debt service will be included in the overhead amount or if he or she must pay debt service from the net guarantee. If the physician has to pay it out of his or her guarantee, then the physician will not be receiving the full $15,000 of the guaranteed net income.

Example of a Net Income Guarantee Calculation

A hospital recruits an orthopedic surgeon and will provide a net income guarantee of $15,000 to the physician each month.

	Month 1	Month 2	Month 3
Practice collections	$ 2,000	$ 6,000	$10,000
Less: Overhead	7,000	7,000	7,000
Net income	(5,000)	(1,000)	3,000
Guaranteed net income	15,000	15,000	15,000
Payment by hospital to practice (guaranteed net income less net income)	$20,000	$16,000	$12,000

In the example, the hospital would be committed to pay $48,000 to the practice in the first three months. Because a hospital generally has to expend larger amounts of funds under the net income guarantee arrangement than under the gross income guarantee method, it may require a cash flow forecast of income and overhead and may even cap the total amount it will pay to the practice. The cash flow forecast provides the hospital with (a) an estimate of how much it may be committed to pay under the recruitment contract and (b) an overview of projected overhead expenditures. Because a physician is basically under no risk with a net income guarantee, the hospital will need to make sure that the physician is not expending funds extravagantly. One way the hospital can do this is by approving all expenditures before they are paid out by the practice.

Finally, the recruitment contract often does not address the advancement of funds. Before a physician signs a contract, he or she will need to know when advances will be made by the hospital under the income guarantee arrangement. For example, if a practice opens August 1 and must pay its employees on August 15, the practice will need funds to make the payroll by August 15. Advances also may be needed to pay bills and overhead at the end of the month.

Other Recruitment Incentives

In addition to the basic income guarantee, hospitals also offer a variety of other incentives. For example, the hospital may subsidize specific overhead items, such as the physician's malpractice insurance premium and ongoing marketing costs. Often, these subsidies do not have to be repaid. The hospital should offer to pay the physician's relocation expenses. If the hospital does not make this offer, the physician should negotiate for its inclusion in the contract.

Up-front Marketing Allowance

One of the most important incentives for a physician is an up-front marketing allowance for the practice. When a hospital recruits a physician to set up a private practice, it will often emphasize how much the community needs the physician and paint a rosy picture of how well the physician is going to do. To be successful, however, a practice must invest time and money in marketing strategies. This is especially true for a primary-care practice, which cannot rely on referrals for business and needs to get its name out to the public. Even a practice that relies on referrals from other physicians must engage in marketing activities. The hospital will generally put advertisements in local newspapers and pay for an open house to promote the new practice. These activities, however helpful, fall short of what is needed to make a serious effort at marketing the practice. At a minimum, the physician should request a marketing allowance of $10,000. This should be enough to develop and implement a marketing plan that will accelerate the volume of patients in the new medical practice. When negotiating the marketing allowance, the physician should ask if the hospital's marketing department can provide assistance, such as logo design and brochure development, thereby reducing the amount needed to market the practice.

Practice Start-up Assistance

A physician who relocates to a new practice area will need help setting up the new practice. If the hospital does not have someone on its payroll to assist the physician, it will need to hire an outside professional. The normal fee for an outside consultant to set up a medical practice is $4,000 to $7,500. This should be included as part of the recruitment contract.

Loans

The physician will need to acquire a loan to pay for furniture and equipment. If the hospital is not willing to provide a start-up loan, the physician will need to apply for a loan with a bank. Without adequate collateral, a bank may deny the financing. The hospital could guarantee the financing by becoming a co-guarantor on the loan. Before signing the recruitment agreement, the physician should determine if the hospital is willing to be a co-guarantor should the physician's loan be denied. Determine the practice's fixed assets when the initial cash flow forecast is prepared. Also, some hospitals will provide interest-bearing or interest-free loans to the new practice. Many do this so the physician will not have to go to a bank for additional financing.

Recruitment Bonuses

To gain a competitive advantage, some hospitals will offer physicians recruitment bonuses as an incentive to sign with the hospital. The typical recruitment bonus ranges from $10,000 to $20,000 but will vary depending on where the hospital is located.

Legal Contract Issues

In addition to the financial contract issues, the legal issues should always be reviewed. The first is the physician's ability to obtain privileges to, and admit patients to, another hospital. Some physicians want to take emergency room calls or even set up offices at other hospitals. If the contract contains a provision prohibiting these activities, the hospital may be in violation of the Medicare illegal remuneration statute as discussed later in this chapter in the section titled "Medicare Fraud and Abuse Issues."

Some contracts provide that the agreement can be terminated by either party with 60 to 90 days' notice. Legal problems may arise if a hospital terminates the agreement and the physician owes the hospital money per the contract. Before signing a contract, you will need to address such issues as how the physician will repay any money owed or if the hospital will immediately forgive the amounts if it voluntarily terminates the agreement.

Repaying Incentives

The physician needs to address the manner in which the financial incentives will be repaid to the hospital after the term of the agreement ends. How money is repaid differs for each hospital and depends on its recruitment philosophy. In some agreements, the contract will state that the hospital amounts will be advanced each month under an income guarantee. If the practice's collections exceed the monthly income guarantee, the difference will be paid back to the hospital. For example, if the hospital offers a monthly gross income guarantee of $18,000 and the practice collects $23,000, $5,000 will have to be repaid to the hospital. After the term of the agreement is complete, any amounts not paid back during the term will have to be repaid to the hospital under a predetermined arrangement. Generally, the incentives are repaid by one of the following standard methods, or by a combination thereof: (a) cash, (b) service, or (c) forgiveness.

Cash Repayment

If the recruitment agreement states that incentives will have to be repaid in cash, the total amount advanced by the hospital becomes a loan payable over time to the hospital. At the end of the recruitment agreement, the physician will sign a note with the hospital, generally payable over three to five years at the prime rate of interest.

Repayment Through Service

Some hospitals will allow the physician to pay back the recruitment advances over time by providing services to or on behalf of the hospital. For example, a physician could provide services to the hospital at a negotiated hourly rate. These services might include community seminars on behalf of the hospital, clinical seminars to the medical staff, and departmental activities. The physician could also provide indigent care or emergency room coverage as a way to pay back the advances. Some contracts will allow the physician to pay back the advances in cash or one-half in cash and one-half in services. If any portion of the incentives is to be repaid in services, the physician should beware of the tax consequences of such a provision in the agreement. (See the discussion concerning the tax consequences of hospital recruitment agreements.)

Forgiveness of Repayment

Because the recruitment of physicians in certain medical specialties is highly competitive, many hospitals will forgive cash advances over time. This often is tied to the length of time the physician remains in active practice and on the hospital's medical staff. For example, assume a hospital advances $60,000 to a physician, and the hospital agrees to forgive this amount over three years. Generally, at the end of the contract's one-year term, the $60,000 will be forgiven in equal amounts over a three-year period. Thus, $20,000 will be forgiven each year, as long as the physician maintains an active practice. If the physician leaves the practice for any reason, the total amount not yet forgiven becomes immediately due to the hospital.

The desire to forgive the advances will often depend on whether the hospital is a for-profit entity or a not-for-profit entity. As discussed in the section on tax issues later in this chapter, a not-for-profit hospital is a tax-exempt Internal Revenue Service (IRS) entity that must conduct itself in a specified manner to maintain its tax-exempt status. Many hospitals tell recruited physicians that they cannot forgive recruitment incentives because forgiveness actions may impair their tax-exempt status. This is not the case, however, if the hospital can show that community need and the incentives are reasonable. The IRS has previously approved forgiveness by a not-for-profit hospital in a 1990 unpublished letter ruling. Based on this letter ruling, the following example suggests language to include in the recruitment agreement if a not-for-profit hospital would like to forgive recruitment incentives.

Sample Wording for Forgiving Recruitment Incentives

Repayment. In order to repay the value of the benefits delivered to Physician under Section(s) , Physician shall repay Hospital in cash according to the following schedule: Within one (1) year from the end of the term of this Agreement, Physician shall pay Hospital one-third (1/3) of the total value of such benefits; within two (2) years from the end of the term of this Agreement, Physician shall pay Hospital one-third (1/3) of the total value of such benefits; and within three (3) years from the end of the term of this Agreement, Physician shall pay Hospital one-third (1/3) of the total value of such benefits.

This cash repayment is subject to the following schedule of forgiveness: If Physician continues to meet all of the requirements under this Agreement for one (1) full year after the term of the Agreement, the first installment owed by Physician will be forgiven; if Physician continues to meet all of the requirements under this Agreement for two (2) full years after the term of the Agreement, the second installment owed by Physician will be forgiven; and if Physician continues to meet all of the requirements under this Agreement for three (3) full years after the term of the Agreement, the third installment owed by Physician will be forgiven.

Tax Issues

A hospital recruitment agreement has obvious tax issues. However, other hidden issues often are overlooked by the physician when negotiating the agreement.

Incorporation and the Phantom Income Principle

The first tax question that a recruited physician often asks is whether to incorporate the practice. The answer to this question will most likely not depend on tax specifics, but rather on the anticipated future behavior of the physician.

The situation illustrated in the following example is called the "phantom income principle." In this particular case, the physician will have to pay taxes when the hospital begins forgiving the $137,000 total advance over the three-year period. Some physicians have the discipline to set money aside for taxes as they receive their income guarantee. Others may have the luxury of planning to defer the taxes as long as possible. These are the exceptions, however, and not the rule. As a way to protect the physician against unexpected tax consequences, the practice may want to incorporate itself and pay the physician a salary at the beginning of the income guarantee. Returning to the example, the physician in an incorporated practice would withdraw the $120,000 in the form of deductible salary. Payroll taxes would be withheld on each payment to the physician. Because payments to the physician would be tax deductible to the corporation, they would, in effect, create a net operating loss that would be carried forward to future years. As the hospital begins forgiving the advances, the related reporting of income would be offset by the net operating loss carryforward.

The phantom income principle would also apply if the practice has to borrow money from a bank to purchase equipment and to use for working capital. The practice will use the income it receives to pay back the loan. The principal part of the loan is not deductible. Depending on what the loan proceeds are used for and whether losses were deducted on the physician's personal income tax return, the physician may have to pay unexpected income taxes. If the physician has the money to pay the taxes, then he or she benefits from not having to take a tax deferral. However, many physicians do not have the money to pay the taxes. The phantom income issue comes down to whether the physician wants to pay taxes at the beginning of the recruitment agreement or later. Personal cash flow planning related to this question will often dictate whether a practice will incorporate or not.

Illustration of Phantom Income

A hospital recruits Dr. Mulligan, a family practitioner. Dr. Mulligan was chief resident of her residency program. The hospital will provide Dr. Mulligan with a net income guarantee of $10,000 per month, to begin July 6 when she opens her private practice. The hospital will forgive any advances over a three-year period. Dr. Mulligan decides not to incorporate and thus will operate as a sole proprietor for tax purposes. Dr. Mulligan's practice statistics after the first year are as follows:

Practice collections	$105,000
Less: Practice overhead	$122,000
Net income	$ (17,000)
Guaranteed net income	$120,000
Payment by hospital to practice (guaranteed net income less net income)	$137,000

Because Dr. Mulligan operates as a sole proprietor for tax purposes, depending on the timing of the income and expenses, she will report a net loss of $17,000 on her personal income tax returns. Because the practice started in July, the net will be split between years. The $120,000 she received is considered proprietor draw and as such is not deductible. The $120,000 is money that is received before taxes. In other words, taxes will have to be paid on this money at some time in the future.

Incentive Repayment Through Service

The second major tax issue related to physician recruitment agreements is when a physician can pay back all or part of the incentives in service.

In the following example, the portion of Form 1099 related to expense subsidies would not be a tax problem for Dr. Thompson, because the practice would have an offsetting deduction when it paid the related expense. However, Dr. Thompson could experience an unexpected tax liability related to advances made under the income guarantee. The hospital would issue Form 1099 at the end of the year for the portion of the total advance to date that the physician would have the election to pay back in service. If the physician spends all of the guaranteed advance, he may not have the money available to pay federal income taxes. Therefore, if the agreement includes a provision related to payback in service, you or the physician should find out when the hospital will issue the related Form 1099 to the IRS and the physician, and attempt to create a debtor/creditor relationship in the contract until the physician elects to pay back the incentives in cash and/or service. When the physician elects the service payback, the income would be reported in that year.

Example of Paying Back Incentives and Issuing Form 1099

Dr. Thompson is given a subsidy for expenses and an income guarantee with the option to repay in either cash or services. If Dr. Thompson elects to repay the subsidy in cash, it is considered to be a loan, and therefore the hospital does not need to issue a Form

1099. If he elects to repay the subsidy in services, it is considered income to the physician at the time the payment is made, and the hospital must issue a Form 1099. Under the recruitment contract, Dr. Thompson is given more than one year to decide to repay in either cash or services.

The issue is if and when a Form 1099 should be issued to the IRS and to the physician reporting the income. Based on the facts in the example, it may appear that the agreement attempts to defer Dr. Thompson's compensation. The tax status when a nonqualified deferred compensation is earned and if it should be reported depends primarily on the **doctrine of constructive receipt.** This is augmented by the basic principle that cash-basis taxpayers are taxed when they receive cash or its equivalent.

When a physician receives cash under an expense subsidy or a minimum income guarantee, the physician has constructive receipt of the income. A determined and calculable amount has been paid to the physician, who has no restriction as to the time or manner of payment or any condition upon which payment is to be made. The funds have been made available to Dr. Thompson, and he has them within his own control and disposition. Because no loan agreement or commitment to treat the funds as a loan existed before receipt of the funds, under the cash basis of accounting required for information reporting, the nonemployee compensation should be reported in the year the cash was constructively or actually paid to Dr. Thompson.

In the event Dr. Thompson decides to treat the payments made as a loan in the following tax year, he might be able to use the claim of right doctrine to mitigate the tax effect of reporting payments as income in the prior year. Use of the claim of right doctrine depends on the physician's individual tax situation.

A Recruitment-Related Tax Ruling in Bankruptcy Court

Monthly draws that a taxpayer physician is entitled to receive from a hospital are to be reported as income in the year they are received, according to a recent Bankruptcy Court tax ruling, *Baer v. United States* (In re Baer, Debtor), U.S. Bankruptcy Court of Western Pennsylvania, No. 97-10454, 119198. This ruling on monthly draws affects new physician hospital recruitment arrangements. The purpose of including monthly draws in a physician agreement is to enable the hospital to attract qualified physicians by providing certain financial assistance. Offering financial incentives to a new doctor in order to recruit the doctor to the hospital's service area is still a common practice today within the health care industry.

The payments in question arose from a Physician Agreement dated December 15, 1992, between the physician and the hospital. Under the agreement, the hospital agreed to provide the doctor $15,000 in moving expenses and $5,000 for office renovations, to pay the debtor's health insurance premiums, and to provide the debtor a monthly draw of up to $10,833.

With regard to the monthly income guarantee, the agreement provided that in the months that the physician's "net practice income" exceeded $10,833, one-half of such excess would be paid to the hospital "to the extent of any outstanding balance in the amount of the draws, bonuses, and advances to be repaid by the Physician to the Hospital." This was a net income guarantee, as opposed to a gross income guarantee arrangement. If any balance remained unrepaid six months following the end of the agreement, either the physician had to repay the balance within one year or "in consideration and recognition of the benefit to the community and the Hospital from the Physician continuing practice in the service area, the amount owed to the Hospital will be amortized and written off in equal monthly amounts, over the next thirty-six months that the Physician remains in active practice in the service area following the expiration of the agreement." In other words, the amount owed to the hospital was forgiven over time in exchange for the physician continuing to practice in the service area.

When the physician resigned from the hospital's medical staff, the hospital had advanced him $131,096. The hospital sued to recover that amount from the physician, obtained a default judgment, and obtained a writ of execution based on the judgment. Two weeks later, the physician filed for bankruptcy under Chapter 7.

The physician-debtor claimed that the funds he received from the hospital constituted a loan and that the hospital did not retain the right to insist upon repayment in cash. The physician argued that he had the right to unconditional use of the funds without an obligation to repay them. If the underlying purpose of the agreement was fulfilled, that is to facilitate a long-term physician-hospital relationship, the hospital was obligated to write off any remaining balance due from the physician following the expiration of the agreement after a period of 36 months. In 1993, when the doctor received payment from the hospital, there was no existing, unconditional, and legally enforceable obligation to repay the sums received. The physician had unconditional use of the funds he received and treated them as belonging to him. (This situation and tax treatment could have changed if the hospital made the physician sign a note each time he received funds.)

It was ruled that the payments were properly included as income in the year received. The court concluded that the physician held the funds received in 1993 under a claim of right. The Claim of Right Doctrine is firmly established in law. *North American Oil v. Burnet,* 286 U.S. 417, 424 (1932), states that "if a taxpayer receives earnings under a claim of right and without restriction as to its disposition, he has received income which he is required to return, even though it may still be claimed that he is not entitled to retain the money, and even though he may still be adjudged liable to restore its equivalent." Other cases concerning the Claim of Right Doctrine include *United States v. Skelly Oil Co.,* 394 U.S. 678 (1969); *Healy v. Commissioner,* 345 U.S. 278 (1953); *Alexander Shokai, Inc. v. Commissioner,* 34 F.3d 1480 (9th Cir. 1994); and *Liddy v. Commissioner,* 808 F.2d 312 (4th Cir. 1980).

The court held that the funds were properly included as income on the debtor's 1993 tax return, even though such payments were subject to repayment at the end of the service agreement, but not to be repaid if the taxpayer continued to practice in the community. Therefore, the doctor was not entitled to a tax refund for the 1993 tax year. The court rejected the doctor's claim that the sum received was a loan and not income and that the Claim of Right Doctrine was inapplicable.

This case illustrates that the accounting and tax treatment of monies received from a hospital pursuant to a hospital recruitment arrangement should be scrutinized very closely. Before setting up the accounting records for the new doctor, obtain a copy of the hospital contract and determine whether or not the monies received should be recorded as income when they are received. In the absence of an executed promissory note, these receipts will most likely be recorded as income under the Claim of Right Doctrine.

For-Profit vs. Not-for-Profit Hospitals

As previously stated, the incentives a hospital offers a recruited physician may depend on whether it is a for-profit hospital or a not-for-profit hospital. Quite often, not-for-profit hospitals will offer fewer incentives because they may lose their tax-exempt status should their recruitment activities be challenged by the IRS. Not-for-profit hospitals are exempted from federal income taxes on the theory that they are organized and operated exclusively for charitable purposes. To maintain their tax-exempt status, not-for-profit hospitals must make sure that their activities are for the benefit of the public as a whole and that no monies are used for private purposes.

Private Inurement and Private Benefit

Two important concepts within the tax code relate directly to physician recruitment activities. The first is the concept of *private inurement*. Section 501(c)(3) of the Internal Revenue Code states that no part of the net earnings of an exempt organization can inure to the benefit of any private shareholder or individual. The inurement concept applies only to insiders. Even though the actual term *insider* does not appear directly in the law and regulations, it has been defined by the Health Care Financing Administration (HCFA) and the Office of the Inspector General (OIG) as a person having a personal and private interest in, or opportunity to influence the activities of, the not-for-profit organization from the inside. The issue then becomes whether a recruited physician could be considered an insider. In General Counsel Memorandum (GCM) 39498 (1986) and GCM 39670 (1987), the IRS stated its opinion that all persons performing services for an organization have a personal and private interest and, therefore, possess the requisite relationship necessary to find private benefit or inurement. In addition, since no part of the earnings can privately inure, it should be taken to mean no type of de minimis exception to the rule exists.

The second important concept is *private benefit*. A hospital is granted tax-exempt tax status if it serves public rather than private interests. Thus, the IRS is mainly concerned with the primary purpose of the hospital's activities. If serving private interests is incidental to the accomplishment of the organization's charitable purpose, however, tax-exempt status may not be affected. If a private benefit is served, it must be in both a qualitative and quantitative sense. In a qualitative sense, it must be a necessary concomitant of the activity that benefits the public as a whole. In other words, the activity must be accomplished only by benefiting certain individuals. To be incidental in a quantitative sense, the private benefit must not be substantial after considering the overall public benefit the activity confers.

The IRS has long been reviewing not-for-profit hospital transactions with physicians. Private inurement may occur if the income guarantee provided a physician is considered unreasonable compensation. Below-market loans and below-market leases are other transactions of potential private inurement and private benefit. Purchases of physicians' practices have also been targeted by the IRS as an area of potential inurement. Private inurement sometimes is quite difficult to prove, however, especially if the transaction is negotiated at arms' length; if the hospital is motivated by a bona fide belief that the transaction furthered its tax-exempt, charitable purposes (and has documentation backing up its bona fide belief); and if the transaction does not violate any other body of law. For example, the IRS has stated in an unpublished letter ruling that whether a particular compensation plan adversely affects an exempt organization's tax-exempt status is an inherently factual question. As long as the arrangement has all the earmarks of being worked out on an arm's-length basis as a means of providing reasonable compensation to employees without any potential for reducing the charitable services or benefits otherwise being provided, the arrangement should not affect the hospital's tax-exempt status.

Hermann Hospital

A settlement with Hermann Hospital clarified the IRS's position with regard to recruitment incentives. In early 1995, Hermann Hospital, located in Houston, Texas, entered into a settlement agreement with the IRS whereby it agreed to pay penalties and fines amounting to one million dollars for recruitment violations. In the settlement, the hospital admitted to participating in questionable recruitment and retention practices involving physicians. The recruitment and retention practices raise questions as to whether inurement and private benefit were conferred upon the individuals in violation of Section 501(c)(3) of the Code. If a new physician is being recruited by a not-for-profit hospital or to assist a not-for-profit hospital itself in the recruitment process, the Hermann settlement agreement provides many interesting insights into what the IRS might now consider to be permissible recruitment activities.

The IRS's settlement with the hospital is binding only upon Hermann Hospital, not any other hospital entity. However, you should know or find out what the IRS might be thinking in regard to any tax matter. Therefore, the ultimate guidance for not-for-profit hospitals will come in the form of published rulings, as in the proposed revenue ruling related to physician recruitment as discussed in the next section. When the IRS inspected Hermann, it found what it considered to be many questionable incentives. These included income guarantees, office personnel salary support, free office space, subsidized parking, malpractice allowances, equipment loans, and loan guarantees. Most of the benefits offered did not include any repayment terms or require the physicians to perform specific duties in exchange for the benefits which they received.

Other alleged violations involved the operation of various hospital outpatient departments in a manner resembling the private practice office of the physicians providing the services. *Note:* The physicians were independent contractors, not hospital employees.

The hospital entered into the settlement agreement and preserved its status as a not-for-profit hospital pursuant to Section 501(c)(3) of the Code. The agreement stated that the hospital would not lose its tax exemption from federal income taxes as a result of the agreement. Further, the hospital agreed not to modify, extend, or renew any of the physician recruitment or retention agreements entered into before the signing of the settlement agreement that do not conform to the *Hospital Physician Recruitment Guidelines*, which were set forth with the closing agreement. The $993,531 penalty is the amount that Hermann Hospital would have paid in income taxes if it were a for-profit hospital. The hospital also agreed to pay $9,720 in penalties for failing to file 1099s or W-2s for the amounts paid to or for the benefits received by the physicians.

The closing agreement with the IRS stipulated the following:

- No retention incentives of any kind can be offered to existing physicians.

- No retention incentives can be offered to new recruits, other than permissible recruits. *Permissible recruits* are those physicians who are recent graduates of a residency or fellowship program, whether or not in the hospital's community; those who have not previously practiced in the hospital's community; or those who have been affiliated with another hospital serving all or part of the hospital's community.

- Recruitment incentives offered to permissible recruits will not be considered permissible unless there is a documented community need for the physician.

Community need can be documented by showing the following:

- Low physician to population ratio in the physician's specialty, as defined in GMENAC reports

- A need for a particular medical service in the community indicated by the lack of availability of a particular service or by long waiting periods for the service

- Evidence that the community is designated a Health Professional Shortage Area

- Reluctance of physicians to relocate to the hospital based on the hospital's physical location. This criterion is meant to be applied to hospitals located in rural or economically disadvantaged inner city areas.

- Expected reduction in the number of physicians in a particular specialty due to anticipated retirement within the next three-year period

- Lack of physicians serving indigent or Medicaid patients within the hospital's service area, provided that the new recruits commit to serving a substantial number of Medicaid and charity-care patients

Using the settlement for guidance, allowable recruitment incentives could include the following:

- Loans and lines of credit with repayment terms, a fair-market interest rate, and adequate security
- Income guarantees with the terms and conditions in written form, with the term not to exceed two years, structured as loans with fair-market interest rates, and if there is to be loan forgiveness, it must be stated in the original agreement and forgiveness of indebtedness should occur only if the physician performs services for the hospital. The amount of compensation that the physician may receive from an income guarantee should be limited to the fair-market value of such services if the services were performed by another physician who did not have this deal. The services should be set forth at the time the loan is made and should be described in the contract.
- Moving costs
- Subsidies for rent and overhead, if no loans or other guarantees were provided (i.e., income guarantees)

Hermann Hospital is not the only case that has been settled for alleged recruitment violations. There were two other cases in which penalties were assessed against hospitals for recruitment violations. The fines in those cases amounted to $75,000 and $50,000 and were levied by the Office of the Inspector General, Department of Health and Human Services.

It appears from all of this activity that federal agencies are now as concerned with the appearance of the transactions as they are with the intent. If it appears that a party might be receiving benefits, directly or indirectly, then the party might be in violation of the rules.

The goal of any new recruit is to get as much financial assistance as possible from the hospital that is recruiting him or her. This definitely helps ease the transition to a new practice. In the process of negotiating with a not-for-profit hospital on behalf of a new physician practice, the hospital may start using the Hermann settlement as a way of getting out of paying certain financial incentives. However, by using this agreement, you can show that the IRS still allows the optimum recruitment package (which should be negotiated), which is:

- A net income guarantee

- Ultimate forgiveness of the guarantee advances
- Payment of relocation costs

If structured correctly, all other financial incentives can flow directly through the net income guarantee arrangement.

IRS Revenue Ruling on Physician Recruitment

The Internal Revenue Service released the final version of the revenue ruling relating to physician recruitment activities of tax-exempt hospitals. Proposed Ruling 95-25 discussed five specific examples of hospital recruitment practices and their potential effect on the tax-exempt status of the hospital. Final Revenue Ruling 97-21 includes the same fact patterns.

Fact Pattern #1   The hospital (Hospital A) is located in a rural area that has been designated by the U.S. Public Health Service as a Health Professional Shortage Area for primary-care professionals. The recruited physician recently completed an OB/GYN residency and is not on Hospital A's medical staff. Hospital A recruits the physician to maintain a full-time OB/GYN practice and become a nonemployee member of its medical staff. Hospital A provides a recruitment package pursuant to a written agreement negotiated at arm's length and approved by the hospital's board of directors or its designees.

In accordance with the agreement, Hospital A pays the physician a signing bonus, pays the physician's malpractice premium for a limited period, provides office space in a building owned by the hospital for a limited number of years at a below-market rent, and guarantees the physician's mortgage on a residence in the county. Hospital A also provides the physician practice start-up financial assistance pursuant to an agreement that is properly documented and bears commercially reasonable terms.

Fact Pattern #2   Hospital B is located in an economically depressed inner city area of City W. Hospital B has conducted a community needs assessment that indicates that there is a shortage of pediatricians in its service area and that Medicaid patients are having difficulty obtaining physician services. Physician N is a pediatrician currently practicing outside of Hospital B's service area and is not on Hospital B's medical staff. Hospital B recruits the physician to maintain a full-time pediatrics practice in Hospital B's service area, to become a member of its medical staff, and to treat Medicaid patients. Hospital B provides a recruitment package pursuant to a written agreement negotiated at arm's length.

Under the agreement, Hospital B reimburses Physician N for moving expenses, reimburses the physician for professional liability tail coverage, and guarantees private practice income for a limited number of years. The private practice income guarantee, which is properly documented and bears commercially reasonable terms, provides that Hospital B will make up the difference to the extent that Physician N practices full-time in its service area and the private practice does not generate a certain level of net income after reasonable expenses of the practice. The amount guaranteed falls within the range reflected in regional or national surveys regarding net income earned by physicians in the same medical specialty.

Fact Pattern #3   Hospital C is located in an economically depressed inner city area of City X. Hospital C has conducted a community needs assessment that indicates that indigent patients are having difficulty obtaining access to care because of a shortage of obstetricians in Hospital C's service area. Hospital C recruits Physician Z, an obstetrician currently on its medical staff, to provide these services and enters into a written agreement with Physician Z. The agreement is in accordance with the guidelines for physician recruitment, which Hospital C's Board of Directors is required to establish, monitor, and review regularly to ensure that recruiting practices are consistent with Hospital C's exempt purpose. Pursuant to the agreement, Hospital C agrees to reimburse Physician Z for the cost of one year's malpractice insurance in return for an agreement by Physician Z to treat a reasonable number of Medicaid and charity-care patients for the year.

Fact Pattern #4   Hospital D is located in City Y, a medium-to-large metropolitan area. Hospital D requires a minimum of four radiologists to ensure adequate coverage and high-quality care for its radiology department. Two of the four diagnostic radiologists currently providing coverage for Hospital D are relocating to other areas. Hospital D initiates a search for diagnostic radiologists and determines that one of the two most qualified candidates is Physician P.

Physician P currently practices in City Y and is a member of the medical staff of Hospital E (which is also in City Y). As a diagnostic radiologist, Physician P provides services for patients receiving care at Hospital E, but does not refer patients to Hospital E or any other hospital in City Y. Hospital D offers Physician P a recruitment incentive package pursuant to a written agreement. Hospital D does not provide any recruiting incentives other than those set forth in the written agreement.

Hospital D guarantees Physician P's private practice income for the first few years that Physician P is a member of Hospital D's medical staff and provides coverage for its radiology department. The private practice income guarantee, which is properly documented and bears commercially reasonable terms, provides that Hospital D will make up the difference between a target amount and Physician P's private practice net income after reasonable expenses of the practice. The target amount guaranteed falls within the range reflected in regional or national surveys regarding net income earned by physicians in the same specialty.

Fact Pattern #5 Hospital F is located in City R. Because of its physician recruitment practices, Hospital F has been found guilty in court of knowingly and willfully violating the Medicare and Medicaid Anti-Kickback Statute for providing recruitment incentives that constituted payments for referrals. The activities resulting in the violations were substantial.

Commentary

This final Revenue Ruling holds that the hospitals in Fact Patterns 1, 2, 3, and 4 have not violated the requirements for exemption as an organization described in Section 501(c)(3) of the Code. In the four Fact Patterns in which recruiting activities were found to be consistent with the hospital's tax exempt-status, the following factors were found: (1) there was objective evidence demonstrating a need for a particular medical specialty; (2) the recruitment incentive was evidenced by a written agreement that included all incentives provided to the physician; (3) the agreement was negotiated at arm's length; (4) the agreement was approved by the hospital's board of directors; (5) total compensation paid to the physician was within a range of reasonableness for the particular physician's specialty; and (6) if financial assistance was provided in the form of a loan or other extension of credit, the agreement was adequately documented and bore commercially reasonable terms. This final Revenue Ruling allows hospitals considerable flexibility in structuring recruitment incentives, provided that they can demonstrate community need. This applies to both metropolitan and rural areas. It is obvious from the fact patterns that recruitment guidelines need to be approved, monitored, and reviewed on an ongoing basis by the hospital's board of directors. Finally, it is important to remember that this ruling does not preclude other incentives that were not specifically mentioned. A Revenue Ruling serves merely as a safe harbor for organizations that desire to fall within the protection afforded in the ruling. Other incentives could be offered if factors 1 through 6 listed in this paragraph are adhered to.

IRS Ruling on Physician Recruitment Incentives to Existing Practitioners

In 1999, the Internal Revenue Service issued a new ruling in response to a hospital's request concerning whether the proposed transaction described below would adversely affect the exempt status of a hospital system under Section 501(c)(3) of the Internal Revenue Code.

This ruling involved a tertiary-care hospital facility that in recent years had focused on establishing a geographically dispersed, integrated health care delivery and financing system. One of the hospital's initiatives called for the development of affiliations with networks of primary-care physicians. The hospital had developed a relationship with a certain group of primary-care physicians employed by a professional limited liability corporation (Group).

The Group was formed by several local primary-care physicians interested in an affiliation with the hospital, but who were not interested in selling or otherwise ceding control over their medical practices. The hospital and Group formed a jointly owned and operated management services organization (MSO). The MSO provided management services to the Group in exchange for fees that had been negotiated at arm's length and which the parties believed represented fair market value. As part of the more formal relationship, the Group committed to recruit additional primary-care physicians to the communities served by the hospital. The hospital agreed to assist in physician recruitment activities subject to compliance with the physician recruitment policy adopted by the hospital's board.

As part of its continuing evaluation of physician needs within its service area, the hospital determined through a formal needs assessment that by the year 2000, its medical staff would need between 202 and 267 additional primary-care physicians and other under-represented physician specialists to serve its patient population. The assessment also determined that additional physicians must be recruited to join the Group and to provide care in the communities served by planned Community Health Centers. To recruit these doctors, the hospital board approved and funded certain physician recruitment incentives.

The hospital board of directors limited the provision of recruitment incentives to physicians whose services were not currently available within its service area or who were graduates of a physician training program (New Physicians). Further, the board required the documentation of a demonstrable community need for the recruitment of the physicians at issue.

Authorized recruitment incentives included income guarantees (not in excess of three years), relocation assistance and signing bonuses, provided that the terms of each physician's recruitment package were reasonable in their entirety and did not confer any prohibited private inurement or more than incidental private benefit upon any physician. All recruitment incentives would be provided pursuant to a written agreement and no "off agreement" incentives or benefits would be offered or provided. Finally, assistance provided to an existing physician practice recruiting a physician would be limited to no more than 50 percent of the total assistance provided to the recruited physician.

The Proposed Transaction

The hospital wanted to expand its recruitment activities to support the recruitment of new physicians, whether those physicians joined the Group or another established physician group; *and to offer support to certain physicians practicing in its service area* (emphasis added) for less than four years to those who had not established a meaningful practice at their current practice site and had expressed an interest in relocating to a practice site in proximity to one of the planned Community Health Centers.

A physician recruitment agreement (Agreement) was negotiated between the hospital and the recruited physician and in the case of a new physician, the recruiting physicians. The hospital would guarantee a new physician a certain level of monthly compensation (income guarantee) for up to three years commencing with the date he or she began employment with the recruiting physicians. *In the case of a currently practicing physician,* the hospital would provide an income guarantee for a year commencing with the date he or she relocated within the service area to a site in proximity to a community health center.

New physicians would receive a signing bonus, reimbursement of reasonable relocation expenses, a one-time marketing payment, and other reasonable incentives. The marketing payment was intended to be a one-time payment to cover the cost of distributing relocation announcements and issuing press releases. Currently practicing physicians would also be given a financial incentive, loan, or advance to permit the currently practicing physicians to terminate any preexisting office space lease obligations.

Amounts advanced under the physician recruitment agreements would be treated as a loan to: (1) in the case of a currently practicing physician, the recruited physician, and (2) in the case of a new physician, the recruiting physicians. Each loan would bear interest at a fixed rate set to a certain federal rate and compounded monthly. If the recruited physician's net income, exclusive of any incentive bonus compensation, exceeded the guaranteed amount in any calendar month, then to the extent there was a balance due under a loan, the recruited or recruiting physician would then repay the hospital the difference between the recruited physician's net income and the guaranteed amount. The loan would be evidenced by (1) in the case of a currently practicing physician, a written promissory note evidencing the recruited physician's obligation to repay the loan, and (2) in the case of a new physician, two written promissory notes ("A" note and "B" note), each of which evidenced the recruiting physician's obligation to repay one-half of the loan.

Under the terms of both of the notes to be used by the recruited physician, the recruited physician or recruiting physicians would be required to repay the hospital the balance due at the end of the guarantee period in equal monthly installments of principal and interest over the succeeding 36 months. With respect to new physicians, the recruiting physician's obligation under the "A" note would be absolute and the obligation to repay the "B" note could be satisfied through the recruited physician's continued maintenance of a full-time medical practice. For each month beyond the guarantee period during which the recruited physician maintained a full-time medical practice in the hospital's community, and during the time the agreement was in effect, the balance due under the notes would be reduced by 1/36.

The hospital sought the following rulings:

- Its forgiveness of the entire amount advanced to recruiting physicians and used to recruit new physician by conforming the terms of an "A" note to the terms of a "B" note would not adversely affect its continuing status as an organization exempt from federal income.

- The extension of the income guarantee and other recruitment incentives set forth above to *currently practicing physicians* would not adversely affect its continuing status as an organization exempt from federal income.

Revenue Ruling 69-545, 1969-2 C.B. 117, holds that a nonprofit organization whose purpose and activity were providing hospital care to the community, promoted health, and had a charitable purpose, could therefore qualify as an organization organized and operated exclusively for charitable purposes if it met the other requirements of Section 501(c)(3) of the Code.

Revenue Ruling 73-313, 1973-2 C.B. 174, holds that attracting a physician to a community that had no available medical services furthered the charitable purpose of promoting the health of the community. In the ruling, residents of an isolated rural community had to travel a considerable distance to obtain care. Faced with a lack of local services, the community formed an organization to raise funds and build a medical office building to attract a doctor to the locality. No hospitals or existing medical practices were involved.

Revenue Ruling 73-313 sets forth the following facts as particularly relevant to the determination whether the recruitment incentives at issue are compatible with the requirements for exempt status: (1) the demonstrated need for a physician to avert a real and substantial threat to the community; (2) evidence that the lack of a suitable office impeded efforts to attract a physician; (3) the arm's-length nature of the arrangements; and (4) the lack of any relationship between persons connected with the organization and the recruited physician. Revenue Ruling 73-313 finds that, under all these circumstances, the arrangements used to induce the doctor to locate a practice in the area "bear a reasonable relationship to promotion and protection of the health of the community" and any private benefit to the physician is incidental to the public purpose achieved. The ruling concludes that the organization's recruitment activity furthers a charitable purpose, and the organization qualifies for exemption as an organization described in Section 501(c)(3).

Revenue Ruling 97-21, 1997-18 I.R.B. 8, analyzes five situations where physician recruitment incentives are offered by an exempt hospital, both with respect to physicians who will perform services for or on behalf of the organization, and physicians who will perform services for members of the community at large. In order to meet the requirements of Section 501(c)(3), a hospital that provides recruitment incentives to physicians must provide those incentives in a manner that does not cause the organization to violate the operational test of Section 1.501(c)(3)-1 of the regulations. The determination of whether the recruitment incentives cause the organization to violate the operational test is based on all relevant facts and circumstances.

Revenue Ruling 97-21 provides that an exempt hospital recruiting a physician for its medical staff, who will provide services to members of the community but not necessarily for or on behalf of the hospital, will be treated as operating exclusively for exempt purposes provided it does not engage in any of the following:

1. Substantial activities that do not further the hospital's exempt purposes or that do not bear a reasonable relationship to the accomplishment of those purposes;

2. Activities that result in inurement of the hospital's net earnings to a private shareholder or individual;

3. Substantial activities that cause the hospital to be operated for the benefit of a private rather than public interest such that it has a substantial nonexempt purpose; and

4. Substantial unlawful activities.

Revenue Ruling 97-21 sets forth guidance concerning the tax consequences of physician recruitment incentives provided by hospitals described in Section 501(c)(3) of the Code. Establishment of community need for particular physician services either for the service area of a hospital or for the staff of a hospital is a favorable criteria listed in the revenue ruling. The revenue ruling provides an analysis of particular incentives that if offered to physicians result in community benefit rather than impermissible private interest.

The IRS Ruling

Based upon the information that was submitted, the hospital provided objective evidence that there is a need for additional physicians to be hired within the area. In order to satisfy this need, the plan on offering various recruitment incentives to new physicians such as an income guarantee, reasonable signing bonus, and reimbursement of relocation expenses was considered reasonable. This was so long as the hospital did not provide recruiting incentives solely to physicians working for the Group.

The IRS also allowed the hospital to offer currently practicing physicians an income guarantee and a one-time payment to cover the cost of distributing relocation announcements and issuing press releases and a financial incentive, loan, or advance to permit the currently practicing physicians to terminate any preexisting office space lease obligations. The ruling also *allows for the recruitment of currently practicing physicians* provided that they have been practicing in that community for less than four years.

The recruitment of currently practicing physicians in the area and providing practice guarantees is similar to Situation 4 of Revenue Ruling 97-21, according to the IRS. This was because the hospital limited the incentives to currently practicing physicians whose practices were floundering and who were practicing in the community for less than four years and who did not have an established patient base. The net income guarantee provided to currently practicing physicians helped to ensure an adequate physician base to care for residents of the service area.

As such, the IRS ruled that the hospital's forgiveness of the entire amount advanced to recruiting physicians and used to recruit new physicians, by conforming the terms of an "A" note to the terms of a "B" note, would not adversely affect its tax exempt status and that the extension of the income guarantee and other recruitment incentives set forth to currently practicing physicians would not do so either.

Physician Recruitment Arrangement Outside a Safe Harbor

On May 3, 2001, the Office of the Inspector General (OIG) of the Department of Health and Human Services (HHS) issued OIG Advisory Opinion No. 01-4, approving a recruitment arrangement between a hospital and a physician in which the hospital was not located within a designated health professional shortage area (HPSA) as required by the safe harbor clause under Medicare's fraud and abuse criminal anti-kickback statute (Anti-Kickback Statute). The Advisory Opinion concluded that given the geographic location of the hospital and the specific circumstances of the parties, the hospital would not be subject to program exclusion or to administrative sanctions under the civil monetary penalties law (CMP Law) or the Anti-Kickback Statute.

The Recruitment Arrangement

The physician recruitment arrangement provided for a tax-exempt, not-for-profit acute-care hospital located in a rural city and county (which was not designated as an HPSA for any medical specialty), to annually lend a physician, who was a recent medical school graduate, a fixed amount during the physician's five-year residency program. Upon completion of the residency, the physician agreed to relocate to the hospital's service area. The physician's residency program was more than 100 miles away from the recruiting hospital. The hospital certified that (a) the hospital's loan was equal to the aggregate monthly payments on the physician's medical school loans, plus an additional amount used to cover other educational expenses; (b) the loan would bear interest; (c) the county in which the hospital was located and all surrounding counties were currently designated as medically underserved areas (MUAs); and (d) pursuant to the hospital's bona fide needs analysis, a shortage existed for the physician's medical specialty and that this shortage would extend into the foreseeable future.

For three consecutive years following the residency, the physician would be obligated to, among other things: (a) establish a full-time private practice in the physician's specialty within a three-mile radius of the city in which the hospital was located; (b) obtain staff privileges at the hospital; (c) accept the hospital's emergency room patients while "on-call" regardless of their ability to pay; (d) assist in the hospital's educational, fund-raising, and recruitment activities; and (e) agree to treat patients receiving Federal health care program benefits in a non-discriminatory manner. The physician was also obligated to repay the loan from the hospital, including accrued interest, in three equal annual payments beginning one year after his relocation. The hospital agreed to incrementally forgive one-third of the loan for each year that the physician fulfilled the above obligations. If the physician defaulted, the outstanding balance of the hospital's loan would then become immediately due and payable.

According to the Advisory Opinion, the hospital certified that: (a) the proposed arrangement would not be renegotiated during its term; (b) the proposed arrangement was not conditioned on the physician making referrals to or otherwise generating business for the hospital; (c) the physician could obtain staff privileges at other hospitals; (d) the value of the proposed arrangement would not vary based on the volume or value of any expected referrals or other business for which payments would be made by a Federal health care program; (e) at least 75 percent of the physician's revenues would be generated from patients residing in a HPSA or MUA, or who were part of a Medically Underserved Population (MUP); and (f) the proposed arrangement would not benefit any potential referral source other than the physician.

Analysis by the Office of Inspector General

The OIG concluded that the proposed arrangement would potentially involve prohibited remuneration under the Anti-Kickback Statute, if the requisite intent to induce or reward referrals of federal health care program business were present. The Anti-Kickback Statute prohibits offering anything of value to any person or entity to induce or reward referrals of items or services paid for by a Federal health care program. Furthermore, the OIG may impose administrative sanctions under the CMP Law for violations of the Anti-Kickback Statute. In the proposed arrangement, the hospital's loan to the physician in exchange for the physician agreeing to relocate to the hospital's service area, at which point he would be in a position to refer to the hospital, would potentially implicate the Anti-Kickback Statute.

Additionally, the proposed arrangement would not come within the recruitment safe harbor under the Anti-Kickback Statute (see the related discussion later in this chapter). This safe harbor sets forth the following nine conditions which any recruitment arrangement must satisfy in order to be immune from prosecution: (1) the arrangement must be in writing, signed by the parties, and specify the benefits and obligations; (2) at least 75 percent of the revenues must come from new patients, not previously serviced by the recruited physician; (3) the benefit period must not exceed three years, and the terms may not be renegotiated during this period; (4) the recruited physician must not be required to make referrals or generate other business for the hospital, provided that the hospital may require the physician to maintain staff privileges at the hospital; (5) the recruited physician may not be restricted from establishing staff privileges at or referring business to any other hospital; (6) the amount or value of the benefits provided may not vary in any manner that takes into account the volume or value of any referrals or other business generated for which payment will be made by a Federal health care program; (7) the physician agrees to treat patients receiving Federal health care benefits or other assistance in a non-discriminatory manner; (8) at least 75 percent of the revenues of the new practice must be generated from patients residing in a HPSA or a MUA, or who are part of a MUP; and (9) the arrangement may not directly or indirectly benefit any potential referral source, other than the physician. In addition, only recruitment into a HPSA can qualify for the exception.

The proposed arrangement failed to meet two of the express conditions of the safe harbor: (1) the hospital was not located in a HPSA, and (2) the benefits of the arrangement did not exceed three years. Since the proposed arrangement didn't satisfy the safe harbor, the OIG made an individual facts and circumstances evaluation of the risk of fraud and abuse posed by the proposed arrangement. The OIG looked at a number of factors, including, but not limited to, the following: (a) whether there was documented evidence of an objective need for the practitioner's services; (b) whether the practitioner had an existing stream of referrals within the recruiting entity's service area; (c) whether the benefit was narrowly tailored so that it did not exceed that which is reasonably necessary to recruit a practitioner; and (d) whether the remuneration directly or indirectly benefited other referral sources (e.g., when a physician is recruited to join an existing practice).

After considering the above factors, the OIG determined that the proposed arrangement would pose a minimal risk of fraud and abuse. The OIG concluded that the hospital provided adequate documentation to address each of the above factors. The hospital demonstrated a current and likely continuation of a shortage of the physician's medical specialty, a reasonable basis for the monetary amount of the benefit, and adequate assurances against the monetary amount benefiting other referral sources. Further, the OIG concluded that upon his relocation the physician would not have a ready stream of referrals, and that even though the duration exceeds the safe harbor three-year period, the period when the physician would be in a position to make referrals is limited to three years. Regarding the latter point, the OIG reasoned that the physician's ability to influence referrals begins once the physician has relocated to the service area, and that the three-year safe harbor time period would run consecutively with the physician's three-year repayment period.

However, it is important to note that in the Advisory Opinion, the OIG expressed no opinion regarding whether the Internal Revenue Service would deem the hospital's needs analysis to be "objective evidence of a demonstrable community need" for purposes of determining whether the proposed arrangement would jeopardize the hospital's tax-exempt status.

Medicare Fraud and Abuse Issues

All hospitals and physicians must concern themselves with fraud and abuse laws, specifically how they might apply to physician recruitment activities. In its simplest form, the fraud and abuse statute prohibits the knowing and willful solicitation, receipt, offer, or payment of any kind in return for the referral of patients or to induce a person to refer a Medicare/Medicaid patient to the hospital. This is known as the *illegal remuneration statute*. The issue of concern regarding physician recruitment is whether the hospital provides incentives to a recruited physician to induce that physician to admit or refer patients into its facility. [See *Polk County, Texas d/b/a Polk County Memorial Hospital v. Kenneth W. Peters M.D.* (CA No. 9:92CV45, E.D. Tex., August 28, 1992), in which the court held the recruitment agreement unenforceable because it violated the Medicare/Medicaid illegal remuneration provision.]

As discussed previously in the section titled "Tax Issues," conflict may arise between the exemption issue and the fraud and abuse issue relative to recruitment activities. The IRS generally holds that it is permissible for a hospital to provide recruitment incentives to achieve its charitable purpose in the community. However, the hospital must at the same time show that it is not providing these incentives to induce referrals.

Arrangements in Violation of Fraud and Abuse Statutes

Enforcement of the fraud and abuse statutes is the responsibility of the Office of the Inspector General. In 1992, the OIG issued a fraud alert of the following arrangements between hospitals and physicians, which violate the fraud and abuse statutes:

- Payment of any incentive when a physician refers a patient to the hospital
- Free or significantly discounted office space or equipment
- Free or significantly discounted billing, nursing, or other staff services

- Free training for the physician's office staff in current procedural terminology (CPT) coding, management techniques, or other areas
- Hospital-provided guarantees to supplement a physician's income if it fails to reach a certain level
- Low-interest or interest-free loans that may be forgiven if a physician refers patients to the hospital
- Payment of a physician's travel costs and expenses to attend conferences
- Providing health insurance to the physician at an inappropriately low cost
- Payment for consulting or other services that require little substantive input by the physician, or payment in excess of fair market value for the services rendered

Safe Harbor Regulations

In 1993, the OIG proposed seven safe harbor regulations describing business arrangements that would be immune from prosecution under the Fraud and Abuse Kickback Statute. One of these safe harbors is directed specifically toward physician recruitment. The physician recruitment safe harbor, however, applies only to rural hospitals and protects only the following two types of physician recruitment activities:

1. Relocation of a physician to a new geographic area to start a new practice
2. Assistance of a physician starting a practice or specialty after completing an internship or residency program

In 1999, the OIG finalized the safe harbor. The final safe harbor regulations protect recruitment agreements between a physician and a hospital if all of the following criteria are met:

1. The arrangement is in writing.
2. If an established practitioner, at least 75 percent of the new practice revenues must be generated from new patients not previously seen at the prior practice.

3. Seventy-five percent of the new practice revenue must be generated from patients residing in a HPSA or a medically underserved area or who are a part of a medically underserved population.

4. The benefits provide for no more than three years, and the terms of the arrangement may not be renegotiated during the three-year period in any substantial respect.

5. There is no requirement for referrals (with an allowance for the requirement that the practitioner maintain staff privileges).

6. There is no restriction against staff privileges at any other facility.

7. The amount or volume of the benefits must not be calculated merely based on the volume or value of expected referrals or other business otherwise generated.

8. The practitioner agrees (i.e., the agreement includes the requirement that) to treat Medicare/Medicaid patients in a non-discriminatory manner.

9. The payment may not directly benefit any other person in a position to make or influence referrals to the entity providing the recruitment payment (e.g., a recruiting practice).

The final safe harbor did away with the 100-mile restriction included in the originally proposed recruitment safe harbor, and added safe harbor protection for underserved places and populations as opposed to simply focusing on non-portable physician practices. The OIG specifically rejected any protection for physician retention, but stated that a safe harbor on physician retention may be the subject of a future rule making. The OIG also addressed recruiting into group practices, interestingly stating in the preamble that:

> We are not persuaded that a safe harbor can be crafted that would protect legitimate joint recruiting arrangements of the type described above without sweeping in sham arrangements that are actually disguised payments for referrals. However, we want to make clear that joint recruitment arrangements are not necessarily illegal and must be evaluated on a case-by-case basis. Parties seeking further guidance about their joint recruitment activities may apply for an advisory opinion.

Payments for Personal Services

In 1991, the OIG issued a series of safe harbor regulations dealing with a variety of fraud and abuse issues. Some affected physician recruitment. The regulations mentioned arrangements involving payments for personal services. While not directly stating so, the safe harbors imply that if a hospital is going to provide income guarantees to physicians, the amounts have to be reasonable. In the settlement of *Inspector General v. Kennestone at Windy Hill, Inc.* (1993), the OIG agreed not to press civil and criminal charges against Kennestone Hospital in Marietta, Georgia. The settlement capped an 11-month investigation into nine recruitment agreements between the hospital and physicians in the Atlanta area. In the investigation, the OIG alleged that the hospital offered income guarantees and free office space to induce the physicians to refer patients to the hospital. For example, one physician was offered a five-year contract worth $1.2 million. The agreement also included free office space for one year. Therefore, when reviewing a hospital's offer that involves an income guarantee, determine the reasonableness of the guarantee. Also, make sure that the hospital can document the reasonableness. Many hospitals review a variety of physician compensation surveys to set their income guarantee levels. The surveys mentioned most often are from the Medical Group Management Association, Medical Economics Publishing, the American Medical Group Association, and the Society of Medical/Dental Management Consultants. (See Chapter 1 for addresses and phone numbers.)

Space and Equipment Rental Rates

When reviewing, pay strict attention to whether the hospital provides office space at below-market rates. If the rate appears to be below market, determine the commercial market rate for medical office space in the area in which the physician's office space is located. Just because a hospital gives out free rent does not necessarily make it below market. Market rate usually can be documented with the help of local commercial rental agents.

The OIG issued a safe harbor regulation in 1991 pertaining to transactions involving space and equipment rental rates. To be protected from potential fraud and abuse prosecution, the physician's office lease must meet all of the following criteria:

- The lease must be in writing and signed by all of the parties.
- The lease must specify the premises covered.
- The lease must be for a term of at least one year.
- The aggregate rental charge must be set in advance, consistent with the area's fair-market value, and it must not take into account the volume of referrals generated between the parties.
- The lease must specify the exact rent and schedule of access if the lease is not for the physician's full-time occupancy.

To emphasize the attack on below-market rental arrangements, a California court ruled that a below-market rental arrangement violates the Medicare anti-kickback statutes. In the case of *Vana et al. v. Vista Hospital Systems* (1993), the hospital attempted to void the long-term lease contracts of various physicians. The hospital charged, and the court agreed, that the contracts were illegal because the rents the physicians were paying were below the market rates for the area. The court stated that the hospital's administration offered the physician's low rental rates in an effort to induce them to refer patients to the hospital, even though the physicians were unaware of the hospital's intent.

Fraud and abuse statutes, proposals, and alerts do have a direct impact on physician recruitment contracts, and CPAs and physicians should review contracts with these rules in mind. Many hospitals have taken them literally and have reduced substantially the array of incentives they provide to a newly recruited physician. This may be taking matters to the extreme, however. The intent of these promulgations is not to eliminate a nationwide industry standard such as physician recruitment agreements. Hospitals must provide incentives to remain competitive; otherwise, they risk losing out on quality primary-care physicians and specialists. Rather, the intent of the promulgations is to detect and stop obvious abuses to the system by health care providers. As long as the agreement is reasonable in its terms and negotiated at arm's length, and the community's need for the physician can be documented, the recruited physician and the hospital should not be in violation of the illegal remuneration statutes.

▼ CHAPTER 21
Medical Practice Consolidations and Office-Sharing Arrangements

Health care executives and physicians today face diverse and complex challenges. During the 1980s and early 1990s, managed care grew significantly in market share and importance. Insurance companies and employers demanded improved utilization management, initiated capitated arrangements, and shifted greater risk to the physician-providers. New government regulations, increased provider competition, and changes in medical technology and payor demands, both for quality outcome information and reduced reimbursement, present constant challenges to physicians. In this century, these forces continue to demand solutions that will improve quality, reduce costs, and meet the needs of local communities.

The Explosion of Group Practices

In addition to the heightened pressures on providers, the nature of medical practice is in constant transition. The number of group practices has increased rapidly since the 1990s. In fact, the majority of graduating residents say they would prefer to practice in a group setting or as employees rather than to set up high-risk solo practices.

Traditional competitive ways of acting (or reacting) no longer work; providers must begin to cooperate as much as they compete. Those practices that want to survive in the twenty-first century must make structural and cultural changes that integrate physicians and hospitals so that medical services can be marketed to payors and the needs of the communities can be served in the most effective manner. Physicians, hospitals, and payors must communicate and collaborate. To be successful in this rapidly changing environment, physicians must be willing and ready to adapt, manage, and lead, rather than resist change.

The recent explosion of group practices can be traced to many factors. First, solo practitioners need to form larger business entities to be competitive, especially in the managed-care arena. Second, it is widely accepted that market forces will continue to drive down physicians' reimbursements. One way to combat this negative force on physicians' income is for physicians to form group practices. When practices merge and operate in a single location, overhead costs can be reduced substantially. Even practices with multiple locations can achieve overhead economies of scale. Also, grouping allows physicians to increase efficiency, improve management, and reduce administrative burdens.

The final factor is the result of a subtle intangible: many physicians, concerned about the future, wonder how they will be able to make the transition out of the practice of medicine. Because it is not easy to sell a medical practice, physicians like the idea of having a safety net that allows for the disposal of their interest in a practice. Buy-out arrangements within group practices fulfill this need.

Advantages of Group Practices

The following are other benefits of group practices:

Increased revenues from same-practice production   Many times revenues can be increased without necessarily increasing production. This is usually due to changes that occur because of a merger. For example, the physicians will want to retain the best employees, which will provide the new group practice with better receivables management, better coding oversight, and improved billing process. Retaining good employees will guarantee improved processes, which will affect the group practice's bottom line.

Computer upgrade capability   Many practices need to upgrade their information systems, which can be quite costly for smaller practices. If the practice has contracted with a managed-care plan, the practice will have to upgrade its computer system. Upgrading a group practice's computer system will not be as costly, because each physician will contribute to the cost. This will reduce each physician's cost.

New revenues   Whenever practices merge, there might be an opportunity to generate new revenues. For example, one practice may have its own in-house clinical laboratory and the other merging practices may not. The other practices might be able to increase their lab revenues by utilizing the in-house lab. Other examples of new revenues are when practices can utilize infusion and home-health services currently being rendered by another practice that is a party to the merger.

Call coverage   Adding physicians to the group practice will usually expand the call group for the physicians in the same medical specialty. This will provide the merging physicians with more free time.

Clinical staff leverage   Some group practices utilize physician extenders that can be incorporated into other practices. For example, the group may be able to utilize a physician assistant or a nurse practitioner from another practice. These professionals may be able to leverage physician time by seeing patients in certain circumstances for the merging practices and thus freeing up the physicians either to see more patients or to render other services. For example, a physician assistant in an orthopedic practice might be able to handle minor surgical follow up, allowing the orthopedist more time in the operating room. The physician assistant also could see a primary physician's patients. For instance, the assistant could see patients with very minor problems and the physician could see patients requiring more care. If the physicians can see more patients during the day, their revenue will increase.

Reduced competition   The degree to which group practices can be competitive depends on both the practices' geographic areas and the impact of the market. As managed care grows, many believe that the multispecialty practice model will dominate. Insurance plans and other payors will look to the gatekeeper concept to control utilization and costs. [A *gatekeeper* is a primary-care physician in a health maintenance organization (HMO) who makes referrals to other physicians. The gatekeeper's function is to reduce health care use and costs.] Driven by primary care, multispecialty groups offer a one-stop-shopping concept that appeals to many payors. To compete and maintain referral patterns, specialists have to meet the needs and desires of the primary-care groups. Specialists who join primary-care groups to form a multispecialty group, however, lose autonomy. The growth of the multispecialty practice model does not mean that opportunities do not exist for single-specialty group practices. Many payors now look to consolidate their enrollee services with only one or only a few groups of physicians. Mental health services are an example.

The formation of any group practice is fraught with problems unless it is planned correctly. If issues such as compensation, buy-out, utilization of hard assets, assumption of debt, and matters involving the practice's employees are not dealt with up front, the initial success of the new group could be threatened. Many mergers set themselves up to fail. However, if properly planned, the merger can be a success and the resulting group practice can be quite rewarding. The major issues that must be addressed during a consolidation of medical practices are discussed in the following sections. A medical practice merger should not take place without the assistance of a CPA or qualified consultant. During the merger process, the CPA or consultant can perform various functions and tasks that are critical to the consolidation procedure.

> ■ **Practice Point:** You must make clear to the physicians early on that for the merger to be successful, each physician must be ready to compromise. You should explain that many issues demand compromise. If physicians believe that they must get their way all of the time, the merger will more than likely fail.

Disadvantages of Group Practices

The following are some of the disadvantages of group practices:

Loss of control   Loss of control is a given fact and a way of life in a group practice environment. As mentioned earlier, physicians must be willing to compromise.

> ■ **Practice Point:** For a merger to be successful, the physicians must begin thinking like a group. In other words, the decisions they make should be in the best interest of the group practice, not necessarily in the best interest of

the individual physician. If a physician cannot develop a group attitude, he or she probably should not participate in the combination.

Personnel decisions   When practices merge, tough personnel decisions will need to be made. For example, if each practice has an office manager, only one manager will be needed for the group practice. The physicians will need to decide who will be kept, who will be reassigned, who will be let go.

Retirement plan   Because of IRS regulations, the new group will need to decide whether or not it has a retirement plan. Usually, the practices that have retirement plans want to continue contributions, and those practices that do not have plans find it difficult to implement them. Again, the physicians will need to decide if their new group practice will have a retirement plan.

Start-up costs   Merging medical practices is not cheap. Lawyers and consultants must be hired, new equipment might have to be purchased, a marketing plan must be implemented, and so on. Most mergers cost a minimum of $50,000, even for mergers of two to five physicians.

Governance   This is tied to the control issue. Physicians in a group practice must make decisions as a group instead of as individuals. Some decisions are placed into the hands of a few individuals, such as the managing physician or the executive committee. Many physicians initially want a strong voice in governance issues.

Lease obligations   Depending on the merger situation, continuing lease obligations may prevent the practices from consolidating office space and/or consolidating equipment usage.

Disruption of referral patterns   Some physicians who join a group practice have experienced problems with their referral relationships because some referring physicians did not like some of the physicians in the group practice.

Physician compensation   A new compensation system will be designed for the new group. It may not be one the physician had in mind and it may cause a decline in take-home pay.

Premerger Assessment (Due Diligence)

After the physicians have decided to merge their practices, their first step is to conduct what generally is termed a *premerger assessment* or *due diligence*. This assessment can be conducted by the CPA or an engaged consultant. It identifies potential problems that might arise during the merger process, some of which could terminate the combination. The assessment also may identify issues the physicians have not considered. Also, preassessment allows the physicians to see the benefits of merging, both operational and financial. Always emphasize and communicate the positives and benefits of the merger.

To conduct an assessment, begin by interviewing each physician and finding out why he or she wants to merge. Never assume that physicians who have decided to merge should. Many mergers that have taken place have been the result of emotion instead of common business sense. When talking with the physician, listen for mention of the advantages of merging that were discussed earlier. If the only reason the physicians are merging is managed care, they will probably not survive as a group practice. If their only concern is managed care, they have other options, such as forming an independent practice association (IPA), which is a good way for the physicians to test the waters and determine if they do want to merge their practices.

> ■ **Practice Point:** If managed care is the physicians' dominant reason for the merger, suggest that they form an IPA first and use this as the vehicle to deal with managed-care issues.

Intangibles

The physicians should make sure that they are comfortable with each other's practice, business, and clinical styles. They should also have the same philosophies about the future of the new practice and the practice of medicine in general. These intangibles often are overlooked, and the physicians should discuss them before the merger takes place.

■ **Practice Point:** Evaluate each physician's clinical and practice style during an on-site visit to each practice participating in the merger. Pay strict attention to clinical styles if practices intend to consolidate offices. Try to see each practice on its busiest patient visit day.

Finances

The preassessment should provide a thorough analysis of each practice's finances. For each practice, compare a history of charges, collections, and adjustments. This information will be used to develop the group's physician compensation formula. You will need to identify the debt of each practice so that the physicians considering consolidation can decide which liabilities the new group practice will assume and which will remain each physician's responsibility. Friction may develop among the physicians if one practice's accounts payable are considerably higher than the other practices'. A final decision on the assumption of accounts payable may depend on how the cash basis overhead will be allocated to the physicians.

■ **Practice Point:** The following are the main reasons to review practice financial information:

- To decide on a proposed compensation system for the new group

- To evaluate each practice's personnel (Good practice management statistics are usually a helpful indication of how competent personnel really are. This information will be used to develop a proposed organizational chart.)

- To draft a proposed group practice cash flow projection (This projection takes every practice's data and shows potential merger adjustments. The purpose of this projection is to see how each physician might fare under the new group and to project the economies of scale the merger might achieve. For example, the projection will indicate potential revenue increases and possible overhead decreases as a result of the merger. However, it will also show all start-up costs related to the merger.)

The following is a sample cash flow spreadsheet:

	Practice A	Practice B	Practice C	Adjustments	Adj. Balance
Revenues: (List Below)					
Expenses: (List Below)					

The CPA should use the following worksheet in the pre-assessment of each practice's finances:

Financial Analysis

Practice Name:	Practice A	Practice B	Practice C	Practice D
Prod-YTD				
Coll-YTD				
Gross Coll %				
Prod-Last Yr				
Coll-Last Yr				
Gross Coll %-Last Yr				
Adj-YTD				
Adj-Last Yr				
Net Coll %-YTD				
Net Coll %-Last Yr				
A/R-YTD				
A/R Ratio-YTD				
A/R-Last Yr				
A/R Ratio-Last Yr				
Overhead-YTD				
% of Collections				
Overhead-Last Yr				
% of Last Yr Collect				
MD Comp-YTD				
% of Collections				
MD Comp-Last Yr				
% of Last Yr Collect				
Fixed Assets				
Current A/P				
Notes Payable				

Payor Mix				
Medicare				
Medicaid				
Commercial				
Managed Care				
Work Comp				
Self-Pay				
Other				

Staff Considerations

Potential group members should compare the number of employees in each practice, their salaries, and the benefits they receive. In most mergers, not all of the employees will be needed in the new practice. For example, if three practices merge and each has an office manager, only one will be needed in the new practice. Unless the remaining office managers can be reassigned to other duties, they will have to be let go. The number of front-desk and billing personnel will also probably be reduced.

If there is a wide disparity in employees' salaries, the physicians will have to decide whether to reduce or equalize the disparity. For example, if one physician's billing clerk makes $27,000 per year and another makes $17,000 per year, the new group will need to decide if it wants to continue the higher pay scale. Comparing fringe benefits is equally important, especially with respect to policies regarding vacation and sick leave.

■ **Practice Point:** Draft a proposed organizational chart for the new group. Distribute the chart to each physician to review and discuss. The organizational chart will help the physicians decide their personnel needs and determine a salary for each job duty.

■ **Practice Point:** Remember that most physicians will want to minimize disruption among the employee group and not lay off anyone initially. More than likely, the physicians will want to let attrition take its course. After the first four to six months of the new group's existence, it will become evident how many employees are needed to operate the group efficiently. However, some physicians will make these personnel decisions early.

Use the following worksheet to analyze staffing needs and salary levels:

Employee Analysis

Practice Name:	Practice A	Practice B	Practice C	Practice D
Office Manager:				
Salary:				
Front Desk:				
Salary Range:				
Billing/Collection:				
Salary Range:				
Clinical:				
Salary Range:				
Technicians:				
Salary Range:				
Physician Extenders:				
Salary Range:				
Secretary:				
Salary Range:				
Administrative:				
Salary Range:				
Other:				
Salary Range:				
Benefits:				
Vacation:				
Sick Leave:				
Retirement Plan:				
Other:				

If all the practices that are merging do not have retirement plans in place, the new group must decide whether to set up a new retirement plan or adopt one of the practice's plans. This issue is often the deal-buster when practices merge. Physicians who do have a retirement plan usually want to continue providing and contributing to a plan, whereas physicians who do not have a plan may not want the financial burden of implementing and contributing to a new one. This is an acute problem in group practices without walls (GPWW), a network of physicians who have merged into one legal entity but maintain each individual practice location, and other groups in which such costs are posted directly to each physician in the group's physician compensation formula. In this type of situation, each physician's compensation will be reduced by the amount contributed to the practice's retirement plan on his or her behalf. If a physician did not contribute to a retirement plan before the merger, he or she could see a drop in his or her personal compensation after the merger because of the contribution the physician will have to make to the retirement plan. This is a point of contention for many physicians.

■ **Practice Point:** If retirement plans become an issue, recommend that there be no retirement plan in the first year but a contribution in the second year as a compromise. Another compromise that works is to establish a retirement plan with a minimal first-year contribution.

Fee Schedule

Each practice's fee schedule must be reviewed before a merger takes place. Because the new group will develop its own fee schedule, the physicians will have to contend with changing their own fees. Physicians whose fees are low may not want to raise them, and physicians whose fees are high may not want to lower them. For example, if a physician charges $45 for an office visit and another physician charges $70 for the same visit, the physicians will have to compromise to determine a new fee. If the physicians cannot compromise, a conflict could arise over a fee schedule for the new group practice. To analyze fees, take the 20 to 25 most common services rendered by each physician and prepare a table showing the fees for each physician. If a wide disparity exists in specific service fees, bring this to the attention of the merging physicians.

■ **Practice Point:** Analyze the top 20 fees for at least the following three CPT categories: evaluation and management, medicine, and surgery. The revenues of most medical practices, except for anesthesiology, will be concentrated in these categories.

Medicare and Coding Practices

The new group will have to make a decision about Medicare. If all of the physicians are not participating providers, the new group could experience some conflict. If a reviewer reviews the coding practices of some of the physicians and finds that some of the practice's revenue is artificially high because it was upcoding its services and had a higher utilization of ancillary services, this could affect all the physicians' compensation in the future because the coding will be corrected after the new practice begins. On the other hand, the coding assessment may identify situations in which a physician is either undercoding or missing coding opportunities. In this situation, revenue should increase in the new practice simply because the group will code the physician's services correctly. To analyze CPT code utilization, prepare a table of each practice's most commonly used codes. Calculate the number of times the code was used during the most current year-to-date period and compare the practices to one another. Most computers can provide this utilization output. If substantial differences exist in how physicians code their services, inform all of the physicians and advise them that they should discuss this at the beginning of the merger process. (See Chapter 10 for a more detailed discussion of CPT and diagnosis-coding rules.)

After the formal assessment of each practice, determine potential problem areas and conflicts. The physicians and the engaged consultant should be able to use the assessment information to provide answers to other merger issues, which will be discussed throughout this chapter. If problems and conflicts exist, discuss them with the merging physicians immediately. The merger cannot proceed until such issues are resolved. If the issues are not discussed and solved, the new group practice could suffer an early breakup.

Financial and Legal Considerations

A number of financial and legal considerations must be addressed by the physicians as the merger process progresses. Many of these considerations are dealt with during the preassessment and contract development phases.

New Practice Entity

After the premerger assessment has been conducted and the physicians decide to go forward with the merger, the next step is for the physicians to choose the type of legal entity under which they will practice. The most common choices are professional corporations and partnerships of professional corporations or individual physicians. The partnership format is most common in states that have enacted limited liability statutes. It is also sometimes chosen because the physicians do not want to dissolve their corporations. Many want to keep their own entity as a fallback in case the merger is not successful. The merging physicians should search for an entity that will simplify the merger, provide liability protection, offer the maximum tax advantages, and be easy to operate on a day-to-day basis. When selecting an entity, the physicians should keep in mind that one or more physicians may opt out of the merger and plan for the anticipated change.

Assignment of Equity Interests

Once an entity is chosen for the new group practice, the physicians will then need to decide how to assign equity interests to each physician. The most common method is to value each practice and assign equity interests based on a ratio of the appraised values. Although this method may seem acceptable in the beginning, mainly because most physicians will bring different practices of different values to the merger, it fails over the long term. This is because as the new group practice integrates over time, the original values tend to blend themselves in. After five to ten years, most physicians cannot say that their practice is still worth the initial equity differentials that were assigned when the group practice began. However, this methodology does take into account an early transition out of the practice, such as one due to a total disability.

> ■ **Practice Point:** Consider initially giving equal ownership to each physician but use the appraised value method for buy-out events and the distribution of proceeds in the event of a sale. This way, the physicians do not have to worry about evening out equity interests in the future as

the practice matures and evolves. All the physicians have to do is revise the buy-out provisions.

Buy-out provisions can be based on appraised values or on a predetermined formula. Some employment agreements state that if the practice is sold, the owners will vote on how to distribute the proceeds. This may eliminate the cost associated with having each practice appraised.

■ **Practice Point:** Each physician must have an equal voice in the management of the new group practice. This is usually accomplished by giving each physician an equal vote, no matter what his or her equity interest might be.

Name of the Group Practice

To establish a new identity, the physicians will want to come up with a name for the new group. Professionals who specialize in marketing for physicians agree that this is an opportunity to reposition the individual physicians as a new group within the service area. Each physician should submit three names for the new group. The physicians should then meet to review the suggested names and select one.

Contribution of Assets by Each Physician

Once the entity is formed, the merging physicians must decide which assets, if any, will be contributed to the new group.

Hard assets The physicians must decide how to disperse hard assets, especially if the practices consolidate into one central location. For example, if three family practitioners merge and each has laboratory equipment, some of the equipment may not be needed at the new location. If all three have computer systems, two of them will not be required in the new practice. If debt is attached to an asset that will be used by the practice, the physicians will have to decide if they want to assume the debt. The contribution of hard assets often requires compromises by the merging physicians.

The physicians will need to decide which equipment to use; whether to assume any related debt, if applicable; and whether to compensate the physician whose equipment is going to be used in the new practice. In addition, the physicians will have to decide on what to do with the equipment that will not be used. They may decide to put it into storage. If it is sold, the proceeds may be contributed to the group, assuming that the physicians whose assets are being used are not being compensated in any way. There are no correct answers to these questions. The answers will depend on how the physicians want to resolve the issues.

For example, six separate OB/GYN practices decide to merge into one single location. Each practice has an ultrasound machine and a good computer system. The physicians will need to decide which of these hard assets will be retained and which will be stored or sold.

Fixed assets   The merging physicians will also have to decide whether to contribute fixed assets to the new practice entity. To facilitate the merger, each physician should retain ownership of his or her own fixed assets. This is one reason the partnership format sometimes is preferred. Retaining ownership of fixed assets safeguards each physician in case the merger does not succeed. If the new group must be dissolved, each owner walks away with his or her fixed assets. If ownership is retained by each physician, the new group will acquire new assets beginning on the actual start date of the new practice.

Each of the merging physicians must assess the tax consequences of retaining ownership of his or her own fixed assets. If the physicians become employees of the new group, an unincorporated merging physician will generally deduct the related depreciation as an employee business expense. An incorporated physician will continue to deduct the depreciation expense on the corporate tax return as long as the corporation is engaged in a trade or business.

Accounts receivable   A new practice will need working capital when it begins, which will come either from a bank loan or from the physicians' existing accounts receivable. Generally, if accounts receivable are contributed to the new practice, the amount of receivable to contribute will depend on how the physicians will be compensated. If the physicians will be compensated based on the direct collections on their own production, then all of the accounts receivable usually are contributed. For other compensation arrangements, the physicians generally agree to contribute an equal amount of their receivables to the new group. The excess is then accounted for separately, and the related collections are paid directly to each physician. Each physician must contribute the same amount of realizable receivables to the new group. Medicaid receivables will pay less than commercial insurance receivables. Thus, the payor detail of each physician's accounts receivable must be analyzed thoroughly by someone before they are contributed.

> ■ **Practice Point:** If accounts receivable are contributed to the new group, the receivables become at risk in the event of litigation, especially in the event of a malpractice lawsuit in which the judgment exceeds the malpractice coverage. Since receivables should turn over quickly, this should not be a major concern for the physicians.

> ■ **Practice Point:** The merging physicians must understand that the group's accounts receivable will always be at risk. For example, a malpractice lawsuit and resulting large judgment could deplete the group's accounts receivable.

Medical records   The new group will become the new owner of each physician's medical records. Therefore, the physicians must contribute these charts to the new group practice. Check with the State Board of Medical Examiners to determine if patients must legally assign their chart over to the new group to establish ownership. The potential problem here is if a physician with a professional corporation liquidates the corporation and recontributes the assets to the new group practice. This would include the medical records, which do have a value. This situation may result in a taxable event to the physician, unless the transaction can be structured as a tax-free reorganization or if the professional corporation became the owner and contributes assets in exchange for an equity interest.

Promotion of the New Group Practice

An often overlooked issue is a marketing program for the new group. The merging physicians should discuss marketing strategies as the group is being created, starting with the image the group wants to present for both the patients and the medical community. Then the physicians should create a marketing plan to increase the practice's combined revenue base. Before developing a plan, review current managed-care contracts to see if any new leverage was created by the merger. If it was, the new group may be able to renegotiate its managed-care contracts. (See Chapter 15 for a more in-depth discussion of marketing considerations.)

Physicians' Issues

The new group must address a variety of physicians' issues. The legal aspects of these issues are discussed in Chapters 17 and 18. For example, the physicians must work out the details of buy-out and employment agreements.

Physicians' Compensation

After all of the practices' financial information has been gathered and analyzed, you will need to create a physician compensation formula. The circumstances of the merger will help you decide which formula to use. Your choice also will be influenced by the philosophies of the merging physicians. For example, the physicians may want to emphasize productivity or they may want to promote a sense of unity and teamwork by splitting income equally. A successful formula is one that each physician believes to be fair and reasonable.

The following are some common compensation formulas:

- Direct physicians' collections and shared overhead
- Fixed compensation plus bonus
- Bonus based on percentage of collections
- Bonus based on percentage of production
- Equal compensation for all physicians
- Fixed compensation plus percentage of net production
- Percentage of net production

Refer to Chapter 18 for a detailed discussion of various compensation formulas.

After the physicians decide how they want to be compensated, they must determine how the compensation methods will pay out in the new group. Thus, you will need to prepare a projection of revenue and expense and apply the income compensation formula for each physician. Inform all the physicians of any likelihood that their income will decrease in the new group setting.

> ■ **Practice Point:** Few physicians want to join a group practice and take a cut in pay. This is why during the assessment stage you need to prepare a revenue and expense projection for the new group and model certain compensation formulas.

In addition to direct compensation, the physicians will need to determine benefit packages. These benefits include vacation time, time off for continuing medical education (CME), CME compensation for each physician, sick leave, and insurance compensation, including which insurance to pay on behalf of the physicians. If the practice has a claims-made malpractice policy, the physicians will have to decide who will be responsible for the malpractice tail-end premium in the event there is a separation of service from the group. As discussed in Chapter 18, under a claims-made policy, the insurance carrier covers malpractice claims or notices of a claim only if they are filed before the policy's termination date. The issue that has to be resolved among the physicians is who is responsible for paying the premium that covers the tail-end period, the period after the policy is terminated. Normally, the physician-owner is responsible for his or her own tail-end premium. The group may actually pay for the premium, however, and any buy-out amount will be reduced by the amount paid.

The physicians also should discuss what will happen if they choose, or are forced, to take extra time off from the practice. For example, how is compensation affected if one physician takes more vacation time than the other physicians? What happens if a physician breaks a leg and is out for seven weeks? What happens if a physician is sued for malpractice and must attend a trial for two months? Unfortunately, these issues usually are dealt with after they occur, rather than discussed beforehand when the new group's legal documents are drafted. Generally, a physician will be personally responsible for the payment of any additional coverage, such as the payment for a *locum tenens* (substitute) physician. Personal time off should be uncompensated, just as it would be for any other employee, unless the physician wants to pay for a *locum tenens* physician or compensate the other physicians in the group out of his or her own pocket. Physician-owners who cover for an absent physician will usually be paid extra compensation if the absence is a long one.

Managing Physician and Group Management

One physician should be appointed the managing physician of the new group. This person interacts with the new group's employees and is responsible for a specific set of duties. In most cases, the employees actually report to the office manager or administrator, who in turn reports to the managing physician.

> ■ **Practice Point:** Not everyone can be the boss. Keep this in mind when the physicians nominate a managing physician. This is a political matter and should be handled with care.

You should be able to identify managing physician candidates during the preassessment phase after the physician interviews have been conducted, on-site practice visits made, and financial data analyzed. For example, the physician whose practice shows excellent practice management statistics is a possible candidate. The managing physician should have the following characteristics:

- Has experience in a group practice environment
- Works well with employees
- Is interested in practice operations
- Can make decisions
- Can interact and communicate well with the other physician-owners

The following list identifies a few of the most common duties of a managing physician:

- Takes responsibility for all day-to-day operations
- Supervises employees
- Supervises billing and collection activities
- Ensures that all insurance required by the group is paid and maintained
- Acquires fixed assets for less than a specific agreed-upon amount
- Enters into contracts on behalf of the group, not in excess of a specific agreed-upon amount
- Maintains bank accounts
- Makes sure all tax returns are prepared and filed in a timely manner
- Pays accounts payable
- Implements the business decisions of the group practice

The managing physician's duties are normally listed in the legal records of the new practice, either in the corporate bylaws or in the partnership agreement. In most group practices, management decisions are made by the physician-owners as a group. Implementation of the decisions is the responsibility of the office manager. The duty of the managing physician is to make sure that the management decisions are implemented.

■ **Practice Point:** There is a tendency to want to "corporatize" the governance of a new group practice (i.e., CEO, board of directors, owners). People sometimes want to consolidate the decision-making process, which can be very dangerous. At the least, initially all of the physicians who are parties to the merger must be involved in making major decisions, otherwise there could be problems. Try to make sure that the physicians are involved.

The group needs to decide if it wants to compensate the managing physician. Often, this will depend on how much time the managing physician spends on administrative duties, especially dealing with physician matters. Most groups, however, do not compensate the managing physician. The new group also must decide if and how the position will be rotated. Some medical practices vote in a new managing physician each year; other practices simply rotate the position among the practicing physicians.

When physicians merge, they usually place great emphasis on making sure the billing and collection operation is working perfectly. Although this function is important, it is equally important for the physicians to create a sense of unity within the organization. Otherwise, the group may end up as physicians who are basically just sharing an office. Physicians need to begin thinking like a group immediately.

There are many ways physicians can become a group. The first way is to develop a strong governance structure. Many practice issues need immediate attention and cannot be left up to the office manager to handle. A physician governance committee should be established to oversee the management of the practice and to take on the strategic issues that cause most physicians to group together in the first place. This committee will also handle all physician complaints and comments. This is a natural part of the group evolution process, especially for a GPWW. Physicians can and do become nervous whenever they join their first group practice. They need a communication forum to air their concerns and doubts. Without this forum, physicians may become disgruntled.

Never overlook the billing and collection process. A group practice will never be successful unless its billing and collection process works. Physicians do not want to join a group practice and then have their salary reduced. This is one of the quickest ways to destroy the confidence of physicians in a new group practice venture.

The best way to get physicians thinking like a group is by developing a system of communication. This starts at the top and trickles down to the bottom. The physicians must hold regular meetings to stay informed about the happenings within the group and to discuss strategic and operational issues. Between these meetings, the office manager must take charge. He or she must begin the process of managing the new office, and the physicians must let this process happen. Some physicians find it difficult to let go of some of the control over their employees. However, the physicians need to do this to allow the new practice to become a group. The physicians should also let the office manager manage the office so that he or she can make sure that all office processes are functioning. For example, if any area of billing or collection is impaired, the administrator must fix it immediately.

Within a GPWW, a centralized business office is established. However, this office is generally faceless to most of the physicians because they do not deal with the office directly. That's why it is important that the office manager have good communication with all of the office administrators and the physicians. A good office manager will keep physicians and office administrators informed. Again, issues should be discussed immediately to ensure the success of the group practice. However, there can never be total success without the cooperation and commitment of all the physician-owners.

Retirement Plan

The decision to implement or not to implement a retirement plan has the potential to cause major conflict, so the physicians should settle that issue during the preassessment phase of the merger process. Regardless of the decision made, however, the physicians who currently have retirement plans must decide either to terminate or freeze their current plans. Otherwise, they risk having their plans disqualified by the Internal Revenue Service (IRS). This is the result of both the affiliated service group and discrimination rules of the IRS Code.

If the new group adopts a new plan, the physicians must select a retirement plan administrator and, usually, an investment counselor. Because retirement dollars will be invested for the employees, the selection of the investment counselor is important. Since each physician will probably have his or her own favorite, you should interview each investment counselor and make a recommendation to the physician-owners.

Operational Issues

Numerous operational issues must be addressed by the physicians during and after the merger process. These issues are similar to those for any new practice (refer to Chapter 7, "Setting Up a New Medical Practice," and Chapter 9, "Basic Medical Office Procedures," for more detailed discussions).

As a general guideline, the following must be accomplished before the group practice can be operational:

- Assess personnel needs.
- Establish common billing and collection policies.
- Develop the new group's fee schedule.
- Design and approve a call schedule.
- Secure a new group provider number.
- Review each physician's insurance coverage.
- Obtain bids for new group health insurance.
- Obtain bids for new group malpractice insurance.
- Obtain bids for new group workers' compensation insurance.
- Obtain bids for any other new group insurance coverage that may be required.
- Obtain bids for new group office equipment and supplies.
- Choose an accountant.
- Choose a lawyer.
- Choose a practice management consultant.
- Choose outside services, such as a laboratory and radiology services.
- Select a bank.
- Buy a centralized computer system.
- Create a new medical charting system.
- Order new office forms, stationery, and business cards.

Personnel

As noted earlier, the new group will need to make personnel decisions before the practice can begin operation. For example, the physicians must decide who is going to be the practice's office manager, which employees are going to stay, which employees may have to be terminated, how much to pay the group's employees, and what benefits to provide to the employees of the new group. Deciding who to keep in the merged practice will depend on the needs of the new group. To ease the transition, most physicians initially try to keep all their employees. After the group has been operating for about four to six months, the physicians can make decisions about employees based on qualifications, the practice's needs, and the satisfaction of the physician-owners. The most common benefits given to employees are two weeks of vacation and five days of sick leave each year. The new group will also have to define the job duties of new employees. (See Chapter 16 for sample job descriptions.)

Billing and Collection

Setting up a centralized billing and collection process is one of the most important issues the new group will face. The new physician-owners will need to choose a computer system that will meet all of their needs, both immediately and in the future. The billing and collection personnel must be selected from the existing employees or hired. In addition, the physicians must develop and implement new billing and collection policies for the group. Potential conflicts related to billing and collection should have been identified during the preassessment phase of the merger. For example, if a physician had a loose collection policy for his or her practice, a conflict might arise with this physician if the new group adopts a more stringent set of collection policies.

When setting up a centralized billing and collection operation, the merging doctors will want to know how much the related start-up costs will be. This is especially true if additional office space has to be rented for these operations. When billing and collection is centralized, the business operations are usually combined with them (e.g., administration, accounting, accounts payable, etc.). Therefore, during the merger process, it is a good idea to prepare a worksheet such as the one below, showing the merging doctors what these (and other start-up costs) might be. The following worksheet is an actual estimate of the start-up cost for an OB/GYN merger of 22 physicians.

	Estimated Cost Per Item	No. of Items Requested	Total Budget
FURNITURE & FIXTURES			
Billing Office			
Staff Chairs	$250	8	2,000
Desk/Credenza	1,000	8	8,000
Guest Chair	200	8	1,600
Partitions			
Kitchen / Break room			
Dinette Set (including chairs)	1,200	1	1,200
Small Refrigerator	800	1	800
Microwave	325	1	325
Coffee Maker	40	1	40
Misc. Kitchen Supplies	150		150
TOTAL ESTIMATED FURNITURE & FIXTURES			**$14,115**
OFFICE EQUIPMENT / SUPPLIES			
Supply/Work Room			
Supply Cabinet	300	1	300
Shelves	300	3	900
Copier	7,000		7,000
Calculator	100	8	800
Typewriter	1,000	1	1,000
Fax Heavy	3,000	1	3,000
Fax	1,000	1	1,000
Misc. Supplies (bulletin boards, supplies, note)	2,000		2,000
TOTAL ESTIMATED OFFICE EQUIPMENT			**$15,200**
COMPUTER EQUIPMENT			
Medical Billing/Mgmt Package (Network)			
Hardware (16 workstations)	**$150,000**		**$150,000**
Misc. Computer Supplies (e.g., power supply)			1,000
Network/Cabling (110 × 18)	2,000	1	2,000
TOTAL ESTIMATED COMPUTER EQUIPMENT			**$153,000**

Summary:

Furniture & Fixtures .... $ 14,115
Office Equipment .... $ 15,200
Computer Equipment .... $ 153,000

Total: **$182,315**

An operational policy manual will help the new practice avoid billing and collection conflicts. The manual should outline all of the policies and procedures for the new practice. These should be reviewed, discussed, and approved by all the physician-owners before they are implemented. Another benefit of a policy manual is that it explains to employees what their job functions are and how they are expected to perform their duties. Generally, the manual addresses issues such as front-desk collections, insurance verification, filing insurance claim forms, preparing and mailing patients' statements, follow up on unpaid insurance claims, and closing out each day.

Major Implementation Issues

The following are the major issues that you should be concerned with during the implementation phase of the merger (i.e., the operational set-up).

Computer Selection

When a new group selects a computer, think of the practice's long-term and short-term needs. Don't let price govern the selection. Make sure that the system will meet the long-term needs of the group in areas such as financial reporting, managed-care contracting, reimbursement analysis, capitation contracting, and clinical data gathering and analysis. Acquiring a new computer system is probably one of the most important operational issues a group will have to address. During due diligence, review each of the practice's computer systems and determine if one is adequate enough to be upgraded. If one isn't, a new system must be acquired.

> ■ **Practice Point:** If a new system must be acquired, create a computer selection committee made up of one staff member or physician from each of the merging practices. The committee members should attend the computer demonstrations and provide input on what they like and don't like about each system. These members will have to work with the system on a day-to-day basis, so their input in invaluable.

■ **Practice Point:** If the merging physicians decide to acquire a new medical billing system for the new group, be
sure to reference (use) the medical practice management
software features checklist in Appendix A.

Computer Training

Make sure that all employees are adequately trained on the selected computer billing system before the new practice opens.
Furthermore, make sure that the computer vendor commits to
adequate training time and secure training time lines. Follow up
after the training and talk to each employee. The employees will
be able to tell you how much more training is needed. Poorly
trained employees will cause major problems to the billing and
collection process during the first few months of the merger. The
result could be a significant drop in cash flow and disgruntled
physicians.

■ **Practice Point:** If you ever believe employees are not
adequately trained on the computer system, push the
start date back a month, if necessary. The practice will
experience big problems in the billing and collection process if employees are unsure of how to use the computer.

Computer Conversion

The patient accounts for all of the physicians must be transferred
to the new computer system. The computer vendor may be able to
write a program that will convert all of the account history and
demographics to the new system. Before proceeding, obtain references of previous conversions and call them to see how the conversion process went. The practice may experience major problems if the conversion does not take place correctly. The biggest
problem usually occurs in the transfer of the patients' demographics. When this happens, a lot of staff time will be needed to correct
the problem, and the billing staff will have difficulty billing the
physicians' services.

The easiest and most conservative way to convert balances is to
do the following:

1. Convert the accounts receivable balances only with the related patient demographic information. This is accomplished by transferring these amounts as a balance forward into the new computer system. These accounts and their demographics are usually input by staff members the weekend before the new practice opens.

2. Have each physician or administrator print detailed account ledgers for each patient or at least make sure that they are available for the business office employees. They will need this information to handle patient account inquiries and to perform collection activities.

3. Have each patient complete a new patient information form in order to obtain demographic data. The front-desk employee should explain to the patients that as a result of the merger, the practice is attempting to update its records. Most patients won't mind filling out the form. By having all patients fill out a new form, the practice is ensured of getting up-to-date demographic information for all of its patients.

Informing Third-Party Payors

When a new group forms, it must get a new federal identification number under its new group practice name. When the new practice opens, its employees will bill out under this new name and identification number. However, unless the payors are informed of the merger, they will have no record of the new name or the related ID number. This could result in insurance claims being denied when the group bills, which will cause a major disruption to cash flow. To prepare the payors, do the following:

1. Send a fax to each payor at least six weeks before the start date of the new practice and inform the payor that the merger has taken place, the new group's name and federal identification number, and the names of the physicians (or practices) participating in the merger and their current identification numbers (these are the names the payor has in its computer).

2. One week before the new practice opens, call at least 20 of the most commonly billed payors. Make sure that the group has been properly set up in the payors' computer systems.

The following is a sample form which can be used to notify the payors.

[Date]
[Address]

Dear_____:

The following list of_____ [city] OB/GYN physicians have formed a group under the name of "_____,"
_____ (address) and will be active under this group name and address as of _____, 20__.
_____ (Physician name) is currently one of your network providers, and as of _____, 20__(date), he will be using the group's tax i.d.# _____ (if applicable) and mailing address.

Please make these changes accordingly to Dr. _____'s (physician name) provider information. We would like to add the other physicians to become network providers as a group for your company. Please contact _____ or _____ ( )_____ , Fax ( )_____, or by mail at the above address to let us know what we need to do for the group as a whole to become a network provider.

(List of physicians)

Thank you.

_____

Health Care Assistant

■ **Practice Point:** The merged group will also have to obtain new group Medicare and Medicaid provider numbers. Use Medicare Form CMS-855 to apply for the new Medicare group provider number.

Setting Up Operational Systems

Concentrate on the following operational systems:

Daily closeout activity   Each day the office manager or billing employee must close the practice's books and reconcile them to the daily bank deposit. For most groups, closeout begins at 4:00 p.m. Patients seen after 4:00 p.m. are posted the next day.

Insurance follow-up Make sure that the proper system is in place to follow up on unpaid insurance.

Physician reconciliation If the compensation formula is productivity-based, the office manager must track each physician's collections. This is important because all physician receipts will not be commingled in one bank account. If ever unsure of the practice's ability to track this, have the office manager deposit receipts in the first month *by physician*. Although this is cumbersome, it guarantees reconciliation.

- ■ **Practice Point:** One week before the new practice opens, conduct a meeting with the office personnel. Walk through the practice's operational policies and procedures to make sure that every employee knows his or her duties.

- ■ **Practice Point:** Monitor implementation of the practice's operational policies for at least two months after the practice opens. For example, make sure that the office manager is closing out the office properly, the billing employee is mailing insurance claim forms in a timely manner, an employee is following up on unpaid insurance claims, and so on.

Facilities

Facility issues mainly involve office leases or building ownership. If the physicians want to consolidate in one location, they need to determine the expiration date of each physician's office lease. If a physician cannot get out of his or her lease, that physician's office may need to become a temporary satellite location. If more than one physician is burdened with an existing long-term lease, the physicians may need to create a group practice without walls instead of consolidating into one office location. A physician who owns his or her office building will have to decide whether to stay in the building, sell the building, or lease the space.

Major Decisions by the Group

The physicians should determine which decisions must be decided by all of the owners instead of allowing the managing physician to make a unilateral decision. Following are some decisions that should be made only after the majority of the physician-owners have approved them:

- Hiring and firing personnel
- Amending the practice's fee schedule
- Purchasing fixed assets in excess of a specific, agreed-upon amount, generally $5,000
- Adopting or amending a retirement plan
- Making any individual expenditure in excess of a specific, agreed-upon amount, generally $2,500
- Designating or changing signatories on group bank accounts
- Borrowing money
- Entering into lease contracts
- Withdrawing from group bank accounts
- Negotiating and settling claims against the group practice
- Determining which expenses of the individual physicians should be paid for by the group practice
- Purchasing insurance
- Selling group practice assets

> ■ **Practice Point:** All of the physician-owners must have a voice in governance decisions. Even physicians who are starting a large group practice should follow this rule. One way the physicians can implement this is by conducting a monthly owner's meeting with a formal agenda. After decisions are made on agenda items, the office manager or the managing physician should implement them.

Dissolution of the Group Practice

Before a new group opens its practice, a method for dissolving the group must be discussed and decided on. Although nobody starts a new venture thinking it might fail, it is prudent to resolve the issues involving dissolution. The group's buy/sell agreement should state the vote necessary to dissolve the group. Generally, it is by majority vote of the owners. The agreement should also outline how the group will be dissolved, such as how assets will be distributed.

Physicians contemplating merging their practices must understand that proper planning is the key to a successful combination. A merger should not take place unless all of the issues presented in this chapter are analyzed, discussed, and decided on. Only then are physicians ensured a smooth transition from solo practice to group practice. (See the medical practice merger checklist in Appendix C.)

Antitrust Concerns When Merging Medical Practices

When physicians decide to merge their medical practices, this issue of whether or not the new group will or might run afoul of antitrust rules should be addressed. Chapter 22 discusses antitrust issues as they relate to integrated delivery systems such as IPAs. However, many of these principles apply to group practice formation as well.

There have been several antitrust rulings regarding group practice formation. The following is a summary of all of the recent business review letters that have been issued by the U.S. Department of Justice. This information also can be found at the following web sites located at:

http://www.usdoj.gov/atr/public/busreview/4579.htm

http://www.usdoj.gov/atr/public/busreview/letters.htm#99

> ■ **Practice Point:** If you are involved in a group practice formation and are concerned about antitrust, go to the detailed discussion of the Allentown Gastroenterology merger ruling discussed at the web sites above. This ruling provides excellent guidance on what the government looks for when practices merge.

Merger of Pulmonary Associates Ltd. and Albuquerque Pulmonary Consultants P.A.

October 31, 1994

Two pulmonary specialist physician groups in Albuquerque, New Mexico, each employing five doctors, four full-time and one part-time, proposed to merge. The combined firm, with 8 full-time and 2 part-time doctors, would be competing against at least 100 other physicians offering similar services in the area.

APPROVED: Because board-certified pulmonologists are not the exclusive providers of the services they provide, but face competition in these services from general surgeons, cardiac surgeons, thoracic surgeons and internists as well as family physicians; because HMOs and other third-party payors in the area currently employ, contract with, or reimburse many non-pulmonologists for the same type of services provided by pulmonologists; and because staff privileges at area hospitals are extended to many non-pulmonologists to perform these services, it appears that the new firm would not be able to exercise market power.

Anne Arundel Medical Center Anesthesiologists

October 17, 1996

The sixteen independent practitioner anesthesiologists who provided anesthesia services at Anne Arundel Medical Center in Annapolis, Maryland, proposed to merge into a single, integrated group to contract with the Medical Center and third-party payors. The Medical Center and payors indicated a preference for a single anesthesia group for a variety of reasons including ease of negotiating contracts, scheduling doctors' time, identifying and budgeting for costs, and establishing and monitoring consistent quality control standards. The proposal would enable the Medical Center to contract with the integrated group about pricing terms in order to offer payers global fee arrangements.

APPROVED: Under any plausible geographic market definition and assumption about the number of market participants, the merger does not raise substantial competitive concern. This conclusion is bolstered by the lack of concern about possible anticompetitive effects by the Medical Center or any third-party payors who utilize the Medical Center. The merged group should face effective competitive constraints on its ability to exercise market power. In addi-

tion, the merger may produce substantial efficiencies to the benefit of consumers.

Orthopaedic Associates of Mobile, P.A., and the Bone Joint Center of Mobile

April 16, 1997

Two groups of orthopedic specialists in the greater Mobile, Alabama, area proposed to merge. The combined entity would be an integrated group practice comprised of 16 of the 50 providers of orthopedic services (32 percent) in the greater Mobile area.

APPROVED: *Such a combination could raise competitive concerns, but no managed-care plan or other third-party payor expressed any concern that the proposed merger would likely cause any substantial anti-competitive effects. Rather, payors were confident that if the merged group attempted to raise prices, they would have adequate substitutes to defeat such a strategy. Therefore, it does not appear likely that the proposed merger would lessen competition substantially in the greater Mobile area.*

CVT Surgical Center (CVT) and Vascular Surgery Associates (VSA) of Baton Rouge

April 16, 1997

A group of six cardiovascular-thoracic surgeons proposed to merge with a group of four peripheral vascular surgeons. The groups were more complementary than competitive, with only 60 procedures performed in common by the two groups—about 15 percent of the procedures performed by CVT were peripheral procedures also performed by VSA. The groups contended that their geographic market was at least as large as an area within one-and-one-half hours' drive from Baton Rouge, including the cities of Hammond, New Orleans, Houma, Lafayette, and Thibodaux. In that area the merged entity would represent significantly less than 20 percent of the surgeons available to perform the relevant procedures. The merging groups accounted for approximately 50 percent of the vascular surgeons listed in the Baton Rouge Yellow Pages.

APPROVED: *While the Department doubted that the geographic market was as large as the parties proposed, the payors in the greater Baton Rouge area (a more probable geographic market) needed very few peripheral vascular surgeons to successfully market their plans* *to consumers. Competing surgeons from the New Orleans area seemed capable of quickly entering the Baton Rouge market, and had in fact begun to do so. Payors in the area were generally confident that the merged group was not likely to acquire market power. The Department concluded that the proposed merger was not likely to have any significant adverse competitive effects and might result in efficiencies benefiting consumers and payors.*

Allentown, Pennsylvania, Gastroenterologists

July 7, 1997

Three practice groups each comprised of four gastroenterologists proposed to merge into a single 12-person firm in Allentown, Pennsylvania. The group would then represent 12 of 14 gastroenterologists in Allentown (85.7 percent) and 12 of 19 gastroenterologists in Allentown and nearby Bethlehem (63 percent). The group suggested that the geographic market area within which to measure the potential market power of the merged firm would be the Greater Lehigh Valley, including Lehigh and Northampton counties and parts of Bucks, Berks, and Carbon counties, because some of the merging physicians regularly traveled to these areas to provide services at outlying hospitals. Within that area, the group would comprise 36 percent of all board-certified gastroenterologists.

REJECTED: Managed-care payors told the Department that they could not market a product that excluded gastroenterologists, and the Department concluded that the medical specialty of gastroenterology was the appropriate product or service market for analyzing the merger. The Department also found the relevant geographic market to be at most the cities of Allentown and Bethlehem, and possibly only the city of Allentown. Managed-care payors told the Department that they could not ask enrollees to travel to distant counties or, in many instances, even from Allentown to Bethlehem, to obtain gastroenterologic services in order to defeat a price increase by the merging firms. Based on its investigation, the Department concluded there was a substantial likelihood that the merging group would cause anticompetitive harm in the market for gastroenterologic services in the Allentown/Bethlehem area. It was not apparent that entry within two years of additional gastroenterologists would occur to defeat a price increase, particularly as it appeared there was already an oversupply of gastroenterologists in the area. The parties demonstrated no merger-specific efficiencies to counteract the potential anticompetitive harm posed by this merger. As a result, the

Department could not state that it would not take enforcement ac-tion against the merger were it consummated as described.

Merger Time Line

Phase One: Preassessment

Generally, the due diligence phase of a practice merger will take approximately two to three months. This time line is directly de-pendent on how quickly the physicians can gather and submit their data for the due diligence process and how quickly on-site visits to each practice can be conducted.

Phase Two: Contract Development

Phase Two will take six weeks to two months to complete, de-pending on how quickly the attorney can get the legal document drafted, how quickly the physicians can get the contract reviewed, and how long it takes to get the contract revised and executed. During this phase, you will usually need to engage a CPA to work carefully with the attorney drafting the contract, because most pro-visions in the document will be financial in nature and because the attorney will need an accountant's input based on findings and recommendations from the preassessment (e.g., physician com-pensation).

Note: The time line for Phase Two depends on one critical is-sue: Making sure the physicians' advisors provide timely and sub-stantive changes. After the contract is initially drafted, a copy will be given to each physician who is a party to the merger so that each physician can review it. Usually, the physician has the docu-ment reviewed by his or her personal attorney, accountant, or con-sultant. If the document drafts are given to advisors, be sure to state the following in an accompanying memorandum: Advisors should provide only substantive comments.

Some advisors tend to make nitpicking revisions when they re-view the drafts. This just delays the process and needlessly in-creases professional fees. Unless their changes are substantive, the physician should not submit them.

Phase Three: Implementation

It will take at least three months to integrate the practices. It can be done more quickly, but this phase of the merger process must never be rushed.

Group Practice Implementation Checklist

The following is a checklist that can be used to implement the formation of a new group practice. This checklist is included on the CD-ROM accompanying this book.

GROUP PRACTICE IMPLEMENTATION INFORMATION CHECKLIST

Practice Name _____

- ❏ Prepare and execute legal entity agreements.
- ❏ Prepare and execute physician compensation agreement.
- ❏ Obtain Federal identification number.
- ❏ Obtain State unemployment tax number.
- ❏ Prepare and file Medicare application.
- ❏ Prepare and file Medicaid application.
- ❏ Draft employee organizational chart.
- ❏ Set up computer demonstrations.
- ❏ Obtain bids from computer vendors.
- ❏ Select computer system.
- ❏ Interview candidates for position of practice administrator.
- ❏ Select practice administrator.
- ❏ Prepare and file Medicare participation agreement.
- ❏ Draft policies and procedures manual for practice.
- ❏ Send RFPs to vendors in selected expense categories.
- ❏ Select practice vendors.
- ❏ Schedule computer training.

- ❏ Select data for and implement computer conversion.
- ❏ Draft master fee schedule.
- ❏ Contact insurance companies to inform each that doctors are merging effective (date) and to find out how new entity needs to be set up in their computer system. **This is very important for all managed-care plans.**
- ❏ Select bank and open up bank account(s).
- ❏ Set up accounts payable system and order computer checks.
- ❏ Set up financial general ledger.
- ❏ Draft and order announcement cards.
- ❏ Order stationery and envelopes.
- ❏ Obtain group health insurance policy.
- ❏ Obtain group disability insurance coverage.
- ❏ Bid out (by RFP) and select malpractice coverage.
- ❏ Obtain group overhead disability coverage.
- ❏ Obtain buy-out life insurance coverage.
- ❏ Draft patient encounter forms.
- ❏ Set up capability to file insurance claims electronically.
- ❏ Make list of managed-care plans and complete applications for those plans any physician is not currently credentialled on.
- ❏ Select physician governance structure and managing physician if applicable.
- ❏ Review all tax issues impacting consolidation.
- ❏ Select and implement retirement plan for practice.

Office-Sharing Relationships

Another way in which solo physicians attempt to reduce overhead, but without the legal matters and philosophical compromises of group practice, is to share office space. In doing so, physicians not only split the rental costs but can also share overhead items such as personnel and supplies. If physicians decide to share an office, they will need to prepare and execute an office-sharing agreement or hire someone to do so. Disputes can arise in office-sharing relationships if the terms of the arrangement are not spelled out entirely beforehand. The following are the basic elements of an office-sharing agreement.

Nonfinancial Issues

In every office-sharing arrangement, both financial and nonfinancial issues arise. Following is a brief discussion of the nonfinancial issues involved with office-sharing arrangements.

Space Allocation

The agreement should first identify the space that will be shared and what portion each physician will occupy. Generally, the agreement states that each physician will have equal access to the space. The agreement should expressly state that the physicians are sharing only office space and in no way are to be considered a partnership. This will protect the uninvolved physician if the other one becomes entangled in legal problems.

Agreement Term and Termination

The term of the agreement should be spelled out, along with how the office-sharing contract can be terminated. Generally, the term is one year and is automatically renewable each year until the contract is terminated. Termination events generally occur when one physician gives written notice or when a physician no longer practices medicine.

Telephone Service

In most office-sharing relationships, the physicians will have separate telephone numbers. This way, each physician can still retain his or her own number should either leave the premises. If the physicians decide to share the same telephone number, the agreement must specify who will keep the number should the office-sharing relationship be terminated.

Rotating New Engagements

The agreement should also state the procedure the front-desk employee should follow when a new patient calls the office for an appointment and does not request any physician by name. In most situations, the agreement will state that new patients not asking for a specific physician will be rotated equally among the physicians. Monitor the front desk, however, to confirm that new patients are actually being rotated on an equal basis.

Financial Issues

To help avoid disputes, the financial arrangements between two or more physicians sharing office space must be spelled out in detail. Following are the major financial issues that should be addressed in the office-sharing agreement.

Overhead Costs

Probably the most important provision in an office-sharing agreement is the one that addresses how the physicians split overhead. The agreement must list each overhead item and specify how each will be split among the physicians. This will prevent a future dispute among the physicians if one physician feels that he or she should not have to pay for an overhead item. In addition, the agreement should specify when the physicians must pay for their share of the overhead. This will prevent a physician from delaying payment.

Personnel

Staffing is a major issue in any office-sharing relationship. The agreement should specify which employees are the responsibility of which physician and which employees will be shared by the physicians. It is also vital that the agreement specify the manner in which shared employees will be hired and fired. Generally, all of the physicians in the office must agree on the final decisions. A physician who has sole responsibility over an employee can terminate that employee's employment as he or she chooses. Likewise, if a physician wants to bear the financial responsibility, the physician can hire his or her own employees.

The CD-ROM contains a sample office-sharing agreement for use in a medical practice. As with all legal documents, the physicians should make sure that an attorney reviews the document before it is executed.

Rental of Space in Physician Offices by Persons or Entities to Which Physicians Refer

A Special Fraud Alert was issued in the year 2000 by the U.S. Office of Inspector General (OIG) focusing on the rental of space in physicians' offices by persons or entities that provide health care items or services (suppliers) to patients who are referred either directly or indirectly by their physician-landlords. In the Alert, the OIG describes some of the potentially illegal practices it has identified in such rental relationships. This Alert is important because physicians are attempting to increase their revenue by any means possible. Much of this activity has been caused by the rapidly reduced reimbursement by managed-care plans over the past two years. However, some attempts to affiliate and generate additional revenue could run afoul of government rules.

Questionable Rental Arrangements for Space in Physician Offices

The OIG Alert states that a number of suppliers who provide health care items or services rent space in the offices of physicians or other practitioners. Typically, most of the items or services provided in the rented space are for patients, referred or sent, either directly or indirectly, to the supplier by the physician-landlord. In particular, the OIG is aware of rental arrangements between physician-landlords and:

- Comprehensive outpatient rehabilitation facilities (CORFs) that provide physical and occupational therapy and speech-language pathology services in physicians' and other practitioners' offices;

- Mobile diagnostic equipment suppliers that perform diagnostic-related tests in physicians' offices; and

- Suppliers of durable medical equipment, prosthetics, orthotics, and supplies (DMEPOS) that set up "consignment closets" for their supplies in physicians' offices.

The OIG is concerned that in such arrangements, the rental payments may be disguised as kickbacks to the physician-landlords to induce referrals. The OIG has received numerous credible reports that in many cases, suppliers, whose businesses depend on physicians' referrals, offer and pay "rents"—either voluntarily or in response to physicians' requests—that are either unnecessary or in excess of the fair market value for the space to access the physicians' potential referrals.

The Anti-Kickback Law Prohibits Any Payments to Induce Referrals

Kickbacks can distort medical decision-making, cause overutilization, increase costs, and result in unfair competition by freezing out competitors who are unwilling to pay kickbacks. Kickbacks can also adversely affect the quality of patient care by encouraging physicians to order services or recommend supplies based on profit rather than the patients' best medical interests.

Section 1128B(b) of the Social Security Act (the Act) prohibits knowingly and willfully soliciting, receiving, offering, or paying anything of value to induce referrals of items or services payable by a federal health care program. Both parties to an impermissible kickback transaction are liable. Violation of the statute constitutes a felony punishable by a maximum fine of $25,000, imprisonment up to five years, or both. The OIG may also initiate administrative proceedings to exclude persons from federal health care programs or to impose civil money penalties for fraud, kickbacks, and other prohibited activities under sections 1128(b)(7) and 1128A(a)(7) of the Act.

Suspect Rental Arrangements for Space in Physician Offices According to the OIG

The questionable features of suspect rental arrangements for space in physicians' offices may be reflected in three areas, according to the OIG:

- the appropriateness of rental agreements;
- the rental amounts; and
- time and space considerations.

The OIG Alert examined the following suspect areas below, which separately or together may result in an arrangement that violates the anti-kickback statute, in order to help identify questionable rental arrangements between physicians and the suppliers to which they refer patients. This list is not exhaustive, but rather gives examples of indicators of potentially unlawful activity.

Appropriateness of Rental Agreements

The threshold inquiry when examining rental payments is whether payment for rent is appropriate at all. Payments of "rent" for space that traditionally have been provided for free or for a nominal charge as an accommodation between the parties for the benefit of the physicians' patients, such as consignment closets for DMEPOS, may be disguised kickbacks, according to the OIG. In general, payments for rent of consignment closets in physicians' offices will be suspect.

Rental Amounts

Rental amounts should be at fair market value, be fixed in advance, and not take into account, directly or indirectly, the volume or value of referrals or other business generated between the parties. Fair market value rental payments should not exceed the amount paid for comparable property. Moreover, where a physician rents space, the rate paid by the supplier should not exceed the rate paid by the physicians in the primary lease for their office space, except in rare circumstances.

Examples of suspect arrangements include:

- Rental amounts in excess of amounts paid for comparable property rented in arm's-length transactions between persons not in a position to refer business;

- Rental amounts for subleases that exceed the rental amounts per square foot in the primary lease;

- Rental amounts that are subject to modification more than annually;

- Rental amounts that vary with the number of patients or referrals;

- Rental arrangements that set a fixed rental fee per hour, but do not fix the number of hours or the schedule of usage in advance (i.e., "as needed" arrangements);

- Rental amounts that are only paid if there are a certain number of federal health care program beneficiaries referred each month; and

- Rental amounts that are conditioned upon the supplier's receipt of payments from a federal health care program.

Time and Space Considerations

Suppliers, according to the OIG, should only rent premises of a size and for a time that is reasonable and necessary for a commercially reasonable business purpose of the supplier. Rental of space that is in excess of suppliers' needs creates a presumption that the payments may be a pretext for giving money to physicians for their referrals.

Examples of suspect arrangements include:

- Rental amounts for space that is unnecessary or not used. For instance, a CORF requires one examination room and rents physician office space one afternoon a week when the physician is not in the office. The CORF calculates its rental payment on the square footage for the entire office, since it is the only occupant during that time, even though the CORF only needs one examination room.

- Rental amounts for time when the rented space is not in use by the supplier. For example, an ultrasound supplier has enough business to support the use of one examination room for four hours each week, but rents the space for an amount equivalent to eight hours per week.

- Non-exclusive occupancy of the rented portion of space. For example, a physical therapist does not rent space in a physician's office, but rather moves from examination room to examination room treating patients after they have been seen by the physician. Since no particular space is rented, the proration of time and space used to calculate the therapist's "rent" will be closely scrutinized.

In addition, rental amount calculations should prorate rent based on the amount of space and duration of time the premises are used. The basis for any proration should be documented and updated as necessary. Depending on the circumstances, the supplier's rent can consist of three components: (1) exclusive office space; (2) interior office common space; and (3) building common space.

1. *Apportionment of exclusive office space*—The supplier's rent should be calculated based on the ratio of the time the space is in use by the supplier to the total amount of time the physician's office is in use. In addition, the rent should be calculated based on the ratio of the amount of space that is used exclusively by the supplier to the total amount of space in the physician's office. For example, where a supplier rents an examination room for four hours one afternoon per week in a physician's office that has four examination rooms of equal size and is open eight hours a day, five days per week, the supplier's prorated annual rent would be calculated as follows:

Physician Office Rent Per Day	% of Physician Office Space Rented by Supplier		% of Each Day Rented by Supplier		No. of Days Rented by Supplier Per Year	
$\dfrac{\text{annual rent of primary lease}}{\text{no. of work days per year}}$	$\times$	$\dfrac{\text{sq. ft. exclusively occupied by supplier}}{\text{total office sq. ft.}}$	$\times$	$\dfrac{\text{4 hours}}{\text{8 hours}}$	$\times$	52 days (i.e., 1 day per week) = Supplier's annual rent for exclusive space

2. *Apportionment of interior office common space*—When permitted by applicable regulations, rental payments may also cover the interior office common space in physicians' offices that are shared by the physicians and any subtenants, such as waiting rooms. If suppliers use such common areas for their patients, it may be appropriate for the suppliers to pay a prorated portion of the charge for such space. The charge for the common space must be apportioned among *all* physicians and subtenants that use the interior office common space based on the amount of non-common space they occupy and the duration of such occupation. Payment for the use of office common space should not exceed the supplier's pro rata share of the charge for such space based upon the ratio of the space used exclusively by the supplier to the total amount of space (other than common space) occupied by all persons using such common space.

3. *Apportionment of building common space*—Where the physician pays a separate charge for areas of a building that are shared by all tenants, such as building lobbies, it may be appropriate for the supplier to pay a prorated portion of such charge. As with interior office common space, the cost of the building common space must be apportioned among *all* physicians and subtenants based on the amount of non-common space they occupy and the duration of such occupation. For instance, in example number one above, the supplier's share of the additional levy for building common space could not be split 50/50.

The Space Rental Safe Harbor Can Protect Legitimate Arrangements

The OIG strongly recommends that parties to rental agreements between physicians and suppliers to whom the physicians refer, or for which physicians otherwise generate business, make every effort to comply with the space rental safe harbor to the anti-kick-back statute. (See 42 CFR 1001.952(b), as amended by 64 FR 63518 (November 19, 1999).)

When an arrangement meets all of the criteria of a safe harbor, the arrangement is immune from prosecution under the anti-kick-back statute. The following are the safe harbor criteria, all of which must be met:

- The agreement is set out in writing and signed by the parties.

- The agreement covers all of the premises rented by the parties for the term of the agreement and specifies the premises covered by the agreement.

- If the agreement is intended to provide the lessee with access to the premises for periodic intervals of time rather than on a full-time basis for the term of the rental agreement, the rental agreement specifies exactly the schedule of such intervals, their precise length, and the exact rent for such intervals.

- The term of the rental agreement is for not less than one year.

- The aggregate rental charge is set in advance, is consistent with fair market value in arm's-length transactions, and is not determined in a manner that takes into account the volume or value of any referrals or business otherwise generated between the parties for which payment may be made in whole or in part under Medicare or a state health care program.

The aggregate space rented does not exceed that which is reasonably necessary to accomplish the commercially reasonable business purpose of the rental. Arrangements for office equipment or personal services of physicians' office staff can also be structured to comply with the equipment rental safe harbor and personal services and management contracts safe harbor. (See 42 CFR 1001.952(c) and (d), as amended by 64 FR 63518 (November 19, 1999).) Specific equipment used should be identified and documented, and payment limited to the prorated portion of its use. Similarly, according to the OIG, any services provided should be documented and payment should be limited to the time actually spent performing such services.

Practice Continuation Agreements

One issue rarely addressed when physicians share an office is what happens to one physician's practice should he or she die, become disabled, or have to leave the practice involuntarily for any other reason. A practice continuation agreement between the physicians, which is very similar to the buy/sell agreement discussed in Chapter 17, basically allows the remaining physician the first right to purchase the departing physician's practice.

The practice continuation agreement safeguards both parties. The remaining physician secures the right to purchase the other practice should he or she so desire. If no practice continuation agreement exists, the departing physician's representatives may not sell the practice or may sell it to another physician. In return, the departing physician will be assured of receiving some value for the practice. When a physician of a solo practice dies or is severely disabled, the value of his or her practice drops dramatically. Without the practice continuation agreement, the remaining physician can rely on a good portion of the departing physician's patients to come to him or her anyway, leaving no need to buy the departing physician's practice. Situations in which physicians share calls or have been together in the same location for a long time are especially vulnerable to this practice of absorbing one physician's client base without compensation. Therefore, for the benefit of both parties, the physicians should make sure that their office-sharing arrangements address the issues of practice continuation.

Stark Rules and Regulations

Whenever practices consolidate or physicians affiliate, government rules and regulations must be considered in every transaction. Medicare fraud and abuse statutes and antitrust laws are just a few of the examples discussed throughout this book. However, one piece of government regulation could affect any physician affiliation, and that is the federal self-referral laws, otherwise known as the Stark Rules. There have been two pieces of self-referral legislation known throughout the industry as Stark I and Stark II. In general, these laws prohibit physicians who have a financial relationship with an entity from referring their Medicare (and Medicaid) patients to the entity for what are called *designated health services*. Stark I addresses clinical laboratory services and Stark II addresses a number of other health services. Each of these laws affects physician consolidations and affiliations.

Stark II

Stark II is a federal statute that became effective January 1, 1995. The first set of final Stark II regulations were published in January 2001. Like Stark I, Stark II is intended to curb the abuses inherent in physician self-referral arrangements. Like Stark I, Stark II prohibits physicians who have a financial relationship with an entity from referring their patients to the entity for designated health services. Stark I dealt with clinical laboratory services. Stark II's ban applies to the following other designated health services:

- Physical therapy
- Occupational therapy
- Radiology services, including MRI, CT scan, and ultrasound
- Radiation therapy
- Durable medical equipment
- Parenteral and enteral nutrients, equipment, and supplies
- Prosthetics, orthotics, and prosthetic devices
- Home-health services
- Outpatient prescription drugs
- Inpatient and outpatient hospital services

A Stark analysis (Stark I or II) involves the following three questions:

1. Is there any financial relationship between the physician and the entity providing a designated health service?
2. Are there any referrals for designated health services to the entity?

3.   Do any exceptions apply?

If the answer to the first or second question is "no," there should be no Stark-related problems. If the answer to both questions is "yes," a Stark problem will arise unless one of the exceptions is met, as discussed below.

What Is a Financial Relationship?

In Stark I and Stark II, a *financial relationship* is defined as either an ownership or investment interest or a compensation arrangement. An ownership interest in an entity may be through equity, debt, or any other means and may include an interest in an entity that holds ownership or investment in any entity providing designated health services. A compensation arrangement exists when there is any remuneration between a physician and an entity. Remuneration includes any payment, direct or indirect, overt or covert, in cash or in kind. The law also prohibits a physician from referring patients to entities that have a financial relationship with one of the physician's immediate family members.

An ownership interest or compensation arrangement can be direct or indirect. An indirect ownership interest may pierce through several "holding companies" or layers of ownership. The final regulations clarify, however, that an indirect ownership interest will trigger Stark sanctions only if the entity furnishing the designated health services has actual knowledge of or acts in reckless disregard or deliberate ignorance of the fact that the referring physician (or an immediate family member) has some ownership or investment interest in the entity.

The final regulations also articulate a test for determining when an indirect compensation arrangement will trigger the Stark referral prohibition. The final regulations create a new exception for indirect compensation arrangements when the compensation received by the referring physician from an intermediate entity with which the physician has a direct financial relationship is consistent with fair market value and does not vary based on the volume or value of the physician's referrals to the entity providing designated health services.

What Is a Referral?

A *referral* is a request by a physician for a patient for an item or service payable under Medicare Part B, according to the statute. Referrals include requests by a physician for a consultation with another physician and any test or procedure ordered or performed by, or under the supervision of, the consultant. If the referral relates to any one of the designated health services, a Stark issue arises.

The final regulations further modify the definition of "referral" by excluding any designated health service personally performed or provided by the referring physician. Thus, a physician does not make a referral when he or she personally performs a service. However, the regulations indicate that a service is not personally performed if it is provided by any other person, including but not limited to, the referring physician's employees, independent contractors, or group practice members.

In-Office Ancillary Exception

The in-office ancillary exception permits referrals of most categories of designated health services (DHS) furnished personally by the referring physician, personally by a physician who is a member of the same group practice as the referring physician, or personally by individuals who are "directly supervised" by the physician or by another physician in the group practice, if specified location and billing requirements are met.

Also keep in mind that the in-office ancillary exception requires that services be furnished in a building in which the referring physician or another member of the group practice furnishes physician services unrelated to the furnishing of DHS or, in the case of a group practice, in another building used by the group for the provision of some or all of its clinical laboratory services or the centralized provision of DHS. Services will be considered furnished in the location where the services are actually performed upon a patient or when an item is dispensed to a patient in a manner that is sufficient to meet Medicare billing and coverage rules. The final regulations clarify specific location issues, such as the "centralized building" and "same building" requirements.

Group Practice Exception

Another Stark exception applies to a transaction or transactions that occur within the confines of a "group practice." This impacts a potential merger because the new merged group must meet the definition of a "group practice" as defined in the Stark II regulations.

In addition, if a group of physicians meets the proposed definition of a "group practice," such physicians may be entitled to avoid the reach of the Stark II prohibition if certain other exceptions are met. For example, Stark II excepts certain referrals for physician services provided personally by or under the personal services of another physician in the same group practice as the referring physician. An in-office ancillary service exception does not include services furnished personally by or directly supervised by either the referring physician or another physician who is a member of the same group practice. Also, income from designated health services cannot be distributed based on the volume or the value of referrals within the group practice.

Under Stark, a "group practice" is defined as a group of two or more physicians, legally organized into a partnership, corporation, faculty practice plan or similar association, where:

1. Each physician who is a member of the group provides substantially the full range of services that the physician routinely provides through the joint use of shared office space, facilities, equipment, and personnel;

2. "Substantially all" services of the physicians who are members of the group are provided by the group and billed under a billing number assigned to the group and amounts so received are treated as receipts of the group. Independent contractors are not considered to be "members" of a group practice;

3. The overhead expenses of and the income from the group practice are distributed in accordance with methods previously determined;

4. Except for payments based on a share of the overall profits of the group or productivity, or bonuses based on services personally performed or incidental to personally performed services, no member of the group directly or indirectly receives

compensation based on the volume of value of referrals by the physicians; and

5. Each member of the group personally conducts at least 75 percent of the physician-patient encounters of the group practice.

Under Stark, a group practice must be one legal entity, even if it is composed of owners who are actually individual professional corporations or who are individually incorporated.

The following structures are among those that may qualify under the final regulations, assuming all other requirements of the group practice definition are satisfied:

- A partnership between two or more physicians.

- A partnership between one physician and another party, provided that the partnership employs at least one other physician. (Similarly, a partnership between two nonphysician parties can qualify if it employs at least two physicians.)

- A corporation or limited liability company with one or more physician shareholders or members, provided that a corporation or limited liability company with only one physician shareholder or member employs at least one other physician.

- A corporation or limited liability company owned by nonphysicians, provided it employs at least two physicians.

- A single legal entity owned by two or more physicians through their individual professional corporations.

- A solo practitioner who is organized as a legal entity (for example, a professional corporation) and employs at least one other full-time physician.

- A single legal entity (whether a corporation, limited liability company, or other form) owned by one or more other legal entities (that is, a multi-entity arrangement) that involves two or more physicians through employment or indirect ownership, provided that the "investing" or "owner" entities are not themselves functioning group practices. (In other words, existing groups may not band together to form a group practice primarily to share in-office ancillary referrals.) The prevalent practice in these kinds of arrangements is for the physicians who own the investing entities to become employees of the new group practice, and for the investing entities themselves to cease functioning as group practices.

In order to be considered a group practice under the concept of "substantially all," physician members must furnish "substantially all" of their patient care services through the group. These services must be billed under a group number, and receipts must be treated as receipts of the group. The final regulations define a member of a group practice as any physician who owns, or is employed by, the group practice. In the case of a group practice owned by professional corporations or defunct group practices, the physicians who own those entities will be considered members of the group practice.

Also, those physicians who own all or part of the group practice through their own professional corporations and who are employed by their own professional corporations (which contract with the group practice to provide physician services) will be considered members of the group. Physicians are members of the group during the time they furnish "patient care services" (as defined in the final regulations) to patients of the group or for the benefit of the group, even if those services cannot be billed by the group (for example, certain administrative services, *pro bono* services). Independent contractors and leased employees will not be considered members of the group.

Income and Overhead

A group practice, under the Stark Law, must distribute its income and overhead according to methods that have been previously determined. The final regulations treat a distribution methodology as "previously determined" if it is determined prior to receipt of payment for the services giving rise to the overhead expense or producing the income. Apart from this limitation, the rule does not prevent group practices from adjusting their compensation methodologies prospectively as frequently as they desire, assuming these methodologies are in compliance with the Stark restrictions on the distribution of designated health service revenues.

These methods must indicate the practice is a unified business. According to the final regulations, to meet the unified business test, a group practice must be organized and operated on a *bona fide* basis as a single, integrated business enterprise with legal and organizational integration. Essential elements are: (1) centralized decision making by a body representative of the practice that maintains effective control over the group's assets and liabilities (including budgets, compensation, and salaries); (2) consolidated billing, accounting, and financial reporting; and (3) centralized utilization review (for example, utilization review conducted on a group-wide basis). This rule was designed to preclude group practice status for loose confederations of physicians that are group practices in name, but not in operation.

Compensation

To qualify as a group practice under Stark, physician compensation cannot be based on the volume or value of referrals by a group physician. Physician-members cannot be compensated directly or indirectly based on their own referrals.

Under the final regulation, group practice physicians can receive compensation directly related to the physician's personal productivity and to services incidental to the physician's personally performed services, provided the "incident to" services comply with related Medicare billing rules. This means that the "incident to" services must be directly supervised by the physician. In other words, the physician (or another clinic physician in the case of a physician-owned clinic) must be present in the office suite and immediately available to provide assistance and direction. Moreover, the person performing the "incident to" services must be an employee of the physician (or the physician-directed clinic).

Other Stark Exceptions

Although there are many Stark exceptions, most are narrowly defined. One exception relates to compensation arrangements. Most of these arrangements are mentioned in both the Stark I regulations and the Stark II law. Remember, most arrangements must be for at least one year.

Rental of office space and equipment Compensation for rental of space or equipment is not a financial relationship for purposes of Stark as long as (a) the lease is in writing, is signed by the parties, and specifies the premises or equipment leased; (b) the equipment or space leased does not exceed what is reasonable and necessary for legitimate business purposes and is used exclusively by the lessee; (c) the term is for one year; and (d) the lease terms are consistent with fair market value and would be commercially reasonable if there were no referrals between the parties. Payment for the use of common areas comes within the exception if such payments do not exceed the lessee's pro rata share of expenses for such space.

Bona fide employment relationships Remuneration for employment that meets the following criteria will not be deemed a financial relationship under Stark II: (a) the employment is for identifiable services; (b) remuneration is consistent with fair market value and is not based on the volume or value of referrals; and (c) the arrangement would be commercially reasonable even if no referrals were made to the employer. To meet this Stark exception, many group practices will have to amend their productivity-based compensation formulas if designated health services are being billed to Medicare and/or Medicaid patients.

Personal service arrangements Remuneration for personal services performed by a physician acting as an independent contractor will not be deemed a financial relationship as long as (a) the agreement is in writing, is signed by the parties, specifies the services covered, and includes all of the services that the physician will be providing; (b) the aggregate services do not exceed what is reasonable and necessary for legitimate business purposes; (c) the term is for at least one year; (d) compensation is set in advance, does not exceed fair market value, and does not take the volume or value of referrals into consideration, except as allowed in certain physician incentive plans; and (e) the services to be performed do not involve counseling or promoting a business arrangement or activity that violates state or federal law.

Physician incentive plans relating to appropriate utilization of services This exception is designed to protect managed-care delivery systems that use capitation or bonuses to reward appropriate utilization. To take advantage of this exception, the plan must meet certain criteria.

Remuneration unrelated to the provision of designated health services   Remuneration paid by a hospital to a physician will not be deemed a prohibited financial arrangement if it does not relate to the provision of designated health services.

Physician recruitment   Remuneration made by a hospital to a physician to assist in relocation is not a prohibited financial relationship as long as the physician is not required to refer patients to the hospital and the amount of remuneration is not based on the volume or value of referrals the physician makes to the hospital.

Specific group practice arrangements with a hospital   Services billed by a hospital but rendered by a group practice to inpatients pursuant to an arrangement for the provision of inpatient hospital services are exempt from Stark if the following conditions are met:

- The arrangement began prior to December 19, 1989.
- Substantially all of the designated health services provided under the arrangement are furnished to patients of the hospital by the group practice under the arrangement.
- The services to be provided and the compensation are specified in writing.
- The compensation is consistent with fair market value, is not based on the volume or value of referrals, and would be commercially reasonable in the absence of referrals between the parties.

Payments by physicians for items and services   Payments made by physicians to a laboratory in exchange for the provision of clinical laboratory services rendered will not be deemed a financial relationship if such remuneration is consistent with fair market value.

Defining Fair Market Value

In the final regulations, the government discusses exactly what is "fair market value." This term is relevant to many Stark requirements, both in the group practice context and elsewhere. In establishing fair market value and general market value of a transaction that involves compensation paid for assets or services, the government will accept any method that is commercially reasonable and provides evidence of the compensation as comparable to what is ordinarily paid for an item or service in the location by parties in arm's-length transactions who are not in a position to refer. However, the volume or value restriction will often eliminate the reliance on comparables involving parties in a position to refer or generate business. In these cases, you must look to alternative valuation methodologies, such as cost plus a reasonable rate of return on investment, to determine fair market value according to the final regulations. While reliance on an independent valuation consultant is not required, the final regulations make note that internally generated surveys do not have strong evidentiary value and may be subject to more intensive scrutiny than an independent survey.

The definition of fair market value under Stark states that the value of rental property is its value for general commercial purposes not taking into account its intended use. The final regulations clarify that it is permissible to take into account costs incurred to develop or upgrade the property or maintain it regardless of why the improvements were added. Further, while the rental rate charged by a physician cannot take into account the value of potential referrals to the lessee from the lessor physican, rental rates may reflect the value of an area being a medical community and its impact on fair market value generally.

▼ CHAPTER 22
Integrated Delivery Systems

Many health care providers are responding to the expansion of managed care and the increase in competition by forming what are known as *integrated delivery systems*. Integrated delivery systems are essentially affiliations of health care providers set up to deliver health care services together. Most of the affiliations are either between hospitals and physicians or among physicians themselves.

These affiliations are developing in the health care marketplace in part because health plans and employers want to contract with just one entity (the integrated delivery system) instead of contracting separately with hospitals and physicians. This leads to another reason for the rapid development of integrated relationships—the need to consolidate the delivery of physicians' and hospitals' services. Physicians and hospitals work together to deliver health care services so that costs can be reduced and the quality of care enhanced.

Other reasons health care plans enter into contracts with integrated delivery systems involve physicians' practice management and physicians' recruitment. Many hospitals use certain types of integrated delivery systems to recruit physicians for their medical staffs. For example, everyone needs primary-care physicians. Thus, a hospital may form a management service organization (MSO) that will handle a medical practice's administrative duties so that the physician will be free to practice medicine. The elimination of administrative duties is quite attractive to many physicians who want to set up a medical practice and affiliate with a hospital.

Integrated delivery systems are also important when a retiring physician's practice must be transferred. When a physician retires, he or she must decide what to do with his or her medical practice. A hospital will want to maintain the physician's patient base to sustain its own revenue stream. An integrated delivery system allows this to happen.

Managed care is fueling the development of many integrated delivery systems, especially independent practice associations (IPAs). Most managed-care plans have leverage over their provider communities. Most providers do not have a negotiation position with these health plans. In this type of environment, many providers form their own delivery system in order to negotiate with managed-care plans.

The main purpose of integrated delivery systems, however, is to obtain insurance contracts. Hospitals or physicians, or both, must offer something attractive to the insurance plans. These incentives generally come in the form of reduced charges to the health plans for the services rendered by the hospitals and physicians. Integrated delivery systems help reduce costs by (a) increasing the cooperation between physicians and hospitals in cost containment, (b) enhancing the quality of care, and (c) developing common treatment protocols.

What Payors Are Looking For

Physicians must begin preparing their practices for the imminent expansion of managed care and changing reimbursement. To do this, physicians must know what payors want. First, the physician should define who a payor is. The payor could be an employer, a preferred provider organization (PPO), an insurance company, a purchasing alliance, or a health maintenance organization (HMO). These are the people the physician will have to market to and contract with—now and in the future. The following is the payor's wish list:

- Physicians must have the ability to assume and manage risk. Payors will want to shift this responsibility onto the physician providers.
- An integrated finance and service delivery system must be in place. Patient care and related financial issues must be connected.
- Comprehensive, integrated clinical and administrative information systems must be in place. Utilization and its related costs can best be managed with these mechanisms.
- Physicians must have demonstrated clinical and value-based outcomes, along with cost-effective patient-care management. This is what keeps health care costs down. Physicians will need to provide this information to those payors with whom they want to contract.

- Payors want clinically, administratively, and financially integrated physicians. This bodes well for group practices and individual practice associations. Payors want cost-effective service management and integrated health care functions. More important, they are focusing on primary care and related preventive care. Primary-care physicians will further ingrain themselves as the gatekeepers of managed care to patients.

- Physicians need to cover a broad geographic base and have a strong financial position. This is because of exclusivity. To obtain an exclusive managed-care contract, the provider must be able to serve all patients within a geographic region and must remain solvent. A payor cannot afford to have one of its delivery systems dissolve.

These are the main items payors are looking for from a provider, provider group, or integrated delivery system. The importance of each item is specific to each individual payor. Therefore, the physician must begin meeting with representatives of the payors who are in the physician's area. The physician should meet with medical directors, people in charge of physician contracts, provider relations personnel, and human resource personnel. Meeting with representatives will help keep the physician on top of the payors' contracting philosophies. Also, the information that the physician receives at the meetings will assist the physician with planning for the medical practice or integrated delivery system.

Should a Physician Network?

Managed care and the related competition for managed-care revenues are growing. In fact, they are developing rapidly in many urban areas throughout the country. Whenever a marketplace changes, it affects most practicing physicians. In the midst of a changing marketplace, a physician should have the following two goals: revenue enhancement and revenue protection. One purpose of revenue enhancement is to expand the practice's patient volume. The main purpose of revenue protection is to make sure that the patients stay. In other words, physicians do not want the marketplace to move their patients to other physicians.

Many physicians are using payor information to compete for managed-care dollars. They are forming integrated delivery systems, such as IPAs, and consolidating physicians into integrated group practices. This type of networking is one solid way to preserve and enhance a practice's revenue base.

When presented with networking opportunities, physicians must seriously consider them. Each service area will be different and the needs of the payors will be different. This is why physicians need to examine network affiliations carefully to determine if they will be valuable for them and their service area. For example, numerous IPAs are failing because they could not get a managed-care contract. Physicians cannot afford to pass up networking opportunities because the physicians could lose patients to another physician's network.

The Affiliation Decision

The health care marketplace is changing rapidly and this is forcing many practicing physicians to consider their future options for the first time. Some physicians fear that their practices' collections are going to decrease in the near future. Many physicians do not believe they have enough leverage to negotiate. The combination of these two items is making physicians nervous. The culprit causing much of this concern is managed care. As managed care continues to gain market share, whether it be in the Medicaid, Medicare, or employer segments, physicians are fearful that either their reimbursements will decrease or their patients will be forced to leave them for other participating physicians or other competing entities, such as IPAs. These reasons, along with other compelling factors, are enough to make some physicians consider selling out to a third party or to begin looking at other possible affiliation opportunities.

Physician Options

As physicians begin to consider the future of their own practice area and attempt to decide what is the best course of action, the first step to an informed decision is knowing exactly what the options are. The following are some common alternatives:

1. Do nothing
2. Sell out
3. Merge
4. Affiliate

Almost overnight, hospitals everywhere have formed physician/hospital organizations (PHOs), physicians have sold their practices to hospitals or practice management companies, physicians have formed IPAs, physicians have merged, and numerous management service organizations (MSOs) have formed. The result of all of this activity has been both good and bad. For example, some PHOs are dormant because they could not get enough managed-care contracts, and some IPAs have successfully obtained contracts. Some physicians regrettably sold their practices prematurely and others are quite happy with their decision.

The Road to an Informed Decision

Before the physician makes a decision about which option to take, the physician must make sure that he or she has enough information to make an informed decision. Any decision should not be based solely on fear about the future, information in a trade journal, or discussions with other physicians. Business conditions, market conditions, and other factors must first be evaluated before any practice decision is even considered.

Step 1: Analyzing the Practice

Before considering any option, a physician must make an assessment of his or her medical practice. This is important because the physician needs to make an informed decision, not one based on fear. The physician must first know exactly where current practice revenues are coming from. You can determine the percentages of practice collections that come from Medicare, Medicaid, commercial payors, self-pay, workers' compensation, preferred provider organizations, and health maintenance organizations. This information is necessary to assess the stability of the practice's own revenue base. It will also help to determine if revenue will remain unaffected in the future or if something could happen that may cause revenues to decline. For example, revenues could be affected by governmental regulations or shifts in payor mix. If the practice's revenue declines, the physician might address the issue by adopting an appropriate affiliation.

Next, determine the percentage breakdown of managed-care revenues by specific managed-care payors. Patient access is the reason this issue is so important. As long as a patient can call up a physician for an appointment, or a referring physician can make a referral to the practice, then the physician's only concern is reimbursement. In some cases, the physician will see the same volume of patients but will get paid less for them. If that is the case, the physician must decide how to improve the bottom line. Even if the physician's reimbursement rate will not be affected in the near future, the physician must always keep an eye on the service area because things can change rapidly. Managed-care penetration may increase rapidly, or Medicare patients may start moving into particular managed-care programs.

For example, if a physician knows managed care represents 23 percent of total practice revenues, should the physician do anything right now about the practice? Depending on the rest of the payor mix, the physician should probably do nothing. In situations where one payor does not represent a large portion of revenues, the best course of action is to do nothing and keep a close eye on the marketplace. Again, any practice cannot afford the involuntary shifting of patients to other providers. The physician must constantly monitor managed-care penetration and related predictions for his or her service area because this is the environment in which patients can be lost. Specifically, when HMOs penetrate a market, patients can shift to an exclusive provider network.

When a practice derives 50 percent of its patients from managed-care plans and 30 percent from one specific payor, the physician can easily lose a significant amount of patients. For example, if the payor with 30 percent of the physician's patients begins to lose patients to another HMO where the physician is not credentialled, the physician has effectively lost the revenue. No physician can afford to lose this kind of revenue. However, if the payor loses patients to a preferred provider organization, and the physician is a participating provider on the plan, reimbursement becomes the primary concern.

Step 2: Analyzing the Service Area

Determining how a physician's service area can change is arguably the hardest part of the decision-making process for the practice. The analysis methods presented in Step 2 are closely intertwined with those in Step 1. Keeping a close eye on the practice's own patient mix is a good first step. Specialists should keep an eye on referral patterns. Both of these could be used as indicators that the service area is shifting its payor mix. Another important step in the process is to answer the following question: What could happen in the practice's service area in the next three to five years that could make practice collections decrease? There are at least three ways the practice's revenue could decrease. The first, and sometimes the most overlooked, is a decline in service reimbursement. For example, many commercial insurance companies are converting to Medicare's RBRVS system of payment. The recent attempt to reform Medicare would have resulted in a decline in revenues for many physicians with a significant volume of Medicare patients. As previously stated, revenues will likely decline as patients shift to any type of managed-care system. This means that most physicians will receive less for seeing the same volume of patients. However, the important point to remember is that the physician gets to see the patient. He or she is not locked out of an appointment or referral availability.

If the physician is experiencing a decline in service reimbursement, the practice might want to look for ways to improve its overall operations and possibly decrease its costs to increase revenue. This can be accomplished through the addition of ancillary services and marketing, which of course requires a capital outlay. Many practices do not have the money to spend on these kinds of activities nor do they desire to borrow capital from a bank to do it. Therefore, partnering up through a practice merger, for example, may make some sense. However, remember that each practice is unique, and so each practice must be analyzed carefully before making any kind of a decision.

The second way collections can go down is through competition. Physicians and other delivery systems are competing for the same block of patients in any given service area. If the practice is vulnerable to competition, it may have to partner up with a third party just to compete. This could mean selling the practice or affiliating with other physicians in one form or another. For example, if a practice has significant market share in a particular area, it may be vulnerable to outside competition. If a well-known competing practice decides to open up an office, revenues could decline over time. The same could happen if a strong integrated delivery system formed and it obtained exclusive managed-care contracts. For example, one IPA secured an exclusive agreement with an HMO for over 200,000 patients. Obviously, most of these patients came from (i.e., were shifted away from) other practices. Practice revenues can be lost in this type of situation. If the physician believes his or her practice is vulnerable to competition, affiliating with another physician or group may make sense. Many physicians are forming IPAs to compete or are merging with other practices to gain leverage in a particular service area. Whether the physician should do this will depend on the diversity of the practice's patient base.

The issue of competition is entangled with the third reason for falling collections and that is the previously discussed concept called "denied access." This means that a patient cannot call and make an appointment with the practice or a referring physician cannot make a referral to the practice. This usually happens (1) if the practice is deselected from a PPO plan or (2) if the practice is excluded from an HMO population. Exclusion is what worries many physicians, because exclusive HMO provider networks are allowed in most states. Physicians fear that, as HMOs gain market share, their patients will get shifted to a provider network with which the physicians are not affiliated. Again, determine how much diversity there is in the practice's practice payor mix before making any kind of a decision. At the same time, attempt to gain knowledge about where the service area is headed in terms of payor penetration. You must analyze the service area to assess the potential for patients shifting to other types of insurance programs, such as PPOs and HMOs. Much of this will depend on the employer base in the practice's service area. Some practice areas have experienced a managed-care penetration of over 50 percent within only two to three years. If you believe patient shifting will occur (resulting most likely in heightened competition), the practice must then look at its patient base.

Antitrust

You must have a good understanding of antitrust issues if you become involved in the development of multiprovider networks or any integrated delivery network. The government defines *multiprovider networks* as "ventures among providers that jointly market their services to help benefit plans or other purchasers." These ventures can cause an antitrust concern except when they involve competing providers. When examining multiprovider networks for antitrust violations, the government generally will focus on the following seven analytical principles:

1. Integration

2. Joint pricing and joint marketing

3. Market definition

4. Competitive effects

5. Exclusivity

6. Exclusion of providers

7. Efficiencies

Generally, unless a network is sufficiently integrated economically, it must avoid price agreements or market or service allocations. The members of the network must substantially share financial risk by providing services under a capitated rate or under a system in which significant financial incentives exist for network members to achieve specific cost-containment goals. There really is no true definition for a market. However, the government has indicated that it would review multiprovider networks with respect to each of the markets that might be affected by the networks' conduct.

Effect on competition is a major antitrust hurdle. Competitive restraints can occur in both horizontal integration and vertical integration situations. Some networks actually create both horizontal and vertical problems at the same time. The question must be asked whether or not the network would foreclose competition by impeding the formation and operation of competing networks. The answer will be based generally on the facts and circumstances of each case. The government has expressed a specific antitrust concern about vertical arrangements that required providers, principally physicians, to be exclusive to the network. Physicians should beware of networks that are nonexclusive in name but are operated in such a way as to be in fact exclusive.

Most networks contract with some, but not all, of the providers in a particular service area. Government agencies responsible for antitrust enforcement have noted that this has pro-competitive benefits in achieving quality and cost-containment goals and enhancing the ability of the network to compete against other providers. However, concerns have been expressed that the exclusion of particular providers not be based on an attempt to reduce competition. This concern arises from the possibility that if the excluded providers do not have another network to join, they might continue competing in the market area. The government has finally noted that it would attempt to balance any potential anticompetitive effect of a multiprovider network against the potential efficiencies associated with its formation and operation. The government has stated that it will focus on the efficiency principle only when it can be shown that, due to the operation of the network, efficiencies were passed on to the consumer in the form of higher quality or lower prices.

On August 28, 1996, the Department of Justice and the Federal Trade Commission issued revised versions of their Statements on Enforcement Policy in Healthcare. The nine 1996 Statements delineate the agencies' official enforcement position with respect to hospital mergers and joint ventures, providers' collective provision and exchange of various information to purchasers of health care services, providers' exchange of price/cost data, joint purchasing arrangements, multiprovider networks, and physician joint ventures. When the Statements were originally issued in 1993, the agencies declared that a physician network would probably not incur antitrust scrutiny if certain safety zones were met. The safety zones are as follows:

1. An exclusive network joint venture whose participants share substantial financial risk and constitute 20 percent or less of the physicians in each specialty with staff privileges in a local market

2. A nonexclusive network joint venture whose participants share substantial financial risk and constitute 30 percent or less of the physicians in each specialty with staff privileges in a local market

The revised Statements indicate the agencies may be willing to accept networks that do not impose substantial financial risk upon network participants. While the sharing of substantial financial risk by network physicians remains a safety zone requirement, the agencies have now determined that "physician network joint ventures that do not involve the sharing of substantial financial risk also may be lawful if the physician's integration through the joint venture creates significant efficiencies and the venture, on balance, is anticompetitive."

Accordingly, networks that do not fall within the safety zones (i.e., because they involve a higher percentage of the physicians in a relative market or do not involve substantial financial risk sharing) may still be lawful if they are not anticompetitive on balance. Generally, the agencies are now more likely to evaluate a network under the *rule of reason,* in which the case analysis includes a determination of the pro-competitive nature of the venture, the efficiencies claimed by the venture, and the ultimate benefit to the consumer. For example, a non-safety zone network that has developed an active cost and quality-control program may survive the agencies' scrutiny. This program should include mechanisms to monitor and control the utilization of services, a process for choosing network physicians to further efficiency objectives, and a significant investment of time and money for creating a program to realize the claimed efficiencies.

The Statements provide further guidance through a specific example of an IPA that has clinical integration but no risk-sharing.

The agencies offered the following as the basis of their decision not to challenge the IPA's joint pricing and marketing functions:

1. The IPA has systems to establish goals relating to quality and utilization of services.
2. Regular evaluations of individual and network performance with respect to those goals are conducted.
3. Processes such as case management, pre-authorization of some services, and concurrent and retrospective review of in-patient days are in place.
4. The IPA made a significant investment of capital to purchase the information systems necessary to gather aggregate and individual data.
5. The IPA has a program to measure the performance of the group against cost and quality benchmarks.
6. The IPA has a program to monitor patient satisfaction.
7. Detailed reports to payor on cost and quantity of services are provided.
8. The IPA has a medical director and support staff to perform the referenced functions.
9. The participating physicians are actively involved in developing standards and protocols.
10. The IPA retains an agent to develop a fee schedule, negotiate fees, and contract on behalf of the network.
11. Information about what participating physicians charge non-network patients will not be disseminated.
12. The physicians will not agree on the prices they will charge patients not covered by IPA contracts.
13. Physician participation in the IPA is nonexclusive.
14. Participating specialists constitute only from 20 to 35 percent of the specialists in each relevant market, depending on the specialty.

The Phoenix Medical Network, Inc.

One way to know more about antitrust and how it applies to provider delivery systems is to read and analyze FTC advisory opinions related to IPAs or any other physician network formation. These opinions are on the FTC's web site at www.ftc.gov. The Advisory Opinion on the CD-ROM is a good summary of what the government looks at when physicians decide to form their own delivery system.

A good example of an advisory opinion regarding integrated delivery systems is the case of Phoenix Medical Network, Inc. (Phoenix). This case shows what the government is looking for from an antitrust standpoint. Phoenix was a planned network of physicians located in Erie, Pennsylvania. According to the facts contained in the advisory opinion, Phoenix would be a for-profit professional corporation owned by physician shareholders, most of whom also would be participants on Phoenix's provider panel. Membership in Phoenix would be limited to licensed medical physicians or physicians of osteopathy engaged in the practice of medicine in a ten-county area, which is the primary service area (PSA) of northwestern Pennsylvania. Phoenix would be governed by a 15-member board of directors, elected by Class A shareholders. Ten of the 15 board members would be primary-care physicians, and 13 of the 15 would be Class A shareholders.

Shares of stock in Phoenix were sold at $1,000 per share; each shareholder held one share. There were two classes of shareholders: Class A common stock was available to independent physicians, defined as those who obtain the majority of their professional income from self-employment or employment by a physician-owned entity. Class B common stock was available to non-independent physicians—those employed by hospitals or other nonprofessional groups. According to the bylaws, Class B shareholders were not entitled to vote for members of the board of directors or on other matters, except as required by law.

Phoenix's purposes were to preserve individual providers' practices by strategically aligning the providers in a manner that would enhance their ability to obtain health care contracts, to establish a vehicle for the providers to accept risk-sharing arrangements, and to develop efficiencies and maintain quality assurance in the provision of comprehensive multi-disciplinary health care.

At the time of the advisory opinion, Phoenix had 218 shareholders, and had stopped admitting new shareholders. It had not yet been determined how many shareholders would sign participation agreements and actually provide services pursuant to Phoenix contracts. However, the opinion assumes that all shareholders would be participating providers.

In addition, Phoenix stated that it might seek to enter into participation agreements with non-shareholders in order to offer comprehensive medical services. Those physicians would not participate in Phoenix on an equity basis, but would participate, along with shareholders, in any risk pools established by Phoenix. Phoenix planned to enter into contracts with third-party payors under which its participating physicians would share substantial financial risk by agreeing to provide all medically necessary services to their enrollees for a percentage of the insurance premiums collected by the payors.

Phoenix also stated that it would pay its primary-care physicians on a capitated basis for primary-care services. Specialty physicians would be paid by Phoenix on a fee-for-service basis, subject to a 15 to 20 percent withhold to be placed into a risk pool. On an annual basis, funds withheld in the risk pool could be distributed to primary-care physicians and specialists upon their meeting or exceeding certain utilization and quality levels. In order to manage the financial risk that it would assume under contracts with payors, Phoenix intended to implement medical management procedures including utilization management, retrospective review, development of standard practice parameters, and sharing of professional expertise. All participating providers would participate in ongoing utilization management review, quality assurance programs, and credentialling programs undertaken by Phoenix. Phoenix intended to employ a paid medical director and a utilization review nurse.

At the time of the advisory opinion, 553 identified physicians were actively practicing in Erie County in the specialties that would be represented in the network, and 1,188 such physicians were practicing in the 10-county PSA. Phoenix had 218 shareholders, who were approximately 40 percent of all the physicians in the represented specialties in Erie County and approximately 18 percent of such physicians in the PSA. The proportion of participation varied widely by specialty.

Phoenix would assume the risk of providing both primary and specialty physician services to those patients who designated a

Phoenix participating physician as their primary-care physician. Phoenix did not intend to attempt to contract to be the sole physician network of any health plan. Rather, Phoenix envisioned that payors would continue to contract with other provider networks, or with physicians individually, in order to provide services to patients whose primary-care physician was not a participant in Phoenix. Participation in Phoenix was nonexclusive. Phoenix also stated that it would not impose any restrictions on the ability of network providers to provide medical services independently or through other organizations, including other physician networks.

The FTC's Analysis of the Physician Network

The analytical framework used by the Federal Trade Commission in assessing physician network joint ventures is set forth in the U.S. Department of Justice and Federal Trade Commission Statements of Antitrust Enforcement Policy in Healthcare (August 1996). You may obtain a copy directly from the FTC's web site.

It was noted that Phoenix would establish the prices at which members sell their professional services through the network. However, these price-related agreements were integral to the financial integration of Phoenix's physicians. Contrast this to a messenger model IPA, whereby in most cases the physicians establish a target negotiation rate before negotiating with managed-care plans. Typically physicians are not financially integrated in a messenger model IPA.

Since Phoenix members would share substantial financial risk through contracts with third-party payors to provide medically necessary services to certain of their enrollees for a percentage of the premiums collected, the government evaluated any likely competitive effects of the formation and operation of Phoenix under a rule of reason analysis.

A rule of reason analysis determines whether the formation and operation of a network may have substantial anticompetitive effects and, if so, whether those potential effects are outweighed by any procompetitive efficiencies resulting from the joint venture. (*Note*: Messenger model IPAs usually must be able to show procompetitive efficiencies to avoid government scrutiny; unfortunately, most operate as a negotiating shell.) In general, a rule of reason analysis involves the definition of the relevant markets within which the entity operates, and evaluation of the likely competitive effects of the venture, procompetitive efficiencies likely to be engendered by the venture, and any anticompetitive collateral agreements among participants or spillover effects outside the joint arrangement.

Geographic/Product Market Analysis

As part of its analysis, the government considered Phoenix's share of the available physicians with respect to each medical specialty practiced by Phoenix members. This is a standard analysis for all physician networks. With respect to the geographic market for Phoenix, there was a ten-county PSA; however, some specialties' physicians compete for patients in an even larger area. However, for each specialty group, the government looked at data provided by Phoenix on practicing physicians in the specialty, both in the PSA and for Erie.

Competitive Effects Analysis

With respect to primary-care physicians, Phoenix shareholders included 41 family practitioners, 15 internists, and 6 pediatricians. These physicians constituted 33 percent of the family practitioners in Erie County (plus 1 of 8 in Venango County and 1 of 28 in Crawford County), 28 percent of the internists in Erie County (plus 2 of 10 in Crawford County), and 35 percent of the pediatricians in Erie County. Even assuming that for these physicians the geographic market is no broader than Erie County, affiliation of this percentage of primary-care physicians with Phoenix, on a nonexclusive basis, did not appear likely to present a significant risk of competitive harm, according to the government. Many other primary-care physicians would be available for contracting with payors.

Moreover, several of the hospitals in Erie employ a number of primary-care physicians. Two hospitals in particular employ a large number of primary-care physicians who are highly regarded in the community and who have large patient loads. The hospitals' physician panels appeared to be capable of providing significant competition to Phoenix, according to the FTC.

With respect to specialty physician services, Phoenix's percentage of participants did not appear likely to raise significant competitive concerns. This is because Phoenix had as participating physicians the following proportion of practicing physicians in Erie County and the PSA:

Specialty	In Erie County	In PSA
Anesthesiology	29 percent	11 percent
Pathology	36 percent	18 percent
Dermatology	33 percent	20 percent
Emergency Medicine	3 percent	3 percent
General Surgery	31 percent	14 percent
Neurosurgery	22 percent	9 percent
OB/GYN	30 percent	13 percent
Orthopedic Surgery	28 percent	11 percent
Plastic Surgery	33 percent	22 percent
Psychiatry	11 percent	4 percent
Radiology	36 percent	18 percent

A problem occurred with other medical specialties. Phoenix's proposed panel had a higher portion of physicians in other specialty areas. The network asserted that those high percentages of specialists and subspecialists are necessary for the success of the network. Some specialty fields had only a few physicians or a few physician group practices, so that enrolling one physician or one major group practice in a panel inevitably would give Phoenix a high percentage of the available physicians in that specialty. It was pointed out by the network that it was not practicable to include fewer than all members of a group practice on the panel for reasons including cross-coverage responsibilities, and that including all of the physicians did not reduce competition among the group members, because they are not competitors of one another in any event. Nonetheless, the government had a concern that a limited number of substitutes were available to other provider panels in these specialties.

In some specialty areas, Phoenix had a high percentage of specialists who were not all members of one group practice. For example, Phoenix had as shareholders the following percentages of physicians:

Specialty	_In Erie County_	_In PSA_
Cardiovascular Disease; 9 physicians in 2 groups	83 percent	66 percent
Cardiovascular/Thoracic Surgery; 9 physicians in 2 groups	69 percent	69 percent
Colon and Rectal Surgery; 3 physicians in 2 groups	100 percent	100 percent
Gastroenterology; 7 physicians in 3 groups	100 percent	50 percent
Infectious Diseases; 4 physicians in 3 groups	80 percent	67 percent
Nephrology; 6 physicians in 2 groups	86 percent	43 percent
Urology; 7 physicians in 3 groups	55 percent	40 percent

The network stated that inclusion of a large number of physicians was necessary for the network to offer coverage at all hospitals, which they stated was necessary because many patients have a strong preference for one or the other of the hospitals, so that a network offering access to only one hospital is not effectively marketable. Because Phoenix would provide all covered services to patients who select a Phoenix provider as their primary-care physician, the network needed to be able to provide specialty services at the hospital selected by the patient or the primary-care physician.

The scope of the participation of these specialty physicians in Phoenix was a cause for concern by the government. The physicians participating in Phoenix constituted such a high percentage of providers in these specialties in Erie County and the PSA that third-party payors seeking to contract with a multispecialty physician panel in Erie County would likely have to contract with many members of the Phoenix network. To the government, this raised a significant potential danger to competition if Phoenix participating physicians refused to participate in other managed-care plans, if they agreed to participate only on terms comparable to those offered by Phoenix, or if they otherwise used Phoenix as a vehicle to coordinate their pricing behavior.

The government determined that it would not challenge the formation of Phoenix based on the size and composition of its proposed provider panel; however, the government did state it reserved the right to take appropriate action if Phoenix does not operate in fact as a nonexclusive network, or if its operation facilitates collusion among network members or otherwise leads to anticompetitive spillover effects, *which is a major concern for all messenger model IPAs.*

Contract Terms

As noted, the participation of primary-care physicians in Phoenix did not appear to present a significant risk of competitive harm. With respect to specialties which have a high representation of area physicians, Phoenix, according to the government, asserted plausible business reasons for inclusion of the physicians that it proposed to have as participating providers. In addition, it was in the network's favor to make sure that physicians who participate in Phoenix would be available to contract with payors or other networks independently, and the structure of Phoenix, as described above, makes it unlikely that the physician participants could, as a result of their participation, refuse to contract with other plans.

Other Considerations

As the network stated, it will contract with health plans only to provide services to patients who have selected one of Phoenix's physicians as their primary-care physician. This will be done on a risk-sharing basis. Because Phoenix includes only about one-third of the primary-care physicians in Erie, there is an inherent limit on the volume of patients that will flow to specialists through the Phoenix network; therefore, it appears unlikely to the government that most specialists could maintain their practice with only Phoenix patients. For example, Highmark, the local Blue Cross plan, has a substantial enrollment in the Erie area and therefore it appears that as a practical matter, specialists will find it necessary to continue to contract with other health plans.

To assess the Phoenix network, government workers spoke to administrators of other health plans servicing the area. The plan administrators did not express concern that the formation and operation of Phoenix as proposed was likely to impede competition by managed-care plans directly, as long as it operates as a nonexclusive network in fact and does not facilitate collusion or lead to anticompetitive spillover.

Finally, the fact that a majority of the members of Phoenix's board of directors must be primary-care physicians (who also will control the flow of patients to specialists) may place some constraints on the ability of groups of specialists to charge supracompetitive prices through the network venture. Since all Phoenix providers would receive compensation from a predetermined percentage of the premium collected by contracting payors, the other physicians should have strong incentives to pay those specialists at competitive levels. Nevertheless, there was a substantial concern that Phoenix participants could use their participation in the network as a vehicle for collusion, in order to *agree covertly with one another on the prices they would accept from payors other than through Phoenix.*

Also, the government had a concern that the operation of Phoenix could alter the opportunity or incentives of certain groups of physicians to act in concert to restrict competition among them. Particularly given the very high representation in some specialties, such conduct could have very serious anticompetitive effects. In fact, the payors to whom the government spoke expressed some concern about this possibility. If Phoenix participants refuse to contract with other plans independently on competitive terms, or if Phoenix becomes a vehicle for collusion with the hospitals' panels of physicians, serious issues would be raised. The government would not hesitate to take appropriate action.

Potential Efficiencies Assessed

The government weighed the significant potential procompetitive benefits that could result from Phoenix's operation against potential dangers to the competition. Phoenix intends to accept risk and to manage the medical care delivered by participating physicians in order to do so. Thus, Phoenix has the potential to inject into the market a type of competition that has not existed before. Moreover, Phoenix may present payors with an alternative to the panels of physicians employed by the two major Erie hospitals.

Conclusions

For the reasons discussed above, the FTC's staff declared that it had no intention to recommend a challenge to the proposed operation of Phoenix. This advisory opinion did a good job of setting out the views of the staff of the Bureau of Competition of the Federal Trade Commission.

From an analysis of this opinion, four things become apparent. Keep these four points in mind if you are ever involved in the formation of a physician network:

1. The government does not like to see more than 30 percent of the physicians of one specialty in a network unless the network can demonstrate why the excess numbers are needed.

2. The government does not like any mechanism in which physicians can collude against third-party payors.

3. The government does not like any mechanism in which physicians have the ability to set (i.e., fix) prices in a marketplace.

4. A network must be able to show potential or actual efficiencies to the marketplace as a result of its formation.

Causes of IDS Failure

It is important to understand why an integrated delivery system (IDS) loses money. Possible solutions to correct these problems will be discussed.

The most common causes of IDS failure fall into three basic categories:

- Purposes, projections, and policies
- Classic revenue and expense issues
- Organizational structures

Purpose, Projections, and Policies

Problems in this category are due to faulty business principles and assumptions in the original formation of the IDS. Here are some common problems that fall in this category.

Problem: Outdated Original Objectives

Many IDSs were formed in order to achieve a certain business objective which is either no longer viable or has been forgotten. Still others never fully developed any real business strategy at all.

The key to preventing this problem is to identify the original strategy and either improve the implementation and execution of it or abandon it for one that is more appropriate. For example, if the IDS was formed in anticipation of an emerging managed-care market that has still not arrived, it may be appropriate to adopt a strategy to compete in a thriving fee-for-service environment. Was the IDS formed to work better with a local practice by providing a full spectrum of specialty care? If specialty care is no longer a commodity, perhaps the IDS should divest itself of specialty care risk.

Problem: Over-Optimistic Projections

Many times it turns out that the financial projections contained in the valuation supporting a practice acquisition were overly optimistic. For example, the purchase price and initial compensation terms could have been based on certain revenue growth that has not occurred due to lack of physician productivity. Alternatively, baseline expense projections may have been too conservative given the actual operating costs and underestimation of start-up expenses.

If the failure to meet the original projections lies solely with physician performance, the IDS may want to consider reevaluating and adjusting the projections to be consistent with performance and impose corresponding adjustments to the original purchase price or physician compensation. Perhaps a portion of the purchase price is being paid over time under a non-compete agreement and a portion of it remains outstanding. The physicians may be willing to forfeit the balance in exchange for being held to less stringent productivity standards. In the alternative, the physicians could agree to repay a portion of the purchase price over time or adjust compensation downward. However, keep in mind that the "any willing buyer" principle still holds true in reviewing the appropriateness of the valuation. If, according to market standards, the practice could have performed better, it will be difficult to question the validity of the valuation and expect any action (i.e., repayment) from the physicians.

If the failure to meet the original projections lies with other components of the IDS, such as management's failure to market the IDS or obtain better contract rates, then reforming the purchase price would not be an appropriate solution. Adjusting physician compensation and reassessing the IDS's business plan, however, should be considered. Many IDSs are in fact attempting to change physician compensation structures, which in turn is leading to conflict with the physician providers. As a result, some physicians are trying to get out of their contracts altogether.

Problem: Lack of Information Systems

One of the cornerstones of successful financial performance is accountability within the network. Many times compensation systems are predicated upon the assumption that the physician members of the IDS will receive regular reports pertaining to utilization and other important issues that will allow them to monitor their performance. Incentive compensation cannot be expected to achieve the desired results unless those individuals eligible for it are able to monitor their actual performance against the applicable performance goals.

The IDS should ensure that it has appropriate information systems in place, which may include devising alternative means to disseminate information.

Problem: Lack of Brand Name Awareness or Market Share

Many times physician members of an IDS complain that they have the capacity to increase productivity, yet neither patients nor payors are sufficiently aware of the service capabilities of the IDS. As a result, the "build it and they will come" philosophy fails to produce the anticipated results. If this is the case, the IDS should develop a plan of action for raising its visibility through increased advertising and community activities. Additionally, in many cases, systems have been shy about "branding" practices with a uniform name, including the name of the hospital or health system, thereby often missing opportunities to increase credibility and awareness of the practices. It may be prudent to establish a marketing plan and budget for this purpose.

Problem: Large Physician Network

Some systems have aggressively recruited to add to their physician base, in addition to acquiring existing practices. As a result, the physician-to-patient population ratio may be too high to support reasonable physician productivity levels.

In these cases, after careful review of marketplace conditions and real potential for growth, downsizing the physician network may be the most appropriate option. This obviously requires a careful review of employment agreements, covenants not to compete, and other transaction documents from the original transaction.

Problem: Expensive and Varied Treatment Protocols

This occurs when the IDS is not integrated from a clinical standpoint. Most IDSs have adopted a mission statement or core value system that includes the concept of quality of care. Few, however, have developed mandatory or permissive uniform treatment protocols. If the IDS has not taken a systematic approach to care, expensive and varied treatment protocols can cause significant financial losses throughout the organization.

One solution to this problem is to adopt uniform clinical practice guidelines. These guidelines can be used to reduce costs substantially, particularly in a managed-care environment. They also can be the basis of an affirmative defense to a medical malpractice claim in many states.

Problem: Indigent Care, Charity Care, and Research Education Activities

An IDS may be losing money because it engages in a substantial amount of research and educational activity or because it provides a significant amount of charity and indigent care when compared to its revenue-generating activities. This may be a characteristic of an IDS that is tax-exempt and nonprofit.

The truth is that if this is the reason the IDS is losing money, it may not be a problem at all. Many times the IDS plays a significant role in satisfying the overall institutional tax-exempt and charitable purposes of the health care system to which it belongs. The solution here is to acknowledge this contribution and accept the fact that subsidizing care is part of the overall goal of the organization. From a legal standpoint, the IDS should adequately substantiate the amount and value of the research and educational activities as well as the charity and indigent care and ensure that these activities provide a material community benefit. In the alternative, the IDS may want to limit less profitable activities in favor of more profitable ones.

Classic Revenue and Expense Issues

The second category of problems focuses on the "cause and effect" of some typical revenue and expense issues affecting integrated delivery systems.

Problem: Fixed Salaries

Fixed salaries can often be the reason an IDS is losing money. This problem may be the one that health care attorneys contributed to most. In the early years of the IDS, it was often recommended that physician compensation be fixed in a way that removed any effective incentives in order to comply with the federal Stark and anti-kickback laws. While these fixed compensation models seemed to make the most sense from a legal standpoint, they often did not work from a business standpoint. Structuring an effective physician compensation package is extremely difficult in today's health care market. While certain physician compensation packages may minimize the applicable legal and tax-exemption risks, their design may actually disincentivize the behavior that is essential to the financial success of the IDS and a long-term stable relationship.

Now that private and government practitioners and regulators have had more experience with the regulatory issues, there are many incentive compensation models which create appropriate performance incentives consistent with the goals of the IDS while minimizing the legal risks. Incentive compensation packages should be redesigned if necessary in order to align compensation with the organization's goals.

Fixed salaries for the IDS administrative staff may also contribute to the failure of an IDS. An IDS may want to consider instituting incentive compensation for the senior management. Many CEOs are being compensated now based on the overall financial performance of the organization as well as other performance measures such as patient service or quality indicators. Compensation based on measurable performance goals may be a powerful tool in turning around the financial performance of the IDS.

Problem: Excessive Overhead

This is one of the most common problems and one of the hardest to alleviate. In some cases, the IDS has managed the practice with a hospital mentality rather than with a small business mentality. This often results in missed opportunities to save on basic expenses, such as supplies, office space, and equipment. However, there are limits to how much appropriate cost-cutting can be implemented and exactly how much impact this cost-cutting will have on the overall financial performance of the IDS. An IDS should continually examine cost categories such as medical supplies, office supplies, office space, staffing, and information systems and cut where possible from a budgetary standpoint.

In analyzing expenses, it is important to determine whether certain costs are being incurred by the IDS on behalf of a related component of the health care system to which it belongs. For example, the IDS may be responsible for paying the salaries of individuals who are providing systemwide services rather than services realized only by the IDS.

Problem: Underpriced and Undercompensated Services

During the formation phase, the IDS may assume existing payor contracts or adopt existing fee schedules of the physicians joining the IDS. While this is appropriate during the start-up phase and many times is the only avenue available from a legal standpoint, it is easy to overlook the fact that the IDS has attained significant market share and that it may be able to demand a higher price than before the integration. Once contracts come up for renewal, an IDS should push the limits with payors and, where possible, adopt uniform rate schedules depending on market share. In evaluating pricing strategies, an IDS should consider the antitrust implications of its conduct and conform accordingly.

An IDS may also find that the types of services it provides are not as profitable as it had anticipated. If this is this case, the IDS may want to consider cutting back or eliminating less profitable services unless there is a countervailing reason to provide such services (i.e., such as providing a "loss leader" service in order to attract other services).

Problem: Poor Collection Procedures

Like any other type of business, an IDS could be losing money because its billing and collection systems are inadequate. The IDS should carefully examine its billing and collection procedures with regard to coding, documentation, bad debts, average rates of collection, IBNR lag, and other factors. The IDS should work on perfecting its collection procedures and, if possible, seek outside assistance in this area. Many times sufficient revenue is being generated but dollars are left on the table because of poor billing and collection efforts. Furthermore, physicians are often not well educated on proper coding and documentation techniques, which raises the double-edged sword of missed charges and/or compliance concerns. (For more information on proper coding, see Chapter 10.)

Problem: Increased Wages and Benefits

Many times the heavy costs of wages and benefits can contribute to poor financial results. Many physicians complain that, because of the institutional nature of the IDS, they can no longer keep the staff costs as low as they could in private practice.

There are basically two solutions. First, the IDS should continually evaluate its salary and benefits package to ensure that it is competitive and attempt to lower the costs wherever possible. This includes shopping around on a regular basis for a reasonably priced benefits package. The other solution is to accept the situation. Providing a competitive salary and benefits package is essential to maintaining competent professional staff necessary to support the business.

Problem: Lack of Productivity

Many times various components of the IDS are not as productive as they could be. This may be true even if incentive compensation has already been put into place. The IDS may want to consider instituting better incentive compensation models to increase productivity, instituting uniform work standards (i.e., standardizing full-time equivalent requirements within provider contracts), or even terminating unproductive members.

Problem: Poor or No Leverage

This is another problem typical of service businesses. The IDS should ensure that it is maintaining both physician and other professional and staffing ratios that will maximize efficiency, quality of care, and profitability. It may be that the care and treatment being provided should be dispensed by allied health professionals rather than by highly compensated senior physicians. It also can be the case that a senior physician could be more productive if she or he had better support staffing.

The solution is to analyze the problem, establish appropriate staffing ratios, and institute a recruitment or hiring plan to achieve the objectives.

Organizational Structures

This final category of problems focuses on how certain organizational models may impact the integrated delivery system's bottom line.

Problem: Accreditation and Licensing Requirements

Many times the organizational model being utilized by the IDS incurs high operating costs because of state licensing or Joint Commission on Accreditation of Healthcare Organizations (JCAHO) requirements. For example, in California, an IDS often will utilize outpatient hospital departments as a method of owning and operating a physician's practice. This model can be an expensive one, given that hospital outpatient departments generally must comply with federal anti-dumping laws, JCAHO staffing requirements, and medical supply standards, as well as certain indigent care requirements. In many cases, an alternative structural model, such as the "community clinic" model, may avoid many, if not all, of these expensive operational requirements.

The IDS should be encouraged to consider other less expensive operational models if they are available in your state.

Problem: Lack of Integration Efficiencies

Often, governance and operations of the IDS are not coordinated in a practical way. This can lead to a lack of valuable integration efficiencies because of the doubling of efforts, which can result in unnecessary losses.

The IDS should assess its governance structure to ensure that all participants have sufficient representation in order to promote accountability, yet eliminate layers of decision-making that are unnecessary. In addition, the IDS should streamline its operational functions to ensure that the integration efficiencies intended are actually achieved.

Problem: Lack of Leadership

It is clear from a review of successful independent medical groups that medical leadership and the development of a group culture are crucial. Too often, physicians are left in isolated, small practices, with no sense of ownership or accountability to the group or the system. This can undermine performance, as well as a commitment to achieving the original goals established for the network. In addition, some systems use displaced hospital administrators as medical practice administrators. This has generally failed, given the distinct differences in hospital vs. medical group management.

Problem: Allocating Revenues and Expenses Among Related Entities

This is a problem of perspective. Many times the IDS, despite its name, is actually only one component of a larger health care delivery system. It may be that, according to its financial statements, the IDS is losing money, but another component of the delivery system is posting record profits due to risk pool splits or the division of revenues and expenses among the related entities. By looking at the system as a whole, and netting the gains and losses, you will be able to assess the true financial performance of the IDS.

The solution is one of perspective. Ensuring proportionality will allow you to assess whether the IDS is really losing money or merely taking on a disproportionate amount of expense revenue within the health care delivery system to which it belongs.

Problem: Outlier Divisions

Sometimes a particular practice location or a particular group of physicians in the IDS operates on a different level, causing the IDS to incur a net loss. It may be appropriate, in certain circumstances, to eliminate that location or group or reorganize it so as to eliminate the loss attributable to it and to put the IDS in an overall positive situation.

Delivery Systems

The remainder of the chapter details various integrated delivery systems and the professional needs of each; related antitrust concerns are also discussed.

Physician/Hospital Organizations

A physician/hospital organization (PHO) consists of a hospital and medical staff (or possibly an IPA) that provide services to patients and negotiate and obtain managed-care contracts. The advantages of a PHO are as follows:

1. It allows the development of an integrated service plan in an effort to provide efficient services and to reduce costs.
2. The hospital and its medical staff work together to deliver care.
3. Managed-care and other health plans can contract with both physicians and hospitals.

A PHO has the following disadvantages:

1. Medical staff relationships may be strained if the physicians believe that the PHO is looking out only for the hospital's interests.
2. The hospital, through the PHO, actually looks out mainly for its own interests in contract negotiations with health plans.
3. The medical staff members may form an IPA because they do not trust the hospital, thus straining the cooperation needed to make the PHO successful.
4. The medical staff is not consulted in the planning of the PHO.
5. The physicians and the hospital may not agree on protocol and services.
6. The PHO may not have the ability to enforce quality and utilization standards needed to control and contain costs.
7. The PHO may not be successful in its ability to contract with health plans, thus creating frustration with the medical staff.

Critical issues in the development of a PHO are as follows:

*   Its governance (equal voice on the board between the physician-providers and the hospital representatives)
*   How the PHO will be capitalized
*   Legal concerns, such as antitrust and monopoly
*   The development of pricing for services
*   The authority of the PHO to bind the hospital and physicians to contracts
*   The development of the physician-provider panel to obtain service efficiencies

SUMMARY TABLE

The following is a summary listing of the reasons an IDS loses money and possible solutions for each:

CAUSES	POTENTIAL SOLUTIONS
1) Outdated original objectives	1) Reevaluate purpose
2) Over-optimistic projections	2) Reevaluate and adjust purchase price and/or compensation; reform original deal
3) Lack of information systems	3) Develop information systems
4) Lack of brand name awareness or market share	4) Increase marketing and community visibility
5) Large physician network	5) Reduce network size
6) Expensive and varied treatment protocols	6) Adopt uniform practice guidelines
7) Indigent care, charity care, and research education	7) Substantiate fair market value and community benefit
8) Fixed salaries	8) Compensate based on measurable performance goals
9) Excessive overhead	9) Analyze costs and cut where possible; develop gain-sharing incentives
10) Underpriced services and undercompensated services	10) Renegotiate rates and eliminate losing services
11) Poor collection procedures	11) Institute new policies; check for coding errors
12) Increased wages and benefits	12) Normalize wages and benefits
13) Lack of productivity	13) Institute incentive compensation models; terminate unproductive members; institute work standards
14) Poor or no leverage	14) Analyze staffing ratios; institute a recruitment/hiring plan

CAUSES	*POTENTIAL SOLUTIONS*
15) *Accreditation and licensing requirements*	15) *Explore alternative operating scenarios*
16) *Lack of integration efficiencies*	16) *Analyze the organizational structure and reorganize governance*
17) *Lack of leadership*	17) *Identify physician leaders*
18) *Allocating revenues and expenses among related entities*	18) *Attain a different perspective*
19) *Outlier divisions*	19) *Terminate the relationship*

A PHO's professional needs include assistance with all aspects of setting up the organization; development of the fee schedule; and development of contracts, accounting, and tax issues. A PHO has needs similar to those of the IPA.

> ■ **Practice Point:** If the practice has a managed-care contract that was negotiated through a PHO, you will need to do the following:
>
> 1. Contact the managed-care plan and see if the physician can be credentialled as an individual provider instead of through the PHO.
>
> 2. If the physician can be credentialled as an individual provider, obtain the reimbursement rates from the plan for the practice's most common utilized services.
>
> 3. Compare these rates with the current reimbursements that were negotiated through the PHO.

Often, the physician will be paid more if he or she executed the contract as an individual provider instead of through the PHO. This is a problem with most PHO contracting. During PHO negotiations, physician reimbursement rates are sacrificed for higher hospital rates, or the individuals negotiating the contract fail to look after the physician's interest.

The physician's contract with the PHO may prevent individual contracting if the physician is a member of the PHO. You will have to perform a reimbursement analysis for all PHO contracted plans to determine if it makes economic sense to remain with the PHO.

Medical Foundations

A *medical foundation* is an integrated delivery system consisting of two components: the foundation itself and a group of physicians. The foundation generally is a not-for-profit, tax-exempt entity that acquires the business and clinical assets of large medical groups. The foundation then provides all facilities, equipment, and administrative support to the physician group. The physician group contracts with the foundation to provide care for its patients. The physicians are either employed by the foundation or remain independent by entering into a professional services agreement with the foundation. If the physicians are independent, the foundation generally pays them a prenegotiated fee to provide the care. The physician group then decides its own method of compensation for its physicians.

The advantages of a medical foundation are as follows:

1. It avoids problems with the corporate practice of medicine laws that exist in some states.

2. It provides an alternative to physicians, because some physicians may not want to be employed by a hospital.

3. It provides a vehicle to retain earnings for funding capital projects or new ventures in the future.

4. It enables the equity of retiring partners to be bought out.

Disadvantages of a medical foundation include the same legal concerns as for other integrated systems, and the physicians generally have less autonomy in a medical foundation.

The professional needs of a medical foundation are as follows:

1. The IRS not-for-profit application under Section 501(c)(3)

2. Budgeting and cash flow planning to determine the present and future capitalization needs of the foundation

3. Analysis of fraud and abuse issues related to the payment for goodwill in the acquisition of medical practices

4. Valuation of the physician's assets that are being acquired by the foundation

Management Service Organizations

A *management service organization* (MSO) is a separate legal entity, generally a subsidiary of a hospital, formed to provide administrative and practice management services to physicians' offices. The hospital uses the MSO to facilitate binding physicians to it, negotiate with managed-care plans, and recruit physicians.

Advantages for physicians that sign with an MSO include the following:

1. Physicians can avoid the problems of managing a practice.

2. Physicians can cash out certain assets if the MSO decides to buy the practice's fixed assets or accounts receivable.

3. Physicians can make more money.

An MSO often is an attractive option to physicians who would like to avoid the headaches associated with operating a medical practice. Other physicians may be interested in an MSO because they see a future that includes a declining income stream and want to cash out assets while they can. Because an MSO can achieve certain economies of scale, it can charge a physician less for overhead. This, in turn, could allow the physician to make more money under an MSO contract.

In the typical MSO model, almost all of the physician's overhead rolls into the MSO. The MSO generally charges the physician a percentage of the practice's collections as its administrative fee. If an MSO wants to charge a percentage of collections, a participating physician should try to get the administrative fee capped. All parties must have a clear understanding of which expenses the MSO will pay and which expenses the physician will continue to pay. Generally, the physician is responsible for costs related to continuing medical education (CME), dues, specific salaries, auto upkeep, entertainment, and debt service. Before a contract is signed, the physician's CPA should project the practice's collections, what will be paid as an administrative fee, what overhead will be paid for by the physician, and how much will be left over. This way, the physician can determine whether he or she will take home more or less with the MSO.

The biggest disadvantage the physician should be concerned with is the loss of administrative control. The physician's employees are employed by the MSO. If the MSO wants to fire one of them, it can do so without consulting the practice or even without contacting the physician. The MSO may also implement certain policies that are disagreeable to the physician. Some MSOs even require physicians to sign with particular managed-care plans, whether they want to or not.

The formation of an MSO requires professional assistance, which a CPA or consultant can provide. Because the MSO needs to be capitalized, detailed cash flow forecasts must be prepared. In addition, all of the MSO's administrative functions have to be set up, including the billing and collection office.

Any physician who wants to sign with an MSO should first have the contract reviewed. Strict attention should be paid to the financial aspects of the contract, along with the MSO's ability to bind the physician to managed-care contracts.

After the MSO relationship begins, the physician should have a professional periodically conduct an independent review to determine how well the MSO is billing and collecting the charges related to the physician's services. The practice must be sure that the MSO is doing a better job at billing and collection than the practice was doing on its own. If it is not, the physician should reevaluate the relationship.

(See Appendix C for a sample MSO contract.)

Group Practices

Group medical practices can be considered a form of integrated delivery systems. The way in which group medical practices are formed and the related need for professional services is discussed in Chapter 21.

Many hospitals around the country are acquiring physician's practices in order to form their own integrated delivery systems. The competition for primary-care practices is great simply because most insurance payors perceive these practices as the ultimate gatekeepers in any managed-care system. To compete for managed-care contracts, hospitals and other integrated delivery systems must have a strong base of primary-care physicians. When a not-for-profit hospital wants to acquire medical practices, it involves many specialized appraisal issues. This is especially true where the Internal Revenue Service (IRS) is concerned.

The IRS has issued guidelines related to tax-exempt entities when such entities acquire medical practices. These guidelines are contained in the IRS's *Exempt Organizations Continuing Professional Education Technical Instruction Program Textbook.* Valuation of assets or medical practices is a key issue in many cases involving tax-exempt health care organizations, whether they be applications for recognition of exemption, requests for private letter rulings, or audit examinations. The IRS has raised areas of concern with respect to appraisal methods used in the acquisition of hospitals, medical practices, and partnerships. Because many tax-exempt hospitals are acquiring physician practices, this should be a major area of concern. Many tax-exempt hospitals are acquiring medical practices in order to integrate them into their delivery systems. Therefore, by working with either a physician practice or a tax-exempt hospital in a sale transaction you should be aware of the IRS guidelines. Chapter 23 discusses these guidelines in more detail.

Physician Practice Management Companies

In previous editions, this book has included a discussion of the "why," "how," and "problems" of medical practices selling out to physician practice management companies (PPMCs). As we now know, the PPM industry is practically dead. Therefore, this portion of the book has changed from looking at "being acquired" to "how do I get out?"

The physician practice management experiment has not lived up to its lofty expectations. There have been many reasons for this; for example, paying for overpriced practices, poor management, failure to integrate, and the inability to increase revenues and cut operating costs. These are just a few. As a result, many medical practices that were acquired by a physician practice management company (PPMC) now want out of this relationship. However, while some PPMCs first approach practices about a buy-back transaction, it is usually the practice that has to make the first move. The following are some issues to be aware of should you ever assist a medical practice with a buy back from a PPMC.

Arguments for a Buy Back

Unless the PPMC approaches the practice first, the practice must find valid arguments why the practice can and should be repurchased from the PPMC. These are usually legal arguments that will need the advice and assistance of legal counsel. The most common argument is that the PPMC breached its management contract with the medical practice. In this situation, the medical practice will claim that it did not get the management services it had contracted for. As such, look at the following:

1. What services are called for under the agreements? Are they being provided? Failure to provide services could be considered a breach of the management contract.

2. Did any turnover of PPMC personnel adversely affect the quality of the services delivered under the management contract? Poor quality or service value could also result in a breach situation.

Another way a medical practice could get out of a PPMC relationship is to claim the relationship is invalid due to regulatory reasons. For example, the Office of the Inspector General has previously indicated in Advisory Opinion 98-4 that payment of a percentage management fee may be illegal, rendering the entire PPMC transaction defective. Another possibility is that the transaction violates the State Corporate Practice of Medicine law or the transaction violated laws against fee splitting. Finally, the medical practice could also claim that the initial payment made to the doctors was excessive and therefore violated Stark and Fraud and Abuse laws.

Reacquisition Issues

If the medical practice can and does enter into a repurchase transaction with the physician practice management company, make sure the following issues are properly addressed:

What exactly is going to be repurchased?   What assets will be repurchased and which assets will not be? For example, will accounts receivable be repurchased or will the PPMC keep them?

Has the PPMC filed for bankruptcy?   If so, you will have to deal with bankruptcy laws, the bankruptcy trustee, etc.

Repurchase price   With respect to the repurchase price, for example, is there any consideration due from the PPMC to the medical practice? If so, is the remaining obligation to pay the notes and deliver PPM stock simply canceled or will it be treated as part of buy-back consideration? Are there any escrow payments that must be considered when developing the repurchase price? Were any liabilities of the medical practice originally assumed by the PPMC? If so, does reacquisition of the practice automatically trigger the reacquisition and assumption by the physicians of these liabilities? Finally, what will be the PPMC's continuing liability with respect to liabilities after the practice is reacquired?

Control of cash accounts   During the relationship, was the PPMC in control of cash receipts or did the medical practice retain control? During the unwinding process, be sure to discuss how cash control will be released by the PPMC to the medical practice once the reacquisition documents are executed.

Inventory   Are there any practice inventories involved? If so, how will this be accounted for in the reacquisition of the practice from the PPMC?

Records   Who will control business records and medical records? How will ownership of these records be transferred to the medical practice?

Public disclosure   Who will control press releases to the public? How will patients be notified of the transaction? Whose expense will this be?

Bank covenants   Does the transaction violate any bank covenants of the PPMC or the medical practice?

Software/technology   Did the PPMC provide any new information systems/software/technology to the medical practice? If so, will the medical practice continue to be able to use this software and technology? How? Is it fair for a physician group to retain ownership of these assets?

Billing   How easy will it be for the practice to continue the billing for its medical services? Must it implement a new billing system?

Real estate   If applicable, make sure all real estate issues are addressed. For example, are there any problems with office space leases?

Employment issues   Which PPMC employees will become employees of the practice after reacquisition? Does the practice have to go out and secure new benefit arrangements, such as health insurance? Must it set up a new retirement plan? Are there any liabilities for accrued vacation and sick leave that must be addressed?

Credentialling   Are there any problems with managed-care credentialling as a result of the repurchase of the practice?

Insurance   Will the doctors' malpractice insurance remain in force after the transaction? Must a tail-end premium be paid? Can any other insurance contracts owned by the PPMC be assigned to the medical practice or the doctors themselves?

Financing the repurchase   Should total consideration be paid at one time? If so, the practice will need to secure bank financing. However, will the PPMC finance a portion of the reacquisition?

Tax issues   Finally, make sure all tax issues are properly addressed during the process of reacquiring the practice from the

PPMC. Make sure all tax issues related to the practice entity and the doctors individually are addressed.

Independent Practice Associations

An independent practice association (IPA) is a separate entity, usually a state not-for-profit corporation or limited liability company, that brings physicians together to facilitate and contract directly with managed-care plans and employers. An IPA often is considered another intermediary in the managed-care process. The IPA contracts directly with health plans on either a capitated or fee-for-service basis. The IPA then contracts with and pays physicians to provide clinical care to the individuals who are enrolled in the individual health plans. Therefore, the IPA bears almost all of the administrative costs associated with delivering care to patients. The IPA can also facilitate directly with managed-care plans on behalf of its providers. In many instances, the providers will continue to bill to, and be paid by, the managed-care plans. In this case, revenues do not flow through the IPA to the providers. Revenues flow most often through an IPA when it contracts with a payor on a capitated basis. In this situation, the IPA receives capitated revenues and in turn is responsible for paying the health care providers for the negotiated covered services.

An IPA provides a way for physicians to affiliate without having to join together legally as a group practice. A physician who joins an IPA must review the IPA contract with the same scrutiny as any managed-care contract. Thus, the physician will need to have a professional review the IPA's provider contract terms, facilitate with the payors, assess the reasonableness of any capitated payments, and perform a related assessment of potential risks. In addition, the physician's office staff will need assistance with the implementation of all specific IPA billing and collection procedures and subsequent monitoring of the office's compliance with these procedures if the physician is going to be reimbursed directly by the IPA for services rendered to IPA patients. If applicable, the physician will also require a proper accounting and possible renegotiation of the capitated payments.

Remember that IPAs are not a group practice without walls, are not an integrated organization through a group practice or other mechanism, and are typically independent of any outside influence other than through its own operating entity, governance, or membership.

An IPA can operate as a corporation, limited partnership, or limited liability company, and it can be owned by a variety of people. The owner could be the physician providers themselves or it could be a limited number of investors. Who will own the IPA depends on many factors. This decision could be tied to the ultimate capital needs of the IPA. If the physician providers will not be the owners, then the IPA will certainly need to charge the providers some sort of membership fee to join the IPA. This is typical in the industry. The rest of the capitalization will have to come from investors or from bank financing. The capital needs of an IPA could be quite substantial. Many IPAs that will enter into risk-sharing contracts will need a minimum capitalization of $300,000 to $400,000 if the IPA will perform all of its own administration.

One important decision will be whether or not the IPA should comprise multispecialty providers or single-specialty providers. The answer will usually depend on the preferences of the payors (i.e., insurance plan). Some insurance plans prefer to contract with single-specialty IPAs. For example, in one area of the country, a managed-care plan is aggressively carving out its services to various single-specialty delivery systems. Other managed-care plans will not talk to a delivery system unless it is a multispecialty and has a ratio of 50 primary-care physicians to 50 specialists.

Equally important is the development of the provider panel within the IPA. The IPA's goal is to develop a product that is salable to a managed-care insurance plan. As stated earlier, a multispecialty IPA will need at least the usual 50–50 split between primary-care physicians and specialists to be attractive to a managed-care plan. Also, many physicians have found that they cannot invite all of their friends onto the IPA panel. Too many physicians dilute the attractiveness of the IPA and create problems regarding how to compensate the physicians who are on the panel.

For example, a multispecialty IPA secures a capitated contract with an initial enrollment of 1,000 members. The IPA subcapitates the orthopedic surgeons at $2 per member, per month. Therefore, the orthopedic physician receives $2,000 per month to care for these enrollees. If the IPA hires two orthopedic physicians, the IPA will have a difficult time splitting the $2,000 between the two physicians, and the physicians will not be able to make a profit under this type of risk sharing.

During the initial development of the IPA, usually only one physician is chosen for each medical specialty other than primary care. In addition, the IPA will need to select physicians who are managed-care efficient. This is difficult in those areas of the country that are just developing a growth in managed care. Physicians in these areas are not used to working in a managed-care environment and are not cost-efficient providers. This will create a problem in service areas in which capitation is growing.

Those who advise physicians wanting to affiliate sometimes forget that the same personality and behavioral traits that lead the physicians to become successful physicians are sometimes obstacles to the successful establishment of an integrated delivery system, such as an IPA. To be a successful clinical physician, one must be intelligent and steeped in a scientific background, often involving training in the sciences in a clinical setting for many years. The physician must be able to work independently, to take charge, and to be decisive, even in life-or-death situations. On the other hand, to develop an integrated delivery system, a physician must think in terms of a collective effort, be able to delegate responsibility, deal in committees, be able to compromise, and make judgments based on gray areas of law and circumstance. In addition, there has been little need to comprehend what a physician's decision or charge does to the overall cost of the course of treatment of an individual, much less a group of individuals. The traits for economic and professional success for physicians are a strong work ethic, high-quality care, and accomplished interpersonal skills with patients and referring providers. There has been little emphasis on understanding the complexities of the business world and the creation of value (highest quality at the lowest cost) within it. This is a major intangible that you should remember as physicians come together as a group in an attempt to secure managed-care contracts. Your objective is to create a salable IPA.

Finally, as with any type of integrated delivery system, address antitrust issues as soon as the IPA begins to develop. Most of these issues were discussed earlier in this chapter.

> ■ **Practice Point:** The problem with physicians wanting to affiliate is that they adopt the "build it and they will come" philosophy. However, it makes much more sense for those physicians wanting to acquire managed-care contracts to meet with the payors in their service area and ask whether or not the proposed delivery system would be an attractive contracting opportunity for them. In other words, physicians should adopt the philosophy of "Tell me what you want and I'll build it for you!"

Obtaining Managed-Care Contracts

Securing a managed-care contract on behalf of an IPA will depend on the market—what managed-care plans are looking for from an IPA in a specific service market area. This applies to primary-care IPAs, single-specialty IPAs, or multispecialty IPAs. In reality, success during the negotiation process often depends on how much bargaining power the IPA has in the marketplace. If the IPA does not have leverage, it must develop a service product that will be attractive to an insurance plan.

The first decision the IPA has to make is whether to facilitate fee-for-service contracts, go after capitated contracts, or both. In states that have a willing provider statute, the IPA should not concentrate its efforts on fee-for-service contracts unless the IPA can obtain an exclusive provider contract or can obtain better rates and terms than those the physicians now have on their own.

> ■ **Practice Point:** At a minimum, the goal of an IPA should be to facilitate a better contract with managed-care payors than the physicians could have facilitated individually.

IPA Goals and Objectives

As previously stated, the main goals and objectives of any IPA are to obtain managed-care contracts (usually HMO/capitated contracts) and/or to facilitate with managed-care payors on behalf of the IPA providers (usually PPO contracting). The first thing the IPA should do is market itself to the payors. This is important because unless an IPA is formed at the request of a specific payor, nobody will know it exists. Therefore, the IPA should first do the following:

1. **Create a marketing packet.** The packet will contain the following sections: (a) general information about the IPA, including any quality assurance and utilization management programs; (b) a listing of the IPA providers; (c) physician CVs; and (d) a map indicating provider locations. The map will show the payor where the offices are located in the area and, ideally, demonstrate that the IPA has geographic coverage.

2. **Issue a press release.** Send a press release about the formation of the IPA to all local newspapers, business journals, and medical-related publications. Key personnel from managed-care payors often read these publications, and it is a good way to make the IPA known quickly within the community.

Next, survey certain plan attitudes about the new IPA. You will want to talk specifically with HMOs because it is HMO contracting that will allow the IPA to obtain an exclusive contract and have revenues flow through the entity. Because many HMO payor negotiations are all-inclusive, many HMO plans are reluctant to contract with one group for just a single medical service. Many plans prefer integrated delivery systems that will contract for all medical services. These systems are usually able to keep the costs of utilization down, since all medical specialties are coordinated within one single delivery system. However, some HMOs will carve out services for a single specialty. For example, an HMO might carve out cardiology services and award the contract to a single IPA in the service area for these services. It does not make sense to form an IPA to secure only HMO contracts when these plans will not be interested in the new IPA. This is why you should survey the HMO plans as soon as possible after the IPA is formed. The best way to survey plans is to set up a meeting with representatives of the managed-care plans who are in charge of physician contracting. Select the plans with the most enrollees in the area. Usually, you will want to meet with at least five HMOs. The representatives of the respective plans will tell you whether or not there is much interest in the IPA. You must take the IPA's marketing packet to each of these meetings.

Coinciding with the HMO payor meetings, the IPA will want to mail out its marketing packet to all payors who sell their insurance products in the service area, including PPOs. The IPA might also want to mail the packet to self-funded employers, because a contracting opportunity may exist. This will alert the payors of the new IPA and will help the IPA when it markets itself and facilitates with a payor in the future, especially with PPO plans.

Points to Remember

During the development process, most IPAs, in particular specialty IPAs, will want to make sure that they have *geographic coverage*. Many managed-care plans will want to contract exclusively with an IPA if it can provide medical services to its members over an entire service area. This service area is generally an entire county but sometimes it can be a certain part of a large city. For example, an IPA made up of OB/GYNs can provide obstetrical and gynecological care for all of the plan's enrollees in a specific county. The ability to provide this kind of geographic coverage should never be underestimated because managed-care plans want to consolidate their contracting with as few delivery systems as possible.

Finally, the IPA must demonstrate to all managed-care plans that it has instituted certain quality-assurance controls. Generally, the managed-care plan follows guidelines established by the National Commission on Quality Assurance (NCQA), known within the industry as *NCQA standards*. A managed-care plan will not contract exclusively with an IPA unless it can show it has instituted NCQA standards. You will have difficulty negotiating reimbursement rates or renegotiating reimbursement rates with PPOs or other discounted fee-for-service contracts if the IPA cannot demonstrate it is making an effort to contain costs and improve quality. As stated in the section discussion on antitrust, this is critical for those IPAs that do not take on substantial risk.

Facilitation of Fee-for-Service Contracts

The IPA members should agree that all discounted fee-for-service contracts will be facilitated through the IPA. This includes the renegotiation of contracts. Be extremely careful here. Under no circumstances should physicians share information with other physicians about fees. The government could easily make a case for price fixing is these circumstances.

Before the IPA receives a discounted fee-for-service contract to facilitate, the first step is to obtain each provider's desired contracting arrangement. This should include both terms and rates. The IPA should have power of attorney to bind the IPA provider if the payor decides to pay the designated rate structure. For example, if the IPA provider states that it would like to receive reimbursement equal to at least 140 percent of current Medicare rates, then the IPA has the right to bind the provider to any payor contract where at least 140 percent of Medicare rates are offered.

Once this is obtained, then the information can be presented to the payor. This is usually done by sending to the payor a messenger-model type letter. An example is in Appendix C and on the CD-ROM.

■ **Practice Point:** Remember to keep contract discussions with each practice separate. Do not discuss in a joint meeting or conversation details of your negotiation. Insulate each practice from the others to avoid antitrust claims.

The next step is to follow up and facilitate the rates if this is the requested action by the payor. You can do this either by phone or during a meeting. The success of the facilitation will depend on the facts and circumstances of the payors' needs and the IPA itself.

■ **Practice Point:** Be sure to get physicians involved separately in the contracting process. This can be done at the outset of negotiations, but physicians usually get involved as the negotiations progress.

The Role of the Messenger

If you form an IPA or you are a consultant who is involved in the formation of an IPA, it is extremely important to know the role of the messenger. The conduct of the messenger is crucial to keeping the IPA out of antitrust trouble.

Based on prior Federal Trade Commission rulings, the following is a list of the duties normally associated with the messenger for a messenger-model IPA:

1. Soliciting or receiving from any participating physician, and conveying to the payor, information relating to reimbursement, outcomes data, practice parameters, utilization patterns, credentials, and qualifications of such individual physician;

2. Conveying to a participating physician any contract offer made by the payor;

3. Soliciting or receiving from the payor, and conveying to a participating physician, clarifications of proposed contract terms;

4. Providing to a participating physician objective information about proposed contract terms, including comparisons with terms offered by other payors;

5. Conveying to a participating physician any response made by the payor to information conveyed, or clarifications sought, by the IPA;

6. Conveying, in individual or aggregate form, to the payor, the acceptance or rejection by a participating physician of any contract offer made by the payor; and

7. At the request of the payor, providing the individual response, information, or views of each participating physician concerning any contract offer made by such payor. Make sure each participating physician makes an independent, unilateral decision to accept or reject each contract offer made by the payor.

Under the messenger model, make sure the IPA does not:

1. Disseminate to any physician information about another physician's proposed or actual reimbursement, or views or intentions as to possible terms of dealing with the payor;

2. Act as an agent for the collective negotiation or agreement by the participating physicians; or

3. Encourage or facilitate collusive behavior among participating physicians; each participating physician should remain free to deal individually with any payor.

Messenger Model IPA Cautions

If you are involved in a messenger model IPA, remain up-to-date on the government's requirements for creating and operating messenger model IPAs. Keep close watch on the activities of the Federal Trade Commission and the Justice Department.

The importance of keeping up with the rules pertaining to IPAs is underscored by a recent government suit. The case involved both a messenger model IPA and the messenger itself. The government brought a civil antitrust suit against a surgical IPA, which was made up of 29 physician shareholders practicing general or vascular surgery in the Tampa area, and its messenger, an accounting and health care practice firm. The suit sought to prevent the physicians from negotiating with managed-care plans jointly on behalf of otherwise competing IPA member physicians to obtain higher fees for their services.

By way of background, seven Tampa hospitals provide general and vascular surgery services. In 1996, the IPA's general and vascular surgeons performed 87 percent of all general and vascular surgeries and constituted over 83 percent of all general and vascular surgeons having operating privileges at five of the seven hospitals (the "Primary Hospitals").

Tampa employers and other payors often use managed-care plans (MCP) to provide health care benefits. An MCP induces its members to obtain their care from doctors in its provider network. Doctors, on the other hand, compete to contract with MCPs by agreeing to lower prices, improve hospital utilization management, and provide care in less costly but medically appropriate settings, such as outpatient surgery facilities. An MCP typically contracts with enough providers (doctors, hospitals, and other health care providers) to offer a marketable plan to employers and a panel of conveniently located, reputable providers to its members and prospective members. The MCPs operating in Tampa include the five Primary Hospitals in their provider networks, plus a number of general and vascular surgeons who provide services at those hospitals.

Background of the Case

Several competing general and vascular surgeons in Tampa formed an IPA in May 1997 to facilitate jointly on their behalf with MCPs.

The IPA, according to the government's complaint, was organized specifically to use the collective strength of its physician share-holders to improve "overall managed-care reimbursement" to the IPA's surgeons. The IPA's objectives consequently included "[o]btain[ing] contract terms more favorable than if each physician contracted separately" and "[p]roactively us[ing] critical mass to obtain contracts at acceptable rates."

The messenger would attempt to facilitate a favorable contract for the IPA's surgeons with a particular managed-care plan. If that failed, the messenger would shift to a "contract-or-no-contract" negotiating strategy. The MCP could either contract through the IPA and have all the general and vascular surgeons belonging to IPA in the MCP's provider network or not contract through the IPA and have none of the IPA's surgeons in the network. The messenger would then recommend that the IPA's board either approve a facilitated contract and recommend that the IPA surgeons agree to it, or, if the messenger was unable to facilitate acceptable terms, reject the contract offered by the MCP.

This is what caused the problems for the IPA. By adopting a "take it or leave it" stance, the IPA was inviting government scrutiny. Under antitrust law, people cannot collude to prevent competition in the marketplace and drive up prices. The messenger also attempted to renegotiate the IPA surgeons' existing contracts with Aetna US Healthcare ("Aetna"). In a letter, the messenger advised Aetna that "a few adjustments to your current fee schedule would allow us to recommend the surgical group [the IPA] accept an agreement with Aetna." In closing, the letter indicated that, if Aetna met the proposed financial and contractual terms, the messenger would recommend that the IPA surgeons accept the Aetna contract.

Aetna later offered a contract that the messenger said was "no improvement" and without "concessions." The messenger advised the IPA's board of directors that "Aetna was unwilling to make changes to their standard contract for the IPA" and recommended that all IPA surgeons notify Aetna of their intent to terminate their contracts. Without an Aetna contract, individual IPA surgeons faced a "potential 30 percent decrease in market share . . . additional risk for bad debts . . . [and] unhappy patients." The messenger, however, advised the IPA board that the termination process would get

Aetna's attention, allow the messenger to negotiate better terms, and "better position the IPA for future discussions."

The IPA's board of directors accepted the messenger's recommendation that every IPA surgeon write a letter terminating the contract with Aetna. Twenty-eight of the twenty-nine IPA surgeons wrote such a letter. Aetna then proposed increased payment levels for the IPA's doctors.

According to the Justice Department, the IPA's and the messenger's joint negotiations and other alleged collusive activities left managed-care plans with two choices: inflated contract rates for the doctors or an unmarketable network without the IPA's surgeons. The MCPs paid the higher rates requested by the IPA. The government contended that, as a result of the IPA's and the messenger's activities, the managed-care plans in the Tampa area faced significantly higher health care costs, ultimately paid by the employers and their employees through higher insurance premiums or co-payments. The government stated that these increased insurance premiums and co-payments may have even led some employers and employees to forgo health care insurance altogether.

According to the government, the conduct of the IPA and its messenger attempted to cloak their alleged antitrust activities as those of a legitimate "third-party messenger." The IPA claimed that it complied with the messenger model. But documentary evidence contradicted this. In the documentation, the messenger stated that the IPA's goal was to get the physicians used to working cooperatively on managed-care contracts and noted that "if you have the majority of physicians in a geographic area, you have clout."

In a legitimate messenger model, the messenger acts merely as an efficient third-party conduit for information and communications between managed-care plans and individual physicians or physician group practices. The messenger does not coordinate or engage in collective pricing activity for competing independent physicians, enhance their bargaining power, or facilitate the sharing of price and other competitively sensitive information among them.

The government charged the IPA with unreasonable restraint of interstate trade and commerce in violation of Section 1 of the Sherman Antitrust Act. The government also charged the messenger as an active participant in this conspiracy.

Lessons to Be Learned

If you will be involved in the formation and operation of a messenger model IPA, keep the following in mind:

- **Monitor developments with respect to IPAs by following the government's Enforcement Statements, especially if many doctors participate in the IPA.**

  The Statements say that a group of doctors can organize in a nonexclusive contracting arrangement if they represent more than 30 percent of the doctors of their medical specialty in their service area. The Statements are explicit about extra activities the IPA must do to remain in compliance. Remember that the government does not like situations in which doctors come together with the sole purpose of trying to increase health care costs. The IPA must be able to show actual efficiencies created for the consumer and the marketplace as a result of the doctors contracting together as an IPA. If there is a termination by the IPA's doctors, and the payor's provider panel can be damaged as a result, the IPA should be concerned about antitrust rules.

- **The IPA must perform utilization management activities.**

  Messenger model IPAs must create and implement utilization management activities. In addition, they should implement internal quality assurance programs, as well as conduct outcome management studies. These benefit consumers and managed-care payors if implemented correctly and maintained.

- **Create a strategy in which fees will not be jointly negotiated on behalf of the IPA.**

  To avoid problems, the messenger should first talk to each doctor and then create a global contracting strategy for the IPA, essentially negotiating on behalf of each doctor. Fees and pricing must never be discussed as a group. Practically speaking, payors will want to contract with a group of doctors at the same rates, especially when the IPA brings tangible benefits to the payors.

- **Hire an experienced messenger.**

  As the Tampa IPA case demonstrates, the wrong messenger can create major problems. The messenger hired by the IPA should be able to demonstrate a working knowledge of antitrust guidelines and have verifiable experience working with other messenger model IPAs.

- **Never threaten a payor.**

  The goal of the IPA should be to work with, rather than against, payors. Making threats may have the effect of pushing the payor into a corner, which can negatively affect negotiations. Successful IPAs look for ways to "partner" with payors to help contain and reduce their medical costs, while at the same time giving the IPA doctors higher rates in return.

- **A contract should not be terminated unless it is necessary to do so.**

  Think carefully before terminating a contract, for several reasons. For one, termination could result in a government investigation for antitrust compliance if the payor reports the IPA to the government alleging violations. For another, termination may burn a bridge with the payor, creating an uncomfortable situation if the doctors need to sign up with the payor at a later date. Instead of terminating, try to find out what the payor really wants from the IPA and try to deliver.

  If a termination must occur, doctors should vote independently rather than as a group. Advise the payor as to which doctors have decided not to accept the contract and that the payor is free to negotiate with those doctors individually. The doctors may also approach the payor individually. This gives each party opportunity to work with the other outside the confines of the IPA format.

- **Be careful about what is put into writing.**

  Warn doctors to be prudent with correspondence and documentation of events, which could be used against the IPA during an investigation. At the end of the IPA's first year of operation and regularly thereafter (perhaps every other year), a qualified attorney should be engaged to review all IPA activities, correspondence, and documentation. This type of independent review should keep the IPA in compliance with antitrust guidelines. Also, make sure that the IPA uses its own attorney on an ongoing basis for this type of review.

- **Guard the IPA's privacy.**

  IPA activities should be kept confidential, even with other professional colleagues. Avoid the temptation to boast about IPA activities, such as successful contract negotiations.

Rio Grande Eye Associates

In a recent ruling, the Antitrust Division of the U.S. Department of Justice (DOJ) gave its blessings to a proposed joint venture by eight ophthalmologists in El Paso, Texas. The doctors wanted the Antitrust Division's opinion on their plan to offer their services as a group to managed care and other third-party payors. The Antitrust Division granted the Rio Grande Eye Associates business review clearance in a letter released by the DOJ on August 29, 2001. The Divison said the operations of the group, which plans to provide utilization review as well as offer services at a discount, are unlikely to substantially reduce competition in the area. It said that since the group would share risk and include fewer than 30 percent of the local ophthalmologists, its operations fall within a safety zone for nonexclusive physician joint ventures that the DOJ and the Federal Trade Commission issued in August 1996. The group may add a ninth ophthalmologist, which would boost its numbers from 28 percent to 31 percent of the eye doctors, but intends to stop there. The Division said that all eight specialists already participate in other physician panels in the El Paso area and third-party payors in the area had raised no objections. The members of the Rio Grande Eye Associates will share risk by withholding 20 percent of fees, and distributing them only if the entire group meets cost containment and quality utilization goals. In other words, this IPA was not intended to be used as a messenger model IPA. However, this does show that the government continues to scrutinize IPAs. To read the business review letter, go to: http://www.usdoj.gov/atr/public/busreview/8973.htm.

HMO Contracting

Generally, when an IPA contracts with an HMO, it will usually do so by submitting a contract proposal or by winning a contract after responding to a request for proposal (RFP). Many times the HMO will issue RFPs and then reward a contract to a provider group or delivery system based on the responses submitted.

The IPA's proposal can address all contract issues or just the major issues the plan wants to see proposed. Usually, the managed-care plan will provide proposal guidelines, and the remainder of the contract issues can be negotiated later. The IPA may be able to issue a proposal immediately or it may have to wait until existing contracts come up for renewal. At that time a proposal may be submitted.

There is no industry format for submitting contract proposals, although some managed-care plans will provide their own format. Generally, a managed-care plan will issue an RFP to selected physician groups it may want to contract with. (A sample proposal made to an HMO by an IPA is provided in Appendix C.)

If the HMO agrees to contract with the IPA or group practice, the next step is to negotiate the actual terms of the contract. The following is a sample of the contract matters that must be addressed and negotiated:

1. Must all providers be credentialled and licensed?
2. Which services are required to be rendered under the contract and related fee structure?
3. What are the precertification requirements?
4. What is the required malpractice coverage for the providers in the IPA?
5. If capitated, will the IPA take on any other risks?
6. What are the noncovered services under the contract?
7. What happens if services are rendered to disenrollees? What is the plan's required notification of disenrollment?
8. Must the IPA providers accept all patients or can they limit the number of patients?
9. Is there a time limit for filing claims?

10. What is the turnaround time for paying claims and how is it enforced?

11. What is the plan's utilization review process?

12. What are the grievance and appeals procedures?

13. How can the contract be terminated?

14. Are second opinions required?

IPA Development

The following is a comprehensive checklist for developing a very structured IPA. This type of IPA should be able to contract with HMOs.

- Assess market conditions and competition.
- Evaluate feasibility for market entry and development options.
- Quantify goals and objectives.
- Determine availability of financial resources.
- Establish IPA legal entity.
- Identify optimal HMO partner or sponsor.
- Secure key management personnel.
- Formalize board committee structure and work process.
- Initiate development of provider group.
- Specify service area parameters.
- Select key provider targets.
- Formulate preferred risk-sharing approach.
- Identify utilization management strategy.
- Prepare budget guidelines and estimates.
- Draft reimbursement policy.
- Review benefit plan design and actuarial assumptions.
- Design plan for compliance with regulatory requirements.
- Formalize terms and conditions for physician agreements.
- Commence physician recruitment activities.
- Determine nomenclature, coding, and claims processing conventions.

- Implement physician credentialling process.
- Collaborate with HMO on hospital and ancillary facilities contracting.
- Formulate medical policy development process.
- Specify utilization control, quality assessment, and related program protocols and particulars.
- Finalize the parameters for financial and risk management information systems.
- Design, test, and implement management information systems.
- Prepare all forms, provider manuals, notices, and related materials for operations.
- Establish provider orientation, training, and professional relations programs.
- Conclude business development details and activate programs.

HMO/IPA Service Agreement

The HMO/IPA service agreement should address the following issues:

- Contractual relationship and provision of services
- Obligations of the IPA
- Obligations of the HMO
- Terms of the agreement
- Capitation compensation arrangements
- Payment and timing provisions
- Proscription against member surcharges
- Hospital risk/incentive sharing formulae
- Claims administration and adjudication
- Physician coverage criteria

IPA/Physician Agreement

The IPA physician agreement should cover the following issues:

- Role of the medical director
- Gatekeeper protocol and physician-patient relationships
- Quality assurance and monitoring responsibility
- Utilization management controls
- Professional selection, credentialling, and peer review processes
- Frequency and content of provider listings
- Description of benefit services, limitations, and exclusions
- Advance review of marketing materials
- Grievances and disputes resolution
- Administrative and reporting responsibilities
- Compliance with state statutes
- Record-sharing and confidentiality
- Term of agreement and termination provisions
- Agreement modification and notification protocols
- Records retention requirements
- Compliance with IPA articles, bylaws, and rules
- Physician services to be provided
- Compensation arrangements
- Collection of member co-payments
- Proscription against member surcharges
- Risk/incentive sharing particulars
- Billing procedures, coding conventions, and reporting times
- Caseload minimums
- Utilization management and monitoring
- Gatekeeper and controlled referrals protocol
- Availability of coverage and continuity of care requirements
- Sanctions and expulsion process
- Professional liability (malpractice) insurance
- Sharing of medical records and confidentiality
- Access to business and finance records
- Permission for use of name in marketing materials
- Compliance with health plan grievance procedures

- Description of benefit plan services, exclusions, and limitations
- Notices and agreement modification protocols
- Binding arbitration for contract disputes
- Credentialled physician panel
- Risk incentive (or capitation) for physicians
- Sanctions for noncompliance
- Structured quality-assurance program
- Provider education and notification/feedback system
- Patient education and wellness orientation program
- Gatekeeper and controlled referrals policy
- Mandatory day-of-surgery admission
- Preadmission outpatient laboratory testing
- Preadmission authorization protocol
- Surgical second opinion program
- Clear documentation by physician
- Admission certification process
- Mandated ambulatory surgery list
- Regular concurrent review on-site
- Early discharge planning
- Alternative to inpatient care
- Ambulatory surgery center
- Home health care
- Skilled nursing facility
- Capitated mental health services
- Ambulatory chemical dependency programs
- Urgent-care centers benefit coverage
- Retrospective review, inpatient and outpatient (management information system [MIS])
- Patterns of care norms for community
- All-inclusive hospital per-diem-by-bed-type contract (or capitation)
- Capitated pharmacy program
- Capitated outpatient laboratory

Other IPA Issues

The IPA itself will have professional needs. A managed-care plan that contracts with the IPA will want continuous assurance about the solvency of the IPA. Thus, the IPA may need a special procedures examination of the IPA's solvency on a periodic basis, and it will need to give the managed-care entity a report on the examination. The report generally is in the form of either an actual audit report or a special procedures comfort letter. In addition to regular accounting and tax work, the IPA needs to make sure that all physician's contract provisions are being complied with, especially any withhold provisions and year-end, look-back provisions. Typically, the year-end, look-back provision gives a physician a bonus payment based on various criteria. The IPA must accrue this contingent liability on its books to reflect economic reality. These, and possibly other issues, will affect the IPA's balance sheet and income statement. The IPA will also need an independent review of the reasonableness of any incurred but not reimbursed (IBNR) accrued liability on its balance sheet. An IBNR liability is accrued to reflect how much the IPA would owe health care providers if it were to cease its activities and pay providers for all services rendered to date. Finally, the IPA may also need to assess the reasonableness of its administrative costs, monitor its internal compliance with established policies and procedures, and confirm that its records agree with any HMO records.

IPA Accounting

The service for an IPA will usually involve financial statement preparation and tax return preparation. If financial statement preparation is involved, it is important to be aware of the specific accounting concepts applicable to these types of entities. The following are the most common accounting concepts for IPAs. Their application will vary and should be tailored to the specific IPA.

Cash vs. Accrual

A brief description of these two methods of accounting is as follows:

- **Cash basis**   Simply stated, this method only considers two issues—cash in and cash out. Revenue is recognized when received (vs. when earned) and expenses are recognized when paid (vs. when incurred). Because IPAs are not a cash-in, cash-out business, cash basis financial statements will not reflect the true financial status of an IPA.

- **Accrual basis**   The accrual accounting method recognizes revenue when earned (vs. when received) and expenses when incurred (vs. when paid). IPAs typically have significant receivables and accruals, which should be represented in the financial statements in order to present an accurate picture of the IPA's financial position.

Because of the nature of IPA financial activity, the accrual method of accounting is strongly recommended to present more accurately the IPA's financial position. For example, the largest balance sheet item on the accrual basis financial statements will most likely be the IBNR reserve. To leave off an IBNR liability from the financial statements would dramatically distort the true financial status of an IPA.

IPAs often receive the bulk of their income in the form of capitation (based on per member, per month predetermined rates). Most of the expenses will be provider-related, such as capitation, claims, and stop-loss premiums. The capitation revenue is received monthly and the intent is that these funds will cover claims incurred within the same time period. Because it can often take six months to a year to receive all claims which are IBNR, the accrual methodology is essential to state the IPA's financial position fairly. To report on a cash basis, not noting a large claims liability that is looming, will be misleading.

Cash

A checking account and money market account should be set up for each IPA. In cases where numerous IPAs are being managed, it is highly recommended that cash for each legal entity be maintained in separate bank accounts. This is because co-mingling cash for numerous IPAs can be extremely confusing (from an accounting standpoint) and typically does not sit well with physicians on the individual IPA boards. Both a long-term and short-term cash budget should be maintained and compared to the daily cash balance.

Cash flow can be improved by accelerating inflows and slowing outflows. For example, receiving deposits electronically, leasing or financing capital purchases rather than paying cash, and paying claims at the end of each month rather than throughout the month will improve cash flow.

Receivables

- *IPA capitation receivables* represent receivables due from the HMO. An IPA typically will not have a receivable from an HMO since capitation is normally prepaid for a given month. Adjustments relating to prior periods are called retroactive adjustments and will usually appear on subsequent capitation checks. Unless these adjustments for retroactive additions (or deletions) are significant, a receivable (or payable) should not be recorded.

- *Third-party receivables* include amounts due from secondary insurance and workers' compensation insurance.

- *Risk pool receivables* typically are not recorded on IPA financial statements because accurate information regarding the settlement of the pools is usually not available on a timely basis. Following conservative accounting principles, receivables should not be recorded in the financial statements until they are estimable and realizable.

A shared risk arrangement is simply defined as risk shared by two or more parties. Usually the shared risk agreement is between the HMO or hospital and an IPA and involves the sharing of hospitalization risk.

- *Stop-loss recovery receivables* represent the anticipated dollar amount of provider claims to be recovered by the IPA from the HMO (or outside insurer). IPAs typically have stop-loss insurance to indemnify them of claims reaching a certain dollar amount. It is recommended that a receivable be booked at the time the stop-loss recovery claim is filed with the insurer by the IPA. This receivable should be conservatively reflected, since the claims often get negotiated (reduced). If needed, an allowance should be booked.

Fixed Assets, Intangibles, and Depreciation

Fixed assets and intangibles of an IPA normally include office furniture, equipment, computer software, and leasehold improvements. A capitalization policy should be in place and followed. This policy should include the capitalization threshold and depreciation method. All purchases should be approved through the budget process or by the appropriate party. A detailed listing of all asset additions and deletions should be maintained.

Custodial Trust Account

In some cases, an IPA will agree to hold in trust amounts payable for monthly capitation to certain provider panels. These funds will be held by the IPA until the panel decides how to allocate the aggregate capitation to the individual physicians who constitute the panel. The capitation should be expensed on the income statement and the related liability should be recorded at the time the capitation is owed to the panel. Accordingly, the cash required to pay out this liability should be segregated on the balance sheet as *restricted cash—trust account*. Note: The custodial cash asset should always equal the custodial trust liability.

Payout from the trust account should occur after the panel head authorizes the payments to the individual physicians who make up the panels.

Incurred but not Reported Liability (IBNR)

IBNR liability is an estimate of costs directly associated with the delivery of non-capitated health care services incurred during a financial reporting period but not yet reported to an IPA. Simply put, the health care service has already been provided, but the fee-for-service claim has not yet been received by the IPA. Most of this liability is associated with services provided by non-capitated specialists who are referred patients through the IPA.

The IBNR is a complex and fairly difficult liability to estimate because the IPA must rely primarily on trends from historical data to project a liability which can take more than six months to reach completion.

Accrued Distributions

Accrued distributions represent the excess funds available to be disbursed to providers and/or management services organizations primarily as a result of effective managed-care methodologies. These distributions are typically a part of a physician incentive or bonus program.

Capitation Revenue

Capitation revenue is the per capita monthly payout that an IPA receives from an HMO. In exchange, the IPA agrees to provide a specific menu of health services to a defined population over a set period of time. IPAs will normally receive, in advance, a negotiated monthly payment from an HMO. This payment is the same regardless of the amount of services rendered.

Risk Pool Revenue

Risk pool income is typically recognized on the financial statements of an IPA when it is received. This is because accurate and timely information regarding risk pool settlements is often difficult to obtain.

One recommendation is to acknowledge the potential risk pool income in a footnote disclosure to the financial statements and then to record the income on the financial statements when the cash is received. Risk pool income is one of the few transactions of an IPA that is typically recorded in the cash basis method of accounting.

Risk pool income should be reflected as *other income* on the financial statements of an IPA (vs. revenue).

Provider Expenses—Capitation

Capitation expense represents the per member, per month fees paid to physicians and other health care providers. The intent of capitation is to prepay a provider based on a predetermined estimate of the volume of services to be performed over a specific period of time.

For physicians or other health care providers that can manage patient care effectively through early diagnosis and treatment, capitation can provide better reimbursement than fee-for-service. The advantages for providers can include increased and consistent cash flow and the elimination of tracking accounts receivable (and write-downs) for their capitated patients.

The most successful provider reimbursement systems will encourage and reward the practice of managed care through physician bonus incentive programs.

Provider Expense—Fee-For-Service Claims (FFS)

The fee-for-service claims expense category on the financial statements contains two items—claims paid and the change in IBNR. Fee-for-service refers to paying providers according to a fee schedule set for each service and/or procedure. The payment to a physician will vary by the number of services/procedures actually performed. The claim (for payment) must be submitted by the provider to the IPA. It can take months for claims to be submitted to the IPA. Because of this lag in the receipt of the claims, claims expense must be, in part, accrued for financial statement purposes.

Stop-Loss Insurance (Reinsurance)

The IPA should obtain stop-loss insurance to provide fiscal protection to the IPA. A stoploss insurance contract indemnifies an IPA by guaranteeing that medical cases above a specific dollar threshold will be insured as a risk of the insuring party. Some forms of stop-loss segregate specific types of medical conditions (e.g., transplant cases or AIDS).

Often, the HMO will include stop-loss provisions within the medical service agreement between the IPA and the HMO. The HMO usually charges for providing this service by deducting a per member, per month rate or a predetermined percentage from the monthly capitation check. In cases in which the HMO does not offer stop-loss coverage, it is absolutely recommended that the IPA seek coverage from another insurance carrier.

When stop-loss coverage is a deduction of the capitation revenue, the IPA's financial statements should provide for recognition of the stop-loss premium costs. One recommendation is to "gross up" the capitation revenue and show an offset called *stop-loss withhold* as a reduction of capitation revenue. When an IPA pays insurance premiums directly to an outside insurance carrier, these amounts should also be shown as a reduction of capitation revenue to reflect the cost in the same area of the financial statements (to compare apples to apples).

Stop-loss recoveries should be reported as a reduction to claim expense. The recording of a receivable for the anticipated recovery is acceptable when there is reasonable certainty of the amount to be recovered and when the insurance carrier has acknowledged this liability. Often, recovery claims filed by the IPA will be negotiated or reduced by the HMO so the actual amount of recovery may change a few times. View anticipated recoveries with an accountants skepticism to avoid the write-down or write-off of a receivable.

General and Administrative Costs

General and administrative costs, if applicable, should be expensed when incurred. These costs will include (but are not limited to) the following:

- Payroll and related costs
- Rent and occupancy costs
- Physician stipends
- Office supplies
- Copying and printing
- Depreciation expense

These costs should be included in the general and administrative expense category of the income statement, following provider expenses.

▼ CHAPTER 23
Medical Practice Valuations

The changes going on within the health care industry today have resulted in a great demand for medical practice valuations. Numerous medical practice acquisitions and mergers are occurring. The most common instance is when the medical practice is acquired by another entity, such as a hospital or physician practice management company. If a physician wants to sell his practice, the practice will have to be valued to determine the sales price.

Another example of a need for a valuation is when a physician transitions out of a group practice and the buy-out price is based on an appraised value. The buy/sell agreement will state how the buy-out price will be determined.

A valuation is usually needed when a physician gets divorced. The practice must be appraised, because its fair market value is usually included as part of the marital estate. Separate practices that merge into a group practice will usually require an appraisal, because the determination of the equity interests might be determined based on the fair market value of each practice.

■ **Practice Point:** When valuing a medical practice because a physician is getting divorced, always refer to related divorce cases. Review cases that involve a professional getting divorced and see how his or her professional practice value was included as part of the marital estate. These cases will give specific guidance on how the courts want a professional practice valued.

Even though valuation formulas are similar across a number of industries, they are different for medical practices. The application of these formulas separates accurate appraisals from those that are not.

Here are two important points to keep in mind as you conduct a medical practice valuation:

1. It is the strength of the practice's income that determines the ultimate value of a medical practice. The income produced by the practice is what creates true value.

2. Make sure that the practice's income will remain unaffected in the future. This can affect the valuation process. With all of the changes going on in the health care industry, and with the health care marketplace directly impacting medical practices, most medical practices will experience a decrease in income or will have constant income, but without growth.

Regulatory Issues

When conducting medical practice valuations, take into account the changes occurring in the health care industry. Depending on their timing, these changes will have a definite impact on the revenue and net incomes of most medical practices. A lack of familiarity with current law can cause a severe overvaluation or undervaluation of the practice.

The following are regulatory issues that you should be aware of when conducting medical practice valuations. Continually monitor these areas of laws for changes.

The Stark Laws

Under fraud and abuse statutes, it is illegal to make payments, offers, or inducements of any remuneration in exchange for patient referrals. The Office of Inspector General (OIG) stated in a letter to the Internal Revenue Service (IRS) that payment for goodwill may violate the *fraud and abuse anti-kickback law*. The OIG believes that hospitals might seek to purchase physician practices as a means to retain existing referrals or to attract new referrals. Such a purchase might constitute illegal remuneration if, to the extent that a payment exceeds fair market value of the practice or the value of the services rendered, it can be inferred that the excess amount paid over fair market value is intended as a payment for the referral of program-related business. Therefore, if a practice is purchased at true fair market value, documented by a written appraisal by an independent third party, the transaction should not violate fraud and abuse statutes.

As discussed previously in this book, the Stark self-referral laws prohibit physicians from making referrals for designated health services if a financial relationship exists between the physicians and the entity to which they are referring. In the context of medical practice valuations, this statute will usually apply to hospital acquisitions of medical practices, because a payment will be made to the physician, and the physician will refer patients to the hospital for designated health services. This might also apply to group practices that purchase another medical practice.

The *Stark II law* contains an isolated transaction exception to the Stark prohibition. An isolated transaction, such as a one-time sale of property or a practice, is acceptable if the remuneration (a) is consistent with fair market value, (b) is not determined in a manner that takes into account the volume or value of referrals, and (c) would be commercially reasonable even if no referrals occurred. Because the isolated transaction allows a one-time sale, the purchaser cannot pay for the practice in installments; the entire purchase price must be paid up front.

Tax-Exempt Earnings

Tax-exempt entities must also be careful not to run afoul of private-inurement issues when they acquire a medical practice. *Private inurement* means that no part of a tax-exempt entity's net earnings may inure to the private benefit of any private individual. Therefore, if a tax-exempt entity pays more than fair market value for a medical practice, it could put its tax-exempt status at risk. The IRS has issued guidelines related to tax-exempt entities when such entities acquire medical practices. These guidelines are contained in the IRS's *Exempt Organizations Continuing Professional Education Technical Instruction Program Textbook* and will be discussed later in this chapter.

Transfer of Medical Records

There is often a distribution of medical records in health care transactions, including in the context of liquidations, mergers, and acquisitions. Does such a transfer result in a taxable event? According to the ruling of the Tax Court in *William Norwalk et al. v. Commissioner,* T.C. Memo. 1998-279, the answer depends on the facts. The ruling should be kept in mind any time medical records—and other customer-based intangibles—are distributed to physician-owners in these various types of transactions.

William Norwalk and Robert DeMarta formed DeMarta & Norwalk CPAs, Inc. (DNCPA) in 1985 and executed five-year employment agreements containing noncompetition clauses. In 1992, after the employment agreements lapsed, Norwalk and DeMarta liquidated DNCPA, distributed its assets and liabilities, and left outstanding shareholder loans of $96,000. Following the distribution, they became partners in another accounting firm, contributing the distributed assets and liabilities in exchange for opening partnership capital account balances. The tangible assets were contributed to the partnership using the DNCPA adjusted basis of $59,000. The partnership did not assume DNCPA's tax liabilities or the shareholder loans.

Many of DNCPA's employees, who had never executed noncompetition agreements with DNCPA, were hired by the partnership. Again, only DeMarta and Norwalk executed noncompetition agreements. Within a few months, two employee-accountants left to start their own practices and clients followed them. Within five years of the liquidation, only about 10 percent of DNCPA's clients remained with the partnership.

The IRS claimed that when the corporation was liquidated, it distributed to its shareholders "customer-based intangibles" in addition to tangible assets. This included the corporation's client base, client records and workpapers, and goodwill, including going-concern value. The IRS said that these intangibles were assets of the corporation that had a specific value and that, when distributed to the shareholders in the liquidation, these triggered a taxable gain to the corporation. Further, the transfer of the customer-based intangibles received by the shareholders generated taxable gain to the shareholders, according to the IRS.

DeMarta & Norwalk maintained that the accountants, rather than the corporation, owned the intangibles in question. Because the accountants personally owned the intangibles, there was no transfer or any corresponding taxable gain attributable to these intangibles.

The Ruling

The court held that at the time of liquidation, any "customer-base intangibles" in the accounting practice belonged to the accountants, not to the corporation. The court agreed with DNCPA that client lists and goodwill have no "meaningful value" absent an effective noncompetition agreement. Therefore, there was no gain realized by DNCPA, Norwalk, or DeMarta on the liquidation of this zero-value asset.

Because there was no enforceable contract which restricted the practice of any of the accountants at the time of the distribution, their personal goodwill did not attach to the corporation, according to the court. Any goodwill transferred to the partnership was that of the individual accountants, not the corporation. Under these circumstances, the court concluded that the value of any "customer-based intangibles" that the corporation may have had was nominal.

Factors That Influence Practice Value

You want to be as sure as possible that the income earned today can continue to be earned in the future by the buyer. If managed care is expected to grow in the future, this will affect the practice's future revenue. If a particular service area has 20 percent managed care today but is expected to reach 50 percent in the future, this fact must be included in the valuation. If this is the case, you may want to stress the discounted future cash flow method in the valuation.

When conducting any medical practice valuation, it is important to identify and analyze certain key factors. All of the factors that will be discussed in this chapter may at some time affect the valuation process and the ultimate determination of fair market value, and they apply to large practices as well as small practices. If these factors are not properly evaluated before and during the valuation process, the result could be an overstatement or understatement of practice value.

Medical Practice Revenues

Practice Years

The first step in the valuation process is to decide which practice years to include in the valuation calculation of excess profits generated by the practice. As we know, profit is created for the practice's owner or owners by the actual revenue "stream" produced by the medical practice. As a valuator, you must decide which practice years best reflect the "true" income and revenue stream of the practice. Is it the current year? Is it a weighted average of prior years? The "years" under review are derived from the practice's financial statements and tax returns. The following is an example of calculating the profit of a medical practice:

	Year 1	Year 2	Year 3
	Amount	**Amount**	**Amount**
Net Revenues	$ 8,735,516	$ 8,698,702	$8,705,293
Physician Payroll/Benefits	1,606,461	1,599,691	1,600,903
Non-Provider Employee Costs	1,117,709	1,112,999	1,113,842
Occupancy and Equipment Costs	383,052	381,438	381,727
Supply Costs	170,779	170,060	170,188
Purchased Medical Service Costs	4,672,628	4,652,936	4,656,461
Other General and Administrative Costs	215,767	214,858	215,021
Total Expenses	8,166,396	8,131,982	8,138,142
Net Operating Income	**569,120**	**$566,720**	**$567,151**

Note: Physician payroll and benefits include adjustment for reasonable physician-owner compensation.

Look at this history of practice earnings, then decide which year best represents the income stream of the practice. In this particular case, the valuator concluded that year 3, the most recent operating year, best reflected the true income stream of the practice. For example, the valuator found out that doctors had been added to the practice in years 1 and 2; doctors also departed during these same years. There were no doctor changes in the year 3 financial year. These are just a few of the reasons for the valuator's conclusion.

When looking at operating history, be sure to see if revenues have declined over time. If so, it might indicate that the most recent operating year is the year that actually reflects the true income stream of the practice. For example, a practice might be experiencing a continuing decline in what it gets paid by insurance companies, which is a common trend these days. But what if a review of the operating history indicates that revenue has been increasing each year? In this case, you might want to take a conservative approach in the valuation calculation and include the current year and the previous three to four years in the valuation, and weigh each year from highest (current year) to lowest. The key issue here is this: When you get a practice's tax returns and financial statements, do not immediately assume all recent years' revenue activity should be included in your valuation calculations. Analyze each year and determine which year or years best reflect the true income stream of the medical practice.

Non-Recurring Income

When analyzing gross revenues, identify non-recurring income items. When taking a first look at the revenue stream of a medical practice, do not blindly assume that all revenue is going to occur each and every year. Since it is the income stream that creates true value, you must make sure that the revenues the practice generates will transfer to a potential buyer or any person or entity taking over the practice. Unfortunately, many inexperienced valuators do not investigate the makeup of the practice's revenue stream and therefore cannot decide whether or not adjustments must be made *before* calculating practice value. Failure to do this often leads to an overvaluation of the practice.

Remember that any buyer would not want to pay for something he or she will not receive or benefit from in the future. This is why non-recurring income should be removed from the practice's revenue stream before calculating net profit and ultimate value. During your analysis, look for the following potential non-recurring revenues:

1. Medical directorships
2. Honorariums
3. Fees for testifying at trials
4. Income related to the review of medical records
5. Special service programs, such as revenues from weight loss programs headed by practice physicians or preventive health program revenues
6. Expense subsidies
7. Receipts from pharmaceutical companies
8. Revenue from ER coverage
9. Royalty income
10. Rental income

Besides interviewing the physician, practice accountant, and office administrator regarding the existence of non-recurring revenues, you can also review month-end computer-generated reports by looking closely at the debit adjustments shown on the report. If the practice is posting these revenues into its medical billing system, it must offset the credit by posting a revenue-based debit adjustment. Review these categories for one-time or non-transferable revenues.

Investigate Revenues Not Included in Practice Revenues

When reviewing the income stream of the practice, check whether there are any additional revenues that should be added to it before performing your valuation calculations. This is in addition to looking for non-recurring revenues. As an independent valuator, it is your objective to include in your valuation process the accurate income stream of the practice. In some situations, revenues must be added to the gross revenues shown on the tax return or the practice's financial statements.

If there are any missing revenues, you must be careful in the decision whether or not to add them to the practice's income stream. Some valuators believe that doing this causes the valuation to reflect "investment value" and not necessarily "fair market value." Remember that fair market value is defined as the price at which property would change hands between a willing buyer and a willing seller when the former is not under any compulsion to buy and the latter is not under any compulsion to sell, with both parties having reasonable knowledge of the relevant facts.

Investment value represents what a medical practice might be worth to a potential investor. It represents individual investment requirements and opportunities (e.g., potential missing revenues) and also reflects the worth of the practice to a particular investor for his or her own reasons. This is why considering this type of adjustment is so important and requires caution during the valuation process. Generally, if a buyer of the practice would obviously make the adjustments necessary to generate the missing revenue, then consider adding the income in your valuation calculations.

Following are a few situations in the medical practice valuation process that most often cause the valuator to make an increase adjustment to the gross revenue figure.

Undercoding of Office and Inpatient Visits

During the valuation, investigate each doctor's coding of evaluation and management (visit) services. In many cases, these services are undercoded, resulting in lost revenues to the practice. To identify possible visit undercoding, obtain a copy of the most recent year-to-date CPT frequency report and the prior 12-month CPT frequency report. If you are experienced in or have a good knowledge of CPT coding, scanning these reports will probably identify an undercoding situation. Create a worksheet comparing each doctor's visit coding patterns and look for possible undercoding situations. You could also obtain Medicare visit coding statistics and use this information as part of your review. These statistics can be found at HCFA's website at http://www.hcfa.gov/stats/resource.htm.

The following is an example of a physician coding comparative worksheet:

CPT Code		Dr. Jones		Dr. Mason	
		# of Times	%	# of Times	%
99201	OV, New, Straightforward	0	0.00	4	2.67
99202	OV, New, Expanded	0	0.00	53	35.33
99203	OV, New, Low	170	76.58	81	54.00
99204	OV, New, Moderate	52	23.42	12	8.00
99205	OV, New, High	0	0.00	0	0.00
	Totals	222	100.00	150	100.00
99211	OV, Est., Minimal	61	2.78	71	4.48
99212	OV, Est., Straightforward	87	3.97	206	13.01
99213	OV, Est., Low-Expanded	1607	73.28	992	62.63
99214	OV, Est., Moderate-Detailed	379	17.28	283	17.87
99215	OV, Est., High-Comp.	59	2.69	32	2.02
	Totals	2193	100.00	1584	100.00
99241	Consult, Brief	0	0.00	2	0.84
99242	Consult, Expanded	2	0.55	49	20.68
99243	Consult, Detailed	311	86.15	165	69.62
99244	Consult, Moderate	43	11.91	20	8.44
99245	Consult, High	5	1.39	1	0.42
	Totals	361	100.00	237	100.00

Fee Schedule

There may be a situation where the practice does have a substandard fee schedule. This can be found out by conducting an EOB review and looking for billed charges that were 100 percent approved for payment by third-party payors. If managed-care plans are approving the entire billed charge, this would be an excellent indication of a substandard fee schedule since a managed-care plan's approved charge is a "discount" off the physician's normal fee schedule.

Overstated and Missing Revenues

Look for overstated revenues as well as missing revenues. If overstated revenues are included in the calculation of practice value, it could create an overvaluation of the medical practice. The following are three common types of overstatement situations: (a) the commitment of fraud and abuse by the practice, (b) utilization abuse by the practice, and (c) upcoding of visit services normally due to a lack of coding education by the doctors.

It is difficult to detect fraud and abuse situations in a medical practice, except for intentional upcoding of visit services. For example, it would be almost impossible for a valuator to detect the billing of services that were never rendered. This is a classic form of health care fraud. Therefore, make sure the representation letter includes language stating that the practice is not aware of any fraud and abuse violations and is currently not under investigation for the same. This representation letter must be executed before releasing the valuation report.

Utilization abuse by a practice is a little easier to detect, but still can be quite difficult to see. Use the same analysis tools as those mentioned above in the discussion on undercoding of evaluation and management services (comparative worksheet, comparison to published Medicare statistics, etc.). As with missing revenues, if an overstatement situation is detected, decide whether or not to record a reduction adjustment to gross revenues. Failure to do so might result in an overstated fair market value of the medical practice.

Overhead Expenses

Determining the net profits of a medical group also includes reviewing and analyzing the practice's operating costs as well as its gross revenues. In your valuation calculations, include only reasonable and necessary practice operating expenses; that is, identify those costs in the financial statements and tax returns that exceed standard expense norms.

As such, do the following as part of the valuation process:

1. Distinguish overhead expenses that appear to exceed what would be considered normal for a medical practice;

2. Identify personal and other non-operating expenses;

3. Find possible missing operating costs; and

4. Make the appropriate adjustments to operating costs so that the appraisal reflects true, normalized operating overhead expenses for the practice.

To begin the overhead review, obtain industry surveys on medical practice operating overhead. The American Group Practice Association and the Medical Group Management Association have excellent surveys to utilize in determining the expense norms. A worksheet is usually prepared comparing actual operating costs to these related survey amounts. If any expense category appears out of line, the appraiser will want to investigate each further to determine if an adjustment is warranted.

The following is a brief discussion of the operating costs to emphasize in your overhead review:

Physician continuing medical education   This expense category is often overstated. Physicians at times take their family members and relatives on CME trips and charge the entire trip to the practice. Some doctors take extravagant education trips. A reasonable CME expense is about $2,500 per physician.

Retirement plan expenses and contribution   The conservative approach is to assume a buyer of the practice will continue or implement a retirement plan. Often, no adjustment is made to this expense category. In a divorce valuation, obviously you would not make an adjustment because the doctor or doctors with the plan retain the practice.

What if you know that the buyer does not have and will not implement a retirement plan? In that case, you may want to eliminate by adjustment the retirement plan expense in the calculation of excess earnings and in the discounted cash flow calculations. The buyer may have a different retirement plan from the practice's and, as a result, retirement contributions will either increase or decrease after the purchase. For example, the practice may have a simplified retirement plan while the buyer has an age-weighted retirement plan. A hospital may acquire a practice and, as a result, contributions for practice employees and physicians will decrease. These are common issues in acquisition transactions.

In these situations, it is often recommended that no adjustment be made if it is known that plan contributions will increase or decrease after the acquisition. The fact that these expenses may increase or decrease after an acquisition is an economic issue assumed by a buyer, and an independent appraiser should not take this into account in the valuation process.

Auto expenses   This expense category is often overstated. The financial records of the practice could list multiple automobiles, including those of family members. A very expensive automobile may be on the books of the practice, resulting in maintenance and operating costs that are higher than what is considered to be the norm.

Salary costs   To assess salary costs, obtain a listing of all employees, their job duties, and their salaries. The first step is to see if any employees are obviously not necessary to the daily operations of the practice. Look for paid family members and/or relatives. These salary figures and their benefits should be eliminated from each related expense category if the job duty is not necessary. Remember that it is the job duty of each employee that drives this analysis. Just because a wife is employed as the office manager should not make a difference because all practices need an office manager.

The next step is to analyze what each person is currently paid and what each person has been paid in previous years, if multiple practice years have been included in the valuation process. An issue that often arises in the valuation process is what to do when a practice has employees who are getting paid at a rate higher than what is considered the norm for that area or the norm according to salary surveys. Excess compensation often can be tied to employees having long lengths of service at the practice. What about the employee who has been with the practice for 15 years? Some practices give annual salary raises; base compensation of long-time employees at some point will exceed what their counterparts are getting in the marketplace.

In this situation, no adjustment is warranted (*unless* the excess compensation obviously applies to a family member or relative) because a highly paid employee cannot easily be replaced by another person of equal talent at a lower salary. The net earnings of the practice cannot be and should not be changed by adjusting salary expense downward because the physician-owners have decided to pay their employees a certain amount.

The impact of employee changes also has to be considered, since this often affects the operations and eventually the cash flow of the practice. For example, it sounds simple to replace a highly paid front-desk person with someone of equal ability but at a lower salary. Unless the person who gets hired can demonstrate equal ability, most likely front-desk operations will be compromised, which often results in a problem in the billing/collection processes.

Rent expenses Make sure all leased property and equipment are reasonable and are at fair market value. A practice could be paying excess fair market value; for example, the doctor or doctors own the building where the practice operates. In this situation, many times the practice is paying in excess of fair market value because the doctors want to convert what would normally be ordinary taxable income (in the form of salary) into passive income (in the form of rental income). This is a common tax technique used by many doctors.

A similar situation is when certain office medical equipment is owned by a trust which, in turn, rents the equipment back to the practice. This occurs mainly in solo medical practices, but may be found in multiple physician practices as well. This is another common tax technique. The trust is usually owned by the doctor and/or the doctor's family members. This one-way cash flow is transferred to family members to pay for other expenses, such as college education.

When rental expense exceeds fair market value, you should reduce rental expense to this amount and transfer the difference to physician compensation.

Service Transfer

The issue to review here is whether a buyer or transferee can perform the same services as the doctor or doctors who own the practice. If not, an adjustment to revenue might be warranted. This factor will obviously depend on the specific scope of the valuation (i.e., practice sale vs. practice buy-in valuation). In most situations, the doctor will transfer the practice to another doctor or entity that can perform the same services as those indicated on the CPT frequency report. However, this may not occur in some cases, as illustrated by the following example.

A valuator is engaged by a hospital to value a family medical practice consisting of one physician. The reason for the valuation is that the family physician is moving to the West Coast and the hospital is recruiting another family practitioner to buy and take over the practice. When the valuator calculated the profit generated by the practice, it was over and above what is a reasonable compensation figure for family practitioners; the valuator found that profit was more than $400,000. When excess profit appears high, the valuator must immediately investigate why this is so. In this instance, the valuator found that practice production was much higher than the average family practice. A review of the practice's CPT frequency report explained why.

Most family practitioners treat many patients in the office and order ancillary services, such as lab tests and X-rays, but most do not perform many procedures. However, when the CPT frequency report of one family practitioner was reviewed, many procedures were included, such as colonoscopies, endoscopies, and some ear, nose, and throat procedures. In reality, this family practitioner was practicing as an internal medicine physician, one who typically performs these types of procedures. The question presented to the valuator is this: Based on the specific scope of the engagement, can a recruited family practice doctor perform the same services as the practice being valued?

When this was discussed with the hospital administrator and the practicing family physician, the conclusion was that, unless the hospital recruited an internist, a recruited family physician most likely would not perform these procedures. In this situation, based on the specific scope of the engagement (the recruitment of a family practice physician), the procedures would have to be eliminated from the gross revenues of the practice during the valuation process. A failure to do so would have resulted in a large overstatement of practice value and more important, whoever purchased the practice would inherit a major problem. Revenues would automatically decline, simply because the same services could not be rendered by the new doctor servicing the practice.

Physician Production

There may be some practices that do not produce at capacity. For example, a practice that should normally see 20 to 30 patients in the office every day only sees 10 to 15 per day. In this type of situation, it's important to find out why this is happening. In most cases, you won't have to make an adjustment to the gross revenues of the practice. Instead, evaluate whether or not the productivity can be increased and if so, this fact would be used in the calculation of practice value using the discounted future cash flow methodology. Under this model, you might increase *future* gross revenues; physician productivity can easily be increased. The ability to increase production will be based on the facts and circumstances of each practice valuation and also will be based on interviews with practice management, billing personnel, and the doctors.

You should not carelessly increase gross revenues in the valuation calculations simply because it appears the practice is not productive. The following is an example:

A valuator is engaged by a 66-year-old otolaryngologist (ENT physician) to place a value on his practice for purposes of selling the practice to another ENT physician or ENT group practice. During the valuation process, it is found the doctor works three days a week and, due to eye surgery two years ago, no longer does surgery. The doctor states that he still treats patients in the office but if the patients need surgery, he refers them to a fellow ENT physician. This referral pattern has existed since the eye surgery. The doctor's take-home salary the previous year was $100,000.

Since the $100,000 salary is far below current reasonable compensation for this medical specialty, it appears that the practice does not have value beyond book value or possibly hard asset value. The issue the valuator must address is whether or not a new ENT physician will be able to pick up the surgeries the doctor is now referring out. The valuator will be able to find out the number of surgeries being referred out and should be able to quantify this figure. How should this figure be incorporated into the valuation and calculation of final practice value?

In this situation, the valuator must first investigate the current referral patterns, both by the practice primary-care referring physicians and by the doctor to the other ENT physicians for surgeries. This is the type of situation in which an inexperienced valuator may decide to increase the gross revenues, thinking that any ENT physician acquiring this practice will be able to keep and perform the surgeries that are now being referred out. This type of thought process is dangerous, because obviously there is no guarantee that the new doctor can garner the surgeries now being referred out. If not, and an increase in gross revenues is made, there might be a large overstatement of practice value.

In this instance, the first step is to determine whether or not the referrals can be, in fact, garnered by any new ENT physician stepping into the practice. This is done by analyzing carefully what surgeries the doctor is currently referring out and the number of them. Next, assess whether or not the primary-care referrals would continue. If a doctor has not been doing surgeries for two years, it is likely that the primary-care doctors are referring directly to a surgeon if a person needs surgery. Can these referral patterns be switched to the new doctor? To answer these questions, the valuator might interview the following individuals to gain insight into the referral process: the hospital administrator, the doctor selling the practice, billing personnel, the practice administrator, and possibly some of the primary-care referring physicians.

Assuming the valuator is confident that a new doctor can garner the surgeries now being referred out, the valuation report must take into account the fact that productivity might not increase as planned. In this specific situation, the valuator will increase surgical productivity using the future discounted cash flow model. Each year this method will show an increase in practice revenues because the new doctor will be able to perform surgeries that are now being referred out. The valuator will of course have to quantify how many surgeries a new ENT physician will be able to perform. If the surgical assumption is wrong, the result will be an overstatement of value. This is why the valuator must also increase the capitalization rate for some type of utilization risk; in other words, the valuation takes into account the possibility that the number of surgeries shown in the future discounted cash flow calculation might not occur.

Primary Care, Specialty Practice, or Subspecialty Practice

The valuation process should be affected by the medical specialty of the practice you are appraising. For example, the type of medical specialty is taken into consideration as you create your future discounted cash flow or earning model. Based on the specialty, you must assess what could happen now and in the future that could impact the revenues of the medical practice. If external factors affect the income stream, you must take them into account. This could also impact how you build the capitalization.

The most obvious external factor is reimbursement. As part of the interview process, ask the physician(s) and the office administrator about specific current events that are impacting the practice now or could have an impact in the near future. For example, find out about:

1. Actual and expected changes in Medicare reimbursement.
2. Actual and expected changes in managed-care reimbursement.
3. Medicaid managed care.
4. Increase in managed-care penetration.

Could these and other potential events impact reimbursement and the future income stream of the practice? Future events are hard to predict, but they must be considered as part of the valuation process. Again, a detailed practice interview is critical to finding out this information. Knowledge of the health care industry and its current and future trends are also important.

Physician Referrals

If a practice relies on referrals from other doctors to generate its production, assess whether these referral patterns will continue into the future if the practice is transitioned to another doctor or doctors. When assessing this factor, always keep in mind the particular scope of your valuation. This factor specifically impacts medical specialists because they receive most of their patients by referral from other doctors. The first step is to obtain a copy of the year-to-date and 12-month prior year Referring Doctor Report. Almost all medical software billing systems can produce this report. Next, review the report to see where the referrals come from and whether or not the majority of referrals are concentrated in a small number of doctors. The objective here is to make sure these referrals will continue into the future; if not, the practice's future revenue stream could be at risk and this risk must be included in the valuation, if it is applicable.

For example, 80 percent of the practice's production is generated from patient referrals coming from only five doctors. It would appear that the practice might be at risk because if anything happened to one of the five doctors (death or disability, for example), future referrals could decline. You might want to include a referral risk factor as part of your capitalization rate. In addition, you would probably also want to get the ages of each of these referring doctors. This is important to make sure there is not a risk of one of the doctors retiring and the practice losing his or her referrals. Referrals could be lost if the doctor retired, sold his practice to the hospital, and the hospital moved the referrals to other, similar specialists who were not as busy.

As stated, the reason for (or scope) of the valuation is important. If the reason for the valuation is the sale of the practice, the valuator will need to find out who potential buyers might be in order to assess whether the purchaser of the practice will be able to maintain the current practice's referral patterns. For example, some referring physicians may not want to refer their patients immediately to a much younger physician unless the older physician assists in the transition for a period of time (see the discussion of the transition factor below). Any doubt on the valuator's part about the ability of the practice to maintain the current referral pattern will most likely impact the development of an appropriate capitalization rate. The rate will take into account some sort of future referral risk.

Combination of Third-Party Payors

The source from which a practice derives its revenue (i.e., who it bills) impacts the valuation process. Therefore, it is critical to conduct a review of the practice's payor mix and determine what impact, if any, this may have on the future income stream of the practice or whether certain risks exist. This is important because the source from which a practice receives its revenues often defines its financial performance. For example, suppose a practice treats mainly Medicare patients. Knowing this, you could assess the impact on the practice if Medicare payment methodologies and billing rules change.

The following is a sample breakdown of a practice's payor mix. The total should equal 100 percent. The figures should be based on production generated, not production collected.

Percentage of patients in each insurance class:

Medicare	_____%
Medicaid	_____%
Champus	_____%
Workers' Comp.	_____%
HMO Fee for Service	_____%
PPO Fee for Service	_____%
Capitation	_____%
Blue Cross	_____%
Commercial (indemnity)	_____%
Self-pay	_____%
	_____100%

Most medical software billing systems can produce some type of report that can give an actual or good idea of the practice's payors. If not, ask the administrator or a billing person for a "guesstimate" of the payor mix breakdown; as part of your analysis, keep in mind that some information is better than none.

First determine if practice revenues are derived from only a few payors and assess related risks, especially any risks associated with actual and possible changes in reimbursement. Likewise, see if the percentage above is high for managed-care payors, such as PPOs and HMOs; if so, find out if the production is concentrated in a few managed-care plans. If yes, assess any related reimbursement risks and the associated potential decline in future revenues as a result. For example, suppose the majority of the practice's production is concentrated in the PPO fee for service plans. You then find out that the majority of these revenues come from one plan—Blue Cross/Blue Shield. After further investigation, you become aware that Blue Cross has just adopted Medicare's payment methodology to pay its contracted doctors and reimbursement is expected to decline 20 percent. In the valuation, this fact would impact the modeling of future practice revenues in the future discounted cash flow methodology.

If a large portion of practice production is from capitated plans (usually received from HMOs or similar third-party payor), you will need to assess past profitability on the contract or contracts. If profitability has been declining over a number of years, this might impact the figures placed in the future discounted cash flow method. Profitability can be assessed by comparing the capitated payments to the related fee for service equivalent for services rendered to these patients. Profitability also can be assessed by comparing the total capitation payments received to the costs incurred to render these same services.

Finally, if a large portion of the practice's production is from capitation contracts, find out if any of these contracts are exclusive arrangements between the medical practice and the payor. In this situation it's important to assess risks associated with the exclusive contract ending and the practice's ability to keep the patients (i.e., keep the revenues). While you cannot assume that a contracting relationship will ever end, the amount of revenue generated by the relationship might cause you to include some sort of contract risk as part of your capitalization rate build up.

Competitors in the Marketplace

Competition, or lack thereof, can impact the future income stream of a medical practice. As such, it's important to assess whether or not the practice's future income could be affected by an increase in current competition and if it is at risk from future competition. The following is an example: Suppose a specialty practice's (e.g., cardiology) service area is underserved, and the physician treats most of the patients in the area. If another physician of a similar specialty is recruited into the area, he or she could take patients (i.e., income) away from the current physician. This might impact the development of the capitalization rate by possibly including some of the competition risk. It might also impact how you model future revenues as part of your discounted cash flow or earnings calculations. Your interview with the physician(s) and practice administrator should identify actual and potential competitors. Also, a decline in practice revenues and/or a decline in physician referrals could also indicate competition is increasing.

Third-Party Payments (Reimbursement)

Medical practices receive payments from third-party insurance companies (e.g., Aetna and Cigna) and government entities (e.g., Medicare and Medicaid). Any actual or potential change in physician reimbursement must be accounted for in the valuation process. This specific issue has been talked about throughout this discussion on key factors to analyze as part of your medical practice valuation. If reimbursement declines, practice revenues will decline accordingly. Therefore, any actual predicted changes must be taken into account in the discounted cash flow or earnings model, or at least it should be taken into account as part of the capitation rate buildup. In the buildup, consider inserting some type of reimbursement risk exposure.

Billing and Collection

What if the practice you are appraising is doing a poor job with its billing and collection efforts and, as such, practice revenues are not being maximized? For example, what if the accounts receivable aging categories, the gross collection percentage, the net collection percentage and other financial indicators are less than industry standards? In my opinion, this kind of a situation cannot and should not impact the valuation process. How a future buyer or anyone taking over the practice might handle the billing and collection process is pure speculation. Any changes would result in an investment value calculation and not a fair market value calculation.

Practice Transition

If you are valuing a medical practice because it is going to be sold to a third party, you must assess ease of transition to the third party. How easy a practice can be transitioned has a potential impact on the future income stream of the practice. Therefore, determine if the physician selling or transitioning out of the practice will help the new doctor or owner with the transition into the practice. My experiences have indicated that if a doctor transitions out of the practice quickly and does not help out with the transition, revenue in the near term has a tendency to decline anywhere from ten to twenty percent. Without transition, patients and possibly referring doctors will need to get acquainted with the new doctor. With little or no transition assistance, the new buyer of the practice is asking the patient to make an appointment with a doctor he or she does not really know much about.

If the departing doctor will transition the practice, usually by staying around for at least three to six months, you probably would not make too many adjustments either to the capitalization rate or to the future discounted cash flow or earnings method. This is because most patients and referrals will continue with the practice and the revenue stream should remain intact.

You might be asked to value a medical practice that is transitioning as a result of a physician's death. The analysis of this situation will depend on whether the doctor is a medical specialist or a primary-care physician, as well as if the doctor is in a solo practice or in a group practice. Transition issues affect a solo medical specialist the most. This is because this physician most likely derives most of his or her revenue from referrals from other doctors. Upon a death, there is no one in the practice to "take over" these referral patterns and, as such, the referring doctors will immediately start to refer their cases to the other doctors in the area of the same medical specialty. In this situation, it will be hard to find any intangible value for the practice.

On the other hand, if the medical specialist is a member of a group practice, and if the group has in it another doctor of the same medical specialty, the impact is lessened because the practice can keep the referral patterns intact. In this situation, you should be able to find and calculate intangible value. The same applies to a primary-care physician in a group practice, as long as there is another doctor in the practice of the same medical specialty.

There is a greater likelihood that value can be retained by a solo primary-care practice than by a solo specialist. This is because most primary-care practices do not generate their patients from referrals by other doctors. Most of these patients will make an appointment with the doctor when they feel sick or at the time of their next scheduled checkup. In this situation, a large part of practice goodwill (i.e., the intangible) could be retained if you determine that the practice could be transitioned quickly to a third party. If not, value decreases dramatically because patients will start finding other primary-care physicians for treatment.

Instead of a death situation, what if the physician becomes permanently disabled? The same issues as the one previously discussed above should also apply. The only difference is that the disabled doctor might somehow be able to assist in the transition of a solo physician medical practice. The retention of value will obviously depend on whether or not the practice could be sold to a third party fairly quickly. The longer it takes to transition a practice, the more likely patients and referral patterns will be lost for good. If the practice can be transitioned quickly, and if the disabled doctor can participate in the transition, a greater portion of practice value can be retained.

At times you will be asked to value a solo practice when other doctors in the same medical specialty are in the service area. You may think that there is a ready market for the practice and you might then place full or near full value to the practice. This is a common mistake. In almost all of these types of situations, a competing practice is not going to pay full value for a patient base or a referral pattern that it might get anyway. This is especially the case for referral-based practices. However, in some situations a competing practice may want to procure the medical charts and try to transition some or all of these patients. In this situation, the competing practice will try to buy the practice for chart value but little else.

Finally, there may be a time when you are asked to value the practice of a doctor who has been diagnosed with a terminal illness. As in the case of death and disability, full value will most likely be retained if the doctor is a member of a group practice and the patients or referral sources can successfully be transitioned to another doctor in the group of the same medical specialty. This is not the case for the solo physician. This is because as long as the terminal illness has not been disclosed, there is an opportunity to place a full value on the practice because the doctor will continue in business as usual and will be able to assist with any transition of the practice. However, as soon as the illness is disclosed or known, practice value will begin to decline. When patients or referral sources find out about the illness, they will continue with the doctor as long as the doctor is able to practice. However, as soon as the illness is known, any potential market for the practice begins to dwindle because any doctor or practice wanting to acquire the doctor's practice will use the issue of the illness as leverage in the negotiations. Again, why would you buy something at full value that you are probably going to get anyway once the physician finally quits practicing medicine?

Technology, Drugs, and Other Related Clinical Issues

Every year, new drugs and technologies are being developed to enhance the wellness and increase the life expectancies of individuals. So, the issue here is whether or not these drugs, technologies, and other related clinical issues could have an impact on the future revenue stream of the medical practice. While this would be extremely difficult to quantify, it is a good idea to include some related risk factor in the development of a capitalization rate. One clear example of this is heart disease. Numerous drugs and technologies have been and will be developed that reduce an individual's susceptibility to heart disease and even prevent a worsening of a person's already current problems with heart disease. This might impact the future revenue stream of a cardiology practice or a cardiothoracic surgeon's practice. Will people be having fewer heart problems in the future? Could heart catherizations and angioplasties decline? Could heart bypass surgeries decline? So when valuing any medical practice, be sure to take a look at technology, drugs, and other related clinical issues that could have an impact on the future revenue stream of the medical practice being valued.

Information Needed to Conduct a Medical Practice Valuation

The following is a list of the information you will need to conduct a medical practice valuation:

Financial Items

- Financial statements and tax returns for the past five years
- Charges, collections, and adjustments for the past five years
- Practice's fee schedule
- Prior-year and year-to-date CPT frequency report
- List of employees and current salaries
- Current aging of accounts receivable
- Aged accounts payable list
- Listing of notes payable
- Detailed listing of practice's fixed assets
- Number of patients seen per day in the office
- Physician's referral list
- Practice's payor mix
- Comparable compensation figures (Sources: Medical Group Management Association, Medical Economics, American Medical Association, Modern Healthcare's Annual Physician Compensation Survey)

Nonfinancial Items

- Copy of office lease
- Copy of equipment leases
- List of managed-care contracts
- Vendor price lists
- Copies of previous practice assessments/reviews
- Copy of any prior valuation reports
- Existing buy/sell agreement
- List of competing practices
- List of competing delivery systems

Developing the Capitalization Rate

Most formulas used in medical practice appraisals use a capitalization rate in their calculations of value. A *capitalization rate* converts income into an indication of a value for the medical practice. It generally is defined as the sum of (a) the annual rate of return currently available from investments offering maximum security and the highest degree of liquidity (often the Treasury Bill rate or the rate on a certificate of deposit) and (b) a risk premium, which takes into account the risk that the predicted amount of future income will not be realized by the medical practice and the risk of unforeseen changes in the health care industry in the area in which the practice is located. Besides items (a) and (b), the physician may add his or her own adjustments when building the capitalization rate.

A capitalization rate considers the rate that would constitute a reasonable rate of return. In other words, it determines the rate of return a potential investor (i.e., buyer) would want to receive as a return on his or her investment. Often, the rate is higher for high-risk businesses and lower for low-risk businesses. Therefore, a primary-care medical practice will usually have a lower capitalization rate than other medical specialties, generally because its earnings are not expected to be affected negatively by any changes within the health care industry and the marketplace that may occur in the future. The following is an example of building a capitalization rate for a family practice:

Risk Factor Impact

Risk-free rate	6.25%
Small business/medical specialty risk	4.00%
Competition risk	3.00%
Managed competition impact/change in reimbursement risk	3.00%
Capitalization rate	16.25%

There are a number of risk factors to be aware of related to medical practice appraisals. The most common are:

1. Specialty risk
2. Competition risk
3. Reimbursement risk
4. Payor risk

All of these risk factors should be considered when developing the capitalization rate. Remember, the strength of a practice's income is what creates true value. As an appraiser, you must make sure the income the practice has today will still be there in the future. However, the changes occurring in the health care industry right now will have a direct impact on a practice's future income.

The appraisal must take into account the practice's medical specialty. Because of the changes in the health care industry, the revenues of specialty practices are riskier than those of primary-care practices. For example, national Medicare reform would affect the revenues of specialty practices more than those of primary-care practices. Payors are trying to reduce costs and, in order to do so, are targeting the specialists. Also, in some areas, there is an oversupply of specialists. If managed care is growing in these areas, the specialists' revenue will decrease, especially as capitation grows, because in a managed-care environment only a limited number of specialists are needed.

The appraiser must also consider competition risk and assess how vulnerable the practice's revenue stream is to competition. How easily could the practice's income be taken away by competition? Competition can take many forms. It could come from another physician setting up a competing practice, from a group practice recruiting a physician of the same specialty, or even from physicians and delivery systems competing for exclusive managed-care contracts. Likewise, changes in reimbursement can affect the medical practice's revenue. There is tremendous pressure on payors to reduce costs, and one way they can reduce costs is to cut physician fees. Payors are, therefore, continually revising their reimbursement schedules. For example, many payors are starting to use the Medicare RBRVS payment system to set physician fees. In addition, as managed care grows, physicians are getting paid less. As more patients join managed-care programs, physicians will still treat the same patients but will get paid less for their services. An example of this is when states move their Medicaid enrollees to managed-care plans.

Finally, payor risk must be assessed. This mainly pertains to the growth of managed-care programs in a particular service area. You must assess the potential for managed-care growth in the service area and its related impact on the practice's future income. As previously mentioned, as managed care grows, there is the real likelihood that reimbursements and related practice revenues will decline. All payor classifications must be assessed. This includes the potential for managed care to impact both the Medicare and Medicaid sectors in a particular area. It also includes the potential for more HMOs to enter a particular market and for employers to begin shifting to managed-care insurance products. Some service areas have had managed-care penetration of 20 percent one year and 50 percent the next year.

Calculating Excess Earnings

The first step in a medical practice valuation is to calculate the common valuation principle of excess earnings. Excess earnings represent the portion of the practice that creates its true value. In other words, excess earnings are the earnings above a reasonable level of physician's compensation for a particular medical specialty. This is because most physician-owners pay out all of the practice's profits at year end (and even during the year) as compensation to avoid paying federal and state income taxes.

Something special about the practice allows it to earn these excess earnings. This is what creates value. Excess earnings are calculated as follows:

Step 1: Gross collections − Overhead = Net income

Step 2: Net income + Addbacks − Adjustments = Excess earnings

Addbacks include owners' compensation, extraordinary expenditures, and optional expenditures. Extraordinary or optional expenditures are not connected with the normal operating overhead of the practice. The best illustration is a physician's costs that are more personal in nature than they are business in nature. For example, a physician may spend $15,000 on continuing medical education (CME) for a year, whereas the norm is around $2,500. The difference should be added back when calculating excess earning. Adjustments include comparable owner compensation and extraordinary revenue items.

Extraordinary revenue is revenue that is nonrecurring or would not stay with the practice if the practice were sold outright. Examples include expense subsidies and one-time, nonrecurring contract payments. Another example is free rent. If the practice currently receives free rent but will shortly have to begin remitting rental payments, the future income stream will be affected. To reflect economic reality, most appraisers subtract an amount for reasonable rent for the years used in the appraisal calculation.

Excess earnings should be calculated for the current year and for the past four years. Net income generally is derived from either the practice's corporate tax return or the partnership tax return. Extraordinary expenditures and revenue are then added back or subtracted from the excess earnings calculation.

The main factors contributing to the excess earnings calculation are the addition of physician's compensation and the subtraction of comparable compensation. Most medical practices are said to have value when their physicians earn more than is considered the norm in the industry for that medical specialty. For a truly comparable compensation figure, compute the average of the physician's earnings from each of the compensation surveys. If you have a number of clients in a particular medical specialty, you can also include another practice's compensation figures in the calculation.

> ■ **Practice Point:** The revenue the practice produces that is above what is considered reasonable compensation for that practice's medical specialty represents the true net earnings of the medical practice.

Once excess earnings are calculated for each year, you must decide which years to include in the appraisal and how much weight to give each year. Answer this simple question for every medical practice appraisal: Will the practice continue its past gross and net earnings trend?

To determine this, answer the following questions:

- What will be the future reimbursement trend for the practice?

- Could insurance demographics change?

- Could the patient demographics change?

- Will there be a strong switch toward managed care?

If you believe that the practice's revenue will decrease in the future, you may want to include any past activity in the appraisal. The figures may need to be restated based on current reimbursement and economic conditions. The main point is to not rush out and perform, nor rely on, an appraisal based mainly on past performance. This is especially true when the future may indicate a decline in earnings. By carefully studying the health care industry, you should be able to determine a practice's future income potential. Therefore, more importance is usually placed on the most current year, and less emphasis is placed on prior years if they are included in the appraisal calculation.

Example of Excess Earnings Calculation

	12-31-98	*12-31-99*	*12-31-00*
Revenue	*599,287*	*662,662*	*702,116*
Expenses	*579,830*	*601,075*	*666,378*
Net income	*19,457*	*61,587*	*35,738*
Reductions:			
Comparable comp	*120,998*	*127,366*	*133,734*
Entertainment tax			
disallowance	*62.00*	*191.00*	*0.00*
Other income	*0.00*	*40,444*	*37,333*
Interest income	*11,015*	*8,730*	*784*
Addbacks:			
Owner comp	*346,875*	*375,000*	*425,000*
Depreciation	*16,339*	*13,171*	*11,176*
Interest expense	*3,003*	*1,487*	*1,093*
ODC	*253,599*	*274,514*	*301,156*
Weights	*1*	*2*	*3*
Weighted Avg. Owner's Discretionary Cash			*$284,349*
Weighted Avg. Revenue			*$671,827*

Valuation Methods

Use a number of valuation methods when appraising a medical practice. Most of the following methods are specific for medical practice valuations. The key issue is to determine which valuations to use and what emphasis to place on each formula. Rate each formula's importance in the valuation process. Weights will differ depending on a variety of factors, such as the medical specialty being valued and the demographics of the practice's area. The following are the most common formulas used in medical practice valuations.

Capitalization of Weighted Excess Earnings

The basic theory is that the ultimate intangible value of a medical practice is the earnings that the practice generates. This approach

is based on the theory that an investment will yield a return sufficient to recover its initial cost and to justly compensate the investor for the inherent risks of ownership. Thus, the capitalization
rate represents the rate of return required to compensate for the
risk inherent in the particular medical practice specialty.

Example of Capitalization of Weighted Excess Earnings

Average owner's discretionary cash	284,349
Capitalization rate	24.60%
Intangible indicated	1,155,890
Fair market value of assets	30,900
Gross valuation	1,186,790
Net premium	0.00
Other adjustments	0.00
Net valuation	1,186,790
Current fair market value of assets	30,900
Intangible indicated	1,155,890

Historically, professional practices have generally been valued
by using the *excess earnings method*. This approach makes sense
in the professions and service businesses, because acquisition of
an equity interest leads to higher income than earned as an employee (all things being equal, of course).

This method is commonly used in many types of business valuations and is accepted by the courts and the Internal Revenue Service. However, the *Friendly Hills* and *Harriman Jones* tax exemption rulings, in addition to public statements issued by the IRS and
the *Continuing Education Handbook*, have made the *discounted
free cash flow method* the standard. Does the excess earnings
method remain relevant?

The underlying difficulty with use of the excess earnings method
in a medical practice acquisition by a hospital or other institution
with continued employment is the salary and benefits paid to the
selling physician. Many transactions provide that the seller will be

paid a salary equivalent to the amount that he or she earned in the period preceding the sale. This raises the specter of zero excess earnings and no value.

Valuators typically determine excess earnings by subtracting a base earnings number from actual earnings. *Base earnings* are determined by reference to statistical sources such as the Medical Group Management Association. Often, the median or mean earnings are used, as would be the case in a traditional sale to another physician. This is most likely the core of the IRS objection to the method. This objection can be cured by using compensation negotiated as part of the transaction to compute the excess earnings. This certainly seems consistent with what the IRS desires, though it may run afoul of the fair market value standard.

A better approach may be to examine carefully what the buyer expects to receive in additional revenue from the transaction. Historical earnings should then be normalized for these additional future earnings. Excess earnings could then be based on compensation paid post-transaction or, preferably, on a statistical measure of compensation for an experienced physician, such as the seventy-fifth percentile earnings, or whatever the valuator finds relevant to the analysis. Therefore, it would be best to try to normalize historical earnings for future increases, then use fair market value earnings for the seller. (The normalization adjustment should be determined by reference to market factors, such as capitation profits, especially in Medicare, and other sources of growth in the practice. Additional revenue to the buyer, which would be in violation of Stark or fraud and abuse statutes and regulations, should *never* be considered.)

Another issue in the use of this method is whether or not an allowance for a return on tangible assets should be deducted in computing excess earnings. The standard application of the excess earnings method requires such a reduction (refer to related IRS Revenue Rulings for additional guidance). However, physicians generally take all of their income out of the practice as compensation. Statistical sources therefore reflect the return of tangibles as part of physician compensation. Deducting it again would be double-counting.

Since every valuation should be prepared with the expectation that it will be reviewed by a court, you may want to consider a deduction for the allowance for a return on tangibles. If so, the statistical physician earnings should be adjusted to avoid the double-counting of tangible asset return. The presentation of the method will then be consistent with the generally accepted manner of performing it.

What should the rate of return on tangible assets be? This is often a difficult question. According to the opinions of many appraisers, the required rate of return should be determined by reference to the practice's cost of debt, with a potential adjustment to reflect personal guarantees or collateral. The rationale for this approach is as follows: The principal tangible assets in a medical practice are accounts receivable and furniture and equipment. If the practice has debt, it will typically have been incurred to get working capital loans or to finance furniture and equipment. Working capital loans are usually on demand at a rate floating with prime, secured by the accounts receivable. Furniture and equipment can often be financed on a fixed-rate, fixed-term basis of 24 to 60 months, with the lender taking a collateral interest. In the author's experience, the interest rates on both types of loans range from 9.25 percent to 12 percent. If the presence of personal guarantees is critical to the loan, the valuator should consider adding to the rate a charge for the personal guaranty, similar to that for a letter of credit accommodation.

If properly prepared with normalization adjustments and relevant base earnings, the excess earnings model should represent a useful valuation tool. The normalization process in an excess earnings model can be likened to the forecast of future earnings required in the discounted free cash flow method. Ideally, both methods should be used to provide a cross-check of the other's results.

Market Approach

This method measures value based on the purchase price paid in the marketplace for similar assets. One source of comparable sales is based on a weighted average of intangible multipliers from the *Goodwill Registry*, published by The Health Care Group, Inc., for the medical specialty in question. The *Registry* has tracked medical practice's sales from 1985 through 2000, and it currently contains information on more than 3,000 transactions.

Example of Market Approach

Weighted average revenues	*671,827*
Intangible multiplier	*31.00%*
Estimated intangible	*208,266*
Current fair market value of assets	*30,900*
Gross valuation	*239,166*
Net premium	*0.00*
Other adjustments	*0.00*
Net valuation	*239,166*
Current fair market value of assets	*30,900*
Intangible indicated	*208,266*

■ **Practice Point:** Make sure there is adequate history in the *Goodwill Registry* for the medical specialty being valued. If not, this method should not be used. In addition, many appraisers do not like to use this source because it includes in its database a compilation of appraisals prepared for a variety of situations. For example, there are appraisals for divorce cases, buy-outs, and outright practice sales. In other words, there is a mix and match of values. So if you are preparing a valuation pertaining to just a practice sale transaction, the goodwill percentage used in the *Registry* will not be for practice sale transactions only.

The market approach is familiar to home buyers who compare the value of homes they are interested in purchasing to recent prices paid for similar homes. The market approach tracks actual sales of comparable assets or businesses. Projections and estimates, necessary parts of the income approach, are not used. The only subjective component of this approach involves determining appropriate adjustments for comparability.

The market approach is an excellent technique to value buildings and real estate (including leases). Generally, a market valuation analysis starts by describing the community. The description provides important information about its economic, social, transportation, and environmental strengths and weaknesses.

Next, the building and land being appraised are compared to actual sales of comparable buildings and land in the community.

The appraiser lists recent sales transactions for office buildings and land. The history of recent transactions compares the property being appraised to that sold in recent transactions, in terms of such factors as building square footage, lot square foot/acre, location, acre, condition, quality of construction and design, and access to transportation. The appraiser visually inspects comparable properties to better evaluate their comparability to the subject property. After all important information is gathered, the appraiser estimates the value of the property being appraised by making appropriate comparability adjustments to the sales prices of the comparable properties. A final fair market value is determined using the impartial data based on the actual sales of comparable buildings and real estate in the community. Because this method relies on data derived from actual transactions, it is less subjective than the income approach.

The market approach is also used to determine the value of a whole business, not just its buildings and real estate. In the market approach to practice value, a meaningful (though approximate) comparison must be made of the seller's business to similar businesses.

In selecting comparable companies for the medical practice being appraised, the appraiser should first look to the public marketplace, because more information is available on public companies than on private businesses. The universe of possible comparable companies starts with all companies that provide health care services; it thus would exclude HMOs and other managed-care entities, since managed care involves assuming health care provider risk whereas physician practices are primarily oriented to providing health care services and generally assume little provider risk. In "heavily capitated" markets, where physicians are compensated primarily through capitated arrangements, managed-care companies might be appropriate "comparables." Hospitals and home health care services would also be excluded, because they provide specialty inpatient medical services or in-home secondary health care services, respectively.

Publicly traded physician practices do not exist. However, publicly traded physician practice management companies are buying physician practices, and such practice acquisitions are detailed in annual reports and reports to the Securities and Exchange

Commission. Obtaining this information may be one way to begin compiling and analyzing comparable practice sale information on a per-physician basis. For example, you may find that, on average, Physician Resource Group is buying ophthalmology practices at $200,000 per physician.

An additional potential source of market information on medical practices is private local or contractual markets. The sale of medical practices is a relatively new phenomenon. Unlike real estate, for which actual sales information is readily available, little accurate data exists on prices paid for medical practices. Because medical practices are not public companies, and physicians generally view sales information as confidential, sales information is difficult to obtain. Even where such information is accessible, information demonstrating the comparability of the practices sold may not be available. Where information about private sales of physician practices is used in the market approach, it should be substantiated by appropriate documentation.

The following two ways to look at the market are useful when using the market approach:

Market established by actual sales   Actual sales of physician practices in the same community as the subject practice may be used in the market approach. Where market information is included in a valuation, actual purchase prices paid for comparable physician practices should be evaluated, adjusted, and applied to the operating data of the seller's business to arrive at fair market value. The factors affecting comparability between the market and the seller's business should be discussed.

Factors affecting comparability include markets served, practice and specialty type, competitive position, profitability, growth prospects, risk perceptions, financial composition (capital structure), physician compensation, physician health and reputation, physician productivity, average revenue per physician, cost structure, and average revenue per visit or covered life to revenue mix (capitated versus fee-for-service).

Market established by offers   Market information involving letters of intent or memoranda of understanding to purchase medical practices could be used in a market approach. Because offers are not actual sales transactions, however, this information is inferior to actual sales transactions. Also, "comparable" information based on offers is relevant only when the offers are legally binding and contain detailed information about the terms and conditions of sale (e.g., price, financing, assets purchased, compensation to be paid for sellers' services as employees or independent contractors after the sale). Factors affecting comparability must be discussed in the appraisal report.

Income Approach (Discounted Cash Flow)

The discounted cash flow (DCF) method focuses on incorporating the specific operating characteristics of the seller's business into a cash flow analysis. Estimate cash flow that could be taken out of the practice without impairing operations and profitability. The cash flow available for distribution is then discounted to present value at the indicated discount rate and is totaled. The DCF method is based on the fact that a sum of money expected to be received some time in the future has a lower present value than the same amount of money in hand today. Thus, a valuation will project the cash flows of a business for some future time period to determine present value.

This approach is an after-tax, debt-free cash flow model. That is, there is no provision in the model for either periodic debt service payments or for periodic interest expense. Therefore, the discounted cash flow method produces a value that is equal to total assets less current liabilities (excluding maturities of long-term debt); alternatively stated, it is the value of tangible and intangible assets and net working capital.

A DCF analysis estimates the cash flow that could be taken out of the practice being valued without impairing operations and profitability. The cash flow available for distribution is then reduced to a present value by applying a discount rate.

Estimation Period

The income approach to business enterprise value (BEV) is based on the fact that money received in the future has a lower present value than the same amount of money received today. The future time period over which cash flows are projected—generally five years in a medical practice valuation—is referred to as the *estimation period* or *projection period*. Thus, a valuation will project the cash flow of a medical practice to determine its present value as of the date of the appraisal. The sum of the present value of annual cash flows is added to the present value of the terminal year or reversion (the value of the cash flows at the end of the estimation period) to arrive at BEV.

Normalized Financial Statements

The first step in a DCF analysis involves developing financial statements for the estimation period. These data are derived from the historical financial information of the medical practice. Historical information should be adjusted ("normalized") for any unusual or nonrecurring items that were included in the medical practice's financial results. The resulting financial information is called "normalized financial information." Expected unusual occurrences or known changes in revenues or expenses for years included in the estimation period should be reflected only in the results of the year or years affected.

Assumptions

After normalized financial statements are developed, reasonable assumptions are made about events affecting future cash flow such as: rates of revenue increase/decrease, patient volume, and rates of expense increase/decrease based upon, for example, current market conditions, growth, and inflation trends. Overvaluation problems often emerge at this stage. For example, projections of revenue growth may appear to be at odds with known market conditions in a particular area. Thus, revenue projections require scrutiny to test their assumptions and to make appropriate adjustments to normalized financial information. The following factors are examples used in assessing the assumptions underlying revenue projections for a medical practice:

1. Who owns the patient base—payor or physician? In a managed-care arrangement, the patient goes where the payor directs, affecting the base upon which revenues are projected.

2. What is the mix of managed care and fee for service? The larger the percentage of income generated by managed care, the greater the possibility of a guarantee of revenues. Thus, the mix of managed-care and fee-for-service arrangements is an important factor in revenue projections, as are the length of managed-care contracts and the probability of their renewal.

3. A description of the physician practice. This description should include a description of the medical community environment (primary service area of the practice and local medical competition, including number of practitioners in the specialty of the subject practice and in other specialties). It should also thoroughly analyze the patient base. This may include a discussion of the volume and quality of patient charts, patient age mix and demographics, and payor source. The age of physicians and number of years in practice should be stated. Are necessary adjustments made to the income stream? Future cash flows/income may need to be adjusted. For example, in a surgical specialty, only the portion of payments reflecting the surgical component should be included in revenue projections. There could be increases or decreases in fees or capitation because of competition and the possibility of a change in referral.

4. Are expenses appropriate? Expense projections and assumptions should also be carefully reviewed to ensure they are reasonable and appropriate.

Earnings Before Depreciation, Interest, and Taxes

After projecting reasonable levels of revenue and expense, the restated figure is earnings before depreciation, interest, and taxes, or EBDIT. Sometimes valuations include amortization (depreciation of intangible assets) in the formula. Thus, the formula sometimes appears as EBDITA—earnings before depreciation, interest, taxes, and amortization. EBDITA is often used as a measurement to compare one business investment with another. Valuation analysts will often divide EBDITA by revenues to obtain a EBDITA/revenue ratio. This ratio is then compared to industry averages to determine how the proposed investment compares with the industry at large.

Earnings Before Taxes

EBDIT is then adjusted by subtracting depreciation/amortization. The restated figure is earnings before taxes, or EBT. A tax rate is then applied to determine net income after taxes. After-tax cash flows must always be incorporated in a DCF analysis.

Cash Flow Available for Distribution

Net income after taxes is then adjusted for depreciation/amortization, changes in working capital, and capital expenditures. The result is debt-free cash flow available for distribution.

Discount Rate

The discount rate is an essential component of a valuation based on a DCF analysis. The rate should reflect the risk of the investment in the business. Investment risk represents the probability of failure.

Choosing a correct discount rate is an important component of a valuation. The discount rate determines the value of the cash flows during the estimation period and the terminal year. The methodology most commonly used to determine the discount rate in a DCF analysis is the *weighted average cost of capital* (WACC). The theory behind cost of capital discounting techniques is that they allow alternative potential investments to be compared by using an identical set of yield performance standards.

The health care entity's business enterprise value (i.e., total invested capital) is the sum of the entity's interest-bearing debt, both current and long-term, plus preferred stock plus common stock. In order to establish the fair market value of the entity's equity, all interest-bearing debt that is expected to be paid must be deducted from the indicated value of the health care entity's capital structure. The result is the entity's business enterprise value.

Cost of Capital

The cost of capital is the minimum rate an investment must yield to provide a required return to all sources of capital. Sources of capital include common and preferred stock, long-term debt, and retained earnings. Debt has a lower cost of capital than equity because it has a priority claim on earnings and assets in liquidation. The overall cost of capital is a function of the relative proportions of debt and equity. As more debt is added, the cost of capital declines.

Cost of Equity

The capital asset pricing model (CAPM) is the traditional approach to determine the cost of equity capital in a BEV determination. CAPM is based on the principle that a business enterprise's required rate of return (cost of equity capital) is related to the current interest-rate environment, the expected volatility of investment returns, and the market equity risk premium in excess of the current risk-free rate of return.

Weighted Average Cost of Capital (WACC)

Once the cost of equity is calculated, the discount rate can be determined. As noted above, the weighted average cost of capital (WACC) methodology is commonly used for this purpose.

Discount Rate Example

Weighted Average Cost of Capital

Equity:		
Cost	16.97%	
Weight	85.00%	
		14.42%
Debt:		
Cost After Tax	05.36%	
Weight	15.00%	
		00.80%
		15.22%

Terminal Value Exit Multiples

The terminal value is a very important calculation in a DCF analysis. It is an estimate of the worth of the medical practice's cash flows beyond the estimation period. The terminal value can represent between 50 percent and 150 percent of the total value determined by a DCF analysis. Exit multiples ranging from 3 to 8 are generally seen in valuations of medical providers. Lower multiples within that range might be seen in a medical practice consisting of older physicians in a specialty affected by managed care, whereas a valuation of a practice consisting of younger, primary-care practitioners who will benefit from managed care might use a somewhat higher multiple. An exit multiple at the high end of the range might be seen in an appraisal of an established ambulatory surgery center, for example, which is positively affected by favorable reimbursement policies and managed care.

Given the exit multiple's influence on the bottom line in a DCF analysis, it is important to examine critically the criteria used in selecting it. Factors that might be relevant in selecting an exit multiple include: (a) the growth and stability of the local market environment as suggested in the financial forecast, (b) the long-term growth expectations for the health care industry, (c) the perceived quality and composition of the medical practice, (d) exit multiples used in similar transactions, (e) the interest rate environment at the time of valuation, and (f) the financial and business risk related to the revenue stream of the practice.

Example of Income Approach

Calculation of Value:

Sum of present value (5 years)	*$599,551*
Add: Present value of terminal year	*317,788*
Unadjusted business enterprise value	*917,339*
Net premium	*0.00*
Indicated adj. business enterprise value	*917,339*
Current fair market value of assets	*(30,900)*
Intangible indicated	*886,439*

Premiums and Discounts

During the valuation process, it may be necessary to account for any premiums and/or discounts that could exist. After the preliminary valuation calculations of value are completed, the next step is to review the interest being valued and the market for that interest.

Two important questions should be considered at this point in the valuation process:

- Is the interest being valued a controlling interest or a minority interest?

- Is the interest being valued a marketable interest?

These questions are essential in determining whether the value conclusion will need to be adjusted upward or downward to reflect the value of the specific interest subject to the valuation.

Elements of Control

In all valuation engagements related to medical practices, the degree of control exercised by the interest being valued is important to the overall value of that interest. Control can be defined as the ability of the owner of the interest being valued to adopt, change or discontinue the specific operational aspects of the business. In other words, can the owner of the interest being valued exercise any control over the medical practice, by changing the legal structure of the business entity, selling the practice, setting physician compensation, committing the practice to debt, or adding new owners? If the owner of the interest being valued has the ability to exercise these and other elements of control, this owner is said to have a "controlling interest." In a solo practice, the physician-owner has complete control over these elements; therefore, control is a less critical issue in this structure. However, the relative degree of control exercised by one member of a group practice plays an important role in the valuation of that interest relative to the value of the practice.

Consider the role of Dr. Phil Wheat, a single physician in a three-owner practice. Assuming the owners share equally in the ownership of the practice and in the division of profits, this physician basically has a one-third interest in the practice. Given this set of facts, is the value of the physician's one-third interest in the practice equal to one-third of the value of the practice taken as a whole? Generally, the answer is "no."

Suppose that this one-third owner has no greater or lesser influence on the operational aspects of the practice than does his co-owners. Would a hypothetical willing buyer pay exactly one-third of the value of the entire practice, when the one-third interest does not yield any majority control over the management of the practice? Likewise, would three unrelated purchasers pay as much in the aggregate for three one-third interests as a single purchaser would pay for the entire practice? The answers to these questions obviously vary depending upon the specific facts and circumstances of the practice being valued. Generally, however, it is most often the case that the whole is greater than the sum of its parts, meaning that complete control is more valuable than three-thirds' worth of control. The degree to which the interest owner can exercise control affects the difference between the value of that interest on a controlling or minority basis.

When the value conclusion obtained for a medical practice results in a controlling interest value, the underlying assumption is that the hypothetical purchaser is buying the rights to exercise complete control over the operational aspects of the practice, using the elements of control described above. When this controlling interest value is applied to an interest less than 100 percent, you must determine to what extent the value of that interest is lessened by the lack of complete control. This is quantified in the use of the minority interest discount. In the above example of the one-third owners, given a value of $300,000 for the practice as a whole, how much should the value of one physician's interest be discounted for this lack of control?

To determine this, the analysis should include specific facts about the elements of control exercised by the owner of the interest being valued. Can the owner exert such significant influence as to control the direction of the practice? Can he set policy and compensation amounts? Can he add a new owner? In some cases, a one-third owner has such influence over the practice that a minority interest discount is not appropriate or significant. In other cases, the control exercised by the owner is so small as to warrant a more significant discount. Furthermore, the simple ownership of an interest greater than 50 percent does not eliminate the need for a minority interest discount. Owners with a smaller interest may have a "swing vote" which could effectively reduce the control of the majority owner. And a 50/50 interest does not necessarily translate to equal control, which may result in a greater minority discount for one owner's interest.

Quantifying the minority interest discount requires judgment and a clear understanding of the elements of control exercised by the owner of the valued interest in the medical practice. Unfortunately, there exists no mathematical formula for determining the percentage discount to be applied to a given interest in any business, although there is published data documenting studies of publicly traded companies and the relative amounts of discounts for minority interests. As a rule, the typical minority interest discount often ranges between 20 and 30 percent, although wide variances from this range are commonly found. In valuing a minority interest in a medical practice, the calculation of the minority interest discount should include a thorough analysis of the data gathered during interviews of the physicians regarding the elements of control, while considering the control afforded by the percentage of ownership interest in the practice. In majority ownership situations, the baseline discount is often in the 5 to 10 percent range, and higher for smaller ownership interests. Of course, the baseline rate should be adjusted for specific elements of control exerted by the owner.

Marketability

Assessing the relative market for a medical practice is also important to completing the valuation. In considering the value of a practice, the valuator must be concerned with the existence or absence of a ready market for the practice, and the effect of these factors on value. For obvious reasons, a practice with a readily available market generally commands a higher value than a practice without a market. Furthermore, a partial ownership interest in a practice may be less marketable than the practice as a whole.

The specialty of the medical practice is also an important consideration in the evaluation of marketability, especially given the activity surrounding primary-care practices. Obviously, an understanding of the marketability of the practice and the application of an appropriate discount for lack of marketability is critical to an accurate representation of value.

Many of the approaches commonly used in valuing medical practices today assume a readily available market for the medical practice. Published studies of medical practice transactions show dozens, if not hundreds, of medical practice sales transactions for comparative purposes. But some practices, or fractional interests in medical practices, may require an adjustment to value to reflect a lack of marketability.

Again, no mathematical formula exists to apply to a specific practice to obtain a discount for lack of marketability. However, studies of initial public offerings are readily available that yield information on implied marketability discounts. Of course, no public market for physician practice interests exists, leaving the valuator to the use of judgment. Experience shows that any necessary minority interest discount is usually small, usually less than 15 percent, because of the lack of significant impact on value resulting from the lack of a public market for physician practice interests.

Valuing Fixed Assets and Accounts Receivable

In a medical practice appraisal, you need to value fixed assets and accounts receivable. Fixed assets may be valued in a number of ways. If assets are substantial, the physician should consider hiring an independent appraiser to value them. Value could be based on book value amortized over a reasonable period (such as five to ten years). If the assets are not material to the practice, you may take inventory and ask the physician what the assets could be sold for on the open market. If real estate is involved, an independent appraiser should be engaged. Accounts receivable must be valued as closely as possible to the amount that actually will be collected in the future. Thus, the net realizable value for accounts receivable should be based on the following factors:

1. Insurance receivables multiplied by the practice's gross collection percentage for the past 12 months
2. Patient receivables that are 90 days old or less
3. Patient receivables that are more than 90 days old when the patients have consistently made installment payments

The practice's gross collection percentage should take into account the contractual allowances from the various insurance companies. The appraiser may also want to multiply the patients' receivables by some percentage (e.g., 90 percent) to take into account potential bad debt write-offs.

Weighing the Methods

After making the calculations for each method, the appraiser must decide which ones to use and the weights to place on each method. The results are *weighted average values* for the medical practice. After calculating the weighted average values, you need to assess the reasonableness of the amounts. This is normally done by determining if, after paying out reasonable physicians' compensation, the practice's excess earnings are sufficient to pay out the value of the practice over a number of years. To perform this calculation, first determine the yearly amounts due if the practice's value was financed over five years at an interest rate close to the prime rate of interest. This total is compared to the practice's excess earnings. If the excess earnings are sufficient to cover the installment amounts, the calculated values should be reasonable. The appraiser must also assess whether the excess earnings of the practice will remain close to the same in the near future. If not, the appraiser will need to recalculate excess earnings based on the expected earnings potential of the practice and compare this number to the practice's calculated value. If the practice is potentially high-risk, the appraiser may choose to calculate the installment amount based on a period less than five years. A high-risk medical practice's earnings could fluctuate substantially in the future. In this situation, the physician would want to pay out the values as quickly as possible before the practice is affected economically.

The Impact of Transaction Contracts on Fair Market Value

There are some subtle nuances of transaction contracts that people performing valuations of small medical practices may want to consider, according to Mark Dietrich, CPA. Dietrich is a highly respected medical practice appraiser who believes that advisors to buyers (in particular) and sellers should be cognizant of these matters, as well.

When valuing a medical practice, the valuator must specify the interest being valued. Typically, this is 100 percent of the tangible and intangible asset value, free and clear of any debt. Small businesses and medical practices are typically sold in asset transactions, not stock transactions. The sale to a hospital, physician practice management company, or other entity is generally a 100 percent interest, which, of course, means a controlling interest.

Valuation theory attaches significance to the presence of a controlling interest, and this significance should be considered by the valuator. Consider that the value of a share of a publicly traded company reflects a noncontrolling, freely traded, minority interest. If a single buyer were to acquire a controlling number of shares, he or she would likely pay a control premium. That control premium might be quite large.

The valuation techniques typically employed in medical practices, such as the excess earnings and discounted free cash flow methods, generally calculate values of controlling interests. Look carefully at the method used to develop the discount and capitalization rate. Be sure that there is not an explicit or implicit inclusion in the rate of a discount for lack of marketability or a minority discount. Many, if not most, transactions also include an employment contract or services contract between the selling physician(s) and the buyer. Should this contract be a factor in computing the value?

The engagement letter should carefully spell out the nature of the interest being valued and the standard of value employed (typically fair market value). This specification should be repeated in the report letter and/or in the value conclusion. In this manner, the valuator makes clear the precise nature of the engagement. If the buyer subsequently consummates a transaction that is inconsistent with the terms of the engagement, the valuator (it is hoped) will not be liable.

Fair Market Value

The hypothetical "any willing buyer, any willing seller" is the hallmark for medical practice valuations and is the standard required by the IRS and the Office of Inspector General. Investment value—the value of a business to a specific buyer—is not the standard employed. How much consideration should the valuator give to the specifics of a particular transaction?

Valuation engagements vary. In some cases, the valuator is retained, performs the analysis, and issues a report. There is no interaction with the buyer and the seller. In other cases, the valuator may sit at the table and play an integral role in quantifying the effect of different assumptions on the valuation model. This is particularly true when someone prepares a valuation using the discounted free cash flow model. A representation letter is required from the practice in support of, and in concurrence with, the assumptions in the forecast. A valuator sitting at the table may become aware of proposed post-transaction employment terms that affect the buyer's ability to exercise control (as that term is used in controlling interest) or otherwise affect the valuation. Typical provisions in physician practice transactions might include the following:

1. Physician salary guarantees not requiring minimum productivity

2. Guarantee of employment for nonphysician employees

3. Agreement not to relocate practice

4. Approval authority granted to selling physicians for annual budgets, hiring and firing, capital asset acquisitions, resale of practice

5. Compensation and benefits negotiated that differ from those of the valuation model

It should be clear that the buyer and seller understand the risks of consummating a transaction that causes the fair market value standard to be violated. The principal regulatory risk is that the IRS or OIG will reject the valuation as being inconsistent with the actual transaction. The buyer, of course, relying on fair market value, may not end up getting what he or she bargained for; the seller in this case would get more.

Another infrequent but important potential occurrence is the use of an asset valuation in a stock transaction. The author is aware of several circumstances in which valuation reports specifically citing asset values were then used by the buyer to effect a stock sale. There are considerable differences in the approach used to value assets as opposed to stock, including the following:

1. Additional depreciation deductions that result from a step-up in basis in an asset purchase reduce taxes and increase cash flow and value.

2. Purchased intangible asset value can be amortized over 15 years, increasing value as with depreciation.

3. Valuation of stock is only an equity interest while assets may be both equity and debt. An asset purchase may therefore use a weighted average cost of capital, including debt, which is always less than the equity-only discount rate. It is not clear that the WAAC can be used to value an equity-only (stock) interest, unless the computation is of business enterprise value, and the long-term debt is subtracted from the total to arrive at equity value.

4. A tax-exempt buyer of stock cannot liquidate the target without paying a tax on the unrealized value of the underlying assets (IRC Section 337). This is the difference between the purchase price of the stock and the basis of the assets. As a defense against use of an asset valuation in a stock transaction, you may want to include a specific statement in your report that taxes on the sale proceeds are assumed to be an obligation of the seller and are not accounted for in the valuation.

5. A stock transaction means that the underlying debts of the corporation are acquired as well. If the valuation is for assets only, the value needs to be reduced by debt assumed.

Other Impacts of Transaction Contracts

The health care industry is heavily regulated and affected by a myriad of statutes and regulations. Uninformed, poorly represented, or simply dishonest parties to a transaction may include terms that violate the Stark or Medicare Fraud and Abuse laws. For example, parties may include compensation based upon ancillary test productivity or requirements to refer patients to a particular institution. These terms may be in writing (not likely) or oral. The statement of limiting conditions in the report should explicitly state that the valuator assumes compliance with all applicable federal, state, and local regulations. This *should* shift the burden of noncompliance away from the valuator and onto the buyer and seller.

■ **Practice Point:** You cannot guarantee that a practice will not misuse a valuation report. It is important that the engagement letter and report are consistent and clear about the nature of the interest being valued and the standard of value employed.

IRS Tax-Exempt Appraisal Guidelines

As stated in Chapter 22, the IRS issued appraisal guidelines for tax-exempt delivery systems or other entities that acquire physician practices. According to the IRS, whether the valuation placed on an asset represents fair market value depends on the quality of the appraisal. The IRS defines *fair market value* as the "price on which a willing buyer and a willing seller would agree, neither being under any compulsion to buy or sell, and both having reasonable knowledge of the relevant facts." (Refer to Revenue Ruling 59-60, 1959-1 C.B. 237, for an expanded explanation.) The IRS has included the following language in all favorable Internal Revenue Code (IRC) Section 501(c)(3) integrated delivery system (IDS) exemption letters:

Applicant represents that all assets acquired will be at or below fair-market value (FMV) and will be the result of independent appraisals and arm's-length negotiations. The applicant's representations must include an appraisal that details the market price of the assets. Appraisals, according to the IRS, are pivotal in determining if a price represents FMV, and whether an applicant establishing an IDS by purchasing a physician's practice may receive exemption. Thus, a critical issue is whether the appraisal is correctly performed.

The IRS National Office of Appeals, Office of Appraisal Services, in reviewing valuations submitted in IDS cases at the request of exempt organizations, has stated generally that fair market value is determined within the framework of the business enterprise value to the most likely hypothetical purchaser. In this situation, the hypothetical purchaser, according to the IRS, usually is assumed to be a commercial health care corporation. The *business enterprise value* (BEV) is defined by the IRS as the total value of the assembled assets that make up the entity as a going concern (the value of a practice's capital structure). BEV can be defined in other ways, too. Another definition of a more technical nature states that the BEV is the capital structure of the business, the components of which are common equity, preferred equity, and long-term debt. By removing long-term debt from the business enterprise, you obtain shareholders' (or partners') equity, or the net worth of the business. The BEV is the basis for most appraisals submitted to the IRS.

How Is BEV Determined?

The IRS has requested in all IDS applications that the valuation provide all recognized approaches for estimating BEV, including the income approach, market approach, and cost approach. The income approach is considered the most relevant method by the IRS, as it includes the excess earnings method described in Revenue Ruling 68-609, 1968-2 C.B. 327, and was approved for the valuation of intangible assets in Revenue Ruling 76-91, 1976-1 C.B. 149. According to the IRS, in many valuations of medical groups, the seller places a substantial value on intangible assets. Intangibles are often difficult to measure in terms of real value and are often a likely place to inflate the valuation.

Income Approach

The income approach focuses on incorporating the specific operating characteristics of the seller's business into a cash flow analysis. The discounted cash flow (DCF) method will be employed in this particular discussion. The DCF often is used in the income approach to valuation. In this analysis, cash flow that could potentially be taken out of the practice or business without impairing operations and profitability is estimated. The cash flow available for distribution is then discounted to present value at a selected discount rate and totaled.

The DCF method of estimating economic value is based on the fact that a sum of money expected to be received in the future has a lower present value than the same amount of money in hand today. Thus, a valuation will project the cash flows of a medical practice for a future time period to determine present value. This future time period, usually five to ten years, is referred to as the *estimation period*. The sum of the present yearly value of cash flow available for distribution is added to the terminal value or reversion (the selling price of the practice or business at the end of the estimation period) to arrive at the indicated BEV. (See James Zukin, *Financial Valuation: Businesses and Business Interest*, page 1618.)

According to the IRS, the term *income* does not refer solely to income in the accounting sense. Income includes cash flow earned from assets and also such future benefits as synergy, growth, or expansion. Determine what the practice or business is worth today and tomorrow in terms of earnings, and add or subtract from this amount the value of the practice's competitive position and its future growth to determine the practice's worth in five years. This future value must be discounted to arrive at today's FMV.

The key to understanding the income approach is to recognize that the value of an asset or medical practice or business is equal to the present worth of the future benefits of ownership. In other words, an organization purchasing a medical practice must ascertain if today's sales price is equal to its future earnings. Following is an explanation of the income approach as provided by the IRS.

First develop financial statements for the estimation period. These data are usually derived by using historical information from prior reporting periods. Then adjust or normalize the historical information for any extraordinary occurrences during the estimation period or for known changes in revenues or expenses that will be sustained into the future. The resulting financial statements are called the "normalized financial statements." After preparing the normalized financial statements, make reasonable assumptions about rates of revenue increase, patient volume, and overhead increases based on current market conditions, growth, and best estimates of inflation trends. In all cases, use reasonable assumptions with respect to the rate of revenue increases and patient volume combined with common inflationary increases.

After you have calculated a reasonable level of revenue and expense, you can then calculate earnings before depreciation, interest, and taxes (EBDIT). EBDIT is then adjusted for changes in depreciation, changes in net working capital, changes in capital expenditures, and new capital. The formula can be expressed as follows:

+	Depreciation and amortization
+/–	Changes in net working capital
+/–	Changes in fixed assets
+/–	Changes in capitalization
=	Earnings before Taxes (EBT)

The next step is to determine earnings after taxes, using the applicable tax rates. The number remaining after the adjustment for taxes represents debt-free cash flow available for distribution. Multiply this number by the discount rate factor to determine the unadjusted business enterprise value. (See the example in the income approach section that was included within the IRS's *Exempt Organizations Continuing Professional Education Technical Instruction Program Textbook.*)

Market Approach

The second preferred method of estimated BEV of the IRS is the market approach. This approach measures value based on the purchase price paid in the marketplace for similar assets. This approach, familiar to most home purchasers, compares the value of one home with that of other, similar homes to determine FMV. However, with the sale of a business it is more difficult to find comparable entities. Therefore, actual purchase price multiples paid for similar companies are evaluated, adjusted, and applied to the operating data of the seller's business to arrive at FMV. According to the IRS, factors affecting comparability include geographic markets served, competitive position, profitability, growth prospects, risk perceptions, and financial composition. One resource for the market approach is the *Goodwill Registry*. The *Registry* has been tracking sales of medical practices for ten years and has developed its own set of comparables.

Cost Approach

The last method for estimating BEV is the cost approach. The method measures value by determining the cost to replace or reproduce an asset, less an allowance for physical deterioration or obsolescence. The cost approach uses the FMV of the individual corporate assets as a starting point. After the FMV of all assets has been estimated, the book value of liabilities is subtracted to arrive at an indication of the cost of the business. The adjusted net asset method of determining cost takes into consideration the potential for monetary and tangible asset value greater than the enterprise value. According to the IRS, intangible assets, if any, typically are not valued under this method unless their value be estimated reasonably. However, for a medical practice, always consider including a value for intangible assets. Because most medical practices have a very low cost structure, excluding the intangible would result in a value too low to represent a true FMV.

Summary of Approaches

The IRS expects all three of the methods discussed in this section to be included in any appraisal of a medical practice when that practice is being acquired at FMV by a tax-exempt entity. The most common situation now is the acquisition of medical practices by not-for-profit hospitals. The IRS suggests that when the discounted cash flow method is appropriate to value the practice or business being sold, the valuation must be based on a discount rate supportable by current market conditions. To ensure a correct valuation, test the results of the income approach against other approaches, such as market and cost.

▼ GLOSSARY

Accounts receivable ratio   Current accounts receivable balance divided by the average monthly gross production for the prior 12-month period.

Addbacks   Include owner compensation, extraordinary expenditures, and optional expenditures. Applies to an appraisal of a medical practice.

Adjustments   Include comparable owner compensation and extraordinary revenue items. Applies to an appraisal of a medical practice.

Age/sex rating   A method of structuring capitation payments based on enrollee/member age and sex.

Alternative delivery system (ADS)   A method of providing health care benefits that departs from traditional indemnity (commercial insurance) methods. A health maintenance organization (HMO), for example, is an alternative delivery system.

Ancillary services   Services in addition to the physician's personal clinical treatment of the patient (e.g., laboratory and X-ray services).

Anniversary   The beginning of a subscriber group's benefit year. A subscriber group with a year coinciding with the calendar year would be said to have a January 1 anniversary.

Attrition rate   Disenrollment expressed as a percentage of total membership. An HMO with 50,000 members experiencing a 2 percent monthly attrition rate would need to gain 1,000 members per month in order to retain its 50,000 member level.

Basic health services   Benefits that all federally qualified HMOs must offer.

Benefit package   A collection of specific services or benefits that the HMO is obligated to provide under terms of its contracts with subscriber groups.

Benefit year A 12-month period that a group uses to administer its employee fringe benefits program. A majority of subscribers use a January through December benefit year.

Break-even point The HMO membership level at which total revenues and total costs are equal and therefore produce neither a net gain nor loss from operations.

Buy/sell agreement Legal agreement that spells out the manner in which an owner can buy into the practice and how the practice will buy out an owner.

C corporation Corporation that does not elect Subchapter S status. Rules under Subchapter C of the Internal Revenue Code govern the taxation of this entity.

Capitalization rate Rate used to convert an income stream into some indication of a value for the medical practice. It is the sum of the annual rate of return currently available from investments offering maximum security and the highest degree of liquidity and a risk premium.

Capitation The per capita cost of providing a specific menu of health services to a defined population over a set period of time. The capitated payment is generally a fixed payment received each month by the physician provider. This payment is the same regardless of the amount of service rendered by the physician or physician group.

Cash indemnity benefits Sums that are paid to insureds for covered services and that require submission of a filed claim.

Catchment area The geographic area from which an HMO draws its patients.

Charge ticket *See* Superbill.

Claims processing edits Part of a Medicare carrier's automated claims processing system that allows the carrier to compare situations where two or more services are provided to one beneficiary in a single day, and to identify situations, for example, where outdated codes are being used, CPT definitions for services may have been misunderstood or misinterpreted, mutually exclusive procedures have been coded together, or simply a coding mistake has been made.

Claims-made malpractice policy Type of malpractice policy in which a doctor is covered only if the alleged malpractice claim or notice of a claim is made before the coverage is terminated.

Clinical Laboratory Improvement Amendment (CLIA) Amendment enacted by Congress to govern and police laboratories located in physicians' offices.

Closed panel A managed-care arena in which members are required to see the physicians with which the plan has contracted and cannot see physicians outside of this set of providers for routine care covered by the plan.

Coinsurance The portion of the cost for care for which the insured is financially responsible. This usually is determined by a fixed percentage, as in major medical coverage. Often coinsurance applies after a specified deductible has been met.

Comfort letter A special procedures letter generally issued to an individual practice association (IPA).

Community rating A method for determining health-insurance premiums based on actual or anticipated costs in a specific geographic location as opposed to an experience rating that looks at individual characteristics of the insured.

Composite rate A uniform premium applicable to all eligible members by a subscriber group regardless of the number of claimed dependents. This rate is common among labor unions and large employer groups and usually does not require any contribution by the union member or employee.

Consultation The advice or opinion that one physician provides in response to another physician's request.

Continuing medical education (CME) A requirement of state law that a physician must fulfill each year to maintain his or her medical license.

Contract An HMO agreement executed by a subscriber group. The term may be used in place of subscriber when referring to penetrations within a given subscriber group. The term is also used to designate an enrollee's coverage.

Contract mix The distribution of enrollees according to contracts classified by dependency categories, for example, the number or percentage of singles, doubles, or families. It is used to determine average contract size.

Contractual adjustment The difference between what a practice bills and what it is legally entitled to collect.

Contractual percentage Contractual adjustments divided by gross production.

Coordination of benefits Establishes procedures to be followed in the event of duplicate coverage thus assuring that no more than 100 percent of the costs of care are reimbursed to the patient.

Co-payment A modest payment made by an HMO or preferred provider organization (PPO) enrollee at the time that selected services are rendered.

Critical care visit A visit in which a medical emergency requires the constant attendance of the physician.

Current procedural terminology (CPT) codes Numerical codes adopted by all insurance companies that physicians must use to report their services to the insurance companies. These codes explain what clinical services the physician performed.

Current procedural terminology (CPT) modifiers Numerical descriptors that are added to a CPT code to provide further detail about a patient's encounter.

Deselection When a health plan cancels a practice's provider agreement, usually because the health plan perceives that a physician has overutilized the plan's services.

Diagnosis codes Also called ICD-9 codes. Numerical codes that explain in more detail to the insurance company what particular service a physician performed on a patient.

Direct contracting The situation that results when individual employers or business coalitions contract directly with providers for health care services with no HMO or PPO intermediary. This enables the employer to include in the plan the specific services preferred by its employees.

Direct overhead　Expense items that can be costed to one physician directly.

Enrollment　The process of converting subscriber group eligible members into HMO members or the aggregate count of HMO enrollees as of a given time.

Excess earnings　Net income plus addbacks, less adjustments.

Experience rating　A method to determine an HMO premium structure based on the actual utilization of individual subscriber groups. Age, sex, and utilization experience are the principal determinants in rate setting using this method.

Explanation of benefits (EOB)　An accompaniment to the check from the insurance company that indicates how much of the charged fee was approved for payment, how much was applied to a deductible, how much was applied to a co-payment, and how much was applied to other sources, such as a withhold.

Extraordinary expenditures　Expenditures not connected with the normal operating overhead of the practice.

Extraordinary revenue　Revenue that is nonrecurring or would not stay with the practice if the practice were sold outright.

Fee for service　The amount the patient is charged according to a fee schedule set for each service or procedure to be provided.

Fee profile　*See* Usual, customary, and reasonable fee.

Fee schedule　The normal fee a doctor would charge a commercial insurance carrier.

Fixed costs　*See* Shared overhead.

Gatekeeper　A primary-care physician in an HMO who makes referrals to other physicians. The gatekeeper's function is to reduce health care use and costs.

Goodwill　The intangible value of a medical practice. Goodwill is an indicator that a particular medical practice performs better than the typical practice in its medical specialty. Typical usually is defined by industry surveys and employment opportunities.

Gross collection percentage Collections divided by gross production.

Gross income guarantee A type of income guarantee that provides the practice with a minimum level of collections each month.

Group practice without walls (GPWW) A network of physicians who have merged into one legal entity but maintain each individual practice location.

HCFA common procedure coding system (HCPCS) codes Alpha numerical codes developed by the Health Care Financing Administration for physicians to use when reporting certain services to Medicare.

Health maintenance organization (HMO) An organization of health care personnel and facilities that provides a comprehensive range of health services to an enrolled population for a fixed sum of money paid in advance.

Incidental surgical procedures Services insurance companies believe are *casual* to the other surgical procedures that were performed and thus are not considered to be medically necessary.

Income guarantee A hospital recruitment incentive that provides the practice with its working capital to pay both general operating overhead and compensation to the doctor.

Incurred but not reimbursed (IBNR) liability Liability accrued to reflect how much an IPA would owe health care providers if it were to cease its activities and pay noncapitated providers for all services that have been rendered to date.

Indemnity carrier Usually an insurance company that offers selected coverage within a framework of fee schedules, limitations, and exclusions as negotiated with subscriber groups.

Indemnity plans Type of insurance plan that generally pays for all reasonable health care costs. The patient usually pays 20 percent of the costs under this type of plan.

Independent practice arrangement (IPA) A separate entity, usually a state not-for-profit corporation, that brings physicians together to contract directly with managed-care plans and employers.

Individual practice association (IPA) An entity of physicians formed to obtain insurance contracts or negotiate with managed-care plans or integrated delivery systems.

Integrated delivery systems Affiliations of health care providers, usually between hospitals and physicians or among physicians, that deliver health care services.

International Classification of Diseases, 9th Revision, Clinical Modification (ICD-9) codes *See* Diagnosis codes.

Limiting charge The maximum amount nonparticipating physicians can charge for covered services. It is calculated as a percentage above the national fee schedule amount for nonparticipating physicians.

***Locum tenens* physician** A physician hired, generally through an agency, to work on a temporary basis.

Managed care A planned and coordinated approach to providing quality health care at lower cost.

Management service organization (MSO) A separate legal entity, generally a subsidiary of a hospital, formed to provide administrative and practice management services to physicians' offices.

Managing physician The physician in a group practice who interacts with the employees and is responsible for a specific set of duties.

Market area The targeted geographic area or area in which the principal market potential is located.

Market share That part of the market potential that an HMO or PPO has captured. Usually market share is expressed as a percentage of the market potential.

Medicaid Government program that allows individuals below an income threshold to receive medical care. Services are paid for by the government.

Medical foundation An integrated delivery system consisting of a nonprofit, tax-exempt entity that acquires the business and clinical assets of large medical groups and the group of physicians themselves.

Medicare Government program that allows eligible individuals to receive medical care paid for by the government. Generally, persons age 62 or older qualify for Medicare benefits. The individual pays a Medicare health insurance premium, which is deducted from his or her Social Security benefits.

Medicare abuse Activities that, while not considered fraudulent, may directly or indirectly cause financial losses to the Medicare program or the beneficiary.

Medicare compliance program A program a practice develops to ensure that physicians, billing clerks, upper management, corporate officers, and others within its organization know the laws and requirements to be in compliance with Medicare.

Medicare fraud Knowingly and willfully making or causing a false statement or representation of a material fact made in application for a Medicare benefit or payment.

Medicare Part A insurance Medicare reimbursement that applies to hospital and other specific services. It does not apply to physicians.

Medicare Part B insurance Medicare reimbursement that covers physicians' services and other specific services.

Medicare supplement Also called Medigap. A health-insurance plan specifically designed to supplement Medicare's benefits by filling in some of the gaps in Medicare coverage.

Medigap *See* Medicare supplement.

National Correct Coding Initiative Initiative implemented by the Health Care Financing Administration to identify and eliminate incorrect coding of medical services. Implemented via the installation of a set of new edits into Medicare carriers' automated claims processing systems.

Net collection percentage Collections divided by the sum of production less contractual adjustments.

Net income guarantee A type of income guarantee that provides the doctor with a guaranteed level of compensation after the payment of overhead and, sometimes, debt service.

Nonparticipating physicians Physicians who do not elect to participate in the Medicare program. These physicians are not required to accept as full payment what Medicare allows for reimbursement for a particular service.

Occupational Safety and Health Administration (OSHA) Subsidiary of Congress that governs workers' safety rules and regulations.

Office of the Inspector General (OIG) Established under the Department of Health and Human Resources in 1976 for the purpose of identifying and eliminating fraud, abuse, and waste in Health and Human Services programs and to promote the efficiency and economy in departmental operations.

Open enrollment period The period of time stipulated in a group contract in which eligible members of the group can choose a health plan alternative for the coming benefit year.

Open panel A managed-care arena in which private physicians contract with a plan to provide care in their own offices.

Out-of-area benefits The scope of emergency benefits available to HMO and PPO members while temporarily outside their defined service areas.

Participating physicians Physicians who elect to participate with Medicare. These doctors legally agree to accept as full payment for their services the amount Medicare allows for a particular service. These amounts can be found on the physician's Medicare disclosure report.

Patient's encounter form *See* Superbill.

Payor mix The various percentages of revenue derived from particular insurance classes. For example, a practice may derive 20 percent of its revenue from Medicare, 10 percent from Medicaid, 10 percent from self-paying patients, 40 percent from commercial insurance, and 20 percent from managed care.

Peer review Evaluation of a physician's performance by other physicians, usually within the same geographic area and medical specialty.

Penetration   The percentage of business that an HMO is able to capture in a particular subscriber group or in the market area as a whole.

Per member, per month   The cost or revenue from each plan's member for one month.

Personal service corporation   Type of defined service corporation designated by the Internal Revenue Service to be taxed at a separate tax rate.

Phantom income principle   Income generated without the corresponding cash flow to pay related federal or state income taxes.

Physician extenders   Nurse practitioners and other employees who directly assist the physician.

Physician/hospital organization (PHO)   An organization consisting of hospital and medical staff to provide services to patients and to negotiate and obtain managed-care contracts.

Physician practice management company (PPMC)   A company that acquires the nonmedical assets of a physician practice and then manages all of the practice's affairs, including billing, managed-care contracting, asset acquisition, personnel, and physician compensation.

Preferred provider organization (PPO)   Contractual arrangements between physicians and insurance companies, employers, or third parties in which physicians provide services to a designated area with set fee schedules.

Private benefit   Tax code provision that requires that serving private interests is incidental to the accomplishment of the organization's charitable purpose. If an organization violates this provision, its tax-exempt status may be affected.

Private inurement   The tax code provision that states that no part of the net earnings of a tax-exempt organization can inure to the benefit of any private shareholder or individual. If an organization violates this provision, its tax-exempt status may be affected.

Relative value unit   Measurement of value. When it is multiplied by a conversion factor, it results in a proposed fee to be paid over to the physician for services rendered.

Resource-based relative value scale (RBRVS)   Payment system developed by Medicare and implemented in 1992 to pay for services rendered to Medicare beneficiaries.

Responsibility grid   Grid indicating the specific services a managed-care health plan includes within the capitated rate for a physician's medical specialty.

Retained earnings   Money needed to pay debt service and capital expenditures or be retained as future working capital.

Retroactive adjustments   Adjustments to the monthly capitation payment to reflect new enrollees in a managed-care health plan.

Revenue Ruling 97-21   A ruling by the IRS addressing the circumstances under which a not-for-profit hospital can be said to have violated the requirement for tax exemption under Code Section 501(c)(3) when it provides incentives to recruit private physicians to join its medical staff and provide services on its behalf.

S corporation   Corporation with a limited number of shareholders, which has elected subchapter S status. For federal income tax purposes, taxable income is taxed at regular income tax rates. S corporations usually avoid the corporate income tax, and corporate losses can be claimed by the shareholders.

Secondary insurance   Insurance coverage obtained by Medicare beneficiaries to cover any amount they may be personally responsible for after Medicare makes its payments to the health care provider(s).

Shared overhead   Also fixed costs. Overhead items that are shared equally among physicians. These expenses, such as rent and payroll, keep going regardless of how much revenue a physician generates.

Shareholder agreement   *See* Buy/sell agreement.

Superbill The document on which a physician records his or her services, normally for services rendered to patients in the office.

Tail-end premium Premium paid to an insurance company if a claims-made policy is in force and the physician leaves the employment of the practice. The premium is used to purchase coverage in the event a claim is made against the physician for services rendered during the time the physician was employed by the practice.

Twenty percent rule A rule to assess financial risk regarding managed-care contracts: Of a practice's total managed-care revenue, no more than 20 percent should come from one managed-care plan.

Unique provider identification number (UPIN) Issued by the Medicare carrier to all physicians who apply for a Medicare provider number.

Usual, customary, and reasonable (UCR) fee The maximum fee an insurance company will pay for a particular service. Also called the fee profile or the charge ticket.

Utilization The frequency with which a benefit is used, for example, 3,200 doctor's office visits per 1,000 HMO members per year. Utilization experience multiplied by the average cost per unit of service is capitated costs.

Utilization management A process that measures use of available resources to determine medical necessity, cost-effectiveness, and conformity to criteria for optimal use.

Variable overhead Overhead items that are split among physicians, generally on the basis of productivity. These expenses cannot be costed directly to any one physician.

Withhold An amount withheld by a managed-care plan from a doctor's reimbursement that may or may not be reimbursed depending on the plan's criteria for reimbursement.

Write-offs Receivable balances that are deemed no longer collectible.

▼ APPENDIX A

Part I: Medical Practice Financial Management

Chapter 2

Chapter 4

Chapter 5

Chapter 7

Chapter 8

APPENDIX ITEM 02-01
MEDICAL PRACTICE STATISTICAL REPORT

	Current	Year-to-Date	Prior Y-T-D
Patient activity			
Office			
Hospital care			
Procedures			
Radiology			
Laboratory			
% of practice income			
Office			
Hospital care			
Procedures			
Radiology			
Laboratory			
Production			
Collections			
Gross collection %			
Contractual write-offs			
Contractual %			
Net collection %			
Accounts receivable			
Current			
30 days			
60 days			
90+ days			
A/R ratio			

APPENDIX ITEM 02-02
REGULAR FINANCIAL STATEMENT FOR A MEDICAL PRACTICE

STATEMENT OF ASSETS, LIABILITIES, & EQUITY
INCOME TAX BASIS

ASSETS

Current Assets

Cash—Source #1	3,132.81
Cash—Source #2	1,022.47
Cash—Source #3	264.87
Cash—Source #4	3,518.71
Cash—Source #5	1,296.00
Funds	50.00
Total Current Assets	9,284.86

Fixed Assets

Furniture & Fixtures	1,825.23
Medical Equipment	1,524.76
Office Equipment	10,492.00
Computer Equipment	53,172.85
Accumulated Depreciation	(49,659.64)
Total Fixed Assets	17,355.20

Other Assets

Total Other Assets	.00
Total Assets	26,640.06

LIABILITIES AND EQUITY

Current Liabilities

Accrued P/S Contributions	41,989.14
401K Contributions	769.68
Total Current Liabilities	42,758.82

Long-Term Liabilities

Notes Payable	6,379.37
Total Long-Term Liabilities	6,379.37
Total Liabilities	49,138.19

Equity

Partner's Capital	(27,816.39)
Current Year Profit (loss)	5,318.26
Total Equity	(22,498.13)
Total Liabilities and Equity	26,640.06

STATEMENT OF REVENUE & EXPENSES
INCOME TAX BASIS

	├─Period to Date─┤		├─ Year to Date ─┤	
	Actual	%	Actual	%
Revenue				
Fee Income	147,804.36	101.6	299,321.16	101.5
Med. Records Inc.	70.00	.0	120.00	.0
Patient Refunds	(2,388.33)	(1.6)	(4,612.89)	(1.6)
Total Revenue	145,486.03	100.0	294,828.27	100.0
Expenses				
Advertising	2,879.42	2.0	3,333.98	1.1
Acctng. & Prof.	1,982.54	1.4	3,232.54	1.1
Ans./Paging Svc.	369.74	.3	573.98	.2
Auto Expense	287.99	.2	468.43	.2
Bank Charges	13.86	.0	23.88	.0
Collection Service			42.22	.0
Computer Usage	165.88	.1	896.66	.3
Contract Labor	85.00	.1	235.74	.1
Contract Payroll Svc.	131.40	.1	235.74	.1
Contributions	530.00	.4	530.00	.2
Credit Card Process.	18.84	.0	34.89	.0
Delivery Services			44.00	.0
Depreciation	596.33	.4	929.67	.3
Dues & Subs.	301.37	.2	326.37	.1
Education			195.00	.1
Equipment Rental			124.08	.0
Entertainment/80%			1,269.06	.4
Gifts			610.62	.2
Insurance—General	15,446.10	10.6	16,525.78	5.6
Insurance—Malprac.	7,211.02	5.0	14,422.04	4.9

	⊢— Period to Date —⊣		⊢— Year to Date —⊣	
	Actual	%	Actual	%
Interest	53.44	.0	115.53	.0
Licenses & Fees			15.00	.0
Maint. Agreements	534.00	.4	1,178.55	.4
Medical—Dues			175.00	.1
Medical—Pubs.	411.02	.3	470.97	.2
Medical—Supplies	530.76	.4	550.30	.2
Office Expense	1,239.94	.9	3,862.37	1.3
Mobile System	429.77	.3	912.44	.3
Pension Plan Contrib.	295.25	.2	885.75	.3
Pension Plan Exp.	1,575.00	1.1	1,900.00	.6
Postage	300.00	.2	629.00	.2
Prof. Services	1,277.88	4.3	12,392.76	.8
Rent	6,196.38	4.3	12,392.76	4.2
Repairs & Maint.			152.65	.1
Salaries—Other	23,195.43	15.9	45,236.14	15.3
Security	44.06	.0	44.06	.0
Seminars			210.00	.1
Stationery & Printing			116.91	.0
Taxes—Other	57.74	.0	5,981.25	2.0
Taxes—Payroll	2,319.55	1.6	4,623.46	1.6
Telephone	2,264.95	1.6	3,397.91	1.2
Travel & Lodging	153.27	.1	429.78	.1
Total Expenses	70,898.03	48.7	129,843.81	44.0
Other Income & Exp.				
Interest Income	(2.18)	.0	(4.42)	.0
Physicians Comp.				
Physician #1	26,000.00	17.9	56,598.98	19.2
Physician #2	26,000.00	17.9	53,839.59	18.3
Physician #3	25,450.67	17.5	49,232.05	16.7
Total Other Inc. & Exp.	77,448.49	53.2	159,666.20	54.2
Total Expenses	148,346.52	102.0	289,510.01	98.2
Net Income (Loss)	(2,860.49)	(2.0)	5,318.26	1.8

APPENDIX ITEM 02-03

COMPARATIVE FINANCIAL STATEMENT SHOWING CURRENT RESULTS AND PRIOR-YEAR RESULTS FOR THE SAME PERIOD FOR A MEDICAL PRACTICE

COMPARATIVE STATEMENT OF REVENUE & EXPENSES
INCOME TAX BASIS

| | Period to Date | | | | Year to Date | | |
	Actual	%	Prior Year	%	Actual	%	Prior Year	%
Revenue								
Fee Income	147,804.36	101.6	122,379.20	100.4	299,321.16	101.5	280,601.91	101.0
Medical Records Income	70.00	.0	60.00	.0	120.00	.0	210.00	.1
Patient Refunds & Returns	(2,388.33)	(1.6)	(582.98)	(.5)	(4,612.89)	(1.6)	(2,902.41)	(1.0)
Total Revenue	145,486.03	100.0	121,856.22	100.0	294,828.27	100.0	277,909.50	100.0
Expenses								
Advertising	2,879.42	2.0	1,051.90	.9	3,333.98	1.1	2,482.33	.9
Accounting & Professional	1,982.54	1.4	477.00	.4	3,232.54	1.1	1,507.00	.5
Answering/Paging Service	369.74	.3	151.08	.1	573.98	.2	266.43	.1
Auto Expenses	287.99	.2	244.14	.2	468.43	.2	381.40	.1
Bank Charges	13.86	.0	18.25	.0	23.88	.0	28.28	.0
Collection Service					42.22	.0		
Computer Usage	165.98	.1	2,500.00	2.1	896.66	.3	6,113.78	2.2
Contract Labor	85.00	.1	535.00	.4	255.00	.1	1,235.00	.4

	Period to Date				Year to Date			
	Actual	%	Prior Year	%	Actual	%	Prior Year	%
Contract Payroll Service	131.40	.1	96.23	.1	235.74	.1	250.48	.1
Contributions	530.00	.4	135.00	.1	530.00	.2	285.00	.1
Credit Card Processing	18.84	.0	31.28	.0	34.89	.0	44.10	.0
Delivery Services					44.00	.0		
Depreciation	596.33	.4	333.34	.3	929.67	.3	666.68	.2
Dues & Subscriptions	301.37	.2	318.72	.3	326.37	.1	2,011.72	.7
Education			38.10	.0	195.00	.1	134.44	.0
Equipment Rental					124.08	.0		
Entertainment/80%	3,309.71		2.7		1,269.06	.4	4,651.59	1.7
Gifts			133.34	.1	610.62	.2	1,099.02	.4
Insurance—General	15,446.10	10.6	4,451.98	3.7	16,525.78	5.6	9,645.37	3.5
Insurance—Malpractice	7,211.02	5.0	6,703.00	5.5	14,422.04	4.9	13,406.00	4.8
Interest	53.44	.0	152.64	.1	115.53	.0	313.11	.1
Licenses & Fees					15.00	.0	65.00	.0
Maintenance Agreements	534.00	.4	252.00	.2	1,178.55	.4	252.00	.1
Medical—Dues					175.00	.1		
Medical—Pubs	411.02	.3			470.97	.2		
Medical—Supplies	530.76	.4	669.25	.5	550.30	.2	1,938.49	.7
Miscellaneous			8.03	.0			8.03	.0
Office Expenses	1,239.94	.9	1,166.89	1.0	3,862.37	1.3	2,882.33	1.0
Mobile System	429.77	.3	493.28	.4	912.44	.3	1,003.46	.4
Pension Plan Contributions	295.25	.2	416.48	.3	885.75	.3	851.21	.3
Pension Plan Expenses	1,575.00	1.1	291.39	.2	1,900.00	.6	291.39	.1
Postage	300.00	.2	300.00	.2	629.00	.2	605.80	.2
Patients' Education			327.40	.3			696.78	.3

	Period to Date				Year to Date			
	Actual	%	Prior Year	%	Actual	%	Prior Year	%
Professional Services	1,277.88	.9	3,045.67	2.5	2,490.04	.8	3,045.67	1.1
Rent	6,196.38	4.3	5,258.38	4.3	12,392.76	4.2	10,823.51	3.9
Repairs & Maintenance					152.65	.1		
Salaries—Other	23,195.43	15.9	22,819.81	18.7	45,236.14	15.3	46,860.41	16.9
Security	44.06	.0	44.06	.0	44.06	.0	88.12	.0
Seminars			253.00	.2	210.00	.1	253.00	.1
Stationery & Printing	57.74	.0	81.19	.1	116.91	.0	633.27	.2
Taxes—Other			312.07	.3	5,981.25	2.0	742.39	.3
Taxes—Payroll	2,319.55	1.6	1,996.73	1.6	4,623.46	1.6	4,100.28	1.5
Telephone	2,264.95	1.6	2,283.34	1.9	3,397.91	1.2	4,491.83	1.6
Travel & Lodging	153.27	.1	310.47	.3	429.78	.1	685.10	.2
Total Expenses	70,898.03	48.7	61,010.15	50.1	129,843.81	44.0	124,839.80	44.9
Other Income & Exp.								
Interest Income	(2.18)	.0	(28.62)	.0	(4.42)	.0	(30.51)	.0
Physicians' Comp								
Physician #1	26,000.00	17.9	26,000.00	21.3	56,598.98	19.2	52,000.00	18.7
Physician #2	26,000.00	17.9	26,000.00	21.3	53,839.59	18.3	52,000.00	18.7
Physician #3	25,450.67	17.5	20,000.00	16.4	49,232.05	16.7	40,000.00	14.4
Total Other Income & Exp.	77,448.49	53.2	71,971.38	59.1	159,666.20	54.2	143,969.49	51.8
Total Expenses	148,346.52	102.0	132,981.53	109.1	289,510.01	98.2	268,809.29	96.7
Net Income (Loss)	(2,860.49)	(2.0)	(11,125.31)	(9.1)	5,318.26	1.8	9,100.21	3.3

APPENDIX ITEM 02-04

COMPARATIVE FINANCIAL STATEMENT SHOWING CURRENT RESULTS WITH BUDGET NUMBERS AND RELATED VARIANCE FOR A MEDICAL PRACTICE

STATEMENT OF REVENUE & EXPENSES
INCOME TAX BASIS

	Period to Date				Year to Date			
	Actual	%	Curr. Budget	%	Actual	%	Curr. Budget	%
Revenue								
Fee Income	22,194.19	58.0	33,240.00	100.0	61,507.93	79.7	93,920.00	100.0
Refunds	(300.93)	(.8)			(697.06)	(.9)		
Overhead Income	16,374.85	42.8			16,374.85	21.2		
Total Revenue	38,268.11	100.0	33,240.00	100.0	77,185.72	100.0	93,920.00	100.0
Operating Expenses								
Advertising	100.00	.3	275.00	.8	1,848.21	2.4	825.00	.9
Accounting			330.00	1.0	1,000.00	1.3	990.00	1.1
Amortization	17.69	.0			53.07	.1		
Ans./Paging Svc.	178.61	.5	170.00	.5	466.67	.6	510.00	.5
Bank Charges	10.43	.0	40.00	.1	19.00	.0	120.00	.1
Contract Labor	195.00	.5			641.25	.8		
Credit Care Fees	97.90	.3	100.00	.3	266.95	.3	300.00	.3

	Period to Date				Year to Date			
	Actual	%	Curr. Budget	%	Actual	%	Curr. Budget	%
Delivery Services	32.00	.1			63.00	.1		
Depreciation	500.00	1.3			1,500.00	1.9		
Dues & Subscriptions			170.00	.5			510.00	.5
Equipment Rental	351.69	.9	175.00	.5	675.17	.9	525.00	.6
Entertainment	198.89	.5	220.00	.7	320.30	.4	660.00	.7
Gifts	71.21	.2			71.21	.1		
Ins.—General	199.00	.5	1,868.00	5.6	199.00	.3	5,604.00	6.0
Ins.—Malpractice			841.00	2.5			841.00	.9
Ins.—Officer's Liab.	858.70	2.2			986.70	1.3		
Interest Expense	658.00	1.7			2,098.75	2.7		
Laboratory Expense			2,750.00	8.3	1,177.83	1.5	7700.00	8.2
Laundry	224.26	.6			442.84	.6		
Licenses & Fees	100.00	.3	121.00	.4	405.00	.5	363.00	.4
Medical—Pubs.			100.00	.3	944.55	1.2	300.00	.3
Medical—Supplies	3,015.16	7.9	1,463.00	4.4	6,200.72	8.0	4,133.00	4.4
Miscellaneous			910.00	2.7	110.00	.1	2,730.00	2.9
Office Expense	999.25	2.6	2,200.00	6.6	1,426.11	1.8	6,600.00	7.0
Postage	735.00	1.9			1,175.07	1.5		
Rent	1,026.00	2.7			2052.00	2.7		
Repairs & Maint.			200.00	.6	2.50	.0	2,026.00	2.2
Salaries—Officer	5,000.00	13.1			5,000.00	6.5	600.00	.6
Salaries—Other	7,838.14	20.5	10,190.00	30.7	19,595.35	25.4	30,570.00	32.5

	Period to Date				Year to Date			
	Actual	%	Curr. Budget	%	Actual	%	Curr. Budget	%
Stationery & Print.	146.60	.4	—	—	146.60		—	—
Supplies					235.00	.2		
Taxes—Payroll	1,431.42	3.7	815.00	2.5	3,089.95	4.0	2,445.00	2.6
Telephone	476.53	1.2	390.00	1.2	1,448.82	1.9	1,170.00	1.2
Waste Removal	48.00	.1	85.00	.3	96.00	.1	255.00	.3
X-Ray Expense			250.00	.8			750.00	.8
Total Operating Exp.	24,509.78	64.0	23,663.00	71.2	53,757.62	69.6	70,527.00	75.1
Other Inc. & Exp.								
Other Inc.	.00		.00		60.00	.1	.00	.1
Total Other Inc. & Exp.	.00		.00		60.00			
Total Exp.	24,509.78	64.0	23,663.00	71.2	53,817.62	69.7	70,527.00	75.1
Net Income (Loss)	13,758.33	36.0	9,577.00	28.8	23,368.10	30.3	23,393.00	24.9

APPENDIX ITEM 04-01
MEDICAL PRACTICE INTERNAL CONTROL CHECKLIST

❑ Check that Superbills (patient encounter forms) are prenumbered and accounted for on a daily basis.

❑ Ensure that the person who posts payments to patient accounts does not open the mail or prepare the deposit slip.

❑ Reconcile the patients listed on the sign-in sheet to the appointment book and either the daily report of charges (computerized system) or the daysheet (pegboard system).

❑ Review the daily report of payments (computerized system) or the daysheet (pegboard system) to detect any payments by patients that may not have been posted.

❑ Review the practice's contractual adjustments for the period and year-to-date. Does the amount appear to be reasonable after taking into account the practice's payor mix?

❑ Take a sample of patient charges and trace the information on the related explanation of benefits (EOB) to each individual ledger sheet. Trace payment per EOB to the deposit slip. Investigate any discrepancies.

❑ Review all patients' ledger cards to detect if any balances were written off in their entirety.

❑ Make sure that the practice has a policy in place so that an account cannot be written off as a bad debt without the authorization of a physician.

❑ Implement a password into the computer system. Supply the password only to authorized practice personnel.

❑ For a pegboard system, reconcile the accounts receivable balance per the daysheet to the individual ledger cards.

❑ Are all practice employees bonded?

❑ Is a physician the only one who is authorized to sign checks?

❑ Does a physician review and approve vendor invoices before signing checks?

❑ Review endorsements of canceled checks and investigate any irregularities.

APPENDIX ITEM 05-01

CASHFLOW FORECAST FOR A MEDICAL PRACTICE

New General Surgery Practice—Initial Cash Flow Forecast

Cash Flow Projection Year 1	Start-Up	Month 1	Month 2	Month 3	Month 4	Month 5	Month 6	Month 7	Month 8	Month 9	Month 10	Month 11	Month 12	Total
Total Charges		18,525	39,580	39,225	39,225	39,525	39,525	39,975	39,975	41,080	40,425	40,875	40,875	458,810
Total Cash Receipts per Mo.		584	10,173	21,893	24,372	26,028	27,161	27,504	27,937	28,227	28,871	28,681	28,899	280,330
Cash Requirements														
Salaries		5,190	5,190	5,190	5,190	5,190	5,190	5,190	5,190	5,190	5,190	5,190	5,190	62,285
Employee Benefits		598	598	598	598	598	598	598	598	598	598	598	598	7,179
Employer Tax (8.00%)		415	415	415	415	415	415	415	415	415	415	415	415	4,983
Supplies	3,000	556	1,187	1,177	1,177	1,186	1,186	1,199	1,199	1,232	1,213	1,226	1,226	16,764
Rent	1,500	1,500	1,500	1,500	1,500	1,500	1,500	1,500	1,500	1,500	1,500	1,500	1,500	19,500
Tele./Communic.		390	390	390	390	390	390	390	390	390	390	390	390	4,680
Acct./Legal	3,000	500	500	500	500	500	500	500	500	500	500	500	500	9,000
Pro. Fees/Dues		121	121	121	121	121	121	121	121	121	121	121	121	1,452
Ins.—Malpractice		841	0	0	841	0	0	841	0	0	841	0	0	3,364
Ins.—Business		770	770	770	770	770	770	770	770	770	770	770	770	9,240
Mrktng./Ads.	5,000	275	275	275	275	275	275	275	275	275	275	275	275	8,300
Travel/Promotion		0	0	0	0	0	2,200	0	0	0	0	0	0	2,200
Pro. Entertainment		220	220	220	220	220	220	220	220	220	220	220	220	2,640
Utilities		0	0	0	0	0	0	0	0	0	0	0	0	0
Other	2,200	2,200	2,200	2,200	2,200	2,200	2,200	2,200	2,200	2,200	2,200	2,200	2,200	26,400
Cash Req. from Operations	12,500	13,577	13,367	13,357	14,198	13,366	15,566	14,220	13,379	13,412	14,234	13,406	13,406	177,987
Cash Position from Operations	(12,500)	(12,993)	(3,194)	8,537	10,174	12,662	11,595	13,284	14,558	14,815	14,637	15,275	15,493	102,343
Computer	20,000	0	0	0	0	0	0	0	0	0	0	0	0	20,000
Furnishings & Equipment	40,000	0	0	0	0	0	0	0	0	0	0	0	0	40,000
Phone System	5,000	0	0	0	0	0	0	0	0	0	0	0	0	5,000
Leasehold Improvements	0	0	0	0	0	0	0	0	0	0	0	0	0	0
Physician Compensation		10,000	10,000	10,000	10,000	10,000	10,000	10,000	10,000	10,000	10,000	10,000	10,000	120,000
Hospital Subsidy	(12,500)	(23,342)	(14,543)	(2,812)	(1,175)	0	0	0	0	0	0	0	0	(55,372)

Financing & Debt Service

Financing & Debt Service	Month 1	Month 2	Month 3	Month 4	Month 5	Month 6	Month 7	Month 8	Month 9	Month 10	Month 11	Month 12	Total
Loan Requested	65,000												65,000
Debt Service	1,349	1,349	1,349	1,349	1,349	1,349	1,349	1,349	1,349	1,349	1,349	1,349	16,191
Cash Position for Period	0	(0)	(0)	(0)	1,313	246	1,934	3,209	3,466	3,288	3,926	4,143	21,523
Beg. Cash Position for Per.	0	(0)	(0)	(1)	(1)	1,311	1,557	3,492	6,701	10,166	13,454	17,380	0
End. Cash Position for Per.	(0)	(0)	(1)	(1)	1,311	1,557	3,492	6,701	10,166	13,454	17,380	21,523	21,523

Volume & Revenue Projection Year 1

Volume

	Month 1	Month 2	Month 3	Month 4	Month 5	Month 6	Month 7	Month 8	Month 9	Month 10	Month 11	Month 12	Total
1 Office Visit—NP	5	5	5	5	5	5	5	5	5	5	5	5	60
2 Office Visit—NP	5	5	5	5	5	5	5	5	5	5	5	5	60
3 Consultations	15	17	19	19	21	21	24	24	27	27	30	30	274
4 Consultation—IP	3	3	3	3	3	3	3	3	3	3	3	3	36
5 Hosp. Admit.	0	2	0	0	0	0	0	0	2	0	0	0	4
6 Hosp. Visit	0	3	0	0	0	0	0	0	3	0	0	0	6
7 Hosp. Discharge	0	2	1	1	1	1	1	1	1	1	1	1	12
8 Procedure	1	1	1	1	1	1	1	1	1	1	1	1	12
9 Procedure	1	1	1	1	1	1	1	1	1	1	1	1	12
10 Procedure	1	1	1	1	1	1	1	1	1	1	1	1	12
11 Procedure	1	1	1	1	1	1	1	1	1	1	1	1	12
12 Procedure	1	1	1	1	1	1	1	1	1	1	1	1	12
13 Procedure	1	1	1	1	1	1	1	1	1	1	1	1	12
14 Procedure	1	1	1	1	1	1	1	1	1	1	1	1	12
15 Procedure	1	1	1	1	1	1	1	1	1	1	1	1	12
16 Procedure	1	1	1	1	1	1	1	1	1	1	1	1	12
17 Procedure	1	1	1	1	1	1	1	1	1	1	1	1	12
18 Procedure	0	1	1	1	1	1	1	1	1	1	1	1	11
19 Procedure	0	1	1	1	1	1	1	1	1	1	1	1	11
20 Procedure	0	1	1	1	1	1	1	1	1	1	1	1	11
21 Procedure	0	1	1	1	1	1	1	1	1	1	1	1	11
22 Procedure	0	1	1	1	1	1	1	1	1	1	1	1	11
23 Procedure	0	1	1	1	1	1	1	1	1	1	1	1	11
24 Other	20	45	45	45	45	45	45	45	45	45	45	45	515

Gross Revenue	Charge	Month 1	Month 2	Month 3	Month 4	Month 5	Month 6	Month 7	Month 8	Month 9	Month 10	Month 11	Month 12	Total
1 Office Visit—NP	75	375	375	375	375	375	375	375	375	375	375	375	375	4,500
2 Office Visit—NP	125	625	625	625	625	625	625	625	625	625	625	625	625	7,500
3 Consultations	150	2,250	2,550	2,850	2,850	3,150	3,150	3,600	3,600	4,050	4,050	4,500	4,500	41,100
4 Consultation—IP	150	450	450	450	450	450	450	450	450	450	450	450	450	5,400
5 Hosp. Admit.	125	0	250	0	0	0	0	0	0	250	0	0	0	500
6 Hosp. Visit	75	0	225	0	0	0	0	0	0	225	0	0	0	450
7 Hosp. Discharge	90	0	180	0	0	0	0	0	0	180	0	0	0	360
8 Procedure	2,500	2,500	2,500	2,500	2,500	2,500	2,500	2,500	2,500	2,500	2,500	2,500	2,500	30,000
9 Procedure	2,250	2,250	2,250	2,250	2,250	2,250	2,250	2,250	2,250	2,250	2,250	2,250	2,250	27,000
10 Procedure	2,000	2,000	2,000	2,000	2,000	2,000	2,000	2,000	2,000	2,000	2,000	2,000	2,000	24,000
11 Procedure	1,800	1,800	1,800	1,800	1,800	1,800	1,800	1,800	1,800	1,800	1,800	1,800	1,800	21,600
12 Procedure	1,500	1,500	1,500	1,500	1,500	1,500	1,500	1,500	1,500	1,500	1,500	1,500	1,500	18,000
13 Procedure	1,200	1,200	1,200	1,200	1,200	1,200	1,200	1,200	1,200	1,200	1,200	1,200	1,200	14,400
14 Procedure	1,000	1,000	1,000	1,000	1,000	1,000	1,000	1,000	1,000	1,000	1,000	1,000	1,000	12,000
15 Procedure	800	800	800	800	800	800	800	800	800	800	800	800	800	9,600
16 Procedure	500	500	500	500	500	500	500	500	500	500	500	500	500	6,000
17 Procedure	275	275	275	275	275	275	275	275	275	275	275	275	275	3,300
18 Procedure	100	0	100	100	100	100	100	100	100	100	100	100	100	1,100
19 Procedure	3,000	0	3,000	3,000	3,000	3,000	3,000	3,000	3,000	3,000	3,000	3,000	3,000	33,000
20 Procedure	3,500	0	3,500	3,500	3,500	3,500	3,500	3,500	3,500	3,500	3,500	3,500	3,500	38,500
21 Procedure	3,750	0	3,750	3,750	3,750	3,750	3,750	3,750	3,750	3,750	3,750	3,750	3,750	41,250
22 Procedure	4,000	0	4,000	4,000	4,000	4,000	4,000	4,000	4,000	4,000	4,000	4,000	4,000	44,000
23 Procedure	4,500	0	4,500	4,500	4,500	4,500	4,500	4,500	4,500	4,500	4,500	4,500	4,500	49,500
24 Other	50	1,000	2,250	2,250	2,250	2,250	2,250	2,250	2,250	2,250	2,250	2,250	2,250	25,750
Total Charges (Maps to Cash Flow)		18,525	39,580	39,225	39,225	39,525	39,525	39,975	39,975	41,080	40,425	40,875	40,875	458,810

Cash Receipts Year 1 Payer Mix		Month 1	Month 2	Month 3	Month 4	Month 5	Month 6	Month 7	Month 8	Month 9	Month 10	Month 11	Month 12	Total
Self-pay	11.0%	2,038	4,354	4,315	4,315	4,348	4,348	4,397	4,397	4,519	4,447	4,496	4,496	50,469
Blue Shield	9.0%	1,667	3,562	3,530	3,530	3,557	3,557	3,598	3,598	3,697	3,638	3,679	3,679	41,293
Medicare	35.0%	6,484	13,853	13,729	13,729	13,834	13,834	13,991	13,991	14,378	14,149	14,306	14,306	160,584
Medicaid	18.0%	3,335	7,124	7,061	7,061	7,115	7,115	7,196	7,196	7,394	7,277	7,358	7,358	82,586
Commercial	26.0%	4,817	10,291	10,199	10,199	10,277	10,277	10,394	10,394	10,681	10,511	10,628	10,628	119,291
Workers' Comp	1.0%	185	396	392	392	395	395	400	400	411	404	409	409	4,588

Item	%													
HMO	0.0%	0	0	0	0	0	0	0	0	0	0	0	0	0
0	0.0%	0	0	0	0	0	0	0	0	0	0	0	0	0
0	0.0%	0	0	0	0	0	0	0	0	0	0	0	0	0
Total Charges	100.0%	18,525	39,580	39,225	39,225	39,525	39,525	39,975	39,975	41,080	40,425	40,875	40,875	458,810
(Maps to Cash Flow)														
Timing of Cash Receipts														
% of Paying at Time of Visit:														
Self-pay	5.0%	102	218	216	216	217	217	220	220	226	222	225	225	2,523
Blue Shield	0.0%	0	0	0	0	0	0	0	0	0	0	0	0	0
Medicare	0.0%	0	0	0	0	0	0	0	0	0	0	0	0	0
Commercial	10.0%	482	1,029	1,020	1,020	1,028	1,028	1,039	1,039	1,068	1,051	1,063	1,063	11,929
Workers' Comp	0.0%	0	0	0	0	0	0	0	0	0	0	0	0	0
HMO	2.0%	0	0	0	0	0	0	0	0	0	0	0	0	0
0	0.0%	0	0	0	0	0	0	0	0	0	0	0	0	0
0	0.0%	0	0	0	0	0	0	0	0	0	0	0	0	0
Total at Time of Visit		584	1,247	1,236	1,236	1,245	1,245	1,259	1,259	1,294	1,273	1,288	1,288	14,453
Insurance Proceeds														
Assumes Bad Debt Allowance of:														
Medicaid	50.0%	0	1,334	3,183	3,537	3,530	3,552	3,557	3,590	3,598	3,677	3,650	3,671	36,878
Blue Shield	20.0%	0	934	2,262	2,680	2,827	2,839	2,844	2,868	2,875	2,934	2,917	2,938	28,917
Medicare	30.0%	0	3,631	8,212	8,885	9,361	9,673	9,676	9,768	9,783	10,005	9,909	9,995	98,898
Commercial	10.0%	0	2,731	6,225	7,006	7,832	8,312	8,311	8,384	8,400	8,572	8,508	8,584	82,867
Workers' Comp	20.0%	0	104	266	315	314	315	316	319	320	326	325	326	3,245
HMO	25.0%	0	0	0	0	0	0	0	0	0	0	0	0	0
0	100.0%	0	0	0	0	0	0	0	0	0	0	0	0	0
0	0.0%	0	0	0	0	0	0	0	0	0	0	0	0	0
Total Insurance		0	8,733	20,147	22,423	23,864	24,692	24,705	24,929	24,975	25,514	25,309	25,514	250,805
Self-pay (Billed)	50.0%	0	194	510	713	918	1,223	1,540	1,749	1,958	2,083	2,084	2,098	15,072
Total Cash Receipts per Month		584	10,173	21,893	24,372	26,028	27,161	27,504	27,937	28,227	28,871	28,681	28,899	280,330
(Maps to Cash Flow)														

APPENDIX ITEM 05-02
COLLECTION RECONCILIATION LETTER

[Date]

[Name]
[Address]
[City, State, Zip]

Dear [Name]:

In preparing your balance sheet and income statement for the period ended [Date], we noticed the following discrepancy:

Total patient receipts per your internal records	$_____
Total miscellaneous or other income	$_____
Total	$_____

The total deposits recorded on your cash basis income statement were $[dollar value], resulting in a difference of $[dollar value]. Your practice's records must always agree with what was actually deposited into the bank account.

Please review your records and report to us why the difference occurred. You may complete the lines below to reconcile.

Explanation	*Amount*
_____	$_____
_____	$_____
_____	$_____
_____	$_____
Total difference	$_____

Please do not hesitate to contact me if you have any questions or comments.

Sincerely,
[Signature block]

APPENDIX ITEM 05-03
ACCOUNTS RECEIVABLE
RECONCILIATION LETTER

[Date]

[Name]
[Address]
[City, State, ZIP]

Dear [Name]:

While preparing your practice's balance sheet and income statement, we noticed the following discrepancy related to the practice's accounts receivable.

Beginning accounts receivable as of [Date] was $[dollar value]. During the period, the practice had charges of $[dollar value], debit adjustments of $[dollar value], received total payments of $[dollar value], and credit adjustments of $[dollar value].

Based on this information from your internal records, the ending accounts receivable balance should be $[dollar value]. The total accounts receivable balance, however, per [report name] was $[dollar value].

The difference in these accounts receivable balances is $[dollar value].

Please investigate this discrepancy immediately and report back to us your findings.

Do not hesitate to call if you have any comments or questions.

Sincerely,
[Signature block]

APPENDIX ITEM 05-04
ACTUAL-TO-BUDGET COMPARISON

[Name of medical practice]

Current month: [Month, Year]

	Actual	*Budget*	*Variance*
Collections			
Overhead			
Net			

Year-to-date: [Month, Year] through [Month, Year]

	Actual	*Budget*	*Variance*
Collections			
Overhead			
Net			

APPENDIX ITEM 07-01
CHECKLIST FOR A NEW MEDICAL PRACTICE

[Name of medical practice]

To Do Item	Person Responsible	Date Started	Date Completed	Comments
Practice location				
Hospital privileges				
Recruitment				
Incentives				
Arrange for coverage				
Sign up with managed-care programs				
Sign office lease				
Design office layout				
Incorporate practice?				
Cash flow projection				
Arrange for working capital loan				
Open business checking account				
State medical license				
Federal narcotic license				
State narcotic license				
State unemployment #				
Federal I.D. #				
Medicaid #				
Medicare #				
Medical equipment				
Office equipment				
Medical supplies				
Office supplies				
Office furnishings				
Business cards				
Business stationery				
Medical record filing system				
Medical software				

To Do Item	Person Responsible	Date Started	Date Completed	Comments
Computer hardware				
Pegboard system?				
Office telephone #				
Answering/paging service				
Office policy and procedures manual				
Group health insurance				
Liability insurance				
Workers' comp. ins.				
Life insurance				
Disability insurance				
Overhead disability ins.				
Fidelity bond insurance				
Malpractice insurance				
Select lab				
OSHA compliance				
CLIA compliance				
Practice fee schedule				
Practice Superbill				
Personnel policies				
Employee job descriptions				
Seek job candidates				
Interview job candidates				
Make job offers				
Select collection agency				
Select method of appointment schedule announcement cards				
Announcement in newspaper				
Announcement mailing				
Other direct mail?				
Practice marketing plan				
Medicare participation?				
Prepare participation agreement				

To Do Item	Person Responsible	Date Started	Date Completed	Comments
Employee computer training				
Patient info. booklet				
Reception room periodicals				
Physician dues				
Employee CPT training				
Physician CPT training				
Develop accounts payable system				
Prepare employee personnel files				
Payroll tax deposit training				
Petty cash policy				
Bank reconciliation training				
Front-desk collection training				
Physician/billing staff communication of hospital charges				
Insurance verification training				
Insurance follow-up training				
Patient A/R collection training				
Select list of referring physicians				
Select open house date				
Open house planning				
Who will prepare practice financial statements and when?				
Who will prepare payroll tax reports?				

To Do Item	Person Responsible	Date Started	Date Completed	Comments
Cellular telephone				
Pager				
Other:				

APPENDIX ITEM 07-02

MEDICAL PRACTICE MANAGEMENT SOFTWARE FEATURES CHECKLIST

ACCOUNT/PATIENT RECORD STRUCTURE

1. Describe how the system allows the practice to number its patient accounts:

   _____

   _____

   _____

2. Is it acceptable?   ❑ Yes   ❑ No

3. A patient's account can be accessed by: ❑ Chart number
   ❑ X-ray number   ❑ Name search

   ❑ Other: _____

4. The system can accept the following patient account information:
   ❑ Name   ❑ Address   ❑ Home phone   ❑ Office phone
   ❑ Pharmacy phone   ❑ Accept assignment   ❑ Referral
   source   ❑ User definable fields

5. The system can accept the following patient information:
   ❑ Name   ❑ Address   ❑ Home phone   ❑ Sex   ❑ Relation to
   account holder   ❑ Date of birth   ❑ Provider   ❑ Signature on
   file   ❑ Comment   ❑ Continuing diagnosis   ❑ Referral to
   ❑ Referral from   ❑ Guarantor   ❑ Medical profile   ❑ User
   definable fields

6. What is the maximum number of patients that can be set up per
   account?   ❑ 1 to 5   ❑ 6 to 10   ❑ More than 10   ❑ Unlimited

7. What employment information can be entered into the system?   ❑ Guarantor employer name   ❑ Guarantor employer
   address   ❑ Spouse employer name   ❑ Spouse employer address

8. The system accepts the following primary insurance company
   information: ❑ The insured (self, spouse, or guarantor)
   ❑ Insured's ID   ❑ Insured's birthdate   ❑ Name of insurance
   company   ❑ Group health insurance ID number   ❑ Participant
   ID number   ❑ Group name

9. Can the system accept a secondary insurance carrier?   ❑ Yes
   ❑ No

10. Can the system accept more than three insurers?   ❑ Yes   ❑ No

11. The system has the capability of issuing delinquency notices to the patient by: ❏ Allowing messages on patient account statement ❏ Messages on fee slips ❏ Issuance of separate collection letters

12. The system can display a current account aging by: ❏ Current 30/60/90 ❏ User defined aging categories

13. Account aging can be based on: ❏ Date of posting ❏ Date of service

14. A report listing of patient information can be sorted by: ❏ Account number ❏ Name ❏ Account type ❏ Employer ❏ Insurance company ❏ Range of accounts ❏ Range of names ❏ New accounts ❏ Delinquent accounts ❏ Provider name ❏ User defined fields

GENERAL SYSTEM REQUIREMENTS

15. System is: ❏ Patient/account oriented—uses hot keys to switch tasks for a single patient ❏ Task/function oriented— all functions must be accessed off a menu; may have to return to menus to access tasks

16. Reports can be printed to: ❏ Multiple printers ❏ Screen ❏ File

17. The system provides the user with online help: ❏ Yes ❏ No
Is it useful: ❏ Yes ❏ No
Comment:_____

18. The system allows direct access to the following information through pop-up windows: ❏ Accounts ❏ Patients ❏ Procedure codes ❏ Diagnosis codes ❏ Patient types ❏ Employer listing ❏ Insurance companies ❏ User defined fields ❏

19. Does the system integrate with an accounting software package? ❏ Yes ❏ No
If yes, which one?: _____

20. Does the system offer an online tutorial? ❏ Yes ❏ No

21. Does the system provide for password protection? ❏ Yes ❏ No
If yes, the system allows passwords to limit access to:
❏ Practice site ❏ Specific physician ❏ Subsystem (e.g., scheduling or billing) ❏ Functions (e.g., ability to enter cash receipts) ❏ Other:
(List)_____

22. The system is capable of backing up and restoring data files:
    ❏ Yes ❏ No

    To back up data files, the system uses: ❏ Tape backup system ❏ Only floppy disks

    To recover data, you must: ❏ Restore last backup ❏ Run a recovery routine ❏ No special requirements ❏ Other:

    (List)_____

OTHER FEATURES

23. Can the system print customized forms? ❏ Yes ❏ No

24. Does the software include a letter writer? ❏ Yes ❏ No
    ❏ If yes, is it capable of using patient information to print the following?: ❏ Labels ❏ Envelopes ❏ Recall letters
    ❏ Any other type of letter designed by the practice to send to patients

25. Can the system export its data? ❏ Yes ❏ No ❏ If yes, in what formats?_____

26. Does the system purge patient and account history by
    ❏ Cut off date ❏ All paid transactions ❏ Other method

27. Are purged histories archived within the system? ❏ Yes ❏ No

MANAGEMENT REPORTS

28. The system is capable of automatically raising its fee schedule by asking it to: ❏ Increase all fees by a certain dollar amount
    ❏ Increase all fees by a given percentage

29. The system is able to produce the following management reports:

    CPT code frequency report

    Summary of charges, payments, and adjustments—total for practice

    Summary of charges, payments, and adjustments by provider

    Summary of charges, payments, and adjustments by individual payor

    Summary of charges, payments, and adjustments by designated account type

    Accounts receivable aging by patient

    Accounts receivable aging by payor

Accounts receivable aging by designated account type

CPT realization by payor

CPT realization by referral source

CPT realization by provider

Referring doctor report

General referral report by activity

Any report by zip code

Any report by employer name

Capitation analysis

Comparative reports

MASTER FILES

30. Is the software capable of identifying separate practice sites for reports?: ❏ Yes ❏ No

31. Is the software capable of identifying each separate service site, such as hospitals, clinics, outpatient surgery, etc.?: ❏ Yes ❏ No

32. Is the software capable of setting up multiple providers?: ❏ Yes ❏ No

33. Can referral sources be set up in the system, including related identification and UPIN numbers, if applicable?: ❏ Yes ❏ No

34. Is the system capable of setting up the following information for individual insurance companies?: ❏ Name ❏ Identification Number ❏ Insurer Type ❏ Electronic Claims Submission ID Number ❏ Fee Schedule ❏ Benefit Structure, such as deductibles and co-payments

35. Is the system capable of establishing receipt codes by the following?: ❏ Description ❏ Code ❏ Type ❏ Service Sites ❏ CPT Code ❏ Patient Type ❏ Employer

BILLING

36. Is the system capable of printing an insurance claim form?: ❏ Yes ❏ No

37. Is the system capable of printing a statement for a patient when he or she leaves the office?:

❏ Yes ❏ No

38. Is the system capable of printing monthly patient statements?:
    ❑ Yes   ❑ No

39. Is the system capable of performing "cycle account billing"?:
    ❑ Yes   ❑ No

40. Is the system capable of placing dunning messages on each statement?:   ❑ Yes   ❑ No

41. Is the system capable of dunning messages according to age of the account?:   ❑ Yes   ❑ No

42. Can the system track patient installment agreements to pay?:
    ❑ Yes   ❑ No

43. Does the system have electronic billing capabilities?:
    ❑ Yes   ❑ No

44. Can the system print audit and/or submission verification reports?:   ❑ Yes   ❑ No

45. Is the system capable of handling secondary insurance claim filing?:   ❑ Yes   ❑ No

46. Can the system print a report listing all unpaid insurance as of the current date?:   ❑ Yes   ❑ No
    If yes, can this report be printed by individual insurance companies?:   ❑ Yes   ❑ No

RECEIPTS AND CREDITS

47. Can the system handle capitation payments?:   ❑ Yes   ❑ No
    If yes, explain how:

    _____

48. Is the system capable of batch posting?:   ❑ Yes   ❑ No
    If yes, does the system display the following?:
    ❑ Batch numbers   ❑ Batch totals   ❑ Number of items

49. Is the system capable of line item posting?:   ❑ Yes   ❑ No

50. Can the system post receipts by the following?:   ❑ Individual charges   ❑ To all charges in a day   ❑ In proportion to charges   ❑ To oldest charges first

51. If there are multiple providers, does it appear easy to post payments to each individual provider?:   ❑ Yes   ❑ No
    Assess how easy it is to reconcile the day's posting to the actual deposit to the bank:

    _____

52. Can the system print a deposit slip?: ❑ Yes ❑ No
53. Can the system print a credit balance report?: ❑ Yes ❑ No
54. How are refund checks to patients posted in the system?:

_____

_____

PATIENT-RELATED ISSUES

55. Does the system have a patient scheduling feature?:
    ❑ Yes ❑ No
    If yes, can the system schedule a patient with minimal information, such as name only?
    Must the system first have an account for the patient?
56. Patient scheduling can locate an available slot for a patient:
    ❑ By day of week ❑ By time of day
    ❑ By length of appointment ❑ Within a date range
57. The system has a patient recall system: ❑ Yes ❑ No
    If yes, the system is capable of tracking recalls by:
    ❑ Weeks ❑ Months within a year ❑ Reason or instruction
    ❑ Procedures to be performed
58. Is the system capable of automatically determining the next recall?: ❑ Yes ❑ No
59. The following recall notices can be printed: ❑ By letter ❑ By card ❑ Labels ❑ Other _____
60. Can the system track patient hospitalization?: ❑ Yes ❑ No
    If yes, hospitalization can be tracked by:
    ❑ Date of admission ❑ Hospital ❑ Room number ❑ Reason patient was hospitalized ❑ Provider ❑ Discharge date
61. Can the system print a hospital rounds list for a provider?:
    ❑ Yes ❑ No

OTHER ISSUES:

APPENDIX ITEM 08-01
FREQUENCY REPORT REVIEW

Statistics for [number of months], from [month, year] to [month, year].

Office Visits: Fill in the total number of times performed.

CPT Code	Times Performed	Percentage
99201		
99202		
99203		
99204		
99205		
Total		100%
99211		
99212		
99213		
99214		
99215		
Total		100%
99221		
99222		
99223		
Total		100%
99231		
99232		
99233		
Total		100%
99241		
99242		
99243		
99244		
99245		
Total		100%

APPENDIX ITEM 08-02

MEDICINE AND LAB FEE WORKSHEET

CPT	Service Description	Practice Fee	Medicare Par Fee	Workers' Comp	Managed Care	Managed Care	Survey Fee

APPENDIX ITEM 08-03
REVENUE ANALYSIS WORKSHEET
[Use this worksheet to quantify revenue gains from fee schedule revision.]

CPT	New Fee	Old Fee	Difference	Frequency	$ Impact

Total Impact

% of Practice
Affected by
Change

Total Est.
Increase in
Cash Flow

[**Note:** Percentage of practice affected by change in fee schedule is the estimated percentage of the practice's revenue that can be expected to result in an increase in related cash flow. Generally, this is the percentage of the practice's revenue from commercial or indemnity-type insurance. For example, a change in fees will not affect Medicare reimbursement, because the Medicare fee schedule is fixed. The same can be said for managed-care plans, unless the current fees are below what the managed-care plan or plans are reimbursing.]

▼ APPENDIX B

Part II: Medical Office Operations, Policies, and Procedures

Chapter 9

Chapter 12

APPENDIX ITEM 09-01
NEW PATIENTS' INFORMATION SHEET

For Office Use Only: ☐ Std ☐ Med ☐ Mcd ☐ HMO/PPO ☐ Thn ☐ Cash	
X-Ray:	Diagnosis:
Test:	Referring Physician:

Please print clearly. Please complete all information so that your claim can be processed quickly and efficiently. Thank you!

PATIENT INFORMATION

Name: (First) _____ (MI) ____ (Last) _____

Date of Birth: _____ Age: _____ Sex: ☐ M ☐ F Marital Status: ☐ S ☐ M ☐ W ☐ D

Address: (Street) _____

(City, State, ZIP) _____

Phone #: _____ Social Security #: _____ Driver License #: _____

Work #: _____ Employer: _____

Employer's Address: _____

Referring Physician: _____ If Student, School Name: _____ Full/Part Time _____

RESPONSIBLE PARTY OR SPOUSE INFORMATION

Name: _____ Relationship to Patient: _____

Address: (Street) _____

(City, State, ZIP) _____

Phone #: _____ Social Security #: _____ Driver License #: _____

Work #: _____ Employer: _____

Employer's Address: _____

Friend or Relative Not Living with You: _____ Phone #: _____

INSURANCE INFORMATION

Medicare #: _____ Medicaid #: _____

Insurance Co: _____ Phone #: _____

Insurance Address: _____

Group #: _____ Certificate or I.D. #: _____

Insured's Name: _____ Relationship to Patient: ☐ Self ☐ Spouse ☐ Dependent

Insured's Employer: _____ Phone #: _____

Employer's Address: _____

Insured's Social Security #: _____ Date of Birth: _____ Sex: ☐ M ☐ F

If the patient is covered by another insurance policy, please complete the following information for coordination of benefits. This information will enable your insurance company to process you claim more quickly. Thank you!

INSURANCE INFORMATION

Insurance Co: _____ Phone #: _____

Insurance Address: _____

Group #: _____ Certificate or I.D. #: _____

Insured's Name: _____ Relationship to Patient: ❑ Self ❑ Spouse ❑ Dependent

Insured's Employer: _____ Phone #: _____

Employer's Address: _____

Insured's Social Security #: _____ Date of Birth: _____ Sex: ❑ M ❑ F

I hereby assign, transfer, and set over to [Name of Practice] all of my rights, title, and interest to my medical reimbursement benefits under my insurance policy. I authorize the release of any medical information needed to determine these benefits. This authorization shall remain valid until written notice is given by me revoking said authorization. I understand that I am financially responsible for all charges whether or not they are covered by insurance.

Patient's Signature _____ Date _____

APPENDIX ITEM 09-02

DAILY CONTROL SHEET

Number of insurance claim forms prepared: _____
Superbills used (list numbers): [beginning #] to [ending #]

Charges:
    Per claim forms: _____ Office visits: _____ Total: _____

Payments:
    By mail: _____ By patients in office _____ Total _____
    Total deposit:_____

Petty cash reconciliation:
    Beginning petty cash balance   _____
    Additions   _____
    Disbursements   _____
    Ending balance   _____

Comments: _____
_____
_____
_____
_____

APPENDIX ITEM 09-03
DAILY STATUS REPORT

Day of week: _____ Date: _____ Prepared by: _____

Total number of patients seen in the office: _____
     Number of new patients: _____
     Number of established patients: _____

Breakdown of specific patient activity:
     Number of walk-ins seen: _____
     Number of Medicare seen: _____
     Number of Medicaid seen: _____
     Number of managed-care seen: _____
     Number of workers' comp seen: _____
     Number of private pays seen: _____
     Number of personal injury accidents seen: _____
     Number of cancellations: _____
     Number of rescheduled: _____
     Number of no-shows: _____

Total charges: _____

Total collected: _____
     Cash pay total: _____ Check total: _____ Credit card total: _____

Numerical sequence of superbills used on this date:
     From: _____ To: _____

List voided superbill numbers: _____

Cash on hand at end of day: _____

Counted by: _____

A copy of this report is to be given at the end of each business day to:
     1. Billing department
     2. Physician
     3. Other: _____

APPENDIX ITEM 09-04
PATIENTS' SIGN-IN SHEET

Practice Name: _____

Date: _____

Patient's Name	Address Changed?	Appointment Time	Arrival Tme	Doctor today?	New Insurance?
	Yes or No				Yes or No
	Yes or No				Yes or No
	Yes or No				Yes or No
	Yes or No				Yes or No
	Yes or No				Yes or No
	Yes or No				Yes or No
	Yes or No				Yes or No
	Yes or No				Yes or No
	Yes or No				Yes or No
	Yes or No				Yes or No
	Yes or No				Yes or No
	Yes or No				Yes or No
	Yes or No				Yes or No
	Yes or No				Yes or No
	Yes or No				Yes or No
	Yes or No				Yes or No
	Yes or No				Yes or No
	Yes or No				Yes or No
	Yes or No				Yes or No
	Yes or No				Yes or No
	Yes or No				Yes or No
	Yes or No				Yes or No
	Yes or No				Yes or No
	Yes or No				Yes or No
	Yes or No				Yes or No

APPENDIX ITEM 09-05
VERIFICATION OF INSURANCE COVERAGE

Insurance Company: _____

Address: _____

Contact: _____ Telephone: _____

1. Name of the insured: _____

2. Name of the patient: _____
   Relationship: _____

3. Diagnosis: _____
   Est. in-patient days: _____

4. Member I.D.: _____
   a. Effective date: _____ (of Patient)
   b. Paid to date: _____

5. Subject to pre-existing? ❑ YES ❑ NO

6. Waiver on policy? ❑ YES ❑ NO
   Waiver reads: _____

7. Pre-certification required? ❑ YES ❑ NO
   If required—Phone: _____
   (If precertification is required but not done, benefits may be reduced.)

8. Benefits:
   Deductible: $ _____ per _____ Out of pocket: $ _____
   Co-payment: $ _____
   Percentage: _____ of $ _____ for diagnosis above.
   Lifetime maximum: $ _____

9. Comments: _____
   _____
   _____
   _____
   _____
   _____

Signed: _____ Date: _____

APPENDIX ITEM 09-06
WORKSHEET FOR ANALYSIS OF PATIENTS' WAITING TIME IN RECEPTION AREA

Date: _____

Patient's Name	Time Arrived	Time Escorted to Exam Room	Number of Minutes Elapsed

Total number of elapsed minutes: _____

÷ Total number of patients: _____

= Average waiting room time
   calculated per patient: _____

APPENDIX ITEM 09-07
PHYSICIAN REFERRAL TRACKING FORM

Physician's Name	Referrals This Month	Referrals Year-to-Date	Total Referrals Year-to-Date Last Year

APPENDIX ITEM 09-08
NEW PATIENT TRACKING FORM

Activity	New Patients This Month	New Patients Year-to-Date	New Patients Year-to-Date Last Year
From Physicians			
From Patients			
Yellow Pages			
Direct Mail			
Physician Referral Service			
Newspaper Ad.			
Other Advertising			
Speeches			
From Other People			
Emergency Room			
Other:			

APPENDIX ITEM 09-09
HEALTH INSURANCE CLAIM FORM

PICA							
MEDICARE ☐	MEDICAID ☐	CHAMPUS ☐	CHAMPVA ☐	GROUP HEALTH PLAN ☐	FECA BLK LUNG ☐	OTHER ☐	1a. INSURED'S I.D. NUMBER (FOR PROGRAM IN ITEM 1)
(Medicare #)	(Medicaid #)	(Sponsor's SSN)	(VA File #)	(SSN or ID)	(SSN)	(ID)	

PATIENT AND INSURED INFORMATION

2. PATIENT'S NAME (Last Name, First Name, Middle Initial)

3. PATIENT'S BIRTH DATE MM DD YY SEX M ☐ F ☐

4. INSURED'S NAME (Last Name, First Name, Middle Initial)

5. PATIENT'S ADDRESS (No., Street)

6. PATIENT RELATIONSHIP TO INSURED Self ☐ Spouse ☐ Child ☐ Other ☐

7. INSURED'S ADDRESS (No., Street)

CITY | STATE

8. PATIENT STATUS Single ☐ Married ☐ Other ☐

CITY | STATE

ZIP CODE | TELEPHONE (Include Area Code) ( )

Employed ☐ Full-Time Student ☐ Part-Time Student ☐

ZIP CODE | TELEPHONE (INCLUDE AREA CODE) ( )

9. OTHER INSURED'S NAME (Last Name, First Name, Middle Initial)

10. IS PATIENT'S CONDITION RELATED TO:

11. INSURED'S POLICY GROUP OR FECA NUMBER

a. OTHER INSURED'S POLICY OR GROUP NUMBER

a. EMPLOYMENT? (CURRENT OR PREVIOUS) YES ☐ NO ☐

a. INSURED'S DATE OF BIRTH MM DD YY SEX M ☐ F ☐

b. OTHER INSURED'S DATE OF BIRTH MM DD YY SEX M ☐ F ☐

b. AUTO ACCIDENT? YES ☐ NO ☐ PLACE (State)

b. EMPLOYER'S NAME OR SCHOOL NAME

c. EMPLOYER'S NAME OR SCHOOL NAME

c. OTHER ACCIDENT? YES ☐ NO ☐

c. INSURANCE PLAN NAME OR PROGRAM NAME

d. INSURANCE PLAN NAME OR PROGRAM NAME

10d. RESERVED FOR LOCAL USE

d. IS THERE ANOTHER HEALTH BENEFIT PLAN? YES ☐ NO ☐ If yes, return to and complete item 9 a-d.

READ BACK OF FORM BEFORE COMPLETING & SIGNING THIS FORM.
12. PATIENT'S OR AUTHORIZED PERSON'S SIGNATURE I authorize the release of any medical or other information necessary to process this claim. I also request payment of government benefits either to myself or to the party who accepts assignment below.

SIGNED _____ DATE _____

13. INSURED'S OR AUTHORIZED PERSON'S SIGNATURE I authorize payment of medical benefits to the undersigned physician or supplier for services described below.

SIGNED _____

14. DATE OF CURRENT: MM DD YY ILLNESS (First symptom) OR INJURY (Accident) OR PREGNANCY(LMP)

15. IF PATIENT HAS HAD SAME OR SIMILAR ILLNESS GIVE FIRST DATE MM DD YY

16. DATES PATIENT UNABLE TO WORK IN CURRENT OCCUPATION FROM MM DD YY TO MM DD YY

17. NAME OF REFERRING PHYSICIAN OR OTHER SOURCE

17a. I.D. NUMBER OF REFERRING PHYSICIAN

18. HOSPITALIZATION DATES RELATED TO CURRENT SERVICES FROM MM DD YY TO MM DD YY

19. RESERVED FOR LOCAL USE

20. OUTSIDE LAB? YES ☐ NO ☐ $ CHARGES

21. DIAGNOSIS OR NATURE OF ILLNESS OR INJURY. (RELATE ITEMS 1,2,3 OR 4 TO ITEM 24E BY LINE)
1. _____ 3. _____
2. _____ 4. _____

22. MEDICAID RESUBMISSION CODE _____ ORIGINAL REF. NO. _____

23. PRIOR AUTHORIZATION NUMBER

PHYSICIAN OR SUPPLIER INFORMATION

24. A DATE(S) OF SERVICE From MM DD YY To MM DD YY	B Place of Service	C Type of Service	D PROCEDURES, SERVICES, OR SUPPLIES (Explain Unusual Circumstances) CPT/HCPCS MODIFIER	E DIAGNOSIS CODE	F $ CHARGES	G DAYS OR UNITS	H EPSDT Family Plan	I EMG	J COB	K RESERVED FOR LOCAL USE
1										
2										
3										
4										
5										
6										

25. FEDERAL TAX I.D. NUMBER ☐ SSN ☐ EIN

26. PATIENT'S ACCOUNT NO.

27. ACCEPT ASSIGNMENT? (For govt. claims, see back) YES ☐ NO ☐

28. TOTAL CHARGE $

29. AMOUNT PAID $

30. BALANCE DUE $

31. SIGNATURE OF PHYSICIAN OR SUPPLIER INCLUDING DEGREES OR CREDENTIALS (I certify that the statements on the reverse apply to this bill and are made a part thereof.)

SIGNED _____ DATE _____

32. NAME AND ADDRESS OF FACILITY WHERE SERVICES WERE RENDERED (If other than home or office)

33. PHYSICIAN'S, SUPPLIER'S BILLING NAME, ADDRESS, ZIP CODE & PHONE #

PIN# _____ GRP# _____

(APPROVED BY AMA COUNCIL ON MEDICAL SERVICE 8/88)

PLEASE PRINT OR TYPE

FORM HCFA-1500 (12-90)
FORM OWCP-1500 FORM RRB-1500

APPENDIX ITEM 09-10
EXPLANATION OF BENEFITS

Participant Information:
Check #   0123456789
Participant: Last, First
SS #:   987-65-4321
Group #:   00000

To assist us in serving you, please include participant information and patient's name when you direct inquiries to:

Claims Office
P.O. Box 00000
Anywhere, USA 00000
Telephone (999) 888-9999

EXPLANATION OF BENEFITS

FOR SERVICES PROVIDED BY: Iwill Fixit, M.D.

Patient/ Service	Service Date(s)	(A) Total Charge	(B) Excluded Amounts	(C) Not Payable by Plan	(D) Coins. Amount	%	(E) Plan Paid Amount	%
Last, F								
Office Visit	02/17/94	56.00	11.00 EM	10.00 CA	35.00	100%		
X-Ray	02/17/94	268.00		250.00 DD	3.60	20%	14.40	80%
Lab	02/17/94	20.00		15.00 CA			5.00	100%
TOTALS		344.00	11.00	275.00	3.60		54.40	

Payments made to:

03/04/96	Iwill Fixit, M.D.	54.40

Codes and Remarks

EM: This amount represents the discount which resulted from the patient using a preferred provider. The patient is not responsible for this amount.

CA: This is the patient's co-payment amount for this charge. The patient is responsible for this amount.

DD: This amount was applied to the patient's deductible.

APPENDIX ITEM 09-11

MEDICARE DISCLOSURE REPORT

*   Transition amount is below the full fee schedule amount

**   Transition amount is above the full fee schedule amount

	LOC	PROC	MOD	PAR AMOUNT	PAR SOS AMOUNT	NON-PAR AMOUNT	NON-PAR SOS AMOUNT	LIMITING CHARGE	LIMITING CHARGE SOS
*	18	11441		72.38	60.14	68.76	57.13	79.07	65.70
*	18	11442		90.36	73.92	85.84	70.22	98.72	80.75
*	18	11443		106.82	87.76	101.48	83.37	116.70	95.88
*	18	11444		141.33	.00	134.26	.00	154.40	.00
*	18	11446		158.08	.00	150.18	.00	172.71	.00
*	18	11450		185.23	.00	175.97	.00	202.37	.00
*	18	11451		207.52	.00	197.14	.00	226.71	.00
*	18	11462		167.26	.00	158.90	.00	182.74	.00
*	18	11463		179.62	.00	170.64	.00	196.24	.00
*	18	11470		158.19	.00	150.28	.00	172.82	.00
*	18	11471		208.38	.00	197.96	.00	227.65	.00
	18	11600		90.86	71.18	86.32	67.62	99.27	77.76
	18	11601		119.18	94.84	113.22	90.10	130.20	103.62
	18	11602		140.66	108.89	133.63	103.45	153.67	118.97
	18	11603		166.63	127.27	158.30	120.91	182.05	139.05
	18	11604		187.72	.00	178.33	.00	205.08	.00
**	18	11606		337.71	.00	320.82	.00	368.94	.00
	18	11620		95.72	72.42	90.93	68.80	104.57	79.12
*	18	11621		133.34	102.97	126.67	97.82	145.67	112.49
*	18	11622		162.51	124.50	154.38	118.28	177.54	136.02
	18	11623		199.62	154.56	189.64	146.83	218.09	168.85
	18	11624		241.51	.00	229.43	.00	263.84	.00
**	18	11626		305.38	.00	290.11	.00	333.63	.00
	18	11640		114.59	85.76	108.86	81.47	125.19	93.69
*	18	11641		154.21	119.18	146.50	113.22	168.48	130.20
	18	11642		198.81	153.93	188.87	146.23	217.20	168.16
**	18	11643		237.67	184.78	225.79	175.54	259.66	201.87
*	18	11644		274.78	.00	261.04	.00	300.20	.00
	18	11646		375.99	.00	357.19	.00	410.77	.00
	18	11700		23.15	17.62	21.99	16.74	25.29	19.25
**	18	11701		18.75	14.26	17.81	13.55	20.48	15.58
**	18	11710		25.03	19.06	23.78	18.11	27.35	20.83
**	18	11711		17.79	13.59	16.90	12.91	19.44	14.85
**	18	11730		64.50	55.67	61.28	52.89	70.47	60.82
	18	11731		39.07	30.09	37.12	28.59	42.69	32.88
	18	11732		22.64	18.32	21.51	17.40	24.74	20.01
	18	11740		27.58	20.85	26.20	19.81	30.13	22.78
**	18	11750		160.81	117.99	152.77	112.09	175.69	128.90
**	18	11752		432.13	.00	410.52	.00	472.10	.00
	18	11755		84.35	.00	80.13	.00	92.15	.00
*	18	11760		64.19	52.59	60.98	49.96	70.13	57.45
*	18	11762		195.69	151.26	185.91	143.70	213.80	165.26
*	18	11765		37.13	29.21	35.27	27.75	40.56	31.91
**	18	11770		322.20	.00	306.09	.00	352.00	.00
**	18	11771		509.59	.00	484.11	.00	556.73	.00
**	18	11772		592.74	.00	563.10	.00	647.57	.00
	18	11900		23.63	20.25	22.45	19.24	25.82	22.13
	18	11901		37.63	31.79	35.75	30.20	41.11	34.73
**	18	11960		546.81	.00	519.47	.00	597.39	.00
**	18	11970		1,014.26	.00	963.55	.00	1,108.08	.00
**	18	11971		549.69	.00	522.21	.00	600.54	.00
*	18	12001		59.50	.00	56.53	.00	65.01	.00
*	18	12002		78.77	.00	74.83	.00	86.05	.00
**	18	12004		114.34	.00	108.62	.00	124.91	.00
*	18	12005		122.02	.00	115.92	.00	133.31	.00
*	18	12006		169.05	.00	160.60	.00	184.69	.00
*	18	12007		192.76	.00	183.12	.00	210.59	.00
*	18	12011		70.15	.00	66.64	.00	76.64	.00
*	18	12013		94.60	.00	89.87	.00	103.35	.00
*	18	12014		105.42	.00	100.15	.00	115.17	.00
*	18	12015		142.44	.00	135.32	.00	155.62	.00
*	18	12016		168.78	.00	160.34	.00	184.39	.00
	18	12017		273.71	.00	260.02	.00	299.02	.00
	18	12018		388.68	.00	369.25	.00	424.64	.00
**	18	12020		140.88	.00	133.84	.00	153.92	.00
**	18	12021		161.16	.00	153.10	.00	176.07	.00
*	18	12031		73.23	.00	69.57	.00	80.01	.00
*	18	12032		96.37	.00	91.55	.00	105.28	.00
*	18	12034		117.74	.00	111.85	.00	128.63	.00
*	18	12035		184.41	.00	175.19	.00	201.47	.00
*	18	12036		194.35	.00	184.63	.00	212.32	.00

APPENDIX ITEM 09-12

SUPERBILL

Initial Visit

✓	Code	
	99201	Prob. Focus-H&E-St. Fwd. (10)
	99202	Expanded-H&E-St. Fwd. (20)
	99203	Detailed-H&E-Low Complex. (30)
	99204	Comp.-H&E-Mod. Complex (45)
	99205	Comp.-H&E-High Complex (60)

Injection/Aspiration

✓	Code	
	20550	Injection, Trigger Points
	20600	Injection/Aspiration, Small Joint
	20605	Injection/Aspiration, Medium Joint
	20610	Injection/Aspiration, Large Joint
	90782	Therapeutic Injection
	J0810	Injection, Cortisone up to 50mg

73140	Finger 2v	R/L	73620	Foot 2v WB	R/L
73130	Hand 3v	R/L	73630	Foot 3v	R/L
73100	Wrist 2v	R/L	73650	Heel 2v	R/L
73110	Wrist 3v	R/L	73600	Ankle 2v	R/L
73090	Forearm 2v	R/L	73610	Ankle 3v	R/L
73070	Elbow 2v	R/L	73590	Tib-Fib 2v	R/L
73080	Elbow 3v	R/L	73560	Knee 2v WB	R/L
73060	Humerus 2v	R/L	73562	Knee 3v	R/L
73020	Shld 1v	R/L	73564	Knee 4v	R/L
73030	Shld 3v	R/L	73564	Knee 5v	R/L
73030	Shld 4v	R/L	73564	Knee 6v	R/L
73660	Toe(s)	R/L	73565	Knees AP WB	
			73550	Femur 2v	R/L

Follow-Up Visit

✓	Code	
	99211	Eval. & Mgmt. (No Physician) (5)
	99212	Prob. Focus-H&E-St. Fwd. (10)
	99213	Expand.-H&E-Low Complex (15)
	99214	Detail-H&E-Mod. Complex (25)
	99215	Comp.-H&E-High Complex (40)
	99024	Post-Op

Special Services

	99199	IME
	99199	No. Show Worker's Comp.
	99075	Deposition/Medical Testimony
	99080	Preparation of Medical Report
	99199	Copy of Office Records

RADIOLOGY

73510	Hip 2v	R/L	72052	Cervical 7v
72170	Pelvis AP WB/NWB		72070	Thoracic 2v
72190	Pelvis Obliques	R/L	72080	Thoracolumbar 2v
73520	Pelvis AP/Frogs	R/L	72100	Lumbar 2v
73630	Clubfoot Series	R/L	72110	Lumbar 5v
76065	LE AP Telegram	R/L	72114	Lumbar 7v
76040	LE Scanogram	R/L	72010	36" Spine 1v
71020	Chest 2v	R/L	72020	36" Spine 2v
73000	Clavicle 2v	R/L	72090	Scoliosis / New
71100	Ribs uni	R/L	76020	Bone Age
72220	Sac / Cocx	R/L	99080	Xray Copies
72040	Cervical 2v		76140	Xray Interp
72050	Cervical 5v			

Office Consultations

✓	Code	
	99241	Prob. Focus-H&E-St. Fwd. (15)
	99242	Expanded-H&E-St. Fwd. (30)
	99243	Detailed-H&E-Low Complex (40)
	99244	Comp.-H&E-Mod.Complex (60)
	99245	Comp.-H&E-High Complex (80)
	99003	TRC
	99199	Extended Consultation

Follow Up Consultation

	99261	Level 1
	99262	Level 2
	99263	Level 3

Confirmatory Consultations (2nd Opinion)

✓	Code	
	99271	Conf. Consult, Brief
	99272	Conf. Consult, Limited
	99273	Conf. Consult, Intermediate
	99274	Conf. Consult, Extended
	99275	Conf. Consult, Comprehensive

OTHER E/M SERVICES

Y	N	
☐	☐	Cast/Splint
☐	☐	Injection
☐	☐	X-rays _____

TOTAL OFFICE CHARGE

TOTAL RADIOLOGY CHARGE

CAST ROOM

Cast Application

CPT Code	Description	Qty.	FEE
29065	Long Arm		
29075	Short Arm		
29065	Muenster Cast		
29305	Unilateral Spica		
29345	Long Leg		
29355	Long Leg Walking		
29358	Long Leg Cast Brace		
29405	Short Leg		
29425	Short Leg Walking		
29425	Patellar Tendon Bearing		
29450	Serial Cast Uni.		
29450	Serial Cast BIL.		

Cast Removal / Repair

CPT Code	Description	Qty.	FEE
29705	Removal-Full Arm or Leg		

Splint Application

CPT Code	Description	Qty.
29105	Long Arm	
29125	Short Arm	
29130	Finger Splint	
29515	Short Leg	

General Supplies

CPT Code	Description	Qty.
A4460	Ace Bandage - 2", 3"	
A4460	Ace Bandage - 4", 6"	
E0100	Cane	
A4580	Cast Shoe	
L0120	Cervical Collar	
E0114	Crutches, pair	

General Supplies

Code	Description	Qty.	Fee
99070	Dressing Change, Major		
99070	Dressing Change, Minor		
99070	Elbow Brace, Tennis Elbow		
99070	Kerlix Roll		
99070	Kling Roll		
L3002	Plastazote		
99070	Post-Op Shoe, each		
A4565	Shoulder Immobilizer		
A4560	Sling		
A4580	Tubigrip		
A4570	Wrist Support		

Knee Brace

Code	Description	Qty.	Fee
L1845	ACL / PCL		
L1832	Post Op Universal		

Knee Supplies

Code	Description	Qty.	Fee
E1399	Cryo/Cuff & Cooler, Knee		
L1830	Knee Immobilizer		
99070	Miracle Wrap Knee Support		

Ankle Supplies

Code	Description	Qty.	Fee
L4350	Ankle Sport Stirrup 02D		
99070	Anklet, Double Wrap		
L4360	Fracture Walker, Aircast		
L2116	Fracture Walker, Universal		
L2114	Fracture Walker, Mid Calf		
99070	Viscoheel N		
L1906	Malleotrain Ankle Sup		

Cast / Splint Application Performed By: ☐ Physician ☐ Cast Room ☐ Right ☐ Left   DOI: _____

PHYSICIAN'S SIGNATURE

DATE	TIME	PATIENT	APPOINTMENT NOTES	D.O.B./AGE
TICKET NO.	DOCTOR	FACILITY		PHONE NO.
PATIENT I.D.	RESPONSIBLE PARTY		CITY/STATE/ZIP	

SEX M / F   ADDRESS

CURRENT	OVER 30	OVER 60	OVER 90	OVER 120

ALLOCATION TYPE   FINANCIAL CLASS

INSURANCE CARRIER 1 | INSURANCE CARRIER 2 | INSURANCE CARRIER 3

RECALL APPOINTMENT INFORMATION | DAYS | WEEKS | MONTHS

PRIOR BALANCE	LAST VISIT DATE

PRIOR DIAGNOSIS

TOTAL CAST ROOM CHARGES

TODAY'S TOTAL CHARGES

NOTES

ADJUSTMENTS

TODAY'S PAYMENT

BALANCE DUE

PAYMENT TYPE ☐ CHECK # _____ ☐ CASH ☐ VISA/MC

ENTERED BY

L97SF022871M 8/98

APPENDIX ITEM 09-13
SURGERY CHARGE CARD

Patient's Name _____

Date of Service _____ Diagnosis No. _____

Surgery Assistant _____

☐ Place of Service: _____

☐ Right   ☐ Left

CODE	TREATMENT	FEE	CODE	TREATMENT	FEE	CODE	TREATMENT	FEE	CODE	TREATMENT	FEE	CODE	TREATMENT	FEE
	GENERAL			SPINE (cont'd)			FOREARM-WRIST (cont'd)			PELVIS-HIP JOINT (cont'd)			TIB/FIB-ANKLE (cont'd)	
20000	Incision Abscess		63035	Add Lami Level		25240	Darrach Procedu		27176	SCFE in situ pin		27696	Rpr Both Coil Ligam	
20005	Deep/Com		63042	Laminotomy/Re-Do		25260	Rpr Flexor Each		27177	SCFE ORIF		27698	Sec Rpr Both Ligament	
20200	Biopsy Muscle		63047	Laminectomy/Decom		25270	Rpr Extensor Ea		27187	Prophyla Tr Fem		27705	Osteotomy Tibia	
20205	Deep		63048	Add Lami Level		25400	Rpr NoUn Rad/Ul		27284	Arthrodesis Hip		27707	Osteotomy Fibula	
20206	Biopsy Mus. Needle			SHOULDER		25405	w/graft		27236	Gilberty/FX		27709	Osteotomy Tib/Fib	
20240	Biopsy Bone		23040	Arthrotomy G-H Jt		25440	Rpr NoUn Navicu					27870	Arthrodesis Ankle	
20245	Deep		23044	Arth A-C, S-C Jt		25800	Arthrodesis, Wr			FEMUR KNEE JOINT		27880	BK Amputation	
	FB/PRODUCT REMOVAL		23120	Claviculectomy, Pt		25820	Intercarpal Fus		27310	Arthrotomy Knee		27888	Amputation Syme	
20650	Insert/Skel Tx		23130	Acromioplasty		25900	Amp Forearm		27332	Menisectomy One		27889	Ankle Disartic	
20680	Rem of Implant		23160	Saucerz Clavicle		64719	Ulnar Nerve Wri		27333	Menisectomy Both		29894	M-A Loose Body	
20690	External Fixation		23182	Saucerz Scapula		64721	Carpal Tunnel		27334	Arth Synovectomy		29895	M-A Synovec-Partial	
	I&D ABSCESS HEMATOMA		23184	Saucerz Prox Hum			HAND-FINGERS		27340	Exe Prepat Bursa		29897	M-A Debride-Limited	
10060	SO Abscess		23410	Rep Rot Cuff/Acute		26055	Rel Trig Finger		27345	Exe Baker's Cyst		29898	M-A Debride-Extensi	
10140	SO Hematoma		23412	Chronic		26121	Fasclectomy Pal		27350	Patellectomy		27892	Fasciotomy-Ant &/or Lat	
23030	Shoulder, deep		23415	Rel Cor-Acro Lig		26123	Fasciectomy Fin		27380	Rpr Intrapatel Ten		27893	Fasciotomy-Post Comp.	
23930	Upper Arm/Elbow		23420	Rep Cuff Avulsion		26125	add finger		27385	Rpr Quad/Ham Rup		27894	Fasciotomy Ant &/or Post	
25028	Forearm/Wrist		23430	Tenodesis Bicep		26135	Synovectomy M-P		27403	Meniscal Repair			FOOT	
26011	Finger		23450	Magnuson/Put Plat		26350	1° Flexor Repair		27405	Repair MCL, LCL		28003	I&D Subascial	
26990	Pelvis/Hips		23455	Bankart		26356	1° Flex RepNoMan		27418	Maguel Epip Arr		28005	I&D/Osteomyelitis	
27301	Thigh/Knee		23462	Bristow		26410	Ext Ten Rep Hand		27425	Lateral Release		28008	Fasciotomy	
27603	Leg/Ankle		23470	Neer Implant		26418	Ext Ten Rep Fing		27427	X Art Rpr ACL		28035	Tarsal Tunnel	
28001	Foot		23472	Total Shoulder		26432	Mallet Fin Perc		27428	intr-art open		28060	Fasciectomy Plantar	
			23332	Rom Total Shoulder		26433	Mallet Fin Open		27447	TKA		28080	Morton Neuroma	
			23700	Manipulation		26450	Tenotomy Fir/Palm		27486	Rev TKA 1 comp		28090	Exc Ganglion/Cyst	
									27487	Rev TKA all				

	SKIN DEBRIDEMENT				
		24356	w/ostectomy	26843	Fusion Q-M Other
11040	Partial Thickness	24400	Osteotomy, Humerus	26850	Fusion M-P
11041	Full Thickness	29534	M-A Loose Body	26860	Fusion L-P
11042	Skin & SQ	29835	M-A Synovec-Partial	26951	Amp Fin/Thumb
11043	Skin, SQ, Muscle	29837	M-A Debride-Limited		PELVIS-HIP JOINT
11044	Skin, SQ, Musc, Bone	29838	M-A Debride-Extens	27001	Tenotomy Addur
		64718	Ulnar Nerve Transfer	27030	Arthrotomy/Sep
	SPINE		FOREARM-WRIST	27060	Coccygectomy
22625	Fusion-Lumbar	25000	Release DeQuervens	27130	THA
22520	Harvest Bone Gr	25101	Arthrotomy Wrist	27132	THA Conversion
22840	Harrington Rod	25111	Exc Ganglion	27134	Revision THA
22842	Segmental Fixation	25115	Synovec Rheums	27137	Acetabulum Univ
22852	Rem Post Seg Inst	25118	Synovectomy Wri	27138	Femoral Only
62292	Chemonucleolysis				
63010	Gill Type Opera				NOTES/COMMENTS
63030	Laminotomy/l-1				

29888	M-A ACL Repair	28755	Fusion Gr Toe 1-P
29889	M-A PCL Repair	28810	Amp Metatarsal
29850	Knee FX w-w/o Man	28820	Amp M-P
29851	Knee FX w-w/0 I or E Fix	28825	Amp 1-P
29855	Tib FX-w-w/0 I or E Fix		
29856	Condyle FX-w-w/0 I or E		
	TIB-FIB-ANKLE		
27600	Decom Fasciotomy Ant		
27601	Posterior Compart		
27602	Both Compartments		
27610	Arthr Ankle-Sepsis		
27620	Arthr Ank/Loose Body		
27650	Repair Achilles		
27652	w/graft		
27695	1 Rep Rup Ligament		

7-10 or _____ DOI _____

F/U appt. _____ Ins. _____

PAYMENT _____

TYPE _____

APPENDIX ITEM 09-14
HOSPITAL CHARGE CARD

PATIENT: _____ HOSP: _____ ADMIT DATE: _____

DATES OF SERVICE:	INITIAL HOSP. CARE:	INITIAL CONSULTS:	F/U CONSULTS:	EMERGENCY ROOM:
1. ___ / ___ / ___	☐ 99221	☐ 99251 ☐ 99254	☐ 99261	☐ 99281 ☐ 99284
2. ___ / ___ / ___	☐ 99222	☐ 99252 ☐ 99255	☐ 99262	☐ 99282 ☐ 99285
	☐ 99223	☐ 99253	☐ 99263	☐ 99283

		1	2	3	4	5	6	7	8	9	10	11	12	13	14	15	16	17	18	19	20	21	22	23	24	25	26	27	28	29	30	31
SUB.	99231																															
HOSP.	99232																															
CARE	99233																															
DISCHARGE	99238																															
C. CARE	99291																															
C. CARE	99292																															
TELEPHONE-BRIEF	99371																															
TELEPHONE-INTER.	99372																															
TELEPHONE-COMP.	99373																															

TYPICAL PT. EXAMPLES	**1** STABLE, RECOVERING OR IMPROVING	**2** INADEQUATE THERAPY RESPONSE OR MINOR COMPLICATION	**3** UNSTABLE, OR SIGNIFICANT COMPLICATION OR NEW PROBLEM

DATE		PROCEDURE	CODE	DIAGNOSES	CODE
	1				
	2				
	3				
	4				
	5				

DR. NO.: _____   NO.: ___5376

APPENDIX ITEM 12-01
FRONT DESK COLLECTION ANALYSIS WORKSHEET

[Name of Medical Practice]

Prepared By:_____

Day of Month	Office Visits	Office Visits Paid

Total _____

Percentage Paid _____

[**Note:** Only include office visits at which the patient could have made a payment, even if it was only $1. Exclude visits at which the office could not legally accept payment from the patient at the time of the office visit (e.g., Medicaid).]

APPENDIX ITEM 12-02
COLLECTION LETTER NUMBER 1

[Date]

[Patient's name]
[Address]
[City, State, ZIP]

Account Balance:	$[Dollar value]
Account Number:	[Account number]
Date of Service	[Date]

Dear [Name]:

We recently received a payment from your insurance company. The balance listed above is not payable by your insurance and our records indicate that you do not hold secondary insurance. Therefore, this amount needs to be paid by you.

When submitting your payments, please write the account number on the face of the check or money order.

If you have any questions regarding your account, or might have difficulty making immediate payment, please call our office as soon as possible. Thank your for your cooperation.

Sincerely,
[Office manager or collection clerk
signature block]

APPENDIX ITEM 12-03
COLLECTION LETTER NUMBER 2

[Date]

[Patient's name]
[Address]
[City, State, ZIP]

Account Balance:	$[Dollar value]
Account Number:	[Account number]
Date Last Paid:	[Date]

Dear [Name]:

This is a reminder that your account is now 30 days old and that full payment on your account is now due. Please remit your payment as soon as possible, along with our office's account statement.

If you have any questions or may have difficulty making full payment at this time, please call our office as soon as possible.

If your payment has already been sent, please disregard this notice. Thank your for your cooperation.

Sincerely,
[Office manager or collection clerk
signature block]

APPENDIX ITEM 12-04
COLLECTION LETTER NUMBER 3

[Date]

[Patient's name]
[Address]
[City, State, ZIP]

Account Balance: $[Dollar value]
Account Number: [Account number]
Date Last Paid: [Date]

Dear [Name]:

Our records indicate that you have an outstanding balance with our office in the amount indicated above. Also, according to our records, your balance is now over 60 days old.

In an effort to settle this account in a most reasonable way, we are asking that you remit full payment as soon as possible. If you cannot pay the full amount at this time, please contact our office immediately to discuss a payment arrangement.

Failure to contact our office or remit full payment will result in more severe collection efforts. If your payment has already been sent, please disregard this notice. Thank you for your cooperation.

Sincerely,
[Office manager or collection clerk
signature block]

APPENDIX ITEM 12-05
COLLECTION LETTER NUMBER 4

[Date]

[Patient's Name]
[Address]
[City, State, ZIP]

Account Balance: $[Dollar value]
Account Number: [Account number]
Date Last Paid: [Date]

FINAL NOTICE

Dear [Name]:

We have sent a number of previous notices advising you that your account is seriously delinquent. We have not received any response to these letters.

A payment must be made within ten (10) days from the date of this letter to prevent severe collection action.

Please indicate your desired form of settlement and return a copy of this letter to our office within the 10-day period:

❑   I prefer to settle the account. Please find full payment enclosed.

❑   I prefer to make monthly payments of $____ until this balance is paid in full. I understand that no interest will be charged for this delayed payment schedule.

Patient's Signature: _____

It is our sincere wish to avoid collection action. Please contact us immediately. If your payment has already been sent, please disregard this notice.

Sincerely,
[Office manager or collection clerk
signature block]

APPENDIX ITEM 12-06
COLLECTION LETTER NUMBER 5

[Send this letter to patients when their accounts reach 90 days old.]

[Date]

[Patient's Name]
[Address]
[City, State, ZIP]

Dear [Name]:

Our records indicate that your account is now 90 days past due. This letter is your final notice. If we do not hear from you within ten (10) days from the date of this letter, your account will be turned over to collection.

If you cannot pay the balance of your account now, we still want to work with you to set up a mutually agreeable payment arrangement; however, our cooperation is available only if you contact us within the next 10 days.

Please ask for me when you call. Thank you for your prompt attention to this matter.

Sincerely,
[Office manager or collection clerk
signature block]

APPENDIX ITEM 12-07
COLLECTION LETTER NUMBER 6

[Use this letter immediately after the insurance company pays its portion of services rendered.]

[Date]

[Patient's Name]
[Address]
[City, State, ZIP]

Dear [Name]:

According to our records, we have filed a claim with your insurance company for medical services provided. Your insurance company has paid its portion of the claim. The amount you owe is now due and is payable by you.

We would appreciate your immediate remittance of this balance to our office. If you need further information or you would like to make special payment arrangements, please contact our office.

Sincerely,
[Office manager or collection clerk
signature block]

APPENDIX ITEM 12-08
COLLECTION LETTER NUMBER 7

[Use this form when the office discovers that the insurance company is waiting on the claim statement or signed authorization of benefits from the patient before it pays the insurance claim.]

[Date]

[Patient's Name]
[Address]
[City, State, ZIP]

Dear [Name]:

Your insurance company requires a completed claim statement or signed authorization of benefits. According to the company's records, it has not yet received this form from you. Please contact your employer or the insurance company immediately if you are unfamiliar with the required form. As always, please do not hesitate to contact our office for assistance.

We also want to remind you that although we file your insurance for you as a courtesy, it is ultimately your responsibility to provide your insurance company with this information. Please do not delay in contacting either your employer or the insurance company.

Your prompt attention to this matter would be greatly appreciated.

Sincerely,
[Office manager or collection clerk
signature block]

APPENDIX ITEM 12-09
COLLECTION LETTER NUMBER 8

[Date]

[Patient's Name]
[Address]
[City, State, ZIP]

Dear [Name]:

We recently received a check in our office in the amount of $[dollar value], which was returned to our office for insufficient funds on your account.

Please contact our office immediately to settle this matter. If we do not hear from you, our office will pursue other collection efforts.

Sincerely,
[Office manager or collection
clerk signature block]

APPENDIX ITEM 12-10
COLLECTION LETTER NUMBER 9

[Check with your state's collection laws before using this letter.]

[Date]

[Patient's Name]
[Address]
[City, State, ZIP]

PAYMENT AGREEMENT

This notice is given as evidence and acknowledgment of indebtedness for medical care.

For value received, and in consideration of the extension granted me by [Name of practice], I hereby agree to the following payment schedule:

$[Dollar value] per month on my account balance until paid in full. Payments are due by the [Date] of each month and will begin on [Date].

I agree that if payments are not made in the full amount stated above or if the payments are not received in a timely manner, the entire balance will be considered delinquent and will be due and payable immediately unless a new agreement has been approved by [Name of practice].

I agree to be responsible for reasonable collection costs or attorneys' fees incurred in collecting a delinquent balance.

I understand and accept the above.

Patient:
[Signature block]
[Date]

Guarantor:
[Signature block]
[Date]

Witness:
[Signature block]
[Date]

APPENDIX ITEM 12-11
INSURANCE FOLLOW-UP TELEPHONE CALL CHECKLIST

Patient's Name: _____ Policy #: _____

Insurance Carrier: _____

Account #: _____

1. Name of person with whom you spoke: _____

2. Was the claim received? _____

3. Did the insurance company receive assignment of benefits or other patient forms? _____

4. When will the claim be processed? _____

5. Payment will be sent on_____to_____for the amount of $_____.

6. Insurance coverage was denied or charges reduced because:

   _____

   _____

   _____

7. Other remarks: _____

   _____

   _____

APPENDIX ITEM 12-12
COLLECTION SYSTEM MONITOR

Month: _____

Collection Activity	Monthly Target	Date Printed	Date Mailed	Number of Calls	Employee Initials
Monthly Statements	25th to 30th		N/A		
Collection Letters Sent	1st	N/A	N/A	N/A	N/A
30-day letter			N/A		
60-day letter				N/A	
90-day letter			N/A		
Final notice				N/A	
Unpaid Insurance Follow up	Weekly	N/A	N/A	N/A	N/A
Week 1		N/A	N/A		
Week 2		N/A	N/A		
Week 3		N/A	N/A		
Week 4		N/A	N/A		
Patient A/R Follow up	Weekly	N/A	N/A	N/A	N/A
Week 1		N/A	N/A		
Week 2		N/A	N/A		
Week 3		N/A	N/A		
Week 4		N/A	N/A		
Payment Plan Reminder	Monthly				
Accounts Sent to Collection Agency	Monthly			N/A	

Date Mailed to Accountant:_____

Signature:_____

APPENDIX ITEM 12-13
BAD DEBT CONTROL CHECKLIST

Do written guidelines exist on the collection of self-pay accounts? ❑ yes ❑ no

Are collection guidelines reviewed and revised periodically? ❑ yes ❑ no

Are collection guidelines clear, concise, and sufficiently detailed to serve as a working reference to personnel? ❑ yes ❑ no

Do business office personnel receive formal training on collection guidelines before beginning work? ❑ yes ❑ no

Do employees receive formal training on collection guidelines after any revision or otherwise at least annually? ❑ yes ❑ no

Does management solicit employee suggestions for changes in policies and procedures? ❑ yes ❑ no

Do exceptions to approved guidelines require the approval of management on a case-by-case basis? ❑ yes ❑ no

Do self-pay guidelines allow monthly payments on certain accounts? ❑ yes ❑ no

Do self-pay guidelines specify the maximum number of payments that will be accepted? ❑ yes ❑ no

If so, how many? _____

Do self-pay guidelines specify the minimum monthly payment amount that will be accepted? ❑ yes ❑ no

If so, how much? _____

Do collection guidelines specify what action should be taken if a patient misses a payment? ❑ yes ❑ no

Does management support the collection guidelines, even when a patient complains? ❑ yes ❑ no

APPENDIX ITEM 12-14
CLAIM INQUIRY FAX FORM

Attn: Provider Assistance Department
Attn: Claims Department

This is a claim status request. Please complete the box below and fax back to our office as soon as possible. Your prompt attention to this matter would be greatly appreciated.

Physician Name: _____

Federal Identification Number: _____

Phone Number: _____

Fax Number: _____

Name of person submitting inquiry: _____

❑ Check here if claim was electronically filed.
❑ HCFA 1500 attached to this form.

PAYOR RESPONSE

❑ Claim not on file (refile to claims department for processing)
❑ Claim receivable but not yet paid
❑ Claim sent to medical review
❑ More information is needed to process claim (see comments below)

Comments:

_____

_____

_____

_____

APPENDIX ITEM 13-01
INSURANCE CLAIMS FILING ANALYSIS WORKSHEET

Date per Claim	Last Date of Service	Number of Days	Type of Patient	Type of Service

Total Days

# of Claims

Average Days

APPENDIX ITEM 13-02
LETTER TO THE INSURANCE COMMISSIONER

[Use this letter when all attempts have failed to obtain payment from the patient's insurance company. Check your state's insurance laws to determine whether the patient or the physician has the jurisdiction to file the formal complaint with the Insurance Commissioner.]

[Date]

[State] Insurance Commissioner
[Address]
[City, State, ZIP]

Dear Insurance Commissioner:

My physician filed the attached insurance claim form over thirty (30) days ago. Even after repeated attempts by my physician's office to contact the insurance company regarding the payment status of this claim, to this date, my insurance company has not paid this claim and has provided no explanation to my physician for its nonpayment.

Please accept this letter as a formal written complaint against the insurance company. Your prompt attention to this matter would be greatly appreciated.

I am providing the insurance company and my physician with a copy of this notice.

Sincerely,
[Patient's name]

APPENDIX ITEM 13-03
PAYMENT POSTING AUDIT FORM

Patient's Name	Amount Billed	Amount Approved	Contractual Write-off	Other Write-offs	Amount Due from Patient
	$	$	$	$	$

Place a checkmark to the right of each column to indicate that the amount was traced to the patient's detailed account ledger.

APPENDIX ITEM 16-01
EMPLOYEES' ANNUAL PERFORMANCE REVIEW

[Complete this annual review form on or before the employee's anniversary date of hire.]

Employee Name: _____

Employee No.: _____

Date: _____

Supervisor's Name and Title: _____

Rate employee performance by circling "E" for excellent; "G" for good; "A" for average; and "P" for poor in the following areas:

1. Knowledge of Work: Understands the duties and
   procedures of the job.   E G A P
   Comments: _____
   _____

2. Quantity of Work: Completes tasks.   E G A P
   Comments: _____
   _____

3. Quality of Work: Completes work and pays attention to
   detail.   E G A P
   Comments: _____
   _____

4. Adaptability: Learns rapidly and reacts well to new
   situations.   E G A P
   Comments: _____
   _____

5. Personal: Has tact and poise and is even-tempered,
   dependable, and confident.   E G A P
   Comments: _____
   _____

6. Attitude: Shows interest in work. Is enthusiastic and
   cooperative and strives to do good work.   E G A P
   Comments: _____
   _____

7. Judgment: Can be trusted to make appropriate
   decisions.   E G A P
   Comments: _____

   _____

8. Initiative: Seeks solutions, acts independently, tries
   to improve the job.   E G A P
   Comments: _____

   _____

9. Responsibility: Follows rules and instructions and is
   accountable for the job.   E G A P
   Comments: _____

   _____

10. Expression: Communicates clearly in speech and
    writing.   E G A P
    Comments: _____

    _____

11. Interpersonal: Works well with others, and accepts
    criticism and instruction.   E G A P
    Comments: _____

    _____

12. Health and Vitality: Is of sound mind and body and has
    stamina.   E G A P
    Comments: _____

    _____

13. Leadership Ability: Inspires trust and confidence
    in others.   E G A P
    Comments: _____

    _____

14. Punctuality and Attendance: Is punctual and has a good
    attendance record.   E G A P
    Comments: _____

    _____

15. Strongest points: _____
16. Weakest points: _____
17. Short-range goals (next 3 months): _____
18. Long-range goals (next year): _____
19. Employee comments: _____

Employee's signature: _____Date: _____
Supervisor's signature: _____Date: _____

APPENDIX ITEM 16-02

EMPLOYEES' TIME-OFF REQUEST FORM

Date: _____

Employee's name: _____

Time off requested: _____

Reason for time off: _____

Comments: _____

Employee's signature: _____

❑   Time off granted as vacation leave.

❑   Time off granted as sick leave.

❑   Time off granted without pay.

❑   Time off granted with pay.

❑   Time off not granted.

Signature: _____

Date: _____

▼ APPENDIX C

Part III: Physicians' Contracts, Relationships, and Related Issues

CHAPTER 21

CHAPTER 22

APPENDIX ITEM 17-01
BUY/SELL AGREEMENT CHECKLIST

❏ Agreement addresses the following events requiring a buy-out:
  Death
  Disability
  Retirement
  Voluntary and involuntary termination

❏ Agreement specifies the number of months of disability after which an owner is required to give up ownership in the practice.

❏ Agreement specifies (if owners so desire) the age requirement before a physician can retire from the group (for example, to qualify for retirement, a physician must be at least 62 years old; otherwise the withdrawal is considered voluntary).

❏ In the case of a voluntary withdrawal, agreement specifies how much notice is required.

❏ In the case of a voluntary withdrawal, agreement specifies whether there will there be penalties to the buy-out price if the owner forms a competing practice, joins a competing practice, or violates the employment contract.

❏ In the case of an involuntary withdrawal, agreement specifies how much notice is required.

❏ Agreement specifies the required vote to admit a new physician into the group.

❏ Reasonableness of the buy-out price of an ownership interest has been reviewed.

❏ If the buy-out price is to be based on an appraised value, the qualifications of the appraiser have been assessed.

❏ Agreement specifies, based on the current practice environment, whether goodwill should be paid to a departing owner.

❏ The manner in which the buy-out price will be paid has been established and reviewed.

❏ The tax consequences of the buy-out provisions have been reviewed.

❏ The buy-out amount has been calculated for each owner using the current formula in the agreement.

❏ Each owner has reviewed the calculations.

❏ All parties agree to the reasonableness of the buy-out amounts.

APPENDIX ITEM 17-02
BUY/SELL AGREEMENT

STOCK PURCHASE AND OPTION AGREEMENT

This stock purchase and option agreement ("Agreement"), made and entered into as of the [Date] day of [Month, Year], by and among [Name of practice] ("Company"), and [First physician's name], M.D., [Second physician's name], M.D., [Third physician's name], M.D., and [Fourth physician's name], M.D. being all of the shareholders of Company (jointly and severally, "Shareholders").

WITNESSETH

WHEREAS, Company has issued shares respectively of its one dollar ($1.00) par value common stock ("Stock") to Shareholders; and

WHEREAS, Company further desires to insure the continuity of harmonious management of Company and to effect a method of controlling the respective ownership of Company to the extent possible and not in violation of the requirements of [Appropriate state act(s)]; and

WHEREAS, Company and all Shareholders are now desirous of placing certain restrictions on transfer and option to purchase such shares of Stock.

NOW, THEREFORE, in consideration of the foregoing and the mutual covenants, conditions, stipulations, and agreements hereinafter contained, and other good and valuable consideration, the adequacy and receipt of which are forever irrevocably acknowledged and confessed, the parties hereto do mutually covenant and agree as follows:

ARTICLE I: TERM AND TERMINATION
OF EMPLOYMENT

1.1 **Term** Unless terminated at an earlier date, this Agreement shall terminate twenty-one (21) years after the death of the last survivor of the parties hereto and their now living lineal descendants.

1.2 **Termination** Should Shareholder terminate employment with Company, and provided such termination of employment is not attributable to the death or disability of Shareholder and the termination is not related to the disposition of Stock pursuant to other provisions of this Agreement, such Shareholder ("Terminated Shareholder") and Terminated Shareholder's spouse, shall, within ten (10) days from the termination date, be obligated to give notice pursuant to Paragraph 10.1 hereof to the other Shareholders ("Other Shareholders") and Company to sell all (but not less than all) of Terminated Shareholder's Stock first to Other Shareholders (in proportion to their then existing ownership of Stock to all Stock issued and outstanding other than that of Terminated Shareholder and his or her spouse), and then to Company. The notice shall be in force and effect collectively for a period of thirty (30) days. Other Shareholders shall have ten (10) days from the effective date of the notice to exercise their option to purchase or provide for the purchase of Stock of Terminated Shareholder and his or her spouse for "Option Price" as set forth in Paragraph 5.3 below. Those Shareholders electing to purchase the offered Stock shall be permitted to purchase that portion of the offered Stock that the number of shares held by such electing Shareholder bears to the number of shares held by all of Other Shareholders electing to purchase the offered Stock. To the extent some or all of Other Shareholders elect not to so purchase Stock owned by Terminated Shareholder, Company shall have the lesser of (a) twenty (20) days from the date of receipt of such written notice of refusal or (b) the remainder of the Option Period, to exercise the option to purchase the remainder of Stock of Terminated Shareholder (and his or her spouse) for Option Price.

ARTICLE II: CHANGE OF SHAREHOLDERS

2.1 **Divorce of Shareholder**   If the spouse ("Divorced Spouse") of any Shareholder ("Divorced Shareholder") becomes entitled to any shares of Stock owned by or registered in the name of Divorced Shareholder by virtue of a divorce or a property settlement agreement executed pursuant thereto, Divorced Spouse will be obligated to offer in writing, within thirty (30) days from acquiring such Stock, to sell to Divorced Shareholder all of the shares of Stock so acquired. Divorced Shareholder will have thirty (30) days from the date of the offer to give written notice of his or her intention to purchase all (but not less than all) of the shares of Stock so offered. If Divorced Shareholder fails to so exercise this option to purchase all of the offered shares, Other Shareholders will have until thirty (30) days from the effective date of written notice thereof received from Divorced Spouse within which to exercise their option (in proportion to their then existing ownership of Stock to all Stock issued and outstanding) to purchase such Stock by giving written notice of such intention. If Other Shareholders fail or refuse to exercise their option to purchase the offered Stock or to the extent a portion of Stock is not so purchased, Company will have thirty (30) days from the effective date of written notice thereof from Divorced Spouse within which to exercise its option to purchase such Stock by giving written notice of such intention. If Company fails or refuses to exercise its option to purchase such Stock, Divorced Spouse shall be entitled to retain any shares of Stock not so acquired as provided herein; provided, however, Divorced Spouse shall be considered to be a new Shareholder and shall be required to execute a stock restriction agreement governing Stock acquired, containing the same provisions as included within this Agreement, and in a form to be provided by Company; otherwise, such Stock shall be deemed void and therefore in the treasury of Company without any additional consideration to Divorced Spouse. The price to be paid for any shares transferred pursuant to the terms hereof, whether by Divorced Shareholder, Other Shareholders, or Company, shall be for Option Price (based on shares owned by Divorced Spouse). Furthermore, Divorced Spouse, by his or her signature below, understands this provision, is not acting under coercion, and has had the opportunity to retain independent counsel to represent and explain the legal consequences of this provision.

2.2 **Marriage of Shareholder or New Shareholder** If Shareholder marries subsequent hereto or a new Shareholder receives, purchases, or otherwise obtains Stock by or through the terms of this Agreement or otherwise, such Shareholder shall immediately thereupon execute a substitute stock restriction agreement with Company and the new spouse, if applicable, thereof, containing substantially the same provisions as this Agreement, and properly reflecting Shareholder's then changed status and Shareholder's changed obligations vis-à-vis Company and Other Shareholders; provided further that Shareholder shall cause such spouse, if applicable, to also execute said substitute agreement.

2.3 **Death of Shareholder** Upon the death of a Shareholder ("Deceased Shareholder"), Company or Other Shareholders shall purchase all Stock of Deceased Shareholder, including such shares as may be owned by his or her spouse, within the sooner of (a) thirty (30) days after the date of qualification of a legal representative of the estate of Deceased Shareholder or (b) ninety (90) days after the date of death of Deceased

Shareholder, and Deceased Shareholder obligates his or her estate or the personal representatives of his or her estate to the sale of all of Deceased Shareholder's interest in Stock, and Deceased Shareholder's spouse hereby agrees to such sale of his or her interest in such Stock. The total purchase price of all shares of Deceased Shareholder's Stock, including any interest owned by Deceased Shareholder's spouse, shall be an amount equal to the proportionate Stock interest as it relates to Option Price as of the date of death.

2.4 **Death of Spouse** If the spouse ("Deceased Spouse") of a Shareholder ("Surviving Shareholder") dies, and it is determined that (a) Deceased Spouse had an interest in Stock on the date of Deceased Spouse's death and (b) all or any portion of Deceased Spouse's shares of Stock did not thereby vest in Surviving Shareholder (outright or as the primary, beneficiary, and trustee of a trust created for his or her beneficial interest), then Deceased Spouse's personal representative will be required to offer all (but not less than all) of such shares in turn, first to Surviving Shareholder, secondly to Other Shareholders, and thirdly to Company, in the manner provided for such offers to be made in the case of a divorce of Shareholder and his or her spouse. If Surviving Shareholder, Other Shareholders, and Company all fail to exercise the option hereby given to purchase collectively all (but not less than all) of the offered shares pursuant hereto, such Stock will be deemed to have properly passed to the heirs or legatees of Deceased Spouse, who will be considered new Shareholders, but as such, will be required to execute a stock restriction agreement containing the same provisions as this Agreement, in a form to be provided by Company; otherwise, such Stock shall be deemed void and therefore in the treasury of Company without any additional consideration thereto. The price to be paid for any Stock transferred pursuant to the terms hereof, whether by Surviving Shareholder, Other Shareholders, or Company, will be the value calculated in the same manner as if Shareholder and his or her spouse had divorced.

ARTICLE III: DISABILITY OF A SHAREHOLDER

Each Shareholder may apply for and pay the premiums on disability insurance for Other Shareholders for purposes expressed in this Agreement. Alternatively, Company may apply for and pay the premiums on disability insurance for all or some Shareholders for the purposes expressed in this Agreement. Any disability policy so obtained shall be attached hereto and incorporated herein as Exhibit A.

3.1 **Sale by Disabled Shareholder** In the event either Shareholder becomes "Disabled" under the definition of the applicable insurance policy (attached hereto as Exhibit A) or if no disability policy is then in effect, the inability to permanently perform medical services and provide treatment for patients and ninety (90) days thereafter, that Disabled Shareholder and his or her spouse will be required to offer to sell to Other Shareholders (in proportion to their then existing ownership of Stock to all Stock issued and outstanding) all Stock owned or registered in the name of Disabled Shareholder and Disabled Shareholder's spouse for a period of thirty (30) days. Following the thirty- (30) day period, should Other Shareholders fail or refuse to exercise this option, Company may purchase Stock so offered. The purchase price shall be an amount equal to the proportionate Stock interest of Disabled Shareholder and his or her spouse as it relates to Option Price.

3.2 **Reimbursement of Proceeds** Should Company expend funds for the purchase of Disabled Shareholder's and his or her spouse's Stock interest and such funds are covered by an insurance policy that reimburses Disabled Shareholder for such expenditure, Disabled Shareholder shall reimburse Company for the funds outlayed for the purchase of such Stock interest.

ARTICLE IV: OPTION TO PURCHASE IN CERTAIN OTHER EVENTS

4.1 In the event of the transfer, gifts, disposition, or encumbrance of all or any part of Shareholder's Stock and that of his or her spouse in any manner whatsoever, whether voluntarily or involuntarily, including, but not limited to, a transfer or disposition under a sales agreement at a time in which Other Shareholders or Company had or should have had an exercisable option to purchase Stock so sold, an attachment, a petition or transfer in bankruptcy, a foreclosure proceeding, the perfection of a judgment lien, the enforcement of a pledge, the transfer for the benefit of any creditor or prospective creditor, a transfer in trust, a mortgage, a pledge, a hypothecation, or any other encumbrance of Stock, or otherwise, or a sale under any of them, Other Shareholders shall first, and Company thereafter, have the option to purchase or redeem all or any part of Stock so encumbered or so passing to a purchaser, transferee, or other recipient, within thirty (30) days after Company has actual notice of the transfer, disposition, or encumbrance, or within thirty (30) days after Stock is presented for transfer on the books of Company, whichever shall last occur. Those Other Shareholders electing to purchase the offered Stock shall be permitted to purchase that portion of the offered Stock that the number of shares held by such electing Shareholder bears to the number of shares held by all of Other Shareholders electing to purchase the offered Stock, by giving written notice of their election to purchase Stock to the encumberee, purchaser, transferee, or one to whom such Stock passes, by certified mail, return receipt requested. In the event that Other Shareholders fail to exercise said option, together or individually, Company may exercise said option to purchase or redeem Stock by giving written notice of its election to purchase or redeem Stock to the encumberee, purchaser, transferee, or one to whom such Stock passes, by certified mail, return receipt requested. The price of each share of Stock so purchased or redeemed shall be the lesser of (a) net book value (on the accrual basis of accounting excluding accounts receivable and goodwill) of Company as determined by Company's accountant, or (b) the price, if any, paid by the encumberee, purchaser, transferee, or one to whom Stock passes. If Other Shareholders and Company fail to exercise said option within such period, the restrictions imposed by this Agreement upon Stock shall automatically terminate at the end of such period.

ARTICLE V: OPTIONS

5.1 **Exclusiveness of Options**   Shareholders hereby agree that the provisions of this Agreement shall in all events be the sole method of disposition of Stock. Notwithstanding the foregoing, in the event that Company shall enter into any plan of merger or consolidation to which Company is a party and Company is not the surviving entity or shall enter into any transaction for the sale, lease, exchange, or other disposition (not including any pledge, mortgage, deed of trust, or trust indenture) of all, or substantially all, of the property and assets of Company, Shareholders hereby waive and renounce all rights of dissent and appraisal that may exist under the laws of the state of incorporation of Company.

5.2 **Endorsement on Stock Certificates**   All certificates representing the shares of Stock shall be endorsed appropriately to comply fully with any articles of incorporation or bylaws of Company and any applicable laws so that this Agreement shall be fully effective to bind any transferee of Stock. The parties hereto shall take all necessary and appropriate actions to accomplish the foregoing.

5.3   **Option Price**   The term "Option Price," unless otherwise defined by later agreement as indicated hereinbelow, shall mean the amount, per share, equal to the net book value per share of Company computed on the accrual basis of accounting, excluding accounts receivable and goodwill as determined by Company's accountant. Each party to this Agreement agrees that annually, Shareholders may negotiate and agree upon, by unanimous vote, a different value for Option Price. Such agreement altering the value hereunder shall be attached to and become part of this Agreement.

A.   **Payment of Option Price at Death and Disability**   All payments of all or some percentage of Option Price shall be paid, at the option of Company or Other Shareholders, by one of the following methods:

1. To the extent that insurance proceeds are available, all such proceeds shall be payable immediately to the estate of Deceased Shareholder and his or her Spouse or to Disabled Shareholder and his or her spouse

2. In cash

3. By installment payments as set forth in Paragraph 5.3.B.2 below

4. By any method of payment agreeable to Company and the selling Shareholder or his or her estate

B.   **Payment of Option Price under All Other Circumstances**   All payments of all or some percentage of Option Price shall be paid, at the option of Shareholders or Company, whichever party is the purchaser or redeemer, by one of the following methods:

1. All in cash

2. By installment payments. If the purchaser or redeemer elects to pay Option Price in installments, the payments shall be represented by a promissory note providing for the payment of the balance of the purchase price in equal monthly installments, over a period of five (5) years from the date of the note, together with

interest thereon at one (1) point above the prime rate of interest charged from time to time by [Name of bank] of [City, State], as established by the President or any Vice President of the Bank ("Stated Rate") with a cap of ten percent (10%). Notwithstanding the foregoing, if during any period Stated Rate exceeds the nonusurious maximum rate of interest that could be charged ("Maximum Rate"), the rate of interest in effect on this note shall be limited to Maximum Rate during each such period, but at all times thereafter the rate of interest in effect on the note shall be Maximum Rate until the total amount of interest accrued on the note equals the total amount of interest which would have accrued thereon if Stated Rate had at all times been in effect, at which time Stated Rate shall then be applicable. Said promissory note shall be secured by either a pledge of Stock for which said note is given as consideration or by other assets having an unencumbered value at least equal to the amount of the promissory note given hereunder, as the parties shall mutually agree.

3. Any method of payment agreeable to the purchaser, Shareholders, Company, and the selling Shareholder.

C. **Release from Indebtedness**   Upon the death of Shareholder or disposition of Stock by Shareholder during his or her lifetime pursuant to Paragraphs 1.2 and 2.3 and Article III, Company hereby agrees to attempt to secure the release of Shareholder, Shareholder's estate, and Shareholder's spouse from any and all indebtedness that was incurred on behalf of Company directly or which was personally guaranteed by Deceased Shareholder or selling Shareholder, or spouse thereof, as the case may be. Should Company be unable to secure a release of such personal indebtedness, whether represented by a personal guarantee or otherwise, Company and Other Shareholders, at the closing of the sale or exchange of Stock, shall enter into an indemnification agreement agreeing to indemnify and hold harmless Deceased Shareholder's estate or the selling Shareholder and his or her spouse, as the case may be, from any and all personal liability that may exist attributable to Shareholder's association with Company.

5.4   **Exercise of Option and Closing**   The exercise of an option created hereunder shall be deemed exercised at the time written notice of exercise is given by the exercising party to the selling party or his or her representative. The closing of a sale or exchange of Stock pursuant to this Agreement shall be held at the office of Company at 10:00 a.m. on such date, not later than thirty (30) days after the date notice of exercise is given, as may be agreed upon by the parties to the sale, or at such other time and place as may be agreed to by the parties to the sale.

ARTICLE VI: INSURANCE

6.1 **Life Insurance** Each Shareholder or Company may purchase life insurance on the life of Other Shareholders ("Insured Shareholders") under a policy or policies issued by an insurance company or companies ("Insurer") which is attached hereto and incorporated herein as Exhibit A. In addition, Shareholders agree to review periodically the sufficiency of such policy in light of changing circumstances affecting amounts payable under the terms and conditions contained herein. It is further agreed that each Insured Shareholder shall do any and all acts and things, and execute and deliver any and all instruments, papers, and documents, which shall be reasonably required by Company for the purpose of applying for, obtaining, maintaining, converting, or canceling such insurance policies or collecting the proceeds thereof, including, but not limited to, such as shall be necessary to vest in Company any and all rights, powers, privileges, options, or benefits to and under such insurance policies. All such insurance policies shall be listed on Exhibit A attached hereto and made a part hereof, as amended from time to time.

6.2 **Transfer of Life Insurance** At any time Stock of Shareholder is purchased by Company or Other Shareholders pursuant to Section 5.3 of this Agreement, such Shareholder whose Stock was so purchased will have the right to all life insurance policies on the life of such Shareholder, if any, then owned by Company or Other Shareholders.

ARTICLE VII: CONFLICTING PROVISIONS

7.1 If Shareholder dies under the following conditions, then in any of such events, it shall be deemed for all purposes that all offers, acceptances, and options made or required to be made under this Agreement have terminated and are of no force and effect and Company shall instead proceed in accordance with the provisions of Paragraph 2.4 of this Agreement:

a. There is outstanding an offer to purchase Stock owned or registered in the name of such Shareholder under Paragraph 1.2 of this Agreement; or

b. There is outstanding an offer by such Shareholder to purchase Stock owned or registered in the name of Other Shareholders under Paragraph 1.2 of this Agreement; or

c. An offer to sell or purchase Stock under Paragraph 1.2 of this Agreement has been accepted but not closed.

Likewise, should a Shareholder become disabled within the meaning of the provision of Article III of this Agreement at a time in which Stock has been offered (or is required to be offered) under Paragraph 1.2 of this Agreement, and when such offer has not yet been accepted, or if accepted or required to be accepted, has not been closed, then all actions taken or required to be taken under Paragraph 1.2 of this Agreement shall not be required and shall not be taken but instead, the provisions of Article III shall be complied therewith.

ARTICLE VIII: ENFORCEMENT

8.1   Shareholders acknowledge that a remedy at law for any breach by any Shareholder of the provisions of this Agreement will be inadequate and Shareholders hereby agree that Other Shareholders or Company shall be entitled, without the necessity of posting a bond of cash or otherwise, to injunctive relief in case of any such breach in addition to all other relief that may be available to Other Shareholders or Company.

ARTICLE IX: BENEFIT

9.1   No transfer or attempted transfer of Stock in violation of this Agreement shall be valid and Shareholders agree with Company, for its benefit, that Company shall not be required to transfer Stock on the books of Company or recognize any voting or other rights of any purported transferee, if such transfer or attempted transfer is in violation of this Agreement. This Agreement shall be binding upon and shall operate for the benefit of, the parties hereto and their respective heirs, executors, administrators, or other legal representatives, successors, and assigns, and shall be binding upon any person, partnership, or corporation to whom any

Stock is transferred, whether voluntarily or involuntarily, and whether or not in violation of the provisions of this Agreement.

ARTICLE X: MISCELLANEOUS

10.1 **Notice**   All notices under this Agreement shall be mailed certified mail, return receipt requested to the parties hereto at the following respective addresses:

Company:
    [Company name], P.A.
    [Address]
    [City, State, ZIP]

Shareholders:
    To the most recent addresses appearing on Company's books and records.

Any party may change its mailing address by serving written notice of such change and of such new address upon the other party. Whenever written notice is served by certified mail, it shall be deemed to have been given on the date such notice is posted.

10.2 **Joinder of Spouses**   For the reasons set forth in this Agreement, the spouses of Shareholders have executed this Agreement, and by such execution, the spouse of each Shareholder hereby binds himself or herself, and his or her heirs, assigns, and legal representatives to the terms and provisions hereof.

10.3 **Further Assurances**   Each party hereto agrees to perform any further acts and to execute and deliver any further documents that may be reasonably necessary to carry out the provisions of this Agreement.

10.4 **Severability**   In the event that any of the provisions, or portions thereof, of this Agreement are held to be unenforceable or invalid by any court of competent jurisdiction, the validity and enforceability of the remaining provisions, or portions thereof, shall not be affected thereby.

10.5 **Governing Law**   This agreement has been executed in and shall be governed by the laws of the State of [State].

10.6 **Amendment**   This Agreement may only be amended by the written consent of all parties to this Agreement.

10.7 **Terms Used in This Agreement**   Pronouns, nouns, and terms used in this Agreement shall include the masculine, feminine, neuter, singular, and plural form thereof wherever appropriate to the context.

10.8 **Entire Agreement**   This Agreement contains the entire understanding between the parties hereto concerning the subject matter contained herein. There are no representations, agreements, arrangements, or understandings, oral or written, between or among the parties hereto, relating to the subject matter of this Agreement, which are not fully expressed herein.

10.9 **Divisions and Headings**   The division of this Agreement into sections and subsections and the use of captions and headings in connection therewith are solely for convenience and shall have no legal effect in construing the provisions of this Agreement.

IN WITNESS WHEREOF, the parties have set their hands and seals as of the date and year first above written.

[INSERT SIGNATURE BLOCKS ACCORDINGLY]

SPOUSAL CONSENT

The undersigned spouses of Shareholders, having read the provisions of this Agreement, and particularly the provisions of Paragraphs 1.2, 2.1, 2.3, 2.4 and Article III, do specifically affirm that although they are not and will not become Shareholders pursuant to the foregoing Agreement solely by reason of the stock ownership of their respective spouses, they do, as current Spouses, each hereby specifically accept and agree to be bound by the provisions of the Agreement to the extent such provisions may ever be applicable to any community property or other interest which they may have or obtain in Company or Company's assets. The undersigned Spouses, as evidenced by execution hereinbelow, understand the foregoing provisions, are not acting under coercion, and have had the opportunity to retain independent counsel for personal representation purposes and to explain the legal consequences of this provision.

[INSERT SIGNATURE BLOCKS ACCORDINGLY]

DEATH VALUATION SCHEDULE

Date	Shareholder	Value	Signature
__/__/__	_____, M.D.	$_____	_____
__/__/__	_____, M.D.	$_____	_____
__/__/__	_____, M.D.	$_____	_____
__/__/__	_____, M.D.	$_____	_____

EXHIBIT A

DISABILITY INSURANCE POLICIES

Insurance Co.: _____ Policy No.: _____
Owner: _____
Insured: _____

Insurance Co.: _____ Policy No.: _____
Owner: _____
Insured: _____

Insurance Co.: _____ Policy No.: _____
Owner: _____
Insured: _____

Insurance Co.: _____ Policy No.: _____
Owner: _____
Insured: _____

LIFE INSURANCE POLICIES

Insurance Co.: _____ Policy No.: _____
Owner: _____
Insured: _____

Insurance Co.: _____ Policy No.: _____
Owner: _____
Insured: _____

Insurance Co.: _____ Policy No.: _____
Owner: _____
Insured: _____

Insurance Co.: _____ Policy No.: _____
Owner: _____
Insured: _____

APPENDIX ITEM 18-01
NEW PHYSICIAN LETTER OF INTENT

[Used to make an offer of employment to a new physician.]

[Date]

PERSONAL & CONFIDENTIAL
[Name of Physician]
[Address]
[City, State, ZIP]

Dear Dr. [Name of Physician] :

On behalf of [Name of practice] (hereinafter called the "practice"), this letter sets out a proposed agreement for your initial employment in Dr. [Name of physician]'s medical practice. After both you and Dr. [Name of physician] have agreed upon all issues related to your employment, a formal physician employment agreement will be prepared for your review and signature.

1. **Term**   You will be an employee of the practice for an initial [Duration]-month period starting [Month, Date, Year]. Should you and the practice want to proceed past this initial employment period, an offer of co-ownership may be made to you as described in item nine below.

   Your employment with the practice will essentially be "at will," since you or the practice may voluntarily terminate it at any time upon 30 days' written notice to the other. However, the following are conditions under which the practice may terminate your employment immediately: (*a*) upon your death or disability for three (3) consecutive months; (*b*) upon the suspension, revocation, or cancellation of your right to practice medicine in the State of [State]; (*c*) if you should lose privileges at any hospital at which the practice regularly maintains admission privileges; (*d*) should you fail or refuse to follow reasonable policies and directives established by the practice; (*e*) should you commit an act amounting to gross negligence or willful misconduct to the detriment of the practice or its patients; (*f*) if you are convicted of a crime involving moral turpitude, including fraud, theft, or embezzlement; and (g) if you breach any of the terms of your employment contract.

2. **Compensation**   Your salary for the initial 12-month period will be $[dollar value] and $[dollar value] in the second 12-month period, each year payable in monthly installments. You will also be entitled to an incentive bonus calculated as follows: [Percentage]% of your collected production when such collections exceeds $[dollar value] in the first year and $[dollar value] in the second year. The bonus each year will be calculated and paid on a semiannual basis. You will also be entitled to receive a one-time signing bonus of $[dollar value] if you sign your employment contract before [Month, Date, Year].

A portion of your compensation may be paid for by proceeds received from [Name of hospital] under the terms and conditions of a hospital recruitment agreement. The parties to this agreement will be the hospital and the practice only. However, forgiveness of any advances made by the hospital will be directly contingent upon the length of time you remain with the practice. Therefore, should your employment terminate for any reason, the practice will require you to repay to it any amounts the practice repays the hospital, in no matter what form, per the terms and conditions in the hospital recruitment agreement. [**Note:** Use this if the practice signs a hospital recruitment agreement with the hospital.]

3. **Benefits**   In addition to your base compensation and incentive bonus, the practice will pay for the following: (a) health insurance, (b) malpractice insurance, (c) continuing medical education (CME) costs, (d) medical license fee, (e) board certification exam fee, (f) reasonable cellular phone costs, and (g) a pager. You will also be entitled to a moving cost allowance for relocating to [Location.]

You will be entitled to two weeks of paid vacation, 10 working days as paid sick leave, and four days paid time off for CME or the board certification exam.

4. **Disability Leave**   In case of absence because of your illness or injury, your base salary will continue for a period not exceeding 30 days per calendar year, plus any unused vacation time and sick leave. You will be entitled to any incentive bonus payments that may be

due to you as collections are received on your prior production. Absence in excess of 30 days would be without pay. Unused sick leave cannot be carried over to succeeding years, nor will it be paid for at any time.

5. **Exclusive Employment**   As an employee, you will be involved full-time in the practice and you may not take any outside employment during the term of your employment agreement without the practice's written approval. However, you will be entitled to keep compensation from honorariums, royalties, and copyrights if approved by the practice in writing. If the practice does not give approval, then the income from such activities shall remain the property of the practice.

6. **Termination Compensation**   Should your employment terminate for any reason, you will be entitled to accrued but unpaid base compensation, earned but unpaid incentive bonus, and unused vacation leave.

7. **Nonsolicitation**   During the course of your employment, the practice will introduce and make available to you its contacts and referring physician relationships, ongoing patient flow, general hospital sources, business and professional relationships, and the like. Since you have not been in private practice in the area previously, you acknowledge that you currently have no established patients following you. If there should be a termination, the practice will not restrict your ability to practice medicine in the area; however, it will require you to enter into a nonsolicitation agreement in which you agree not to solicit the employees of the practice nor its patients to follow you into your new medical practice. [**Note:** Insert Covenant Not to Compete here, if applicable.]

8. **Employee-Only Status**   During the term of your employment, you will not be required to contribute any money toward the practice's equipment or operations, but likewise your work will give you no financial interest in the assets of the practice. However, the practice intends to offer you the opportunity to buy into the ownership of the practice as set forth in item 9 below.

9. **Ownership Opportunity**   At the end of your employment period, the practice will evaluate your relationship and may offer you the

opportunity to become a co-owner in the practice (or enter into an office-sharing relationship). This offer is not mandatory and is at the total discretion of the practice. Should an offer not be tendered for some reason, the practice will wait until the end of your next 12-month employment period to decide whether to tender an offer of co-ownership.

If an offer of co-ownership is made, Dr. [Name of physician] will discuss with you the following: (*a*) what percentage of the practice you will be allowed to acquire, (*b*) how best to value such interest, and (*c*) how you will pay for the acquisition of such interest. The practice hopes to achieve mutually agreeable solutions to these ownership issues.

We hope this offer meets with your approval. If so, please contact Dr. [Name of physician] as soon as possible. This letter is not intended to be a legally binding agreement; it is, rather, a tool to be used to prepare your formal physician employment agreement. If you should have any questions, please do not hesitate to contact myself or Dr. [Name of physician] at your convenience.

Sincerely,
[Name], CPA

APPENDIX ITEM 18-02

PHYSICIAN EMPLOYMENT AGREEMENT OUTLINE

I. DURATION OF THE CONTRACT

A. Length of the contract

    1. Option: Annual with automatic renewal

B. Effective date of the contract

II. CONDITIONS UNDER WHICH CONTRACT CAN BE TERMINATED

A. Voluntary termination by employee or employer with thirty (30) days' written notice

B. Death of employee

C. Suspension, revocation, or cancellation of employee's right to practice medicine in the State of [State]

D. Employee loses privileges to any hospital at which practice regularly maintains admission privileges

E. Employee fails or refuses to follow reasonable policies or directives established by the practice

F. Employee commits acts amounting to gross negligence or willful misconduct to the detriment of the practice or its patients

G. Employee is convicted of a crime involving moral turpitude, including fraud, theft, or embezzlement

H. Employee breaches terms of the employment contract

I. Employee becomes and remains disabled in excess of three (3) consecutive months

III. COMPENSATION

A. Amount of annual salary

B. Incentive bonus, calculated as follows: [formula]

C. Determine how long physician will be paid during period of disability and how much

IV. BENEFITS

A. Health insurance

B. Retirement plan contribution

C. Malpractice insurance

    1. Malpractice tail-end premium?

D. Dues, books, and periodicals

E. Licenses

F. CME expenses

    1. Annual allowance of $[dollar amount]

G. Entertainment

H. Automobile

I. Relocation

J. Vacation leave

K. Sick leave

L. Life and disability insurance

M. Cellular phone

N. Pager

O. Other

V. OUTSIDE INCOME

A. Decide on the type of outside income the physician can retain and the type of outside income earned by the physician that the practice will be entitled to retain.

B. At the same time as (A), discuss the physician's restrictions on outside employment.

VI. PHYSICIAN'S DUTIES

A. Required work hours

B. Required on-call schedule

C. Discuss any restrictions on the acceptance of new patients by the physician.

D. Discuss any provision if the physician is called to jury duty or related duty.

VII. TERMINATION COMPENSATION

A. Determine how much the physician will be paid if employment is terminated.

VIII. OPPORTUNITY TO BUY INTO PRACTICE OWNERSHIP

A. How long after joining the practice?

B. What exactly will the physician be allowed to buy into?

    1. Accounts receivable

    2. Hard assets of the practice

    3. Goodwill

C. How will the assets be valued?

    1. By independent appraiser

    2. By fixed formula

D. If applicable, how will accounts receivable be valued?

E. How will fixed assets be valued?

F. How will the buy-in price be paid for?

IX. REASONABLENESS OF COVENANT NOT TO COMPETE

X. OTHER ISSUES

APPENDIX ITEM 18-03
SAMPLE PHYSICIAN EMPLOYMENT AGREEMENT

This PHYSICIAN EMPLOYMENT AGREEMENT (this "Agreement") is made and entered this _____ day of _____, 2001 (the "Effective Date"), by and between Mason Otolaryngology Associates, P.L.L.C., a Texas Limited Liability Company ("Company") and Phil Wheat, M.D., ("Physician").

RECITALS

A. The Company desires to retain the services of Physician and Physician desires to be employed by the Company;

B. Physician is duly licensed to practice medicine in the State of Texas and is highly experienced in the field of Otolaryngology;

C. Company desires that its patients receive the highest quality medical services; and

D. Company desires to retain Physician to provide professional medical services for the Company's patients pursuant to the provisions of the Agreement, and Physician agrees to provide the services.

AGREEMENTS

NOW, THEREFORE, for and in consideration of the premises and of the mutual covenants and agreements hereinafter stipulated, the parties agree and covenant as follows:

ARTICLE I: EMPLOYMENT

1.01 **Engagement** The Company employs Physician, and Physician accepts employment with the Company, to render professional medical services to the patients of the Company, as determined by the Members of the Company ("Members") in the manner and to the extent permitted by law and the applicable canons of professional ethics. Physician shall maintain regular full-time office/work hours and on-call rotation in accordance with Company policies that are uniformly applied to all physician employees of the Company. Except as may be otherwise provided for in this Agreement, during the term of the Agreement, Physician shall not, without the prior written consent of the Company, engage in the practice of medicine except as an employee of the Company or directly or indirectly engage in any professional or business activity that competes with the business of the Company, that duplicates a service provided by the Company or that is adverse to the business of the Company, unless the Company agrees otherwise. In the performance of professional medical services under this Agreement, Physician shall employ his own means and methods, shall exercise his own professional judgment, and shall not be subject to the control or direction of any other person.

1.02 **Right to Fees** Any and all Professional Fees generated during the term of this Agreement shall belong to the Company. "Professional Fees" shall include, but not be limited to, fees or remuneration generated by the provision of professional medical services by Physician in his capacity as an employee of the Company, the compensation received for administrative services provided to hospitals or other health care providers, and any royalties, honoraria, or the like from similar professionally related activities. The Company, at its sole discretion, shall establish the fees to be charged for professional services. It is specifically understood and agreed that Physician shall have no right or claim to any portion of Professional Fees, except as otherwise provided in this Agreement. The decision of the Company shall be final and binding in the event of a disagreement concerning the application of this Section.

1.03 **Managed-Care Agreements** From time to time, the Company may enter into managed-care or network agreements with third-party payors, employers, or governmental entities that may require the Company and/or Physician to engage in utilization review or peer review activities. Physician will fully cooperate in such activities and will comply with any and all requirements of any managed-care or network agreement to which the Company becomes a party. If required by any managed-care entity or network, Physician will execute the managed-care or network agreement individually, notwithstanding that all fees generated by such agreement during the term of this Agreement will belong to the Company. Physician shall have no authority to, and shall not, execute agreements binding Company unless Physician is duly authorized to do so by the

Company. During the term of this Agreement and thereafter, Physician shall refrain from interfering with or disturbing the contractual relationships between the Company and any managed care organization.

1.04   Patients and Records of the Company   Without superseding any patient's right to choose a provider of health or medical services, Physician acknowledges that all patients for whom professional services are provided by Physician shall be patients of the Company and not of the Physician. During the term of this Agreement or any time thereafter, Physician shall not induce, solicit, or encourage any patient who has received or is receiving health or medical services from the Company to seek such services from another provider, including Physician. Subject to applicable law regarding medical records, all medical, patient, business, financial, or other records, papers and documents generated by Physician, the Company, or employees or agents of the Company shall belong to the Company, and Physician shall have no right to keep or retain such records, papers, or documents after this Agreement is terminated; provided, however, that Physician shall have reasonable access to such records, papers, or documents when reasonably required, including the ability to make copies thereof (including records kept in electronic media) at Physician's expense, provided that proper patient consents have been given. In addition, Physician shall be given copies of such records in the event of any action, claim, inquiry, investigation or litigation. This paragraph does not restrict a patient's right to obtain copies of his or his medical records from the Company. Upon termination of this Agreement, any outstanding accounts receivable shall belong solely to the Company and shall not be billed or collected by Physician even if the patient leaves the Company and continues to see the Physician.

1.05   Physician Recruitment Agreement   For the initial twelve- (12) month term of this agreement, Physician and Company acknowledge that Physician is a party to that certain Physician Recruitment Agreement by and between Physician and Mason Healthcare System within an initial one- (1) year term. Pursuant to such Physician Recruitment Agreement, Mason Healthcare System will be paying Physician certain sums on a monthly basis for one (1) year. The Parties understand that such agreement is a material basis for Company and Physician to enter into this Employment Agreement. Physician's salary herein is based upon Company receiving all funds paid by Mason Healthcare System pursuant to section ___ of the Physician Recruitment Agreement. Physician, as a condition of employment, agrees to immediately turn over to Company all sums received from the guaranteed minimum income payment as stated in section _____ of the Physician Recruitment Agreement. Physician shall endorse over to Company all such sums, which shall become the property of the Company.

ARTICLE II: DUTIES

2.01 **Professional Duties** Physician shall provide professional medical services exclusively for the Company at facilities used by the Company or at other locations as the Company determines. Physician shall not engage in the practice of medicine except as an employee of the Company. Physician agrees to use his best efforts in performing his duties. The Physician's essential duties shall also include, but not be limited to:

a. Keeping and maintaining, or causing to be kept and maintained, appropriate records, reports, claims, and correspondence necessary and appropriate in connection with all professional services rendered by Physician under this Agreement, all of which records, reports, claims, and correspondence shall belong to the Company;

b. Promoting, to the extent permitted by law and the applicable canons of professional ethics, the professional practice of the Company;

c. Attending, to the extent required by policies of the Company and the applicable canons of professional ethics, the administrative duties of the professional practice of the Company;

d. Performing all acts reasonably necessary to maintain and improve Physician's professional skills;

e. Assisting the Company in fulfilling its contractual obligations, if any; and

f. Providing professional medical care to patients of the Company in accordance with the Company's professional standards of quality and practice protocols and policies adopted by the Company from time to time that protocols and policies shall be uniformly applied to all physician employees of the Company.

2.02 **Representations/Warranties** Physician represents and warrants that:

a. He has and during the term of this Agreement shall maintain a valid and unrestricted license to practice medicine in the State of Texas;

b. He has and during the term of this Agreement shall maintain in good standing and without restriction all state and federal certificates and registrations necessary to prescribe drugs, medications, or controlled substances in the State of Texas;

c. He has, or shall use his good faith efforts to, seek and obtain, and during the term of this Agreement shall maintain medical staff privileges at health care facilities as required by the Company; and

d. He has not been disciplined by any professional or peer review organization, governmental agency, or hospital medical staff for any action or omission based on quality of care.

2.03 Reporting Obligation Physician has an affirmative obligation as a condition of employment to report to the Company any investigation or inquiry by any regulatory agency, governmental authority, or professional society regarding any item or activity listed in Section 4.2(A) of this Agreement.

ARTICLE III: COMPENSATION

3.01 Salary During the initial term of this Agreement, Physician's annual base salary shall be two hundred thousand dollars ($200,000) for the first year of this Agreement. Payment for professional services shall be paid in equal monthly installments or in the manner and on the timetable in which the Company's payroll is customarily handled, in no event less frequently than monthly, or at such more frequent intervals as the Company and Physician may hereafter agree to from time to time.

3.02 Bonus Physician shall be entitled to a bonus during the initial twelve- (12) month period of this Agreement. In the event that during the initial twelve- (12) month period of this Agreement, the net collections attributable to the professional services rendered by Physician are greater than $510,000, then Physician shall receive thirty percent (30%) of any such collections exceeding the $510,000 collected within the initial twelve-month period.

The bonus, if any, shall be calculated and paid within one (1) month following the end of the initial twelve- (12) month period, so long as such payment does not render the Company insolvent. Upon termination of this Agreement for any reason, except for termination with cause, the Company shall calculate and pay Physician any bonus that accrued and was earned prior to the termination of this Agreement, if such termination occurs within the initial twelve-month period.

3.03 **Vacation Time** Physician shall be entitled to two (2) weeks' paid vacation during the first year of the Agreement. In the second year, Physician shall be entitled to three (3) weeks' paid vacation.

3.04 **Sick Leave** Physician shall be entitled to sick leave, which accrues each month for a total of ten (10) working days per year.

3.05 **Continuing Medical Education** Physician shall be entitled to five (5) days per year of continuing medical education leave and an annual allowance of $2,500 for reasonable continuing medical educational expenses. Any unused portion of the continuing medical education allowance shall belong to the Company.

3.06 **Professional Liability Insurance** During the term of this Physician Employment Agreement, the Company shall maintain at its sole cost and expense professional liability insurance in an amount of at least $200,000 per occurrence and $600,000 annual aggregate, or other amounts as determined by the Company, covering Physician for his acts and omissions in the performance of his professional duties under this Agreement. In the event Physician ceases to be an employee of the Company, or otherwise ceases to practice medicine, the Physician shall be responsible for obtaining "tail" professional liability insurance coverage in an amount equal to the malpractice insurance carried during the term of the Agreement or in such an amount and for such a period of time determined by mutual agreement of Physician and the Company. The Company shall be named as an additional insured under the "tail" professional liability policy. Physician shall be responsible for paying all premiums for "tail" insurance coverage. During the term of this Agreement, the Company may maintain professional liability insurance covering the Company for the acts and omissions of its physicians.

3.07 **Business Expenses** Subject to approval of the Company, Physician shall be entitled to reimbursement for all reasonable and necessary business expenses incurred by him hereunder upon presentation of appropriate documentation of such expenses.

3.08 **Insurance** The Company shall provide to Physician group medical insurance coverage, life insurance coverage, and short-term disability coverage consistent with the coverage the Company is providing to its other physician employees similarly situated.

3.09 **Dues and Licenses** The Company shall provide to Physician all medical society dues, association dues, and all necessary licenses.

3.10 **Retirement Plan** Physician will be eligible to participate in the Company's retirement plan one year after employment.

ARTICLE IV: TERM AND TERMINATION

4.01 **Term** The term of this Agreement shall commence on the Effective Date and shall continue for a period of twenty-four (24) months, unless sooner terminated by the Company or Physician in accordance with the terms of this Agreement.

At the end of your initial twelve- (12) month employment period, the Company will evaluate your production and relationship and shall make a new offer of compensation for the second year of employment.

4.02 **Termination for Cause**

a. By the Company The Company may terminate this Agreement immediately upon written notice to Physician, which notice shall describe the reason for termination, for any of the following reasons, which shall be deemed to be "cause":

   i. The suspension, surrender, revocation, or cancellation of Physician's right to practice medicine in the State of Texas or to prescribe controlled substances;

   ii. The discipline of Physician by final action of any professional medical organization;

   iii. The reduction, suspension, surrender, non-renewal, or revocation of Physician's membership on the medical staff of any hospital or other health care provider or any adverse action against

Physician's clinical privileges at any hospital or other health care provider taken as a result of professional quality or competence issues related to Physician's practice of medicine;

iv. Physician's resignation from any professional medical organization under threat of disciplinary action;

v. The imposition of any restrictions or limitations by any governmental authority having jurisdiction over Physician to such an extent that he can not engage in the professional practice for which he was employed;

vi. Physician's failure or refusal to perform the duties required under this Agreement or to comply with the policies, standards, and regulations of the Company that may be established from time to time and of which he has written notice; Notwithstanding the foregoing, all such policies, standards and regulations shall be uniformly applied to all physician employees of the Company;

vii. Physician is found guilty of unprofessional or unethical conduct by any board, institution, organization, or professional society having any privilege or right to pass upon the professional conduct of the Physician;

viii. Physician's conviction in a court of competent jurisdiction of any felony offense or any misdemeanor offense involving moral turpitude;

ix. Physician, for reasons other than illness, disability, family emergency, vacation scheduled and approved in advance by Company, holidays, or other reasons outside of the Physician's control, devotes less that his full time to his duties under this Agreement;

x. The commission by Physician of an act of fraud upon, or materially evidencing bad faith, dishonesty, or material disloyalty toward the Company during the term of this Agreement;

xi. The commission by Physician of (i) any criminal offense other than minor traffic violations, (ii) any public or private conduct that offends decency or morality, causes Physician to be held in public ridicule or scorn, or causes a public scandal, or (iii) any conduct that may harm the reputation or operations of the Company or that is detrimental to the interests of the Company;

xii. The misappropriation of any funds or property of the Company by Physician during the term of this Agreement; or

xiii. Physician takes any action, fails to take any action, or engages in any activity, the result of which is contrary to the interest of Company.

Notwithstanding the foregoing, prior to terminating the Physician's employment under Section 4.2(A)(6) or 4.2(A)(10), Company shall first give Physician written notice specifying the alleged breach under these subsections and thirty (30) days following the receipt of such notice to correct such alleged breach(es).

b. Reporting Obligation   Physician has an affirmative obligation as a condition of employment to report to the Company any investigation or inquiry by any regulatory agency, governmental authority, or professional society regarding any item or activity listed in Subsection (A) above.

c. By Physician   The Physician may terminate this Agreement immediately upon written notice to Company, which notice shall describe the reason for termination, for either of the following reasons:

   i. The Company dissolves;

   ii. The Company loses any certification or otherwise becomes unable, due to any act or omission, to continue to operate under Texas law;

   iii. In the case of a non-monetary breach, the Company materially fails to perform its duties under this Agreement and such failure continues for thirty (30) days after receipt of written notice;

   iv. In the case of a monetary breach, the Company materially fails to perform its duties under this Agreement and such failure continues for ten (10) days after receipt of written notice; or

   v. The Company becomes insolvent, makes an assignment for the benefit of creditors or is subject to any bankruptcy filing or procedure.

4.03   Termination Without Cause   This Agreement may be terminated by Physician or the Company without cause upon ninety (90) days' prior written notice. In the event of such notice, the Company may limit Physician's activities during the notice period to participation on the call schedule or to treatment of only those patients that Physician has treated prior to the notice date, or the Company may impose any other restrictions it deems necessary and reasonable, provided the Company must still continue to pay Physician his full base salary specified in Section 3.1.

4.04 Termination upon Death or Disability This Agreement shall automatically terminate upon Physician's death. Any compensation or fringe benefits due at the time of death shall be paid on a pro-rata basis. This Agreement shall also be deemed to terminate upon the commencement date of Physician's disability that does continue for ninety (90) days. For purposes of this Agreement, the term "disability" means a documented illness or incapacity that keeps Physician from resuming Physician's full-time medical practice for at least ninety (90) days; provided, however, that such ninety- (90) day period shall not be deemed to be broken if Physician returns to work for no more than three (3) consecutive working days during any given attempt to resume his regular work schedule. Physician's base salary will continue for a period not exceeding sixty (60) days during the disability period, plus any unused vacation time and sick leave.

4.05 Effect of Termination Upon any termination of this Agreement, except for termination with cause, the Company shall pay Physician the compensation and any accrued but unpaid bonus specified under Section 3.2 due through the date of termination. Physician shall not be entitled to receive any accounts receivable of Company except for amounts due to Physician as compensation under Sections 3.1 and 3.2 of this Agreement. The payments hereunder shall constitute the full and final satisfaction of the terms of this Agreement, and Physician shall have no further claims against the Company for compensation under any section of this Agreement.

ARTICLE V: ASSIGNMENT OF RIGHT TO BILL

As a condition of the Physician's employment, Physician assigns to the Company any right the Physician might have from time to time, during the term of this Agreement, to bill and receive payment from any individual or third-party payor, including, without limitation, the Medicare and Medicaid programs and any managed-care payor, for professional services rendered by Physician under this Agreement. Physician acknowledges that the Company shall submit these billings in its own name and that Physician is precluded from billing any individual or third-party payor for Physician's professional services under this Agreement unless required by a third-party payor, in which event Physician shall bill such services with the understanding that all fees generated for services performed during the term of this Agreement from such billings shall belong to the Company.

ARTICLE VI: CONFIDENTIALITY OF INFORMATION

Physician agrees to keep confidential and not to use or to disclose to others during the term of this Agreement and for any time thereafter, except as expressly consented to in writing by Company or as required by law, any secrets or confidential technology, proprietary information, patient lists, or trade secrets of the Company, or any matter or thing ascertained by Physician through Physician's affiliation with the Company, the use or disclosure of which matter or thing might reasonably be construed to be contrary to the best interest of the Company. Physician further agrees that should Physician leave the employment of the Company, Physician will neither take nor retain, without prior written authorization from the Company, any papers, patient lists, fee books, patient records, files, other documents, copies thereof, or other confidential information of any kind belonging to the Company pertaining to the Company's patients, business, sales, financial condition, services, or products.

Without limiting other possible remedies to the Company for the breach of this covenant, Physician agrees that injunctive or other equitable relief shall be available to enforce this covenant, such relief to be without the necessity of posting a bond, cash, or otherwise. Physician further agrees that if any restriction in this paragraph is held by any court to be unenforceable or unreasonable, a lesser restriction shall be enforced in its place and the remaining restrictions in this paragraph shall be enforced independently of each other.

ARTICLE VII: MISCELLANEOUS

7.01 **Notices** All notices hereunder by either party to the other shall be in writing, delivered personally, by certified or registered mail, return receipt requested, or by Federal Express or Express Mail, and shall be deemed to have been duly given when delivered personally or when received by the United States mail, postage prepaid, at the last known respective addresses of the Company and Physician. Either party may change from time to time by written notice transmitted in the manner prescribed above, the address to which notices are to be sent.

7.02 **Assignability** Physician shall not assign or transfer this Agreement or any of his rights, duties or obligations under this Agreement without the prior written consent of the Company. The Company may assign this Agreement to a successor medical practice upon notice to Physician.

7.03 **Enforceability** Should any provisions of this Agreement be held invalid or unconstitutional by any governmental body or court of competent jurisdiction, that holding shall not diminish the validity of any other provision of this Agreement.

7.04 **Governing Law** This Agreement shall be governed by and interpreted in accordance with the laws of the State of Texas.

7.05 **Construction** Common nouns and pronouns and all other terms shall be deemed to refer to the masculine, feminine, neuter, and singular and/or plural, as the identity of the person or persons, firm, or Company may in the context require.

7.06 **Binding Effect** The provisions of the Agreement shall insure the benefit of and shall be binding upon the heirs, personal representatives, successors, assigns, estates, and legatees of each of the parties.

7.07 **Multiple Counterparts** This Agreement and its exhibits, if any, shall be in writing and shall be executed in multiple copies. Each multiple copy shall be deemed an original, but all multiple copies together shall constitute one and the same instrument.

7.08 **Waiver of Breach** The waiver by either party of a breach or violation of any provision of this Agreement shall not operate as, or be construed to be, a waiver of any subsequent breach of the same or another provision.

7.09 **Entire Agreement** The making, execution, and delivery of this Agreement by the parties has not been induced by any representations, statements, warranties or agreements other than those expressed in this Agreement. This Agreement constitutes the entire agreement in effect between the parties pertaining to the employment relationship between the Company and Physician and supercedes all prior or contemporaneous agreements, understandings, or negotiations of the parties. THIS AGREEMENT REPRESENTS THE FINAL AGREEMENT BETWEEN THE PARTIES AND MAY NOT BE CONTRADICTED BY EVIDENCE OF PRIOR OR CONTEMPORANEOUS AGREEMENTS BY THE PARTIES. THERE ARE NO UNWRITTEN ORAL AGREEMENTS BETWEEN THE PARTIES AS OF THE SIGNING OF THIS AGREEMENT.

7.10 **Amendments** This Agreement shall not be modified, amended, or supplemented except in a written instrument executed by both parties.

IN WITNESS WHEREOF, the parties have executed this Agreement in duplicate originals effective as of the Effective Date.

The Company: Mason Otolaryngology Associates, P.L.L.C.

By: _____

Name: Reed Tinsley, M.D.

Title: _____

Physician:

_____

Phil Wheat, M.D.

APPENDIX ITEM 18-04
INCENTIVE BONUS RECOMMENDATION

Memorandum

To: Dr. Roger Hutchison
From: Phil Wheat
CC: File
Date: October 8, 2001
Re: Bonus Program/Dave Thompson

Per your request, here is my recommendation for a bonus plan for Dave Thompson. It is my understanding he is currently making $60,000 per year and in the past has received a $10,000 bonus each year. Since your overhead and A/R are already well below industry averages and your collection ratios look good too, the plan suggested below is based largely on maintaining and growing the practice.

5 percent of current base salary

Incentive bonus if operating expenses at the end of the year equal 52 percent to 58 percent of practice collections. Operating expenses do not include physician-related expenses and physician compensation.

10 percent of current base salary

Additional incentive bonus if operating expenses at end of year are less than 52 percent of practice collections.

5 percent of current base salary

Incentive bonus is practice's net collection ratio equals or exceeds 95 percent.

5 percent of current base salary

Incentive bonus if accounts receivable ratio at end of year is equal to or less than 1.5 times average monthly production for the immediate 12-month period.

Collections Growth Incentive

Dave needs incentives for increasing the collected revenues of the practice. I suggest giving him 3 percent of all collections exceeding a designated collection target. In developing the target, you would start with practice collections for the prior year and add a targeted growth rate (for example, 10 to 25 percent). If Dave can get collections over the targeted growth rate, he will receive 3 percent of the excess.

For example, if practice collections for the prior 12-month period were $1,000,000 and you wanted to target a 10 percent increase in the next year, Dave would get 3 percent of all collections exceeding $1,100,000.

Discretionary Bonus

You can allocate a $2,500 discretionary bonus. This bonus will be based upon a designed grade point system and each doctor will complete the "Administrator Satisfaction Grading Form." Based on how each doctor individually grades Dave, he will receive all or part of the $2,500 bonus.

These are just a few ideas. I look forward to talking with you about them at a later time.

APPENDIX ITEM 18-05
PHYSICIAN QUESTIONNAIRE

Compensation Plan

Physician's Name:_____Date _____

1. How would you rate your medical practice's distribution plan?
   ❑ Generous ❑ Reasonable ❑ Marginal
   ❑ Unfair ❑ Disastrous

2. How would you rate your level of compensation?
   ❑ Extremely overcompensated
   ❑ Overcompensated
   ❑ Basically fair
   ❑ Undercompensated
   ❑ Extremely undercompensated

3. Do you understand the present income distribution plan? ❑ Yes ❑ No

4. How would you rate the level of complexity of your existing income distribution plan?
   ❑ Extremely complex
   ❑ Complex
   ❑ Moderate
   ❑ Simple
   ❑ Very simple

5. Do you feel that your income distribution or compensation plan is adequately achieving its goals?

   _____

6. What do you like most about your existing plan?

   _____

7. What do you like least about your existing plan?

   _____

8. What would you recommend as a change to the existing income distribution or compensation plan?

   _____

APPENDIX ITEM 19-01

SUMMARY OF MANAGED-CARE PLAN REQUIREMENTS

[Use this form to summarize specific billing requirements of managed-care plans.]
Prepare for each managed-care plan with which the practice is a provider.

Name of plan					
Phone number					
Address					
Name of provider's representative					
Precertify services?					
List specific services that must be provided					

Filing deadline for claim submission to the plan			
Required forms that must be filed with the plan			
Hospital referral*			
Diagnostic referral*			
Lab referral*			
Surgical clinic referral*			
List other requirements:			
1.			
2.			
3.			

*List all hospitals, diagnostic centers, labs, and surgical clinics to which the patient can be admitted or referred.

APPENDIX ITEM 19-02
WITHHOLD STATUS LETTER FOR MANAGED-CARE CARRIERS

[Date]
[Insurance Carrier Name]
[Address]

Attn: Chief Financial Officer

Dear Sir or Madam:

I am a contract provider in your [Name the plan] managed-care product and as such have been subject to a withhold of [percent] for the past year. As of the anniversary date of the plan [show date] my records indicate that $[amount] has been withheld from health-care service payments due to me. Please provide me with an analysis of my provider account, if your records differ from mine with respect to amounts withheld from my payments. In addition, please provide me with an analysis of the withhold due to me based upon my utilization in the plan, along with an explanation of the calculation and an estimate of when I can expect payment of these funds.

Thank you for your cooperation in this matter.

Sincerely,

[Signature]

APPENDIX ITEM 19-03
HMO CHECKLIST

1. What services is the provider obligated to provide under the capitated fee?

2. Is the provider bound by the insurer's interpretation of the policy (particularly with respect to high cost, new, and experimental techniques)?

3. Is the provider bound to the insurer's amendments to the policy?

4. Is the provider obligated to treat pre-existing illnesses under the capitation fee?

5. Can the provider provide all the services allocated to it under the capitation rate? Does the insurer limit the provider's ability to subcontract those services it cannot provide?

6. Who is responsible for out-of-area coverage of members assigned to the provider? The provider or the insurer?

7. To whom are covered services due?

8. When is a person deemed to be eligible (for payment purposes)?

9. How are member eligibility disputes handled?

10. What fee schedule was used to build the payment rate? What utilization predictions were used to build the payment rate? Are they based on historical data of the same population? What information exists regarding the health, age, and sex of the expected membership population? Will the insurer share its information, including actuarial assumptions, with the provider? May the provider renegotiate the capitation rates if the risk status of the enrollee population changes, for example, if the insurer begins to sell its product to the Medicare and Medicaid population?

11. What information will the insurer give the provider during the contract year?

12. When and how will the provider be paid? Will the capitation rates reflect adjustments for age, sex, plan benefits, and co-payment levels?

13. Who is entitled to bill other health insurers in coordination of benefit cases? In subrogation cases? If the insurer is entitled to do so, is it "chase and pay" or "pay and chase"?

14. What protection is available to the provider for unexpected utilization?

15. What protection is available to the provider if it has an unexpectedly small membership population?

16. Is there contract language made non-negotiable by legislation or regulation?

17. Will the provider offer "most favored nation" prices?

18. How are the risk pools constructed?

APPENDIX ITEM 19-04
MANAGED-CARE CONTRACT

PHYSICIAN SERVICES AGREEMENT

This Physician Services Agreement ("Agreement") is entered into this [date] day of [month] by and between [Name of managed-care organization], a [type of corporation] organized and existing under the laws of the State of [State], ("MCO"), and [Name of Physician], a physician licensed to practice medicine in the State of [State], as appropriate ("Physician").

PREAMBLE

WHEREAS, MCO has executed or will execute one or more written Service Agreements with employers, individuals, or their organizations, to provide health care coverage to individual subscribers and their dependents (hereinafter called "Members)"; and

   WHEREAS, Physician desires to provide health services to Members; and

   WHEREAS, MCO desires to enter into an Agreement with Physician relating to the provision of health care services to Members through MCO prepaid health care products.

   NOW, THEREFORE, the parties hereby agree as follows:

ARTICLE I: DEFINITIONS

1.01 **"Agreement"** shall mean this Physician Services Agreement and any attachments hereto.

1.02 **"Benefit Year"** shall mean the fiscal year beginning January 1, and ending December 31 of each year. The term of this Agreement shall be the remainder of the Benefit Year for the year in which it is mutually executed, and then each successive Benefit Year thereafter unless it is duly terminated. Risk or surplus sharing arrangements shall be calculated with respect to Covered Services performed during a Benefit Year.

1.03 **"Covered Services"** shall mean those health care services specified in a service agreement between MCO and a subscriber group or individual, which shall be made available to MCO Members on a prepaid basis, subject to applicable co-payments or deductibles, by a health care provider contractually affiliated with MCO.

1.04 **"Emergency"** shall mean a life-endangering bodily injury or sudden serious illness that requires a Member to seek immediate attention under circumstances which effectively preclude the Member from seeking such care from or through a Participating Physician.

1.05 **"Hospital"** shall mean a hospital that has agreed contractually to serve as an MCO-affiliated provider of hospital services to MCO Members and means an acute general hospital that provides inpatient diagnostic and therapeutic facilities for surgical or medical diagnosis, treatment, and care of injured and sick persons by or under the supervision of a staff or one or more duly licensed Physicians; which provides continuous nursing service by or under the supervision of registered professional nurses; and is not a federal hospital or a place primarily for the aged, or a skilled nursing facility, or a nursing home, or an institution of rehabilitation; and is an institution that operates as an acute general hospital pursuant to applicable state or local laws.

1.06 **"Independent Practice Association"** ("IPA") shall mean an incorporated or otherwise organized group of independently practicing physicians that has admitting privileges with at least one Hospital and which has contracted with MCO to provide medical services to Members.

1.07 **"Member"** shall mean any individual and his or her eligible dependents, if any, enrolled with MCO for the provision of Covered Services.

1.08 **"MCO Service Area"**   The area approved by the State Department of Insurance which shall be the counties of [list counties].

1.09 **"Out of Area"** shall mean, in the context of Emergency care and risk/surplus sharing, the geographic area outside a thirty (30) mile radius of MCO Service Area.

1.10 **"Participating Physicians"** shall mean all Primary-Care Physicians and Specialist Physicians, generally.

1.11 **"Physician"** shall mean the party hereto named in the Preamble to this Agreement who shall be a Physician duly licensed to practice medicine and who has privileges to admit patients to the acute care facilities of at least one Hospital.

1.12 **"Physician Group"** shall mean an unassociated group of independently practicing Physicians that has admitting privileges with at least one Hospital and that has contracted with MCO to provide medical services to Members.

1.13 **"Primary-Care Physician"** shall mean any physician who has contracted with MCO to provide primary care and is practicing medicine in the primary-care field of internal medicine, family practice, general practice, or pediatrics.

1.14 **"Specialist Physician"** shall mean any physician who practices in a specialty area other than primary care (internal medicine, family practice, general practice, or pediatrics) and has contracted with MCO to provide specialty services upon referral from a Primary-Care Physician.

1.15 **"Participating Provider"** shall mean any physician, hospital, health professional, home health agency, laboratory, alcohol dependence treatment center, or such other provider or entity that has contracted with Provider to provide health care services to Members.

ARTICLE II: PHYSICIAN'S GENERAL OBLIGATIONS

2.01 **General** Physician agrees to provide medically necessary services as indicated by his or her specialty to Members, including care under Emergency conditions. Physicians shall be available and accessible during regular business hours, and shall be available and accessible for services twenty-four (24) hours a day, seven (7) days a week, through shared call or other arrangements satisfactory to Provider.

2.02 **Referrals**   Physician shall use his or her best efforts when consistent with sound medical practice to refer Members to Participating Physicians and Participating Providers, except in cases of Emergencies, or in cases in which no Participating Provider is available to perform the appropriate service. A referral authorization form shall be prepared by the Primary-Care Physician to all other Participating Physicians and Participating Providers and processed in accordance with MCO quality assurance and medical management programs.

2.03 **Admissions**   Physician represents and warrants that for purposes of providing services to Members pursuant to this Agreement, Physician is affiliated with the Hospital listed under his or her signature, and is thereby a member of an Independent Practice Association (IPA) or a Physician Group associated with such Hospital. Physician shall share in the Physician Fund and Hospital Fund established by MCO for his or her IPA or Physician Group, as outlined in Article IV herein. Physician shall use his or her best efforts when consistent with sound medical practice to admit Members requiring hospital services to a Hospital with which he or she is associated. If services required by a Member are not available at such Hospital, or if such Hospital is at full capacity, Physician shall use his or her best efforts to admit such Members to another participating Hospital. Physician shall seek authorization from MCO for Hospital admission except in the case of Emergency admissions.

2.04 **Risk-Sharing and Medical Management Participation**   Physician agrees to participate in the risk-sharing arrangements as set forth in Article IV herein ("Reimbursement Methods") in order to facilitate effective medical management of Covered Services. Physician further agrees to comply with the medical management directives of the medical advisory committee (MAC), which will be composed of the medical directors of each IPA or risk-sharing pool in MCO's system of health care providers.

2.05 **Records**   Physician agrees to maintain standard medical records for Members and to provide such records and other information to MCO as may be requested and as permitted by law. Physician agrees that all records kept in connection with Physician's participation in MCO are subject to review and audit at any reasonable time by authorized MCO administrative staff.

2.06 **Promotional Material** Physician shall display promotional materials provided by MCO within Physician's office.

2.07 **Claims and Encounter Data** Physician agrees to furnish to MCO on a timely basis, on forms acceptable to MCO, claims or other data necessary to evaluate actual IPA or Physician Group/MCO utilization compared with MCO capitation and rating assumptions.

2.08 **Quality Assurance Participation** Physician agrees to cooperate with, participate in, and comply with medical management utilization review, quality assurance, peer review, and audit procedures of MCO or other programs that may be established by MCO to promote high standards of medical care. Physician agrees to the review of the medical, financial, administrative, and other records required for the above procedures, and to comply with all final determinations rendered by such procedures.

2.09 **Malpractice Coverage** Physician shall provide, and maintain at his or her own cost, medical malpractice insurance in adequate amounts as necessary to comply with [State] state law and good business practices. Physician shall provide evidence of such coverage to MCO upon request. Physician shall give MCO at least fifteen (15) days' advance notice of cancellation of such medical malpractice insurance.

2.10 **Nondiscrimination** Physician agrees, within the limits of his or her specialty: (*a*) not to differentiate or discriminate in the treatment of patients who are Members nor to differentiate or discriminate in the treatment of Members because of race, color, national origin, ancestry, religion, sex, marital status, or age and (*b*) to render health care services to Members in the same manner, in accordance with the same standards, and within the same time availability as offered his or her other patients.

2.11 **Grievance Resolution** Physician agrees that any dispute between Members and Physician or between Physician and MCO shall be resolved in accordance with MCO's Grievance Resolution Procedure, a copy of which is attached hereto as Exhibit 4.

2.12 **Out-of-Area Transfers** Physician shall assist MCO in facilitating the transfer of MCO Members receiving services in Out-of-Area health facilities to a Hospital if Member's condition warrants such transfer, subject to review by MCO's medical director. Subject to the approval of the transfer by MCO's medical director, MCO shall be responsible for the cost of transferring MCO Members from Out-of-Area health facilities to a Hospital.

ARTICLE III: MCO'S GENERAL OBLIGATIONS

3.01 **Marketing** MCO shall market its prepaid health care products and shall arrange to have Physician's name, office address, and specialty included in the list of Participating Physicians distributed to eligible Members, including marketing brochures and other marketing literature.

3.02 **Utilization and Peer Review Systems** MCO shall structure appropriate utilization review and peer review procedures as necessary to achieve and maintain cost-effective delivery of quality health care services by Participating Physicians and Hospitals.

3.03 **Organization of Risk-Sharing Pools** MCO agrees to assist Participating Physicians in the organization of individual practice associations or similar risk-sharing pools (hereafter generally referred to as "IPAs") for the purpose of facilitating effective medical management of health care services and risk-sharing arrangements. Each IPA will have its own Physician Fund and Hospital Fund, as described in Section 4.07 herein.

ARTICLE IV: REIMBURSEMENT METHOD FOR PROVISION OF COVERED SERVICES

4.01 **Physician to Seek Payment from MCO Only** For those health services determined by MCO to be Covered Services, Physician agrees that in no event, including but not limited to nonpayment by MCO, MCO insolvency, and breach of this Agreement, shall Physician bill, charge, collect a deposit from, seek compensation, remuneration, or reimbursement from, or have any recourse against subscriber, enrollee or persons other than MCO acting on their behalf for services provided pursuant to this Agreement. This provision shall not prohibit collection of supplemental charges or co-payments on MCO's behalf made in accordance with the terms of applicable Agreement between MCO and Members.

Physician further agrees that (*a*) this provision shall survive the termination of this Agreement regardless of the cause giving rise to termination and shall be construed to be for the benefit of Members and (*b*) this provision supersedes any oral or written contrary agreement now existing or hereafter entered into between Physician and Member or persons acting on their behalf.

Any modification, addition, or deletion to the provisions of this section shall become effective on a date no earlier than fifteen (15) days after the Commissioner of Insurance has received written notice of such proposed changes.

4.02 **Establishment of Physician Fund and Hospital Fund**   MCO shall establish a Physician Fund for each IPA or Physician Group in MCO's provider network. MCO shall establish a Hospital Fund to correspond with each Physician Fund. MCO shall deposit an actuarially determined portion of each Member's monthly premium payment, as set forth in Schedule II, into each Physician Fund, Physician Reserve Fund, and Hospital Fund (sometimes collectively referred to herein as "Funds"), except the amount deposited into the Physician Reserve Fund shall not be less than five percent (5%) of the amount deposited into Physician Fund. MCO shall pay Participating Physicians and Hospitals for Covered Services rendered to MCO Members from money collected by each of the Funds in accordance with the division of claims as set forth in Section 4.07 herein.

4.03 **IPA-Approved Fee Schedule**   Each IPA or Physician Group may submit its own schedule of current "Usual, Customary, and Reasonable" fees to MCO for approval or adjustments. MCO reserves the right to adjust the IPA's approved fee schedule rates. MCO shall review the approved fee schedule for adjustment at least once per Benefit Year.

4.04 **Physician Claims Submissions**   Physician agrees to submit to MCO, or its disbursing agent(s), statements for Covered Services rendered to Members, including a full itemization of services charges and treatment given. Physician understands that failure to submit proper statements may result in delayed reimbursement for services rendered. Statements must be submitted within (60) days from the date of service for payment to be made.

4.05 MCO Payment of Claims from Funds   MCO shall satisfy claims from Physicians for the provision of Covered Services to Members within a reasonable period of time, less any applicable deductible or co-payments due by Member. Payment for services shall be:

A. Primary-Care Physicians

1. The fee-for-service rate, according to the service or procedure indicated by the standard Current Procedural Code (CPT), such reimbursement to be at a Usual, Customary, and Reasonable rate in accordance with Schedule I and paragraph 4.03 herein or the billed charge, whichever is less, if Physician is assigned less than fifty (50) MCO Members;

2. An actuarially determined amount, as indicated in Schedule II, if Physician is assigned fifty (50) or more MCO Members;

3. The Usual, Customary, and Reasonable, fee-for-service rate in accordance with paragraph 4.03 herein, or the billed charge, whichever is less, for those services not indicated in Schedule I;

B. Specialist Physicians

1. The fee-for-service rate, according to the service or procedure indicated by CPT code, such reimbursement to be the Usual, Customary, and Reasonable rate in accordance with paragraph 4.03 herein, or the billed charge, whichever is less.

Furthermore, MCO, may, with thirty (30) days prior notification, reduce fees Schedule I, the actuarially determined amounts in Schedule II, or the fee schedule compiled in accordance with paragraph 4.03 by no more than thirty percent (30%) if ongoing utilization indicates a loss or deficit in the Funds at the end of Benefit Year.

4.06 MCO reserves the right to change or otherwise update fee Schedules I and II on an annual basis, to coincide with each Benefit Year.

4.07 Allocation of Covered Services to Funds

A. Physician Fund

1. The following Covered Services, rendered to an MCO Member shall be paid from the Physician Fund with which such Member's Primary-Care Physician is affiliated, regardless of whether the Covered Service was performed by Primary-Care Physician, a Participating Physician, or a physician who has not contracted with MCO but renders services to Members as authorized by MCO:

   a. All professional Covered Services, including but not limited to Emergency services required within MCO Service Area;

   b. All outpatient laboratory, X-ray, and other outpatient diagnostic or therapeutic procedures;

   c. Emergency room charges, both professional and facility;

   d. Amounts necessary to fund stoploss reinsurance (per Member per Benefit Year);

   e. Prosthetics, durable medical equipment and ambulance service;

   f. Any services deemed to be payable from the Physician Fund by MCO's Grievance Resolution Procedure.

2. Expenses which shall *not* be paid from the IPA's or Physician Group's Physician Fund are the following Covered Services:

   a. All surgical fees for procedures for which MCO's dental providers are capitated, including fees for such dental services that are provided on an inpatient basis if the IPA or Physician Group is otherwise responsible for medically necessary Covered Services. The professional anesthesia expense related to inpatient dental surgery is payable from the Physician Fund if such expense is not included in the Hospital charges.

   b. Speech therapy expenses for learning disorders or slow speech development. Speech therapy following an accident or stroke, however, is payable from the Physician Fund.

   c. Services rendered by any physician not affiliated with the IPA or Physician Group without authorization by Participating Physicians affiliated with the IPA or Physician Group except for medically necessary Emergency services received by a Member within MCO Service Area and except for those services deemed payable by MCO's Grievance Resolution Procedure.

d.　Outpatient dialysis, home health care, and Out-of Area Emergency services.

3.　When a Member, who has chosen Physician as his or her Primary-Care Physician, receives services from a Participating Physician who is not affiliated with Physician's IPA or Physician Group, the cost for such services shall be paid from the Physician Fund with which the Physician is affiliated to the Physician Fund with which the Participating Physician who rendered such services is affiliated. The Participating Physician shall then be paid out of his or her Physician Fund in accordance with Section 4.05 above.

B.　IPA or Physician Group's Hospital Fund

1.　Each Hospital shall participate with MCO and its referring IPA or Physician Group in the management of utilization of the IPA's or Physician Group's total Hospital Fund. The IPA's or Physician Group's total Hospital Fund available for payment of the Covered Services listed below shall be comprised of capitation amounts from premiums collected by MCO from each of its different health care coverage plans, less the capitation amounts necessary to fund a thirty thousand dollar ($30,000) stoploss provision offered by an insurance carrier to MCO. The stoploss provision protection applies to inpatient Hospital expenses incurred in the aggregate per Member per Benefit Year in excess of thirty thousand dollars ($30,000).

2.　Expenses which shall be paid from the IPA or Physician Group's Hospital Fund are the following Covered Services:

a.　Inpatient Hospital expenses incurred during IPA- or Physician-Group-authorized bed days. "IPA- or Physician-Group-authorized bed days" shall mean:

i.　Bed days in any Hospital or institution directly authorized by a Participating Physician affiliated with the IPA or Physician Group; or

ii.　Hospital bed days incurred incident to medical care rendered by a physician not affiliated with the IPA or Physician Group but authorized by a Participating Physician affiliated with the IPA or Physician Group; or

      iii. Emergency Hospital admissions that were medically necessary which occurred within MCO Service Area.

   b. Skilled Nursing Facility bed days authorized by a Participating Physician;

   c. Day surgery expenses authorized by a Participating Physician at any Hospital or surgical center;

   d. Home health care;

   e. Outpatient dialysis;

   f. Preadmission testing charges if admission subsequently occurs within forty-eight (48) hours of such testing.

3. When a Member, who has chosen Physician as his or her Primary-Care Physician, receives authorized services from a Participating Hospital that is not the Hospital with which Physician is affiliated, the cost for such services shall be paid by the Hospital Fund established for the Hospital with which Physician is affiliated, to the Hospital Fund established for the Participating Hospital that rendered the services.

4.08 Benefit Year-End Settlement

A. General

1. In any risk-sharing or surplus-sharing calculations, MCO will use an incurred date-of-service-received method of determining actual utilization with an appropriate factor added for incurred-but-not-yet-reported expenses for services rendered during Benefit Year.

2. Each individual Participating Physician's share of the surplus funds in either the IPA's or Physician Group's Physician Fund or the IPA's or Physician Group's Hospital Fund shall be equal to that individual Participating Physician's utilization from the Physician Fund for his or her services directly rendered to MCO Members during Benefit Year divided by the total utilization of all Participating Physicians affiliated with the IPA or Physician Group for services directly rendered to all MCO Members.

B. Benefit Year-End Surplus Sharing

1. **Physician Fund Surplus** MCO shall distribute one hundred percent (100%) of any surplus of the Physician Fund to Partici-

pating Physicians. Fifty percent (50%) of this amount shall be distributed to Primary-Care Physicians, and fifty percent (50%) shall be distributed to Specialist Physicians. Determination of the existence of a surplus shall be made subject to the satisfaction of any deficit in the Hospital Fund, if one exists, as set forth in Section 4.08.C herein.

2. **Hospital Fund Surplus** MCO will distribute fifty percent (50%) of any surplus remaining in the total Hospital Fund at the end of Benefit Year to Participating Physicians. Thirty percent (30%) of the Hospital Fund surplus will be distributed to Primary-Care Physicians, and twenty percent (20%) will be distributed to Specialist Physicians. The total amount deposited in the Hospital Fund is based upon an actuarially determined amount calculated according to utilization and expected costs.

3. **Physician Reserve Fund Surplus** MCO will maintain in an interest bearing account the amounts allocated to Physician Reserve Fund, and will distribute one hundred percent (100%) of any surplus to Participating Physicians. This surplus will be distributed on a *pro rata* basis according to each individual Participating Physicians' utilization from the Physician Fund for services rendered to MCO Members during the Benefit Year divided by the total utilization of all Participating Physicians affiliated with the IPA for services rendered to all MCO Members. Physician Reserve Fund shall be deemed to have a surplus if it exceeds five percent (5%) of the total Funds for the Benefit Year just ended. Upon termination of this contract, Physician shall be paid his or her *pro rata* share of this reserve at the end of Benefit Year during which the contract obligations expire.

C. **Benefit Year-End Hospital Fund Deficit Sharing** Fifty percent (50%) of any Benefit Year-end deficit in Hospital Fund shall be charged to Physician Fund at the end of Benefit Year. If the amount of surplus in Physician Fund is inadequate to fully satisfy this deficit, funds from Physician Reserve Fund referred to in paragraph 4.08.B.3 will be applied.

D. Catastrophic Loss Protection

1. **Physician Fund** Catastrophic losses shall be paid on the following basis:

a. The Physician Fund shall pay for the first five thousand dollars ($5,000) of nonprimary-care charges normally paid from the Physician Fund per Member per Benefit Year.

b. MCO shall pay for all nonprimary-care Covered Services normally paid for by the Physician Fund in excess of five thousand dollars ($5,000).

2. **Hospital Fund** MCO's stoploss reinsurance policy will pay for all claims over thirty thousand dollars ($30,000) per Member per Benefit Year that are normally paid from Hospital Fund.

E. Benefit Year-End Settlement Stages

1. The Benefit Year-end settlement shall be accomplished in two stages:

a. An interim settlement shall be completed within one hundred twenty (120) days of the close of Benefit Year.

b. A final settlement shall include paid claim expenses through the first six (6) months following the end of the Benefit Year but incurred in the Benefit Year, with an incurred-but-not-yet-reported factor added. MCO and the IPA or Physician Group will make any retroactive payments to each other within thirty (30) days of this final settlement, subject to the provisions of Section 4.08.C herein.

4.09 Claims for Nonmembers In the event MCO fails to inform Physician that a patient is no longer a Member, and Physician has submitted a claim for payment, MCO will provide Physician payment for Covered Services in accordance with Article IV, subject to a determination by the utilization and peer review committee of MCO that the service rendered by Physician was medically necessary.

4.10 Coordination of Benefits Physician agrees to cooperate in implementing the provisions of a Member's agreement with MCO relating to the coordination of benefits. Physician will notify MCO of any additional third-party coverage for Member. Physician may bill and collect any additional funds relating to coordination of benefits without adjustment by MCO.

ARTICLE V: MUTUAL AGREEMENTS

5.01 **Term** This Agreement shall become effective on the date first written above and shall continue in effect so long as Physician shall continue in the private practice of medicine in the area served by MCO unless terminated by either Physician or MCO.

5.02 **Automatic Termination** This Agreement shall terminate automatically in the event Physician dies, becomes incapable of rendering services hereunder, or the license to practice medicine in [State] is revoked or suspended, or if the privileges of Physician at any of MCO's Participating Hospitals are suspended or revoked, or malpractice coverage as required by paragraph 2.09 herein is terminated.

5.03 **Termination with or without Cause** Either Physician or MCO may terminate this Agreement at any time, with cause, by giving thirty (30) days' prior written notice to the other party by certified mail, or without cause by giving ninety (90) days' prior written notice to the other party by certified mail, but MCO may require Physician to continue to provide services to Members during the thirty- (30) or ninety- (90) day notification period.

5.04 **Six Months of Participation Necessary before Surplus Sharing** This Agreement must be in effect for at least six (6) months of any Benefit Year for Physician to participate in any surplus sharing otherwise payable during that year.

5.05 **Payments after Termination** In the event of lawful termination of this Agreement by either party for whatever reason, MCO shall make appropriate payment for Covered Services actually provided by Physician prior to termination of this Agreement, after processing, if the claim for payment is appropriately submitted by Physician.

5.06 **Nonexclusivity** This Agreement is nonexclusive and Physician may contract with preferred provider organizations, health maintenance organizations or other alternative provider arrangements.

5.07 **Independent Contractors** None of the provisions of this Agreement is intended to create nor shall be deemed or construed to create any relationship between the parties hereto other than that of independent entities contracting with each other hereunder solely for the purpose of affecting the provisions of this Agreement. Neither of the parties hereto, nor any of its respective employees, shall be construed to be the agent, employee, or the representative of the other.

5.08 **Mutual Indemnification** Each party to this Agreement respectively assumes responsibility for liability, real or alleged, arising from their respective activities performed pursuant to this Agreement.

5.09 **Notification of Change in Physician's Staff Privileges** Physician will advise MCO promptly and in writing if Physician's status as an active staff member of any Hospital is changed for any reason.

5.10 **MCO to Give Prior Authorization of Use of Names and Status** MCO's name and Physician's status under this Agreement will not be used by Physician in any form of advertisement or publication without the prior written permission of an officer of MCO.

5.11 **Waivers of Default** The waiver by either party of one or more defaults on the part of the other party in the performance of obligations under this Agreement will not be construed as a waiver of any subsequent defaults.

5.12 **Controlling Law** This Agreement shall be governed in all respects by the laws of the State of [State]. The invalidity or unenforceability of any terms or conditions hereof shall in no way affect the validity or enforceability of any other term or provision.

5.13 **Nonassignability without Prior Mutual Consent** This Agreement may not be assigned by either party without the prior written consent of the other party.

5.14 **Notices** All notices which are, or may be required to be given by any party to the other(s) in connection with this Agreement and the transactions contemplated thereby shall be in writing and shall be deemed to have been properly given if and when delivered personally or sent by certified mail, return receipt requested, addressed to the below indicated address of the party to be notified, or at such other place or places as a party may from time to time designate by written notice to the other party.

5.15 MCO's Board Approval Formal acceptance of this Agreement and all attachments are subject to approval by MCO's Board of Directors.

IN WITNESS WHEREOF, the parties have executed this Agreement intending to be bound as of the date set forth on the first page.

[INSERT SIGNATURE BLOCKS ACCORDINGLY]

EXHIBIT 1
TABLE OF DEFINITIONS

Covered Individual An employee or an employee's eligible dependent who is covered under the terms of a Plan to which this Agreement pertains.

Covered Services Medical care services rendered to a Covered Individual that are reimbursable under the terms of a Plan to which this Agreement pertains, subject to any applicable deductible, co-payment, and limitation provisions of that Plan, and under which the individual receiving services is a Covered Individual.

Usual, Customary, and Reasonable Fee Fee for a medical service rendered to Covered Individual that is reimbursable under the terms of a Plan to which this Agreement pertains, subject to any applicable deductible, co-payment, and limitation provisions of that Plan, and under which the individual receiving services is a Covered Individual.

Managed-Care Organization Network (MCO Network) Health care provider network that is used for a type of preferred provider program which requires Participating Physicians to comply with the provisions of Exhibit 3 of this Agreement.

Managed-Care Organization Specific Network (MCO Specific Network) Health care provider network that is used for a type of preferred provider program which does *not* require Participating Providers to comply with the provisions of Exhibit 3 of this Agreement.

Participating Hospital Hospital that has contracted to participate in MCO Network.

Participating Physicians All Personal Primary-Care Physicians and Specialist Physicians who have contracted to participate in MCO Network.

Physician Party to this Agreement who is a physician or allied practitioner duly licensed, certified, or otherwise authorized to practice within the scope of such license or authorization, and who has privileges to admit patients to the acute care facilities of at least one Participating Hospital.

Personal Primary-Care Physician Any physician who has contracted to participate in MCO Network and who is practicing medicine in the areas of internal medicine, family practice, general practice, or pediatrics or who is designated by MCO as a Personal Primary-Care Physician.

Specialist Physician Any physician who has contracted to participate in MCO Network to provide specialty services upon referral from a Personal Primary-Care Physician.

EXHIBIT 2
FEE SCHEDULES

[Insert Fee Schedules Here]

EXHIBIT 3
MANAGED-CARE NETWORK

1. **General** It is understood that this Exhibit pertains to those Employers' Plans that contain programs which include the Managed-care organization Network (MCO Network).

2. Personal Primary-Care Physician's and Specialist Physician's General Obligations

   a. **Referrals**   Physician agrees to refer Covered Individual to other Participating Physicians and other providers participating in MCO Network unless the required medical services are not available through a Participating Physician or such providers, or in the case of Emergencies. Except in the case of Emergencies, Physician shall seek authorization from the Plan designee for referrals to physicians who are not Participating Physicians and providers which are not participating in MCO Network.

   b. **Admissions**   Physician agrees to admit Covered Individuals requiring hospital services to Participating Hospitals unless the necessary hospital services are not available from a Participating Hospital or in the case of Emergencies. Except in the case of Emergencies, Physician shall seek authorization for the Plan designee as required under an Employers' Plan prior to admitting any Covered Individual to Hospital.

   c. **Specialist Physician**   Specialist Physician agrees to see Covered Individuals on referral from Primary-Care Physician. Specialist Physician will advise Covered Individual of additional costs to individual if seen without a primary-care referral. Specialist Physician will promptly inform Covered Individual's Personal Primary-Care Physician about any referrals to other Specialist Physicians or admissions to Hospital.

3. **Failure to Comply with Utilization Review**   Physician shall not attempt to collect from the Covered Individual the amount of any benefits either denied or reduced because of Physician's failure to comply with the utilization review provisions of a Plan.

EXHIBIT 4
MCO'S GRIEVANCE RESOLUTION PROCEDURE

Complaints must be filed in writing to:

[MCO's Name and Address, City, State, ZIP]

MCO will promptly investigate the complaint and a written response will be provided to the Covered Individual, Physician, or Physician's organization within thirty (30) days after the date of receipt of the complaint.

This mechanism provides for an advisory role only by a physician panel of not less than three (3) physicians selected by MCO from those physicians who have contracted with MCO in the service area.

EXHIBIT 5
MCO AGREEMENT

WHEREAS, the Employers that have established employee welfare benefit plans ("Plans") for Covered Individuals identified according to the terms of paragraph 5 of this Exhibit 5, have each incorporated into its Plan a program that includes one of two types of networks of participating health care providers (individually referred to herein as the Managed-Care Organization Network ("MCO Network") and the Managed-Care Organization Specific Network ("MCO Specific Network"); and

WHEREAS, MCO either provides administrative services for the Employer's self-funded Plan or provides insurance benefits under the Plan (pursuant to an insurance policy), as the case may be; and

WHEREAS, Physician desires to participate in both MCO Network and MCO Specific Network (collectively referred to herein as "the Network").

NOW, THEREFORE, the parties hereto in consideration of the mutual covenants and agreements herein contained, do hereby agree as follows:

1. **Definitions**   The following terms used in this Agreement are defined in the Table of Definitions, Exhibit 1, hereto: Covered Individual; Covered Services; Usual, Customary, and Reasonable Fee; Managed-Care Organization Network; Managed-Care Organization Specific Network; Participating Hospital; Participating Physicians; Physician; Personal Primary-Care Physician; and Specialist Physician.

2. **Payment**   For those health care services determined by MCO to be Covered Services, Physician agrees to accept as full payment the lesser of the applicable amount in the Schedule of Allowed Fees set forth in Exhibit 2 hereto and the Physician's Usual, Customary, and Reasonable Fee. Unless Physician does not accept benefit assignment from an individual covered under a Plan which contains a

program which includes MCO Specific Network, Physician will not, under any circumstances, seek payment from any Covered Individual, except as follows: after MCO pays benefits for Covered Services, either on behalf of a self-funded Plan or pursuant to the insurance policy issued to an insured Plan, as the case may be, Physician may seek payment from the Covered Individual of (*a*) any applicable deductible and co-payment amounts, which shall be calculated on the basis that the lesser of the amount of the Schedule of Allowed Fees and the Usual, Customary, and Reasonable Fee is the full amount of Physician's fee and (*b*) any of the amounts due for any services that are determined by MCO not to be Covered Services.

Additional Payment—MCO Network   Within one hundred twenty (120) days of the end of each calendar year, Physician will be eligible for an additional payment. The decision to make additional payment and the amount of any such payment rests solely at the discretion of MCO. This additional payment is only available in connection with Physician's participation in MCO Network. Accordingly, the additional payment determination will only be based upon those Plans containing programs that include MCO Network.

Physician further agrees that this provision supersedes any oral or written contrary agreement now existing or hereafter entered into between Physician and Covered Individual, or persons acting on their behalf.

3. **Records**   Physician agrees to maintain standard medical records for Covered Individuals and to provide such records and other information to MCO and/or its designee(s) as may be requested and as permitted by law for the performance of their utilization review activities.

Physician agrees that all records kept in connection with Physician's participation in the Network are subject to review and audit at any reasonable time by authorized MCO administrative staff or a designee.

4. **Nondiscrimination**   Physician agrees to render health care services to patients who are Covered Individuals in the same manner, in accordance with the same standards, and within the same availability as offered his or her other patients.

5. **Identification Cards**   MCO will provide each Covered Individual with an identification card. If the individual is covered under a Plan

that contains a program which includes MCO Network, Physician shall also comply with the requirements provided in Exhibit 3 hereto.

6. **Utilization Review**   Physician agrees to cooperate with, participate in, and comply with the utilization review, peer review, and/or audit procedures that are applicable to the Network as established by MCO or a Plan to which this Agreement pertains.

7. **Nonexclusivity**   This Agreement is nonexclusive and Physician may contract with other preferred provider organizations, health maintenance organizations, or other participating provider arrangements.

8. **Assignment of Benefits**   If a Covered Individual is covered under a Plan that contains a program which includes MCO Network, Physician shall accept assignment of benefits to the extent permitted by law and subject to the terms of the Plan under which the individual is a Covered Individual.

    If a Covered Individual is covered under a Plan that contains a program which includes MCO Specific Network, Physician will not discourage the individual from assigning benefits when permitted by the Plan.

    Upon acceptance of such benefit assignment, Physician shall submit to MCO all claims within sixty (60) days of the date of service for which payment is claimed. Such claim shall include standard utilization codes and a full itemization of charges and services rendered. Physician may request payment from the Covered Individual as provided in paragraph 2 of this Exhibit 5 only after receipt of MCO's claim determination with respect to said services.

9. **Liability Coverage**   Physician shall obtain, at his or her own cost and keep in force, professional malpractice insurance in an amount agreeable to MCO. Evidence of such coverage shall be provided to MCO upon request. Physician shall give MCO at least fifteen (15) days' advance notice of cancellation or any modification of such medical malpractice insurance.

10. **Service Area**   The Network Service Area is the [specify service area].

11. **Assignment**   No assignment of this Agreement or delegation of the duties or obligations set forth herein shall be made by either party without the express written approval of the other party. Notwithstanding the foregoing, MCO may, at any time, assign this Agreement or any of its rights, or delegate any of its duties or obligations set forth

herein, without the express written approval of Physician, to any of MCO's affiliated companies, and subsequently, any such affiliated company shall also have the right to so assign or delegate its duties under this Agreement.

12. **Independent Contractors**   None of the provisions of this Agreement is intended to create or shall be deemed or construed to create any relationship between the parties hereto other than that of independent entities contracting with each other hereunder solely for the purpose of affecting the provisions of this Agreement. Neither of the parties hereto, nor any of its respective employees, shall be construed to be the agent, employee, or the representative of the other.

13. **Physician's Responsibility for Medical Services**   It is hereby understood that Physician is solely responsible for all decisions regarding the medical care of Covered Individuals as well as their treatment and that the traditional relationship between Physician and patient shall in no way be affected by or interfered with by any of the terms of this Agreement. Physician understands that claim determinations made by MCO and determinations in connection with the utilization review provisions of a Plan are solely for purposes of determining whether services are covered under the terms of that Plan and the extent to which such determinations shall in no way affect the responsibility of Physician to provide appropriate services to Covered Individuals.

14. **Term**   This Agreement shall become effective on the date first written above and shall continue in effect unless terminated in accordance with paragraph 15 of this Exhibit 5.

15. **Termination**   This Agreement may be terminated by either party at any time, with or without cause, by giving thirty (30) days' prior written notice to the other party by certified mail.

In addition, this Agreement shall terminate automatically in the event Physician dies or becomes incapable of rendering services; Physician's license or privilege to practice is revoked or suspended or Physician is placed on probation, reprimanded, fined, or Physician's practice privileges are restricted by any state agency; Physician's privileges at any Hospital are revoked, suspended, or reduced from full active status; Physician is expelled or suspended from Medicare/Medicaid; Physician is convicted of a felony; or Physician fails to maintain malpractice insurance in the amounts required by this Agreement.

Physician (or a representative of Physician in the case of death) agrees to advise MCO in writing of any of the above listed occurrences within five (5) days.

In the event of termination of this Agreement, the payment provision set forth in this Agreement will continue to apply to all claims for Covered Services rendered on dates prior to the effective date of termination.

16. **Authorization to Use Name and Status**   MCO shall market the Network and shall arrange to have Physician's name and address included in the directory of Participating Providers distributed to individuals covered under those Plans for which Physician is a Participating Provider. MCO may also use Physician's name in marketing brochures and other marketing literature.

    MCO's name and Physician's status as a participant in the Network will not be used in any form of advertisement or publication without the prior written permission of an officer of MCO.

17. **Waivers of Defaults**   The waiver by either party of one or more defaults on the part of the other party in the performance of obligations under this Agreement will not be construed to operate as a waiver of any subsequent defaults.

18. **Controlling Law**   This Agreement shall be governed in all respects by the laws of the State [State]. The invalidity or unenforceability of any terms or conditions hereof shall in no way affect the validity or enforceability of any other term or provision, provided the intent of the parties in entering into this Agreement can reasonably be given effect without the invalid or unenforceable term(s) or condition(s).

19. **Entire Agreement**   This Agreement includes the Exhibits attached hereto and such Exhibits are incorporated as part hereof. The terms set forth in this Agreement contain the entire agreement between the parties. Except as otherwise provided in this Agreement, it can be altered or amended only by written agreement signed by Physician and an officer of MCO.

20. **Notices**   All notices that are, or may be, required to be given by either party to the other in connection with this Agreement and the transactions contemplated hereby shall be in writing and, except as otherwise provided in this Agreement, shall be deemed to have been properly given if and when delivered personally or sent by certified

mail, return receipt requested, to the below indicated address of the party to be notified, or at such other place or places as either party may from time to time designate by written notice to the other party:

If to Physician:

[Name of Physician]
[Address]

If to MCO:
[Name of MCO]
[Address]

21. **Complaints**   MCO will provide a mechanism for the resolution of any complaints initiated by Covered Individual and/or health care providers as described in Exhibit 4.

IN WITNESS WHEREOF, the parties have executed this Agreement to be bound as of the date set forth on the first page.

[INSERT SIGNATURE BLOCKS ACCORDINGLY]

APPENDIX ITEM 19-05
RESPONSE TO CAPITATION PROPOSAL

VIA HAND DELIVERY

[Date]

Ms. Karen Carkhuff
Director of Ancillary Contracting
Universal Health Plans
3500 Main Road, Suite 300
Metropolitan, USA 12345

Dear Karen:

We are pleased to enclose a response to Universal Health Plan's request for proposal to provide obstetrical and gynecological services to its members on behalf of
the Women's Healthcare Network (WHN). At the present time, WHN's core group
is made up of 75 physicians located through the greater Metropolitan area who
share the common goal of improving quality of care while becoming more cost-
effective providers.

As requested, we have prepared a comprehensive proposal to provide an
obstetrical case rate as well as a gynecological capitation rate. WHN's OB package
is comprehensive—starting with the initial diagnosis of pregnancy and extending
through delivery and post-partum care consistent with ACOG guidelines. Both
normal and high-risk patients are addressed as requested. The gynecological capitation rate is inclusive of all GYN professional services, both medical and surgical,
performed by panel members.

We have developed a quality network that will clearly address the needs of Universal Health Plan and its members. Our OB/GYNs are committed to providing
accessible, cost-effective services based on uniform standards of high-quality care.
In addition, many of WHN's physicians are already participating with one or more
of Universal's plans which should help facilitate a smooth transition for your
patients and primary-care physicians.

We look forward to your positive response to our proposal. Please contact us if
you need additional information or have any questions. The WHN leadership is
available to meet with you or Dr. Cuevas to discuss this proposal in detail. In
addition, we can arrange site visits at any of the participating physicians' offices
if needed.

Sincerely,

Willard Third-Party, Ph.D.

Enclosures

Proposal to Provide Obstetrical and Gynecological Services

Table of Contents

Section I: Overview of Network

Women's Healthcare Network (WHN) is a network of prominent, well-established obstetricians and gynecologists strategically located throughout the Metropolitan area. WHN was organized to provide high-quality, cost-effective patient care in response to managed-care environments. WHN's participants are carefully selected and share the common goal of maintaining high standards of quality while practicing medicine in a cost-effective manner.

WHN members share common goals with managed health care programs as evidenced by their participation in existing managed-care plans, including those of Universal Health Plans (UHP). A total of forty-three (43) of WHN's seventy-five (75) core network physicians (57.3%) currently participate with UHP in one or more programs.

WHN has a strong commitment to provide UHP with a diverse panel which will provide maximum accessibility for UHP members. Minority representation among the core panel is 20 percent of the total, while female physicians account for 25.3 percent. In concert with UHP, WHN will continue to recruit qualified minority and female applicants.

As a result of their commitment to shared goals and their experience with managed care, WHN members are premier physicians in their respective Metropolitan communities. Two of WHN's board members (Dr. Ellis and Garcia) have participated as advisers to UHP for a number of years.

Except for seven (7) Board Qualified physicians, all WHN physicians are Board Certified. WHN bylaws require that participating physicians be Board Certified or Board Qualified. Board Qualified physicians must become Board Certified within four years to remain a WHN member working with UHP.

WHN will provide the following:

- A highly qualified OB/GYN panel with members that are geographically accessible throughout the Metropolitan area and that have excellent relationships with UHP's primary-care physicians and preferred hospitals.

- An improvement in the quality and utilization rates of OB/GYN services through participation in utilization management and quality improvement advisory panels and the progressive development and application of clinical protocols.

- A willingness to work toward win-win financial relationships that will benefit UHP, primary-care physicians, and network physicians.

- The ability and willingness to expand the WHN panel as required to meet UHP's specific needs.

- The willingness to assume 100 percent of the professional fee risk under a capitation arrangement for gynecological services and case rate reimbursement for obstetrical services. WHN will also work with UHP to develop case and capitation rates for subspecialty, OB/GYN services based on the needs of UHP.

- The willingness to share financial risk with UHP for facility and pharmaceutical costs.

There are a number of key factors that differentiate WHN from other networks. These factors substantially increase the likelihood that WHN will be successful and provide a sound basis for a long-term relationship with UHP.

a. WHN is organized as a collaborative, physician-directed endeavor. Each physician is personally motivated to become actively involved in managed health care. WHN has organized and forged a consensus and collective effort among its member physicians to positively respond to the dynamic health care environment. The active involvement and participation of WHN members will invariably produce a stronger, more viable business partner.

b. WHN is based on a positive, patient-oriented approach to cost containment. To this end, each practice in the network is equally represented with regard to cost and quality issues and each practice is represented on the Board of Directors, as well as the utilization management/quality improvement (UM/QI) committee. The physicians are developing clinical protocols that will meet or exceed the standards, guidelines, and criteria established by the American College of Obstetricians and Gynecologists and other national medical organizations. Participation in UM/QI is a requirement for WHN membership.

c. WHN's physicians have a long history of participation with managed-care plans. They have worked within the managed-care system and understand how to appropriately manage utilization while maintaining high standards of quality.

d. WHN medical directors will pre-certify all admissions and will include an approved length of stay in coordination with UHP. A utilization nation management coordinator for the network will monitor each admission to verify that treatment protocols are followed.

e. WHN will share in the risk for hospital and outpatient facility costs. WHN providers understand that they can impact these costs by: (i) deciding to operate or to follow a more conservative treatment option; (ii) selecting cost-effective facilities; and (iii) managing the intensity of care provided and overall length of stay.

f. WHN has contracted with Third-Party Advisory Services/Physicians Health Corporation (TAS/PHS), a network administrator, to organize the network and to provide administrative and technical support. TAS/PHS will handle financial management of the network, as well as physician relations, credentialling, quality improvement, and related areas.

g. WHN has contracted with Third-Party Advisory Services/Physicians Health Corporation (TAS/PHS) to provide claims administration and related utilization management services. TAS and PHC personnel have significant experience in claims processing, utilization management, reporting, and staff training.

h. WHN is being organized as a U.S. not-for-profit corporation whose share-holders are the practices (professional corporation, partnership, or solo prac-tice). The practices are represented by the physicians involved in WHN. Each shareholder has a vote in policy decisions, and each shareholder appoints a member of their group to the WHN board of directors. The board of directors elect an executive committee to manage the network on a day-to-day basis. The board has appointed a regional medical director, area medical directors, and a utilization management/quality improvement committee. They are devel-oping referral and clinical protocols.

i. WHN physicians have privileges at most of UHP's participating hospitals in Metropolitan, including: [Include list of hospitals.]

The WHN physician leadership will work with UHP to establish affiliations with physicians in other hospitals.

Section II: Proposed Financial Terms

Women's Healthcare Network (WHN) proposes to contract with Universal Health Plans (UHP) to provide obstetrical services to its members on a case-rate basis and gynecological services on a capitated basis. Under the proposed contract, WHN will provide services to UHP's Select Choice and MC-1 members. WHN is committed to meeting UHP's expectations and requirements regarding panel size, geographic distribution, credentials, and any other necessary factors.

Proposed Obstetrical Case Rate

Consistent with the Universal Select Choice benefit plan, WHN has developed a comprehensive global professional package for obstetrical services starting with initial diagnosis of pregnancy and extending through delivery and post-partum care following standards as set forth by the American College of Obstetricians and Gynecologists. WHN is willing to assume the responsibility and financial risk for these services for Universal based on a mutual understanding of the characteristics of UHP's population, as well as agreement to the specific services enumerated herein.

Basic Obstetrical Package

1. Patient Education
   a. Comprehensive Prenatal Education—WHN will provide individualized counseling to each OB patient upon initiation of care and treatment as needed throughout the entire term of pregnancy. WHN understands and appreciates the patient's lifestyle and attitude can have a material effect on the outcome of the pregnancy and the health of the mother and infant. Consistent with ACOG guidelines, WHN recognizes that the obstetrician has an obligation during the prenatal period to detect potentially harmful influences and to reinforce positive behavior both during and after pregnancy, recognizing, of course, that the patient is ultimately responsible for her own behavior and lifestyle.

   Recognizing the considerable variation in UHP's particular population, WHN shall make all attempts to provide appropriate patient information and prenatal information consistent with the patient's level of knowledge and understanding, as well as an awareness of the patient's social, cultural, religious, ethnic, and economic background. Pertinent educational information including nutrition, exercise, work, sexual activity, and the need to refrain from using alcohol, tobacco, and drugs will be included.

    b.   Nutritional Counseling—All patients will be seen by a nurse or other qualified health professional to counsel them regarding proper diet and nutrition during the term of pregnancy.

2.   Laboratory Tests

The basic OB package rate includes the cost of the following laboratory tests performed in the offices of the participating physicians on each obstetrical patient:

    a.   Urinalysis, and hematocrit (or hemoglobin). These tests will be performed on each obstetrical patient throughout the term of the pregnancy, as required.

    b.   Blood Glucose Screening. All patients will be screened for gestational diabetes usually on or about 26 to 28 weeks of gestation.

    c.   Drawing fees for reference laboratory services

    d.   Other tests. Other clinical laboratory tests will be ordered and/or performed as indicated for each patient's unique needs based on current ACOG guidelines. Reference laboratory costs are not included in the WHN global fees for obstetrical management but will be referred to UHP's participating reference labs for processing and direct billing to UHP. Medical consultations and laboratory testing for concomitant diseases or complications not related to the pregnancy are not included in the global rate.

3.   Normal Vaginal Delivery

Routine obstetrical care including antepartum care, vaginal delivery (with or without episiotomy and/or forceps), and normal postpartum care (CPT 59400) is included.

4.   Vaginal Birth After Cesarean (VBAC)

Routine obstetrical care including antepartum care, vaginal delivery (with or without episiotomy and/or forceps) and postpartum care after prior cesarean (CPT 59400) is included.

5.   Cesarean Section

Routine obstetrical care including antepartum care, cesarean delivery and normal postpartum care (CPT 59510) is included.

6.   Induction of Labor

Induction of labor by attending OB physician by any method and for any reason is included in the basic OB global rate.

7.   Diagnostic Ultrasound

    a.   Each obstetrical patient will receive a complete diagnostic ultrasound (CPT 76805) and follow-up studies (CPT 76816) as indicated throughout the pregnancy, whether performed in the attending obstetrician's office or in other network locations, if ordered by a network obstetrician. The cost of the necessary screening Ultrasounds is included in the global rate.

b. Fetal biophysical profile, if indicated, may be referred to the consulting perinatologist upon approval by the medical director for complex cases.

8. Amniocentesis

Screening amniocentesis may be performed as indicated for possible high-risk patients as identified by ACOG and Universal's established screening criteria (advanced maternal age, complicated obstetrical history, etc.). This service will include the amniocentesis procedure, as well as the related ultrasonic guidance and radiologic interpretation. Genetic testing of the amniotic fluid by the Universal designated reference lab is not included in WHN's global rate.

9. Fetal Non-Stress Tests

Fetal non-stress tests will be performed as indicated.

10. Management of False Labor

Services related to physician observation or management of false labor OB Rate. Management of documented pre-term labor will be included in high-risk global rate.

11. Prolonged Detention Related to the Pregnancy or OB Care

Services of attending physician during extended labor, false labor, or other OB related incidences.

12. Fetal Scalp Monitoring

Fetal scalp monitoring during labor by the attending OB physician is included in the global OB fee. Fees for fetal monitoring by a consulting physician (e.g., perinatologist, neonatologist) are not included in the global fee.

13. Rhogam Injections

Rhogam injections will be administered as indicated. Typical indications will include:

a. Rh negative mother with Rh positive infant,

b. Rh negative mother with sub (1) amniocentesis, sub (2) miscarriage or ectopic pregnancy,

c. Bleeding in pregnancy, as indicated.

14. Any Anesthesia Given Directly by OB Physician

Services include local blocks and epidural anesthesia administered by attending OB physicians.

WHN proposes a fee of $1,925 for the Basic Obstetrical Package. Pregnancies which do not carry to term or for those patients who transfer out-of-network or to another health plan will be reimbursed on a pro-rata basis.

High-Risk OB Package

In addition to the basic services included in the normal OB global rate, the following services are included in the proposed global fee for management of high-risk pregnancies.

1. Inpatient Management for Complications of Pregnancy

   Inpatient management for conditions such as pregnancy induced hypertension, premature rupture of membranes, placenta previa and pre-term labor will be managed either medically or surgically, as follows:

   a. Medical management by the network obstetrician to include admission, daily visits, critical care, and discharge management in the global package. Services of perinatologists or consultants outside the network are specifically excluded from the rate.

   b. Surgical management is limited to D&C's for spontaneous abortions and surgical cerclage during pregnancy. Again, services of perinatologists or other non-obstetrical consultants are specifically excluded from the global package. The global rate for patients who experience spontaneous abortions will be prorated based on a formula to be agreed upon by WHN and UHP.

2. Coordination and Review of Uterine Monitoring Services

   Indications for uterine monitoring include: pre-term labor and pre-term pregnancy, previous pre-term delivery, multiple gestation, uterine anomalies, cervical incompetence, etc. Services usually include uterine management with or without oral tocolytics, as well as appropriate utilization of the terbutaline pump. Patients on uterine monitoring programs will receive daily monitoring by home health care nurses, as well as 24-hour nursing support and reporting from the UHP designated home health provider. The attending physician will work within guidelines as mutually established by UHP and WHN and consistent with ACOG recommended standards of care.

3. Additional Visits to Obstetrician's Office

   Usually 1 to 2 additional visits to attending OB physician per week beginning at 26 weeks or as otherwise required by patient's condition, including additional hematocrits, hemoglobins, urinalysis, NST'S, and glucose screens during additional visits.

4. Additional Target Ultrasounds

   If additional ultrasounds are required beyond the basic OB package related to a verified high-risk pregnancy, the cost of the additional ultrasounds will be included in the high-risk global rate when performed in a network physician's office. Biophysical Profiles and other specialized sonography will be referred to approved perinatologists.

5. Profession Fees for Amnio-Infusion

    Indicated for ruptured membranes w/ fetal distress

6. Oxytocin Stress Test

    Possible fetal distress or post-term pregnancy without labor.

7. Medical Management of Ectopic Pregnancies

    Pregnancies resulting in surgical intervention of ectopic pregnancy will be paid under gynecology capitation rate.

WHN proposes a fee of $2,200 for the management of high-risk patients. This fee is inclusive of the basic and high-risk package services. Pregnancies which do not carry to term or for those patients who transfer out of network or to another health plan will be reimbursed on a pro-rata basis.

Services Excluded from OB Package Rate

1. Circumcision

    Circumcisions are not included in the basic OB package rate as:

    a. It will not be necessary to circumcise all babies delivered and

    b. To also allow for differences between hospital communities as to whether the OB physician or the pediatrician will perform the procedure.

2. Specialized Ultrasound

    a. Fetal Biophysical Profile—In addition, high-risk patients will receive a fetal biophysical profile as indicated. These tests will be paid by WHN if performed in a network obstetrician's office. If referred to a perinatologist, the cost will be paid by Universal consulting perinatologist (indicated for diabetes, cardiolipin antibody syndrome, intra-uterine growth retardation, post-term pregnancy, threat to fetal well-being during labor, pregnancy-induced hypertension, hypertension).

    b. Other target ultrasound as indicated.

3. Elective Termination of Pregnancy (Abortion)

4. Services of Perinatologists or Other Non-OB Specialists

5. Genetic Testing

6. Surgical Intervention for Ectopic Pregnancies (Included in GYN Cap Rate)

7. Laboratory Tests Other than Hemoglobins, Glucose Screenings, Urinalysis, and Hematocrits.

Proposed Gynecological Capitation Rate

WHN proposes a capitation rate of $6.48 per female member per month (equivalent to $2.75 per member per month) to cover all professional fees for all gynecology services the WHN panel provides to UHP members.

Services Covered in Capitation Rate

*   The proposed capitation rate was determined on the basis of our analysis of the utilization data provided by UHP for the period from July 1, 1993 to June 30, 1994. WHN believes that it can provide gynecological services at uniform high standards of quality at the proposed capitation rate through a combination of decreased fees per unit of service and highly managed utilization.

*   A listing of specific CPT and HCPCS codes will be constructed for all services to be covered by the capitation payment based on the final agreement between UHP and WHN. In general, the covered services will include those professional services billed by WHN network physicians as appropriate to the practice of gynecology. Subject to the specific levels of benefits provided by UHP to a covered member, these services shall include:

*   Annual "Well-Woman" examinations (excluding mammograms) per UHP guidelines.

*   Other office and hospital medical services such as office visits, consultations, hospital visits and emergency room services.

*   Infertility counseling.

*   Professional fees for surgery performed in the WHN physician's office, hospital or ambulatory surgery center (with some exclusions as detailed herein). Most of the network physicians' offices are fully equipped to perform colposcopy, cryosurgery, LEEPs, and hysteroscopy.

*   Routine in-office laboratory including hematocrits, hemoglobins, and urinalyses.

*   Gynecologic ultrasound procedures performed in WHN physicians' offices.

- Other gynecological supplies, including injections and medical supplies provided in the physician's office unless specifically excluded.
- Second surgical opinions.

Services Not Covered by the Capitation Rate

The following services are not included in the capitation rate:

- Professional services provided by out-of-network gynecologists.
- Reversals of tubal ligation.
- Elective terminations of pregnancy.
- Estrogen treatments.
- Norplant insertion and removal.
- Assisted reproductive technology, such as in vitro fertilization and artificial insemination.
- Gynecological oncology services and procedures.
- Urodynamics.
- Obstetrical services and related procedures, including antepartum and postpartum care.
- Mammography. However, a number of the WHN physicians provide mammography services at strategic locations throughout Metropolitan and are willing to provide mammography services to UHP patients at a reduced fee for service.
- Facility and professional fees of reference laboratories, radiology and imaging facilities, except as otherwise included.
- UHP approved procedures performed by WHN physicians, but not listed on the approved list of CPT and HCPCS codes. These services will be negotiated on a fee-for-service basis. Additional services can be included at the capitation rate if and when clarified by UHP.
- Services of a non-gynecological provider requested by a WHN physician and approved by the primary-care physician (e.g., consultations by other UHP specialists).
- Durable medical equipment, e.g., breast prosthesis.

Section III: The Physician Panel

Exhibit 1: Women's Healthcare Network Physicians and Credentials [Example]

Physician Name & Address	County	Hospital Affiliation c-Courtesy p-Pending	Board Certified	Sex	DEA Exp. Date	SC-Select Choice OC-Open Choice EC-Elect Choice MC-Managed Choice
Alice C. Monroe, M.D. [address] Phone: 555-7717 Fax: 555-9729 [address] Phone: 555-4500 Fax: 555-4444 [address] Phone: 555-3010 Fax: 555-3030	One	Hospital	Yes	F	1-31-96	SC
William S. Davis, M.D. [address] Phone: 555-7717 Fax: 555-9729 [address] Phone: 555-4500 Fax: 555-4444 [address] Phone: 555-3010 Fax: 555-3030	One	Hospital	Yes	M	6-30-95	SC

Exhibit 2: Office-Based Services

WHN physicians perform a variety of services in their offices. Exhibit 2 indicates, by practice, the procedures and services performed and summarizes what percentage of WHN practices perform each service. Nearly 100 percent of member practices perform the most common services. A minimum of 25 percent of the practices perform less common procedures, such as laser and mammograms.

The UM/QL committee has agreed to recommend to the board for discussion that member physicians refer patients within the panel for required services that are not performed in their office. This will help to further reduce facility costs. Pro rata reimbursement for refunded services will be handled internally.

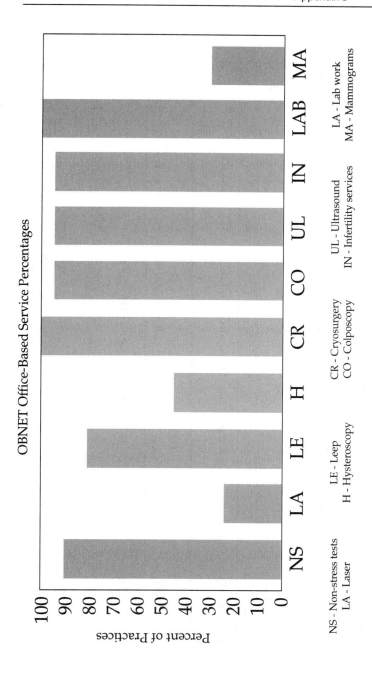

OBNET Office-Based Service Percentages

Percent of Practices

NS - Non-stress tests
LA - Laser

LE - Leep
H - Hysteroscopy

CR - Cryosurgery
CO - Colposcopy

UL - Ultrasound
IN - Infertility services

LA - Lab work
MA - Mammograms

WHN Office-Based Services [Example]

	Non-Stress Tests	Laser	LEEP	Hysteroscopy	Cryosurgery	Colposcopy	Ultrasound A-abd V-vag	Infertility Services	Lab Work	Mammograms
Eva Allen, M.D., P.C.			X		X	X	A&V	X	X	
John S. Barker, M.D.	X	X		X	X	X	A&V	X		
Atlanta Center for Obstetrics & Gynecology, P.C.	X		X	X	X	X	A&V	X	X	
Mike M. Andres, M.D.	X		X	X	X	X	A&V	X	X	
William L. Rhoades, Jr., M.D.	X		X	X	X	X	A&V	X	X	
Kimberly S. Carroll, M.D., P.C.	X		X	X	X	X	A&V	X	X	
Kimberly S. Carroll, M.D.	X		X	X	X	X	A&V	X	X	X
Camille Davis-Williams, M.D.	X		X	X	X	X	A&V	X	X	X
Peter Miller, M.D.	X		X	X	X	X	A&V	X	X	X

[Note: Complete for all physicians.]

Section IV: Contractor Organization

Exhibit 3: Women's Healthcare Network— Organizational Guidelines and Principles

Women's Healthcare Network (WHN) is in the process of finalizing its incorporation as a not-for-profit corporation. The following outline has been sent to the network's attorney to utilize in developing the final legal agreements.

Legal Entity

- A not-for-profit corporation whose shareholders include OB/GYN practices composed of sole proprietorships, partnerships and professional corporations (PC).

- A "shareholder" refers to the individual practice, partnership or PC.

- A "physician affiliate" refers to the physicians who practice within a shareholder.

- One vote per shareholder.

- Board of directors (the Board) comprises one representative from each of the shareholders.

- The Board shall elect a chairperson (the chairperson) who shall serve on the executive committee and shall be the chairperson of the executive committee.

- The Board shall elect a regional medical director who shall also serve on the executive committee.

- The regional medical director will appoint area medical directors who will represent defined geographic areas or medical communities as required by UHP to serve its members.

- The Board shall meet at reasonable intervals determined by its members. The chairperson may also call ad hoc meetings as required.

- An executive committee (the Committee) comprises no more than nine (9) members and shall be elected by the Board to review and make recommendations to the Board on certain administrative issues and to operate the network on a day-to-day basis. The term of office for the members of the Committee shall be established by the Board.

- The Committee shall include the following:

  Chairperson of the board (Committee Chairperson)

Regional medical director

Utilization management/quality improvement committee

Chairperson

All area medical directors

- Utilization management/quality improvement committee (the UM/QI Committee) is a standing committee of the Board and shall address clinical issues. Each shareholder shall designate one physician to the UM/QI Committee. The chairperson of the UM/QI Committee shall have the authority to appoint subcommittees to study specified issues (e.g., maternal health, GYN clinical).

Responsibilities of the Board of Directors

[Insert responsibilities]

Responsibilities of the Executive Committee

[Insert responsibilities]

Responsibilities of UM/QI Committee

- Establish UM/QI review criteria for Board approval and monitor authorization review activities.
- Conduct concurrent and retrospective monitoring of authorization review activities.
- Develop and recommend to the Board quality-improvement criteria and sanctions for non-compliance.
- Conduct peer review and report findings to the Board.

Managed-Care Contracting Provisions

- Approval of contracts with managed-care plans requires the agreement of at least seventy-five percent (75%) of the Board. Any contract approved by the required majority of the Board shall be binding on all shareholders and their physician affiliates.
- Exclusion of a shareholder or physician affiliate from participating in a managed-care agreement, for reasons other than failure to meet the credentialling standards of the plan, or per managed-care plan request, will require a seventy-five percent (75%) majority vote of the Committee. The share-

holder or physician affiliate will be offered an opportunity to meet with the Committee or its designee prior to a vote to exclude the shareholder or physician affiliate.

Insurance Coverage

- WHN corporate is not a direct provider of services and will not procure or maintain any professional liability insurance.

- Each shareholder shall obtain and maintain, at the shareholder's expense, professional liability coverage. Coverage will be $1,000,000/$3,000,000 level or the minimum required by UHP for each physician affiliate, whichever is greater. Each shareholder shall provide WHN written proof of such coverage. Such coverage shall not be canceled or restricted without written notification to OBNET. If possible, each shareholder shall list WHN as an additional insured.

- Errors and omission insurance will be obtained for the Board and its officers (and other lines of coverage necessary to minimize financial risk).

- Credentialling insurance may be obtained for WHN if, in the judgment of the Board, such coverage is necessary.

Disclosure of Other Interests

[Insert disclosure requirements]

Addition of New Shareholders to WHN

[Insert requirements]

Termination of Shareholders from WHN

[Insert termination provisions]

Notices

- Shareholders agree to give WHN notice within ten (10) days of the following events:

    1. Suspension, restriction, probation, or revocation of shareholder's medical staff privileges or memberships, including any change in shareholder's status at admitting hospitals;

    2. Suspension, revocation, probation, or other formal actions taken against the shareholder's right to practice medicine;

3. Suspension, restriction, probation or revocation of shareholder's or physician affiliate's professional license;

4. Charges against shareholders or physician affiliates by a licensing or hospital board alleging gross misconduct of either a professional or personal nature;

5. Conviction of a Class A misdemeanor or felony;

6. Court-appointed guardianship or conservatorship of shareholder,

7. Impairment or disability of shareholder or physician affiliate to the extent shareholder or physician affiliate is unable to perform the duties required by this agreement.

- The occurrence of such events, or failure to give WHN notice of such events, may be grounds for involuntary termination.

- Shareholders agree to give WHN notice within fifteen (15) days of the following events:

1. Addition or deletion of physician affiliates.

2. Change or addition to practice locations or hours of operations

3. Change in hospital affiliation of any physician affiliate.

4. Notice of any malpractice/legal action.

Exhibit 4: Credentialling Requirements

Application

A. Application Form. Each applicant must complete an application form that includes:

   1. An unlimited release granting WHN or its appointed credentialling entity permission to review the records of and to contact any professional society, hospital, insurance company or other entity, institution or organization that does or may have records concerning the applicant;

   2. A release from liability for any such entity, institution or organization that provides information as part of the application process; and

   3. A statement that a report may be submitted to the appropriate state licensing board and/or the National Practitioners Data Bank in the event that the application is rejected for reasons pertaining to the applicant's professional conduct or competence.

B. Required Documents. Each application must be accompanied by:

   1. A copy of the applicant's current professional license(s);

   2. A copy of the applicant's current Drug Enforcement Agency (DEA) registration (narcotic license), if applicable;

   3. A copy of the face sheet of the applicant's current professional liability insurance policy;

   4. A copy of Board Certification or documentation clarifying Board Eligibility status with expected date that the physician will sit for Board; and

   5. A check for $750 which will be refunded if application is not approved by the executive committee (the Committee).

Administrative Requirements

Before forwarding an application to the Committee, the credentialling entity staff will refer application to WHN regional medical director to determine in his/her sole discretion whether an applicant meets administrative requirements. The regional medical director may base his/her determination on any requirements he/she deems appropriate. These requirements may include, but are not limited to, the following:

   1. With respect to physicians, the applicant graduated from an acceptable school of medicine or osteopathy; this is defined as a school listed in the then-current *AAMC Directory of American Medical Education*, published by the American

Association of Medical Colleges, or in the then-current *World Director of Medical Schools,* published by the World Health Organization.

2. Completion of a post-graduate training program in obstetrics and gynecology that is appropriate for the type of participation being sought.

3. Current licensure, without restrictions or conditions, to practice the applicant's profession in the state(s) included in the WHN's and UHP's service area.

4. Current and valid DEA registration unless the provider's practice does not require registration.

5. Current Board Certification in OB/GYN or Board Eligibility status with expectation of completing Board Certification within four years after completion of fellowship training.

6. Active staff privileges at an accredited area UHP approved hospital if the provider's practice requires hospital staff privileges.

7. Applicant's specially and practice location meet WHN's credentialling entity's needs, as determined by WHN's board of directors.

8. Applicant's level of liability insurance or remaining level of policy coverage meets the current minimum limits of $1,000,000/$3,000,000 currently established by the Committee, or any additional amount as may be required by the Committee.

9. Adequate on-call coverage for provider's patients. Applicant must have twenty-four (24) hour, seven (7) day per week coverage available to patients through an answering service or machine and a beeper or paging system. If physician(s) covering emergency and after-hours service for applicant are not part of WHN, applicant must have covering physician agree to abide by utilization review and quality improvement committee's policies and procedures. This agreement must be in writing to WHN's executive committee.

10. Applicant's practice is not substantially oriented toward experimental or unproven modalities of treatment.

11. Credentialling entity has not denied applicant participation within the preceding 24 months or terminated participation within the preceding 48 months.

12. Applicant demonstrates a willingness to allow credentialling entity to conduct a review, satisfactory to credentialling entity, of applicant's practice, including office visits, staff interviews and medical record reviews.

13. Applicant has no history of denial or cancellation of professional liability insurance warranting denial of participation status.

Professional Criteria

Upon referral of an application from the designated regional medical director, the executive committee, in its sole discretion, will determine whether the applicant meets the following professional criteria. Physicians must also continue to meet credentialling criteria to maintain participation in the network. Specific criteria include:

1.   The absence of conduct that violates state or federal law or standards of ethical conduct governing the applicant's profession.

2.   The absence of any felony convictions or other acts involving dishonesty, fraud, deceit or misrepresentation.

3.   The absence of a history of involuntary termination of professional employment that warrants the restriction or denial of participation status.

4.   The absence of a history of professional disciplinary action by a managed-care plan, hospital, medical review board, licensing board or other administrative body or government agency that warrants the restriction or denial of participation status.

5.   The absence of a National Practitioner Data Bank "adverse action" report that warrants the restriction or denial of participation status.

6.   The absence of misrepresentation, misstatement or omission of a relevant fact on the application.

7.   The absence of the wasteful use of medical resources.

8.   The absence of a current physical or mental condition, including chemical dependency and substance abuse, interfering with the ability to practice the applicant's specially or that jeopardizes a patient's health.

9.   Demonstrated willingness to practice in a managed-care environment and to cooperate with credentialling entity with respect to administrative procedures and other matters.

Additional Criteria

Acceptance of an application for participation in the Women's Healthcare Network does not imply acceptance of the applicant by any specific managed-care plan or other third-party payor. Applicant must also meet credentialling criteria as established by UHP in order to participate in that agreement.

Exhibit 5: Board of Directors and Executive Committee

[Provide names and addresses of board of directors and executive committee]

Exhibit 6: Executive Committee Curricula Vitae [Example]

John M. Matua, M.D.
Board Certified

Personal Data

Address: 2801 North Road
Metropolitan, USA 12345
Telephone: (123) 555-8899

Education

Undergraduate:	State University, Metropolitan, USA B.A., Chemistry, 1974
Medical School:	State University School of Medicine, Metropolitan, USA, M.D., 1978

Post-Graduate Medical Training

Internship:	Memorial Hospital, Elsewhere, USA 1978-1979
Residency:	Memorial Hospital, Elsewhere, USA 1979-1982

Certification

American Board of Obstetrics and Gynecology

Memberships

Diplomat, American Board of Obstetrics and Gynecology, 1984
Fellow, American College of Obstetrics and Gynecology
American Association of Gynecologic Laparoscopists
Metropolitan Obstetrics/Gynecology Society
Metropolitan OB/GYN Society
City Medical Society
Publications and Research information Available Upon Request
[Note: Add a curriculum vitae for each physician]

Exhibit 7: Description of Network Administrator

[Insert description here if applicable]

Exhibit 8: Claims Administration and Utilization Management

[Insert information about any third party that is being contracted to handle these duties]

Exhibit 9: Service Authorization, Claims Administration, and Reporting

Service Authorization Process

As Universal Health Plans (UHP) patients present at a network provider's office, initial evaluations are performed. All surgical procedures and hospitalizations must be pre-authorized by WHN's regional medical director (RMD) or area medical director (AMD) using the service authorization request form included in the UM/QI plan (Exhibit 13). If the service request is not consistent with referral or clinical protocols, the request will be denied by the medical director or RMDs. All service denials will be retrospectively reviewed by the UM/QI committee to ensure that decisions made by the medical director or RMDs are clinically appropriate and consistently applied.

All services approved by any of the medical directors are submitted to UHP for confirmation of benefit coverage. Once UHP notifies the medical director of the patient's coverage and authorization number, he contacts the treating physician's office with service authorization. These communications typically occur via facsimile.

Service Authorization Flow

1. Patients present to an WHN physician.
2. Attending physician faxes a completed "service authorization request" form to the clinical services coordinator.
3. The clinical services coordinator gives the form to the medical director/RMD to review for clinical appropriateness and to verify that the case meets protocol(s).
4. If approved, the clinical services coordinator faxes the "request" form to UHP for an authorization number. If denied, the medical director/RMD contacts the attending physician and explains the reason for denial. The medical services coordinator also follows up the denial with a letter.

5. If the patient is eligible for services, UHP returns the form to the clinical services coordinator with an authorization number.

6. The clinical services coordinator contacts the attending physician and gives him/her the authorization number.

Examples of system data entry screens for this process can be found in Attachments 1 and 2.

Claims Administration

Claims administration is conducted by Third-Party Corporation (TPC) in coordination with WHN. Treating physicians submit claims for services to TPC for processing. TPC confirms service authorizations and prepares explanation of payment statements for each physician/group using the claims processing information system. Claims review is conducted to ensure that policy guidelines established by WHN are followed. Each claim is also reviewed to determine if the listed CPT codes are appropriate for the listed diagnoses. If found to be inappropriate, the claims are denied.

Claims Processing Flow

1. Match service authorization number with the submitted claim to properly adjudicate the claim.

2. Verify patient eligibility for services.

3. Perform diagnosis and procedure compatibility edits on each claim prior to payment.

4. Perform customized edits on each claim prior to payment.

5. Coordinate physician inquiries regarding claim status.

6. Print explanation of payment reports for physicians.

7. Prepare physician reimbursement checks.

8. Coordinate the resolution of claim issues between WHN, physicians and UHP.

9. Maintain accounting of payments due from UHP for distribution to WHN.

10. Submit all patient encounter data to UHP.

Examples of system data entry screens for this process are found in Attachments 3 through 7.

Reporting

Third-Party Corporation (TPC) uses a mainframe system [Name of system] for claims processing. Claims are accepted either electronically through the physician's existing system or manually. A customized utilization management information system, developed by TPC, assesses and manages financial and utilization components of WHN. Through this system, multiple utilization reports are prepared on a monthly basis. Sample reports customarily generated by the system are attached and include:

- Provider profile summary;
- Provider analysis by procedure category;
- Provider procedure analysis;
- Provider diagnosis analysis; and
- Paid claims per member per month.

Reports are reviewed by the UM/QI committee and network administrators for medical appropriateness, cost effectiveness, and protocol adherence. Information contained in these reports aids in the retrospective review of each provider's clinical activities and the resulting financial impact on WHN. Each physician may receive personalized reports detailing his or her activity with respect to the entire network. Physicians are then able to monitor their own practice patterns and investigate significant deviations from the norm. Variance from defined norms is routinely investigated by the UM/QI committee and physicians are notified and educated to assure appropriate compliance.

Since the database is relational, ad hoc reports can be developed as needed. Patient encounter data can be captured to meet any of UHP's specifications and sent to UHP via any medium (modem, disk, tape or paper).

Third-Party Corporation
990 Road Drive, PO Box 12
Metropolitan, USA 12345
Phone (123) 555-0373 Fax (123) 555-9567

REQUEST FOR PRIOR APPROVAL FOR SURGERY/HOSPITALIZATION

Today's Date _____ Office Contact Person _____

Phone ( ) _____ Fax( ) _____

Physician Name _____ Physician Phone Number ( ) _____

Physician Address _____ UHC Provider # _____
　　　　　　　　　　Street　　　　City　　　State　Zip

Patient Name _____ Patient Birthdate _____

Patient's Address _____
　　　　　　　　　Street　　　　　　　　　　City　　　　　State　　　Zip

HMO or Plan Name _____ Group and Policy # _____

Proposed Date of Surgery _____

Diagnosis(es) with ICD-9-CM codes (must provide). (Use additional page if more than 3 diagnoses.)

Use A Separate Line For Each Diagnosis

　　1) _____ ICD-9 _____

　　2) _____ ICD-9 _____

　　3) _____ ICD-9 _____

Proposed Procedure(s) with CPT Code (must provide). (Use additional page if more than 3 procedures.)

Use A Separate Line For Each Procedure

　　1) _____ CPT _____

　　2) _____ CPT _____

　　3) _____ CPT _____

PROPOSED LOCATION OF SURGERY

❑ Your office _____ Licensed ambulatory surgical center (Name _____)

❑ Hospital (Name _____) ❑ Inpatient ❑ Outpatient

Is this facility approved by HMO/Plan? ❑ Yes ❑ No

Proposed length of stay if inpatient _____

If hospital, name of co-admitting physician _____

Is he/she a Plan Provider? ❏ Yes ❏ No

If you are requesting hospital use (inpatient or outpatient), justify why this is necessary ____

If you are requesting surgery IN YOUR OFFICE OR YOUR OWN licensed ambulatory surgery center, will an Anesthesiologist or Certified Registered Nurse Anesthetist be utilized? ❏ Yes ❏ No

Approximate Fee _____

If yes, is he/she an HMO/Plan Provider? ❏ Yes ❏ No

_____
Attending Doctor Signature

_____
Approving Doctor Signature

JHCGA/Plan Approval Number _____

WHN OFFICE USE ONLY

Date _____ Second Opinion:- Telephone _____ IP _____

Result of second opinion _____

Name of physician rendering second opinion _____

_____
Signature

Surgery Approved ❏   Surgery Denied ❏

If Denied give reasons: _____

_____

_____
Signature

Site of Surgery:

Physician's office ❏

Licensed ambulatory surgery center (Name _____)

Hospital _____ Inpatient ❏ Outpatient ❏

Location _____ WH Length of Stay ___ Outpatient Days __ Inpatient Days _____

Section V: Utilization Management and Quality Improvement

Exhibit 10: NCQA Compliance Plan

Women's Healthcare Network NCQA Compliance Plan
[Brief example]

NCQA Standard	WHN Support of Compliance
1. Quality Improvement	1. Quality Improvement
Universal must have a written quality improvement (QI) program with procedures and accountable personnel clearly defined demonstrating that:	• WHN's regional medical director, area medical directors, and the chairman of the UM/QI committee will assist Universal's QI committee in drafting Universal's QI program to include interaction with Universal's medical director and QI committee at appropriate points.
• A senior executive is responsible for implementation.	
• Universal medical director has substantial involvement in QI activities.	• WHN's UM/QI committee chairman could also serve as a specially representative on Universal's UM/QI committee.
• There is a QI committee with a defined structure and function, known frequency of meetings, and with Universal providers involved.	• WHN's UM/QI committee will meet at least quarterly to consider issues presented by Universal and those identified as part of WHN's data collection and review process. These issues will form the basis of the annual work plan.
• An annual work plan must include objectives, planned activities, monitoring of previously identified issues, and evaluation of the QI process.	
QI program must be approved by and be accountable to a governing body of Universal to demonstrate Universal's active oversight	Final QI program and subsequent changes recommended by WHN's UM/QI committee will be referred to Universal's governing board for approval.
QI function must be coordinated with other management activity to demonstrate linkage between results of QI findings and appropriate changes to provider network, benefit design, patient education, and so on.	WHN's structure allows the network to adjust panel or procedures to comply with changes or corrective actions recommended by Universal's QI committee.
Provider contracts must require participation in QI process.	WHN requires participation in QI activities. Each practice is represented on the UM/QI Committee.

[Note: Reference all relevant NCQA standards]

Exhibit 11: Utilization Management and Quality Improvement Plan

Women's Healthcare Network (WHN) provides the foundation upon which member physicians can improve the delivery of quality medical care in an efficient manner. This is accomplished through a process of establishing and/or reevaluating treatment protocols and developing expertise in the management of a wide variety of health care costs that can be controlled by physicians. The application of the utilization management and quality improvement program (UM/QI) through creating and monitoring such protocols will help prevent inappropriate care, as well as identify potential quality issues. In addition, traditional retrospective case review and analysis of utilization trends will be conducted.

Purpose

The purpose of the UM/QI program of WHN is to design and implement a comprehensive, integrated process to evaluate practice patterns. The program will also develop and monitor policies and procedures employed in the prospective authorization and retrospective review process, as well as monitor the prospective review approval of the provision of medical services.

Structure and Function of Utilization Management/Quality Improvement Committee

The cornerstone of WHN's approach to effective delivery of health care services within a capitated reimbursement system is to define the expectations of the network related to delivery of high-quality, cost-effective patient care. WHN believes that the best way to establish and maintain quality while managing utilization is to prospectively establish standards that are uniformly understood and followed by the entire panel. To establish these standards, all network practices are required to participate in the development of treatment protocols, clinical pathways, and other areas relevant to progressive quality management.

Utilization Management/Quality Improvement (UM/QI) Committee

Each shareholder is required to designate a physician affiliate as a member of the UM/QI committee. Each member so appointed shall hold office until such shareholder is no longer a shareholder, or until such shareholder designates another physician affiliate to serve on such committee.

The UM/QI committee has been organized with the following duties:

- Establish and monitor criteria for utilization review, on a concurrent and retrospective basis;

- Develop and recommend to the Board quality improvement criteria and sanctions for noncompliance;

- Conduct peer review and report its findings to the Board; and

- Hear complaints and grievances from payors, patients, physicians, and shareholders, and to make recommendations to the Board.

The chairman of the UM/QI Committee shall be a member of the executive committee.

The committee will meet at least once per quarter or as frequently as deemed necessary by the chairman or as directed by the Board.

The UM/QI committee fulfills its duties through a peer-based monitoring and evaluation process, by developing protocols, performance standards and review criteria, as well as sanctions for non-compliance, and by establishing and presiding over the grievance process. The current composition of this committee is found in Exhibit 12. The UM/QI committee will be separated into subcommittees to address each function in detail.

Establishment of Clinical Protocols and Review Standards

The establishment and acceptance of uniform clinical criteria within multiple medical communities will assist in assuring consistently high-quality care across all socioeconomic groups covered by Universal Health Plans (UHP). In this regard, WHN has expended a considerable amount of time and effort developing clinical protocols and standards. WHN started from a clinical perspective. The philosophy was and is to develop the standards first and then proceed with development of capitation contracts using those standards as a basis for carefully managing utilization while improving quality.

Medical appropriateness criteria as determined by the UM/QI committee are developed using a wide range of information, criteria and resources. These include, but are not limited to, the following:

- Severity of illness/intensity of service criteria;

- Criteria established by the UM/QI committee;

- Quality screens;

- UHP's coverage policy manual;

- Relevant standards, guidelines and criteria developed by the American College of Obstetricians & Gynecologists and other appropriate national medical specially boards; and

- Other medical criteria and guidelines reviewed and approved by the UM/QI committee in conjunction with UHPs existing policies and procedures.

The UM/QI committee is developing clinical indicators for a number of high volume procedures. These indicators will be approved by the Executive Committee and distributed to all WHN members for implementation prior to implementation of the UHP contract.

Assignment of Responsibility for Monitoring UM/QI Programs

WHN's regional medical director and area medical directors (AMD) are selected by and report to the board of directors. They are responsible for day-to-day utilization management decisions. Their duties include the establishment of and monitoring of:

- Primary care referral protocols to network specialists;
- Clinical protocols and treatment plans;
- Normative medical criteria;
- Prospective and concurrent review of specific procedures;
- Initial review of all denials of procedures based on clinical issues;
- Retrospective review of claim utilization data; and
- Coordination and review of outcomes studies.

Additionally, elements of the first two duties listed are integrated into the third-party utilization management information system, which will provide timely reports to the regional medical director/area medical directors and UM/QI committee. These reports will identify variances from established criteria for later retrospective review.

WHN has selected Dr. M.D. to serve as its regional medical director. Area medical directors are as follows: [List area medical directors]

To assist the regional medical director and area medical directors, a clinical services coordinator will be assigned to:

- Coordinate the requests for service approvals;
- Respond to questions from network physician offices regarding services;
- Distribute information and notices to the network physicians;

- Coordinate transfers of patients to network physicians at contracted facilities;

- Communicate regularly with the UHP regarding patients, eligibility and benefit levels.

Preauthorization of Services

The process for preauthorization of services will be as follows:

1. Attending physician faxes a completed "request for service" form attached to the clinical services coordinator.

2. Clinical services coordinator gives the form to the area medical director/regional medical director (AMD/RMD) to review for clinical appropriateness and to verify that the case meets established protocol.

3. If approved, the clinical services coordinator faxes the "request for service" form to UHP for an authorization number. If denied, the AMD/RMD contacts the attending physician explaining the reason for denial. The medical services coordinator forwards to the physician a letter containing the reasons for the denial.

4. The managed-care organization sends the form back to the clinical services coordinator with an authorization number.

5. The Clinical Services Coordinator contacts the attending physician with the authorization number.

6. Appeals to any denial of services may be submitted to the medical director/ RMD using the appeal of claim denial form.

Based on UHP's reported utilization statistics, services to be initially reviewed include, but are not limited to: [List services]

Other aspects of patient care to be included in the review process are as follows:

- Review of non-elective hospital admissions within a limited time after notice of admission in order to adequately plan for possible transfer and/or discharge and contain costs.

- Prospective and retrospective utilization review for medical necessity. These will include evaluations of the appropriateness of admission to a hospital, the appropriateness of the level of care provided, and continuing evaluations of the inpatient stay to assist in preventing untimely discharges.

Denials and Appeals Process

Denial of Authorization of Services

Any service submitted for preauthorization which is subsequently denied may be appealed by the treating physician or UHP member. Notice of service denial is formally documented on the preauthorization form and returned to the requesting physician within seven days. The RMD or an AMD document the reason for service denial and inform the treating physician of the appeals process. Members may request documentation outlining service denial and the appeals process.

Billing for Services Denied by WHN

Any service not covered through the member's benefits or any service not covered by UHP will be denied. The treating physician will be notified of the reason for service denial in a standardized report. The treating physician may request an appeal of the decision. The patient may not be billed for any service denied by WHN or UHP based on failure to meet clinical guidelines. Treating physicians may bill patients directly for services not covered in the member's benefits if the patient consents to the charge prior to service provision.

Physician Appeals

The treating physician may appeal any service denial by requesting a second opinion. If the second opinion is in conflict with the treating physician's opinion, he may submit a request for case review to the network regional medical director. Upon receipt, the network regional medical director may deny the service, approve the service, or refer the case to a physician consultant from the appropriate specialty area who is certified by the applicable American Board of Medical Specialties. Denials after such review may be appealed to the full UM/QI committee.

Patient Appeals

A patient may appeal any service denial or treatment regimen by requesting a second opinion. If the second opinion confirms the original treatment regimen, the patient is referred back to the original treating physician for care. This process will be completed within 72 hours.

Retrospective Review

In addition to the prospective review criteria, the utilization management and claims administration system contains normative medical criteria which are used in conjunction with the developed protocols. The reports generated by this system, as well as periodic patient and provider satisfaction surveys, will also help identify any "over- or under- utilization" patterns and patient access problems.

The retrospective review program is a comprehensive integrated process that has the objective of controlling and monitoring the utilization of resources within the organization. The first level of utilization management includes reviews and evaluations of both medical necessity and appropriateness of care delivered to patients on a case-by-case basis. Data from the claims administration system will be used to evaluate physicians' utilization. Trends and patterns will be compared with other physicians in the network, generally recognized community standards of care, and the utilization criteria and the standards which have been established by the network's UM/QI committee and the Board, as well as by the individual managed-care plans.

The UM/QI committee and medical director will be integrally involved in the review and approval process. The plan will be reviewed and updated on a periodic basis, but not less than annually.

Standard utilization management and retrospective review functions will include, but not be limited to:

- Evaluation of utilization of high-cost diagnostic testing procedures in both hospital and alternative or ambulatory settings.

- Collection, review and evaluation of inpatient, outpatient, and other utilization data to evaluate individual provider performance in comparison to targeted goals, group norms, and other published standards.

- Review of claims for adequacy of information, accuracy and appropriateness of charges, as well as determinations of compliance with precertification criteria.

- Collection of data and information to identify opportunities for continuous improvement.

- Plan for the direction and improvement of the utilization management process by targeting areas for special studies regarding utilization, promoting investigation of specific trends, or maintaining standards and criteria of credentialling, utilization management, and internal operations.

- Monthly meetings of executive committee to review and monitor network performance.

- Monthly meeting between the WHN regional medical director and UHP medical director (frequency may change based on the mutual agreement of UHP and WHN).

- Quarterly meeting of UM/QI committee to review utilization trends, service denials, adverse outcomes and specific cases not meeting network protocols.

- Periodic meetings with primary-care physicians in coordination with UHP to review and discuss PCP referral criteria.

- Periodic meetings of UM/QI subcommittees for review and development of additional outcome measures and clinical pathways. Current QI goals are described in Exhibit 14.

In addition, selected indicators will be collected from participating hospitals and through the utilization management and claims administration system. As the indicators identify adverse outcomes, these will be investigated by the medical director and UM/QI committee. Among the adverse outcomes to be monitored are:

- Death
- Return to the operating room prior to discharge
- Re-admission to hospital within two weeks after discharge
- Unscheduled ICU admissions
- Operating room time greater than twice the expected length of surgical case
- Procedure not specified on initial consent form
- Outpatient procedure subsequently admitted to hospital
- Other outcomes as agreed with UHP

Patient and Physician Satisfaction Studies

The effectiveness of the utilization management program is further reinforced by evaluations of member satisfaction, provider satisfaction, and other means. It is the goal of WHN and its affiliated physicians to provide UHP members the same high quality of care expected by any other patient in terms of scheduling, waiting time, and examination content. Results of these surveys will also be referred to the QI committee to study as related to achievement of overall QI goals.

In addition to programs requested by UHP, WHN will provide an ongoing program to measure patient satisfaction with the physician services rendered by members of WHN. These programs will include:

- A telephone call to all UHP members within 24 hours (or next physician office work day) of a hospital discharge, emergency room visit, or outpatient procedure to determine patient's condition, as well as understanding of, and compliance with, after-care instructions.

- Periodic surveys of UHP patients treated by WHN physicians to measure overall satisfaction of services received. These surveys will be conducted on a quarterly basis initially and will be based on a sample of UHP patients seen by each WHN physician. This information will be shared with UHP after review by the UM/QI committee for use in UHPs annual patient survey statistics.

- Periodic surveys of primary care or other referring physicians to measure overall satisfaction of specialty care received, including accessibility to the system and diagnostic quality. These surveys are conducted on a regular basis and are based on a sample of all patients referred to WHN physicians.

- Periodic "Patient Relations Audits" based upon responses from the patient surveys. A third-party will make recommendations to the medical director based on tabulated results from the patient survey and/or primary-care physician survey. The medical director may then request a "Patient Relations Audit" at that time. The cost of the audit will be borne directly by the practice that has received the unsatisfactory rating. The purpose of an audit is to document the typical encounter with a provider through the use of a trained "informed consumer." This person will schedule an office visit as an UHP member, not as an auditor.

Program Communication and Continuing Education

Timely notification of policies and procedures, as well as general communication between network physicians and UHP's administrative staff, is essential to its initial success. We recommend that the following steps be taken:

- WHN will arrange a meeting between the office managers of the network physicians and UHP's provider relations and medical services staff prior to the effective date of the contract in order to clarify administrative procedures among all appropriate parties.

- The medical director will meet with all physicians in the network prior to the effective date of the contract in order to review clinical and administrative procedures applicable to UHP's contract.

- UHP will have customer service and provider service representatives available to answer questions about WHN when the program is implemented.

- Quarterly meetings during the first year (and as required thereafter) with practice administrative staff (recommended for office manager and insurance personnel) to review network systems and procedures. Written standards for preauthorizations, procedural and diagnostic coding, claims submission, appeals and patient relations will be provided to each practice in the network.

- UHP must provide a medical release form to UHP members to request medical records from physicians being terminated from UHP as a result of panel reduction. The medical director and the UM/QI committee of WHN will assist UHP in the evaluation of these records to determine appropriateness of transfers of patients under active treatment or in a post-operative status at the time WHN's contract becomes effective.

Exhibit 12: Utilization Management/Quality Improvement Committee

[List names and addresses of committee members]

Exhibit 13: Clinical Indicators

WHN's UM/QI committee is currently drafting clinical indicators and utilization management guidelines. The draft example of one high-volume procedures is provided for reference purposes The committee is continuing to refine criteria and will publish for all physician affiliates clinical indicators and guidelines as well as referral criteria for primary-care physicians and clinical pathing guidelines as appropriate.

Dilation and Curettage (D&C) [Example]

Indications

1. History—one or more required
    Confirmation of:
        Abnormal uterine bleeding (persisting for two or more cycles).

2. Physician examination—required
    Retained I.N.D.
    Prolapsed Fibroid

3. Tests—required and dated with three months of surgery
    a. Endometrial sample in office, if possible.
    b. Current Pap results
    c. CBC
    d. Hematocrit
    e. Pregnancy test (as indicated)
    f. Ultrasound (as indicated)

Length of Stay (if appropriate)

Outpatient

Post-Operative Observations (Instructions for nurses and residents)

1. Return to normal activity as soon as possible.
2. Monitor any post-operative bleeding.

Outcome Review

1. One Week
    Treatment for any inflection or bleeding

2. Beyond One Week
    Follow-up in office—2 to 3 weeks

Exhibit 14: Quality Improvement Program and Goals

Purpose

The Quality Improvement (QI) Program of WHN is designed to ensure the timely and continuous process of improving, monitoring, and evaluating the quality of patient care and promoting its cost-effective delivery. To this end, the board of directors, physicians and administration have developed an initial draft of the quality improvement program outlined below.

Program Objectives

1. To assure the quality of patient care through performance analysis, review and evaluation to improve patient care and resolve identified opportunities/processes for improvement.

2. To ensure cost-effective expenditure of resources and efficient utilization of services.

3. To ensure optimal interaction of all professional, managerial, technical and support personnel engaged in the delivery of patient care.

4. To promote a process that maximizes the participation of all physicians, allied health professionals, medical assistants, and others in outcome identification and responsiveness to all opportunities for improvement.

5. To assure communication and reporting of all QI activities to the QI committee and to the Board.

6. To conduct ongoing communication related to quality improvement activities.

7. To ensure prompt identification and analysis of opportunities for improvement to include implementation resolution and follow-up of actions.

8. To ensure member's rights and responsibilities are defined, communicated, and respected.

9. To ensure the performance of preventative services when applicable.

Program Guidelines

1. The general policies and processes to be utilized will be developed by obstetricians and gynecologists. The degree of professional performance will be scrutinized objectively and impartially administered by the quality improvement committee serving under the direction of the board of directors of WHN.

2. Any remedial quality improvement activity related to an individual practice should be triggered by concern for that individual's overall practice patterns, rather than by deviation from specific criteria in any single case. Only in exceptional circumstances should isolated single cases be considered.

3. The institution of any remedial activity will be preceded by discussion with the practitioner involved. There should be ample opportunity for the practitioner to explain observed deviations from accepted practice patterns to professional peers, before any remedial or corrective action is decided upon.

4. Emphasis will be placed on education and modification of unacceptable practice patterns rather than on sanctions. The initial thrust of any quality improvement activity should be toward helping the practitioner to correct deficiencies in knowledge, skills or technique, with practice restrictions or disciplinary action considered only for those not responsive to remedial activities.

5. The quality improvement system will make available the appropriate educational resources needed to effect desired practice modifications that may be necessary. Consistent with the emphasis on assistance rather than punitive activity, whether these be pure consultation, continuing education or self-learning, self- assessment programs.

6. Feedback mechanisms will be established to monitor and document the need for change in practice patterns. These will be decided on a case-by-case basis by the quality improvement committee and instituted by the committee.

7.   Restrictions or disciplinary actions should be imposed on those practitioners not responsive to remedial activities, whenever the appropriate professional peers deem such action necessary to protect the public. These will be reviewed by the quality improvement committee, presented before the board of directors and a decision made at that point. The restrictions may include loss of membership, revocation of privileges or suspensions from WHN.

8.   The imposition of restrictions or discipline should be timely and consistent with due process. Before a restriction or disciplinary action is imposed, the practitioner affected should have full understanding of the basis for the action, ample opportunity to request reconsideration and to submit any documentation relevant to that request and the right to meet with those considering its imposition, being the quality improvement committee or the board of directors of WHN. However, in cases where those considering its imposition deem the practitioner to pose an imminent hazard to the health of patients, such restrictions or disciplinary actions may be imposed immediately. In such instances, the due process right noted above should be provided on an expedited basis. This action will be taken only by the board of directors.

Organization

The QI program is conducted through the QI committee under the direction of the full UM/QI committee and the board of directors. The QI committee is responsible for the overall coordination and implementation of the QI program.

The QI committee consists of physicians and other patient care staff (i.e., physician assistants/nurse practitioners, and nurses) who will ensure the program is implemented, opportunities for improvements are focused and resolutions are effective. All data generated by the QI activities will be reviewed by the QI committee. The QI program will be evaluated annually and reviewed as necessary.

The QI Committee will be comprised of the following:

- Physician shareholder, elected by the full UM/QI committee to be, who will serve as chairman
- A patient-care representative
- Network administrator
- Physicians at large
- Additional members may be appointed by the chairman
- Medical directors of Universal Health Plans and WHN.

The QI committee will meet quarterly and perform the following functions:

- Receive and review information which deals with the quality of care delivered by the network.

- Assure that the ongoing process for identification/acknowledgment of opportunities for improvement is conducted in all clinical and non-clinical areas.
- Monitor the effectiveness of the program.
- Perform periodic reassessments of previously identified issues to ensure problem resolution.
- Identify areas in need of patient/staff education.
- Develop and apply clinically valid criteria that are reviewed for updates annually.
- Ensure participation by all members of the professional staff.
- Credential all professional staff.

Key Areas of Review

- Treatment indications
- Treatment review
- Evaluation of clinical outcomes
- Physician utilization
- Patient/physician satisfaction
- Patient access to care
- Appropriateness of care
- Medical records to reflect all aspects of patient care. Standards established by the managed-care organization will also be implemented.
- Top 10 volume procedures

Forms and Tools

- Medical performance chart review
- Quality improvement study
- Patient evaluation survey report
- Clinical guidelines
- Clinical pathways and treatment protocols

Other forms will be added as necessary.

Methods of Identification

Activities utilized for problem identification may include, but are not limited to, the following:

- Clinically based outcomes
- Medical records review
- Direct observation
- Results of patient and staff surveys
- Data from patient telephone interviews
- Results of surveys by external organization, such as insurance company, HMO
- Results of quarterly information system reports
- Suggestions of members

Scope of the Program

- All reports related to evaluation of care will be reported to the QI committee
- All physicians shall report to the QI committee
- Each network provider's clinical and non-clinical departments will participate in the review of the services provided if required
- Issues monitored and evaluated will reflect the demographics of the population serviced

Each study will include, but is not limited to, the following:

- Evidence of review of opportunities for improvement identification, performance criteria and prioritizing
- Stated objectives
- Standard of expected performance
- Assessment and analysis
- Problem resolution
- Outcome measurement
- Evidence of sustained quality improvement.

The QI committee will review reports for identification of opportunities for improvement, patterns and trends and call attention to items requiring immediate action.

- Minutes of each meeting will be kept and be available to any network member and the managed care organization
- Results of all QI focus studies will be reported to all physicians involved
- Summary reports of QI activities will be presented on a regular basis to the board of directors

- Reports will be made available to managed-care organizations on request
- Reports will be made available to the re-credentialling and quality improvement committees

Guidelines and Standards

Monitoring the quality of patient care provided to patients by WHN will be based on currently available standards, guidelines and criteria established by the appropriate medical specially boards and national specially organizations.

Women's Healthcare Network 1995–1996
Quality Improvement Goals [Example]

The following is a list of the initial quality improvement goals identified by the Women's Healthcare Network (WHN) utilization management/quality improvement committee (UM/QI) for implementation during 1995/1996. Additional goals can be added at the request of Universal Health Plans (UHP) or based on specific issues identified by the UM/QI committee or the medical director.

I. Network Goal: Review each practice yearly for compliance with NCQA standards for documentation of clinical data.

Methodology

WHN participants will be divided into four groups, one of which will be reviewed each quarter. A review schedule will be sent to each physician stating when he/she will be responsible for submitting ten UHP patient charts to the UM/QI committee for review. In special instances, charts may be reviewed on-sight by a physician or nurse designated by the UM/QI committee. This review will address the format of the medical records, not clinical content.

The patient charts will be randomly selected from a group of UHP members. Patients must have been treated for one of the ten most frequent diagnoses from the prior year. Five charts must represent patients with chronic conditions. The remaining five will represent patients with acute conditions. Each chart must be 75 percent complete to be deemed acceptable. Charts will be reviewed for completeness using the standards for managed-care plans established by NCQA.

Physicians with less than 75 percent compliance will be notified and their charts will be re-reviewed the following quarter. If they fail to improve by this review, they will be required to meet with the UM/QI committee for education. They will again be reviewed the next quarter. If they fail to improve by this third review, they will be suspended from the network for one quarter.

II. Network Goal: Review each practice yearly for compliance with clinical indicators established by the UM/QI committee and/or current specially standards of care.

Methodology

WHN physicians are developing guidelines for the high-volume diagnoses. Each year, the top three to five diagnoses, in terms of volume and costs, will be reviewed for guideline compliance. A minimum of five charts representing one of these diagnoses will be randomly selected from each physician's practice and reviewed to ensure compliance with the guidelines.

On an annual basis, the UM/QI committee randomly selects and reviews charts representing the following patient conditions and issues for review. A minimum of 75 percent of the charts must be 100 percent compliant for each category of chart review unless specific outcomes dictate a higher threshold. If the appropriate threshold is not met, the issue will be referred to the UM/QI committee for peer review and a corrective plan established. Timely follow-up chart review will be scheduled and completed within three months of the time the deficiency is identified.

Monitoring the appropriateness and quality of patient care provided to patients by WHN is based on currently available standards, guidelines and criteria established by appropriate medical specialty boards and national specialty organizations. These treatment guidelines have been approved by the UM/QI committee. They are reviewed annually and distributed to every physician panel member. A satisfactory review of at least 75 percent of the charts will be acceptable. This percentage will be reassessed annually.

Physicians below the 75 percent satisfactory chart review will be notified and failure to improve to 75 percent compliance by the next quarterly review will result in discussion between the UM/QI committee and the physician. Failure to achieve at least a 75 percent satisfactory chart review within six (6) months will result in temporary suspension from the panel. Additional reviews will be conducted on an as-needed basis as identified by the UM/QI committee based upon the pre-authorization and retrospective review processes or complaints.

III. Network Goal: Survey patients of network physicians on a semi-annual basis to determine levels of satisfaction with access and quality of care.

Methodology

Semi-annually, patient satisfaction surveys will be mailed to all UHP patients seen at all WHN locations during a one-week period. A twenty percent (20%) return rate is expected. Between the mailings, the survey forms will be available in each physician's office. Any patient satisfaction survey with rankings below good or any with a negative response will be reviewed by the UM/QI committee on a quarterly basis.

Periodic "Patient Relations Audits" may be requested by the UM/QI committee based upon responses from the patient satisfaction surveys. Recommendations will be made by the UM/QI committee to the medical director based on tabulated results from the patient survey and/or referral physician surveys and any patient or provider complaint. The medical director may then request an audit. The cost of the audit will be borne directly by the practice that has received the unsatisfactory rating. The purpose of these audits is to document the typical encounters with a provider through the use of a trained "informed consumer." This person will schedule an office visit as an UHP member, not as an auditor, to assure that the practice follows its normal patterns related to patient interaction and treatment and will submit a written report of his/her findings and recommendations.

IV. Network Goal: Review all denials of procedures or admissions by medical director based on medical appropriateness.

Methodology

All denied procedures and admissions will be reviewed by the UM/QI committee at least quarterly to ensure appropriate decisions by the medical director. A member of the UM/QI committee will also be available on a rotating basis to review any urgent appeal of denials made by a patient or other provider. Any denial overturned by appeal will also be reviewed by the UM/QI committee as part of the periodic appraisal of the medical director's performance. The findings will be submitted to the board of directors for any additional review or action.

Exhibit 15: Outcomes Review

Adverse Outcome Review. As the indicators identify adverse outcomes, the utilization management/quality improvement committee (UM/QI) will conduct a thorough investigation. The committee will review selected indicators from participating hospitals, the utilization management and claims administration system. Among the adverse outcomes to be monitored are as follows:

1. Death

2. Return to the operating room prior to discharge

3. Re-admission to hospital within two weeks after discharge

4. Unscheduled ICU admissions

5. Operating room time greater than twice the expected length of surgical case

6. Procedure not specified on initial consent form

7. Outpatient procedure subsequently admitted to hospital

8. Other outcomes as agreed with UHP

These adverse outcomes will be examined in the quarter they occur and any actions deemed necessary will be taken immediately by the UM/QI committee through peer review. [Add graphics, charts, and so on to this section if needed.]

Exhibit 16: Educational Services

Patient Education

Each of the practices in the network provide patient education in an attempt to fully explain the indications, benefits, and risks of surgical and diagnostic procedures in education and healthy lifestyles. All of the physicians in the network counsel their patients prior to any procedure and preoperatively obtain a written "informed consent" as required. In addition, many of the practices use handouts, brochures, videos and training aids to provide in-depth information to their patients. In this regard, the following attachments present a summary of the patient education materials provided by the practices, along with examples of those materials. WHN has recently formed a patient education committee to review the educational materials used by each practice and to make recommendations for improvement to the network.

The physicians involved with WHN have a strong commitment to patient communication and education, with a strong focus on prevention of disease and early diagnosis and effective treatment. WHN members appreciate the value and importance of high-quality information and its impact on their patients' health, lifestyle, and medical outcomes. WHN will provide comprehensive education and counseling services to each patient consistent with the patient's level of knowledge and understanding, as well as an awareness of the patient's social, cultural, religious, ethnic, and economic background.

The physicians of WHN are all involved in their communities and teach community and hospital-based classes on topics of concern. Many are also well published in the professional literature.

Several WHN physicians have authored or produced individualized patient education materials for use in their practices. [Include examples of education materials created by physicians.]

Physician Education

Physician education is a product of the work done by the UM/QI committee. The continuing development of clinical indicators and protocols will provide guidelines. The collection and analysis of experience-based data will allow WHN to further define normative criteria, and identify outer behavior. Through a variety of educational functions, WHN will continue to improve on its overall goal: To provide high-quality patient care in a cost-effective manner.

Primary-care physicians are often involved with the treatment of routine gynecological cases. One of the primary goals of the UM/QI committee is to develop, in conjunction with UHP's medical director, referred criteria for primary-care physicians. Early detection and appropriate pathing and referral will contribute significantly to improve patient outcomes and reduce costs.

Section VI: Representative Procedure Listing

The following is a representative listing of gynecological services covered under the proposed GYN capitation rate and included and excluded procedures related to the obstetrical case based rate.

Other services may be added based on experience and in keeping with Universal Health Plan's covered benefits. [Add list of gynecological services.]

Section VII: Attachments

[Insert any other attachments required by the RFP or any others that would be beneficial.]

APPENDIX ITEM 19-06
PHYSICIAN CAPITATION CONTRACT PROPOSAL

To: Contracting Representatives
ABC Health Plans
[City, State]

American Eye Associates (AEA) is pleased to respond to ABC Health Plans' request for proposal to provide [specialty] services to its members. At the present time, AEA is made up of practicing physicians and therapeutic [specialists] with offices throughout the [location] region. Each physician shares in the common goal of providing quality care, improving the quality of care, and becoming more cost-effective providers.

AEA looks forward to your positive response to this proposal. Please contact one of the following individuals if you need additional information or have any questions:

[Provide names and phone numbers of individuals.]

AEA providers and representatives are available to meet with representatives of ABC to discuss this proposal in detail. In addition, we can arrange site visits at any of the participating provider offices if needed.

INTRODUCTION

American Eye Associates is a network of prominent, well-established [physician specialties] and [physician specialties] located throughout the [region] region. AEA was organized to provide high-quality, cost-effective patient care in response to managed-care environments. AEA's provider panel was carefully selected and shares the common goal of maintaining high standards while practicing medicine in a cost-effective manner.

In developing AEA, there were two main goals for provider selection. First, to form a strong alliance with quality [specialty] professionals to build a stable network that is geared toward satisfying the needs of the payors and their members. Second, to create a network of comprehensive [specialty] services with convenient patient access. The physicians and [physician specialty] selected to participate in AEA have training in areas of subspecialty, such as [list specialties].

AEA intends to provide ABC with the following:

- A highly qualified [specialty] panel with members who are geographically accessible throughout the [region] region and have excellent relationships with ABC primary-care physicians and preferred hospitals

- An improvement in quality and utilization rates of [specialty] services through participation in utilization-management and quality-improvement programs and the progressive development and application of clinical protocols

- A willingness to work toward win-win financial relationships that will benefit ABC, primary-care physicians, and AEA providers

- The ability and willingness to expand the AEA panel as required to meet ABC's specific needs

- The willingness to assume 100 percent of the professional fee risk under a capitation arrangement for covered [specialty] services

There are number of key factors that differentiate AEA from other [specialty] networks in the [region] area. These factors substantially increase the likelihood that AEA will be successful and provide a sound basis for a long-term relationship with ABC.

- Dr. [name], the founding member of AEA, has a provider history with ABC Health Plans. Dr. [name] has worked with ABC on a capitated basis, and such experience will be transferred to the operations and knowledge base of AEA. As a result of this relationship, ABC Health Plans should be aware of both primary care and patient satisfaction with Dr. [name]'s past services.

- The providers selected by AEA have met strict standards regarding the delivery of health care services. AEA believes this will lead to cost effectiveness for both AEA and ABC.

- AEA has selected providers in both adult and pediatric [specialty]. This allows AEA to provide [specialty] coverage for all ABC enrollees.

- AEA will cover [service] services in its network. AEA intends to cover subspecialty services as outlined in the covered services sections of this proposal document.

- A payor, such as ABC Health Plans, must be concerned regarding the financial stability of any provider network it contracts with. Specifically, a payor cannot afford to have its contracted provider network get into financial difficulties. This could interrupt the delivery of health care services to the payor's enrollees. Unfortunately, many physicians who create provider networks do not have the knowledge or experience in managing capitated dollars. AEA has engaged [region] Regional Clinic to provide administration services to its network. AEA has also engaged the services of [CPA company] to provide network consulting services. The CPA company has a long history of working with capitated provider networks in [state] and out of the [state] area. As such, AEA believes it is well served from the standpoint of network and financial administration. Proper financial controls will be instituted and monitored on an ongoing basis to ensure the ongoing financial success and viability for the network.

- AEA can meet the geographic coverage requirements as it relates to patient access by ABC enrollees.

- Eighteen board certified physicians are a part of the network. Provider quality is of utmost importance to the AEA network.

- AEA has begun the process of implementing its own quality-assurance and utilization-management programs even though it is submitting this bid with no guarantee of acquisition. This demonstrates the network's commitment to quality and cost effectiveness.

PROVIDER PANEL

The following is a list of physicians and [physician specialists] who have agreed to participate with American Eye Associates through an IPA arrangement. All members of AEA have been credentialled to verify their appropriateness for participation in this network. The network's credentialling process is comprehensive and provider credentialling files are open for review by representatives of ABC Health Plans and other contracting health plans. It is the policy of AEA to recredential members of the network at least every two years.

Specialists

[List physicians.]

Satellite office locations for the above physicians:

[List addresses.]

Physician Specialists

[List physicians.]

OTHER PROVIDER INFORMATION

Curricula Vitae

Curricula Vitae for the physicians listed above are provided in the Attachment Section of this proposal document. You will notice the [specialists] and [physician specialists] who constitute AEA are well experienced and have distinguished themselves throughout their training and practice.

Appointment Scheduling

Appointments for the providers that constitute AEA are handled by each individual office. For non-emergency [service], appointments can be scheduled within one week and emergency [service] appointments are typically the same day or within 24 hours.

Call Coverage

Call coverage for the network will be coordinated by the management with all [specialists] participating on a rotating basis. General [specialists] will be available to ABC members 24 hours a day as well as specialty [specialists] for [services]. Due to the size of ABC's service area, we will have 3 to 4 geographically dispersed general [specialists] on call at any given time to ensure ease of patient access.

GEOGRAPHIC COVERAGE

Located in the Attachment Section of this proposal document is a chart comparing the location of ABC enrollees under this proposed contract and network provider locations. Also included is a chart showing the total county geographic area and where the network provider offices are located. As you can see, AEA meets the geographic coverage area requirements deemed essential by ABC Health Plans. ABC enrollees should have no problem with access to network office locations.

After reviewing the charts in the Attachment Section, ABC contracting representatives may have two areas of concern, which AEA would like to address at this point. This first is provider access by enrollees in or around the [area] area. Per a review of patient demographic records supplied by AEA providers, the providers with offices located in the [area 2] and [area 3] areas see quite a few patients from the [area] area. Therefore, AEA believes enrollees in this part of the geographic region would not have a problem traveling to either [area 2] or [area 3] for their specialized [service specialty] needs. The second area of concern involves enrollees located in or near the [area 4] area. Since the closest providers in the AEA network are located in [area 5] and south [region], patient access may be considered a problem. AEA providers have voted that if the ABC contract is awarded to the AEA network, an office would be established in [area 4] to serve the needs of the enrollees in the area. Equipment has already been secured to furnish this office. Therefore, the opening of this office should remove this concern from ABC contracting representatives and also indicate AEA's commitment to providing the services needed under this contract.

PROPOSED FINANCIAL TERMS

American Eye Associates (AEA) proposes to contract with ABC Health Plan to provide [specialty] services on a capitated basis. AEA is committed to meeting ABC's expectations and requirements regarding panel size, geographic distribution, credentials, and any other necessary factors.

AEA proposes a capitation rate of 89 cents per member per month (PMPM) to cover all covered adult and pediatric [specialty] services except as noted below. This proposed capitation rate takes into account the services to be covered, both general and subspecialty [specialty], and the fact ABC Health Plans will shift a significant portion of its administrative burden to AEA.

Services Covered in Capitation Rate

A listing of specific CPT and HCPCS codes will be constructed for all services to be covered by the capitation payment based on the final agreement between ABC and AEA. In general, the covered services will include those professional services billed by AEA providers as appropriate to the practice of [specialty] and [specialty 2]. Subject to the specific levels of benefits provided by ABC to a covered member and subject to final construction of covered services with ABC, these services shall include:

[List services.]

The following services are *not* included in the proposed capitation rate:

[List services not covered.]

Assumption of Financial Risk

AEA is willing to engage in discussions with ABC regarding sharing an outpatient facility risk. Such discussions can take place in the future should the contract be awarded to AEA.

CONTRACTOR ORGANIZATION: ADDITIONAL INFORMATION

American Eye Associates is an incorporated entity in the State of [state]. The official corporate name is AEA-American Eye Associates.

Each physician and [specialist] has executed, or is in the process of executing, a Provider Agreement with AEA. A copy of the provider agreement is included in the Attachment Section of this proposal document. The following is a summary of the Provider Agreement:

Credentials

Every physician providing services on behalf of AEA must have a current [state] physician's license in good standing, a current unrestricted DEA certificate, and [state] Department of Public Safety license; must be board certified or board eligible in [specialty]; must have appropriate clinical privileges in good standing at a participating provider hospital; must be able to provide 24 hour coverage; and must have in force medical malpractice coverage as defined below.

Every [specialist] providing services on behalf of AEA must have a current [state] [specialty] license in good standing.

Utilization Management and Quality Management

All providers are required to participate in all quality-management and improvement activities conducted by either ABC or AEA. Each provider must also participate in and cooperate with AEA's utilization-management activities.

Provider Compensation

Every provider will be reimbursed at a scheduled discounted fee for covered services. The fee schedule is based on the current Medicare RBRVS payment system.

Withhold

A 20 percent withhold will be withheld from each provider payment by AEA.

Malpractice Insurance

Each provider is required to maintain malpractice liability coverage with limits of at least $200,000 per occurrence or claim and $600,000 as an annual aggregate.

Termination

A provider can only terminate the Provider Agreement voluntarily by giving 90 days' notice prior to the end of the Agreement's anniversary period. AEA may terminate the Agreement at any time by giving provider 90 days' written notice. The Agreement may be terminated automatically upon the occurrence of specific acts.

NETWORK ADMINISTRATOR

[Region] Regional Clinic (the Clinic) will provide administration services on behalf of AEA. Beginning in 1980 with three physicians, [region] Regional Clinic has grown to one of the largest multispecialty medical groups in the greater [region] area. Today, with more than 140 physicians and other health care providers, the Clinic continues to grow and serve the health care needs of the greater [region] community. The Clinic began as [region]'s first independent medical group to provide services to a managed-care plan. Since that time, the Clinic has developed an experienced team to manage both the clinical and operational aspects of its business, in particular its managed-care business. The Clinic today is a highly respected, managed-care-based medical group and it is regarded as the leader in this arena by both the medical and employer communities.

The Clinic's managed-care philosophy, which is the foundation of its practice, is based on the belief that managed care should be physician directed. In 1992, the Clinic established its own utilization review organization, to perform the traditional pre-certification functions, and an intensive-care management program. These services are performed by a subsidiary of the Clinic called Mediview. The utilization-review program is informally known as C3V, which stands for Cost of Care Contracting Vehicle. In 1995, the Clinic's quality advancement services, contracting, credentialling, and claims functions were added to Mediview. The nine directors and supervisors of UR, QAS, contracting, and claims have over 150 years of combined experience in health care from the nursing, hospital, private practice, HMO, and self-insured perspective.

The Clinic will provide C3V services to the AEA network as described below.

NETWORK ADMINISTRATOR SERVICES

The following services will be rendered to AEA by [region] Regional Clinic:

Claims

- Load/maintain benefits plans/co-payments.
- Load/maintain provider fee schedules.
- Load/maintain provider and vendor files.
- Load/maintain eligibility information.
- Enter encounter data.
- Enter and adjudicate claim.
- Issue claims payment checks and EOBs.
- Produce 1099 forms at year's end.
- Pay subcapitation to providers when applicable.
- Produce reports.

Contracting/Provider Relations

- Compile/update the network provider manual and directory.
- Assist quality assurance and utilization management on site visits/ provider education.
- Serve as liaison with provider network on problem issues.

Credentialling

- Establish process to credential and re-credential providers, including:
    — Primary source verification
    — Licensure updating
    — Filing/retention procedures

Quality Assurance

- Assist in the development of QA processes, policies, procedures, and documentation for assuming delegated functions and assuring NCQA accreditation. This includes the following:
  — Formal peer review
  — Risk management processes
  — Basic medical record standards
  — On site surveys
  — Development of practice guidelines
  — Guideline development process
  — Patient satisfaction surveys
  — Newsletters (e.g., provider, patient, employee)
  — Other surveys (e.g., clinician satisfaction, employee satisfaction)
  — Clinician performance appraisal process
  — Regulatory agencies' standards

  The Clinic will also provide:

- Policies and procedures (e.g., release of information, informed consent)
- Patients' rights and responsibilities
- "How to Use Your Medical Group" brochure
- "Welcome to the Practice" letters
- New-patient packet
- Patient care handbook
- Protocols/guidelines

Utilization Management

- Telephonic precertification
- Telephonic (inpatient and outpatient) case management
- Physician advisory support
- Referral and denial statistics
- Monthly and YTD hospital and other service statistical reporting

Reporting to Network

The Clinic will provide the following reports to AEA (refer to following section on reporting for more information):

- Line item cost of care reporting
- Risk pool management
- Capitation/membership reporting
- Stop-loss reporting
- Catastrophic case reporting, when applicable
- Capitation analysis
- IBNR (incurred but not reported) reporting
- PMPM analysis per contract (upward and downward)
- Capitation reconciliation
- COB/Subrogation coordination
- Referral analysis
- Length of stay analysis

SERVICE REFERRAL, AUTHORIZATION, AND CLAIMS ADMINISTRATION

Referral Process

If a patient is in need of [service], the primary-care physician will make a referral to an AEA provider. AEA will follow the current ABC protocol for specialty referrals.

Service Authorization Process

After a proper referral has been made to an AEA provider by a primary-care physician, the ABC patient will go to a network provider's office, where the physician will conduct an initial evaluation on the patient. All surgical procedures and hospitalization must be preauthorized by all AEA providers. An AEA provider will be required to contact a Clinical

Services Coordinator at the Clinic for proper authorization. An authorization number will be assigned to each respective clinical episode and this authorization number must be used by each provider when submitting claims to AEA for payment. Authorization will be granted on a diagnosis basis and a treatment plan basis. For example, only one authorization will be required for the full treatment of [service]. The following is the expected flow for service authorization:

1. Patient goes to a AEA provider.

2. Attending provider faxes a completed service authorization request form to the Clinical Services Coordinator at the Clinic.

3. The Clinical Services Coordinator reviews the form for clinical appropriateness and to verify that the case meets certain protocols, if applicable. The Clinical Services Coordinator will contact Dr. [name] if clarification is needed before authorization is granted.

4. If approved, an authorization is assigned and communicated to the provider.

Claims Administration

Claims administration will be conducted by the Clinic in coordination with AEA. Treating providers submit claims for services to the Clinic for processing. The Clinic confirms service authorizations and prepares explanation of payment statements for each provider. Claims review is conducted to ensure that policy guidelines established by AEA are followed. Each claim is also reviewed to determine if the listed CPT codes are appropriate for the listed diagnoses and all coding protocols are followed. If found inappropriate, the claims are denied. The following is the expected flow for claims processing:

1. Match service authorization number with the submitted claim to properly adjudicate the claim.

2. Verify patient eligibility for services.

3. Perform diagnosis and procedure compatibility edits on each claim prior to payment.

4. Perform customized edits on each claim prior to payment.

5. Coordinate provider inquiries regarding claim status.

6. Prepare provider reimbursement checks.

7. Coordinate resolution of claim issues between AEA, providers, and the Clinic.

8. If requested, submit all patient encounter data to ABC.

REPORTING

The Clinic will use the EZ-CAP software system for administration and claims adjudication. EZ-CAP is currently used by over 300 IPAs, multispecialty medical groups, and hospitals for more than three million HMO enrollees. The following is a listing of the sample reports produced by EZ-CAP (Sample reports are included in the Attachments Section of this proposal document.):

- Requested Authorization Log
- Check Register
- Claims Paid Report
- Eligibility Listing
- Explanation of Benefits Report
- IBNR Claims Lag Analysis
- Member Month Audit Report
- Claims Expense Per Member Per Month
- Provider Claims Stoploss Summary
- Case Events Sorted by Event Type and Subtype
- Hospital Claims Report

Reports will be reviewed by utilization personnel at the Clinic and by assigned AEA members. The reports will be reviewed for medical appropriateness, cost effectiveness, and protocol adherence. Information contained in these and other reports aids in the retrospective review of each provider's clinical activities and the resulting financial impact on AEA. Each provider will receive personalized reports detailing his or her activity with respect to the entire network. Providers are then able to monitor their own practice patterns and investigate significant deviations from the norm.

Variance from defined norms will be routinely investigated by utilization personnel at the Clinic and by assigned members of AEA. Providers will be notified and educated to assure appropriate compliance with network standards and guidelines.

UTILIZATION MANAGEMENT AND QUALITY ASSURANCE

The cornerstone of any provider network is its ability to police itself clinically. Costs must be managed by developing a comprehensive utilization-management and quality-assurance program. Otherwise the network may put itself at risk financially, which could impair the long-term survival of the network.

AEA, in partnership with the Clinic, has developed its own utilization-management and quality-assurance program. This program will be implemented and monitored on an ongoing basis by the Clinic personnel and assigned members of AEA. Utilization and quality-assurance committees have been established. The program will also develop and monitor policies and procedures employed in the prospective authorization and retrospective review process, as well as monitor the prospective review approval of the provision of medical services. This program is intended to meet all NCQA guidelines.

The following is a brief description of AEA's program:

Quality Management

Purpose

The quality-management program is designed to objectively and systematically monitor and evaluate the quality, appropriateness, and outcome of care and services and the processes by which they are delivered to ABC members, and to continuously pursue opportunities for improvement and problem resolution.

Scope

The scope of the program is comprehensive and includes all activities that have a direct or indirect influence on the quality and outcome of clinical care and service delivered to all ABC members.

Goals and Objectives

- To continuously improve the quality of care and service delivered to ABC members.

- To develop, implement, and coordinate all activities that are designed to improve the processes by which care and service are delivered.

- To ensure a system of quality-management communication that is timely and reports through appropriate channels, to appropriate individuals.

- To facilitate documentation, reporting, and follow-up of quality-management activities in order to prevent duplication and facilitate excellence in clinical care, service, and outcome.

The following are sample sections from AEA's quality-management program:

Provider Care and Service Review

The following is the review of provider care and service policy and procedure for AEA:

Policy

- The Quality Management Committee is responsible, as delegated by the Board of Directors, for monitoring and evaluating the quality, appropriateness, and effectiveness of the care and service provided to health plan members with the goal of continuous improvement.

- The Chairman of the Quality Management Committee is responsible for assuring the implementation of this policy/procedure and for evaluating the quality, appropriateness, and effectiveness of the clinical performance of Provider Panel Members.

- The Quality Management Committee meets at least quarterly and follows a prescribed agenda. Minutes of the meeting are recorded and submitted to the Board of Directors for review and approval. Confidentiality is maintained.

- The minimum monitoring and evaluation process includes but is not limited to:

  a. Member clinical care review

  b. Internal quality management sentinel events

  c. Health plan reports of quality and/or service problems

  d. Member complaints/grievances

  e. Patient Satisfaction Survey results

  f. Peer concerns and reports

  g. Utilization Management Reports

  h. Quality Coalition Study findings

  i. Quality and/or service problems identified through the recredentialling of providers

  j. Patient care site visit deficiencies

  k. Results of quality and/or service studies

  l. Problems reported by recognized monitoring organizations (e.g., NPDB, MBT, OSHA)

  m. Malpractice claims

  n. Quality Management Notices

  o. Other items/issues as determined by the Quality Management Committee

Procedure

1. Information pertaining to the above indicators is collected and analyzed by the Quality Management Committee.

2. If a problem or opportunity to improve care or service is identified, the cause is determined and action is taken to resolve the problem or improve the care/service provided.

3. After a period of time, predetermined by the Quality Management Committee, the effectiveness of the action(s) taken is assessed. Monitoring and evaluation of effectiveness of actions taken are continued until the problem is resolved.

4. Possible opportunities to improve care/service are identified by Utilization and Quality Management personnel, utilizing indicators established by the Quality Management Committee. These are docu-

mented on the appropriate review form and held for review by Quality Management Committee members.

5. If the Committee reviewer identifies no opportunities to improve care or service, the reasons for these findings are documented on the review form and an appropriate review category is assigned. These cases are not referred to the Quality Management Committee for discussion, unless the reviewer refers them for educational purposes.

6. If the reviewer identifies possible opportunities to improve care or service, the case is referred to the Quality Management Committee with a specific question for discussion.

7. Cases identified for further review are placed on the Quality Management Committee Agenda for discussion, conclusion, recommendation, and action. A date for follow-up and evaluation of action and improvement is determined and calendared at the time of review by the Committee.

8. The Chairman of the Quality Management Committee or his/her designee is responsible for carrying out the recommendations of the Committee with the provider(s) involved in the opportunity to improve care or service.

9. A record of the discussion, conclusions, recommendations, and actions are documented in the minutes of the Committee meeting and included in the Provider(s) Quality Profile File in order to document, track, and trend provider performance.

10. When patterns or trends are identified by the Quality Management Committee, an intensive evaluation of the provider's knowledge, judgment, and skill by appointed peers may be initiated.

11. Review findings are utilized as part of the assessment of provider care and service at the time of reappointment to the Provider Panel.

Reporting and Follow-up

The Quality Management Committee reports on the quality, appropriateness, and effectiveness of care and service provided to members, usually monthly but at least quarterly, to the Board of Directors. Recommendations for further action and follow-up are made as indicated by the Board of Directors and carried out by the Quality Management Committee.

Access to Care and Service

Purpose

To ensure that health services are available and accessible to ABC members and that they are able to obtain services within a reasonable period of time.

Policy

The Quality Management Committee is responsible for the development or adoption and communication of Guidelines for the availability and accessibility of care.

Monitoring and Evaluation

1. Access to care is monitored through member surveys and tracking member complaints.

2. Access and availability studies are included as an ongoing part of the Annual Quality Management Work Plan.

3. If an opportunity to improve care or a problem is identified additional telephone or mail surveys may be conducted to further evaluate a particular problem (e.g., accessibility for after-hours telephone consultation).

Reporting and Follow-up

The findings of monitoring and evaluation and action(s) taken, as indicated, are reported to the Quality Management Committee and the Board of Directors. Recommendations for further action are made and follow-up is carried out as directed until the issue is resolved.

Medical Record Guidelines

Purpose

To ensure that the care rendered to patients is consistently documented and that the documentation is of high quality and includes all information necessary to make medical determinations readily available at all times.

To ensure that the medical record is complete and that it includes all of the elements of the member's health history, treatment rendered, and response to treatment.

To ensure the safe and effective transfer of care between the primary-care provider and the specialty provider, in the interest of excellence in patient care and to enhance service between providers.

To ensure the protection of confidentiality of patient medical records is maintained at the provider's practice site.

Policy

- Patient providers are required to maintain a centralized medical record for each member. The individual record includes care provided within and referred outside the network.

- Providers are required to maintain policies and procedures that address release of patient information to any internal or external person. Each patient care site must have a copy of the policy.

- The patient's medical record is maintained in a current, detailed organized manner that permits effective patient care and facilitates quality review.

- The medical record is a legal document and its contents are confidential.

Medical Record Review

- Quality Management Committee reviews medical records to determine compliance with standards.

- Findings, including conclusions, recommendations and follow-up, are reported to the Board of Directors.

- Opportunities to improve care/service are included in the provider's Quality Profile for use at the time of recredentialling.

- Providers are given information regarding medical record guidelines and standards at the time of appointment to the Provider Panel and at the time of any Medical Record Guideline revision.

Practice Guidelines

Purpose

To provide a method of systematically developing statements to assist providers and ABC members to make decisions about appropriate health care for specific clinical circumstances.

To assess the appropriateness of specific health care decisions, services, and outcomes and to provide methods or instruments to monitor and evaluate the extent to which the actions of a provider conform to practice guidelines, medical review criteria, and /or standards of quality to provide optimum clinical outcomes.

Scope

Selection of topics for guideline development will consider high-volume, high-risk services and procedures and those with the potential for reducing clinically significant and unexplained variations in services and procedures used in the prevention, diagnosis, treatment, management, or outcomes related to the clinical condition and the cost of the condition to all payors, including members.

Policy

- The Quality Management Committee is responsible for arranging for the development, periodic review, and updating of clinical practice guidelines that may be used by providers to determine how specific conditions can most effectively and appropriately be prevented, diagnosed, treated, and managed.

- Based on the guidelines produced, the Quality Management Committee develops medical criteria and performance measures for the monitoring and evaluation of care provided to members.

- Guidelines are based on established national guidelines (where available), scientific literature, and prudent practice. Guidelines are peer reviewed and developed by consensus.

- Guidelines are reviewed at least annually and revised if necessary to ensure that they are consistent with current literature and national guidelines as well as the outcomes and experiences of the network.

- Guidelines are provided to providers as they are developed and/or revised through educational sessions, mailings, newsletters, and updates to provider manuals.

- The Quality Management Committee monitors and evaluates the consistency with which providers follow the guidelines, through defined studies, risk and utilization-management reports, patient and provider reports, and applicable quality-management information.

Guideline Development

Guideline development includes the following basic steps:

1. Clearly define the major questions regarding the clinical condition to be addressed, including the desired outcome as well as potential variation in outcomes.

2. Review and analyze the available scientific data for each question.

3. Assess clinical benefits and disadvantages of each intervention.

4. Review estimates of important member outcomes for each intervention being considered.

5. Review current and potential health care costs associated with the guideline. Where cost information is available and reliable, provide costs of alternative strategies for the prevention, diagnosis, treatment, and management of the condition.

6. Invite information and comments on guidelines from providers and patients.

7. Prepare guideline draft based on the available experience evidence or professional judgment, where experience evidence is insufficient.

8. Submit draft guideline to peer review and other experts.

9. Revise draft guideline based on analysis of comments and information received.

10. Obtain Board of Directors approval.

11. Prepare the guideline in a format appropriate for use by providers and members.

12. Distribute guideline to providers per policy.

13. Monitor and evaluate the appropriateness and outcome of guideline use and revise as indicated.

UTILIZATION MANAGEMENT

The Utilization Management (UM) Program is designed to monitor, evaluate, and manage the cost and quality of health care services delivered to all patients of the ABC providers. Whether delegated or non-delegated, this program will ensure that:

- Services are medically necessary and are delivered at appropriate levels of care.

- Authorized care matches the benefits defined in the patient's health plan.

- Services will be provided by providers or health plan contracted providers (e.g., hospital network) unless authorized by the Utilization Management Committee. The health-plan staff will be notified immediately to discuss the use of a non-contracted (non-credentialled) provider based on the health-plan contract.

- Hospital admissions and length of stay are justified.

- Services are not overutilized or underutilized.

- Appropriate care is offered in a timely manner and is quality-oriented.

- Scheduling is efficient for services and resources.

- Costs of services are monitored, evaluated, and determined to be appropriate.

- Guidelines, standards, and criteria set by governmental and other regulatory agencies are adhered to as appropriate.

- AEA will maintain compliance with the regulations set for the specific contracted patient populations.

- AEA utilizes standard criteria and informational resources to determine the appropriateness of health care services to be delivered (e.g., Milliman and Robertson, InterQual, CMRI, Health Plan).

- The utilization management team of providers, licensed staff, and unlicensed staff carry out the responsibilities designated for their level of expertise.

- A written Utilization Management Plan will be submitted annually to the contracted health plans if requested.

- The Utilization Management Program's plan, policies, and procedures will be reviewed and approved, and if necessary, revised on at least an annual basis by the Utilization Management Committee.

- The Utilization Management Program will be integrated with the Quality Management Program to ensure continuous quality improvement.

- New and existing technology will be evaluated according to network policy and procedure.

- The Utilization Management Program will be approved annually by the Governing Body of AEA.

Goals and Objectives

- Provide access to the most appropriate and cost-efficient health care services.

- Ensure that authorized services are covered under the patient's health plan.

- Develop systems to evaluate and determine which services are consistent with accepted standards of medical practice.

- Perform peer review in conjunction with the Quality Management Program when it is necessary.

- Coordinate thorough and timely investigations and responses to patient and provider grievances that are associated with utilization issues.

- Initiate necessary procedural revisions to prevent problematic utilization issues from reoccurring.

- Ensure that services that are delivered are medically necessary and are consistent with the patient's diagnosis and level of care required.

- Facilitate communication and develop positive relationships between patients, physicians, and health plans by providing education related to appropriate utilization.

- Evaluate and monitor health care services provided by IPA contracted providers by tracking and trending data.

- Monitor continuity and coordination of care.

- Identify overutilization and underutilization of services.

- Enhance the delivery of care by rewarding physicians and providers for sound utilization practices and exceptional quality of service.

- Identify high-risk patients and ensure that appropriate care is delivered by accessing the most efficient resources.

- Reduce overall health care expenditures by developing and implementing effective health promotion programs.

- Use Utilization Management data when re-credentialling providers.

The following are sample sections from AEA's Utilization Management Program:

Retrospective Review

Purpose

The Utilization Management Committee (UM Committee) conducts retrospective reviews of patient encounters by network providers. The retrospective review also includes tracking and trending and analysis of utilization statistics.

Policy

The Utilization Management Committee will retrospectively review a sample of patient encounters and make sure authorization requirements were adhered to on all cases that require authorization.

Determine if referrals by the IPA provider were medically necessary.

Utilization statistics will be tracked, trended, and analyzed by the UM Committee and reports will be presented to the Board of Directors at least on a quarterly basis.

Provider Profiling

Purpose

Individual AEA performance is reviewed in order to give the Utilization Management Committee a greater understanding of the problem areas concerned with the utilization of services.

Scope

Utilization statistics are accumulated on the individual providers. The information is reviewed to determine whether services have been utilized appropriately. AEA approved practice guidelines, health plan report cards, and national statistics are included in the comparative data analysis process. The data and results of the analysis are shared with the providers and education is implemented as necessary.

Sample quality assurance and utilization management forms are included in the Attachments Section of this proposal document.

ACCOUNTING

The network will maintain its books and records on the accrual basis of accounting in accordance with generally accepted accounting principles. A balance sheet and income statement will be prepared monthly and reviewed by the Board of Directors.

ABC representatives may have access to these books and records upon request.

The following are specific accounting issues that will be addressed by AEA on an ongoing basis:

Withholds

Provider withholds will be accounted for on a monthly basis and reconciled to each provider. The total amount withheld from providers will be shown as a liability on the balance sheet of the network until such time the withhold pool is disposed of. Disposal will occur within 90 days following the end of AEA's operating year.

IBNR

The obligation to pay a claim occurs when the referral is authorized or when an eligible member has received services for a valid emergency. There can, at times, be a significant lag between incurring the obligation to pay a claim and actually receiving the invoice from the provider's office. The cost of these services should be expensed as they are rendered, including an estimate of incurred but not reported (IBNR) costs. A cash reserve must be established to pay these outstanding claims.

The accrual of IBNR will be shown as an expense on the statement of income and a related liability on the balance sheet. AEA expects to use the Claims Lag Analysis method to account for IBNR. However, it shall also consider the following other acceptable methodologies if appropriate:

1. Analysis of open referrals
2. Projection from historical costs
3. Actuarial data analysis

Reinsurance Proceeds

AEA will acquire appropriate stoploss coverage as part of servicing the ABC contract. Reinsurance proceeds will be accounted for when filings are made to the reinsurer.

ATTACHMENTS

[Provide the following attachments: provider C.V.s, geographic coverage of provider network, sample quality assurance documents, sample utilization management documents, provider agreement, and sample reports.]

APPENDIX ITEM 19-07
COMMON INFORMATION FOR MANAGED-CARE APPLICATION

- Copy of all state medical certificates and licenses
- Copy of State Controlled Substances Registration Certificate (DPS)
- Copy of Controlled Substances Registration Certificate (DEA)
- Clinical Laboratory Improvement Amendment (CLIA) I.D. # (if applicable)
- ECFMG Certificate (if applicable)
- Copy of medical school diploma
- Copy of Internship, Residency and Fellowship diplomas (if applicable)
- Copy of the face sheet of Malpractice Insurance Policy
- Malpractice claims information for past 10 years (if applicable)
- Copy of physician's C.V.

  Include the month and year for all medical training; type (i.e. clinical, research), department and chief of department; and complete addresses for all medical training.

- Copy of board specialty licenses / board eligibility information
- Copy of hospital documents evidencing privileges (date and type of appointment)
- Three physician references who will not be associated in practice

  Include complete addresses with telephone numbers and the physician's specialty.

- List of all office addresses, phone numbers, hours (and billing address if different)
- Name of office manager
- Name and credentials of any nurses, physicians assistants, and medical assistants
- Copy of the firm's W-9 Form (Request for Taxpayer Identification Number and Certification)
- Physician's tax identification number
- Physician's home address

- Physician's Social Security number
- Physician's date and place of birth
- Medicare I.D. number
- Medicaid I.D. number
- UPIN number
- Copy of articles of incorporation

APPENDIX ITEM 19-08
DESELECT APPEAL

Date
[Name of HMO]
Address
City, State, Zip

To Whom It May Concern:

I received your notice of deselection on [date], from [name of network(s)]. I am concerned about this action because many patients in your network(s) have selected me as their physician and wish me to continue as their primary-care physician. Some of my patients will be adversely affected medically if they are forced to change physicians now. [Include examples.] Future patients covered by your network(s) will be denied the opportunity to select me as their physician if I am not able to remain in the network. [Cite examples of how your practice may benefit patients.]

I wish to appeal this decision. Please provide me with a copy of your process for appeal of this decision.

I request a review of the proposed termination by an advisory review panel, composed of physicians, including at least one representative in my specialty or similar specialty, who are appointed to serve on the standing quality assurance committee or utilization review committee of the [name of HMO]. Laws passed and enacted by the Texas Legislature provide that before terminating a contract the plan shall provide the physician with a review process. 20 A TEX. INS. CODE ANN. §18A (West 1997).

I will need, and I request, a copy of all of the information used in making the deselection decision so that I can have a fair opportunity to provide relevant information to the panel in writing, prior to its meeting. Also, I request that I be allowed to meet with the panel to discuss the deselection matter. At the time the panel makes its recommendation to the HMO, I request an opportunity to review that recommendation and to file a statement with [name of HMO] prior to its making a decision to retain or terminate me from the network.

I also request a copy of the recommendation of the advisory review panel and [name of HMO]'s determination.

In addition to the above minimum process rights, I request all other contractual procedural rights to which I am entitled.

Additionally, [name of HMO] may not notify patients who have chosen me as their physician of [name of HMO]'s intentions to terminate until the review panel has made a formal recommendation and [name of HMO] has made its determination based upon that recommendation. To do so would be a violation of the Insurance Code 20a TEX. INS. CODE ANN. §18A(d) (West 1997).

Thank you for your prompt attention to these requests.

Sincerely,

[Physician name]

APPENDIX ITEM 20-01
SPACE AND EQUIPMENT RENTAL AGREEMENT AND PERSONAL SERVICES AGREEMENT

THIS AGREEMENT is made and entered into as of [Date] (hereinafter the "Effective Date") by and between [Name] having its principal place of business at [Address] (hereinafter "Lessee"), and [Corporation], having its principal place of business at [Address] (hereinafter "Lessor").

WITNESSETH:

WHEREAS Lessor is a medical practice that is engaged in the practice of medicine and surgery, specializing in [specialty] and desires to provide expanded practice capabilities for its patients and all patients in Lessor's service area;

WHEREAS Lessee is a medical practice that employs qualified professional employees and agents and is engaged in the practice of medicine and surgery, specializing in [specialty] surgery and related services; and

WHEREAS Lessor is located in [address] and is unable to locally obtain [specialty] surgery services of a quality deemed desirable for all patients in Lessor's service area;

WHEREAS Lessee desires to provide [specialty] surgical and related services to all patients in Lessor's service area under the terms and conditions hereinafter set forth; and

WHEREAS in the course of the relationship described above, Lessee will gain knowledge of the business, affairs, employee and consultant names, finances, management, confidential information, trade secrets, patients, methods of operation of Lessor, programs, procedures and other knowledge of the individual patients, consultants and employees of Lessor; and

WHEREAS Lessor would suffer immediate and irrevocable harm if Lessee were to use such knowledge, information, business or trade secrets, or the procedures, business or trade secrets, or other procedures, business and personal relationships in competition with Lessor; and

WHEREAS Lessor desires to protect its legitimate business, patronage and goodwill without undue hardship to Lessee;

WHEREAS Lessee desires to lease from Lessor on a predetermined periodic basis a portion of Lessor's medical office space (hereinafter "Premises") and certain medical equipment (hereinafter "Equipment") and Lessor desires to lease the Premises and Equipment to Lessee;

NOW, THEREFORE, for and in consideration of the mutual promises and covenants contained herein, the parties agree as follows:

ARTICLE I: PRIMARY OBLIGATIONS OF LESSEE

1.1 Lessee's Use of Premises, Lease of Premises and Equipment Lessee shall provide [specialty] services to any and all patients in need of Lessee's services at Lessor's location. Such services shall be provided by Lessee through one or more of Lessee's partners, associates or physician employees licensed to practice medicine and surgery in the state in which Lessor is located. Lessee hereby leases from Lessor and Lessor hereby leases to Lessee the Premises and Equipment, all as more fully described on the annexed Attachment "B." Lessee shall have the unrestricted right to the use and enjoyment of the Premises and Equipment for the periods of [time and day] of each week and [time and day] of each alternate week. Lessee's use of the Premises and Equipment shall be limited to one or more of Lessee's employees who are licensed to practice medicine in the State of [state] and shall be further qualified in the medical specialty of [specialty] medical and surgical services. Lessor further agrees to provide the appropriate non-physician personnel during the time periods set forth above. Although Lessee's provision of medical services shall be at Lessee's and its physicians' sole discretion, Lessee agrees not to refuse services to any patient because of patient's race, color, sex, age, religion, national origin, handicap, or status as a beneficiary of a particular health benefit plan.

1.2 Designation of Physician Lessee shall have the sole right and responsibility for designation of the individual physician or physicians who are to provide services to patients at Lessor's location under this Agreement, provided, however, that (1) Lessor is informed of Lessee's selection of physician and apprised of the credentials of such individual and (2) if Lessor is for any reason dissatisfied with the physician or physicians designated by Lessee to provide such services, Lessor may request that Lessee provide a different physician or physicians to deliver services at Lessor's location under this Agreement. This request for replacement of physician is completely in the discretion of Lessee on behalf of Lessor and shall be the obligation of the Lessee to respond immediately upon his request.

1.3   **Availability of Non-Physician Personnel**   Lessor shall be responsible for supervision of some non-physician personnel utilized by Lessee in the performance of its obligations under this Agreement, regardless of whether such non-physician personnel are for contract, tax or other purposes employees or agents of Lessor, except to the extent that such non-physician personnel are executing direct orders given by Lessee. Lessee agrees to hold Lessor and Lessor's employees harmless for vicarious liability resulting in injury or damages due to acts or omissions in Lessee's direction of Lessor's non-physician personnel. Lessor shall provide a [specialty] technician and other designated office personnel to assist Lessee's physicians in providing services on site at Lessor's location. Lessor shall provide additional personnel from time to time to assist Lessee in providing services at Lessor's location, as necessary and appropriate and agreed to by Lessor and Lessee.

1.4   **Insurance**   Lessee shall maintain throughout the term of this Agreement and for a period of not less than three years commencing on the date of termination of this Agreement, at its sole expense, professional and comprehensive general liability insurance with a financially sound insurance carrier whose A.H. Best's rating is A or better covering the acts or omissions of Lessee, its employees or agents, in performing services under this Agreement. Lessee shall provide Lessor copies of applicable policies of insurance to Lessor and shall immediately notify Lessor of any actual or anticipated change in the terms of such policies or the rating of the respective insurance company. Lessee shall maintain professional liability insurance coverage in the amount of at least one million ($1,000,000) per occurrence, three million dollars ($3,000,000) annual aggregate. The provisions of this section 1.4 shall survive termination of this Agreement.

1.5   **Disclosures**   Lessee shall disclose to patients serviced by Lessee at Lessor's location that Lessee's relationship with Lessor is as tenant and that they practice medicine independently of each other.

ARTICLE II: PRIMARY OBLIGATIONS OF LESSOR

2.1 **Lease of Space and Equipment** Lessor shall provide such clinical and office accommodations as may reasonably be required by Lessee in providing its services including but not limited to reasonable access of examining rooms and general office space, office and general medical supplies, medical equipment, housekeeping services, building maintenance, and other services and materials as are normally required to conduct a clinical office practice or as are specifically required to provide vitreoretinal services.

2.2 **Availability of Personnel** Lessor shall provide all office personnel and [specialty] technicians and other personnel which are reasonably necessary for the performance of services by Lessee while on-site at Lessor's location.

2.3 **Insurance** Lessor shall maintain throughout the term of this Agreement and for a period of not less than three years commencing on the date of termination of this Agreement, at its sole expense, professional and comprehensive general liability insurance with a financially sound insurance carrier whose A.H. Best's rating is A or better covering the acts or omissions of Lessor, its employees or agents, in performing services under this Agreement. Lessor shall provide Lessee copies of applicable policies of insurance to Lessee and shall immediately notify Lessee of any actual or anticipated change in the terms of such policies or the rating of the respective insurance company. Lessor shall maintain professional liability insurance coverage in the amount of at least one million ($1,000,000) per occurrence, three million dollars ($3,000,000) annual aggregate. The provisions of this section 2.3 shall survive termination of this Agreement.

2.4 **Disclosure** Lessor shall disclose the following information to each patient referred by Lessor to Lessee: (1) that Lessor has entered into lessor-lessee relationship with Lessee; (2) names or other persons or entities, if any, besides Lessee, that are capable of providing Lessee's services to the patient; and (3) that patient has the right to choose freely among these alternative providers of services.

2.5 No Requirement for Referral Lessor and Lessee expressly agree that the payments due Lessor hereunder are not payments for Lessor's referral or patients to Lessee nor are the amounts of such payments in any way conditional upon or related to the amount, if any, of patient referrals. The parties agree that any patient referrals made by either of them shall be made by such party's independent medical judgment and only with regard to the best interest of the patients.

ARTICLE III: NON-SOLICITATION

3.1 Non-Solicitation In consideration of all matters contained herein, the parties agree:

(a) Lessor shall not, at any time throughout the term of this Agreement and for a period of one (1) year following termination of this Agreement for any reason, directly or indirectly solicit the services of, offer employment to, or otherwise enter into any business relationship with any employee or physician of Lessee, whereby such employee is employed, engaged, or otherwise obligated to provide services to or through Lessor of the same or similar nature as the services previously provided by the employees to or through Lessee;

(b) Lessee shall not, at any time throughout the term of this Agreement and for a period of one (1) year following termination of this Agreement for any reason, directly or indirectly solicit the services of, offer employment to, or otherwise enter into a business relationship with any employee or physician of Lessor, whereby such employee is employed, engaged, or otherwise obligated to provide services to or through Lessor of the same or similar nature as the services previously provided by the employees to or through Lessor;

For purposes of this section 3.1, the term of "employee" shall include any person or entity who is at any time during the term of this Agreement an employee or independent contractor of, or owner of any equity interest in, the named party.

3.2 Injunctive Relief The parties hereby acknowledge and agree that in the event of a breach of any provision of this Article III by either party, the non-breaching party would suffer irrevocable injury for which there is no adequate remedy at law and for which money damages would be inadequate or impossible to determine. Accordingly, the parties hereby agree that in the event of a breach of any provision of this Article III by either party, the non-breaching party shall be entitled to immediate, temporary and permanent injunctive relief without the necessity of specific proof or injury or damages, and the parties shall be entitled to damages and such relief as a court of competent jurisdiction shall deem appropriate.

3.3 **Survival of Terms** Neither termination of this Agreement, nor the existence of any claim, demand, action or cause of action by either party, whether predicated on this Agreement or otherwise, shall constitute a defense to the enforcement by either party of the provisions of this Article III, which shall survive the termination of this Agreement for any reason.

ARTICLE IV: LEASE PAYMENTS, BILLING FOR SERVICES, REGULATORY COMPLIANCE

4.1 **Comprehensive—Premises, Equipment, and Personnel** Lessee shall monthly pay to Lessor for premises and equipment rental plus use of Lessor's personnel as follows: Lessee shall pay Lessor $[amount] per month for premises, equipment and personnel covered by this Agreement. The apportionate of payments among those components is specified in Attachment "A." Payment shall be made on the first day of the month and shall be delivered to Lessor at the address of the Premises. All supplies directly used by Lessee in rendering its services and paid for by Lessor shall be added to Lessee's monthly rental rate by Lessor.

4.2 **Billing and Collection** Billing and collection for services provided by Lessee under this Agreement shall be the responsibility of the Lessee. Lessor shall have no right to receive, nor shall lessor attempt to bill for or collect, payment from the patient or from any third party for services provided by Lessee under this Agreement.

4.3 **Compliance with Medicare Regulations** Each party hereby represents and warrants that, to the best of its knowledge and understanding all obligations pertaining to and benefits derived under this Agreement are in full compliance with applicable federal law, including but not limited to all regulations pertaining to the Medicare, Medicaid, and other federally funded state entitlement programs promulgated by the United States Department of Health and Human Services, including its office of the Inspector General and the Health Care Financing Administration. Each party covenants and agrees to maintain compliance with such laws, as presently existing and as hereafter amended, throughout the term of this Agreement, and to use its best efforts to notify the other party of any change in the law of which it becomes aware that may effect the obligations of either party under this Agreement.

ARTICLE V: MEDICAL RECORD MAINTENANCE, AVAILABILITY, INSPECTION AND AUDIT

5.1 Preparation and Maintenance of Medical Records Lessee and Lessor agree to cooperate to assure the preparation of appropriate medical records involving services provided by Lessee under this Agreement. Lessor shall maintain such records at Lessor's location in accordance with prudent record keeping procedures and as required by law. Each party shall maintain, on its premises, a fax machine for purposes of transmitting medical records and other clinical information to the other party, and shall provide such information as required herein.

5.2 Access to Records Each party agrees to allow review and duplication by the other party of any medical records or other clinical information maintained by that party with regard to services provided by Lessee under this Agreement. Such review and duplication shall be at the cost of the requesting party and shall be allowed upon reasonable notice during regular business hours and shall be subject to all applicable laws concerning the confidentiality of such medical records or other information.

5.3 Confidentiality Lessee and Lessor each agree to take all reasonable precautions to prevent the unauthorized disclosure of any and all records required to be prepared and/or maintained by this Agreement and to keep such records confidential.

5.4 Government Access to Records To the extent required by section 1861(v)(1)(1) of the Social Security Act, the parties shall, upon proper request, allow the United States Department of Human Services, the Comptroller General of the United States, or their duly authorized representatives access to this Agreement, and to all books, documents and records necessary to verify the nature and extent of the cost of services provided by either party under this Agreement at any time during the term of this Agreement and for an additional period of four (4) years following the last date services are furnished under this agreement. In the event that either party carries out any of its obligations under this Agreement through an agreement with an organization related to it, such party shall require that a clause substantially to the effect of this section be included in that agreement.

ARTICLE VI: TERM AND TERMINATION

6.1 **Term** This Agreement shall commence on the effective date set forth below and shall continue for one year until [Date]. Thereafter, the Agreement may be renewed by the written consent of the parties for additional terms of one year each.

6.2 **Termination with Cause** This Agreement may be terminated immediately by either party upon the occurrence of any of the following events:

(i) the prohibition or sanction of any physician associated with Lessee or Lessor in the practice of medicine in the States of [States]; or

(ii) the cessation of business of Lessee, or Lessor; or

(iii) any misrepresentation set forth with respect to the declarations set forth in Article VIII herein; or

(iv) loss of Medicare certification

This Agreement may be terminated by either party thirty (30) days after the date of notice to the other party of the occurrence of any of the following events constituting a breach of any covenant or condition, provided that the non-terminating party has not cured said breach to the reasonable satisfaction of the terminating party within such thirty-day period:

(i) the termination, limitation or suspension of privileges of any physician associated with Lessor or Lessee at a hospital; or

(ii) the breach by Lessee or Lessor of any terms of, or failure to perform any covenant or obligation contained, in this Agreement.

ARTICLE VII: GENERAL PROVISION

7.1 Trademarks and Trade Names Nothing in this Agreement shall give either party the right to use the name, symbols, trademarks, trade names, service marks, or copyrights of the other party. Any permitted use shall terminate upon the termination of such consent or termination of this Agreement, whichever first occurs.

7.2 Taxes and Other Employment-Related Expense Lessor shall be solely responsible for all taxes, benefits and other employment-related expenses arising out of the employment of Lessor of any and all non-physician personnel involved in providing services to Lessee. Employment-related expenses shall include, but not be limited to, the taxes imposed by the Federal Insurance Contribution Act (FICA) or the Federal Unemployment Tax Act (FUTA), federal income tax withholding, workers' compensation insurance, disability insurance, unemployment compensation, health insurance, and any other employment-related tax or expense.

7.3 Independent Parties Lessee and Lessor are independent legal entities. Nothing in this Agreement shall be construed to create the relationship of employer and employee or principal and agent or any relationship other than that of independent parties contracting with each other solely for the purpose of carrying out the terms of this Agreement.

7.4 Notices Any notice required or permitted under the terms of this Agreement shall be in writing and shall be sent by United States Certified Mail, postage prepaid, return receipt requested, to the persons at the addresses which follow:

(a) Notices to Lessee.

_____

_____

_____

(b) with a copy to:

_____

_____

(c) Notices to Lessor.

_____

_____

_____

(d) with a copy to:

_____

_____

_____

Any notice given pursuant to the terms of this Section 7.4 shall be effective when mailed. The party giving the notice should retain a post-marked Receipt for Certified Mail as evidence of the mailing date.

7.5 **No Third-Party Beneficiaries** Nothing in this Agreement is in-tended to be construed, nor shall it be deemed to create, any right or remedy in any third party.

7.6 **Entire Agreement** This Agreement contains the entire agreement between the parties relating to the subject matter addressed herein. Any prior or contemporaneous agreement, promise, or representation, whether oral or written, relating to the subject matter of this Agreement and not expressly set forth or referenced in this Agreement or an amendment hereto shall be of no force or effect.

7.7 **Modification or Amendment** This Agreement shall not be modi-fied or amended except by written agreement signed by the parties, and no oral modification or amendment shall be permitted.

7.8 **Applicable Law** Except to the extent preempted by applicable federal law, this Agreement shall be governed by and construed in accor-dance with the law of the state in which Lessor is located.

7.9 **Captions** The captions or heading which precede the various articles, sections, and subsections of this Agreement are included for reference purposes only, are not a part of this Agreement, and shall in no way affect the meaning or interpretation of this Agreement.

7.10 **Assignment** The benefits conferred under this Agreement may not be assigned, nor may the duties of the respective parties otherwise be delegated, without the express written consent of the other party.

7.11 **Severability** If any portion of this Agreement is held to be invalid or unenforceable by any court of law or equity, the remaining provisions shall not be affected thereby, but shall remain in force.

ARTICLE VIII

8.1 **Declarations** Lessee and Lessor, by execution of this Agreement, hereby declare and represent that each has conscientiously reviewed the credentials of physicians currently associated with or employed by them respectively to determine, and further represent to each other, that no physician has a history of arrest or criminal record, has been involved in allegations of abuse of controlled substances, has ever forfeited his/her license to practice medicine in any State or territorial jurisdiction authorized to grant licensure, has ever been suspended from any hospital or other health care entity, has any pending claims against him or her for professional liability and knows of no incidents which may lead to a professional liability claim other than that which is fully disclosed in writing herein or has any knowledge of an actual or threatened action or investigation by a regulatory agency related to the provision of services to Medicare or Medicaid patients. Lessee and Lessor further declare and represent to each other that the execution, delivery and performance of this Agreement will not violate or result in a default under, or breach of, any other agreement to which Lessee or Lessor is a party or is bound, including but not limited to, any noncompetition or other post-employment covenant.

IN WITNESS WHEREOF, the parties have executed this Agreement, effective as of the 1st day of [Month, Year].

LESSEE: _____ LESSOR: _____

By: _____ By: _____

ATTACHMENT A

Space $ _____

Equipment $ _____

Personnel $ _____

Total $ _____

APPENDIX ITEM 20-02

HOSPITAL RECRUITMENT AGREEMENT CHECKLIST

❏ Does the agreement provide the following incentives to the physician?

Income guarantee	YES	NO
Recruitment bonus	YES	NO
Relocation assistance	YES	NO
Marketing allowance	YES	NO
Expense subsidy	YES	NO
Loan guarantee	YES	NO
Practice start-up assistance	YES	NO
Other: _____	YES	NO
Other: _____	YES	NO

❏ If the agreement provides the physician with an income guarantee, determine if incentive is a gross income guarantee or a net income guarantee.

❏ Determine if the physician can obtain a net income guarantee, since this type of arrangement removes risk from the physician.

❏ Under the income guarantee arrangement, determine who will be responsible for the payment of any debt service.

❏ If the agreement provides for a gross income guarantee, assess the following:

> Must physician pay for his or her own debt service out of gross income guarantee?   YES   NO
>
> Is amount of guarantee reasonable?   YES   NO
>
> After paying expenses and debt service, is net amount enough to pay the physician reasonable compensation?   YES   NO

❏ If the agreement provides for a net income guarantee, assess the following:

> Must the physician pay for debt service out of the net amount? YES   NO
>
> Are there any limitations on practice expenses?   YES   NO
>
> Is amount of net guarantee reasonable for the physician's medical specialty?   YES   NO

❏ Determine when advances will be needed by the physician under the income guarantee arrangement. Make sure that the contract provides for such advances. For example, if the physician starts practice on the first of the month, he or she will need money to make payroll on the fifteenth of the same month. Thus, make sure that the hospital will make a necessary advance in this and possibly other situations.

❏ Determine how incentives will be repaid (cash, service, forgiveness). [Attempt to secure repayment in the following order: (1) forgiveness, (2) service, (3) combination of forgiveness and service, (4) combination of forgiveness and cash, (5) combination of service and cash, and (6) cash.]

❏ Assess tax consequences, both immediate and future, related to the repayment option in the agreement. Pay strict attention to immediate tax consequences related to any repayment in service.

❏ Determine when Form 1099s will be issued by the hospital and for how much.

❏ Based on an assessment of tax consequences, determine if the practice should incorporate.

❏ If the hospital is not providing certain incentives because it is a not-for-profit hospital, have the hospital answer the following questions:

Is there a documented community need for the physician?

Are the incentives reasonable?

Were incentives negotiated at arm's length?

Are state benefits going to the hospital by securing the physician's services?

(If the hospital can favorably answer the above questions, it should not be limited in the number and amount of incentives it can provide to the physician.)

❏ Does the agreement restrict the physician's ability to obtain privileges at other hospitals? If so, would this restrict his or her ability to open a satellite office or take emergency calls at other hospitals at some time in the future? Attempt to negotiate the physician's right to obtain other hospital privileges.

❏ Determine if the agreement violates any Medicare fraud and abuse statutes.

❏ Other issue: _____

❏ Other issue: _____

APPENDIX ITEM 20-03
HOSPITAL RECRUITMENT AGREEMENT

PHYSICIAN AGREEMENT

This Physician Agreement ("Agreement") executed this [date] of [month], [year], but effective for all purposes as of the first (1st) day of [month, year], is entered into by and between [hospital name], (hereinafter referred to as "Hospital"), a [State and type of organization], and [Name of Medical Practice], a [State and type of organization], (hereinafter referred to as "Provider").

WITNESSETH

WHEREAS, Hospital owns and operates an acute-care hospital facility located in [City, State].

WHEREAS, Hospital has determined that there is an insufficient number of family practice specialists on Hospital's medical staff to meet the primary-care medical needs of the community in Hospital's service area;

WHEREAS, Hospital seeks to enhance the quantity and quality of the skills of physicians within the medical staff who are available to participate and share in the rotational programs and other functions associated with the medical staff's performance of quality improvement and general administrative duties performed on behalf of Hospital;

WHEREAS, Hospital has determined that in order to meet the primary-care medical needs of the community in Hospital's service area, it is necessary to recruit a family practice physician;

WHEREAS, [Physician's Name] (Physician) specializes in family practice and upon completion of his or her family practice residency program, desires to commence the practice of [specialty], in the [City, State] area, pursuant to a contractual relationship with Provider, to provide primary-care medical services to members of the community in Hospital's service area;

WHEREAS, Provider desires to enter into a contractual relationship with Physician to provide family practice services in the [City, State] area, but requires financial assistance to establish such Physician's practice;

WHEREAS, Hospital finds that expanding the availability of family practice services by assisting Provider to establish Physician's medical practice in Hospital's service area furthers the mission of Hospital;

WHEREAS, Hospital finds that the expenditures to assist Provider Physician's family practice in Hospital's service area are directly and substantially related to Hospital's organizational purposes and are necessary to satisfy Hospital's and the community's need for qualified physicians in primary care; and

WHEREAS, Hospital finds that it will receive adequate return for its expenditures through the services Physician will provide directly to Hospital as a consultant and to persons in the community needing family practice services;

NOW, THEREFORE, In consideration of the promises and mutual covenants contained in this Agreement, the parties hereto agree as follows:

ARTICLE I: COVENANTS OF PHYSICIAN

1.1 **Representations and Warranties** Provider represents and covenants that, as of the effective date of this Agreement and throughout its term, Physician: (*a*) shall maintain valid and unlimited licenses to practice medicine in the State of [State], (*b*) shall hold a valid Drug Enforcement Administration certificate; (*c*) shall hold valid and current Medicare and Medicaid provider numbers; (*d*) shall maintain insurance coverage consistent with the amounts specified in Hospital's medical staff bylaws; (*e*) shall obtain and maintain membership in good standing in the medical staff of Hospital, with appropriate clinical privileges, all in accordance with Hospital and medical staff bylaws, rules and regulations, and policies; and (*f*) shall enter into and maintain a contractual relationship with Physician, whereby Physician shall provide family practice services to the members of the [City, State] community.

1.2 **Establishment of Office** Physician has heretofore entered into an agreement with Provider. Pursuant to this Agreement with Provider, Physician shall establish an office suitable for the practice of family practice medicine and shall engage in the full-time private practice of medicine, specializing in family practice at such office throughout the term of this Agreement. During the term of this Agreement, Physician's "full-time private practice of medicine" shall mean Physician's commitment of an average of forty (40) hours per week to the practice of medicine and the maintenance of regular office hours five (5) days per week; provided, however, that it is recognized that Physician may be absent from the practice for a reasonable period of time for vacation, illness, and continuing medical education purposes. Physician shall practice exclusively in the [City, State] area and shall not furnish professional, administrative, consultative, or other services at other locations outside the [City, State] area, except when, upon prior notice from Provider, Hospital determines that such outside activities do not detrimentally affect Physician's ability to provide family practice services in [City, State], and Hospital shall not unreasonably withhold such determination.

1.3 Medical Staff and Administrative Responsibilities Physician shall perform the following medical staff and administrative duties:

a. Comply fully with all bylaws and rules and regulations of the medical staff and discharge all administrative and professional responsibilities of a member of the medical staff of Hospital, including but not limited to, emergency room and other rotational call duty and participation in *ad hoc* and standing medical staff and Hospital committees;

b. Develop and maintain ongoing dialogue with other members of the medical staff; and

c. Perform such other administrative duties as may from time to time be mutually agreed upon by Provider and Hospital.

1.4 Required Disclosures Provider shall notify Hospital in writing within three (3) days after any of the following events occurs:

a. A malpractice proceeding or any similar legal proceeding against Physician is seriously threatened or filed against Physician or Provider in any federal, state, or local court of law;

b. Physician's license to practice medicine in the State of [State] is suspended, revoked, terminated, or made subject to terms of probation or other restrictions;

c. Physician becomes the subject of a disciplinary proceeding or action before the [State] State Boards of Medicine, the subject of any investigation, sanction, or similar action by a peer review organization, or the subject of any other audit or similar proceeding by any federal, state, or local agency; or

d. An event occurs that substantially interrupts all or a portion of Physician's professional practice or that materially adversely affects Physician's ability to carry out his or her duties hereunder.

ARTICLE II: COVENANTS OF HOSPITAL

2.1 Collection Guarantee In order to enable Provider to establish Physician's medical practice in the service area of Hospital, Hospital guarantees that, for the twelve- (12) month period commencing with the initiation of Physician's office practice, Physician's Gross Fee Revenue (as defined in Appendix A hereto) will not be less than two hundred forty thousand dollars ($240,000) (Guaranteed Amount). The method by which Guaranteed Amount payable by Hospital shall be computed and the method by which such payments shall be repaid by Provider are set forth in Appendix A hereto.

2.2 Start-Up Expense Reimbursement Hospital shall reimburse Provider the reasonable expenses incurred by Provider in establishing the practice of Physician in the [City, State] area, including reasonable marketing, advertising, promotional, practice management, legal, and accounting expenses incurred by Provider, not to exceed the total amount of ten thousand five hundred dollars ($10,500). As a condition to such obligation by Hospital, Provider shall deliver copies of documents evidencing such expenses, along with a request for reimbursement, on or before the expiration of one (1) year from the effective date of this Agreement.

2.3 Referrals The parties expressly agree and do hereby state that the sums paid to Physician pursuant to this Agreement are not payments for patient referrals or admissions by Physician or Provider nor is compensation dependent or conditioned on a certain level of referrals or admissions by Physician or any employee or shareholder of Provider. Physician shall use his or her independent medical judgment in choosing or recommending a hospital or other health care facility for any inpatient care, outpatient care, or ancillary services, including, but not limited to, laboratory and radiology services. Hospital understands and expects that the choice of services and the choice of service suppliers that Physician makes on behalf of patients must be, and will be, made only with regard to the best interests of patients.

ARTICLE III: STATUS OF PHYSICIAN

3.1   It is mutually understood and agreed that in the performance of professional services under this Agreement, Physician is at all times acting as an independent contractor with respect to Hospital in the practice of the profession of medicine. Physician shall employ his or her own means and methods and exercise his or her own professional judgment in the performance of such services, and shall not be subject to the control or direction of Hospital with respect to such means, methods, or judgments, or with respect to the details of such services. The sole concern of Hospital under this Agreement or otherwise is that, irrespective of the means selected, such services be provided in a competent, efficient, and satisfactory manner. It is expressly agreed that Physician shall not for any purpose be deemed to be an employee, agent, ostensible or apparent agent, servant, partner, or joint venturer of Hospital. Provider understands and agrees that (*a*) Hospital will not withhold on behalf of Physician pursuant to this Agreement any sums for income tax, unemployment insurance, Social Security, or any other withholding pursuant to any law or requirement of any governmental body relating to Physician or make available to Physician any of the benefits afforded to employees of Hospital; (*b*) all of such payments, withholdings, and benefits, if any, are the sole responsibility of Provider or Physician; and (*c*) Provider will indemnify and hold Hospital harmless from any and all loss or liability arising with respect to such payments, withholdings, and benefits, if any. In the event the Internal Revenue Service should question or challenge the independent contractor status of Physician, the parties hereto mutually agree that both Provider and Hospital shall have the right to request participation in any discussion or negotiation occurring with such agency or agencies irrespective of with whom or by whom such discussion or negotiation is initiated.

ARTICLE IV: TERM AND TERMINATION

4.1   **Term**   This Agreement shall be binding as of its effective date, on [Month, Date, Year] for a term of one (1) year.

4.2   **Termination**

A.   **Expiration of Term**   Unless otherwise extended by the parties, this Agreement shall terminate at the expiration of the term.

B. **Loss of Medical Staff Membership and Privileges** This Agreement shall automatically terminate if Physician fails to maintain medical staff membership and appropriate clinical privileges at Hospital throughout the term of this Agreement.

C. **Loss of License** This Agreement shall terminate immediately if Physician fails to maintain his or her license to practice medicine in the State of [State].

D. **Death of Physician** This Agreement shall automatically terminate if Physician dies during the term of this Agreement.

E. **Termination for Good Cause** Hospital may terminate this Agreement for good cause upon seven (7) days written notice to Provider. For purposes of this section, "good cause" shall include, but shall not be limited to, fraud, moral turpitude, Physician practicing medicine not in conformance with generally accepted medical standards in Hospital's service area, consistent nonperformance of the obligations set forth in this Agreement, or if this Agreement is required to be renegotiated or revised by any third-party payor, governmental agency, or other agency that may have control over physician contracts or control over any part of this Agreement. Prior to notice of termination for consistent nonperformance, Hospital shall notify Provider in writing at least fourteen (14) days in advance of Hospital's complaint(s) in this regard and provide Provider the opportunity to cure the default within the fourteen-day period.

F. **Effects of Termination** Except as may be otherwise provided in a more specific termination agreement between the parties, upon termination of this Agreement, as provided herein, neither party shall have any further obligation hereunder except for (*a*) obligations accruing prior to the date of termination, and (*b*) obligations, promises, or covenants contained herein that are expressly made to extend beyond the term of this Agreement, including, but not limited to, repayment obligations.

ARTICLE V: MISCELLANEOUS

5.1. **Access to Books and Records** Notwithstanding anything to the contrary in this Agreement, if it shall be determined or asserted that this Agreement is a contract between a provider and a subcontractor within the meaning of Section 1861(b)(1)(I) of the Social Security Act or any rules, regulations, or judicial or administrative interpretations or discussions promulgated or made pursuant thereto, then Provider agrees that until the expiration of four (4) years after the furnishing of any service pursuant to this contract, Provider shall make available, upon written request to the Secretary of the Department of Health and Human Services or upon request to the Comptroller General or any of their duly authorized representatives, this contract, and books, documents, and records of Provider that are necessary to certify the nature and extent of the cost incurred by Hospital with respect to this Agreement.

5.2 Representatives

A. **Hospital Representative** Hospital shall act with respect to all matters hereunder through its President or designee.

B. **Physician Representative** Provider shall act with respect to all matters hereunder through its President or designee.

5.3 **Notices** Any notices, demand, or communication required, permitted, or desired to be given hereunder shall be deemed effectively given when personally delivered or mailed by prepaid certified mail, return receipt requested, addressed as follows or to such other address, and to the attention of such other person(s) or officer(s) as either party may designate by written notice:

Provider: [Name and Full Address]
Hospital: [Name and Full Address]
Attn: Administrator

5.4 **Governing Law** This Agreement has been executed and delivered in, and shall be interpreted, construed, and enforced pursuant to and in accordance with the laws of the State of [State]. [County, State], shall be the sole and exclusive venue for any litigation, special proceeding, or other proceeding between the parties that may be brought or arise out of or in connection with or by reason of this Agreement.

5.5 **Assignment** No assignment of this Agreement or the rights and obligations hereunder shall be valid without the specific written consent of both parties hereto, except that this Agreement may be assigned to any successor entity operating Hospital.

5.6 **Waiver of Breach** The waiver by either party of a breach or violation of any provision of this Agreement shall not operate as, or be construed to be, a waiver of any subsequent breach of the same or other provision hereof.

5.7 **Enforcement** In the event either party resorts to legal action to enforce the terms and provisions of this Agreement, the prevailing party shall be entitled to recover the costs of such action so incurred, including, but not limited to, reasonable attorneys' fees.

5.8 **Gender and Number** Whenever the context hereof requires, the gender of all words shall include the masculine, feminine, and neuter, and the number of all words shall include the singular and plural.

5.9 **Additional Assurances** The provisions of this Agreement shall be self-operative and shall not require further agreement by the parties except as may be herein specifically provided to the contrary.

5.10 **Force Majeure** Neither party shall be liable nor deemed to be in default for any delay or failure in performance under this Agreement or other interruptions of service or employment deemed resulting, directly or indirectly, from Acts of God, civil or military authority, acts of public enemy, war, accidents, fires, explosions, earthquakes, floods, failure of transportation, strikes, or other work interruptions by either party's employees, or any similar or dissimilar cause beyond the reasonable control of either party.

5.11 **Severability** In the event any provision of this Agreement is held to be unenforceable for any reason, the unenforceability thereof shall not affect the remainder of this Agreement, which shall remain in full force and effect and enforceable in accordance with its terms.

5.12 **Conflict** In the event of any conflict between the provisions of this Agreement and Hospital's medical staff Bylaws, this Agreement shall control.

5.13 **Confidentiality** Physician and Hospital agree to keep the terms of this Agreement confidential and not to divulge the terms hereof to third parties except with the prior consent of the parties to this Agreement.

5.14 **Article and Other Headings** The article and other headings contained in this Agreement are for reference purposes only and shall not affect in any way the meaning or interpretation of this Agreement.

5.15 **Amendments and Agreement Execution** This Agreement and amendments hereto shall be in writing and executed in multiple copies on behalf of Hospital by any official of Hospital authorized by the Board of Directors and any Physician. Each multiple copy shall be deemed an original, but all multiple copies together shall constitute one and the same instrument.

5.16 **Entire Agreement** This Agreement supersedes all previous contracts and constitutes the entire Agreement between the parties. Neither Physician nor Provider shall be entitled to benefits, other than those specified herein. No oral statements nor prior written material not specifically incorporated herein shall be of any force and effect and no changes in or additions to this Agreement shall be recognized unless incorporated herein by amendment as provided herein, such amendment(s) to become effective on the date stipulated in such amendment(s). Provider specifically acknowledges that in entering into and executing this Agreement, Provider relies solely upon the representations and agreements contained in this Agreement and no others.

IN WITNESS WHEREOF, the parties have executed this Agreement in multiple originals as of the date above first written.

[INSERT SIGNATURE BLOCK ACCORDINGLY]

EXHIBIT A: COMPUTATION, PAYMENT, AND
REPAYMENT OF GUARANTEED AMOUNT

A.1   The term "Gross Fee Revenue" shall mean the aggregate in any relevant period of (*a*) the total collections by Provider for all billable professional services of Physician (excluding only courtesy allowances, employee allowances, other customary charitable allowances, and any nonpatient care revenue), and (*b*) any other compensation for professional services to patients rendered by Physician at any location. On or before the fifteenth (15th) day of each month, Provider shall forward to Hospital a statement of Gross Fee Revenue from the preceding month.

A.2   If Provider does not realize Gross Fee Revenue of at least the monthly *pro rata* portion of the Guaranteed Amount [twenty thousand dollars ($20,000)], Hospital will pay to Provider the difference between (*a*) Provider's Gross Fee Revenue for the previous month and (*b*) the monthly *pro rata* portion of the Guaranteed Amount [twenty thousand dollars ($20,000)]. Monthly payments to Provider shall be made within fifteen (15) days following receipt of Provider's statement of Gross Fee Revenue. If, however, during any month during the term of this Agreement, Provider's Gross Fee Revenue is equal to or more than twenty thousand dollars ($20,000), Hospital shall have no obligation hereunder to pay Provider any amount for such month. Furthermore, if during any month Provider's Gross Fee Revenue exceeds twenty thousand dollars ($20,000), Provider shall be required to pay such excess amount to Hospital in repayment of amounts previously advanced by Hospital. In the event that, during the term of this Agreement, Provider's Gross Fee Revenue totals two hundred forty thousand dollars ($240,000), Hospital shall have no further obligation to pay Provider any amounts hereunder.

A.3   Upon termination of this Agreement for any reason prior to the expiration of the term, Hospital shall reconcile all amounts paid to Provider under Section A-2, and any other amounts paid to Provider under Article II and compute the amount owed to Hospital by Physician as repayment of the Guaranteed Amount, which amount shall be referred to hereinafter as the "Guaranteed Amount Balance." The Guaranteed Amount Balance shall be treated as a loan subject to repayment by Provider to Hospital in twelve (12) equal monthly installments commencing on the first (1st) day of the next whole month following the termination of this Agreement. Commencing on the first (1st) day of the next whole month following the termination of this Agreement, any outstanding amount owed shall accrue interest at the then current Applicable Federal Rate as set by the Internal Revenue Service in accordance with section 7872(f) of the Internal Revenue Code of 1986, as such may be amended from time to time, compounded monthly as of the first (1st) day of each month, and payments by Provider to Hospital shall consist of equal installments including (a) principal and (b) accrued interest.

A.4   Upon completion of the term of this Agreement, Hospital will reconcile all amounts paid to Provider under Section A-2 above, and any other amounts paid to Provider under Article II, subtract amounts repaid by Provider, if any, and compute the amount owed to Hospital by Provider as Guaranteed Amount Balance. Provider shall repay to Hospital the Guaranteed Amount Balance by virtue of Physician's continued maintenance of an active private practice in the [City, State], area pursuant to his or her contract with Provider, for a period of three (3) years following the end of the term of the Agreement. Specifically, for each month beyond the term of this Agreement that Physician maintains an active medical practice in the [City, State], pursuant to his or her contract with Provider, the Guaranteed Amount Balance shall be reduced by one thirty-sixth (1/36). Amounts forgiven by Hospital pursuant to this Section A-4 shall be reported annually by Hospital on an Internal Revenue Service Form 1099 as income to Provider for federal income tax purposes.

A.5   If Physician for any reason terminates his or her active medical practice in the [City, State], area pursuant to his or her contract with Provider during the three- (3) year period following the end of the term of this Agreement, Provider is obligated to repay to Hospital the amount of Guaranteed Amount Balance that has not been repaid to date pursuant to Section A-4 above. Repayment shall be in no more than twelve (12) monthly installments commencing on the first (1st) day of the next whole month following termination of Physician's active medical practice in the [City, State], area. Commencing on the first (1st) day of the next whole month following such termination, any outstanding principal owed shall accrue interest as set forth in Section A-3 hereof, and payments by Provider to Hospital shall consist of (a) equal installments of the outstanding principal and (b) the accrued interest.

APPENDIX ITEM 21-01
PREASSESSMENT CHECKLIST

To conduct the merger preassessment, I will need the following information:

- Charges, collections, and adjustments for the year [Year]
- Charges, collections, and adjustments for each month and year-to-date of [Year]
- Business tax returns for the last 4 years
- Current aging of accounts receivable
- Listing of all employees, their related salaries, and their job duties
- Practice's policy for employee vacation and sick leave
- Estimated patient payor mix (i.e., percent of practice that is Medicare, Medicaid, and so on)
- Current practice fee schedule
- CPT frequency report of the year [Year] and year to-date [Year]
- Copies of 20 filed but unpaid insurance claim forms
- Copies of 20 managed-care explanation of benefits
- Copies of 30 non-managed-care explanation of benefits (Do no submit Medicare/Medicaid.)
- Year-end balance sheet and income statement
- Most recent balance sheet and income statement
- Detailed tax depreciation schedule
- Copy of practice superbill (patient encounter form)
- Example of insurance appeal letters
- Copy of practice insurance verification form
- Copy of practice insurance follow-up form
- Type of retirement plan the practice currently has, if applicable

Please mail this information to:

[Name of CPA]

[Address]
[Phone number]
[Fax number]

APPENDIX ITEM 21-02
MEDICAL PRACTICE MERGER CHECKLIST

PREMERGER ASSESSMENT

❏ Review each practice's finances.

❏ Review employee payroll and benefits for each practice.

❏ Review coding practices.

❏ Review fee schedules.

NEW PRACTICE ENTITY

❏ Partnership of corporations?

❏ Professional association?

ASSETS THAT WILL BE CONTRIBUTED TO NEW ENTITY BY EACH PRACTICE

❏ Hard assets

Accounts receivable:

    ❏ What amount will be contributed?

    ❏ How will remainder of physician A/R be accounted?

NEW PRACTICE'S ASSUMPTION OF DEBT OF EACH PRACTICE

Review physician's existing debts:

    ❏ Accounts payable

    ❏ Notes and other payables

    ❏ Lease obligations

FORMULA FOR COMPENSATION OF THE DOCTORS (USUALLY BASED ON PREASSESSMENT)

❏ Physician collections and share overhead

❏ Fixed compensation plus bonus

❏ Bonus based on percentage of collections

- ❏ Bonus based on percentage of net production
- ❏ Equal compensation for all physicians
- ❏ Fixed compensation plus percentage of net production
- ❏ Percentage of net production

PERSONNEL

- ❏ Determine practice's administrator
- ❏ Review current compensation of employees
- ❏ Decide which employees stay and which may have to leave
- ❏ Establish new fringe benefits
- ❏ Establish job duties for each employee
- ❏ Identify potential employee conflicts

FACILITIES

Review current lease obligations of each practice:

- ❏ Office leases
- ❏ Equipment leases
- ❏ Determine if offices will consolidate into one location
- ❏ Decide how specific equipment will be used in the practice
- ❏ Review issues related to physician ownership of office building, if applicable

MANAGING PHYSICIAN

- ❏ Who will be managing physician?

Decide on duties of managing physician:

- ❏ Manage day-to-day operations
- ❏ Supervise employees
- ❏ Supervise billing/collection activities
- ❏ Ensure that all insurance as required by the group is paid and maintained
- ❏ Acquire fixed assets for less than $[dollar amount]
- ❏ Authorize contracts on behalf of the group not in excess of $[dollar amount]

- ❏ Maintain bank accounts
- ❏ Make sure all tax returns are prepared and filed timely
- ❏ Make sure all licenses are renewed
- ❏ Supervise payment of accounts payable
- ❏ Implement business decisions of the group practice
- ❏ Call to order regular meeting of the physicians
- ❏ Other duties

❏ Will managing physician be compensated? If so, how much?

How will managing physician be elected each year?

- ❏ Vote of the physicians
- ❏ Annual rotation

OPERATIONAL ISSUES

- ❏ Call schedule
- ❏ Billing/collection policies
- ❏ Computer system
- ❏ Appointment scheduling
- ❏ Office forms
- ❏ Medical charts
- ❏ Superbill
- ❏ Fee schedule
- ❏ Notification of insurance carriers of new entity, if applicable
- ❏ New group provider number
- ❏ Banking

Insurance:

- ❏ Group health
- ❏ Malpractice
- ❏ Office contents
- ❏ Other

- ❏ Office hours
- ❏ Telephone number

❑ Purchasing

❑ Professional assistance

❑ Choose practice's accountant

❑ Choose practice's attorney

❑ Other operational issues

ASSESS HIDDEN COSTS TO MERGE

❑ Nonproductive time (lost patient billings)

❑ Marketing costs

❑ Professional fees to merge

❑ Moving costs, if applicable

❑ Malpractice tail premium

❑ Cost to equalize fringe benefits

❑ Cost to develop common operational policies

❑ Possible facility costs

❑ Buy-out of existing leases

❑ Additional leasehold improvements

❑ Other hidden costs

PRACTICE'S RETIREMENT PLAN

❑ Will there be a new plan?

❑ Decide what to do with current plan(s).

❑ Choose retirement plan administrator.

❑ Choose investment counselor.

NEW NAME OF THE GROUP PRACTICE

❑ Adopt name of one of the practices or decide on name of the new practice

SPECIFIC PHYSICIAN CONTRACT ISSUES

Voluntary withdrawal by an owner:

❑ Required notice

Involuntary termination of an owner:

❏ Death

❏ Suspension, revocation, or cancellation of owner's right to practice medicine in the state of [State]

❏ Owner loses privileges to any hospital at which the practice regularly maintains admission privileges

❏ Owner fails to follow reasonable policies or directives established by the practice

❏ Owner commits acts amounting to gross negligence or willful misconduct to the detriment of the practice or its patients

❏ Owner convicted of a crime

❏ Owner breaches the terms of his or her employment agreement

❏ Physician becomes uninsurable for medical malpractice coverage

❏ Disability of an owner:

  ❏ Owner becomes and remains disabled for [number] months

  ❏ Continued compensation to a disabled owner

    ❏ How long?

    ❏ How much?

  ❏ Permanent vs. temporary disability

Physician fringe benefits:

  ❏ Vacation

  ❏ Sick leave

  ❏ Effect on compensation if physician chooses to take extra time off for vacation, CME study, etc.

  ❏ Expenses (CME, etc.)

Malpractice tail-end premium:

  ❏ Who pays in event of owner's withdrawal?

Buy-out of an owner:

  Address these events requiring a buy-out:

    ❏ Death

    ❏ Disability

    ❏ Retirement

    ❏ Withdrawal from the practice

How will ownership interest be valued?

- ❏ Appraisal
- ❏ Fixed formula
- ❏ Will a goodwill calculation be required?

Pay out of ownership interest

Death

- ❏ Insurance proceeds
- ❏ How much insurance to obtain
- ❏ Proper structure for "key man" insurance

Disability, retirement, withdrawal

- ❏ Installment payments or lump sum
- ❏ Interest rate for installment payments
- ❏ When will installment payments begin?

Admission of a new owner:

- ❏ Required vote

How to value buy-in amount

- ❏ Appraisal
- ❏ Fixed formula

DISSOLUTION OF THE GROUP PRACTICE

- ❏ Required vote of the current owners
- ❏ Method of dissolution

MAJOR DECISIONS BY THE GROUP

- ❏ Majority or unanimous approval?
- ❏ Hiring and firing of personnel
- ❏ Amending practice fee schedule
- ❏ Purchase of fixed assets in excess of $[dollar amount]
- ❏ Adopting or amending retirement plan
- ❏ Any expenditure in excess of $[dollar amount]

❑ Designating or changing signatories on group bank accounts
❑ Borrowing money
❑ Entering into lease contracts
❑ Offering ownership to a physician
❑ Terminating a physician's ownership
❑ Withdrawals from group bank accounts
❑ Negotiating and settling claims against the group practice
❑ Determining which expenses of the individual physicians should be paid for by the group practice
❑ Dissolution of the group practice
❑ Purchase of insurance
❑ Sale of group practice assets
❑ Other

PROMOTION OF THE NEW GROUP PRACTICE
❑ Develop marketing strategy
❑ Budget costs for marketing implementation

APPENDIX ITEM 21-03
GROUP PRACTICE INFORMATION IMPLEMENTATION CHECKLIST

Practice Name _____

❑ Prepare and execute legal entity agreements.

❑ Prepare and execute physician compensation agreement.

❑ Obtain Federal identification number.

❑ Obtain State unemployment tax number.

❑ Prepare and file Medicare application.

❑ Prepare and file Medicaid application.

❑ Draft employee organizational chart.

❑ Set up computer demonstrations.

❑ Obtain bids from computer vendors.

❑ Select computer system.

❑ Interview candidates for position of practice administrator.

❑ Select practice administrator.

❑ Prepare and file Medicare participation agreement.

❑ Draft policies and procedures manual for practice.

❑ Send RFPs to vendors in selected expense categories.

❑ Select practice vendors.

❑ Schedule computer training.

❑ Select data for and implement computer conversion.

❑ Draft master fee schedule.

❑ Contact insurance companies to inform each that doctors are merging effective (date) and to find out how new entity needs to be set up in their computer system. **This is very important for all managed-care plans.**

❑ Select bank and open up bank account(s).

❑ Set up accounts payable system and order computer checks.

❑ Set up financial general ledger.

❑ Draft and order announcement cards.

❑ Order stationery and envelopes.

❑ Obtain group health insurance policy.

❑ Obtain group disability insurance coverage.

❑ Bid out (by RFP) and select malpractice coverage.

❑ Obtain group overhead disability coverage.

❑ Obtain buy-out life insurance coverage.

❑ Draft patient encounter forms.

❑ Set up capability to file insurance claims electronically.

❑ Make list of managed-care plans and complete applications for those plans any physician is not currently credentialled on.

❑ Select physician governance structure and managing physician if applicable.

❑ Review all tax issues impacting consolidation.

❑ Select and implement retirement plan for practice.

APPENDIX ITEM 21-04

MANAGEMENT ORGANIZATION'S PROPOSAL TO PROVIDE DUE DILIGENCE SERVICES

PERSONAL AND CONFIDENTIAL

Date
Name
Name of PPMC
Address
City, State, Zip

Dear _____:

As requested, the following is our proposal to provide due diligence services to and on behalf of APS Practice Management, Inc. This proposal, if accepted in whole or in part, will also serve as an engagement letter detailing our understanding of the services we will provide, the terms and limitations of this engagement, and the responsibilities of both parties.

OUR UNDERSTANDING OF YOUR NEEDS

We understand APS Practice Management, Inc. is beginning the initial due diligence phase of the practice acquisitions for the Physician Practice Management Company's (PPMC) targeted practices. In this stage, the PPMC needs to perform an initial assessment of the operations of the targeted practices, in particular, all related billing and collection functions and activities. As such, APS Practice Management, Inc. has requested O'Neal, McGuinness & Tinsley, PLLC (OMT) to submit a proposal for assistance in carrying out this due diligence.

DESCRIPTION OF PROPOSED SERVICES

Billing and Collection Assessment

Based upon our conversations, we expect the due diligence to focus on the following areas:

- Assessment of all practice billing and collection activities. This includes the following:
- Review of financial performance, including all related statistical analysis
- Review of physician production and related volumes
- Assessment of doctor referral patterns
- Detailed review of all billing and collection processes
- Interviews with, and assessment of, all business-related personnel. This includes front-desk personnel
- Review of current detailed accounts receivable aging
- Explanation of benefits (EOB) review
- Fee schedule review
- Sample testing of front-desk collections
- Sample testing of insurance claim filing turnaround time
- Sample testing of insurance company payment turnaround time
- Sample testing of EOB posting

Coding and Documentation Assessment

- Review of utilization patterns for evaluation and management codes by individual physician. The purpose of reviewing E & M coding by physician is to identify unusual trends in the selection of CPT codes for office visits. This analysis will be used as the basis for selecting samples of medical records to review for office visits.
- Review of practice's entire CPT frequency report, along with a review of individual doctor coding patterns.
- Review of medical record documentation—This would include a review of compliance with Medicare and Medicaid rules and regulations for billing and medical records documentation. We would draw a sample of 30 medical charts for this review.

REPORTING

We will provide a report to you for each assessment performed. Before we prepare our first report, we will work with you to create a reporting format that would be useful to you. The report will include all of our financial analysis spreadsheets documenting the historical and practice specialty comparative information, where applicable. Analytical comparisons of practice data to specialty averages will be provided in areas such as production, adjustments, collections, overhead, staffing levels, physician productivity and earnings. The report will also address all of the other issues listed above, regarding our billing and collection assessment.

Attached is a sample report for your review.

INFORMATION REQUIRED

To conduct the review, we will provide you with a detailed checklist of the information we would need access to, or completion of, for practice assessment engagement:

POLICY ON SETTING FEES—FEE PROPOSAL

Our fee for the practice due diligence assessment will be as follows:

> $3,000 per physician per practice. If, in our opinion, the assessment engagement should require a more detailed due diligence review, we will notify you prior to starting such intensive due diligence and our fee will be capped at $5,000 per physician per practice.

USE OF SUPPLEMENTAL INDEPENDENT SPECIALISTS

From time to time, we may employ the expertise of other independent specialists to assist us in the execution of the services to be provided in this engagement. These specialists will be in the employ of our Firm and there will be no extra charge to you for their services, unless specifically agreed upon beforehand.

BILLING POLICY

OMT will invoice once per month for services rendered and expenses incurred since the last invoice. All invoices shall be paid within fifteen days after the date thereof. Any invoice not paid as specified shall bear interest from its due date at the rate of 1.5% per month or the maximum rate permitted by the applicable usury law, whichever is less. In the event any invoice is not timely paid, then OMT may terminate its performance hereunder.

In such event OMT shall still be entitled to full payment for all fees and expenses incurred before the date of such termination and OMT shall have no liability to client or any third party due to such termination. Once OMT's performance hereunder is terminated, they shall have no obligation to resume performance hereunder, even when all amounts owed are paid in full.

If any amounts due hereunder are placed in the hands of attorneys for collection, collected by suit, through the Probate Court, or through a court of Bankruptcy, client agrees to pay 25 percent additional on the amount (including interest) then due as collection or attorney's fees.

RENEWAL OF AGREEMENT

This agreement shall automatically renew for an additional year from the approval date of this agreement unless otherwise canceled.

TIMELINESS OF SERVICES

We intend to provide our services on a timely basis. However, our performance depends, in part, on your cooperation. In order to have timely management, advisory services, and reports from us on a regular basis, we must receive requested information from your office on a timely basis.

COMPLIANCE RESPONSIBILITY

While we may assist you and your practices in areas such as coding and complying with government rules and regulations, the ultimate responsibility for compliance lies with the practices themselves.

COMMUNICATION CHANNELS

The establishment and retention of communication channels between our Firm and you are vital for our relationship to remain workable. Our experience shows that problems can continue undetected, important data can be misdirected or delayed, and mix-ups can occur more easily when direct communication or personal accessibility is somehow restricted. Therefore, we view communications as a matter of serious concern.

We expect that our direct discussion with you will involve myself and other assigned professional personnel in our Firm. The table below will serve to establish the communication channels between us. We realize personnel changes are inevitable, so these assignments will change accordingly:

[INSERT ENGAGEMENT TEAM MEMBERS HERE]

Any questions or contacts as our engagement progresses can be directed to these people from our Firm assigned to your account.

RESPONSIBILITY FOR FRAUD AND EMBEZZLEMENT

Our engagement cannot be relied upon to detect and disclose any errors, irregularities, or illegal acts, including but not limited to, fraud, embezzlement, or defalcations. Therefore, we cannot be held liable for any errors, irregularities, liability for new or current personnel evaluations or recommendations, or illegal acts. However, should any such problems be detected in the course of our specific engagement, we will discuss them with you.

TERMINATION OF THIS AGREEMENT

This agreement can be terminated at any time by either you or us, without reason or cause, and without advance notice. Notice can be given either orally or in writing. Once the agreement is terminated, our obligations to you cease and any unpaid and accrued fees become immediately payable.

APPROVAL OF SERVICE AGREEMENT

If this proposal agrees with your understanding of the terms, nature, scope, and limitations of our services we intend to provide to APS Practice Management, Inc. and associated medical practices, your signature and date on this agreement will indicate your approval so we may begin your work. A copy of this agreement is enclosed for your files.

Thank you for allowing our Firm to propose on this engagement and I look forward to our possible client relationship.

Very truly yours,

Reed Tinsley, CPA

CLIENT APPROVAL:

_____

Signature

_____

Print Name

_____

Date

APPENDIX ITEM 22-01
MANAGEMENT SERVICES ORGANIZATION AGREEMENT

MANAGEMENT, SERVICES, AND
FACILITY AGREEMENT

This management, services, and facility agreement ("Agreement") is made and entered into effective as of the [Date] day of [Month, Year], by and between [Physician's name] ("Physician") and [Name of hospital] ("Manager").

RECITALS

WHEREAS, Manager operates a [number of beds]-bed licensed general acute care hospital located at [Address, City, State, ZIP];

WHEREAS, Physician is duly licensed to practice medicine in the state of [State] and is experienced in the rendering of general medical services and treatment;

WHEREAS, Physician and Manager desire to enter into a written agreement for Manager to provide Physician with certain medical office space located at [Address, City, State, ZIP], as more fully described in Exhibit A attached hereto and incorporated herein by this reference ("Medical Office") and, in connection therewith, for Physician to retain Manager's services for management, supervisory, and administrative services required to operate Medical Office on the terms and conditions set forth in Agreement;

WHEREAS, Physician and Manager desire to enter into a written agreement to provide a full statement of their respective rights and responsibilities during the term of Agreement.

NOW, THEREFORE, in consideration of the above recitals, the terms and conditions hereinafter set forth, and other good and valuable consideration, the receipt and sufficiency of which are hereby acknowledged, and for their mutual reliance, the parties hereto agree as follows:

ARTICLE I: NATURE OF RELATIONSHIP

1.1   Physician hereby engages Manager to provide Medical Office with equipment, certain personnel, and services necessary to operate Medical Office, and Manager hereby accepts such engagement in accordance with the terms and conditions contained in Agreement. Notwithstanding anything in Agreement to the contrary, Physician shall remain the holder of all licenses, accreditations, and certificates in connection with Medical Office.

ARTICLE II: TERM AND TERMINATION OF AGREEMENT

2.1   The term of Agreement shall commence on the date first set forth above, and shall continue for three (3) years, and shall be automatically renewed upon the same terms and conditions for successive one- (1) year terms, unless terminated sooner pursuant to the terms and provisions of Agreement or unless either party gives at least sixty (60) days' notice of nonrenewal to the other party prior to the expiration of the then current term of Agreement.

2.2   **Events of Termination**   In addition to the expiration of Agreement in accordance with Paragraph 2.1 above, Agreement may be terminated upon the occurrence of any of the following events:

A.   **Mutual Written Agreement**   Mutual written agreement of the parties;

B.   **Material Breach**   In the event of a material breach of Agreement by either party, the other party shall provide written notice upon the defaulting party ("Default Notice") specifying the nature of the breach. In the event such breach is not cured to the reasonable satisfaction of the nondefaulting party within ten (10) days after service of Default Notice, Agreement shall automatically terminate at the election of the nondefaulting party upon giving a written notice of termination to the defaulting party not later than thirty (30) days after service of Default Notice;

C.   **Insolvency**   If either party shall apply for or consent to the appointment of a receiver, trustee, or liquidator of itself or of all or a substantial part of its assets, file a voluntary petition in bankruptcy or admit in writing its inability to pay its debts as they become due; make a general assignment for the benefit of creditors; file a petition or an answer seeking reorganization or arrangement with creditors or take advantage of any insolvency law; or if an order, judgment, or decree shall be entered by a court of competent jurisdiction or an application of a creditor, adjudicating such party to be bankrupt or insolvent or approving a petition seeking reorganization of such party or appointing a receiver, trustee, or liquidator of such party or of all or a substantial part of its assets, and such order, judgment, or decree shall continue unstayed and in effect for a period of thirty (30) consecutive days, then the other party may terminate Agreement upon ten (10) days' prior written notice to such party;

D. **Immediate Termination**   Notwithstanding any other provision hereof, Agreement may be terminated by Manager for cause, upon one (1) day prior written notice to Physician, upon the occurrence of any of the following events:

1. The termination or suspension of Physician's license to practice medicine in the state of [State];

2. The final conviction of Physician, after all appellate proceedings are taken, of any crime punishable as felony under [State] law;

3. Any act on omission on the part of Physician that results in the cancellation of Physician's malpractice insurance, and Physician does not obtain new or substitute malpractice insurance consistent with Article IX hereof covering Physician as of the cancellation date of the prior malpractice insurance;

4. Any withdrawal by Physician from either Physician's Bank Account or the Joint Account, or any change by Physician in the disposition instructions relating to Physician's Bank Account, in contravention of Section 5.7 of Agreement; or

5. The attempted assignment or other unauthorized delegation of any of Physician's rights or obligations under Agreement.

2.3   **Effect of Termination**   Termination of Agreement shall not release or discharge either party from any obligation, debt, or liability that shall have previously accrued and remain to be performed upon the date of termination.

ARTICLE III: DUTIES AND RESPONSIBILITIES
OF PHYSICIAN

3.1 **Qualifications and Credentials** At all times hereunder, Physician shall be duly licensed to practice medicine in the State of [State].

3.2 **Standards of Practice** Physician shall comply with all applicable laws and governmental regulations concerning the licensure and practice of medicine in the State of [State].

3.3. **Hours of Operation** The hours of operation of Medical Office shall be during normal business hours, Monday through Friday, but in no event less than forty (40) hours a week or less than forty-six (46) weeks per year, plus such extended weekday and such additional weekend and holiday hours as may be determined by Physician from time to time.

3.4 **Managed-Care Agreements** At the request of Manager, Physician shall participate in all managed-care agreements, including but not limited to Medicare capitated contracts entered into by Manager; provided, however, that Physician shall not be obligated to enter into any managed-care agreement that would require Physician to discount his or her usual, customary, and reasonable charges by a percentage greater than the percentage discount given by Manager under such managed-care agreement, unless Physician and Manager mutually agree that such managed-care agreement is not in Physician's best interests.

ARTICLE IV: INDEPENDENT CONTRACTORS

4.1 In the performance of Agreement, it is mutually understood and agreed that Physician is at all times acting and performing as an independent contractor with, and not an employee, joint venturer, or lessee of, Manager. Physician shall have no claim under Agreement or otherwise against Manager for workers' compensation, unemployment compensation, sick leave, vacation pay, pension or retirement benefits, Social Security benefits, or any other employee benefits, all of which shall be the sole responsibility of Physician. Manager shall not withhold on behalf of Physician any sums for income tax, unemployment insurance, Social

Security, or otherwise pursuant to any law or requirement of any government agency, and all such withholding, if any is required, shall be the sole responsibility of Physician. Physician shall indemnify and hold harmless Manager from any or all loss or liability arising out of or with respect to any of the foregoing benefits or withholding requirements.

ARTICLE V: MANAGER'S OBLIGATIONS

For each month during the term of Agreement, Manager or its affiliates, designees, employees, or agents shall provide the following space, items, and services in a competent, efficient, and reasonably satisfactory manner:

5.1 **Medical Office** Manager shall provide Medical Office described on Exhibit A to Physician for Physician's use for so long as Agreement is in effect. Physician shall use and occupy Medical Office solely as a medical office during normal business hours, Monday through Friday, but in no event less than forty (40) hours a week or less than forty-six (46) weeks per year, plus such extended weekday and such additional weekend and holiday hours as may be designated by Physician from time to time. The amounts payable by Physician to Manager for use of Medical Office shall be in accordance with Article 6 of Agreement. The Medical Office provided by Manager may not be changed without the prior written consent of Physician, which consent shall not be unreasonably withheld. Any such substitute space shall thereafter be deemed to be Medical Office for purposes of Agreement.

5.2 **Equipment, Fixtures, Furniture, and Improvements**

A. Manager shall furnish to Physician all medical equipment, office equipment, fixtures, furniture, and leasehold improvements (collectively, "the Equipment") as may be deemed reasonably necessary by Manager for the proper and efficient operation of Medical Office. Manager shall consult regularly with Physician regarding the selection of the Equipment for Medical Office.

B. Manager shall maintain the Equipment in good repair, condition, and working order, and shall furnish all parts, including, but not limited to, all preventative and routine maintenance as may be necessary and appropriate to maintain the Equipment in a proper state of repair and serviceability.

C. The Equipment provided under Agreement shall at all times be and remain the sole property of Manager. Physician shall not cause or permit the Equipment to become subject to any lien, levy, attachment, encumbrance, or charge, or to any judicial process of any kind whatsoever, and shall not remove any Equipment from Medical Office.

5.3 **Management Services and Administration** Physician hereby appoints Manager as his or her sole and exclusive manager and administrator of all nonphysician functions and services at Medical Office, and Manager agrees to accept full responsibility for such management and administration as hereinafter provided:

A. **General Administrative Services** Manager shall provide all accounting and related financial support services required in connection with the operation of Medical Office. These services shall include, but are not limited to, budgeting, financial record keeping, and accounts receivable and accounts payable processing, to the extent that such services are required for, and directly related to, the provision of professional medical services at Medical Office.

B. **Maintenance** Manager shall be responsible for the proper maintenance and cleanliness of Medical Office.

C. **General Financial Services** Manager shall render such financial management, consultation, and advice as may be reasonably required in connection with the operation of Medical Office.

5.4 **Supplies** Manager shall furnish such supplies as may be deemed reasonably necessary by Manager for the proper and efficient operation of Medical Office, including, but not limited to, stationery, statement forms or invoices, office supplies, copier paper, and medical supplies (including pharmaceuticals). Manager shall consult regularly with Physician regarding the selection of the supplies for Medical Office.

5.5 **Utilities** Manager shall make all arrangements for, and pay all costs incidental to, all utilities necessary for the effective operation of Medical Office, including, but not limited to, gas, electricity, water, telephone, trash collection, and janitorial services.

5.6 **Patients' Records** Manager shall provide all services related to the maintenance of patients' records, including, but not limited to, record retrieval services located at Medical Office. All patients' medical records located at Medical Office shall be Physician's property.

5.7 Billing and Collection

A. **Billing Agent** To relieve Physician of the administrative burden of handling the billing and collection of fees for professional medical services, ancillary services, pharmaceuticals, injectibles, and other drugs rendered by or on behalf of Physician during the term of Agreement, Manager shall be responsible, on behalf of Physician and on the billhead of Physician as his or her agent for billing and collecting the charges made with respect to all professional medical services, ancillary services, pharmaceuticals, injectibles, and other drugs rendered by or on behalf of Physician during the term of Agreement.

B. **Documentation and Collection** Physician agrees to keep and provide to Manager all documents, opinions, diagnoses, recommendations, and other evidence and records necessary for the purpose of supporting fees charged for professional medical services, ancillary services, pharmaceuticals, injectibles, and other drugs from time to time. Manager shall maintain complete and accurate records, consistent with the general practices of Manager, of all fees, charges, and billings of all services contemplated hereby. It is expressly understood that the extent to which Manager will endeavor to collect such fees, the methods of collecting, the settling of disputes with respect to charges, and the writing off of fees that may be or appear to be uncollectible, shall at all times be at the reasonable discretion of Manager, and Manager does not guarantee the extent to which any fees billed will be collected. Physician or Physician's duly authorized agent shall have the right at all reasonable times and upon the giving of reasonable notice to examine, inspect, and copy the records of Manager pertaining to such fees, charges, billings, costs, and expenses.

C. **Fee Schedule** Physician shall deliver to Manager an initial schedule of fees for all of Physician's charges ("Fee Schedule"), a copy of which is attached hereto as Exhibit B and incorporated herein by this reference, which Fee Schedule shall not exceed the usual, customary, and reasonable charges for professional medical services, ancillary services, pharmaceuticals, injectibles, and other drugs provided in the community surrounding Medical Office. Thereafter,

Physician shall give Manager at least thirty (30) days' prior written notice of any changes in such Fee Schedule.

D. **Bank Accounts** The parties shall open a bank account ("Physician's Bank Account") at a bank or other suitable financial institution ("Agent") to be chosen by the parties to be used solely for depositing "Net Collections" (as defined in Paragraph 6.2 below) and transferring such Net Collections as hereinafter provided. Physician shall instruct Agent to transfer, at the end of each business day, all Net Collections deposited into Physician's Bank Account to such separate second bank account in the joint name of Manager and Physician ("Joint Account"), as Manager may designate to Agent from time to time.

E. **Sole Control** Physician shall at all times have sole control over Physician's Bank Account and may at any time make withdrawals from Physician's Bank Account or otherwise change the disposition instructions Physician may have given to Agent; provided, however, that Physician shall not make withdrawals from either Physician's Bank Account or Joint Account or otherwise change the disposition instructions given to Agent without the prior written consent of Manager. In the event that Physician makes any withdrawals from either Physician's Bank Account or Joint Account or changes the disposition instructions given to Agent in contravention of Agreement, Manager shall have the right to terminate Agreement in accordance with Paragraph 2.2.D above. Physician shall execute such documents as Agent may reasonably require, including, but not limited to, a limited power of attorney to permit Agent to receive Net Collections, endorse any checks, drafts, notes, money orders, cash, insurance payments, and other instruments relating to such Net Collections, deposit Net Collections into Physician's Bank Account, and transfer Net Collections from Physician's Bank Account into Joint Account.

F. **Disbursements** On or before the tenth (10th) day of each calendar month during the term of Agreement, commencing with the second (2nd) such month, and continuing on or before the tenth (10th) day of each calendar month thereafter until seven (7) months following the expiration or earlier termination of Agreement, Manager is hereby expressly authorized to, and Manager shall, disburse from Joint Account all amounts owed by Physician for the preceding month to Manager in accordance with Article 6 of Agreement and to disburse the remainder to Physician.

G. **Monthly Report** On or before the tenth (10th) day of each calendar month during the term of Agreement, commencing with the second (2nd) such month, and continuing on or before the tenth (10th) day of each calendar month thereafter until seven (7) months following the expiration or earlier termination of Agreement, Manager shall furnish Physician with a statement of all Net Collections for the previous calendar month.

H. **Survival of Collection Obligation** For a period of seven (7) months following the expiration or earlier termination of Agreement, Manager shall continue to be obligated to bill the charges made with respect to all professional medical services, ancillary services, pharmaceuticals, injectibles, and other drugs rendered by or on behalf of Physician during the term of Agreement and to collect Net Collections billed by Manager prior to the expiration or earlier termination of Agreement; provided, however, that Manager shall have no obligation to bill or collect the charges for any professional medical services, ancillary services, pharmaceuticals, injectibles, and other drugs rendered by or on behalf of Physician after the expiration or earlier termination of Agreement. Following the expiration or earlier termination of Agreement, Manager shall continue to bill and collect Net Collections in accordance with the terms and conditions set forth in this Section 5.7 of Agreement.

5.8 **Staffing of Medical Office** Manager shall, on behalf of Physician, provide such nonphysician personnel as reasonably may be necessary to enable Physician to carry out and perform his or her professional medical services at Medical Office, subject to the following:

A. Manager shall, on behalf of Physician, provide all nonphysician support personnel (excluding those physicians' assistants, nurse practitioners, and technicians who provide services that are reimbursed by the Medicare program), including, but not limited to, all receptionists, administrative assistants, clerks, management and purchasing personnel, janitorial and maintenance personnel, and such other personnel as may be deemed reasonably necessary by Manager for the proper and efficient operation of Medical Office (collectively, "Support Personnel").

B. Manager shall, on behalf of Physician: (i) train, manage, and supervise all Support Personnel; (ii) hire and fire all Support Personnel; (iii) determine the salaries, fringe benefits, bonuses, health and disability insurance, workers' compensation insurance, and any other benefits for all Support Personnel; and (iv) be responsible for any appropriate disciplinary action required to be taken against Support Personnel.

C. In recognition of the fact that personnel provided by Manager to Physician under Agreement may perform similar services from time to time for others, Agreement shall not prevent Manager from performing such similar services or restrict Manager from using the personnel provided to Physician under Agreement to perform services for others. Manager will make reasonable efforts consistent with sound business practice to honor the specific requests of Physician with regard to the assignment of Support Personnel by Manager.

5.9   General Limitation on Manager's Services   Manager is hereby expressly authorized to subcontract with other persons or entities for any of the services Manager is required to perform under Agreement; provided, however, that Manager shall remain responsible for all services performed by such other persons or entities. Manager may disclose any term of Agreement to any subcontractor of Manager who performs services to Physician at Medical Office.

ARTICLE VI: MANAGEMENT FEE

Physician and Manager hereby mutually recognize and acknowledge that Manager will incur substantial costs and expenses in fulfilling Manager's obligations to Physician, and that such costs and expenses may vary during each month of Agreement. Manager and Physician further recognize and acknowledge that Net Collections also may vary during each month of Agreement. In connection therewith, the following provisions shall apply:

6.1   Compensation   On or before the tenth (10th) day of each calendar month during the term of Agreement, commencing with the second (2nd) such month, and continuing on or before the tenth (10th) day of each calendar month thereafter until seven (7) months following the expiration or earlier termination of Agreement, Physician shall pay to Manager [Spell out percentage] ([Number]%) percent of Net Collections (as defined in Paragraph 6.2 below) as a fee for the use of Medical Office, and for the management and administrative services, Equipment, supplies, Support Personnel, and other services furnished by Manager to Physician during the term of Agreement. Manager agrees that the payment of such monthly fee shall constitute full and complete compensation to Manager for all of Manager's obligations to Physician for each month that Agreement is in effect.

6.2   **Net Collections**   As used herein, the term "Net Collections" shall be defined as all amounts received by Manager or Physician during the preceding calendar month relating to any and all professional medical services, ancillary services, pharmaceuticals, injectibles, and other drugs rendered by or on behalf of Physician to patients either at Medical Office or elsewhere each month during the term of Agreement, whether such revenues are received in cash from patients, private or prepaid insurance, or other third-party payors for such medical services. If Physician directly receives any Net Collections, Physician shall immediately turn over to Manager any and all such Net Collections.

ARTICLE VII: CONDUCT OF MEDICAL PRACTICE

7.1   Physician shall be solely and exclusively in control of all aspects of the practice of medicine and the provision of professional medical services to their patients, including all medical training and medical supervision of licensed personnel, and Manager shall neither have nor exercise any control or discretion over the methods by which Physician shall practice medicine. Manager's sole function is to render to Physician in a competent, efficient, and reasonably satisfactory manner, all nonphysician services necessary to operate Medical Office. The rendition of all professional medical services, including, but not limited to, diagnosis, treatment, the prescription of medicine and drugs, and the supervision and preparation of medical records and reports shall be the sole responsibility of Physician. Manager shall have no authority whatsoever with respect to such activities and shall have no authority whatsoever with respect to the establishment of fees nor the rendition of such professional medical services by Physician.

ARTICLE VIII: PATIENTS' RECORDS

8.1   All patients' records and charts maintained by Manager in connection with the professional medical services provided by Physician at the Medical Office shall be Physician's property. The parties shall maintain and safeguard the confidentiality of all records, charts, and other information generated in connection with the professional medical services provided hereunder in accordance with all applicable federal and state laws.

ARTICLE IX: INSURANCE

9.1   Physician shall obtain and maintain, in full force and effect during the term of Agreement, at his or her sole cost and expense, comprehensive professional liability insurance coverage, including, but not limited to, malpractice insurance coverage with an insurance carrier reasonably acceptable to Manager, under which Physician shall be named as the insured and Manager as an additional insured, to protect against any liability incident to the rendering of professional medical services at Medical Office. Such insurance coverage shall not be less than one hundred thousand dollars ($100,000) for any one person and three hundred thousand dollars ($300,000) for any one occurrence. If such insurance is on a claims-made basis, it shall include a "tail" covering acts or occurrences during the term of Agreement as to which claims may be asserted after the expiration or earlier termination of Agreement. Such policies of insurance shall provide that Manager shall receive written notice not less than thirty (30) days prior to the cancellation or material change in coverage. At Manager's request, Physician shall furnish certificates, endorsements and copies of all insurance policies to Manager.

ARTICLE X: INDEMNIFICATION

10.1 Each party shall indemnify, defend and hold harmless the other party from any and all liability, loss, claim, lawsuit, injury or cost, damage or expense whatsoever (including reasonable attorneys' fees and court costs) arising out of, incident to or in any manner occasional by the performance on nonperformance of any duty or responsibility under Agreement by such indemnifying party, or any of its employees, agents, contractors or subcontractors; provided, however, that neither party shall be liable to the other party hereunder for any claim covered by insurance, except to the extent that the liability of such party exceeding the amount of such insurance coverage.

ARTICLE XI: ASSIGNMENT

11.1 Except as otherwise provided in Agreement, Physician shall not assign any of his or her rights or delegate any of his or her duties under Agreement without the prior written consent of Manager. Any unauthorized attempted assignment by Physician shall be null and void and of no force or effect.

ARTICLE XII: NONCOMPETITION

12.1 During the term of Agreement, Physician shall not, without the prior written consent of Manager, directly or indirectly, including by or through any corporation or any entity that is an affiliate of Physician (a corporation or entity is an "affiliate of Physician" if Physician owns more than a ten percent (10%) equity interest in such corporation or entity), invest in or participate in the ownership, management, operation or control of any entity within ten (10) miles of Medical Office that is or will be in competition with any of the services provided under Agreement or at Medical Office. Notwithstanding the preceding sentence, nothing in this Article XII shall be construed to either restrict the provision of professional medical services by Physician at, or the referral of patients by Physician to, any location. Physician specifically acknowledges and agrees that the foregoing restriction is a condition precedent to Manager entering into Agreement, and that such restriction is reasonable and necessary to protect the legitimate interest of Manager and that Manager would not have entered into Agreement in the absence of such a restriction. Any violation on this Article XII would result in irreparable injury to Manager, and the remedy at law for any breach of this Article XII would be inadequate. In the event of any such breach, Manager, in addition to any other relief available to it, shall be entitled to temporary injunctive relief before trial from any court of competent jurisdiction as a matter of course upon the posting of not more than nominal bond and to permanent injunction relief without the necessity of proving actual damages. Physician further specifically acknowledges and agrees that

Manager shall be entitled to an equitable accounting of all earnings, profits, and other benefits arising from such breach and further agrees to pay the reasonable fees and expenses, including attorneys' fees, incurred by Manager in enforcing the restrictions contained in this Article XII. In the event that the provisions contained in this Article XII shall ever be deemed to exceed the time or geographic limits or any other limitation permitted by applicable law in any jurisdiction, then such provisions shall be deemed reformed in such jurisdiction to the maximum extent permitted by applicable law.

ARTICLE XIII: CONFIDENTIALITY

13.1 Neither party shall disclose Agreement or the terms thereof to a third party, except as provided herein or as otherwise required by law, without the prior written consent of the other party.

ARTICLE XIV: CONFIDENTIAL INFORMATION AND TRADE SECRETS

14.1 **Proprietary Information** Physician recognizes that because of the nature of Agreement, Physician will have access to information of a propriety nature owned by Manager, including, but not limited to, any and all documents bearing a Manager form number, any and all computer programs (whether or not completed or in use), any and all operating manuals or similar materials that constitute the nonmedical systems, policies, and procedures, methods of doing business developed by Manager, administrative, advertising, or marketing techniques, financial affairs, and other information outlined by Manager. Consequently, Physician acknowledges and agrees that Manager has a proprietary interest in all such information and that all such information constitutes confidential and proprietary information and the trade secret property of Manager. Physician herein expressly and knowingly waives any and all rights, title, and interest in and to such trade secrets and confidential information and agrees to return all copies of such trade secrets and confidential information related thereto to Manager at Physician's expense, upon the expiration or earlier termination of Agreement.

14.2 **Nondisclosure** Physician further acknowledges and agrees that Manager is entitled to prevent Manager's competitors from obtaining and utilizing its trade secrets and confidential information. Therefore, Physician agrees to hold Manager's trade secrets and confidential information in strictest confidence and to not disclose them or allow them to be disclosed, directly or indirectly, to any person or entity other than those persons or entities that are employed by or affiliated with Manager or Physician, without the prior written consent of Manager. During the term of Agreement, Physician shall not disclose to anyone, other than persons or entities who are employed by or affiliated with Manager or Physician, any confidential or proprietary information or trade secret information obtained by Physician from Manager, except as otherwise required by law. After the expiration or earlier termination of Agreement, Physician shall not disclose to anyone any confidential or proprietary information or trade secret information obtained from Manager, except as otherwise required by law or upon the prior written consent of Manager.

14.3 **Equitable Relief** Physician acknowledges and agrees that a breach of this Article XIV will result in irreparable harm to Manager and that Manager cannot be reasonably or adequately compensated in damages, and therefore, Manager shall be entitled to equitable remedies, including, but not limited to, injunctive relief to prevent a breach and to secure enforcement thereof in addition to any other relief or award to which Manager may be entitled.

ARTICLE XV: FORCE MAJEURE

15.1 Notwithstanding any provision contained herein to the contrary, Manager shall not be deemed to be in default hereunder for failing to perform or provide any of Medical Office Equipment, supplies, management services, Support Personnel, or other obligations to be performed or provided by Manager pursuant to Agreement if such failure is the result of any labor dispute, act of God, inability to obtain labor or materials, governmental restrictions, or any other event that is beyond the reasonable control of Manager.

ARTICLE XVI: THIRD-PARTY BENEFICIARY

16.1 None of the provisions contained in Agreement is intended by the parties, nor shall it be deemed, to confer any benefit on any person not a party to Agreement.

ARTICLE XVII: MEDIATION AND ATTORNEYS' FEES

17.1 The parties shall first attempt to resolve any dispute concerning Agreement or arising in any way out of the performance of Agreement through nonbinding mediation. In the event the dispute cannot be resolved within thirty (30) days by the parties in good faith through nonbinding mediation, the prevailing party in any litigation or other legal proceeding brought by either party to resolve any dispute concerning Agreement or arising in any way out of the performance of Agreement shall be entitled to recover reasonable attorneys' fees and court costs from the opposing party. The foregoing provisions of this Article XVII shall not be interpreted to require either party to submit to mediation prior to exercising either party's right to pursue equitable relief from a court of competent jurisdiction at any time or to terminate Agreement in accordance with Article II of Agreement.

ARTICLE XVIII: GENERAL PROVISIONS

18.1 **Governing Law**   This Agreement shall be governed by and interpreted under the laws of the state of [State].

18.2 **Entire Agreement**   This Agreement constitutes the entire Agreement between the parties with respect to the subject matter hereof and supersedes all prior documents, representations, and understandings of the parties that may relate to the subject matter of Agreement. No other understanding, oral or otherwise, regarding the subject matter of Agreement shall be deemed to exist or bind either party.

18.3 **Amendment**   No modification, amendment, addition to Agreement, or waiver of any of its provisions shall be valid or enforceable unless in writing and signed by both parties.

18.4 **Headings**   The headings set forth herein are for the purpose of convenient reference only, and shall have no bearing whatsoever on the interpretation of Agreement.

18.5 **Notices**   Any notice or other communication required or permitted by Agreement shall be in writing and shall be delivered personally or by United States first class mail, postage prepaid, certified or registered, return receipt requested, addressed as follows or to such other addresses or persons as may be furnished from time to time in writing by the parties. If personally delivered, such notice shall be effective upon delivery. If mailed in accordance with this Paragraph 18.5, such notice shall be effective as of the date indicated on the return receipt, whether or not such notice is accepted by the addressee:

If to Physician:
[Name of physician]
[Address, City, State, ZIP]

If to Manager:
[Name of manager]
[Address, City, State, ZIP]

18.6 **Waiver** Any waiver of any provision hereof shall not be effective unless expressly made in writing and executed by the party to be charged. The failure of any party to insist on performance of any of the terms or conditions of Agreement shall not be construed as a waiver or relinquishment of any rights granted hereunder or of the future performance of any such term, covenant, or condition, and the obligations of the parties with respect thereto shall continue in full force and effect.

18.7 **Counterparts** This Agreement may be executed in two or more counterparts, all of which shall, in the aggregate, be considered one and the same instrument.

18.8 **Severability** If any provision or portion of any provision of Agreement is held to be unenforceable or invalid by a court of competent jurisdiction, the validity and enforceability of the remaining provisions of Agreement shall not be affected thereby.

18.9 **Additional Documents** Each of the parties hereto agrees to execute any document or documents that may be requested from time to time by the other party to implement or complete such party's obligations pursuant to Agreement and to otherwise cooperate fully with such other party in connection with the performance of such party's obligations under Agreement.

IN WITNESS WHEREOF, the parties have executed Agreement effective as of the date first written above.

[INSERT SIGNATURE BLOCKS ACCORDINGLY]

EXHIBIT A
MEDICAL OFFICE

[Insert full name and address of Medical Office]

EXHIBIT B
FEE SCHEDULE

[Insert fee schedule]

Very truly yours,

[Firm]

[Engagement Partner]

CLIENT APPROVAL:

_____

Signature

_____

Print Name

_____

Date

APPENDIX ITEM 22-02
INDEPENDENT PRACTICE ASSOCIATION AGREEMENT

PHYSICIAN AGREEMENT

This Physician Agreement ("Agreement") is between [Name of IPA] ("IPA"), whose principal place of business is located at [Address, City, State, ZIP], and [Name of physician] ("Physician"), whose principal place of business is located at [Address, City, State, ZIP].

RECITALS

WHEREAS, IPA intends to enter into contracts with preferred provider organizations, health maintenance organizations, exclusive provider organizations, and other payors ("Plan(s)") to provide medical services to persons enrolled as enrollees ("Enrollees") of Plans; and

WHEREAS, IPA and Physician desire to enter into an agreement whereby Physician agrees to provide medical services on behalf of IPA to Enrollees of Plans, which contract with IPA;

NOW, THEREFORE, IPA and Physician agree as follows:

ARTICLE I: DEFINITIONS

1.1 **"Coordination of Benefits" ("COB")** shall mean how two or more Plans will cover the medical services rendered to Enrollee. Such coordination is intended to preclude Enrollee from receiving an aggregate of more than one hundred percent (100%) of charges for medical services. When primary and secondary benefits are coordinated, determination of liability will be in accordance with the usual procedures employed by the [State] Department of Insurance and applicable state laws.

1.2 **"Co-payment or Deductible"** shall mean those charges which shall be collected directly by Physician from Enrollee in accordance with Enrollee's Evidence of Coverage.

1.3 **"Covered Services"** shall mean those services, equipment, and supplies that Enrollee is entitled to receive under a Plan's benefits program.

1.4 **"Emergency"** shall mean the sudden onset of a symptom or injury, which, if not treated immediately, could result in the loss of life or limb, or permanent disability.

1.5 **"Enrollee"** shall mean a person, including an enrolled dependent, who is enrolled in a Plan that has contracted with IPA, and who is entitled to receive Covered Services.

1.6 **"Evidence of Coverage"** shall mean the document issued by a Plan that describes Covered Services Enrollee is entitled to receive.

1.7 **"Medically Necessary"** or **"Medical Necessity"** shall mean medical services that Enrollee requires as determined by Participating Provider in accordance with accepted medical practices and standards prevailing at the time of treatment and in conformity with the professional standards adopted by IPA's utilization management committee.

1.8 **"Noncovered Services"** shall mean those services, equipment, and supplies that Enrollee is not entitled to receive under a Plan's benefits Program.

1.9 **"Participating Provider"** shall mean a Participating Physician, Participating Hospital, or other licensed health-care provider that has entered into an agreement with IPA to provide Covered Services to Enrollees.

1.10 **"Primary Hospital"** shall mean [Name of hospital].

1.11 **"Primary Physician"** or **"Primary-Care Physician"** shall mean a Participating Physician selected by Enrollee to render first-contact medical care. "Primary Physician" or "Primary-Care Physician" may include, but are not limited to, as determined by IPA, internists, pediatricians, family practitioners, and general practitioners.

1.12 **"Specialist Physician"** shall mean a Participating Physician who is professionally qualified to practice his or her designated specialty and whose agreement with IPA includes responsibility for providing Covered Services in his or her designated specialty.

1.13 **"Subscriber"** shall mean a person or entity that is responsible for payment to a Plan or a person whose employment or other status, except for family dependency, is the basis for eligibility for enrollment in a Plan.

ARTICLE II: SERVICES TO BE PERFORMED BY PHYSICIAN

2.1 **Services** Physician agrees to provide Covered Services in [Specialty] to Enrollees. If Physician is not a Primary-Care Physician, then Physician shall only provide Covered Services not designated as Emergency services to Enrollee upon receiving a prior written authorization to treat Enrollee from IPA's utilization management committee. Failure of Physician to receive such prior written authorization may result, at IPA's option, in IPA not paying Physician for those Covered Services provided to Enrollee.

2.2 **Service Report** If Physician is a Specialist Physician, then Physician agrees to submit a written report to the Primary-Care Physician who is responsible for the ongoing care of Enrollee. The report shall describe the plan of treatment proposed by Physician and any proposed hospitalization or referral and shall be submitted within fourteen (14) days of examination of Enrollee.

2.3 **Consultation** If Physician is a Specialist Physician, then the responsible Primary-Care Physician shall agree on the plan of treatment proposed by Specialist Physician for Enrollee prior to implementation of the plan of treatment. If the responsible Primary-Care Physician and Specialist Physician cannot agree on the proposed plan of treatment, the disagreement regarding the plan of treatment shall be submitted to IPA's utilization management committee for resolution in accordance with the rules and regulations established by IPA's Board of Directors.

2.4 **Covering Physician** If Physician is temporarily unable to provide Covered Services, Physician may secure the services of a qualified *locum tenens* or covering physician who shall render those Covered Services otherwise required of Physician; provided, however, that the *locum tenens* or covering physician so furnished must be a physician approved by IPA to provide Covered Services to Enrollees. Physician shall solely be responsible for securing the services of the *locum tenens* or covering physician and for informing the *locum tenens* or covering physician that he or she will be compensated by IPA in accordance with this Agreement. It will be Physician's responsibility to ensure that the *locum tenens* or covering physician: (*a*) looks solely to Physician for compensation; (*b*) will accept IPA's peer review procedures; (*c*) will not bill Enrollees for Covered Services, except for Co-payments and Deductibles; (*d*) will obtain, prior to all admissions and referrals not designated Emergencies, authorization from IPA's utilization management committee; and (*e*) will comply with the terms of this Agreement, including Paragraphs 6.4, 6.5, 6.6 and 6.7 regarding insurance.

2.5 **Performance** Subject to the provisions of Article XI of this Agreement, Physician will determine the methods and means of performing Covered Services under this Agreement. If IPA so requires, Physician shall submit to IPA a statement or medical report in the form prescribed by IPA of all capitated services rendered each month to Enrollees no later than the fifth (5th) day following the end of each month in which the services were rendered. IPA shall at all times have the right to refer and not to refer Enrollees to Physician based on Physician's ability to treat such Enrollees; provided, however, that if Physician is a Primary-Care Physician, he or she agrees to accept a minimum of two hundred fifty (250) Enrollees unless he or she obtains the written consent of IPA. In addition, IPA will use its best efforts to refer Enrollees who have a pre-existing relationship with Physician to Physician, if appropriate.

2.6 **Assistants** Physician shall, at Physician's sole expense, employ such nonprofessional assistants or employees as Physician deems necessary to comply with this Agreement. IPA shall not control, direct, or supervise Physician's assistants or employees.

2.7 **Hospital Admissions** Physician shall admit Enrollees only to Primary Hospital unless an appropriate bed or service is unavailable. Physician must receive prior written authorization from IPA's utilization management committee before admitting any Enrollee to any hospital, except in an emergency.

2.8 **Referrals** Physician shall refer Enrollee to a health care provider only upon receiving the prior written authorization of IPA's utilization management committee. Failure of Specialist Physician to obtain prior written authorization may result in IPA deducting the full amount of all monies due and owing to the treating health care provider from the amounts owed to Specialist Physician. Physician acknowledges that IPA has the right to contract with other Participating Providers for radiology, laboratory, or other ancillary services for Enrollees. Physician agrees to refer Enrollees to such Participating Providers if requested by IPA, except in an Emergency or if Physician customarily performed such services in Physician's office prior to the date this Agreement was signed by Physician.

2.9 **Eligibility** Physician shall use his or her best efforts to determine the eligibility of all Enrollees prior to rendering services under this Agreement. If Physician renders services to an ineligible person, Physician should make a claim in writing to IPA's Board of Directors and the Board shall approve or deny the claim in its sole and absolute discretion. Physician shall have no right to payment for services rendered to an ineligible person after IPA gives Physician notification of the ineligibility. IPA agrees that Physician shall not be under any obligation to render services to any Enrollee without reasonable assurance that Enrollee is eligible for services and that services required are Covered Services under the applicable Plan.

ARTICLE III: REPRESENTATIONS

3.1 **Representations by IPA** IPA hereby warrants and represents that it is a(n) [State] corporation in good standing with the [State] Secretary of State.

3.2 **Representations by Physician** Physician hereby warrants and represents that Physician is a physician or [State] professional corporation licensed to practice medicine in the State of [State] and is in good standing with the [State] Board of Medical Quality Assurance. Physician warrants and represents that Physician is currently, and for the duration of this Agreement shall remain, a member in good standing of the medical staff of Primary Hospital with privileges in [physician's medical specialty].

ARTICLE IV: COMPENSATION

4.1 **Compensation Formula** If Physician is a Primary-Care Physician, IPA shall pay him/her those amounts set forth in Exhibit A, which is attached hereto and incorporated by reference, for those Covered Services rendered by him/her to Enrollees. If Physician is a Specialist Physician, IPA shall pay him/her those amounts set forth in Exhibit B, which is attached hereto and incorporated by reference, for those Covered Services rendered by him/her to Enrollees.

4.2 **Timing of Payment of Compensation** IPA shall pay Physician those amounts set forth in Exhibits A and B of this Agreement within forty-five (45) days following IPA's receipt of the monthly invoice(s) provided by Physician to IPA.

4.3 **Billing Procedures** Physician shall bill IPA for all Covered Services rendered to Enrollee, less any Co-payments and Deductibles collected or to be collected from Enrollee. Physician shall submit to IPA a written statement (approved as to form and content by IPA) enumerating all Covered Services rendered by Physician to Enrollee within sixty (60) days following the provision of Covered Services. The statement must include a copy of Primary-Care Physician's written authorization to treat Enrollee. Failure of Physician to submit the written statement and copy of Primary-Care Physician's written authorization to treat Enrollee within sixty (60) days of service may result, at IPA's option, in IPA not paying Physician.

4.4 **Billing Patients** Physician shall look only to IPA for compensation of Covered Services rendered to Enrollees and shall not seek any compensation from Enrollees for Covered Services, except for Co-payments and Deductibles.

4.5 **Patients' Responsibilities** Physician shall bill and collect from Enrollees those Co-payments and Deductibles specifically permitted by a Plan. Physician shall use his or her best efforts to collect applicable co-payments from Enrollees. Physician may bill and collect from Enrollees charges for Noncovered Services provided to Enrollees.

4.6 **Surcharges** Physician understands that surcharges against Enrollees are prohibited and IPA in its sole and absolute discretion may terminate this Agreement immediately if Physician utilizes such surcharges. A "surcharge" is an additional fee that is charged to Enrollee for a Covered Service but which is not approved by the Commissioner of Corporations of the State of [State] or allowed by a Plan.

4.7 IPA's Expenses IPA may be required by Plans to perform certain services such as claims processing, billing and collections, record keeping, or utilization review services. In the event that IPA performs such services, IPA shall be entitled to deduct from the gross revenues it receives from Plans the reasonable costs of the services.

ARTICLE V: COORDINATION OF BENEFITS

5.1 Coordination of Benefits (COB) Obligations of Physician Physician agrees to perform COB with IPA and to bill and collect from other Plans the charges the other Plans are responsible for paying. Physician shall report all collections received in accordance with this Paragraph 5.1 to IPA. IPA shall reduce the amounts owed to Physician by IPA under Paragraph 4.1 of this Agreement by the amount collected by Physician under this Article V.

5.2 COB Obligations of IPA IPA will cooperate in providing COB information to Physician by collecting appropriate data from Enrollees and supplying such information to Physician.

ARTICLE VI: OBLIGATIONS OF PHYSICIAN

6.1 Nonexclusivity IPA and Physician agree that:

a. Physician may continue to provide medical services to Physician's own patients and to patients of plans not contracting with IPA.

b. In rendering medical services to Physician's own patients or to the patients of plans not contracting with IPA, Physician shall neither represent nor imply in any way that such medical services are being rendered by or on behalf of IPA.

c. Physician shall be responsible for providing the insurance required under this Agreement.

d. Any medical services rendered by Physician outside the scope of this Agreement shall not be billed by or through IPA.

6.2 **Hours** Physician agrees to be available to render Covered Services or to provide coverage for Covered Services twenty-four (24) hours per day, seven (7) days per week, three hundred sixty-five (365) days per year.

6.3 **Personnel, Equipment, and Supplies** Physician will supply all necessary office personnel, equipment, and supplies required to perform services under this Agreement provided; however, that IPA may require Physician to purchase certain equipment and supplies for Enrollees from Participating Providers.

6.4 **Workers' Compensation Insurance** Physician agrees to provide, at Physician's sole expense, workers' compensation insurance for Physician's agents, representatives, and employees throughout the entire term of this Agreement in accordance with the laws of the State of [State].

6.5 **Malpractice Insurance** Physician shall provide, unless otherwise agreed to by Physician and IPA, at Physician's sole expense, throughout the entire term of this Agreement, a policy of professional malpractice liability insurance with a licensed insurance company admitted to do business in the State of [State] in a minimum amount of one million dollars ($1,000,000) per claim and three million dollars ($3,000,000) in the annual aggregate, to cover any loss, liability, or damage committed or alleged to have been committed by Physician or Physician's agents, representatives, or employees.

6.6 **Comprehensive Insurance** Physician shall provide, unless otherwise agreed to by Physician and IPA, at Physician's sole expense, throughout the entire term of this Agreement, a policy or policies of insurance covering Physician's principal place of business insuring Physician against any claim of loss, liability, or damage committed or arising out of the alleged condition of Physician's office(s) or the furniture, fixtures, appliances, or equipment located therein, together with standard liability protection against any loss, liability, or damage as a result of Physician's, Physician's agent's, Physician's representative's, or Physician's employee's operation of a motor vehicle, both in a minimum amount of one hundred thousand dollars ($100,000) per claim and three hundred thousand dollars ($300,000) in the annual aggregate.

6.7 **Proof of Insurance** Physician shall provide IPA with a minimum of thirty (30) days' prior written notice in the event any of the insurance policies required under this Article VI are canceled, changed, or amended. Physician shall from time to time, at the request of IPA, furnish to IPA written evidence that the policies of insurance required under this Article VI are valid and in full force and effect.

6.8 **Performance** Physician shall devote the time, attention, and energy necessary for the competent and effective performance of Physician's duties to Enrollees under this Agreement.

6.9 **Compliance with Law and Ethical Standards** Physician shall at all times during the term of this Agreement comply with all applicable federal and state laws, all applicable rules and regulations of the [State] Board of Medical Quality Assurance and the ethical standards of the American and [State] Medical Associations.

6.10 **Physician's License** If at any time during the term of this Agreement, Physician shall have his or her license to practice medicine in the State of [State] suspended, conditioned, or revoked, this Agreement shall terminate immediately and become null and void without regard to whether or not such suspension, condition, or revocation has been finally adjudicated.

6.11 **Hospital Privileges** During the entire term of this Agreement, Physician shall be and remain a member of the medical staff of Primary Hospital. Loss of such medical staff membership or loss, impairment, suspension, or reduction of privileges at Primary Hospital shall, at the option of IPA, immediately terminate this Agreement, whereupon it shall become null and void without regard to whether or not such loss of membership or loss, impairment, suspension, or reduction of privileges has been finally adjudicated.

6.12 **Continuing Medical Education** During the entire term of this Agreement, Physician shall maintain his or her professional competence and skills commensurate with the medical standards of the community and all laws by attending and participating in approved continuing medical education courses.

6.13 **Compliance with IPA Articles, Bylaws, Rules, and Regulations** Physician agrees to be bound by IPA's articles of incorporation, bylaws, and rules and regulations, copies of which shall be provided to Physician upon request. Physician recognizes that these documents may be amended from time to time. Physician agrees to cooperate with any administrative procedures adopted by IPA.

6.14 **Physician Roster** Physician agrees that IPA and Plans may use Physician's name, address, telephone number, type of practice, and willingness to accept new patients in their rosters of participants.

6.15 **Cooperation with IPA** Physician agrees to cooperate with IPA so that IPA may meet any requirements imposed on IPA by state and federal laws. Physician agrees to maintain such records and provide such information to IPA, Plans, and applicable state and federal regulatory agencies as may be required. Such obligations shall not be terminated upon termination of this Agreement. Physician agrees to give IPA or IPA's authorized representative and Plans access upon request to books, records, and other papers relating to Covered Services rendered by Physician, to the cost thereof, and to payments received from Enrollees or from others on Enrollees' behalf. Physician agrees to retain such books and records for a period of at least five (5) years from and after the termination of this Agreement. Physician further agrees to give the [State] Department of Corporations, the [State] Department of Health, the United States Department of Health and Human Services, and the Comptroller General of the United States access upon request to those facilities, books, and records maintained or utilized by Physician in the performance of Covered Services under this Agreement.

6.16 **Nondiscrimination** Physician agrees: (*a*) not to differentiate or discriminate against Enrollees because of race, color, national origin, ancestry, religion, sex, marital status, sexual orientation, or age and (*b*) to render Covered Services to Enrollees in the same manner, in accordance with the same standards, and within the same time availability as offered to non-Plan patients consistent with existing medical ethical/legal requirements for providing continuity of care to any patient.

6.17 **Cooperation with Plan Medical Directors** Physician understands that Plans will place certain obligations upon IPA regarding the quality and Medical Necessity of care received by Enrollees and that Plans in certain instances will have the right to oversee and review the quality and Medical Necessity of care administered to Enrollees. Physician agrees to cooperate with Plans' medical directors when they review the quality and Medical Necessity of care administered to Enrollees.

6.18 **IPA Opportunities** By signing this Agreement, Physician agrees to accept all Plan contracts signed by IPA; however, IPA shall make available to Physician all Plan contracts signed by IPA. IPA shall be entitled to the reasonable costs of copying a contract for Physician. Notwithstanding any other provision of this Agreement, IPA is authorized to enter into any contract of any kind with a Plan for the provision of Covered Services to Enrollees by Physician.

6.19 **Workers' Compensation Cases** Physician agrees to be the primary assignee on workers' compensation cases. In addition, Physician shall make every effort to ascertain whether the nature of the injury or illness of Enrollee occurred within the scope of his or her employment and is thereby covered by workers' compensation insurance. Physician shall not pursue additional compensation from IPA, Plan, or Enrollee in such cases. Physician shall report to IPA all workers' compensation cases involving Enrollees on a monthly basis.

ARTICLE VII: MEDICAL RECORDS

7.1 **Record Retention** Physician shall maintain for each Enrollee receiving medical services under this Agreement a single standard medical record in such form, containing such information, and preserved for such time period(s) as are required by state and federal law. To the extent permitted by law, in accordance with procedures required by law, and upon receipt of three (3) business days prior written notice from IPA, Physician shall permit IPA to inspect and make copies of Enrollee records and shall provide copies of such records to IPA upon request.

7.2 **IPA Patients** Physician acknowledges that all Enrollees to whom Physician renders medical services under this Agreement are and will remain patients of IPA. A copy of any Enrollee's medical records created, compiled, or supplemented by Physician during the term of this

Agreement shall be delivered to IPA upon written request. IPA acknowledges that Enrollees' medical records are and shall remain the property of Physician; however, IPA shall have the right to copy all medical records of those Enrollees who have been treated by Physician during the term of this Agreement.

ARTICLE VIII: TERM

8.1   This Agreement will become effective on [Date] and will continue for a period of one (1) year thereafter. This Agreement will automatically be renewed for successive periods of one (1) year each on the same terms contained herein, unless terminated pursuant to the terms of the Agreement.

ARTICLE IX: TERMINATION

9.1   **Immediate Termination**   Notwithstanding any other term of this Agreement, IPA shall have the right in its sole and absolute discretion to terminate this Agreement immediately in the event that Physician fails to comply with any of the terms of the Agreement or is incapable of performing his or her duties or responsibilities under the Agreement.

9.2   **Termination with Notice**   This Agreement may be terminated by Physician without cause by giving one hundred twenty (120) days' prior written notice to IPA. This Agreement may be terminated by IPA without cause by giving ninety (90) days' prior written notice to Physician.

9.3   **Responsibility for Enrollees at Termination**   Physician shall continue to provide medical services to any Enrollee who is receiving medical services from Physician on the effective termination date of this Agreement until (*a*) the medical services being rendered to Enrollee by Physician are completed (consistent with existing medical ethical/legal requirements for providing continuity of care to a patient) or unless IPA or a Plan makes reasonable and medically appropriate provisions for the assumption of such medical services by another provider and (*b*) his or her responsibility is completed pursuant to the applicable Plan contract. IPA shall compensate Physician for those Covered Services provided to Enrollee pursuant to this Paragraph 9.3 in accordance with Exhibits A and B of this Agreement.

9.4 **Physician's Rights upon Termination** Physician agrees that any of IPA's decisions to terminate this Agreement shall be final. Physician further agrees that he or she shall have no right(s) to appeal the decision of IPA through any formal or informal administrative hearing or review process nor shall he or she have any other due process rights to appeal IPA's decision to terminate this Agreement.

ARTICLE X: DOCUMENTATION

10.1 **Documentation** IPA shall provide Physician with a copy of any document that a Plan requires Physician to sign and which has been approved by IPA's Board of Directors. If Physician does not sign and return the document within ten (10) calendar days, then this Agreement shall, at the option of IPA, terminate immediately and become null and void.

10.2 **List of Participating Physicians** IPA shall supply to Physician a list of those physicians with which IPA has executed physician agreements. IPA also shall supply to Physician current information about Enrollees who are eligible for services under Plans as well as information about limitations of coverage, if any, for such Enrollees.

ARTICLE XI: UTILIZATION REVIEW/QUALITY ASSURANCE PROGRAMS AND GRIEVANCE PROCEDURE

11.1 **Utilization Review/Quality Assurance Programs** Utilization review/quality assurance programs shall be established to review the Medical Necessity of Covered Services furnished by Physician to Enrollees. Such programs will be established by IPA in its sole and absolute discretion, and will include prospective, concurrent, and retrospective reviews and will be in addition to any utilization review/quality assurance programs required by a Plan. Physician shall comply with and, subject to Physician's rights of appeal, shall be bound by such utilization review/quality assurance programs. Physician shall, if requested, serve on IPA's utilization management committee. Failure to comply with the requirements of this Paragraph 11.1 may be deemed by IPA to be a material breach of this Agreement and may, at IPA's option, be grounds for immediate IPA termination of this Agreement. Physician agrees that decisions of IPA's utilization management committee may be used by IPA to deny Physician payment for Covered Services and Noncovered Services provided to Enrollee.

11.2 **Grievance Procedure**   A grievance procedure shall be established for the processing of Enrollee complaints. The procedure will be established by IPA in accordance with the requirements of Plans. Physician shall comply with the procedure and, subject to Physician's rights of appeal under the procedure, shall be bound by it.

ARTICLE XII: GENERAL PROVISIONS

12.1 **Notices**   Any notices required or permitted to be given under this Agreement may be given by personal delivery in writing or by registered or certified mail, postage prepaid, return receipt requested. Notices shall be addressed to the parties at the addresses appearing in the introductory paragraph on the first page of this Agreement, but each party may change its address by giving notice in accordance with this paragraph 12.1. Personally delivered notices will be deemed communicated as of actual receipt. Mailed notices will be deemed communicated as of three (3) days after mailing.

12.2 **Entire Agreement of the Parties**   This Agreement supersedes any and all agreements, either written or oral, between the parties with respect to the subject matter contained in this Agreement. Each party to this Agreement acknowledges that no representations, inducements, or promises have been made by either party nor anyone acting on behalf of either party that are not embodied herein. Except as otherwise provided herein, any effective modification must be in writing and signed by the party to be charged with the modification.

12.3 **Severability**   If any term of this Agreement is held by a court of competent jurisdiction or applicable state or federal law to be invalid, void, or unenforceable, the remaining terms will nevertheless continue in full force and effect.

12.4 **Arbitration**   Any controversy or claim arising out of this Agreement will be settled by arbitration in accordance with the rules of commercial arbitration of the American Arbitration Association, and judgment upon the award rendered by the arbitrator(s) may be entered in any court having jurisdiction. Such arbitration shall occur within the County of [County], State of [State], unless the parties mutually agree to have the proceeding in some other locale. The arbitrator(s) may in any such proceeding award attorneys' fees and costs to the prevailing party.

12.5 Governing Law This Agreement shall be governed by and construed in accordance with the laws of the State of [State].

12.6 Assignment Neither Physician nor IPA may assign any of its respective rights or delegate any of its respective duties under this Agreement without receiving the prior written consent of the other party.

12.7 Independent Contractor Under this Agreement, Physician is and shall be construed to be an independent contractor practicing Physician's profession and shall not be deemed the agent, representative, or employee of IPA.

12.8 Confidentiality The terms of this Agreement are confidential and shall not be disclosed, except to perform the Agreement or as required by law.

12.9 Waiver The waiver of any term or the breach of any term of this Agreement must be set forth specifically in writing and signed by the waiving party. Any such waiver shall not operate or be deemed a waiver of any prior or future breach of such term or any other term.

12.10 Headings The headings of this Agreement are included for purposes of convenience only and shall not affect the construction or interpretation of any of its terms.

12.11 Amendment This Agreement may be amended by IPA to comply with any Plan contract, state or federal law, or government requirement. Any other amendments must be mutually agreed to in writing by IPA and Physician.

[INSERT SIGNATURE BLOCKS ACCORDINGLY]

EXHIBITS A AND B

PRIMARY AND SPECIALIST PHYSICIANS' COMPENSATION

Partners senior health plan compensation is currently the only plan wherein the physician is capitated. Capitation amount is approximately twenty-three percent (23%) of IPA's total capitation payment per member per month.

Compensation is based on the following fee for service formula for all other plans:

$$\text{(Conversion factor) x (RVS No.) x (80\%)}$$

The Conversion Factors are as follows:

Medicine	$ 6.00
Surgery	140.00
Anesthesiology	31.00
Radiology—Total	12.50
Radiology—Professional component	1.95
Pathology	1.55
Obstetrics—Normal vaginal	1,106.00
Caesarean section	1,596.00

The Unit Value shall be determined by reference to the [Year, State] Relative Value Study, as adopted by the [State] Medical Association on [Date]. If not so provided, Unit Value(s) shall be determined by the Board of Directors of IPA, in its sole and absolute discretion, based on the report of Physician.

Risk Reserve Pool: There shall be withheld from each payment due Physician for his or her services, an amount set by the Board of Directors in its sole discretion ("Withhold"). The initial Withhold shall be equal to twenty percent (20%) of each payment to Physician by IPA. If the Board of Directors changes the amount of Withhold, the fee-for-service formula in the above paragraph shall be changed proportionately.

The amounts withheld shall annually be placed in two risk reserve pools, designated as follows:

Pool A: This pool shall contain seventy percent (70%) of the Withhold from the payments to Participating Physicians who are not Primary-Care Physicians.

Pool B: This pool shall contain one hundred percent (100%) of the Withhold from the payments made to Participating Physicians who are providing primary-care services plus thirty percent (30%) of the payments made to physicians who are not providing primary-care services.

IPA shall maintain individual accounts for each physician of the amounts in the pool credited to each such physician. The pooled amounts shall not bear interest.

Amounts placed in Pool A for any fiscal year will be credited to Participating Physicians according to the amount withheld from payments made to the Participating Physicians during that fiscal year.

Amounts placed in Pool B will be credited to physicians providing primary-care services in proportion to the number of Enrollee Months each such participant has during that fiscal year. An "Enrollee Month" means an enrollee of the payor organization contracting with IPA for which the participant was the Primary-Care Physician for one month.

Amounts credited to the pools are not assignable and are not payable to participants until and unless a surplus is declared as hereinafter provided and then only as distributed. Termination of this contract shall not entitle a participant to withdraw funds from any pool.

The pooled amounts shall be kept on a fiscal year basis with new pools commencing on January 1 of each year.

The pooled funds shall be used by IPA to meet expenses of IPA arising out of or in connection with operations of IPA, contracts with Participating Physicians, and contingencies and liabilities arising out of independent practice agreements.

To the extent possible, the Board of Directors will charge funds drawn from the pools to the pool for the year in respect of which the expense or liability arose. Draws for operating expenses in a particular fiscal year shall be charged to the pools for that year.

In the event the draw is to meet an expense or liability incurred as result of the acts or failure to act of a Participating Physician, the draw shall be charged to that physician's pool account.

Distributions from Reserve Pools: If, at any time the Board of Directors of IPA determines that the total in all pools exceeds the amount necessary to provide for contingencies and normal operations, the Board shall declare the amount of such excess and shall distribute such excess to Participating Physicians. Such distribution shall be made as follows:

1. No distribution shall be made to any Pool A participants for any fiscal year until all Pool A participants in all previous fiscal years have been paid in full.

2. No distribution shall be made to any Pool B participants for any fiscal year until all Pool B participants in all previous fiscal years have been paid in full.

3. Distributions shall be divided between Pool A and Pool B participants in such a manner as to achieve and thereafter maintain a ratio of seven (7) in all existing Pool A's participants for every three (3) in all existing Pool B's participants.

No amounts from the risk reserve pools shall be distributed to shareholders of IPA except pursuant to contract with IPA as Participating Physicians.

IPA will furnish each participant in a Risk Reserve Pool written notification of the credit of such participant in the pool at the close of the pool and each subsequent adjustment or distribution from the pool.

APPENDIX ITEM 22-03
PROPOSED IPA IMPLEMENTATION CHECKLIST

I. **Managed-Care Contracting**

    A. Establish contracting committee

    B. Review current PPO arrangements—Opportunities to facilitate

        1. Identify payors

        2. Review contract terms

        3. Review reimbursement schedule

        4. Meet with payor representative to facilitate

    C. Review and facilitate new PPO arrangements

        1. All new PPO contracts are run through the IPA

        2. IPA used to facilitate favorable contract terms and rates

    D. Identify payors for potential contracting

        1. Identify payors

        2. Develop marketing packet

        3. Mail marketing packet to managed-care plans

        4. Follow up with managed-care representatives

        5. Set meetings with managed-care representatives

            a) Attempt to negotiate new contracts for IPA

            b) Attempt to position IPA for new contracting opportunities

            c) Execute contracts

II. **Utilization Management**

    A. Develop utilization committee

    B. Begin development of clinical pathways and guidelines

    C. Decide how to capture utilization data

    D. Begin process of reviewing utilization data

    E. Begin implementation of NCQA standards

III. Overhead Reduction
A. Identify vendors to consolidate
B. Issue bids
C. Review bids
D. Select vendors

IV. Shared Billing
A. Select location of central billing office
B. Negotiate lease
C. Prepare organizational chart
D. Select employees
E. Select billing system
F. Furnish central business office
G. Convert account balances to new system
H. Design billing and collection policies

V. IPA Contract Development
A. Select legal counsel
B. Select IPA entity and draft related legal contracts
C. Draft physician provider agreement

APPENDIX ITEM 22-04
IPA DEVELOPMENT CHECKLIST

- ❏ Hire advisors
- ❏ Recruit providers (Must be within a very wide geographic region according to PCA)
  - ❏ Adult providers
  - ❏ Pediatric providers
  - ❏ Therapeutic providers
  - ❏ Outpatient surgery center
  - ❏ Other _____
  - ❏ Other _____
- ❏ Establish IPA legal entity
- ❏ Initiate development of provider group
  - ❏ Confirm service area parameters (i.e., geographic coverage)
  - ❏ Decide how to compensate providers
  - ❏ Identify utilization management strategy
  - ❏ Prepare budget guidelines and estimates
  - ❏ Draft reimbursement policy specifics
  - ❏ Draft physician reporting requirements to the IPA
  - ❏ Determine and review other legal issues related to providers
- ❏ Draft and execute provider agreement
- ❏ Formalize board committee structure, nominate doctors, and develop written committee guidelines
  - ❏ Quality assurance
  - ❏ Financial and administration
  - ❏ Contracting
- ❏ Prepare contracting proposal to PCA
  - ❏ Decide on "group" capitation rate
- ❏ Negotiate terms of PCA/IPA service agreement
- ❏ Implement physician credentialling process
- ❏ Collaborate with PCA on hospital and ancillary facilities contracting

❑ For PCA, decide on level of hospital risk-sharing, if available

❑ Create utilization control, quality assessment, and related program protocols and particulars (in particular, NCQA standards)

❑ Design, test, and implement management information systems

❑ Prepare all forms, provider manuals, notices, and related materials for operations

❑ Establish provider orientation, training, and professional relations programs

APPENDIX ITEM 22-05

PROPOSAL TO PROVIDE MANAGEMENT SERVICES TO IPA

PERSONAL & CONFIDENTIAL

Date
Name
IPA Name
Address
City, State, Zip

Dear Dr. _____:

Per your request, the following is our proposal of our services to assist with the development and administration of your Independent Physician Association consisting of multiple provider locations. It should be understood that our engagement would be limited to the performance of services related only to this matter. Since we believe it is essential for the both of us to have the same understanding of the consultant/client relationship, we have adopted a standard terms of engagement for this specific matter, as outlined below. We ask that you review the terms and contact me immediately if you have any questions about our relationship.

DESCRIPTION OF AVAILABLE SERVICES

IPA Management — Following are the management services that are available to the IPA.

• Establish and Supervise Committee System—IPA Manager sits ad hoc on all committees and is responsible for presentation of information, scheduling of meetings, and effecting any decisions or directives of the committee. The manager, with the help of each committee, will establish policies and procedures.

• Supervise implementation of quality assurance and utilization management activities.

• Supervise All Subcontracting—IPA Manager is responsible for the administration and supervision of all subcontracting, i.e., legal, accounting, and medical consulting.

- Administration—IPA Manager is responsible for all billing of membership, payment of bills, and day-to-day operations, including data gathering. IPA Manager is to maintain all records and information provided to the IPA by its membership in a confidential manner.

- Financial Management—IPA Manager will maintain all financial records in an orderly manner and generate monthly reports, annual budgets, and financial analyses and projection of future revenues. IPA manager is responsible for effecting overhead reduction, through negotiations with malpractice insurance providers, vendors, employee benefit packages, and other cost-saving opportunities. IPA Manager is to prepare all requests for proposals (RFPs), review, and make recommendations to Executive Committee. IPA Manager is responsible for the filing and compliance with all local, state, and federal regulatory agencies, including, but not limited to, the Internal Revenue Service.

Payor and Primary Care Survey (Payor Marketing)—In consultation with the IPA physicians, we would develop and prioritize the list of third-party payors to be contacted on behalf of the IPA. Our personnel would then personally meet with contracting representatives with each of these entities to determine their receptivity to specific reimbursement and risk-sharing arrangements with your group of doctors (i.e., market the IPA to the payors). We would assess each entity's receptivity to contracting with your specialty IPA, both now and in the future. Additional goals during this step of the process are: (a) Learn the objectives of the managed-care payors and the primary-care practices; (b) Find out how many enrolled members are in the managed-care plans; (c) Determine key employers in the managed-care plans; and (d) Assess timetables, if any, for these entities to enter into exclusive contractual arrangements with physician providers. The development of a marketing document for the IPA that can be submitted to each payor may be a part of this service if requested or needed.

Payor Negotiations—We will negotiate with third-party payors on behalf of the IPA; this includes PPOs, HMOs, and primary-care groups who are responsible for the reimbursement of specialists. It also includes the renegotiation of existing managed-care contracts. Included as part of this process is the development of a minimum IPA discounted fee schedule to be used in payor negotiations. Generally, an outside party must develop this type of fee schedule in order to avoid antitrust issues. Our service will include required payor conferences, the negotiation of reimbursement rates, and the review and negotiation of contract provisions.

Proposal Development—If the IPA is ever required to respond to a Request for Contract Proposal (RFP), a proposal packet will be prepared for the interested payor. A proposal will outline the qualifications and credentials of the Network physicians, the organization of the Network, services to be rendered by the Network, and what the Network proposes to charge for these services. It will also give mention to the Network's ability to monitor clinical protocols and manage utilization. The proposal may outline how the IPA specifically intends to manage capitation revenues.

After the proposal is developed, we will present the proposal document to the payor. The objective here is to convey clearly to the representatives that the Network can meet all of their fundamental contracting needs.

Once the proposals are delivered, the next step is to negotiate the rates and terms of each respective managed-care or provider contract. We will work in concert with the Network's legal counsel during the negotiation process. The negotiation will include, for example, such items as covered services, fee structure and related future adjustments, risk-sharing limits, stoploss levels, hold harmless terms, provider coverage, in-area emergency care, and withhold retention.

IPA Administration—If the IPA happens to receive a contract whereby it must manage revenues, internal administration systems must be set up. Cash and accounting systems will be instituted and monitored unless these services are performed by an independent administration firm. Financial and operational policies and procedures for the IPA will be designed. Insurance claim administration activities by the IPA will have to be created if necessary. A system of preparing monthly management and other reports will also be created. IPA committees will continue to meet and execute their duties. Many of these items may be addressed in the creation of the organizational structure.

POLICY ON SETTING PROPOSED FEE STRUCTURE

Our Firm sets its proposed fee structure contained herein based upon a balance of the client's best interests and the anticipated value to the client. It also takes into account the unique expertise and service capabilities our Firm does and can provide you, when compared to other accounting and consulting firms.

In determining the amount to be charged for our professional services, we consider the following:

a) The time and effort required, based upon our standard hourly rates

b) The amount of money involved and the results obtained

c) Time constraints that may be imposed on us

d) The experience, reputation, out-of-pocket costs, and expertise of our professional staff

The following is our proposed fee structure:

Ongoing IPA Management

A flat fee of $3,000 per month, payable each month in advance, plus any out-of-pocket expenses.

All Other IPA Services

Fees will be billed at our standard hourly rates plus out-of-pocket costs. Based on our experience with other IPAs, our Firm's monthly billings will generally run between $800 and $2,500. The fees will tend to be higher in the beginning since we must establish the minimum IPA fee schedule and possibly begin the process of renegotiation of certain managed-care contracts. **THESE ARE ESTIMATES ONLY**; THE LEVEL OF BILLED CHARGES WILL DEPEND ALMOST ENTIRELY ON THE NUMBER OF PAYOR NEGOTIATIONS AND THE DIRECTION PROVIDED US BY THE CONTRACTING COMMITTEE. In the first year you can expect to pay consulting fees (not including management fees described above) of between $15,000 and $20,000 based on our extensive experience working with IPAs.

USE OF SUPPLEMENTAL INDEPENDENT SPECIALISTS

From time to time, we may employ the expertise of other independent specialists to assist us in the execution of the services to be provided in this engagement. These specialists will be in the employ of our Firm and we will bill you for their services as an out-of-pocket cost. However, we will not use a supplemental specialist unless specifically authorized by you to do so.

TIMELINESS OF SERVICES

We intend to provide our services on a timely basis. However, our performance depends, in part, on your cooperation. In order to have timely service, we must receive requested information from your and the other offices on a timely basis.

COMMUNICATION CHANNELS

The establishment and retention of communication channels between our Firm and you are vital for our relationship to remain workable. Our experience shows that problems can continue undetected, important data can be misrouted or delayed, and mix-ups can occur more easily when direct communication or personal accessibility is somehow restricted. Therefore, we view communications as a matter of serious concern.

We expect that our direct discussion with you will involve the following assigned professional personnel in our Firm:

[INSERT ENGAGEMENT TEAM MEMBERS HERE]

TERMINATION OF THIS AGREEMENT

Consulting work is personal in nature, not clinical or impersonal. Our work cannot be continued by force when either party no longer feels comfortable with the relationship. To let you know, the following are just a few of the factors and standards we consider when evaluating and determining whether or not to continue our relationship:

- Illegal acts, financial irregularities, or unethical practices
- Failure to pay our fees
- Consistently not following our advice
- Being uncooperative with our Firm's personnel
- Consistently not providing complete data
- Noncompliance with the terms of this agreement

- Constantly complaining about our fees and service
- Unprofessional conduct
- Mistreatment of our Firm's personnel

This agreement can be terminated at any time by either you or us, without reason or cause, and without advance notice. Notice can be given either orally or in writing. Once the agreement is terminated, our obligations to you cease and any unpaid and accrued fees become immediately payable. We will issue you a final billing based on unbilled charges in your client account.

APPROVAL OF SERVICE AGREEMENT

If this service agreement agrees with your understanding of the terms, nature, scope, and limitations of the services we intend to provide, your signature and date on this agreement will indicate your approval so we may begin your work. A copy of this agreement is enclosed for your files.

Thank you for allowing us to propose our services. We are extremely pleased that you are considering entrusting your work to us.

Very truly yours,

_____

CLIENT APPROVAL:

_____
Signature

_____
Print Name

_____
Date

APPENDIX ITEM 22-06
IPA'S CONTRACT PROPOSAL TO IPA

Date
Name
Company
Address
City, State, Zip
Re: **Ear, Nose & Throat Contract Proposal—ENT Affiliates IPA**

Dear _____:

The following is ENT Affiliates' proposal to Aetna HMO for an exclusive ENT (otolaryngology) contracting relationship. I attempted to respond to the categories I feel will make up most of the entire contract. These proposed terms are to be used to form the basis of a final contract between Aetna HMO and the IPA. I am sure we will need to discuss them further in order to arrive at a final contract everyone is comfortable with.

CONTRACT PROPOSAL

Global Exclusivity

Nothing contained in the agreement shall preclude the physicians from participating in or contracting with any other health care provider organization, managed-care plan, health maintenance organization, insurer, employer, or any other third-party payor, or directly with any payor.

In-Area versus Out-of-Area Coverage

IPA members will be responsible for all "in-area" coverage, but "out-of-area" coverage will be <u>excluded</u> from the IPA's capitated rate.

Evaluation and Management Services

All evaluation and management services applicable to otolaryngology care will be <u>included</u> in the capitation rate we propose. This includes the following: Office Visits, Consults, Hospital Care, Nursing Facility Care, Phone Advice, and Emergency Care.

Drugs—In Office

The practice of ENT is dependent on the pharmacist for its prescribed pharmaceutical therapy. Any prescribed drugs would be <u>excluded</u> from our proposed capitation rate. As such, we need to agree on a pharmaceutical source to refer the patient, or a price for specific drugs or items dispensed in the office. The doctors in turn will bill Aetna HMO for specifically identified items on an agreed fee-for-service basis. If prescriptions requiring drugs must be referred to an independent pharmacy contracted with Aetna HMO, such providers will not bill ENT Affiliates and as such, ENT Affiliates will not be responsible for the payment of these costs.

All in-office drugs incidental to the delivery of ENT services will be <u>included</u> in the capitation rate.

Supplies—In Office

Any disposable supplies used during the treatment in a participating ENT office will be <u>included</u> in the capitation rate.

Diagnostics/Laboratory

Any diagnostic or laboratory service <u>performed in the office</u> shall be <u>included</u> in the capitation rate. However, if these tests must be referred to an independent laboratory contracted with Aetna HMO, such providers will not bill ENT Affiliates and as such, ENT Affiliates will not be responsible for the payment of these costs.

Special Procedures and Diagnostics Related to ENT

Audiological studies and testing (professional component only) are integral to the practice of otolaryngology and will be considered to be part of the capitated contract. The IPA would like to ensure that a proper protocol is followed prior to the patients' referral for such procedures. If a patient should need a hearing aid, the hearing aid "evaluation" and the cost of the hearing aids will be <u>excluded</u> from the capitation rate.

Neuro-otological vestibular studies (balance loss profiles), voice studies, specialized otology procedures (i.e., cochlear implants), speech / hearing therapy, allergy testing and immuno-therapy, facial plastics, and head and neck surgeries for cancer are related to but not integral to the practice of otolaryngology and will be <u>excluded</u> from the capitated rate.

ENG and ABR studies will be <u>excluded</u> from the capitation rate.

Procedures—In Office and In Facility (Inpatient)

An agreed-upon list of in-office and inpatient procedures will be included in the capitation rate and the list will be considered as part of the capitation contract. However, tertiary-related services will be <u>excluded</u>. A partial list of some of these exclusions is attached to this letter. Aetna HMO and IPA members will work together to make a complete list of these specialized services the group will contract for outside of the capitation rate. Aetna HMO will be responsible for these costs that are <u>excluded</u> from the capitation rate. Likewise, artificial devices and prosthetics will be carved out until a good utilization history can be captured and priced.

Otolaryngology services related to cochlear implants shall also be <u>excluded</u> from the capitation rate.

Rates

Based upon the utilization data provided to the IPA, we propose a capitation rate of $1.02 per member, per month. **However, until we can gather specific utilization data on our group for one complete year, Aetna HMO will guarantee the IPA in the first year of the contract reimbursement equal to current Medicare rates.** At the end of the initial twelve- (12) month period, the IPA will calculate its utilization at current Medicare rates. Aetna HMO will verify this calculation and agree to immediately pay over to IPA the difference between this fee-for-service calculation and actual capitation payments made during the same time period.

The proposed capitation rate excludes an allowance for Aetna HMO's transference of certain of its administration costs to the IPA. If Aetna HMO intends to transfer claims adjudication and all other contract administration functions to the IPA, **the proposed capitation rate will be $1.08 cents per member, per month.**

After one year, the agreed-upon first-year capitation rate will be reviewed by all parties.

Bonus

The IPA will be eligible for a bonus if certain utilization targets are met and maintained. This can be discussed in greater detail at a later time.

Reimbursement

As mentioned above, we propose to carve out specific services that will be reimbursed on a fee-for-service basis. In addition to the services listed above, Aetna HMO and IPA can work together to create a specific list of carve-out services.

We propose the following fee-for-service reimbursement:

130% Current Medicare Rates for E&M Services

150% Current Medicare Rates for All Other Services

These rate arrangements will be fixed and cannot change unless agreed upon by both parties.

Non-covered services will be the final responsibility of the patient and will be paid at the doctors' current practice rates.

Contract Term

The proposed contract term is for three years.

Quality Assurance/Utilization Management

IPA agrees to work with Aetna HMO on quality assurance and utilization programs related specifically to otolaryngology care. This includes the development of protocols for the primary-care doctors contracted with Aetna HMO.

Operations

IPA will be responsible for the following:

1. Approval (authorization) of initial referral to one of the IPA's physicians

2. Authorization/precertification of additional service requests (e.g., surgeries and testing) by the IPA's physicians
3. Review of submitted charges before a claim is paid
4. Cash administration
5. ENT affiliates' own provider fee schedules and contract

Conclusion

As a reminder, contract terms that are tentatively agreed upon will have to be ratified by the IPA membership before we can execute a final agreement.

The doctors are excited about this contracting opportunity and the development of a win-win relationship with Aetna HMO and its patients. By working together, I am sure we can develop a contract that will be mutually beneficial to all parties.

I look forward to working with you on this project.

Very truly yours,

---

cc: All Members—ENT Affiliates

SPECIALIST CAPITATION SCHEDULE EXCLUSION LIST FOR HMO PLANS FOR OTOLARYNGOLOGY

The Capitation amounts listed in the contract will <u>exclude</u> the following services and procedures that can or could be performed by some of the IPA's contracted providers.

*   Excision, tumor of ear and mastoid, unless benign
*   Partial temporal bone resection
*   Radical temporal bone resection
*   Pinna excision and neck dissection
*   Total parotidectomy with facial nerve dissection
*   Total parotidectomy without nerve graft
*   Total parotidectomy with nerve graft
*   Partial maxillectomy
*   Total maxillectomy

- Radical maxillectomy with orbital exenteration
- Abbe-Estlander flap
- Partial glossectomy
- Partial mandibulectomy
- Composite resection—primary and tumor with RND
- Radical neck dissection
- Extended radical neck dissection (transsternal mediastinal dissection)
- Diverticulectomy (cervical)
- Subtotal laryngectomy
- Thyrotomy (laryngectomy)
- Supraglottic laryngectomy
- Hemilaryngectomy
- Wide field laryngectomy
- Total laryngectomy with neck dissection
- Cervical esophagectomy with neck dissection
- Tracheal resection with repair
- Major vessel grafting
- Arterial infusion procedure
- Resection acoustic neoroma (translabyrinthine, middle cranial fossa, etc.)
- VII Nerve section via middle fossa
- Reconstruction, external ear
- Otoplasty
- Rhinoplasty
- Laryngoplasty
- Tracheoplasty
- Mentoplasty
- Rhytidectomy
- Blepharoplasty
- Pedicle flap procedures
- Implants (including chest, neck, shoulder, foreheads, scalp, cheek)
- Facial sling procedures

- Prognathism correction
- Retrognathism correction
- Cleft lip repair
- Cleft palate repair
- Mediastinoscopy
- Dacryocystorhinostomy
- Hypophysectomy
- Allergy testing and immuno therapy
- Cochlear implants and ALL RELATED Pre/Post TESTING PROCE-DURES
- All neurology service
- Hearing aid dispensing

▼ INDEX

ABOUT THE CD-ROM

▼ CD-ROM INSTRUCTIONS

System Requirements

- IBM PC or compatible computer with CD-ROM drive
- Windows 95 or higher
- Microsoft® Word 7.0 for Windows™ or compatible word processor
- Microsoft® Excel 7.0 for Windows™ or compatible spreadsheet program
- 10 MB available on hard drive

The CD-ROM provided with the *Medical Practice Management Handbook* contains forms, checklists, letters, spreadsheets, and other practice aids.

Subject to the conditions in the license agreement and the limited warranty, which are reproduced at the end of this book, you may duplicate the files on this disc, modify them as necessary, and create your own customized versions. Using the disc in any way indicates that you accept the terms of the license agreement.

Using the CD-ROM

The disc data are intended for use with your word processing software. The documents are provided in RTF (Rich Text Format), Excel Format, and PDF (Portable Document Format). RTF documents can be read by all compatible word processors, including Microsoft Word for Windows and WordPerfect 7 or above, as well as Microsoft Excel 7. Check your owners manual for information on the conversion of the documents as required. PDF documents are viewable through Adobe Acrobat Reader, which is supplied on this CD for users who do not already have Acrobat Reader installed.

Using the Documents

The list of the CD-ROM Contents is available on your disc in a file called _contents.rtf. The listing includes each individual example exhibit, checklist, correspondence, and workpaper and identifies its location in a particular file. You can open the file and view it on your screen and use it to link to the documents you're interested in, or print a hard copy to use for reference.

1. Open the file _contents.rtf in your word processor.
2. Locate the file you wish to access, and click on the hyperlinked filename. Your word processor will then open the file.
3. You may copy files from the CD-ROM to your hard disk. To edit files you have copied, remember to clear the read-only attribute from the file. To do this, select the name of the file in My Computer, right-click the filename, then choose Properties, and clear the Read-only checkbox.

Installing Acrobat Reader

Most users already have Acrobat Reader installed. If you do not have Acrobat Reader 4.x installed, follow the instructions below:

1. In My Computer, double-click the icon for your CD-ROM drive.
2. Double-click the Acrobat folder.
3. Double-click the file ar40eng.exe. The Acrobat Reader 4.x setup will begin. Follow the prompts to install Acrobat Reader 4.x.
4. You may now access PDF documents on this CD-ROM by either clicking the link to the PDF in the _contents.rtf document (see Using the Documents above) or by opening the PDF directly in the Reader.

Software Support

If you experience any difficulties installing or running the electronic files and cannot resolve the problem using the information presented here, call our toll-free software support hotline at (800) 486-9296. Hours of operation are 8 a.m. to 5 p.m. (EST), Monday through Friday.

▼ CD-ROM Contents

File	Title
02-07	ENT Capitation Rate Analysis
02-08	Diagnosis Codes

Chapter 4

04-01	Medical Practice Internal Control Checklist

Chapter 5

05-01	Cash Flow Forecast for a Medical Practice
05-02	Collection Reconciliation Letter
05-03	Accounts Receivable Reconciliation Letter
05-04	Actual-to-Budget Comparison
05-05	Cash Flow Projection—Fully Operational MSO
05-06	5-Year Cash Flow Projection—Fully Operational MSO Year 1
05-07	5-Year Cash Flow Projection—Fully Operational MSO Year 2
05-08	5-Year Cash Flow Projection—Fully Operational MSO Year 3
05-09	5-Year Cash Flow Projection—Fully Operational MSO Year 4
05-10	5-Year Cash Flow Projection—Fully Operational MSO Year 5
05-11	Cash Flow Example
05-12	MSO First Year Start-Up Projection
05-13	MSO Cash Flow Projection (First Year)

Chapter 7

07-01	Checklist for a New Medical Practice
07-02	Medical Practice Management Software Features Checklist

Chapter 8

08-01	Frequency Report Review
08-02	Medicine and Lab Fee Worksheet
08-03	Revenue Analysis Worksheet

File	Title
08-04	Procedure and Radiology Fee Analysis Worksheet
08-05	Payor Review

Part II: Medical Office Operations, Policies, and Procedures

Chapter 9

09-01	New Patients' Information Sheet
09-02	Daily Control Sheet
09-03	Daily Status Report
09-04	Patients' Sign-In Sheet
09-05	Verification of Insurance Coverage
09-06	Worksheet for Analysis of Patients' Waiting Time in Reception Area
09-07	Physician Referral Tracking Form
09-08	New Patient Tracking Form

Chapter 11

11-01	OIG Model Compliance Plan for Medical Practices

Chapter 12

12-01	Front Desk Collection Analysis Worksheet
12-02	Collection Letter Number 1
12-03	Collection Letter Number 2
12-04	Collection Letter Number 3
12-05	Collection Letter Number 4
12-06	Collection Letter Number 5
12-07	Collection Letter Number 6
12-08	Collection Letter Number 7
12-09	Collection Letter Number 8
12-10	Collection Letter Number 9
12-11	Insurance Follow-up Telephone Call Checklist
12-12	Collection System Monitor

File	Title
12-13	Bad Debt Control Checklist
12-14	Claim Inquiry Fax Form

Chapter 13

13-01	Insurance Claims Filing Analysis Worksheet
13-02	Letter to the Insurance Commissioner
13-03	Payment Posting Audit Form
13-04	Insurance Payment Analysis Worksheet
13-05	Close Out Worksheet

Chapter 16

16-01	Employees' Annual Performance Review
16-02	Employees' Time-Off Request Form
16-03	Sample Policy and Procedures Manual
16-04	Sample Office Administrator Job Advertisement

Part III: Physicians' Contracts, Relationships, and Related Issues

Chapter 17

17-01	Buy/Sell Agreement Checklist
17-02	Buy/Sell Agreement

Chapter 18

18-01	New Physician Letter of Intent
18-02	Physician Employment Agreement Outline
18-03	Physician Employment Agreement
18-04	Incentive Bonus Recommendation
18-05	Physician Questionnaire—Compensation Plan
18-06	Comparable Compensation Calculation
18-07	Sample Buy-In Agreement
18-08	Overhead Allocation
18-09	Sample Worksheet to Value Call Coverage

File	Title

Chapter 19

Chapter 20

Chapter 21

File	Title
21-03	Group Practice Information Implementation Checklist
21-04	Management Organization's Proposal to Provide Due Diligence Services
21-05	Sample Evaluation for Due Diligence Assessment
21-06	Due Diligence Information Request Form for Medical Practice Consolidation Engagement
21-07	Merger Implementation Checklist
21-08	Stark II Final Regulations
21-09	Mobile, AL, Surgeons DOJ Business Review Letter
21-10	Allentown, PA, Physician Group DOJ Business Review Letter
21-11	Office Sharing Agreement

Chapter 22

22-01	Management Services Organization Agreement
22-02	Independent Practice Association Agreement
22-03	Implementation Checklist for Proposed IPA
22-04	Development Checklist for Proposed IPA
22-05	Proposal to Provide Management Services to IPA
22-06	IPA's Contract Proposal to IPA
22-07	Sample IPA Profit and Loss Statement
22-08	Antitrust Enforcement Advisory Opinion
22-09	Sample of IPA Seeking Contact with Management Organizations
22-10	Texas Surgeons' IPA FTC Agreement
22-11	OIG Third-Party Billing Compliance Program
22-12	IPA Provider Application
22-13	Sample Asset Practice Sale Agreement

Chapter 23

23-01	Valuation Template
23-02	Sample Valuation Representation Letter
23-03	Valuation Report

ASPEN LAW & BUSINESS SOFTWARE LICENSE AGREEMENT

READ THE TERMS AND CONDITIONS OF THIS LICENSE AGREEMENT CAREFULLY BEFORE INSTALLING THE SOFTWARE (THE "PROGRAM") TO ACCOMPANY *MEDICAL PRACTICE MANAGEMENT HANDBOOK* (THE "BOOK"). THE PROGRAM IS COPYRIGHTED AND LICENSED (NOT SOLD). BY INSTALLING THE PROGRAM, YOU ARE ACCEPTING AND AGREEING TO THE TERMS OF THIS LICENSE AGREEMENT. IF YOU ARE NOT WILLING TO BE BOUND BY THE TERMS OF THIS LICENSE AGREEMENT, YOU SHOULD PROMPTLY RETURN THE PACKAGE IN RESELLABLE CONDITION AND YOU WILL RECEIVE A REFUND OF YOUR MONEY. THIS LICENSE AGREEMENT REPRESENTS THE ENTIRE AGREEMENT CONCERNING THE PROGRAM BETWEEN YOU AND ASPEN LAW & BUSINESS (REFERRED TO AS "LICENSOR"), AND IT SUPERSEDES ANY PRIOR PROPOSAL, REPRESENTATION, OR UNDERSTANDING BETWEEN THE PARTIES.

1. License Grant. Licensor hereby grants to you, and you accept, a nonexclusive license to use the Program CD-ROM and the computer programs contained therein in machine-readable, object code form only (collectively referred to as the "Software"), and the accompanying User Documentation, only as authorized in this License Agreement. The Software may be used only on a single computer owned, leased, or otherwise controlled by you; or in the event of the inoperability of that computer, on a backup computer selected by you. Neither concurrent use on two or more computers nor use in a local area network or other network is permitted without separate authorization and the possible payment of other license fees. You agree that you will not assign, sublease, transfer, pledge, lease, rent, or share your rights under the License Agreement. You agree that you may not reverse engineer, decompile, disassemble, or otherwise adapt, modify, or translate the Software.

Upon loading the Software into your computer, you may retain the Program CD-ROM for backup purposes. In addition, you may make one copy of the Software on a set of diskettes (or other storage medium) for the purpose of backup in the event the Program Diskettes are damaged or destroyed. You may make one copy of any additional User Documentation (such as the README.TXT file or the "About the Computer Disc" section of the Book) for backup purposes. Any such copies of the Software or the User Documentation shall include Licensor's copyright and other proprietary notices. Except as authorized under this paragraph, no copies of the program or any portions thereof may be made by you or any person under your authority or control.

2. Licensor's Rights. You acknowledge and agree that the Software and the User Documentation are proprietary products of Licensor protected under U.S. copyright law. You further acknowledge and agree that all right, title, and interest in and to the Program, including associated intellectual property rights, are and shall remain with Licensor. This License Agreement does not convey to you an interest in or to the Program, including associated intellectual property rights, which are and shall remain with Licensor. This License Agreement does not convey to you an interest in or to the Program, but only a limited right of use revocable in accordance with the terms of the License Agreement.

3. License Fees. The license fees paid by you are paid in consideration of the licenses granted under this License Agreement.

4. Term. This License Agreement is effective upon your installing this software and shall continue until terminated. You may terminate this License Agreement at any time by returning the Program and all copies thereof and extracts therefrom to Licensor. Licensor may terminate this License Agreement upon the breach by you of any term hereof. Upon such termination by Licensor, you agree to return to Licensor the Program and all copies and portions thereof.

5. Limited Warranty. Licensor warrants, for our benefit alone, for a period of 90 days from the date of commencement of this License Agreement (referred to as the "Warranty Period") that the Program CD-ROM in which the Software is contained is free from defects in material and workmanship. If during the Warranty Period, a defect appears in the Program diskettes, you may return the Program to Licensor for either replacement or, at Licensor's option, refund of amounts paid by you under this License Agreement. You agree that the foregoing constitutes your sole and exclusive remedy for breach by Licensor of any warranties made under this Agreement. EXCEPT FOR THE WARRANTIES SET FORTH ABOVE, THE PROGRAM, AND THE SOFTWARE CONTAINED THEREIN, ARE LICENSED "AS IS," AND LICENSOR DISCLAIMS ANY AND ALL OTHER WARRANTIES, WHETHER EXPRESS OR IMPLIED, INCLUDING, WITHOUT LIMITATION, ANY IMPLIED WARRANTIES OF MERCHANTABILITY OR FITNESS FOR A PARTICULAR PURPOSE.

6. Limitation of Liability. Licensor's cumulative liability to you or any other party for any loss or damages resulting from any claims, demands, or actions arising out of or relating to this Agreement shall not exceed the license fee paid to Licensor for the use of the Program. IN NO EVENT SHALL LICENSOR BE LIABLE FOR ANY INDIRECT, INCIDENTAL, CONSEQUENTIAL, SPECIAL, OR EXEMPLARY DAMAGES (INCLUDING, BUT NOT LIMITED TO, LOSS OF DATA, BUSINESS INTERRUPTION, OR LOST PROFITS) EVEN IF LICENSOR HAS BEEN ADVISED OF THE POSSIBILITY OF SUCH DAMAGES.

7. Miscellaneous. This License Agreement shall be construed and governed in accordance with the laws of the State of New York. Should any term of this License Agreement be declared void or unenforceable by any court of competent jurisdiction, such declaration shall have no effect on the remaining terms hereof. The failure of either party to enforce any rights granted hereunder or to take action against the other party in the event of any breach hereunder shall not be deemed a waiver by that party as to subsequent enforcement of rights or subsequent actions in the event of future breaches.